DISCARDED

EARLY ADOLESCENCE
Perspectives on Research, Policy,
and Intervention

The Penn State Series On Child & Adolescent Development

Series Editors:
David S. Palermo and Richard M. Lerner

Palermo • Coping with Uncertainty: Behavioral and Developmental Perspectives

Susman/Feagans/Ray • Emotion, Cognition, Health, and Development in Children and Adolescents

Lerner • Early Adolescence: Perspectives on Research, Policy, and Intervention

EARLY ADOLESCENCE
Perspectives on Research, Policy, and Intervention

Edited by
Richard M. Lerner
Michigan State University

LAWRENCE ERLBAUM ASSOCIATES, PUBLISHERS
1993   Hillsdale, New Jersey   Hove and London

Copyright © 1993 by Lawrence Erlbaum Associates, Inc.
All rights reserved. No part of this book may be reproduced in
any form, by photostat, microform, retrieval system, or any other
means, without the prior written permission of the publisher.

Lawrence Erlbaum Associates, Inc., Publishers
365 Broadway
Hillsdale, New Jersey 07642

Library of Congress Cataloging-in-Publication Data

Early adolescence : perspectives on research, policy, and intervention
  / edited by Richard M. Lerner.
      p. cm.
  Includes bibliographical references and indexes.
  ISBN 0-8058-1164-8
  1. Socially handicapped teenagers—United States. 2. Social work
with teenagers—United States. I. Lerner, Richard M.
HV1431.E25 1993
362.7'083—dc20   92-40286
                                                                  CIP

Books published by Lawrence Erlbaum Associates are printed on acid-free paper, and their
bindings are chosen for strength and durability.

Printed in the United States of America
10 9 8 7 6 5 4 3 2 1

Contents

Foreword
Anne C. Peterson   xi

Preface   xiii

1   Early Adolescence: Toward an Agenda for the Integration of Research, Policy, and Intervention
Richard M. Lerner   1

I   ADOLESCENTS AND THE FAMILY
Editors: *Kevin W. Allison and Richard M. Lerner*

INTRODUCTION: Integrating Research, Policy, and Programs for Adolescents and Their Families
Kevin W. Allison and Richard M. Lerner   17

2   The Demographic Context of U.S. Adolescence
Gretchen T. Cornwell and Samuel M. Curtis   25

3   Adolescents Living in "Nonfamily" and Alternative Settings
Kevin W. Allison   37

4	Diversity: The Cultural Contexts of Adolescents and Their Families *Kevin W. Allison and Yoshi Takei*	51
5	Familial Economic Circumstances: Implications for Adjustment and Development in Early Adolescence *Ann C. Crouter and Susan M. McHale*	71
6	Early Adolescent Family Formation *Lisa J. Crockett*	93
7	Familial Influences on Adolescent Health *Jordan W. Finkelstein*	111

II EARLY ADOLESCENT EDUCATION
Editors: *Lynne V. Feagans and Karen Bartsch*

INTRODUCTION: A Framework for Examining the Role of Schooling During Early Adolescence
Lynne V. Feagans and Karen Bartsch — 129

8	Adolescents' Theoretical Thinking *Karen Bartsch*	143
9	The Role of Community-Based Youth Groups in Enhancing Learning and Achievement Through Nonformal Education *Judith Semon Dubas and B. Alan Snider*	159
10	Academic Achievement Among Early Adolescents: Social and Cultural Diversity *Yoshi Takei and Judith Semon Dubas*	175
11	Curricular Designs That Resonate With Adolescents' Ways of Knowing *Jamie Myers*	191

12	Transferring Literacy Between the Classroom and Life: Metacognition, Personal Goals, and Interests *Lori A. Forlizzi*	**201**
13	Music in the Lives of Adolescents: A Comparison of In-School and Out-of-School Music Experiences and Involvement *Joanne Rutkowski*	**221**

III HEALTH PROMOTION IN EARLY ADOLESCENCE
Editors: *Patricia Barthalow Koch and Elizabeth J. Susman*

INTRODUCTION: Health Promotion for Early Adolescents
Patricia Barthalow Koch, Dolores W. Maney, and Elizabeth J. Susman — **241**

14	Health Promotion in Adolescence: Developmental and Theoretical Considerations *Elizabeth J. Susman, Patricia Barthalow Koch, Dolores W. Maney, and Jordan W. Finkelstein*	**247**
15	Nutrition and Adolescence *Cheryl L. Achterberg and Barbara Shannon*	**261**
16	Promoting Vocational Development in Early Adolescence *Fred W. Vondracek*	**277**
17	Promoting Healthy Sexual Development During Early Adolescence *Patricia Barthalow Koch*	**293**

IV PREVENTIVE INTERVENTIONS IN EARLY ADOLESCENCE
Editors: *Bonnie L. Barber and Lisa J. Crockett*

INTRODUCTION: Preventive Interventions in Early Adolescence: Developmental and Contextual Challenges
Bonnie L. Barber and Lisa J. Crockett — **311**

viii | CONTENTS

18 Pregnancy Prevention in Early Adolescence:
A Developmental Perspective
Bonnie L. Barber and Lisa J. Crockett   315

19 Sexual Activity and Childbearing Among Hispánic
Adolescents in the United States
Katharine Fennelly   335

20 Interventions to Prevent HIV Infections in
Young Adolescents
Anthony R. D'Augelli and C. Raymond Bingham   353

21 Early Adolescent Belief Systems and Substance Abuse
John D. Swisher   369

22 Depression as a Disorder of Social Relationships:
Implications for School Policy and Prevention Programs
Robert E. Kennedy   383

V **ADOLESCENTS AND THE MEDIA**
Editors: *Jerome D. Williams and Katherine Frith*

INTRODUCTION: Adolescents and the Media
Jerome D. Williams and Katherine Frith   401

23 Media, Music, and Adolescents
Keith P. Thompson   407

24 Creating Meaning From Media Messages: Participatory
Research and Adolescent Health
Michael Frith and Katherine Frith   419

25 Minority Adolescents, Alcohol Consumption, and
Media Effects: A Review of Issues and Research
Jerome D. Williams   431

VI	**RESEARCH, POLICY, AND PROGRAMS: TOWARD AN INTEGRATED APPROACH** Editors: *Bea Mandel and Wayne Schutjer*	
	INTRODUCTION: Research, Policy, and Programs: What Works in Today's Society *Bea Mandel and Wayne Schutjer*	449
26	An Agenda for the Integration of Research and Policy During Early Adolescence *Ruby Takanishi*	457
27	Integrating Research, Policy, and Practice: One School District's Approach to Improving Middle-Level Education *Patricia L. Best*	471
28	The Land-Grant University System and 4-H: A Mutually Beneficial Relationship of Scholars and Practitioners in Youth Development *B. Alan Snider and Jeffrey P. Miller*	481

Author Index	501
Subject Index	521

Foreword

Anne C. Petersen
The University of Minnesota

This volume represents a major accomplishment both for scholars of early adolescence at (or related to) Penn State and for the field. For those at Penn State, it represents a multiyear effort to engage about 80 scholars from across disciplines who came together from five colleges and 21 departments. With funding from the Carnegie Corporation of New York, five working groups began in 1989 to focus on education, families, health and health promotion, media, and preventive interventions for young adolescents.

The breadth of this effort required the inevitable challenges of communicating across disciplines. In addition, many of these scholars had not previously studied early adolescence. To complicate things further, we also included in our discussions scholars with expertise on youth from beyond the United States, policy analysts and policymakers, and practitioners. The result was an exciting mix of new ideas that culminated, in part, in the contributions found in this volume.

Our rationale for this broad and potentially high-risk approach was that the overall field of research on early adolescence had been developing rapidly but largely within disciplinary boundaries. Further, some areas such as education for young adolescents were developed to a much greater extent than others, such as media effects. Finally, as is typically the case, there had been insufficient interaction about issues related to early adolescence among researchers, policymakers, and practitioners, depriving research of knowledge about the most important questions, and depriving practitioners and policymakers of current knowledge from research. This volume only begins this dialogue, but we hope that it stimulates further productive interaction.

We are grateful to the Carnegie Corporation of New York for their support of this experimental effort. Foundation President David Hamburg's priority on children in general and early adolescence in particular has had significant impact on research, policy, and practice in the United States and to some extent beyond.

The Penn State efforts were guided by a Steering Committee. Three on this committee have made particularly significant contributions: Wayne Schutjer has facilitated interactions with 4-H, Richard M. Lerner was very active in implementing these along with leading the research component of the effort, and Brian Winston encouraged the faculty in the School of Communications to lend their expertise on the media.

In the initial year of this effort, staff support was provided by Laura Hess and Dolores Maney. In 1990, we were fortunate to recruit Bea Mandel as executive director. All who have been involved have contributed significant creativity and effort.

Early adolescence represents a highly significant transition in the life course. The nature of this transition provides an opportunity to enhance the lives of young people and prevent the development of limiting life trajectories. We hope that the contributions of this volume will advance knowledge and stimulate further linkage with policy and practice.

Preface

Adolescence is a double-edged sword. On the one hand, and especially during the early portion of this period, adolescence is a time of burgeoning possibilities. During early adolescence there occurs an emergence of new capacities for thought and for moral commitment; for self-understanding and definition; for learning about one's sexuality, social skills, and physical abilities; for renegotiating one's relationships with parents, peers, and teachers; and for establishing at least the beginnings of one's entrance into the world of work and careers.

In turn, however, early adolescence is also a period of profound biological, psychological, and social risk—particularly among contemporary cohorts of youth. Indeed, it is apt to say that there is nothing short of a "generational time bomb" involving today's youth in the United States. According to scholars such as Dryfoos (1990), approximately half of U.S. adolescents are at *moderate or greater risk* for engaging in unsafe sexual behaviors, teenage pregnancy, and teenage childbearing; in drug and alcohol use and abuse; in school underachievement, failure, and dropout; and in delinquency, crime, and violence. Fifty percent of today's 10- to 17-year-olds engage in two or more of these types of risk behaviors, and 10% of youth in this age range engage in all of these risks.

In addition to this overall pattern of risk, some of the characteristics of risk behavior involving young adolescents are markedly disturbing. Ten percent of sixth graders have initiated alcohol use, and 25% of 12- to 14-year-olds are current users of alcohol. About 40,000 babies are born each year to unwed mothers less than 15 years of age. In the mid-1990s, 1.7 million arrests occurred among 15 to 17-year-olds. More than 500,000 of those arrested were adolescents 14 years of age or younger, and 46,000 were under 10 years of age. During the 1980s, 4.5 million 10- to 14-year-olds were one or more years behind their modal grade level.

Moreover, in addition to these behavioral instances of risk there is a structural feature of risk that permeates and promotes these behaviors: persistent and pervasive poverty. According to Schorr and Schorr (1988), poverty is the most damaging risk factor affecting outcomes of development of youth. Poverty creates "rotten outcomes" such as early school dropout; lack of preparedness for jobs; arrests for crimes, often of a violent nature; and long-term welfare dependency. And poverty is epidemic among our nation's youth.

Half of the 28 million U.S. residents who lived below the poverty level during the 1980s were children and adolescents. Moreover, there are some groups in our society—for instance, African-Americans—wherein almost half the youth are poor.

It is clear, then, that the United States is faced with widespread destruction of its most precious resource: the human capital represented by our children. The magnitude of the risk threatening U.S. youth involves more than just a decrease in their life chances. This threat decreases adolescents' chances of even having lives.

In the midst of this bleak picture there are reasons for hope: First, it is certain that interventions can prevent the appearance of risk behaviors in adolescence; policies and programs aimed at prevention can avoid the actualization of the sequelae of persistent and pervasive poverty (Dryfoos, 1990; Schorr & Schorr, 1988). Second, members of the scholarly community are beginning to pursue a model of multidisciplinary research that views people's development as reciprocally embedded in the ecology of human development and, as such, conceptualizes policies and programs as "natural experiments" within this ecology (Lerner, 1991, 1992); evaluation of the outcomes of these endeavors provides information, then, both about the utility of these activities for promoting positive changes in the human life course and the adequacy of the model of human development and context (i.e., developmental contextualism; Lerner, 1991) from which the policies and programs were derived (Lerner, 1992)

In other words, developmental contextualism involves collaborative and integrative relationships among professionals involved in research, policy, and program design and delivery with the youth, families, and communities we seek to both understand and serve. This collaboration among science, service, and community is intended to build a partnership that will effectively prevent the actualization of risk in adolescence and, in turn, that will empower youth to embark on lives marked by personal, familial, and work-life productivity and happiness.

Built on a developmental contextual approach to the integration of knowledge about research, policies, and intervention programs during early adolescence, the goal of this book is to enhance the bases for this collaboration. The opportunity to create this book was enabled by the support of the Carnegie Corporation of New York, and specifically by the confidence expressed by President David Hamburg in the abilities of the Pennsylvania State University faculty to create a "flagship" program integrating scholarship and outreach pertinent to the period of early adolescence. To build this program, several dozen representatives from the Penn State faculty, from the Penn State Cooperative Extension Service, and from communities throughout Pennsylvania were brought together through the leadership of Anne C. Petersen. This group spent over a year surveying and discussing the literature pertinent to early adolescence and the family, the media, education, health promotion, preventive interventions, and policy.

One outcome of this work was the design and implementation of a coordinated plan of activities involving research; intervention program design, delivery, and evaluation; professional development; and policy analysis. A second outcome was this book.

The existence of any book, whether it is the product of a single author or of several, is nevertheless a result of the work of many people. This book exemplifies such a collaborative effort. First, and foremost, this book is the result of the scholarship and commitment of the authors of its chapters and of the editors of each of its several sections. The section editors deserve a special note of thanks. Their integrative intellectual abilities and vision of the scholarly and outreach implications of their subject matter provided the operational means for turning good ideas into important products. This volume is theirs.

The authors, section editors, and I are grateful to several colleagues, either within Penn State or within the national and international research, policy, and intervention communities focused on the period of early adolescence, for their helpful reviews of earlier drafts of the chapters in this book. We thank Linda M. Burton, Avshalom Caspi, Lindsay Chase-Lansdale, Gregory Clarke, Natalie Croll, Robert A. Cutietta, Anthony D'Augelli, Glen H. Elder, Jr., Jordan W. Finkelstein, Marian Goldberg, Louise Guerney, Paul Haach, Debra W. Hafner, Anne Heinsohn, Dennis Hogan, Anthony W. Jackson, Reed Larson, Dolores Maney, Susan M. McHale, Gary Melton, Susan Millstein, Ellen Morehouse, Susan Newcomer, Anne C. Petersen, Jon E. Rolf, Lee Anne Roman, Steven P. Schinke, Susheela Singh, Richard St. Pierre, Ruby Takanishi, Trish Torruella, Diane Weissman, Rex Warland, and Brian Winston.

Still other colleagues at Penn State played a vital role in facilitating the creation of this book. At Penn State, the success of any effort to integrate scholarship and outreach for contemporary youth rests on the collegial relations that exist between 4-H and Family Life Extension Agents and their colleagues involved in research. Wayne Schutjer was the catalyst for and the custodian of this collegiality. His vision of the important agenda for integrated research and outreach that could exist through the enhancement of research-extension relationships provided a clear path for the colleagues involved in this book. Bea Mandel coordinated all the myriad professionals activities that were involved in moving from an exciting concept to a final product, and accomplished this with grace, energy, enthusiasm, consummate management skills, and scholarly creativity. Linda Greenawalt provided superb secretarial support. She designed and implemented the clerical and editorial support system required to produce a book of considerable scope and complexity. Last, all of these efforts would not have occurred, indeed this book would not exist, were it not for the intellectual vision and scholarly leadership of Anne C. Petersen. Her scientific eminence and creativity, and her deep commitment to the youth of America, motivated and modeled all the efforts that are reflected in this book.

Finally, and on a personal note, my family was, as always, my source of love and support during my work on this project. I am fortunate and grateful for what they continue to give me.

REFERENCES

Dryfoos, J. G. (1990). *Adolescents at risk: Prevalence and prevention.* New York: Oxford University Press.

Lerner, R. M. (1991). Changing organism-context relations as the basic process of development: A developmental contextual perspective. *Developmental Psychology, 27,* 27–32.

Lerner, R. M. (1992). Diversity. *SRCD Newsletter, 2,* 12–14.

Schorr, L. B., & Schorr, D. (1988). *Within our reach: Breaking the cycle of disadvantage.* New York: Doubleday.

1 Early Adolescence: Toward an Agenda for the Integration of Research, Policy, and Intervention

Richard M. Lerner
Michigan State University

From conception through the adult and aged years human development involves a dynamic synthesis—or fusion—of biological, psychological, and sociocultural factors (Baltes, 1987; Lerner, 1986; Lerner & Spanier, 1978; Tobach, 1981; Tobach & Greenberg, 1984). The processes of behavior and development are ones linking variables across these levels. Unidisciplinary models and reductionistic methodological strategies do not suffice in the analysis of these interlevel relations (Baltes, Reese, & Nesselroade, 1977; Lerner, 1991; Nesselroade & Baltes, 1979; Nesselroade & Cattell, 1988). As a consequence, many scholars have suggested that the character of human development requires a model that promotes both multidisciplinary theoretical analysis and an integrated empirical examination of the dynamic relations comprising human life (e.g., Baltes, 1987; Featherman, 1983; Lerner, 1984; Petersen, 1988). In other words, interdisciplinary conceptual integration and methodological pluralism have been forwarded as optimal avenues for the analysis of the multiple, fused bases of human behavior and development. For many contemporary scholars, the favored theoretical model framing this approach to human development is termed *developmental contextualism* (Lerner, 1986, 1991).

This orientation is the conceptual basis of this book. A key theme is that multidisciplinary theoretical and methodological integration in the study of human development enhances understanding and provides effective and innovative means for the design, delivery, and evaluation of policies and interventions. Moreover, it is the belief of the authors of this volume that the basic and applied usefulness of an integration of "levels of organization" ranging from the biological through the sociocultural can be well documented in the study of adolescence, particularly in the appraisal of the early portion of this period of life. Accordingly, the goal of this book is to demonstrate the current and potential usefulness of integrated multidisciplinary conceptual and methodological approaches for the understanding of development in early adolescence, and for the design, delivery, and evaluation of policies and programs aimed at enhancing the lives of youth during this period.

The integration of multiple levels of organization involves processes both within the young adolescent (e.g., involving genetic and neurohormonal levels with cognitive and affective ones) and between the adolescent and his or her context (e.g., involving the adolescent and peer group, family, school, and community relations). Understanding this integration allows the identification of both normative developmental patterns and the individual differences in change that are emblematic of life during adolescence (Lerner, 1987; Petersen, 1988; Schneirla, 1957; Tobach & Greenberg, 1984). Through attention to interlevel integration of processes during early adolescence, knowledge of both general and specific characteristics of this period can be used to design and deliver more appropriately focused policies and programs for youth.

Global models of development and research that ignore the diversity of youth and of their contexts cannot be adequate bases for policies and programs. Thus, only through scholarship and application that are sensitive to diversity and context can the richness and complexity of the adolescent period be best appreciated and best used to enhance development during this period.

THE IMPORTANCE OF AN INTEGRATED MULTIDISCIPLINARY APPROACH TO DIVERSITY AND CONTEXT FOR RESEARCH, POLICY, AND INTERVENTION

Adolescence has been described as a phase of life beginning in biology and ending in society (Petersen, 1988). Indeed, adolescence may be defined as the period within the life span when most of a person's biological, psychological, and social characteristics are changing from what is typically considered childlike to what is considered adultlike (Lerner & Spanier, 1980). Early adolescence (typically the years between 10 and 15) is the period in which most of these transitions begin. For the young adolescent experiencing these transitions it is a time of dramatic challenge requiring adjustment to changes in self, family, and peer group. In contemporary American society, young adolescents experience institutional changes as well: There is a transition from elementary school to either junior high school or middle school.

Understandably, then, for both adolescents and their parents, early adolescence is a time of excitement and of anxiety, of happiness and of troubles, of discoveries and of bewilderment, and of breaks with the past but also of continuations of childhood behavior. It is a period about which much has been written but, until relatively recently, little has been known. In short, early adolescence can be a challenging time for the adolescent experiencing this phase of life, for the parents who are nurturing the adolescent during progression through this period, and for the adults charged with enhancing the development of youth during this period of life.

The feelings and events pertinent to parents' reactions to their adolescent children are well known to parents, to teachers, and to many writers who have romanticized or dramatized the adolescent experience in novels, short stories, or news articles. Indeed, it is commonplace to survey a newsstand and find magazine articles describing the "stormy years" of adolescence, the new crazes or fads of youth, or the "explosion" of problems with teenagers (e.g., crime or sexuality).

Until the last 20 years, when medical, biological, and social scientists began to study the adolescent period intensively, there was relatively little sound scientific information available to verify or refute the romantic, literary characterizations of adolescence. Today, however, such information does exist, and it is not consistent with the idea that early adolescence is a necessarily stormy and stressful period (Feldman & Elliott, 1990; Lerner, 1988; Lerner, Petersen, & Brooks-Gunn, 1991; Petersen, 1988).

Indeed, today, the more voluminous and sophisticated scientific literature about adolescence indicates that many of the generalizations made about this period are not accurate (e.g., see Lerner, 1988; Petersen, 1985, 1988). Current information indicates, for instance, that:

1. There are multiple pathways through adolescence (e.g., Block, 1971; Offer, 1969). Individual differences in development are the "rule" in this period of life;

2. Most developmental trajectories across this period involve good adjustment on the part of the adolescent, and the continuation of positive parent-child relationships (e.g., Douvan & Adelson, 1966; Offer, 1969);

3. The individual differences in adolescent development and the problems that do occur for many youths involve connections among biological, psychological, and social factors—and not one of these influences (e.g., biology) acting either alone or as the "prime mover" of

change (Magnusson, 1988; Petersen, 1987; Petersen & Taylor, 1980; Stattin & Magnusson, 1990); and

4. The period of early adolescence is one of continual change and transition; however, when these multiple changes occur simultaneously (e.g., when menarche occurs at the same time as a school transition), there is a greater risk of problems occurring in the youth's development (e.g., Simmons & Blyth, 1987).

Thus, the breadth and depth of high quality scientific information that is currently and increasingly available about development in early adolescence underscores the diversity and dynamics of this period of life (e.g., see Lerner et al., 1991). Theoretically interesting and socially important changes of this period constitute reasons that the field of adolescence has garnered increasing scientific attention and has engaged the activities of growing numbers of high quality scholars and students (Petersen, 1988). This academic prominence has been reflected, in part, by the growth in the number of articles about adolescence; by the number of journals devoted specifically to this period of life; by the publication of a handbook (Adelson, 1980) and an encyclopedia (Lerner et al., 1991) focused on this developmental period; and by the establishment and rapid growth of a scholarly society concerned specifically with advancing quality scientific study of this period, the Society for Research on Adolescence.

Burgeoning scientific activity devoted to adolescence has occurred synergistically with the recognition by society of the special developmental challenges of this period (e.g., pubertal changes and the emergence of reproductive capacity; the development of self-definition and of roles that will allow youth to become productive and healthy adult members of society). In addition, there has been a recognition by society emerging in concert with the growing scientific database, that the individual differences that occur in adolescent development and the problems youth encounter in meeting the stressors of this period represent a special intellectual and professional challenge. For those who wish not only to understand the nature of adolescence but who also desire to employ this knowledge for enhancing the lives of adolescents, a synthesis of research, policy, and intervention must exist to secure an optimal future for the invaluable human capital represented by a nation's youth.

Research must be conducted with an appreciation of the individual differences in adolescent development, differences that arise as a consequence of diverse people's development in distinct families, communities, and sociocultural settings. In turn, policies and programs must be similarly attuned to the diversity of people and context in order to maximize the chances of meeting the specific needs of particular groups of youth. Such programs and policies must be derived appropriately from research predicated on multidisciplinary integrative models of human development such as developmental contextualism. The evaluation of such applications should provide both societally important information about the success of endeavors aimed at youth enhancement, and theoretically invaluable data about the validity of the synthetic, multilevel processes presumed to characterize human life.

Meeting the challenge represented by the need to merge research with policy and intervention design, delivery, and evaluation will bring the study of early adolescence to the threshold of a new intellectual era. The linkage between research, policy, and intervention I have envisioned will demonstrate to scientists that the basic processes of human behavior are ones involving the development of relations between individually distinct youth and the specific social institutions they encounter in their particular ecological setting (Lerner, 1991). This demonstration will be a matter of bringing data to bear on the validity of a new conception of what constitutes basic process and basic research. Studying changing relations between diverse peoples and contexts becomes the basic analytic frame in investigations of human development. In turn, the evaluation of the programs and policies aimed at changing developmental patterns of youth becomes a theoretically vital activity, providing critical empirical feedback about the conceptual usefulness of the ideas of multilevel integration from which the policies and programs should have been derived.

In other words, policy and program design, delivery, and evaluation are not "second-class citizens" to basic research. Within the frame of the fused levels of organization that comprise human behavior and development when seen from a developmental contextual perspective, policies and programs constitute necessary and basic empirical tests of the core, relational process of life. Accordingly, if we wish to meet the challenge of youth development, the activities of colleagues whose expertise lies in policy and program design, delivery, and evaluation are not to be set apart from basic scientific activity. The expertise of policy and program professionals must be integrated with that of the researcher, in a fully collaborative enterprise, if we are to make continued progress in the understanding and enhancement of youth.

In short, the knowledge generation–application avenue is not a one-way street. Indeed, just as the practicing physician is often a source of issues that medical scientists then address, colleagues in the policy and program delivery arenas—whose roles emphasize the interface with the individual, family, and community—can provide invaluable feedback both about how the fruits of scholarship are being received and used and about new concerns that might be addressed with this scholarship.

In summary, then, the burgeoning high quality scientific activity in the study of adolescence has involved, first, the recognition of the importance of theory and research aimed at elucidating the relations between individually different, developing youth and their diverse and changing contexts; and, second, there has been an appreciation of the necessary linkage among research, policy, and intervention, which must exist for the nature of youth development to be understood and for best meeting the challenges of this period of life.

However, there is a "double-edged sword" within this literature. As scholars have increased their understanding of the centrality of individual differences, of context, and of research-application linkages, an important limitation of the contemporary scientific literature has become apparent. Despite the value of the extant knowledge base about development in early adolescence, most studies in the literature have involved the study of American, White, middle-class samples (Fisher & Brennan, 1992; Hagen, Paul, Gibb, & Wolters, 1990). There are, of course, some prominent, high-quality investigations that have either studied other than White or middle-class American samples (e.g., Brookins, 1991; Reid, 1991; Spencer, 1990, 1991; Spencer & Dornbusch, 1990; Spencer & Markstrom-Adams, 1990), or that have studied adolescents from national or cultural settings other than America (e.g., Magnusson, 1988; Mead, 1928, 1930, 1935; Stattin & Magnusson, 1990; Whiting & Whiting, 1991). Nevertheless, as a consequence of the sampling that has characterized most of the studies in the literature, scientific generalizations about the nature of adolescent development must be tentative. Perhaps more important, policies and interventions formulated on the basis of this information are also limited in important ways.

I illustrate these points by reference to the history of my own field of specialization, developmental psychology. Within this field it is a fair but unfortunate conclusion that neither human diversity nor contextual variation have been adequately appreciated or understood. Indeed, one might infer from reading the pages of the leading research journals in the field (e.g., *Child Development* or *Developmental Psychology*) that to understand development, it is sufficient to study White, middle-class, school-age, American children in almost exclusively laboratory experimental situations (Fisher & Brennan, 1992; Hagen, Paul, Gibb, & Wolters, 1990). In an analysis of randomly sampled articles published in *Child Development* over the course of more than 50 years, Hagen et al. (1990) found that, among studies that reported the demographic characteristics of the children sampled, the majority appraised groups having the characteristics noted previously. However, Hagen et al. (1990) also pointed out that most of the *Child Development* articles in their sample reported neither the race nor the socioeconomic status of the children. Fisher and Brennan's (1992) analysis of this and other developmental journals confirmed the findings of Hagen et al. (1990).

Thus, scholars publishing in the best journals in the field of developmental psychology have generally acted either: (a) As if they were studying the "generic child," a child whose context was of such little importance that even mention of some of its general characteristics (e.g., socioeconomic status) was not necessary; or (b) as if the only demographic information worth mentioning was about the White middle class.

It may be deemed by some as impolite or impolitic to point to this shortcoming. However, such lack of sensitivity to human diversity and contextual variation cannot continue. Obviously, the absence of this sensitivity is morally repugnant to many people. Moreover, such lack of sensitivity is simply bad science. Even before we reach the next century we will be a nation wherein "minority" children constitute the majority of the youth of our country.

The revised understanding of what constitutes the basic process of human development brings to the fore the cutting-edge importance of continued empirical focus on individual differences, on contextual variations, and on changing person–context relations. Nothing short of these emphases can be regarded as involving a scientifically adequate developmental analysis of human life. And nothing short of data involving these emphases should be used for policies and programs suitable for individually different youth developing in relation to their specific contexts. Put simply, policies and programs that are derived from research on acontextualized and homogenized groups of children are too global and too undifferentiated to be of value for today's youth, or for the young people who will populate our nation tomorrow.

Accordingly, the specific challenge that is now before us is at least twofold. First, we must focus our multidisciplinary research efforts on the diverse people and settings, which we must learn about if we are to obtain an adequate understanding of the range of developmental patterns and of the richness and potential of human life. Our research efforts must not involve only the implementation of a synthesis of ideas and methods from multiple disciplines; in addition, this integration must be employed in research with youth from as wide a range of ethnic, racial, family, community, and sociocultural backgrounds as possible. Second, it is clear that such research will not succeed unless the people from within these diverse settings are engaged cooperatively in the endeavor. Thus, such research must be seen as relevant and important by the youth, families, and communities about whom we wish to learn; such research, then, should be seen as returning, or providing, something of value to these groups.

In offering such service, the policies implemented, and programs delivered, by colleagues working within these settings become central. Accordingly, the knowledge and expertise of these professionals are necessary not only for the critical conceptual reasons noted earlier. In addition, collaboration is vital for reasons relating to the practical issues involved in attempting to actually do the research we see as requisite for advancing knowledge of developmental diversity in adolescence.

In summary, then, the challenge in the study and enhancement of development in early adolescence is to integrate both multiple academic disciplines and multiple professional activities that range from research through application. One attempt to begin to meet this challenge is presented in this book.

GOALS OF THE PRESENT VOLUME

The purpose of this book is to move the literature on early adolescence forward in at least two significant respects. First, we bring together a broad group of scholars from such disciplines as behavioral health, child and adolescent development, communications, counselor education, economics, family studies, health education, marketing, nursing, occupational studies, policy, psychology, and sociology to write integratively about cutting-edge research issues pertinent to various facets of the study of early adolescence. All contributors to this volume speak to the idea of interdisciplinary integration as a means of advancing knowledge in select areas of early adolescence; all approach their topic with an orientation toward integrating levels of organization.

Thus, the first purpose of the chapters in this book is neither to discuss all areas of the field (a task that has recently been approached in the encyclopedia edited by Lerner, Petersen, & Brooks-Gunn, 1991) nor to provide state-of-the-art reviews of major portions of the extant literature (an accomplishment recently achieved in the volume edited by Feldman & Elliott, 1990). Rather, the goal is to focus on select areas of study: Those most illustrative of the use of interdisciplinary integration and/or those most likely to advance significantly through the application of an interdisciplinary orientation. The intent is to discuss the literature from the vantage point of the utility of integrating disciplinary knowledge and of the value of integrating such multidisciplinary research and scholarship with policy and intervention.

We believe the latter integration may be the second significant contribution of this book. The youth of a nation are its most important resource; they are, as noted previously, a country's most vital human capital. Today, there are several significant problems involving young adolescents, problems that demand a vigorous commitment of intellectual and financial resources (e.g., see Dryfoos, 1990). Issues such as homelessness among American families, teenage pregnancy and childbearing, unsafe sex and disease transmission, hunger, a weakened educational system, and deteriorating living and economic conditions among people near or below the poverty line are key instances of these pressing societal issues. It is clear that there are problems involving how young adolescents behave: How they eat, or, in fact, whether they do; how they plan for and attempt to actualize their economic, social, and personal goals; how they plan their environments to live enjoyable, efficient, and safe lives; how they relate to each other, both positively and negatively, within families, within communities, and across national boundaries; and whether society's policies and services allow them to attain lives of quality and enrichment, to maintain a life marked by health, spiritual well-being, and financial security, and to develop successfully with dignity and respect.

However, these problems of early adolescence are not clustered in the ways that academic disciplines are divided. To address these problems we must break them down into manageable elements; and here, certainly, disciplinary research is useful. But, with regard to the ideas of interdisciplinary integration previously noted, it is the conviction of the authors of this volume that the elements of the problems *must* be put together in order to deal with the problems adequately as they actually exist in the ecology of human life. It is only through reliance on such an integrated knowledge base that policies and interventions may be adequately formulated and extended into programs and services for the people of our nation. Indeed, as previously argued, such extension provides a test of the validity of the basic theoretical and substantive research, which, in the ideal situation, should form a basis of applied research and extension.

Accordingly, the authors of this volume speak to issues pertinent to building bridges between colleagues in the research and applied professional communities both in order to help formulate better research and application agendas in the service of the youth of our society and because of the theoretical importance of integrating research activities with policy and program design, delivery, and evaluation. In short, this book speaks to the importance of two interrelated kinds of integration for furthering understanding of young adolescents: multidisciplinary and multiprofessional integration. It is useful to discuss how the organization of this book reflects its authors' attempts to address these types of integration.

The Plan of this Book

This volume is divided into seven sections. This introductory chapter presents the purposes of and rationale for the multidisciplinary and multiprofessional integration of concern in this book. Parts I and II of the book focus respectively on two key contexts of adolescents: Adolescents and the family, and adolescents and schools (or educational settings more generally).

Part III, Health Promotion in Early Adolescence, stresses that in order to promote health within this age period, one must foster individual, contextual, physical, mental, and social well-being. Similarly, Part IV, Preventive Interventions in Early Adolescence, integrates existing research on young adolescents with the available literature on prevention with an emphasis on the synthesis of developmental analysis with contextual diversity.

Part V, Adolescents and the Media, explores the impact of media on adolescent behavior and development. The section emphasizes that any generalization about this influence must be tempered by an understanding of the specific contexts within which adolescents interact with the media.

Finally, Part VI focuses on synthesizing research, policy, and programs for youth in contemporary society. The chapters in this section bring us "full circle" in that they emphasize, as does this chapter, that the integration of research, policy, and intervention represents the best chance of enhancing youth development and breaking the cycle of risk, failure, poverty, and disadvantage. In summary, then, across the sections of this volume a variety of topics, perspectives, and professional orientations are used to underscore the common belief that if we are to understand and serve the youth of our society we must integrate our research in innovative ways with policies and programs.

CONCLUSIONS

It is the hope of the authors in this book that the volume will illustrate for our colleagues in the area of early adolescence, specifically, and in the field of human development, more generally, the potential advancement of science and service that may be attained through the two types of integration we discuss. We believe that through integrating concepts and methods from the multiple disciplines whose expertise is targeted at the several levels of organization comprising human life, a better understanding will be reached of the multilevel processes that relate the individually distinct developing person to his or her specific setting. In turn, by integrating the expertise of professionals engaged in research, policy, and intervention, better tests of these theoretical integrations may be attained, and a more adequate data base will be available for the design, delivery, and evaluation of better programs for the enhancement of our nation's only truly invaluable resource, our youth.

In summary, our task is not just to do more or do better. If we are to significantly advance science and service for the youth of our nation, we must engage in new activities. This is the challenge before us as we approach the next century. And this is the path upon which the authors of this volume have embarked.

ACKNOWLEDGMENT

The preparation of this chapter was supported in part by NICHD grant HD23229.

REFERENCES

Adelson, J. (Ed.). (1980). *Handbook of adolescent psychology.* New York: Wiley.

Baltes, P. B. (1987). Theoretical propositions of life-span developmental psychology: On the dynamics between growth and decline. *Developmental Psychology, 23,* 611–626.

Baltes, P. B., Reese, H. W., & Nesselroade, J. R. (1977). *Life-span developmental psychology: Introduction to research methods.* Monterey, CA: Brooks/Cole.

Block, J. (1971). *Lives through time.* Berkeley, CA: Bancroft.

Brookins, G. K. (1991). Socialization of African-American adolescents. In R. M. Lerner, A. C. Petersen, & J. Brooks-Gunn (Eds.), *Encyclopedia of adolescence* (pp. 1072–1076). New York: Garland.

Douvan, E., & Adelson, J. (1966). *The adolescent experience.* New York: Wiley.

Dryfoos, J. G. (1990). *Adolescents at risk: Prevalence and prevention.* New York: Oxford University Press.

Featherman, D. L. (1983). Life-span perspectives in social science research. In P. B. Baltes & O. G. Brim, Jr. (Eds.), *Life-span development and behavior,* (Vol. 5, pp. 1–57). New York: Academic Press.

Feldman, S., & Elliott, G. (Eds.). (1990). *At the threshold: The developing adolescent.* Cambridge, MA: Harvard University Press.

Fisher, C. B., & Brennan, M. (1992). Application and ethics in developmental psychology. In D. L. Featherman, R. M. Lerner, & M. Perlmutter (Eds.), *Life-span behavior and development* (Vol. 11, pp. 189–219). Hillsdale, NJ: Lawrence Erlbaum Associates.

Hagen, J. W., Paul, B., Gibb, S., & Wolters, C. (1990, March). *Trends in research as reflected by publications in Child Development: 1930–1989.* Paper presented at the Biennial Meeting of the Society for Research on Adolescence, Atlanta.

Lerner, R. M. (1984). *On the nature of human plasticity.* New York: Cambridge University Press.

Lerner, R. M. (1986). *Concepts and theories of human development* (2nd ed.). New York: Random House.

Lerner, R. M. (1987). A life-span perspective for early adolescence. In R. M. Lerner & T. T. Foch (Eds.), *Biological-psychosocial interactions in early adolescence: A life-span perspective* (pp. 9–34). Hillsdale, NJ: Lawrence Erlbaum Associates.

Lerner, R. M. (1988). Early adolescent transitions: The lore and the laws of adolescence. In M. D. Levine & E. R. McAnarney (Eds.), *Early adolescent transitions* (pp. 1–21). Lexington, MA: D. C. Heath.

Lerner, R. M. (1991). Changing organism-context relations as the basic process of development: A developmental-contextual perspective. *Developmental Psychology, 27,* 27–32.

Lerner, R. M., Petersen, A. C., & Brooks-Gunn, J. (Eds.). (1991). *The encyclopedia of adolescence.* New York: Garland.

Lerner, R. M., & Spanier, G. B. (1978). A dynamic international view of child and family development. In R. M. Lerner & G. B. Spanier (Eds.), *Child influences on marital and family interaction: A life-span perspective* (pp. 1–22). New York: Academic Press.

Lerner, R. M., & Spanier, G. B. (1980). *Adolescent development: A life-span perspective.* New York: McGraw-Hill.

Magnusson, D. (1988). *Individual development from an interactional perspective: A longitudinal study.* Hillsdale, NJ: Lawrence Erlbaum Associates.

Mead, M. (1928). *Coming of age in Samoa: A psychological study of primitive youth for Western civilization.* New York: Morrow.

Mead, M. (1930). *Growing up in New Guinea.* New York: Morrow.

Mead, M. (1935). *Sex and temperament in three primitive societies.* New York: Morrow.

Nesselroade, J. R., & Baltes, P. B. (1979). *Longitudinal research in the study of behavior and development.* New York: Academic Press.

Nesselroade, J. R., & Cattell, R. B. (1988). *Handbook of multivariate experimental psychology* (2nd ed.). New York: Plenum.

Offer, D. (1969). *The psychological world of the teenager.* New York: Basic Books.

Petersen, A. C. (1985). Pubertal development as a cause of disturbance: Myths' realities, and unanswered questions. *Genetic Psychology Monographs, 111,* 207–231.

Petersen, A. C. (1987). The nature of biological psychosocial interactions: The sample case of early adolescence. In R. M. Lerner & T. T. Foch (Eds.), *Biological-psychosocial interactions in early adolescence: A life-span perspective* (pp. 35–61). Hillsdale, NJ: Lawrence Erlbaum Associates.

Petersen, A. C. (1988). Adolescent development. In M. R. Rosenzweig (Ed.), *Annual review of psychology* (pp. 583–607). Palo Alto, CA: Annual Reviews.

Petersen, A. C., & Taylor, B. (1980). The biological approach to adolescence: Biological change and psychological adaptation. In J. Adelson (Ed.), *Handbook of adolescent psychology* (pp. 117–155). New York: Wiley.

Reid, P. T. (1991). Black female adolescents, socialization of. In R. M. Lerner, A. C. Petersen, & J. Brooks-Gunn (Eds.), *The encyclopedia of adolescence* (pp. 85–87). New York: Garland.

Schneirla, T. C. (1957). The concept of development in comparative psychology. In D. B. Harris (Ed.), *The concept of development* (pp. 78–108). Minneapolis: University of Minnesota Press.

Simmons, R. G., & Blyth, D. A. (1987). *Moving into adolescence: The impact of pubertal change and school context.* New York: Aldine.

Spencer, M. B. (1990). Parental values transmission: Implications for black child development. In J. B. Stewart & H. Cheatham (Eds.), *Black families: Interdisciplinary perspectives* (pp. 111–130). Atlanta: Transactions.

Spencer, M. B. (1991). Identity, minority development of. In R. M. Lerner, A. C. Petersen, & J. Brooks-Gunn (Eds.), *The encyclopedia of adolescence* (pp. 525–528). New York: Garland.

Spencer, M. B., & Dornbusch, S. (1990). Challenges in studying minority adolescents. In S. Feldman & G. Elliott (Eds.), *At the threshold: The developing adolescent* (pp. 123–146). Cambridge, MA: Harvard University Press.

Spencer, M. B., & Markstrom-Adams, C. (1990). Identity processes among racial and ethnic minority children in America. *Child Development, 61,* 290–310.

Stattin, H., & Magnusson, D. (1990). *Pubertal maturation in female development.* Hillsdale, NJ: Lawrence Erlbaum Associates.

Tobach, E. (1981). Evolutionary aspects of the activity of the organism and its development. In R. M. Lerner & N. A. Busch-Rossnagel (Eds.), *Individuals as producers of their development: A life-span perspective* (pp. 37–68). New York: Academic Press.

Tobach, E., & Greenberg, G. (1984). The significance of T. C. Schneirla's contribution to the concept of levels of integration. In G. Greenberg & E. Tobach (Eds.), *Behavioral evolution and integrative levels* (pp. 1–7). Hillsdale, NJ: Lawrence Erlbaum Associates.

Whiting, B. B., & Whiting, J. W. M. (1991). Preindustrial world, adolescence in. In R. M. Lerner, A. C. Petersen, & J. Brooks-Gunn (Eds.), *Encyclopedia of adolescence* (pp. 814–829). New York: Garland.

I | Adolescents and the Family

Section Editors:

Kevin W. Allison
The Pennsylvania State University

Richard M. Lerner
Michigan State University

Integrating Research, Policy, and Programs for Adolescents and Their Families

Kevin W. Allison
The Pennsylvania State University

Richard M. Lerner
Michigan State University

Adolescence, universally, is a period of marked biological change (Katchadourian, 1977). In many western countries, and particularly in the United States, there is evidence that this period also involves transitions in numerous individual processes (e.g., involving emotions, cognitions, and morals) and in social relationships (e.g., involving peers and the family (Brooks-Gunn & Petersen, 1983; Hamburg, 1974; Lerner & Foch, 1987). Continuities, however, are inextricably commingled with these alterations in individual and social characteristics (Lerner, 1987).

A key case in point occurs in regard to the family. During childhood the family is the major institution for the socialization of the growing person. Research findings (derived primarily from studies of middle-class, White populations in the United States) indicate both constancy and change during adolescence (Belsky, Lerner, & Spanier, 1984). For most youth, the quality of the parent–child relationships existing during the childhood years is maintained during the adolescent years, and core parental values (e.g., about the importance of education) tend to be adopted by their adolescent children (Bandura, 1964; Douvan & Adelson, 1966; Lerner & Knapp, 1975; Offer, 1969). In turn, however, there are changes (i.e., decreases) in the amount of time spent with parents during adolescence; and the salience of peers and the time and emotion invested in peer relationships increases substantially during this period (e.g., Brittain, 1963; Kandel & Lesser, 1972). Nevertheless, existing research evidence suggests that adolescents choose peers who possess values akin to those of the adolescent's own parents (e.g., Douvan & Adelson, 1966).

These generalizations about the nature and the continuity–discontinuity of the role of the family in adolescence are limited, however, by the lacunae existing in the extant research base. As noted earlier, most studies have been conducted in the United States; have focused on White, middle-class populations; and have defined "success" in development by the norms of these populations. These studies have as well explicitly or implicitly defined a *family* as a structural unit involving an intact marriage and as a functional entity wherein the primary socialization of youth occurs. However, great cultural and intracultural variation in the structure and function of families exist (e.g., Kreppner & Lerner, 1989). It is simply the case that research has not attended adequately to this diversity (cf. Magnusson, 1988).

Such limitations of the research literature have implications that extend beyond science. These limitations impose problems for application as well. Policies and programs derived from such research cannot be optimally suited to meet the needs of adolescents living in the array of distinct settings that may be labeled as familial ones.

For instance, presently within the United States there is considerable variation in the living arrangements within which one finds adolescents. Adolescents are not always (or perhaps even modally) found in intact families; indeed, they may not even reside with a representative of their family of origin. Adolescents may be found in a range of informally to formally organized nonfamily-of-origin settings. For example, they may be runaways living on the streets of urban centers; they may live in commune-like settings; or they may reside in foster homes or larger institutional settings. In addition, of course, adolescents may launch their own families, either in the case of teenage childbearing and/or of teenage marriage (see chapters 3 and 4, this volume). Unfortunately, however, the extant demographic database does not provide information about the proportion of U.S. adolescents found in these different contexts. Policy and program planning cannot be done adequately in the absence of information about the range and scope of this diversity.

Complicating these issues is the possibility that there is fluidity (intraindividual changes) across adolescents' lives in the types of family-like structures within which they live. For example, the divorce rate in the United States would result in many youth spending at least a portion of their adolescence in other than an intact family. Given the presence of such changes, we need to generate a developmental demography of adolescence in order to chart the course of the fluid contexts within which youth reside.

Still further complexity is introduced into the study of the adolescent and the family when one begins to consider the diversity of the functional roles of family-like structures. In the United States, for instance, consumer functions are clustered within the family, but general educational and vocational training functions tend to occur in nonfamilial institutions (e.g., schools). In addition, community organizations (e.g., 4-H) function to inculcate leadership and civic responsibility among adolescents. Such role division has not been true of the U.S. setting across history (Parke, 1978), and may not reflect the functional "duties" of the family as they exist in different cultural and intracultural settings (Brooks-Gunn & Furstenberg, 1989). Again, however, there is not a sufficient developmental or demographic research base to describe adequately functions that families perform for particular children across their adolescence. How can policies and programs be planned and targeted appropriately when the functions of families in contemporary society are not completely understood?

In summary, there is insufficient information about the interindividual and intraindividual variation in structural and functional features of adolescent–family relations. Although obtaining such information would provide substance to the claim of considerable plasticity in these relations (Lerner, 1988), and would possibly uncover the variability in the meaning of "success," the absence of this knowledge means that neither researchers nor interventionists can make informed statements or recommendations about how to capitalize on such plasticity to enhance the relations between adolescents and their families.

The presence of potential plasticity, and the existence of transitions in life, mean that the person and the system of relations he or she has with the context are malleable targets of change (Birkel, Lerner, & Smyer, 1989; Lerner, 1984). One way of representing the changing linkage between the developing adolescent, his or her family, and the broader "ecology of human development" (Bronfenbrenner, 1979) is shown in Fig. 1. This figure presents a developmental contextual (Lerner, 1986; Lerner & Kauffman, 1985) model of adolescent-context relations, one wherein the bidirectional arrows linking the components of the model represent relationships in the adolescent development literature specified, theoretically and/or empirically, to be involved in the changes constituting this period of life. The figure underscores both the complexity of adolescent-context relationships and the interpenetration of the levels of organization which comprise this changing system.

However, it must be stressed that a system that is open to change can be altered for better or worse (Ford, 1987); and there are certainly numerous indices of the fact that adolescents and the relations they have with their families are "at risk" for a host of undesired changes. On the

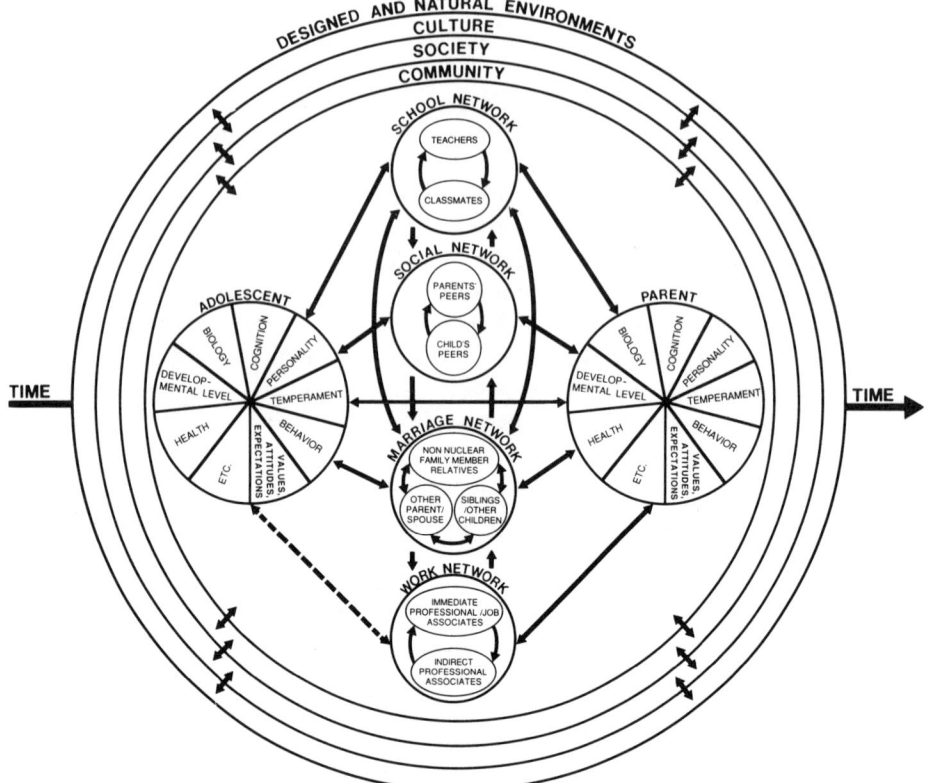

FIG. 1. A developmental contextual model of adolescent-context relations.

other hand, there are both case studies, and some more systematically gathered data as well, that indicate that far from all adolescents who are at risk actualize a negative outcome (e.g., Chess & Thomas, 1984; Werner & Smith, 1982). There are, in other words, several "success stories" in the study of adolescent–family relationships. However, unless the developmental and demographic databases are expanded adequately, we will not have descriptive information sufficient to capitalize on the opportunities for positive growth, and for designing policies and programs, suggested by the presence of diversity along the "success–risk actualization" continuum.

An inability to describe the individual and family conditions associated with different "outcomes" of adolescent–family relations means we will be severely limited in our attempts to evaluate the appropriateness of any given intervention program or policy recommendation (Birkel et al., 1989). In addition, we will not be able to determine why adolescents not perceived as at risk may have a negative outcome. Simply, to intervene appropriately and to propose useful policies for enhancing adolescent life and adolescent–family relations we need to know: (a) What sort of family-related program in relation to; (b) what sort of adolescent and family; (c) is most effective for what sort of individual developmental and/or social relationship outcomes during adolescence.

We must develop, then, a differentiated knowledge base—involving the collection of multiwave (i.e., longitudinal) data. This information must be collected on a diverse array of adolescents, in regard to multiple facets of individual functioning and social relationships that are known to be linked to variation along a success–risk actualization continuum. This information must be appraised in relation to a diverse array of family structural and functional forms.

With such knowledge, the fields of scholarship devoted to the study of adolescence will be able to evaluate the adequacy of existing programs and policies regarding youth. With such knowledge, we will be able to appropriately formulate recommendations for the programs and policies needed to enhance the lives of adolescents and their families into the next century.

The precise features of the research program that will be needed to develop the knowledge base for which we call can be understood best in the context of the more detailed review of the existing literature on adolescents and their families. This review begins, in chapter 2 (by Cornwell and Curtis), by describing the demographic characteristics of contemporary adolescents, emphasizing the range of family settings within which U.S. youth reside. Key features of this section highlight: (a) the need to organize this demographic information developmentally, in order to reflect the changes in family contexts within which youth find themselves across the adolescent years; and (b) the diversity of the settings that may be labeled as *family* ones.

This diversity is the focus of the next two chapters of this section, by Allison (chapter 3) and by Allison and Takei (chapter 4). In chapter 3, data pertinent to adolescents, living outside the "mainstream" context of an intact nuclear family, are discussed. This chapter makes it clear that there exist numerous living arrangements (structures) that may function as a "family," that is, there are several different structures that function to promote or challenge healthy adolescent development. In chapter 4 the issue of diversity in adolescent–family relations is discussed. Through a presentation of the cultural contexts of adolescents and their families, the point is made that several distinct family structures may function to enhance (or detract from) the probability of healthy adolescent development.

Family structures and/or functions may serve, then, as means to create or actualize "risks" in adolescent development or, in turn, to protect or buffer the adolescent from the actualization of risk. These roles of the family are a key focus of chapter 5 by Crouter and McHale, which focuses on familial economic factors as a contributor to adolescent adjustment and development. The individual developmental and contextual resources for, and challenges to, coping with life stresses that exist in families in distinct economic circumstances are emphasized in this chapter.

These functions may exist in different family structures, even in those families created by the young person him or herself through teenage childbearing and parenting. The characteristics and impact of families formed by adolescents themselves are the focus in chapter 6, by Crockett. Adolescent childbearing represents both a source of risk for youth and, nevertheless, a setting within which personal and social competence may be developed. Possible policies and interventions are presented that may increase the likelihood of healthy outcomes of adolescent development. Accordingly, chapter 7 by Finkelstein focuses on a key domain of positive outcomes of adolescent–family relationships: the role of reciprocal adolescent–family relationships in promoting or challenging the maintenance and development of mental and physical health.

REFERENCES

Bandura, A. (1964). The stormy decade: Fact or fiction? *Psychology in the School, 1,* 224–231.

Belsky, J., Lerner, R. M., & Spanier, G. B. (1984). *The child in the family.* Reading, MA: Addison-Wesley.

Birkel, R., Lerner, R. M., & Smyer, M. A. (1989). Applied developmental psychology as an implementation of a life-span view of human development. *Journal of Applied Developmental Psychology, 10,* 425–445.

Brittain, C. V. (1963). Adolescent choices and parent–peer cross pressures. *American Sociological Review, 28,* 385–391.

Bronfenbrenner, U. (1979). *The ecology of human development.* Cambridge, MA: Harvard University Press.

Brooks-Gunn, J., & Furstenberg, F. F., Jr. (1989). Adolescent sexual behavior. *American Psychologist, 44,* 249–257.

Brooks-Gunn, J., & Petersen, A. C. (Eds.). (1983). *Girls at puberty: Biological, psychological and social perspectives.* New York: Plenum Press.

Chess, S., & Thomas, A. (1984). *Origins and evolution of behavior disorders: From infancy to early adult life.* New York: Brunner/Mazel.

Douvan, E., & Adelson, J. (1966). *The adolescent experience.* New York: Wiley.

Ford, D. H. (1987). *Humans as self-constructing living systems: A developmental perspective on personality and behavior.* Hillsdale, NJ: Lawrence Erlbaum Associates.

Hamburg, B. (1974). Early adolescence: A specific and stressful stage of the life cycle. In G. Coelho, D. A. Hamburg, & J. E. Adams (Eds.), *Coping and adaptation* (pp. 101–125). New York: Basic Books.

Kandel, D. B., & Lesser, G. S. (1972). *Youth in two worlds*. San Francisco: Jossey-Bass.

Katchadourian, H. (1977). *The biology of adolescence*. San Francisco: Freeman.

Kreppner, K., & Lerner, R. M. (1989). Family systems and life-span development: Issues and perspectives. In K. Kreppner & R. M. Lerner (Eds.), *Family systems and life-span development* (pp. 1–31). Hillsdale, NJ: Lawrence Erlbaum Associates.

Lerner, R. M. (1984). *On the nature of human plasticity*. New York: Cambridge University Press.

Lerner, R. M. (1986). *Concepts and theories of human development* (2nd ed.). New York: Random House.

Lerner, R. M. (1987). A life-span perspective for early adolescence. In R. M. Lerner & T. T. Foch (Eds.), *Biological-psychosocial interactions in early adolescence: A life-span perspective* (pp. 9–34). Hillsdale, NJ: Lawrence Erlbaum Associates.

Lerner, R. M. (1988). Early adolescent transitions: The lore and the laws of adolescence. In M. D. Levine & E. R. McAnarney (Eds.), *Early adolescent transitions* (pp. 1–21). Lexington, MA: Heath.

Lerner, R. M., & Foch, T. T. (1987). Biological-psychosocial interactions in early adolescence: A view of the issues. In R. M. Lerner & T. T. Foch (Eds.), *Biological–psychosocial interactions in early adolescence* (pp. 1–6). Hillsdale, NJ: Lawrence Erlbaum Associates.

Lerner, R. M., & Kauffman, M. B. (1985). The concept of development in contextualism. *Developmental Review, 5,* 309–333.

Lerner, R. M., & Knapp, J. R. (1975). Actual and perceived intrafamilial attitudes of late adolescents and their parents. *Journal of Youth and Adolescence, 4,* 17–36.

Magnusson, D. (1988). Individual development from an interactional perspective: A longitudinal study. Hillsdale, NJ: Lawrence Erlbaum Associates.

Offer, D. (1969). *The psychological world of the teenager*. New York: Basic Books.

Parke, R. D. (1978). Children's home environments: Social and cognitive effects. In I. Altman & J. R. Wohlwill (Eds.), *Children and the environment* (pp. 33–81). New York: Plenum.

Werner, E. E., & Smith, R. S. (1982). *Vulnerable but invincible: A longitudinal study of resilient children and youth*. New York: McGraw-Hill.

2 | The Demographic Context of U.S. Adolescence

Gretchen T. Cornwell
Samuel M. Curtis
The Pennsylvania State University

Recent U.S. Census Bureau figures indicate that in 1990, there were over 34.6 million children ages 10 through 19 in the United States, a slight decline from the 35.2 million estimated for 1986. The number of children ages 10 through 19 is projected to increase to approximately 38 million by the year 2000 (U.S. Bureau of the Census, 1988a; see Table 2.1). Just as adolescents are characterized by individual differences, the demographic contexts in which they live are characterized by diversity. This chapter describes what is known about the more common living arrangements of children in this age group, identifies several trends in family characteristics related to these living arrangements, and suggests directions for future research.[1]

Much of the information presented here is based on data collected as part of the U.S. Bureau of the Census Current Population Survey (CPS) for March 1988. Because the CPS is a survey in which the household is the sampling unit, it does not provide data describing children who are not living in households. Data from the 1980 Decennial Census provide this information.

---

[1] This discussion limits itself to the demography of adolescents' living arrangements and related trends affecting family composition and experiences. It does not describe numerous other issues sometimes addressed by social demographers including parenthood, alcohol and other drug use, education and employment, or teenage mortality, which is particularly problematic among adolescent men.

Table 2.1
U.S. Population: Children Ages 10–19 in 1980, 1986, 1990, and 2000 (in thousands)

Ages	Census 1980	Estimates 1986	Projections 1990	Projections 2000
10–14	18,242	16,564	17,284	19,208
15–19	21,168	18,610	17,381	19,074

Source: U.S. Bureau of the Census (1988a).

LIVING ARRANGEMENTS OF U.S. ADOLESCENTS

The Census Bureau describes three basic types of living arrangements for children: (a) households headed by a related or unrelated adult, (b) households headed by an adolescent, and (c) group quarters. In 1980, over 99% of children ages 10–14 and approximately 93% of children ages 15–19 lived in households. Table 2.2 describes the living arrangements for children ages 10–17 who were living in households in 1988. Excluded from these counts are adolescents ages 18 and 19, as well as adolescents living in households headed by an adolescent (self, spouse, or unrelated person).

The figures in Table 2.2 show that the two-parent household continues to be the family context for a substantial majority of today's adolescents. About 7 out of 10 adolescents who are living in households, live with two parents. Approximately 21% live with their mothers, whereas 3%–4% live with their fathers. Another 3% live with relatives, such as grandparents, with no parent present. Other data indicate that most one-parent households have no other adults living in them (U.S. Bureau of the Census, 1988d).

Table 2.2
Household Living Arrangements of Children Ages 10–17 by Race, 1988

	Total	White	Black	Hispanic
Living with both parents				
10–14	71.8%	77.7%	42.5%	65.7%
15–17	70.8	76.8	38.8	65.0
Living with mother only				
10–14	21.8	16.9	48.1	28.0
15–17	20.9	15.6	49.1	24.4
Living with father only				
10–14	3.0	3.0	3.1	2.3
15–17	3.6	3.9	2.4	2.5
Living with neither parent				
10–14	3.4	2.5	8.3	4.0
15–17	4.5	3.6	8.7	7.7

Source: U.S. Bureau of the Census (1988b).

Black adolescents are more likely to live in mother-only households (48%–49%) than they are to live in two-parent households (39%–43%). On the other hand, over 75% of White adolescents live with both parents and less than 17% live in mother-only households. Hispanic adolescents are in an intermediate position with 65% of Hispanic teenagers living with both parents, whereas 28% of Hispanics ages 10–14 and 24% of those 15–17 live in mother-only households. The percentages of Black, White, and Hispanic adolescents living in father-only households are similar, with this arrangement being relatively rare—fewer than 1 out of 25 teens live with their fathers, regardless of age and ethnicity.

There are ethnic differences in the proportions of teens living in households without their parents. White teens are least likely to live without their parents, with 2.5% of those ages 10–14 and 3.6% of those 15–17 living in such settings. Approximately 8% of Black adolescents live in parent-absent, adult-headed households. About 4% of Hispanics ages 10–14 and almost 9% of those 15–17 live in parent-absent, adult-headed households.

In 1988, over 200,000 households were headed by adolescents ages 15–19 (Table 2.3), with adolescent females accounting for the majority of household heads. Obviously, the transitions to independent household living and parenthood are closely linked. Fifty-three percent of adolescent married-couple households and 90% of adolescent female-headed households included children under the age of 6.

The third type of living arrangement reported by the Census Bureau is termed *group quarters.* Those living in group quarters are categorized as being either "inmates" or "noninmates." Those who are inmates live in mental institutions, other health-care facilities, correctional institutions, and so forth. Noninmates live in (school) dormitories, rooming houses, military housing, and the like. In 1980, less than 1% of children ages 10–14 were recorded as living outside of households. Among those ages 15–19, about 7.5% of males and 6% of females lived in group quarters. Of these teens living in group quarters, most were noninmates. Over

Table 2.3
Households Headed by Adolescents, 1988

	Married-Couple	Female-Headed
Number of households with head ages 15–19	87,000	101,000
Percent of households with head 15–19 with children under age 6	53%	87%

Source: U.S. Bureau of the Census (1988c).

50% of the males and almost all of the females lived in dormitories. Military housing represented the next largest category of group living arrangements for men. About 5% of men ages 15–19 who were living in group quarters lived in correctional institutions (or 4 of every 1,000 men in this age category).

SIGNIFICANT CHANGES IN FAMILY CHARACTERISTICS

As the preceding section indicates, the family continues to be the primary context in which the U.S. adolescent develops. This family exists in many forms, experiencing and responding to change over time. This section describes several trends in family structure and experience that have pronounced implications for adolescents. The description is statistically based and individual adolescents and their families will differ in their responses to these forces. Among the many changes experienced by the U.S. family in recent decades, four trends are particularly significant for those concerned with the well-being of children and adolescents, including the increase in (a) single-parent households, (b) adolescents' share of childbearing, (c) children and adolescents in poverty, and (d) child-care needs.

Single-Parent Households. The first trend to be addressed is the increase in single-parent households, most of which are headed by women. In 1970, 87% of family groups with children included two parents; however, by 1988 the proportion had declined to 73% (U.S. Bureau of the Census, 1989a). Whether or not living in a single-parent household has negative consequences depends on a variety of factors including the presence of other adults, economic resources, parental background characteristics, and duration and timing of the experience (Bumpass, 1984; McLanahan, 1985; McLanahan & Bumpass, 1988). However, children growing up in single-parent and step-families have been found to be less likely to complete school, even when social and economic background variables are controlled for (Astone & McLanahan, 1989). There is also evidence that women who have had experience living in female-headed households as teenagers are more likely to become single female household heads themselves (McLanahan, 1985).

It is important that we recognize that most studies of single-parent households are cross-sectional and understate the probability that children will at some point experience living in a single-parent household. Based on retrospective histories, Bumpass and Sweet (1989) estimated that more than 4 out of 10 children will spend some time living in a single-parent household before reaching the age of 16. However, Bumpass and Sweet also pointed out the substantial increase in cohabitation among mothers, with approximately one out of four nonmarital births involving cohabiting couples.

It is also important to recognize that fathers not residing in households may have significant contact with their children. Mott (1990) reported that approximately one third of children between the ages of 3 and 7 who were not living with their fathers in 1986, saw their fathers at least once a week.

Adolescent Childbearing. The increase in single-parent households is, in part, associated with the increase in divorce occurring during recent decades (Hernandez, 1988). However, a significant share of the current prominence of mother-headed families is associated with adolescent childbearing: A growing proportion of young women who are giving birth are not married, resulting in single-parent families. This has implications not only for today's adolescents, but also for their children. In 1988, there were over 320,000 births to unmarried teenage women (see Table 2.4). Almost two out of three births to teenagers were premarital, with some population groups experiencing particularly high rates. In 1988, 90% of births to Black teenagers were premarital.

The visibility of adolescent childbearing is increasing, in part, because as fertility drops overall, a higher proportion of all births are first births. Thus, even though rates of adolescent childbearing have decreased, they have not declined as much as overall rates of childbearing. The children born to these women, part of the cohort of tomorrow's adolescents, begin life disadvantaged in multiple ways. Although many of these women will marry eventually, their children are unlikely to grow up with both biological parents. Furstenberg, Levine, and Brooks-Gunn (1990) followed a sample of pregnant adolescents for 20 years, reporting that just one third of the women were married 17 years later and only one sixth were wed to their first child's father.

Women who bear children as teenagers are disproportionately likely to be from low-income families and to be dependent on welfare (Hayes, 1987). They have lower levels of educational aspirations and academic achievement than their non-childbearing counterparts, and this influ-

Table 2.4
Births to Adolescents, 1988

	Under 15	*15–19*
Number of births to women	10,588	478,353
Number of births to unmarried women	9,907	312,499
Number of births to men	376	110,685

Source: National Center for Health Statistics (1990).

ences their life chances. Children born to these mothers are more likely to experience school failure and to have other psychological and social problems, compared to children born to older mothers (Furstenberg et al., 1990). These negative outcomes are not inevitable, as evidenced by recent research demonstrating substantial gains in high school graduation rates among adolescent mothers (Upchurch & McCarthy, 1989).

Poverty Among Adolescents. A third trend involves the increasing proportions of children living in poverty. In 1988, approximately 20% of children ages 6–11 and 16% of children ages 12–17 lived in households having incomes below the poverty line ($12,091 for a family of four). Approximately 6% of married-couple families with children were poor, compared to 42% of female-headed families with children (U.S. Bureau of the Census, 1989b). A child living in a female-headed family is seven times as likely to be poor than is a child living in a two-parent family.

Overall, poverty is experienced most by children living in non-White female-headed families, families that were often initiated while the mother was an adolescent (see Table 2.5). Eleven percent of Black and 16.5% of Hispanic married-couple families with children had incomes below the poverty level in 1988, compared to 53% and 56% of comparable female-headed families.

The age of the household head is also related to family income. As pointed out in *The Forgotten Half* (1988), "More than one of every four young families and sub-families lives below the poverty line. Among those headed by a person under age 25, over one-third live below the poverty line" (p. 22).

Existing data sets do not cover some of the most problematic poor adolescents: Those who are homeless. Children in mother-headed families are particularly vulnerable, as indicated by the finding that four out of five adults living in homeless families are single women with children (Interagency Council on the Homeless, 1990). However, homeless children may live outside any family unit. Adolescent children living on their own are likely to be undercounted as many homeless shelters will not accept minors who are unaccompanied by an adult. These children

Table 2.5
Poverty Status of Children Ages 6–17 by Race, 1988

Ages	Total	White	Black	Hispanic
6–11	19.9%	14.8%	44.8%	37.1%
12–17	16.3	11.6	38.0	32.2

Source: U.S. Bureau of the Census (1989b).

are typically referred to a shelter for "runaways." A recent GAO report that focuses on the special problems of homeless children and youths estimates that between 52,000 and 170,000 unaccompanied youths, ages 12 to 18, could be indentified as homeless in any 1 day (United States General Accounting Office, 1989).

Associated with the poverty status of homeless children are hunger and lack of medical care (U.S. House of Representatives, Select Committee on Children, Youth, and Families, 1986). Children in poverty are much more likely to fall behind in school and the longer the poverty condition exists, the more pervasive the school performance lag. Between 43% and 85% of homeless children living in shelters are estimated to attend school (United States General Accounting Office, 1989). Another survey of 104 shelters for the homeless reported that 34% of their school-age youth were denied an education (Center for Law and Education, 1987). Homeless children are also more likely to have health and behavioral problems and to have experienced child abuse (Interagency Council on the Homeless, 1990).

Child Care. The fourth significant issue discussed here relates to changes in child-care patterns as related to women's labor force participation. In 1988, 63% of both parents in married-couple-with-children families worked, an increase from about 53% in 1980. Women with children who are single-parent household heads are equally as likely to be in the labor force—62% in 1988 (U.S. Bureau of the Census, 1981, 1989c). These women are more likely to need the income generated through regular employment, but family demands and personal characteristics make it less likely that the income earned will be adequate to keep their families out of poverty. Furthermore, although maternal labor force activity has positive implications for the economic welfare of adolescents living in mother-headed households, it may have negative implications for other dimensions of children's well-being. In the Grant Foundation report on *The Forgotten Half* (1988) it is estimated that 2.4 million children ages 5–13 are regularly unsupervised during some part of each day.

CONCLUSIONS

The data described here provide an image of the contexts in which U.S. adolescents develop and function. Although the majority of adolescents continue to live in two-parent households, a substantial minority experience a wide diversity of living arrangements. Little is known about stability and change in these arrangements, how living arrangement transitions are linked to and interact with other transitions, or how these transitions interface with other facets of adolescents' psychological and social experiences and development.

The authors noted several major changes experienced by the family in recent years, including increases in single-parent families, in adolescents' share of childbearing, in child poverty, and in child-care needs related to women's labor force activity. Some of the potentially negative consequences of these changes have been identified. However, these consequences are not experienced uniformly, and many adolescents do not appear to experience negative consequences. To date, research has not adequately addressed the question of why these factors appear to impact some adolescents but not others.

In part, this is because cross-sectional studies have been the major sources of data. For example, the research by Bumpuss and Sweet (1989) cited earlier suggests the extent to which cross-sectional studies tend to understate change, limiting our understanding of family dynamics. Knowing that many more children will at some time live in a single-parent household, than do at any one point in time, greatly expands the population of adolescents for whom research on alternative family forms is relevant. Living in a single-parent household has implications not just for the child during the period he or she lives in this context, but also influences other transitions having long-term consequences. This can be illustrated through the research described earlier that found that children living in one-parent families are less likely to complete school (Astone & McLanahan, 1989). A high school education is a prerequisite not only for further formal education, but also for other types of occupational training programs. Dropping out before completing high school severely constrains economic opportunities, with associated far-reaching implications over the life course.

Although numerous researchers have expressed similar concerns, data limitations have constrained progress in addressing these issues. We suggest several promising avenues of research that could begin to fill these gaps in our knowledge base. The first of these involves using existing cross-sectional data sets more creatively. For example, U.S. Census data lend themselves to the analysis of repeated cross-sections. By looking at trends over time and the manner in which indicators vary with these trends, valuable insights can be gained that point the direction for new data collection efforts. The National Survey of Families and Households (NSFH) is one such recently completed study (Sweet, Bumpass, & Call, 1988). The NSFH focuses on families and households, attempting to collect information that will allow researchers to better understand the structure, functioning, and variability in U.S. family life. Although it is cross-sectional, a great deal of retrospective information is collected and a 5-year follow-up survey is anticipated.

A second avenue to an expanded understanding of process is employing prospective, longitudinal studies. Data sets such as the Youth Panel of the National Longitudinal Surveys (NLSY) are well-suited for research that focuses on the individual, rather than the family, as the unit of analysis. The NLSY is particularly appropriate for looking at adolescents as they make the transition to young adulthood (Center for Human Resource Research, 1987).

Until now the discussion of adolescent-related research has proceeded as if the family is the only contextual unit to be considered, yet a large fraction of adolescent- and family-focused public policies and programs reach their targets via the community and its institutions. This is the very premise of most interventions. Ignoring the community context in which individuals and families act can severely limit understanding. A third approach to enhancing research models involves the incorporation of relevant community and/or other contextual indicators that may directly or indirectly affect the behavior of interest. For example, in the study of the relationship between school completion and family structure that was discussed earlier, the investigators found that the overall dropout rate in the adolescent's school had an effect on school completion, independent of family structure and several other background variables (Astone & McLanahan, 1989). Other influential contextual factors range from peer interactions and norms to educational institutions, residential location, community labor markets, and economic structure. Appropriate analyses that consider contextual effects are becoming more frequent as researchers increasingly merge existing data sets with newly created ones that include community and other contextual indicators.

Finally, the knowledge base can benefit by integrating qualitative with quantitative research, asking qualitative research to help define the research agenda and provide insights into process. Social demographers are increasingly using focus group techniques for these purposes. Focus groups not only allow the researcher to assess individual perceptions, but also to learn from observing interaction within the group.[2] Basically, cross-disciplinary research efforts that combine the strengths of qualitative with quantitative research, using existing data creatively, and supplementing these data through innovative new projects are needed.

REFERENCES

Astone, N., & McLanahan, S. (1989). *The effects of family structure on school completion* (CDE Working Paper 89–6). Madison: University of Wisconsin, Center for Demography and Ecology.

---

[2]A recommended source is Morgan (1988).

Bumpass, L. (1984). Children and marital disruption: A replication and update. *Demography, 21,* 71–82.
Bumpass, L., & Sweet, J. (1989). *Children's experience in single-parent families: Implications of cohabitation and marital transitions* (NSFH Working Paper No. 3). Madison: University of Wisconsin, Center for Demography and Ecology.
Center for Human Resource Research. (1987). *NLS handbook 1987: The National Longitudinal Surveys of labor market experience.* Madison: University of Wisconsin, Center for Human Research.
Center for Law and Education. (1987). *Education problems of homeless children.* Washington, DC: Author.
The forgotten half: Pathways to success for America's youth and young families. (1988). Washington, DC: Youth and America's Future: The William T. Grant Commission on Work, Family and Citizenship.
Furstenberg, F., Levine, J., & Brooks-Gunn, J. (1990). The children of teenage mothers: Patterns of early childbearing in two generations. *Family Planning Perspectives, 22,* 54–64.
Hayes, C. (1987). *Risking the future: Adolescent sexuality, pregnancy and childbearing* (Vol. 1). Washington, DC: National Academy Press.
Hernandez, D. J. (1988). Demographic trends and the living arrangements of children. In E. M. Hetherington & J. D. Arasteh (Eds.), *Impact of divorce, single parenting, and stepparenting on children* (pp. 3–22). Hillsdale, NJ: Lawrence Erlbaum Associates.
Interagency Council on the Homeless. (1990). *The 1990 annual report of the Interagency Council on the Homeless.* Washington, DC: Author.
McLanahan, S. (1985). *Family structure and dependency: Reproducing the female-headed family* (CDE Working Paper 85-23). Madison: University of Wisconsin, Center for Demography and Ecology.
McLanahan, S., & Bumpass, L. (1988). Intergenerational consequences of family disruption. *American Journal of Sociology, 94,* 130–152.
Morgan, D. L. (1988). *Focus groups as qualitative research.* Newbury Park, CA: Sage.
Mott, F. L. (1990). When is a father really gone? Paternal–child contact in father-absent homes. *Demography, 27,* 499–517.
National Center for Health Statistics. (1990, August). *Monthly vital statistics report* (Vol. 39). Washington, DC: Author.
Sweet, J., Bumpass, L., & Call, V. (1988). *The design and content of the National Survey of Families and Households* (NSFH Working Paper No. 1). Madison: University of Wisconsin: Center for Demography and Ecology.
Upchurch, D., & McCarthy, J. (1989). Adolescent childbearing and high school completion in the 1980s: Have things changed? *Family planning perspectives, 21,* 199–208.
U.S. Bureau of the Census. (1981). *Current population reports* (Series P-20, No. 366). Washington, DC: Author.
U.S. Bureau of the Census. (1988a). *Current population reports* (Series P-25, No. 1017). Washington, DC: Author.
U.S. Bureau of the Census. (1988b). *Current population reports* (Series P-20, No. 423). Washington, DC: Author.
U.S. Bureau of the Census. (1988c). *Current population reports* (Series P-20, No. 424). Washington, DC: Author.
U.S. Bureau of the Census. (1988d). *Current population reports* (Series P-20, No. 433). Washington, DC: Author.
U.S. Bureau of the Census. (1989a). *Current population reports* (Series P-23, No. 162). Washington, DC: Author.
U.S. Bureau of the Census. (1989b). *Current population reports* (Series P-60, No. 166, 1989). Washington, DC: Author.

U.S. Bureau of the Census. (1989c). *Current population reports* (Series P-20, No. 437). Washington, DC: Author.
United States General Accounting Office. (1989). *Children and youths—About 68,000 homeless and 186,000 in shared housing at any given time.* Washington, DC: Author.
U.S. House of Representatives. (1986). *Report of Select Committee on Children, Youth, and Families.* Washington, DC: Author.

3 | Adolescents Living in "Nonfamily" and Alternative Settings

Kevin W. Allison
The Pennsylvania State University

The changing context of family life in the United States has brought about a period of challenge for youth; a challenge underlined by evolutions in values, social structures, opportunities, and risks (Conger, 1988). However, when research examines adolescents and their families, an important sector of this age group is most often omitted because these adolescents cannot be located within more traditional family structures (i.e., living with one or both biological or adoptive parents). This missing group includes youth who (a) leave or are removed from their families of origin and are cared for *in loco parentis* by private, state, or other governmental agencies (i.e., psychiatric hospitals, residential treatment facilities, juvenile detention facilities, group homes, foster care, etc.); and (b) those youth who create their own "family" resources independent of their families of origin (e.g., runaways and adolescents living on the streets, including adolescent prostitutes).

Although adolescents who runaway or are in alternative care placements can be viewed as without "real" families, and therefore reasonably omitted from the discussion of adolescent family contexts, this argument severely restricts the conceptualization of family, and the range of contexts available to assist in our understanding of family. Many of these adolescents live in "substitute" families (i.e., foster care families) or have continuing fluid relationships with their families of origin and return intermittently to these families. In addition, these adolescents face a similar range of developmental challenges as do youth in more traditional families, and the social resources marshalled in these traditional homes may be created, re-created, substituted, or potentially lacking for adolescents in alternative living situations. Examining these developmental contexts affords a broader understanding of and alternative perspectives on family functions and adolescent development in those contexts.

These preliminary considerations raise a number of questions relevant to adolescents within both traditional and nontraditional settings. These include: What are the structural and functional components of the family context that are crucial during adolescence? Are these structural and functional aspects found or effectively created by adolescents who do not live with their families of origin? What occurs when adolescents are unable to create these components outside of the family? Do early adolescents seek and/or do societal agents place these youth in alternative care because specific functional components are not present in the family of origin? Although our current research base provides limited answers to these questions, this chapter explores theoretical and research perspectives on the development of early adolescents who live outside the traditional family context.

ADOLESCENTS IN NONFAMILIAL COMMUNITY SETTINGS

Although the vast majority of children are socialized and cared for within one of the many structural variations of a family setting, there are children and adolescents who, because of family dysfunction, including parental physical or mental illness, abandonment, physical and substance abuse (Timberlake, Cutler, & Strobino, 1980), parental death, or the range and intensity of an exceptional child's developmental requirements, live outside a family context. In recognition of and response to these children's need for housing, local, state, and federal agencies have created a series of care institutions for these children and youth—a group recently estimated to number at more than 250,000 (Children's Defense Fund, 1988). At present, these services are most frequently organized as either foster care placements (i.e., where the child lives with a surrogate parent or parents), or group homes (usually a house or cottage arrangement whose staff provides care for a small number of children) within the local community. These accommodations may last one night (e.g., in response to a crisis such as a fire or eviction), or until the child reaches adult status (e.g., in cases where the child has not been adopted or returned to the family of origin). The number of adolescents in foster care has been increasing, associated with larger numbers of children growing up within this care system, the general decrease in social and familial resources, an increase in parents placing troubling children into foster care during adolescence, and diversion of status offenders into child welfare programs (Kadushin, 1980). These services, however, are often fragmented and inconsistent (Fanshel & Shinn, 1978; Hochstadt & Harwicke, 1985). Care may be particularly unstable for adolescents, based on findings that youth entering foster care after age 11 may be at higher risk for multiple placements, and that as the number of these changes increase, placement options tend to become more restrictive (Proch & Taber, 1987). Research has also found that youth who have more severe behavior problems, who have substance-abusing parents, and who were young when first placed into alternative care were more likely to experience multiple moves (Cooper, Peterson, & Meier, 1987). In addition, variables such as the frequency and positive quality of familial contacts have been found to be predictive of shorter stays in foster care (Milner, 1987).

Descriptions of children and adolescents placed in foster care have indicated that they have behavior problems in excess of the general population, and that these problems are more severe in older children and adolescents (Hochstadt, Jaudes, Zimo, & Schacter, 1987). However, reports from foster parents indicate that the majority of adolescents (approximately 75%) function well within their family contexts. Timberlake and Verdieck (1987) proposed that the problems experienced by adolescents in foster families are usually defensive behaviors that serve to distance these youth from the families and protect them from rejection.

In preliminary work by Gil and Bogart (1982), the perspectives of children and adolescents in foster care and group homes have been examined. Although the two groups differed in age and gender composition (i.e., there were more males and older children living in group homes), children in foster homes reported feeling safer, and liking their current placement more often than children in group home care. A related finding from a group home that switched from an 8-hour shift staffing model to the use of an in-house married couple, evidenced positive changes in youth and staff satisfaction, and the adolescents' social skills (Schneider, Kinlow, Galloway, & Ferro, 1982). In examining alternatives to traditional out-of-home placement, interventions such as intensive family therapy, day treatment, or independent living programs have led to shorter stays in placement and less restrictive placements (Rosenthal & Glass, 1986). Relative to examining foster care as a developmental context, Fanshel, Finch, and Grundy's (1989) study of the Casey Family program is one of the few examples of research examining the life course of children and adolescents in foster care placements. The researchers noted continuity in affective and behavioral functioning from entry into foster care to exit, and suggest that placement disruption may not consistently result in negative outcomes. There is a critical need for expanded work along these lines, specifically examining how development takes place within these alternative living situations.

Although the recent paucity of research on children in foster care is acknowledged (Hochstadt et al., 1987), numerous questions are waiting: (a) How are the various physical, cognitive, and socioemotional changes experienced during early adolescence mediated within these nonfamilial living situations? (b) How are attributions about families of origin and foster families mediated by cognitive development during adolescence? (c) Are outcomes (e.g., perceived quality of foster care relationship, length of time in a foster family, etc.) associated with physical, cognitive, or socioemotional development? Considering the movement of adolescents between placement options, there is also a concern that youth learn to manipulate these systems in response to immediate experiences, which might be at the expense of interpersonal and other developmental needs.

ADOLESCENTS IN RESIDENTIAL OR INSTITUTIONAL PLACEMENT

When social control agents (i.e., parents or guardians, schools, and/or juvenile authorities) judge that a child or adolescent cannot be contained within the community due to the severity of behavioral problems or need for intensive services unavailable within the community, the adolescent may be placed into a residential or other institutional setting. These would include psychiatric hospitals, residential treatment facilities, and juvenile correctional institutions. A limited amount of research examines the adolescent's development within these contexts or even examines the movement of adolescents between the various nonfamilial placements. Recent evidence suggests that these placement changes may be multiple and frequent. For example, adolescents in residential treatment programs come from a variety of settings immediately prior to admission (e.g., family of origin, group homes and foster care, psychiatric hospitals, etc.) and the majority have a history of multiple out-of-home placements (Wurtle, Wilson, & Prentice-Dunn, 1983).

In describing the youth in these settings, residential treatment staff report that these adolescents are moderately, rather than severely impaired, and that they primarily manifest social skills deficits (Wurtle et al., 1983). Girls in residential treatment are reported to show interpersonal conflicts, aggression, and distrust (Munson & LaPaille, 1984). Among incarcerated female adolescents, there are more negative perceptions of parents, with teenagers specifically indicating that their fathers were more overprotective, overindulgent, rejecting, and negative compared to fathers of a nondelinquent control group (Kroupa, 1988). In general, the level of family disturbance has been historically associated with outcomes of residential placement (Zimmerman, 1990).

Support for examining structural and functional components of families in relation to various noncommunity settings is found in the conceptualization of numerous therapeutic programs designed for adolescents. Theoretical bases of interventions in residential and psychiatric facilities often stress the parallels between their efforts and family functioning. For example, residential programs have conceptualized treatment as a process of "reparenting" of the child (Soth, 1986) or have described the facilities as providing characteristics of families (i.e., providing emotional support, physical care, and teaching values, skills, and behaviors) (Gurry, 1985). In addition, family involvement in treatment (e.g., home visits and family counseling) are associated with successful treatment outcome (Gilliland-Mallo & Judd, 1986). Of note, running away from the treatment facility has been associated with poor outcomes, and adoptees in psychiatric hospitals who were also evaluated to have weaker ties with adults (including their parents), were more likely to run away (Fullerton, Goodrich, & Berman, 1986). These findings suggest a potential link between attachment (to family) and treatment success.

Although, over 50,000 youth are incarcerated annually (with disproportionately high representation of African-American and Hispanic youth), the general efficacy of juvenile correctional facilities in rehabilitating youth has proved widely disappointing. In fact, many institutions are thought to create deviant ecologies where youth may have the opportunity to learn more criminal career skills.

Unfortunately there are multiple problems in adolescent psychiatric, residential treatment, and juvenile justice research. These difficulties include variability in defining and measuring success and contextual variables (and the use of nonvalidated instruments), limited evaluation of postdischarge adjustment, limited predictor (e.g., intake community risk factors, behavior baseline) and outcome variables, few or no control group studies, poor in-program tracking, and intervention efforts of limited intensity (Pfeiffer, 1989; Whittaker, Overstreet, Grasso, Tripodi, & Boylan, 1987). In addition, these research evaluations seldom take into account the need for continued aftercare and transitional services (Irvine, 1988).

ADOLESCENT RUNAWAYS

Although adults in our society most frequently make the decisions as to minors' living contexts, when children and adolescents perceive that families and/or the institutions created by traditional mental health, educational, and juvenile justice systems have failed them, many leave these settings and are counted among the estimated 733,000 to 1.5 million youth who runaway each year (Children Defense Fund, 1988; Nye & Edelbrock, 1980). Although many of these youth return home after a few hours or an overnight stay, 30% do not return home within a week, and may continue to remain on the streets, staying at youth shelters, with family friends, or in small groups of similarly situated peers. Analysis of Health and Human Service Bureau data from October 1985 to June 1988 indicates that 44,274 homeless and runaway youth were served at federally funded shelters for youth (U.S. General Accounting Office [GAO], 1989). About 21% of these youth were classified by shelter staff as homeless (i.e., a minor who does not have a place of shelter with available adult supervision). According to the GAO report based on these findings, 65% of runaway youth are female. In contrast to 71% of youth ages 10–17, only 66% of runaway youth lived with two parents before coming to a shelter. Only 16% of homeless youth went to a shelter more than 50 miles from their homes. Runaway youth (75%) report primary problems with parents or another adult in the home as the reason for leaving. Other reasons for leaving home (in order of decreasing frequency) were other personal problems (12%), family crisis (6%), and juvenile justice involvement (4%). These results parallel previous findings that suggest that adolescents most often report leaving home because of family problems, conflict, and abuse. However, reasons for running away range from seeking adventure and excitement to escaping problems at school, and may differ between genders. For example, access to resources from boyfriends, overly restrictive environments, or conflicts over unplanned pregnancies may be associated with female adolescents' decisions to leave, whereas males may more often run away from detached, rejecting families (Adams & Munro, 1979; Young, Godfrey, Matthews, & Adams, 1983). That these youth often identify conflict with their parents is positively associated with their perception of their parents as less warm, less supportive, and less restrictive than the parents of nonrunaways (Englander, 1984). These parents are also reported to be less nurturant, more rejecting, and more demanding of conformity (Brennan, Huizinga, & Elliot, 1978). In a study of 47 runaways matched to controls for gender, age, and race, runaways reported their parents to be more punitive and less supportive, although overall they did not report their parents to be higher in controlling behaviors (Wolk & Brandon, 1977).

According to Englander (1984), runaways as a group are described as impulsive, and perceive themselves as higher in socially undesirable and self-oriented traits. Research has also characterized youth who run away as having poorer self-concepts (Wolk & Brandon, 1977), and significant psychiatric needs (Schaffer & Canton, 1984). However, the vast majority of those investigations on runaway youth are correlational, and it is impossible to ascertain whether differences are antecedents or consequences of the behavior causing youths to run away. Limited data suggests that adopted youth are more likely to run away than are those living with both biological parents (Kunfeldt & Nimmo, 1987), that runaways are from large or single-parent families, and that when youth are in families where all other siblings are of the opposite gender, they are more likely to run (Johnson & Peck, 1978). In addition, adolescents who have been the targets of family abuse appear to engage more frequently in escape rather than aggressive behaviors when compared to their siblings and nonabuse adjudicated youthful offenders (Guiterres & Reich, 1981). In a study of child welfare and juvenile records in Arizona, Bolton, Reich, and Guiterres (1977) found children identified by the state child welfare agency due to neglect or physical, sexual, or emotional abuse to have higher rates of "escape" offenses (i.e., changes of runaway, truancy, or missing juvenile) than their siblings. In addition, these abused youth showed lower rates of "aggressive" offenses (offenses such as disturbing the peace, assault, assault with a deadly weapon, armed robbery, etc.) than their siblings. The National Statistical Survey on Runaway Youth (Opinion Research Corporation, 1978) reported that homes of runaways more often provide poor supervision, limited parental assistance with schoolwork or talking about problems, and limited emotional support. Parents of runaway youth are described as showing less "empathetic understanding"; that is, fathers in these families overtly describe these adolescents as "bad and worthless" (Spillane-Grieco, 1984). In addition, in a sample of 144 adolescent runaways who entered shelters in Toronto, 73% of females and 38% of males reported a history of sexual abuse. In females, the abuse was associated with the report of delinquent and criminal activity; in males, a history of sexual abuse was associated with higher rates of suicidal feelings (McCormack, Janus, & Burgess, 1986).

Classification of Runaways

The literature also indicated that there are important distinctions to be made within the population of youths who run away. Kunfeldt and Nimmo (1987), in a study of 489 runaways who were interviewed on the street in Calgary, Canada, classified youth as either *runners* or *in and outers*. Runners tended to leave home without the intention of returning and their absences from the home are of longer duration. Runners report having experienced more physical and sexual abuse (Kunfeldt & Nimmo, 1987). Of these youngsters, 52% had been away from home 2 or more months and 71% had been recruited for illegal activity. In contrast, 51% of in and outers had been on the street for 2 or less weeks and appeared to use running as a means of temporary coping. Of this group, 58% were female, whereas runners were equally male and female. In Kunfeldt and Nimmo's sample, over 50% of runners were from "substitute" (i.e., child welfare care) situations.

An alternative classification of these youth has proposed subgroups identified as: *runaways, throwaways* (also called *castaways* or *pushouts*) and *societal rejects* (i.e., those youth who have no support from peers, family, educational, or social service agencies) (Adams, Gulotta, & Clancy, 1985). Runaways indicated leaving home because of perceived conflict with parents, alienation, or poor social relationships. This group tended to be young (72% were between 11 and 15) and most (85%) had run away more than one time. In contrast, throwaways indicated that they had been encouraged or asked to leave home. These youth were somewhat older (79% were 15–17) and 67% had left home more than once. The third group, societal rejects, were also identified, but so small in number ($n = 2$) that they were not examined further. Adolescents in all three groups frequently indicate family conflict as a reason for leaving home, although throwaways more often perceived their parents wanting them to leave and reported more stress in their interpersonal relationships with their parents.

The severity of family conflict has also been used as a conceptual format identifying adolescents who ran for social pleasure or exploration, those who ran to manipulate the relationship with their parents, those who escape briefly because of conflict, and those who have chronic and severe family problems often characterized by physical or sexual abuse (Roberts, 1982).

Whether an adolescent has run away more than once also seems to be an important dimension in understanding this behavior. *Repeaters* have been characterized as having more severe disturbance (as a group) than nonrepeaters. Difficulties identified in one population of recidivists included more concrete thinking, lower general intelligence, higher risk for delinquent (acting-out) behavior or psychosis (Speck, Gunther, & Helton, 1988). In 12-year, follow-up interviews of 14 adults who had been runaways as youth, Olsen, Ligbow, Mannio, and Shore (1980) found repeaters, in comparison to their siblings, had more court contacts, reported higher job dissatisfaction, and lower job status. The authors reported that repeaters had:

> turbulent and painful relationships in childhood which intensified in adolescence and into adulthood. Today they continue to feel more

pressured by their parents and discouraged by what they have become and how things have turned out. . . . In contrast those who ran away only once appeared to be essentially indistinguishable from their non-runaway counterparts. . . . Sadly for the repeaters, painful and often violent confrontations with parents have had a paradoxical outcome: Those children who yearned most desperately for freedom and independence and ran away repeatedly from their families appear today to be the least free and the most dependent. (p. 185)

Prospective research has also indicated that repeaters (ages 14–15) show higher levels of alcohol and drug abuse at 4-year follow-up as compared to one-time runners and adolescents who never run away (Windle, 1989).

Adjustment Issues for Runaways

Once on their own, these youth appear to develop "street welfare" networks consisting of illegal activities and "helpful friends" (shades of Fagin's den). Functions of these networks may not be dissimilar to those found within juvenile gangs (e.g., providing social and financial resources, allowing for identity contexts and reinforcement, etc.). The illegal activities in which runaways become involved, as suggested earlier, often include drug involvement, encompassing both use and sales, and prostitution. The latter is supported by findings that both male and female adolescent prostitutes are often runaways (Fisher, Weisberg, & Marotta, 1982). Estimates from the early 1980s indicated that there were approximately 600,000 prostitutes between the ages of 6 and 18 (U.S. Department of Health, Education, and Welfare, 1978). In addition, the family lives of adolescent male prostitutes have been marked by conflict, divorce, alcoholism, physical abuse, low incomes (Allen, 1980; Coombs, 1974; MacNamara, 1965), and higher rates of sexual abuse than the general population (Fisher et al., 1982) or runaways not involved in prostitution. Similarly, female adolescent prostitutes report a variety of negative sexual experiences (including incest, molestation, pregnancy, venereal infections, and abortions) prior to their involvement in prostitution. Male runaways who turn to prostitution may have been thrown out or physically abused in response to the disclosure of their homosexuality. Motivations for hustling among these male teens are varied and thought to involve care-taking needs, male affection, excitement and adventure, and identity development (Maloney, 1980). As a subgroup of runaways, teenage male prostitutes are also perceived to develop peer group "family systems" (Fisher et al., 1982).

Despite their attempts to create adequate social resources, runaways appear to more frequently engage in delinquency, and experience incarceration, or youthful pregnancy than nonrunaways. There is also a growing concern of HIV infection within this adolescent group due to the potential for their entry into prostitution, impulsiveness, and early sexual activity. In comparisons with nonrunaway controls, youth sampled from an urban shelter showed higher rates of risk factors related to HIV infection (Yates, MacKenzie, Pennbridge, & Cohen, 1988). Thirty-four percent indicated a history of intravenous (IV) drug use and 26% admitted to prostitution.

In addition, depression is cited as a problem by 61% of youth in shelters, 20% reported problems with drugs and alcohol, and 20% indicated problems with the juvenile justice system. In Schaffer and Canton's (1984) study of youth in New York City shelters, 24% of the shelter residents indicated at least one suicide attempt during their lifetime, an incidence that is greater than that of 10%–12% for psychiatric outpatients. In addition, 82% of these youth scored above the clinical cutoff for serious psychiatric impairment on the Achenbach Child Behavior Checklist.

Although there is ample evidence of problems associated with running away, there is limited knowledge about the resolution of these experiences for adolescents and their families. The GAO (1989) estimates that about one third of adolescents return to their homes, another third move into institutional arrangements, such as foster care homes. However, the remaining third move into situations that appear to offer little stability, such as living with a friend, in a runaway/crisis house, on the street, or in situations unknown to shelter personnel.

The enactment of The Runaway and Homeless Youth Act (RHYA) in 1974 began recent legislative efforts to address the problems of homeless youth. This legislation established a nationwide system of community-based shelters and coordinated services for runaway and homeless youth. Further national efforts such as the Independent Living Programs for Youth in Foster Care established in 1986 and the Transitional Living Grant Program for Homeless Youth, enacted in 1988, supported the development of independent living programs for youth aging out of foster care programs. Despite this legislative activity, runaway and homeless youth continue to be a sector of the adolescent population for whom current policy and programming shows limited effectiveness. This suggests that continued attention to research, and action research in particular, is warranted.

Although recent research has examined causes, descriptions, precipitating events, and the responses of youths' and families, studies have not tended to examine the dynamic interactive quality of adolescents' exchanges with their families. Running away occurs within a family, community, and broader social system. It is therefore more appropriate to conclude that the family and the adolescent are "at risk" (Young et al., 1983). Although research efforts have been further hampered by the transient nature of this population and the resulting difficulty in gaining access to these adolescents in a standard or unbiased fashion, there is a continuing need for understanding the structural and functional social contexts that these youth create on the streets and in shelters. Research can help to clarify whether these resources significantly differ from those available to youth in traditional families. In addition, exploring these differences may suggest potential strategies for runaway youth and their families of origin.

CONCLUSIONS

In considering research on the range and variety of nonfamilial placements, several issues become salient. Adolescents may move between multiple living situations. A family structure is required to adapt as its members enter and exit the system (i.e., families are dynamic). Across the adolescent years, the role that the family plays for the youth may change. Youth may be able to receive or exchange necessary social resources from various places (i.e., outside the traditional family). Therefore, in creating a research base that can address adolescents within their family context, investigators must examine the social and community context of the family and its functional counterparts across time and the span of adolescence. In acknowledging the diversity within foster families, residential treatment programs, and different group homes, and the variability of demands and challenges presented by each individual adolescent, the current research base does not provide much information in identifying the most effective placements for adolescents and their families. We have limited information relative to how adolescents may be selectively chosen for one type of placement versus another. For example, Cohen, Parmalee, Irwin, and Weisz (1990) indicated that there were few differences in measures of emotional and behavioral functioning between adolescents, ages 12–15, placed in a psychiatric as opposed to a corrections facility. In fact, the only placement predictor between these groups was race, with Black adolescents being more likely to be placed in a juvenile facility. Other questions that require further examination include: Does the limited stability of developmental contexts for these youth affect general socioemotional and/or cognitive development? What are the long-term trajectories of adolescents who have had unstable or varied types of placement patterns? Answers to these questions are important in developing a knowledge base from which to develop effective and responsive prevention and intervention programs for adolescents and their families. The answers to these questions must also be considered in the context of legislative mandates and directives (e.g., least restrictive environments under PL 94–142, youth independence as supported by programs under the reauthorization of the Runaway and Homeless Youth Act), and the multiple systems (e.g., juvenile justice, child welfare, education, etc.) which must be coordinated to provide optimal services to adolescents and their families.

REFERENCES

Adams, G. R., Gulotta, T., & Clancy, M. A. (1985). Homeless adolescents: A descriptive study of similarities and differences between runaways and throwaways. *Adolescence, 20*(79), 715–724.

Adams, G. R., & Munro, G. (1979). Portrait of the North American runaway: A critical review. *Journal of Youth and Adolescence, 8,* 359–373.

Allen, D. M. (1980). Young male prostitutes: A psychosocial study. *Archives of Sexual Behavior, 9,* 399–426.

Bolton, F. G., Reich, J. W., & Guiterres, S. E. (1977). Delinquency patterns in maltreated children and siblings. *Victimology, 2,* 349–357.

Brennan, T., Huizinga, D., & Elliot, D. S. (1978). *The social psychology of runaways.* Lexington, MA: D.C. Heath.

Children's Defense Fund. (1988). *A children's defense budget FY 1989: An analysis of our nations investment in children.* Washington, DC: Author.

Cohen, R., Parmelee, D., Irwin, L., & Weisz, J. (1990). Characteristics of children and adolescents in a psychiatric hospital and a corrections facility. *Journal of the American Academy of Child and Adolescents Psychiatry, 29*(6), 909–913.

Conger, J. J. (1988). Hostages to fortune: Youth, values and the public interest. *American Psychologist, 43*(4), 291–300.

Coombs, N. R. (1974). Male prostitution: A psychosocial view of behavior. *American Journal of Orthopsychiatry, 44,* 782–789.

Cooper, C., Peterson, N., & Meier, J. (1987). Variables associated with disrupted placement in a select sample of abused and neglected children. *Child Abuse and Neglect, 11*(1), 75–86.

Englander, S. W. (1984). Some self-reported correlates of runaway behavior in adolescent females. *Journal of Consulting and Clinical Psychology, 52,* 484–485.

Fanshel, D., Finch, S., & Grundy, J. (1989). Foster children in life-course perspective: The Casey Family Program experience. *Child Welfare, 68*(5), 467–478.

Fanshel, D., & Shinn, E. B. (1978). *Children in foster care: A longitudinal analysis.* New York: Columbia University Press.

Fisher, B., Weisberg, D. K., & Marotta, T. (1982). *Report on adolescent male prostitution.* San Francisco, CA: Urban and Rural Systems Associates.

Fullerton, C. S., Goodrich, W., & Berman, L. B. (1986). Adoption predicts psychiatric treatment resistances in hospitalized adolescents. *Jornal of the American Academy of Child Psychiatry, 25*(4), 542–551.

Gil, E., & Bogart, K. (1982). An exploratory study of self-esteem and quality of care of 100 children in foster care. *Children and Youth Services Review, 4*(4), 351–363.

Gilliland-Mallo, D., & Judd, P. (1986). The effectiveness of residential care facilities for adolescent boys. *Adolescence, 21*(82), 311–321.

Guiterres, S. E., & Reich, J. W. (1981). A developmental perspective on runaway behavior: Its relationship to child abuse. *Child Welfare*, 89–94.
Gurry, S. E. (1985). Severely disturbed adolescents in community care. *Adolescence*, *20*(78), 65–79.
Hochstadt, N. J., & Harwicke, N. J. (1985). How effective is the multidisciplinary approach: A follow-up study. *Child Abuse and Neglect*, *9*, 365–372.
Hochstadt, N. J., Jaudes, P. K., Zimo, D. A., & Schacter, J. (1987). The medical and psychosocial needs of children entering foster care. *Child Abuse and Neglect*, *11*(1), 53–62.
Irvine, J. (1988). Aftercare services. Special Issue: Independent-living services for at-risk adolescents. *Child Welfare*, *67*(6), 587–594.
Johnson, N. S., & Peck, R. (1978). Sibship composition and the adolescent runaway phenomena. *Adolescence*, *7*, 301–306.
Juvenile Justice and Delinquency Prevention Act: Runaway and Homeless Youth. (1983). Washington, DC: U.S. Government Printing Office.
Kadushin, A. (1980). *Child welfare services: Sourcebook network*. New York: MacMillan.
Kroupa, S. E. (1988). Perceived parental acceptance and female juvenile delinquency. *Adolescence*, *23*(89), 171–185.
Kunfeldt, K., & Nimmo, M. (1987). Youth on the streets: Abuse and neglect in the eighties. *Child Abuse and Neglect*, *11*(4), 531–543.
MacNamara, D. E. J. (1965). Male prostitution in an American city: A pathological or socio-economic phenomena? *American Journal of Orthopsychiatry*, *35*, 204.
Maloney, P. (1980). *Street hustling: Growing up gay*. Unpublished manuscript.
McCormack, A., Janus, M. D., & Burgess, A. W. (1986). Runaway youths and sexual victimization: Gender differences in an adolescent runaway population. *Child Abuse and Neglect*, *10*(3), 387–395.
Milner, J. (1987). An ecological perspective on duration of foster care. *Child Welfare*, *66*(2), 113–123.
Munson, R. F., & LaPaille, K. (1984). Personality tests as a predictor of success in a residential treatment center. *Adolescence*, *19*(75), 697–701.
Nye, F. I., & Edelbrock, C. (1980). Some social characteristics of runaways. *Journal of Family Issues*, *1*, 147–150.
Olsen, L., Ligbow, E., Mannio, F. V., & Shore, M. F. (1980). Runaway children twelve years later. *Journal of Family Issues*, *1*(2), 165–188.
Opinion Research Corporation. (1978). *National statistical survey on runaway youth*. Princeton, NJ: Author.
Pfeiffer, S. I. (1989). Follow-up of children and adolescents treated in psychiatric facilities: A methodology review. *The Psychiatric Hospital*, *20*(1), 15–20.
Proch, K., & Taber, M. (1987). Alienated adolescents in foster care. *Social Work Research and Abstracts*, *23*(2), 9–13.
Roberts, A. (1982). Adolescent runaways in suburbia: A new typology. *Adolescence*, *17*(66), 387–396.
Rosenthal, J., & Glass, G. (1986). Impacts of alternatives to out of home placement: A quasi-experimental study. *Children and Youth Services Review*, *8*(4), 305–321.
Schaffer, D., & Canton, D. (1984). *Runaway and homeless youth in New York City: A report on the Ittleson Foundation*. New York: The Ittleson Foundation.
Schneider, K., Kinlow, M. R., Galloway, A. N., & Ferro, D. L. (1982). An analysis of the effects of implementing the Teacher-Family Model in two community-based group homes. *Child Care Quarterly*, *11*(4), 298–311.
Soth, N. (1986). Reparenting and deparenting as a paradigm for psychiatric residential treatment. *Child Care Quarterly*, *15*(2), 110–121.
Speck, N., Gunther, D., & Helton, J. (1988). Runaways: Who will runaway again? *Adolescence*, *23*, 881–888.

Spillane-Grieco, E. (1984). Characteristics of a helpful relationship: A study of empathetic understanding and positive regard between runaways and their parents. *Adolescence, 19*(73), 63–75.

Timberlake, E. M., Cutler, J., & Strobino, J. (1980). *A study of the children in foster care in one county department of social services.* Washington, DC: National Catholic School of Social Services.

Timberlake, E. M., & Verdieck, M. J. (1987). Psychosocial functioning of adolescents in foster care. *Social Casework, 68*(4), 214–222.

U.S. Department of Health, Education, and Welfare. (1978). *Juvenile prostitution: A federal strategy for combating its causes and consequences.* Washington, DC: U.S. Government Printing Office.

United States General Accounting Office. (1989). *Homeless: Homeless and runaway youth receiving services at federally funded shelters.* Washington, DC: Author.

Whittaker, J. K., Overstreet, E. J., Grasso, A., Tripodi, T., & Boylan, F. (1987). Multiple indicators of success in residential youth care and treatment. *American Journal of Orthopsychiatry, 58*(1), 143–147.

Windle, M. (1989). Substance use and abuse among adolescent runaways: A four-year follow-up study. *Journal of Youth and Adolescence, 18*(4), 331–344.

Wolk, S., & Brandon, J. (1977). Runaway adolescents' perceptions of parents and self. *Adolescence, 12,* 175–188.

Wurtle, S. K., Wilson, D. R., & Prentice-Dunn, S. (1983). Characteristics of children in residential treatment programs: Findings and clinical implications. *Journal of Clinical Child Psychology, 12*(2), 137–144.

Yates, G., MacKenzie, R., Pennbridge, J., & Cohen, E. (1988). Risk profile comparison of runaway and non-runaway youth. *American Journal of Public Health, 78*(37), 820–821.

Young, R. L., Godfrey, W., Matthews, B., & Adams (1983). Runaways: A review of negative consequences. *Family Relations, 32,* 275–281.

Zimmerman, D. P. (1990). Notes on the history of adolescent inpatient and residential treatment. *Adolescence, 25*(97), 9–38.

4 Diversity: The Cultural Contexts of Adolescents and Their Families

Kevin W. Allison
Yoshi Takei
The Pennsylvania State University

There is an increasing awareness and acknowledgment that development during early adolescence is a period characterized by multiple pathways and individual differences (see Lerner, chapter 1, this volume). Unfortunately, at this point in history, there are considerable limitations to the understanding of this "diversity" within early adolescence, due to limitations in the selection of research populations, the historical focus of developmental researchers on ethic dimensions of development and heavy reliance on reductionistic methodology, and biases affecting the interpretive validity of research findings. Focusing on the family as a developmental context, this chapter examines the issues relevant to the study of ecological and cultural variables that may affect development during early adolescence. This includes a review of issues relevant to the study of cultural issues focusing on adolescents and their families, an analysis of available research, and suggestions for new directions in the study of families and adolescents.

CONCEPTUALIZING DIMENSIONS OF CULTURAL DIVERSITY

In examining adolescents and families within our increasingly pluralistic society, there are multiple cultural dimensions to address. Families may be characterized with respect to their racial and ethnic group membership and the sociocultural history of that group, their immigration status and experience, time in residence, and geographical location, both in terms of specific setting (i.e., urban, suburban, rural, etc.) and region. In turn, these different ecological contexts may each be described based on their individual socioeconomic and racial-ethnic composition, and other dimensions such as population density and stability. In an examination of the literature that focuses on issues of development during early adolescence, there has been an inconsistent and limited examination of these variables, and the resulting literature provides a circumscribed analysis of the effect of contextual and cultural factors on adolescent development. Of these variables, race, ethnicity, and socioeconomic status (SES) are the only dimensions that have been examined with some degree of consistency, although McLoyd (1991) indicated that even this examination has been inadequate. There has been a recent increase of interest in sociocultural issues relevant to racially and ethnically diverse families, reminiscent of the late 1960s and early 1970s. These interests will likely become increasingly important as the demographic portrait of the United States includes larger and increasingly diverse numbers of children and adolescents of color (Wetzel, 1987).

In considering the influence of families on the development of adolescents from various ethnic and racial groups, the vast majority of research has focused on the negative outcomes associated with racial-ethnic status, and has not addressed the broad range of potential developmental topics, except to seek support for ethic perspectives on specific stage theories of development (for discussion and examples see Hoffman, 1980; Nisan & Kohlberg, 1982). Such an approach has left unanswered a plethora of research questions about the development of adolescents from diverse racial and ethnic groups. There are few studies examining the individual and interactive impact of varied cultural norms and standards, potential biological influences, the role of minority status, and the historical and interpersonal effects of racism on adolescent development.

One possible strategy for conceptualizing and organizing research questions relevant to racial and ethnic group adolescents is to consider Bronfenbrenner's (1979) framework examining the role of ecology in human development. The four levels of the ecological context outlined in this model include: (a) the microsystem, that is, the "immediate setting containing that person (e.g., home school, workplace, etc.)" (p. 514); (b) the mesosystem, consisting of the interrelations among major settings (e.g., the relationship of the family to the school, and the family to peers, etc.); (c) the exosystem, that is, the institutions in which the adolescent is not directly involved, yet that have an impact on his or her immediate contexts (e.g., school board, parental work environment, local government, etc.); and (d) the macrosystem, the structures that support the cultural attitudes and ideologies of the society. From this perspective, development occurs, for adolescents who are considered as numerical "minorities" in their most immediate contexts, in a distinctly different ecological base than their "majority" counterparts. For example, in considering the homogeneity of contexts (i.e., the extent to which a context or system is similar to the youth in terms of race, ethnicity, or any other relevant cultural variable in the United States), development for the racial-ethnic group adolescent likely takes place in a setting where the youth are exposed to socialization agents and institutions (e.g., schools, churches, the media, peers) that may demand bi-culturality in order to negotiate the demands of those contexts. According to Chimezie (1985):

> bi-culturality is living by two cultures. To live by two cultures is to share the same values, beliefs, tastes, artifacts (material culture), etc., and to be guided by the same norms, and social expectations as prevail in both cultures. The degree of conflict or dissonance experienced by a bi-cultural individual or group is partly a function of the degree of divergence between the two cultures in values, attitudes, beliefs, tastes, etc. (p. 224)

Within each specific racial-ethnic group or subgroup there may be traditional cultural values and ideologies, including different role expectations and sets of family rules, various cultural practices, and means of marking passage into adulthood that differ from the majority context. Groups may also vary in their perspectives on the relevance and timing of developmental tasks and needs. These differences may be expressed at any of the four levels of context.

This analysis has important implications for racial-ethnic adolescents relative to understanding their development in the family context. For example, what are the demands placed on children and adolescents and families in negotiating these contexts? How well are families equipped to provide socialization experiences that would allow their children and adolescents to be enculturated into two sets of values? What is the level of dissonance between cultural contexts? How are the conflicts between these norms and values resolved? What specific skill demands are placed on ethnic minority adolescents by the needs for bi-culturality? Are there developmental costs exacted by these increased developmental demands? Do majority children show an advantage in certain outcomes because they have less to accomplish developmentally than their minority group peers? What are the costs for the adolescent and the family if these skills are not developed? For example, does the pressure on Black adolescents to succeed in academic (i.e., majority) contexts, as well as in minority settings, result in increasing rates of suicidal behavior

(Spaights & Simpson, 1986)? Does this analysis of bi-cultural demands and the need for socialization relevant to these demands explain findings that Black adolescents whose parents emphasized awareness of racial barriers receive higher school grades than children of Black parents that did not stress this awareness (Bowman & Howard, 1985)?

In this discussion one could begin to examine the relevance of traditional developmental constructs for racial- and ethnic-minority groups. For example, Erikson (1968) suggested that the process of identity development for Black adolescents may be altered by the effects of a racist context and these youth may subsequently develop negative identities. In face of the reality that many adolescents successfully develop positive identities, despite racism and a limited range of role models, how do families socialize their children to counter the impact of these negative cultural images?

The interaction of cultural norms and expectations may also be very important in understanding the impact of cultures on outcomes for adolescents. For example, Mussen and Bouterline-Young (1964) found that personality variables associated with physical characteristics (i.e., timing of physical maturation) were different in Italian versus Italian-American adolescents. The authors indicated that cultural attributions transmitted through the parents account for these differences.

In addition to living in a family context that may be seen as culturally distinct from the ecology of the broader society, many adolescents must also consider factors relevant to the level of dissonance between the demands of their bi-cultural contexts. This has often been defined as the level of a family's acculturation. Yates (1987) indicated that for minority group members in U.S. society, adaptive acculturation may be achieved by two methods, assimilation into the dominant culture, or integration. Yates suggested that the most maladaptive response to minority status is rejection of either the original culture (i.e., complete assimilation) or rejection of the dominant culture (i.e., total segregation). However, many research and popular reports on racial-ethnic minority groups tend to gloss over these intragroup differences and associated changes. Effects of acculturation to the United States on family relationships, educational attainment, and other adolescent outcomes are not discussed. Part of the reason for oversimplification in the depiction of Asian-American, African-American, and other racial-ethnic groups is due to this lack of information. For example, whether acculturation promotes educational attainment among Japanese-Americans (Montero & Tsukashima, 1977) or lowers it (Connor, 1975) is inconclusive. It is likely that outcomes relevant to ethnic and racial-group adolescents will not be adequately understood until these processes are more fully examined.

The struggle to explain the effects of assimilation and acculturation may be particularly important for first-generation immigrant families where adolescents develop between the conflicting values of their parents and those of their peer group. Nguyen and Williams (1989), for example, reported that Vietnamese adolescents may be faced with conflicting demands of the two cultures and the inconsistency in their refugee parent's values. These intergenerational issues may vary with socioeconomic level and other variables. Sue and Nakamura (1984), in proposing a conceptual framework for examining the drinking behavior of Japanese-American youth, provided a promising strategy for examining these variables. Subjects' acculturation to U.S. society is assessed through the comparison of the drinking patterns of first-generation, second-generation and third-generation Japanese-American adolescents. This method of inquiry would allow researchers to examine the differences in socialization experiences and practices while holding certain physiological variables constant. This strategy could be extended and modified for use with other populations and other outcome variables. It would also allow the clarification of research findings where similarities are found between racial-ethnic minority adolescents and majority culture peers. For example, McDermott et al. (1983) report few differences between Japanese-American and White U.S. adolescents in examining the perception of authority and responsibility within families. The authors proposed that the experience of adolescence within this largely middle-class sample may be "so powerful in itself that it overrides cultural differences" (p. 1320). Unfortunately, there is limited information provided to assist in the understanding of this proposition, as the authors did not specify whether the families were first generation, or had lived in the United States (Hawaii) for several generations.

In considering dimensions such as bi-culturality, assimilation, and acculturation, it is also necessary to consider the sociopolitical and historical context of racial-ethnic group families in the United States. For example, there has been a recent trend in this country to view the various Asian groups as "model" minorities. This is somewhat ironic because the two Asian nationalities, the Chinese and the Japanese, who were the first Asian immigrants to this country were considered to be such undesirable people, they were singled out by federal law to be ineligible to become naturalized citizens. Since then, the image of Asians in the public eye has changed from inscrutable, inassimilable people, to that of striving, law-abiding folks. This transformation has no doubt been promoted by articles in the popular press that have been publicizing the educational attainment of Asian-American youngsters.

Although well-intended, such articles again tend to ignore Asian groups such as the Vietnamese and other refugees from Southeast Asia who, on the average, have less formal education than U.S. groups and are encountering considerable difficulty earning incomes above the poverty level. Therefore, these reports usually do not take into account the heterogeneity of the Asian population in the United States. The cultural and situational differences among Asian and other racial-ethnic groups require treating them as separate entities in any scholarly discussion. The historical changes in these cultural and situational differences may have considerable effects on the socialization experiences of adolescents in these families.

RESEARCH ON RACIAL-ETHNIC GROUP ADOLESCENTS AND THEIR FAMILIES

Although there are a number of dimensions available to advance the understanding of diverse adolescents and their families, the research base that examines these factors is restricted. There are some studies in which general family variables (usually structural dimensions, such as size, composition, and marital status, or perceptual evaluation of family) have been found important in the study of racial-ethnic group adolescents. When reviewing the recent research on African-American adolescents and their families, most studies tend to examine negative outcomes (e.g., adolescent pregnancy, drug use, suicide) associated with family variables (see Dawkins, 1986; Gibbs & Hines, 1989). Although there is a developing literature relevant to early adolescents in various racial-ethnic groups, the majority of research examining these variables has focused on African-American adolescents. This review focuses primarily on this population and provides a brief overview of relevant research findings and trends.

Among studies examining the role of structural or perceived family influences on ethnic and racial group adolescents, Dembo et al. (1985) reported that alcohol and marijuana use was directly related to adolescents' perceptions of their relationship with their families in a sample of Black and Hispanic youth from moderate- to low-income families. Research has also suggested that only when the family context of Black adolescents closely parallels those of their traditional White middle-class peers (i.e., when both parents were present and father had at least a high school education) did drinking rates of Black adolescents approach those of their White counterparts (Byram & Fly, 1984). Although White adolescents were more likely to be heavy drinkers when one parent was in the home, for Black adolescents, the opposite was true. Research also seems to suggest that family may play a different role for male as opposed to female adolescents in racial-ethnic groups. For females, stronger family bonds were associated with lower drug use (excepting cigarettes); however, these family bonds were not predictive of cigarette or other drug use for Black males (Ensminger, Brown, & Kellam, 1984). Variables implicated in Black males' initiation of smoking included father absence, sibling smoking, and low social expectation (Brunswick & Messeri, 1983–1984). In contrast, for females, family orientation was important in both the initiation of cigarette smoking and illicit drug use.

Although researchers also suggested that families of specific racial-ethnic groups such as African-Americans, may be organized in structures alternative to the American norm (see Cornwell and Curtis, chapter 2, this volume) and may more frequently incorporate the resources of extended family members, there is limited information in general as to how racial-ethnic adolescents and their families may organize their "human resources" across varied ecological contexts and socioeconomic strata, and how these differences may affect adolescent socialization and related outcomes within these families. For example, Kellam, Ensminger, and Turner (1977) indicated that developmental outcomes in Black families may not be linked solely to the incidence of mother–father dyads. These researchers indicated that Black children in mother–grandmother families have similar outcomes to peers in the nuclear family structure. Farnworth's (1984) exploratory within-group study of Black adolescents using a sample with controls for socioeconomic level, age, and region, similarly found very limited effects for family structure on the types of delinquency examined. In contrast, Matsueda and Heimer (1987) reported that the total effect of broken homes on delinquency is greater for Blacks than non-Blacks, due to the attenuation of parental supervision, which subsequently allows for the increase of more delinquent companions. P. P. Coleman (1986) suggested from his interviews with Black male status offenders and their families, that other variables (such as recent migration of the families, and the discrepancy between the parental and child views on the American Dream) are potentially associated with delinquent status. From an ethnographic study of a White and African-American clique in a working-class community, McLeod (1987) reported that the African-American adolescents, unlike the Whites, believed that there were opportunities for them if they tried to be successful. McLeod attributed their optimism and willingness to avoid deviant acts to the fact that their families had more recently moved into the low-income housing than the Whites and were less affected by the cynicism and hopelessness that characterized the residents who had lived there a longer time.

In addition to living within different structural units, there is the potential that the roles appropriate for adolescents within different racial-ethnic and socioeconomic group families may be different. The expectations for an adolescent Mexican male from a migrant or illegally immigrated family to take a role in the financial survival of the family or the urban Black female in her early teens to assume a primary caretaking role for younger siblings may produce educational and developmental outcomes that when viewed out of context, result in misunderstood values, and pejorative interpretations of family priorities and childrearing practices. These interpretations often blame the family or scapegoat the youth without considering the sociocultural context and the limitations within culture of "disadvantage." For example, Looney and Lewis (1983) found that Black adolescents from working-class families were more likely to have part-time jobs and to begin heterosexual activity earlier than a White comparison group from middle and upper SES groups. Despite the confound (which is consistent with the demographic picture of the United States), the findings raise the unanswered questions as to whether there may be developmental role differences between majority and racial-ethnic group or middle- and working-class adolescents. Researchers often do not take into account the variations in adolescent experiences based on these differing economic demands. Access to family resources due to distribution of human resources in face of socioeconomic needs may limit the time Black adolescents have access to parental figures even when they are present in the home (Brown, Childers, Bauman, & Koch, 1990).

These economic considerations may also be important in understanding a variety of developmental issues. Burton (1988), for example, found that the experience of adolescent pregnancy among different groups of African-Americans from varied sociocultural, political, and historical backgrounds may result in the assumption of different roles by the adolescent and other family members dependent on whether the pregnancy is perceived as subgroup norm appropriate. These perceptions, in turn, may be associated with specific community norms associated with SES. Similarly, Marsiglio (1989) found that parental education level may be related to the choices that Black males make relative to outcomes of an unexpected pregnancy. Black males with high parental education may be less likely to prefer living with their child than Black males from families with lower educational attainment. In other research examining early childbearing, lower maternal education, and better family adjustment was associated with adolescent pregnancy among Black teens (Ralph, Lochman, & Thomas, 1984). Other family variables associated with pregnancy in Black teens has included larger family size (Hogan & Kitagawa, 1985), although parental monitoring significantly reduced rates of pregnancy, and lower rates of communication with mother (Freeman, Rickels, Huggins, & Garcia, 1984). In addition, a tendency toward mother-aloneness has been associated with adolescent pregnancy and a number of related negative child outcomes (Kellam, Adams, Brown, & Ensminger, 1982). In considering early childbearing, it is also important to acknowledge that different racial-ethnic groups may have different values and expectations related to this experience, and subsequently may view the experience in significantly different ways (Smith, McGill, & Wait, 1987).

Other researchers have described general similarities across different racial-ethnic groups of adolescents in their organization of family and other social resources. This is illustrated by Coates' (1987) examination of the social networks of middle- to lower middle-class Black adolescents. She found the social resources of these Black teens to be similar to the networks of White adolescents described by Blyth, Hill, and Thiel (1982), except that the networks of Black female early adolescents (ages 12.9–15.5) may be more kin-dominated (e.g., these respondents nominate family members more frequently as a role model than their male counterparts; Coates, 1987). G. W. Peterson, Stivers, and Peters' (1986) report of familial versus nonfamilial influences on occupational decision making, similarly suggests no differences between use of family resources in a sample of rural Black and White adolescents.

On the other hand, some investigators have suggested that the quality and style of family relationships and the balance between family and peer relationships may differ between racial-ethnic groups. For example, in a sample of young women under 20 who made a first visit to family planning clinics, Black mothers were much more likely to be involved in the clinic visit than were White mothers, whereas the friends and boyfriends of the White respondents were more likely to be involved in the visit, than were the peers of Black respondents (Nathanson & Becker, 1986). Parent–adolescent conflict among other ethnic groups, such as Puerto Ricans has been reported as particularly severe when teenage daughters demand greater freedom. Furthermore, tensions between Hispanic parents and their children can be a result of the children becoming Americanized and speaking English, whereas the parents do not. Therefore, differences in level of acculturation to the United States, are thought to be potential sources of conflict between the older and younger generations among Hispanics. In contrast, the literature on Asian-Americans tends to depict their families as being relatively free from generational conflicts (e.g., see Lyman, 1974; W. Peterson, 1971).

Another focus of research among racial-ethnic adolescents has been an examination of success experiences. In a descriptive study of psychosocial variables associated with academic success in 68 rural Black adolescents, Lee (1985) reported that 79% lived with both parents, and that these home environments were characterized as positive, educationally encouraging, and moderate to highly open. Lee (1984) also found degree of family openness and strong family values were related to academic success.

At present, the literature on structural family variables related to developmental outcomes for racial-ethnic group adolescents is inconsistent. Increasing insight on important process variables in the socialization of youth across racial-ethnic groups has considerable potential to increase the understanding of adolescents in their families and communities (for an example, see Jarrett's, 1990, review of socialization practices in low-income African-American, Chicano, Puerto Rican, and White families). Of the few quantitative examinations of culture and family process, recent research by Steinberg, Mounts, Lamborn, and Dornbusch (1991) suggested that authoritative parenting style is associated with higher self-reliance, and lower psychological distress and delinquency among adolescents across ethnic, socioeconomic, and family structure (i.e., intact vs. nonintact) groups. The relationship between authoritative parenting and academic performance, however, did not hold across ethnic groups. The impact of this parenting style was greater for White and Hispanic youths than for African-American or Asian-American adolescents, similar to earlier findings by Dornbusch, Ritter, Liederman, Roberts, and Fraleigh (1987).

Problems with Current Research on Racial-Ethnic Groups

Although the recent increase in research on racial-ethnic group members is important in building a research base, the interest to date has not been without cost. When the literature on racial-ethnic minority groups is examined, it may be historically classified into one of three models:

1. *Inferiority Models:* Research that focuses on differences between groups and explains these difference through a focus on the inherent inferiority of groups members due to genetics or other internal causes;
2. *Deficit Models:* Research that associates group differences to the deficient environments minorities face due to their disadvantages and experience of discrimination; and
3. *Bi-Cultural Models:* Research that examines the variance within groups and acknowledges the relationship between "minority group" members and the larger culture (and are distinct from *cross-cultural models,* which compare group differences through a culturally relative frame; Sue, 1983).

Unfortunately, the majority of research on racial-ethnic minority adolescents and their families has been framed within the inferiority and deficit models (Cheatham & Stewart, 1990). Numerous research studies conducted on the role of males within the Black family are predominantly negative and from a deficit model perspective (Conners, 1988). In addition, research on Black families where the father is present is sparse. Unfortunately, other racial ethnic groups have received similarly flawed research scrutiny. For example, in a study comparing Caucasian and Navajo children in Grades 5–8, Abraham, Christopherson, and Kuehl (1984) reported that Anglo parents are perceived by their children as showing a more supportive parenting style, whereas Navajo parents are characterized by their children as highly protective and punitive. Although the investigators consider that the differences may be based on social class differences (although no such data was available from the study), lower educational levels among the parents of the Navajo children, and cultural differences in parenting, they fail to fully examine the differences in the enculturation experiences between these two groups of children. For example, whereas the White control group was chosen from the same geographical area as the sample of Navajo youth, the Native American children were selected from a Bureau of Indian Affairs (BIA) boarding school that they had attended since the first grade. These students usually return to their homes at the reservation only over the weekend. Although the reported findings are interesting, they are severely limited in "interpretive validity" (Washington & McLoyd, 1982) due to their failure to take into account how the parenting practices found among the Navajo parents might be influenced by the boarding school and reservation experience of their children, the historical impact of the BIA boarding school and reservation systems on socialization practices within the Navajo families, and the effect of socioeconomic and educational factors, in addition to cultural practices, preferences, and values.

In addition to problems of interpretive validity, research on racial-ethnic adolescents and their families is often unidimensional and frequently does not recognize the considerable diversity (culturally, historically, socioeconomically, geographically, etc.) within racial-ethnic communities. To begin a more than superficial list of racial-ethnic minority categories, one would have to include: Native or aboriginal Americans, of which there are over 450 tribal-national groups; African-Americans, Blacks of Hispanic origin, and other Blacks from the Caribbean; Asian-Americans (which includes Chinese-Americans, Japanese-Americans, Southeast Asians, Filipinos, East Indians, and Pacific Islanders); and Hispanics (encompassing Chicano, Puerto Ricans, Cubans, South, Central, and Latin Americans, and Spanish). Despite the considerable differences within more global group classifications, the general tendency of researchers historically is to use the broader categories (i.e., Black, White, Hispanic, Asian-American, and Native American), without clarifying the specific nature of the sample. Racial-ethnic groups, however, are not monolithic entities, and racial-ethnic group adolescents may develop within a number of multiple ecologies (Bell-Scott & Taylor, 1989). The simplified designation of ethnic families results in the tendency for positivistic and reductionistic methodologies to divert focus from within-group variation. Although treating racial-ethnic group samples in this manner might be the most facile tactic for scientists, the resulting literature may be severely limited in population validity, and ultimately in utility.

In addition to the general concerns of the negative impact of research based on various models, and limited focus on within-group variance, there are other research concerns specific to investigations of racial-ethnic group adolescents and their families. The equivalence of the SES of Black and White families, particularly of groups at or below poverty level, is often suspect even when matching occurs. White families with incomes below the poverty level tend to live in nonpoverty census tracts (70%) more often than Black (15%) or Hispanic (20%) families.

The differences in the socioeconomic quality of Black families is further underlined in Malveaux's (1989) examination of data from the U.S. Bureau of the Census, where the role of the working Black mother within the two-parent family may carry increased socioeconomic significance. White families with working mothers have combined incomes just 27% above the average income for all White families; in contrast, Black families with a working mother have income 186% higher than the income level of the average Black family. This discrepancy may be explained in part by the discrepancy between the wages of White and Black males, the higher proportion of female-headed Black households, and the general discrepancy between the wages of men and women. Therefore, similar status on socioeconomic indices may not reflect the same access to cultural and financial resources within a family or community. The problem is further exacerbated by the general confounding of race and ethnicity with SES in the United States.

In their comprehensive review of the studies on Hispanic populations, Moore and Pachon (1985) similarly pointed out that differences among Chicano, Puerto Rican, and Cuban families are confounded by social class and residential variations. So not only do the Puerto Rican adolescents tend to be from families characterized by lower SES, they tend to live in large cities on the east coast, like New York City.

In addition to concerns regarding the comparability of population samples, there is also a need for adolescent research to address the cultural and contextual relevance of outcome measures. It is often not recognized that the meaning of adolescent outcomes such as academic success, physical health, adolescent mortality, and adolescent pregnancy may differ between various family ecologies. For example, survival may be one of the indices of a "successful" outcome of adolescence for males, but it is not clear how and whether deaths associated with drunk driving or suicide among White males in a rural county are different from the violent deaths associated with drug sales among Black males or gang-related violence among Latino males in inner-city communities. Is marriage associated with early childbirth among urban Black teens the same as that found in rural or suburban settings? Do these experiences have the same cultural meanings? Are they comparable?

NEW RESEARCH DIRECTIONS

In order to further extend our general knowledge of families, it is proposed that additional research on racial-ethnic group families be conducted. Focusing on these groups will permit an examination of various theories about culture and context and their impact on development during early adolescence. One of the many theories that has promise in explaining variations among minority groups is social capital. J. S. Coleman (1988) defined *social capital* as consisting of the mutuality of obligations and expectations that bind people together, the capacity among people to share information and the acceptance of norms regulating behavior. This thesis explains variations in how well different racial-ethnic groups have "succeeded" in this country as the extent to which groups value success, are persistent in work, and are willing to defer gratification—characteristics associated with "middle-class" culture (Glazer, 1975). For example, some people have argued that there is considerable overlap between traditional Japanese values and middle-class culture (Caudill & DeVos, 1956). However, Kitano (1976) concluded that the success achieved by Japanese-Americans is due to their having adopted the values, attitudes, and behaviors of the middle class in this country. On the other hand, Connor (1975) suggested that as Japanese-Americans become more assimilated, their academic achievement orientation is lowered as indicated by lower academic achievement among Japanese-Americans with longer family histories of residence in the United States. J. S. Coleman (1988), in addition, presented data that indicates that adolescents with more social capital are less likely to drop out of school than those with less, even after controlling for financial resources and human capital. This thesis would further suggest that where adolescents and families in financially depressed areas have few social ties and the ties that they do have are of "lesser social worth as measured by the social position of their partners, parents, siblings, and best friends," they would have few resources available to help them move out of these areas (Wacquant & Wilson, 1989, pp. 22–23).

Therefore, the social capital thesis suggests that people differ in the amount of social capital at their disposal and this difference partly accounts for the variation in socioeconomic success among people. Defining social capital to mean the resources available to individuals as a consequence of being socially integrated into solidarity groups, networks, or organizations (Bordieu, 1986), we might explore the possibility that Japanese-Americans' success could be related to their tendency to possess a fairly large amount of social capital in the way of family and group solidarity. Observing the relationship between variations in social capital and academic achievement among Japanese-American adolescents is one way to test the validity of the social capital thesis.

While acknowledging that various theories are not necessarily contradictory and, in fact may overlap to a considerable degree, it seems important to undertake studies that attempt to make a distinction between the various theories and collect relevant data in order to determine which theory is most strongly supported by the data. For example, it can be hypothesized that adolescents with greater amounts of social capital (including "family" capital, i.e., transmitting group ethos and values) will be more likely than those with less to adapt more "successfully" to school (e.g., receive higher grades, are more highly integrated into school activities, etc.) and to have friends who also possess similar levels of social capital. When applied to minority group adolescents, varying levels of social capital may be associated with different ethnic or racial group membership and this approach might prove useful in examining variations in school and other "success" among adolescents of different minority groups. This exercise is important in that there is a long-standing debate in the sociological and psychological literature on the question of how much the differences in educational achievement can be attributed to cultural differences. However, caution must be used to avoid deficit or inferiority applications of the social capital conceptualization. Therefore, we must examine who defines the value and meaning of success across different cultural contexts as it relates to social capital. Is social capital directed at the same goals across different family, community, and peer groups? Are there different sets of social capital necessary for bicultural adolescents? Are there limitations on the impact of social capital for certain minority groups (e.g., see Ogbu's, 1981, discussion of minority status)?

Another interesting area for further research is the examination of differences between parent–adolescent relationships among various ethnic and racial groups in the United States. Most of the research that has been conducted to date tends to have focused on older adolescents and, therefore, little is known about parent–child relationships among younger adolescents. A cross-cultural study conducted on U.S. and Danish families by Kandel and Lesser (1972) revealed that U.S. teenagers were more likely to report their relationships with their parents to be conflictual than Danish teenagers. Kandel and Lesser suggested that this is because U.S. parents are more permissive than are Danish parents while the children are young. Therefore, U.S. parents impose more rules to restrict the activities of their adolescents than do Danish parents. The authors suggest that U.S. teenagers are more likely than Danish teenagers to strain against the parental leash and to complain about it. Kandel and Lesser do not mention the racial identification of the American sample. As such, we have to assume that they were almost all Caucasian because one of their sampling objectives was to achieve as close a match as possible with the Danish sample. We believe that a careful study of parent–adolescent relationships among the various groups in the United States is needed at this time so we will have a better idea of the variations in familial contexts within which U.S. youths are maturing.

To illustrate this with an observation, an intriguing difference by race is reported in the survey conducted among high school seniors in 1986. The report, issued by the survey Research Center at the University of Michigan (see Bachman, Johnston, & O'Malley, 1987), shows that White high school seniors were more likely than African-American students to report conflict with their parents. Of the Whites, 49% admitted that they had argued or had a fight with either of their parents five or more times during the last 12 months; in comparison, only 20% of the African-American adolescents reported a similar level of conflict. On the other hand, 30% of the African-American high school seniors stated that they never argued or fought with either of their parents during the past 12 months as compared to only 7% of the White students who could claim to have had little or no conflict with their parents.

Although these findings focus on older adolescents, the research model provides a point of departure for conceptualizing possible studies in early adolescence. For example, this brief review would suggest the need to conduct further research into two areas. One area is to ascertain whether there are variations in the level and frequency of parent–adolescent conflict by race and ethnicity and to discover the reasons for the variations that do exist. Previous research suggests that there are ethnic and racial differences in relationships between parents and early adolescents. It seems important to find out why those differences exist. The second area of research is partially related to the first. This line of inquiry would ask the question: If families differ in the degree to which the relationships between parent and early adolescent is amicable or conflictual, how will this difference affect the attitudes and behaviors of the adolescent child? Furthermore, will the effects differ by race, ethnicity, and/or world view (e.g., Eurocentrism vs. Africentrism)? Will there be apparent differences in these relationships due to generational status (i.e., second- vs. third-generation American)?

In examining conceptualizations such as the social capital thesis, bi-culturality, or familial conflict, researchers can begin to develop adequate norms for specific racial-ethnic groups and research that takes into account historical and other contextually relevant variables. Although reductionistic research strategies have been criticized for their tendency to minimize the diversity of adolescents and their families, there is a need for "normative" information on different racial-ethnic adolescents. However, the information must address within-group variability, and might make use of qualitative data to assist in making broad-based findings more meaningful. Hopefully these investigations can take place with an increased awareness of the limitations of each type of data.

In addition to providing useful information about specific groups of racial-ethnic adolescents and their families, this research may also begin to address common themes in diversity that may be helpful in examining other "cultural" groups of adolescents. This would include adolescents with disabling conditions and Gay and Lesbian youth whose experiences may be related but unique in that they, in addition, to being a minority within the cultural context, are also a minority within their families. Such work is further warranted due to the pressing need to understand stressors and risk factors facing these adolescents (e.g., see Gibson, 1989).

REFERENCES

Abraham, K. G., Christopherson, V. A., & Kuehl, R. O. (1984). Navajo and Anglo childrearing behaviors: A cross-cultural comparison. *Journal of Comparative Family Studies, 15*(3), 373–388.

Bachman, G. G., Johnston, L. D., & O'Malley, P. M. (1987). *Monitoring the future: Questionnaire responses from the nation's high school seniors—1986.* Ann Arbor, MI: Survey Research Center, Institute for Social Research, University of Michigan.

Bell-Scott, P., & Taylor, R. L. (1989). Introduction: The multiple ecologies of Black adolescent development. *Journal of Adolescent Research, 4*(2), 119–124.

Blyth, D. A., Hill, J. P., & Thiel, K. S. (1982). Early adolescents' significant others: Perceived relationships with familial and nonfamilial adults and young people. *Journal of Youth and Adolescence, 11*(6), 425–450.

Bordieu, P. (1986). The forms of capital. In J. G. Richardson (Ed.), *Handbook of theory and research for the sociology of education* (pp. 241–258). New York: Greenwood Press.

Bowman, P. J., & Howard, C. (1985). Race related socialization, motivation, and academic achievement: A study of Black youths in three generation families. *Journal of the American Academy of Child Psychiatry, 24*(2), 134–141.

Bronfenbrenner, U. (1979). *The ecology of human development: Experiments by nature and design.* Hinsdale, IL: Dryden Press.

Brown, J. D., Childers, K. W., Bauman, K. E., & Koch, G. G. (1990). The influence of new media and family structure on young adolescents televisions and radio use. *Communication Research, 17*(1), 65–82.

Brunswick, A. F., & Messeri, P. (1983–1984). Causal factors in onset of adolescents' cigarette smoking: A prospective study of urban Black youth. *Advances in Alcohol and Substance Abuse, 3*(1–2), 35–52.

Burton, L. (1988). *Creating pathways and timetables: The cultural construction of the intergenerational family life course.* Paper presented at the meeting of the American Sociological Association, Atlanta, GA.

Byram, O. W., & Fly, J. W. (1984). Family structure, race, and adolescents' alcohol use: A research note. *American Journal of Alcohol and Drug Abuse, 10*(3), 467–478.

Caudill, W., & G. DeVos, (1956). Achievement, culture and personality: The case of the Japanese Americans. *American Anthropologist, 58,* 1102–1126.

Cheatham, H. E., & Stewart, J. B. (1990). *Black families: Interdisciplinary perspectives.* New Brunswick, NJ: Transition.

Chimezie, A. (1985). Black bi-culturality. *The Western Journal of Black Studies, 9*(4), 224–235.

Coates, D. L. (1987). Gender differences in structure and support characteristics of Black adolescents' social networks. *Sex Roles, 17*(11/12), 667–687.

Connor, J. W. (1975). Changing trends in Japanese American academic achievement. *The Journal of Ethnic Studies, 2,* 95–98.

Conners, M. E. (1988). Teenage fatherhood: Issues confronting young Black males. In J. T. Gibbs (Ed.), *Young, Black and male in America.* Dover, MA: Auburn House.

Coleman, J. S. (1988). Social capital in the creation of human capital. *American Journal of Sociology, 94*(Supplement), s95–s120.

Coleman, P. P. (1986). Separation and autonomy: Issues of adolescents identity formation among the families of Black male status offenders. *American Journal of Social Psychiatry, 6*(1), 43–49.

Dawkins, M. P. (1986). Social correlates of alcohol and other drug use among youthful Blacks in an urban setting. *Journal of Alcohol and Drug Education, 32*(1), 15–28.

Dembo, R., Grandon, G., Taylor, R. W., La Voie, L., Burgos, W., & Schmeidler, J. (1985). The influence of family relationships on marijuana use among a sample of inner-city youths. *Deviant Behavior, 6,* 267–286.

Dornbusch, S., Ritter, P., Liederman, P., Roberts, D., & Fraleigh, M. (1987). The relation of parenting style to adolescent school performance. *Child Development, 58,* 1244–1257.

Ensminger, M. E., Brown, C. H., & Kellam, S. G. (1984). Social control as an explanation of sex differences in substance use among adolescents. *National Institute on Drug Abuse Research Monograph Series, 49,* 296–304.

Erikson, E. (1968). *Identity: Youth and crisis.* New York.

Farnworth, M. (1984). Family structure, family attributes, and delinquency in a sample of low-income, minority males and females. *Journal of Youth and Adolescence, 13*(4), 349–364.

Freeman, E. W., Rickels, K., Huggins, G. R., & Garcia, C. R. (1984). Urban Black adolescents who obtain contraceptive services after their first pregnancy: Psychosocial factors and contraceptive use. *Journal of Adolescent Health Care, 5*(3), 183–190.

Gibbs, J. T., & Hines, A. M. (1989). Factors related to sex differences in suicidal behavior among Black youth: Implications for intervention and research. *Journal of Adolescent Research, 4*(2), 152–172.

Gibson, P. (1989). Gay male and lesbian youth suicide. In ADAMHA, *Report of the Secretary's Task Force on Youth Suicide* (Vol. 3, pp. 110–142). Washington, DC: U.S. Government Printing Office.

Glazer, N. (1975). *Affirmative discrimination.* New York: Basic Books.

Hoffman, M. L. (1980). Moral development in adolescence. In J. Adelson (Ed.), *Handbook of adolescent psychology* (pp. 295–343). New York: Wiley.

Hogan, D. P., & Kitagawa, E. M. (1985). The impact of social status, family structure, and neighborhood on the fertility of Black adolescents. *American Journal of Sociology, 90*(4), 825–855.

Jarrett, R. L. (1990). *A comparative examination of socialization patterns among low-income African-Americans, Chicanos, Puerto Ricans, and Whites: A Review of the ethonographic ethnopsychic literature.* A report to the Social Science Research Council.

Kandel, D. B., & Lesser, G. S. (1972). *Youth in two worlds.* San Francisco: Jossey-Bass.

Kellam, S. G., Adams, R. G., Brown, C. H., & Ensminger, M. E. (1982). The long-term evolution of the family structure of teenage and older mothers. *Journal of Marriage and the Family, 44*(3), 539–554.

Kellam, S. G., Ensminger, M. E., & Turner, J. (1977). Family structure and the mental health of children: Concurrent and longitudinal community-wide studies. *Archives of General Psychiatry, 43*, 1012–1022.

Kitano, H. (1976). *Japanese Americans: The evolution of a subculture.* New York: Prentice-Hall.

Lee, C. C. (1985). Successful rural Black adolescents. *Adolescence, 20*(77), 129–142.

Lee, C. C. (1984). An investigation of psychosocial variables related to academic success for rural Black adolescents. *Journal of Negro Education, 53*(4), 424–434.

Looney, J. G., & Lewis, J. M. (1983). Competent adolescents from different socioeconomic and ethnic contexts. *Adolescent Psychiatry, 11*, 64–74.

Lyman, S. M. (1974). *Chinese Americans.* New York: Random House.

Malveaux, J. (1989). Transitions: The Black male adolescent and the labor market. In R. L. Jones (Ed.), *Black adolescents* (pp. 267–289). Berkeley, CA: Cobb and Henry.

Marsiglio, W. (1989). Adolescent males' pregnancy resolution preferences and family formation intentions: Does family background make a difference for Blacks and Whites? *Journal of Adolescent Research, 4*(2), 214–237.

Matsueda, R. L., & Heimer, K. (1987). Race, family structure, and delinquency: A test of differential association and social control theories. *American Sociological Review, 52*, 826–840.

McDermott, J. F., Robilland, A. B., Char, W. J., Hsu, J., Tseng, W., & Ashton, G. C. (1983). Reexamining the concept of adolescence: Differences between adolescent boys and girls in the context of their families. *American Journal of Psychiatry, 140*(10), 1318–1322.

McLeod, J. (1987). *Ain't no makin' it,* Boulder, CO: Westview Press.

McLoyd, V. C. (1991). What is the study of African American children the study of? In R. Jones (Ed.), *Black psychology* (3rd ed., pp. 419–440). Berkeley, CA: Cobb & Henry.

Montero, D., & Tsukashima, R. (1977). Assimilation and educational achievement: The case of the second generation Japanese American. *Sociological Quarterly, 18*, 490–503.

Moore, J., & Pachon, H. (1985). *Hispanics in the United States*. Englewood Cliffs, NJ: Prentice-Hall.
Mussen, P. H., & Bouterline-Young, H. (1964). Relationships between rate of physical maturing and personality among boys of Italian descent. *Vita Humana, 7,* 186–200.
Nathanson, C. A., & Becker, M. H. (1986). Family and peer influence on obtaining a method of contraception. *Journal of Marriage and the Family, 48,* 513–525.
Nguyen, N. A., & Williams, H. L. (1989). Transition form East to West: Vietnamese adolescents and their parents. *Journal of the American Academy of Child and Adolescent Psychiatry, 28*(4), 505–515.
Nisan, M., & Kohlberg, L. (1982). Universality and variation in moral judgement: A longitudinal and cross-sectional study in Turkey. *Child Development, 53,* 865–876.
Ogbu, J. U. (1981). Black education: A cultural-ecological perspective. In H. P. McAdoo (Ed.), *Black families* (pp. 139–154). Beverly Hills, CA: Sage.
Peterson, G. W., Stivers, M. E., & Peters, D. F. (1986). Family versus nonfamily significant others for the career decisions of low-income youth. *Family Relations, 35,* 417–424.
Peterson, W. (1971). *Japanese Americans*. New York: Random House.
Ralph, N., Lochman, J., & Thomas, T. (1984). Psychosocial characteristics of pregnant and nulliparous adolescents. *Adolescence, 19*(74), 283–294.
Smith, P. B., McGill, L., & Wait, R. B. (1987). Hispanic adolescent conception and contraception profiles: A comparison. *Journal of Adolescent Health Care, 8*(4), 352–355.
Spaights, E., & Simpson, G. (1986). Some unique causes of Black suicide. *Psychology: A Quarterly Journal of Human Behavior, 23*(1), 1–5.
Steinberg, L., Mounts, N. S., Lamborn, S. D., & Dornbusch, S. M. (1991). Authoritative parenting and adolescent adjustment across varied ecological niches. *Journal of Research on Adolescence, 1*(1), 19–36.
Sue, S. (1983). Ethnic minority issues in psychology. *American Psychologist, 38,* 583–592.
Sue, S., & Nakamura, C. Y. (1984). An integrative model of physiological and social/psychological factors in alcohol consumption among Chinese and Japanese Americans. *Journal of Drug Issues, 84*(2), 349–364.
Wacquant, L. J. D., & Wilson, W. J., (1989). The costs of racial and class exclusion in the inner city. *The Annals, 501,* 8–25.
Washington, E. D., & McLoyd, V. (1982). The external validity of research involving American minorities. *Human Development, 25*(5), 324–339.
Wetzel, J. R. (1987). *American youth: A statistical snapshot*. Washington, DC: William T. Grant Foundation Commission on Youth and America's Future.
Yates, A. (1987). Current status and future directions of research on the American Indian child. *American Journal of Psychiatry, 144*(9), 1135–1142.

5 | Familial Economic Circumstances: Implications for Adjustment and Development in Early Adolescence

Ann C. Crouter
Susan M. McHale
The Pennsylvania State University

Developmental trajectories in the early adolescent years are shaped in part by broader societal conditions and events that impinge upon families (Elder, 1974; McLoyd, 1989; Stewart & Healy, 1989). Economic aspects of social change—such as periods of recession or depression or of rapid economic expansion and opportunity, sector-specific decline and expansion (i.e., service and manufacturing jobs), and changing employment opportunities (e.g., for women and minority groups)—are important features of the ecology of family life. These conditions shape options available to parents and may have important effects on their feelings of competence and self-worth, the quality of their marital relationship, and their childrearing practices. Economic conditions also may influence the ways in which adolescents begin to think about their own future economic roles (Flanagan, 1989; Galambos & Silbereisen, 1987). During rapid social change, family processes play an important mediating role, transmitting effects of broader social context change to the developing adolescent via the roles, relationships, and activities that make up daily family life.

This chapter reviews studies of the effects of economic loss and the effects of maternal labor force participation with a focus on the family processes through which young adolescents experience the effects of changing economic circumstances. A common element in these studies is the recognition that youth are influenced by the world outside the family in large part via parents' socialization practices. For example, when economic strains disrupt parenting, adolescents are at greater risk for problems (Elder, Van Nguyen, & Caspi, 1985; Lempers, Clark-Lempers, & Simons, 1989). Similarly, in regard to maternal employment, effects on adolescent offspring depend on the way parents' work affects family roles, relationships, and activities (Crouter & McHale, in press; Hoffman, 1989).

Our emphasis on the processes through which social change influences developing adolescents emerges from the ecological approach to studying human development (Bronfenbrenner, 1979, 1989; Bronfenbrenner & Crouter, 1983). Bronfenbrenner urged adoption of a "person–process–context" model of development, one specifically proposing that contexts influence individual development via the roles, relationships, and activities that take place within them and in interaction with the characteristics the individual brings to the situation.

Two types of family processes deserve consideration. First is the actual behavior that occurs in families. Examples include how family members divide housework; the extent to which parents and children are involved in joint activities; and parental approaches to the discipline, supervision, and monitoring of offspring. Knowing about these facets of family daily life informs us about the mechanisms through which the economic context may affect adolescents. The second aspect of family process has to do with how family members construct, interpret, and evaluate these behavioral patterns. For example, when adolescent children of employed women are given more household chores do they resent or welcome them? We expect that the implications of such family processes will differ depending on the meaning youth ascribe to their experiences.

Adolescents' personal characteristics are another important component of the person–process–context framework. In most research, the adolescent's gender is the only person characteristic considered. Some studies, however, examine other characteristics, including physical attractiveness (Elder et al., 1985) and sensitivity to peer evaluation (Silbereisen, Walper, & Albrecht, 1990). After reviewing the literature on the family processes that mediate the effects of economic circumstances on the development of youth, we focus specifically on the role of person characteristics, speculating about ones that have not been included in previous studies but that deserve greater research attention. In addition, we explore the role of the cultural context of family and economic life because families in different cultural and subcultural environments may react differently to economic strain.

FAMILY PROCESSES AS MEDIATORS OF ECONOMIC STRESS

Parent–Child Interaction Patterns

Elder's (1974) research on the impacts of The Great Depression on children and adolescents clearly illustrates how family processes serve as mediators between social change and the individual. Elder used data derived from a longitudinal study of child and adolescent mental health, involving a sample of children, born in 1920–1921, living in Oakland, California. Because this study was initiated in 1931, it included pre-Depression information on the functioning of these children and, in a more limited way, that of their parents. It also included extensive follow-up data about development into adulthood. In 1935, at the height of The Depression, these boys and girls were well into adolescence. In *Children of the Great Depression* (1974), Elder argued that economic deprivation actually had positive consequences for many youth in the study, especially for boys; they were thrust into responsible roles (e.g., part-time jobs) and were able to make contributions that were appreciated by their parents.

Elder et al. (1985) subsequently delineated some family processes through which economic strain influenced adolescent development. Fathers who experienced significant drops in income tended to become more rejecting, demanding, and exploitative of their children. This negative parenting was associated with negative outcomes for adolescent girls. Girls whose fathers behaved in this way viewed their fathers less positively than did other girls and were judged by clinical raters to be less socially competent, less goal-oriented, moodier, and less self-confident. This study also illustrates the role of person characteristics in moderating the effects of family processes on adolescents in that physical attractiveness insulated girls from negative paternal behavior. Indeed, it was physically unattractive girls who were the most likely targets of fathers' rejecting and domineering behaviors.

Elder et al. (1985) speculated that daughters were more vulnerable because they were less imposing physically than adolescent sons and because economic deprivation accentuated their domestic role in the family. Whereas boys often worked at paid jobs outside the family, girls helped around the house to relieve mothers who themselves often had one or more paid jobs outside the home. Domestic responsibilities brought daughters into the orbit of fathers, giving fathers an accessible and relatively powerless target upon which to vent their frustrations and anger.

In Elder et al.'s study, fathers' parenting behaviors were vulnerable to the effects of economic stress, but mothers' parenting behaviors were not. The investigators attributed this pattern to the fact that fathers generally experienced the brunt of the Depression, via unemployment or underemployment. To the extent that men are more likely than women to derive a sense of identity from their occupation or provider role, job loss puts them at greater psychological risk than women, who may define themselves more in terms of domestic roles (Simons, Whitbeck, Conger, & Melby, 1990).

Indeed, Simons et al., studying a contemporary sample of families attempting to earn a living in a depressed Midwestern farming community, found that financial stress was associated with increased depression in fathers and a tendency for fathers to perceive their children as "difficult to raise." In turn, these reactions were associated with hostile, demanding behavior on the part of fathers. In addition, the more financial strain, the less likely fathers and mothers were to believe that parenting was consequential for child development. The less fathers showed this belief the less likely they were to exhibit positive, constructive parenting. Given the cross-sectional nature of these data, it is not possible to make conclusions about the causal direction of these linkages. Nonetheless, the similarity of these findings to those of Elder and his colleagues is compelling.

A common theme across studies is the difference in how economic stress affects the parental activities of mothers versus fathers. Simons et al. (1990) found that, for mothers, financial strain was an important influence on parenting because it apparently exacerbated marital tensions. Marital difficulties in turn eroded effective parenting, decreasing the likelihood that mothers would respond to their children with warmth and nurturance. As with fathers, financial strain appeared to increase mothers' sense that their children were difficult, a perception in turn linked to mothers' negative, coercive parenting behavior.

It is possible that a very different set of linkages between economic stress and parenting would emerge for mothers and fathers if economic stress was the result of *maternal* unemployment. Unfortunately, studies of maternal unemployment and its links to family processes are nonexistent. Maternal employment and paternal unemployment have traditionally been seen as risk factors for families, reflecting cultural notions about appropriate roles for men and women (e.g., Kanter, 1977).

Like Simons et al. (1990), Lempers et al. (1989) focused on secondary school students in a Midwestern community hard hit by the declining profitability of farming. Lempers et al., however, included "outcome" data on the adolescents in their sample (i.e., adolescent adjustment), allowing them to examine all the linkages connecting financial strain, parenting, and adolescents' psychosocial functioning. This study found that family economic hardship had both direct and indirect effects on adolescent psychological distress (loneliness and depression) and indirect effects on delinquency and drug use. Although economic hardship had a direct effect on adolescent distress, it also reduced parental nurturance and inconsistent discipline, both of which were linked in turn to increased feelings of depression and loneliness for adolescents. Economic hardship had no direct effect on adolescents' reports of delinquent behavior or drug use, nor was there an indirect path via reduced parental nurturance. Instead, delinquency and drug use were indirectly associated with economic hardship via the effect of hardship on inconsistent discipline, a set of linkages that was significant for both girls and boys, although boys in this study were particularly vulnerable.

Conger et al. (1992) provided strong evidence for the links between economic hardship, parenting, and adolescent psychosocial functioning, in a large sample of boys living in the rural Midwest. The study included extraordinarily rich measures of family process. Family members not only reported on their views of family relationships and processes, but also participated together in several structured interaction tasks that were videotaped and subsequently coded. Using structural equation modeling, Conger and his colleagues developed a model in which economic pressure (operationalized to include not only income loss but also debts and instability in work) was seen as influencing parents' moods that in turn were linked to marital conflict and decreased parental nurturance. These processes in turn were related to adolescents' psychosocial adjustment. It is interesting that, in contrast to Elder et al.'s (1985) research on a Depression-era sample, Conger et al. found very similar links between economic pressure, parents' moods, and parenting behavior for both fathers and mothers. Conger et al. offered two possible reasons for the discrepancy. One is that mothers in the 1990s may play a more important role in the economic life of the family than did mothers in the 1930s. In addition, the Conger research team may have benefited from having better measures of parents' emotional states and parenting than were available for Depression-era researchers.

Related Research on Family Interaction Patterns. A variety of studies have examined parent–child interaction without reference to the economic circumstances of families. The association between inconsistent parenting and delinquent behaviors and drug use is consistent with results from a program of research by Patterson and colleagues on clinical samples of school-age and adolescent boys with conduct problems (Dishion, Patterson, & Reid, 1988; Patterson, 1986, 1988; Patterson & Stouthamer-Loeber, 1984). Patterson (1988) proposed a sequence of stages that lead some children to antisocial careers. The sequence begins with poor discipline and monitoring in the home. Patterson (1986) explained that "parents of problem children have been shown to threaten, nag, scold, bluster, and natter, but they seldom follow through on their threats. . . . As the child learns to be more skillfully coercive, he or she becomes more difficult to discipline" (pp. 436–437). The noncompliant child in turn responds poorly to rules and expectations at school, setting the stage for the possibility of academic failure. Problems in school heighten the chances of peer rejection and parent rejection. Indeed, Patterson (1988) explained that, over time, antisocial children are less likely to choose (and be chosen for) extrafamilial activities such as clubs and sports that might provide positive socialization experiences. With peer and parental rejection, children come to feel increasingly incompetent and depressed, mood states that increase the likelihood that they will seek out similar peers, a group that in turn is likely to encourage delinquent behavior and substance abuse.

Patterson's "stages" represent a series of conditional probabilities, rather than a process of inevitable decline. At any point in the progression, change is possible. Indeed, the focus of much of this research has been to intervene in family systems by teaching parents appropriate family management skills and training them to respond to their children firmly and consistently. Whereas these studies have focused on microprocesses within the family (e.g., coercive exchanges), they have also provided clues about the contextual conditions under which parents face particular problems in maintaining appropriate family management practices. In a study of single mothers, for example, Forgatch, Patterson, and Skinner (1985) concluded that such stressors as financial strain, medical problems, and daily hassles contributed to mothers' ability to discipline their children. Thus, if one superimposes the microprocesses captured by coercive parent–child exchanges onto the more general picture of family process, provided by research examining the effects of income or job loss, a more detailed picture emerges of how economic strain may erode parents' effectiveness as family managers.

Patterson and his colleagues have identified parental monitoring (i.e., the extent to which parents track their children's whereabouts and activities) as an important process underlying antisocial behavior (e.g., Patterson & Stouthamer-Loeber, 1984). Early involvement with drugs also has been associated with poor parental monitoring (Dishion et al., 1988). Moreover, in a study underscoring the importance of parental monitoring, Hogan and Kitagawa (1985) found that parents of a random sample of over 1,000 Black adolescent girls in Chicago significantly reduced the likelihood that their daughters became pregnant by carefully supervising who they dated, where they went, and when they returned home.

Although parental monitoring has not been assessed in studies of economic deprivation, it has recently been examined with regard to maternal employment (Crouter, MacDermid, McHale, & Perry-Jenkins, 1990). In the absence of data on family processes in single- and dual-earner families, Bronfenbrenner and Crouter (1982) speculated that the finding from some studies that middle-class sons of employed mothers may perform less well in school (e.g., Gold & Andres, 1978) could be explained by the possibility that boys in dual-earner families receive lower levels of parental monitoring than boys in families with a full-time homemaker. In this regard, Crouter et al. (1990) found that, although mothers were generally more informed about their youngsters' activities than were fathers, no differences were found in parental monitoring experienced by boys and girls from families with: (a) a full-time homemaker, (b) a mother employed part-time, and (c) a mother working outside the home full-time. Nevertheless parental monitoring had differential effects on boys and girls as a function of family context. Less well-monitored boys received lower grades than other children, although this effect was not seen in girls who received less parental monitoring. Furthermore, the conduct of less well-monitored boys from dual-earner families (families in which mothers worked outside the home at least 15 hours per week) was rated more negatively both by parents and by the boys themselves. Crouter et al. (1990) suggested that boys' vulnerability and the potentially more stressful dual-earner lifestyle may be "person" and "context" factors mediating parental monitoring effects.

Complementary data come from a study of parental supervision patterns of children and young adolescents in the afterschool hours. Steinberg (1986) found that latchkey children (Grades 5–9) who "hung out" after school were more susceptible to peer pressure to engage in antisocial activity than were latchkey children who spent the afterschool hours at home alone. In addition, regardless of the setting in which "self-care" took place (e.g., at home, at a friend's, hanging out), children described themselves as less susceptible to peer influence if their parents were knowledgeable about where they spent their time after school. Thus, Steinberg's work shows that although a simple comparison of children in self-care versus home care is uninformative, differences emerge when the context of self-care is elaborated and when processes such as parental monitoring are included.

The Larger Context of Family Processes

It is probably easier to maintain effective levels of parental monitoring under conditions of family cohesion and support. In the Berlin Youth Longitudinal Study, Silbereisen et al. (1990) linked family processes to economic hardship and adolescent adjustment. Interested in the psychological mechanisms through which family processes influence youth, Silbereisen et al. compared two-parent families who had encountered economic loss during the early 1980s with similar families whose financial circumstances had remained stable. All families lived in West Berlin and had a child aged 10–16. Silbereisen et al. found that economic hardship set a series of processes in motion. First, it tended to decrease family integration. For adolescents who were sensitive to peer evaluation (a person characteristic), lower family integration increased the likelihood of negative self-feelings, which in turn heightened their willingness to misbehave.

Although the Berlin data are consistent with findings from past and current studies of families experiencing economic hardship, it is interesting that the Berlin findings were not replicated in a study of Warsaw youth conducted by Walper, Silbereisen, Albrecht, and Wiszniewska (1989). Here income loss was not associated with increased family friction and discord. Walper et al. suggested that economic hardship is so common in Poland that families have become accustomed to it or that income loss may mean something different in a society plagued with such shortages in basic supplies that income is no guarantee of access to necessary goods. It is also possible, they added, that because men and women work long hours in Poland, families spend less time together; as a result children may be less exposed to the outcomes of economic hardship. The important conclusion of this comparative study is that the meaning of economic hardship is very important. Economic strain has a different meaning depending on the cultural context, a point that highlights the importance of cross-cultural research.

Family cohesion and integration is also a theme in research conducted by Flanagan (1990) in 12 Michigan communities in which automobile manufacturing was the backbone of the economy. This study assessed children from Grades 6 through Grade 7. During this time, unemployment rates in these communities ranged from 8% to 21%. Flanagan categorized her sample into three groups: deprived families (those who reported a layoff or demotion at both the beginning and the end of the study), nondeprived families (no layoffs or demotions), and recovery families (those who were laid off or demoted at the beginning of the study but who had regained their former status by the end of the study). Flanagan hypothesized that family integration would moderate the potentially negative effects of financial hardship on young adolescents.

Boys' perceptions of parent–child conflict were linked to family work status group and to family integration, with the most conflict reported if the boys were in deprived families. Family integration had independent effects; regardless of family work status, boys reported more conflict with parents under conditions of low family integration. For girls, the results were quite different. Parent–child conflict was not associated with financial hardship for girls. Rather, it appeared that mothers in deprived households leaned on adolescent daughters, granting them more autonomy in decision making than did other mothers. These mothers were more likely to involve their daughters in family decision making, to trust them, and to encourage them to think independently. Thus, for daughters in these households, economic stress may have served to push them toward early maturity and responsibility.

Early maturity may come with some costs, however. In another set of analyses based on this data set, Flanagan (1989) found that, compared to children in nondeprived circumstances, girls, but not boys, in deprived households were more likely to report restricted vocational and educational plans. This finding mirrors research by Galambos and Silbereisen (1987) using data from the Berlin Youth Longitudinal Study. Financial hardship increased fathers' pessimism about their daughters' futures, and such pessimism in turn was associated with lowered career expectations among those girls. For many families, education for daughters may be seen as desirable but ultimately as less essential than education for boys. Thus, in a time of economic belt tightening, daughters may receive cues from parents that they should restrain their own ambitions vis-à-vis higher education and plan instead on early entry into the labor force; this decision avoids parental investment in college and provides the family with another source of economic support. Thus, one cost of being enlisted as a full participant in family decision making may be that girls are encouraged to think about the needs of others in the family and, in so doing, they begin to foreclose their own visions for the future.

Children's Family Roles

Other evidence for the effects of parents' economic situations on the assumption of young adolescents of alternative family roles comes from studies of children's involvement in household work. Many parents hold ideas about the importance of involving children in household work; yet, surprisingly little research has linked involvement in housework to children's psychosocial functioning. As mentioned earlier, Elder's (1974) research indicated that adolescent girls responded to Depression-era economic deprivation by taking on more household tasks. Such domestic responsibilities meant that daughters were accessible to fathers, many of whom acted out their own disappointments on their female offspring (Elder et al., 1985). Household work also seemed to put these daughters on a "domestic track." Many married early and had adult lives that centered on spouse and children. The adolescent boys in Elder's study, on the other hand, tended to respond to economic hardship by taking on paid work, a choice that exposed them to adults outside the family. As adolescents, they were characterized as responsible and mature (Elder, 1974).

Unfortunately, more recent studies of economic loss have generally not studied children's roles in the family economy. In early adolescence, however, involvement in housework may be an important source of self-esteem for children, particularly if housework is seen as a valuable and important contribution by parents. With this in mind, McHale, Bartko, Crouter, and Perry-Jenkins (1990) examined the implications of involvement in housework for a sample of children aged 9 to 11, living in single- and dual-earner households. Children living in dual-earner families were predicted to thrive under conditions of high involvement in housework because their contribution would be seen as particularly helpful in these busy, "time-poor" family contexts. The study found no connections between involvement in traditionally masculine tasks and children's psychosocial functioning, perhaps because children were seldom involved in these kinds of activities. For girls, there were some connections between involvement in feminine tasks and psychosocial functioning: Regardless of parental earner status, higher levels of involvement in housework was positively related to psychosocial functioning (e.g., to self-perceived competence). Results for boys, however, were more complex.

The relationship between involvement in traditionally feminine tasks and boys' psychosocial functioning depended on both the context (single- vs. dual-earner) and the "message" communicated by fathers about the acceptability of doing housework, a message conveyed by fathers' gender role attitudes and by their fathers' own level of involvement in housework. Boys functioned least well when their own behavior was not congruent with that of their father and with the demands of the context. Thus, in dual-earner families, when sons of less traditional fathers performed fewer household tasks, boys felt less competent, more stressed, and evaluated their relationships with their parents less positively. In contrast, in single-earner families, when sons of more traditional fathers performed more feminine tasks, they had more negative psychosocial outcomes.

These findings raise several interesting questions. What processes in dual-earner families leave some sons on the periphery of family life, uninvolved in domestic work even when their fathers are heavily involved? For some dual-earner families, stress may be a cause. Goodnow (1989) pointed out that involving children in domestic work is often a more time-consuming endeavor (in terms of teaching and supervision) than parents simply doing the work themselves. The causal arrow may also run the other way; parents may give up trying to involve sons in housework when boys are difficult to deal with. Similarly, what processes in single-earner families pull sons into household work in ways that are inconsistent with their father's level of involvement? Mothers may insist that these sons carry out housework, perhaps because they need the assistance (and are not getting it from husbands) or because they believe in the importance of housework for sons' socialization. It would be helpful to know the extent to which children become involved in household tasks on their own versus the extent to which such involvement is the result of nagging and pushing on the part of parents, particularly mothers. Data on children's own views on housework and their involvement in such tasks would also be useful. Presumably, children benefit most from involvement in household work when it pulls them into positive interactions with their parents, when it provides opportunities to master new skills and experience increasing autonomy, or when they understand (and endorse) the reasons why their parents encourage them to participate in housework.

Summary

There are important parallels among the studies we have summarized. Research studies on both economic downturns and the dual-earner arrangement identify family processes that mediate the effects of family economic circumstances on children and adolescents; in many cases, the processes are the same. For example, warm, consistent parenting and involvement of the adolescent in household roles appear to ameliorate potentially negative outcomes in both situations. Other family processes have been examined less thoroughly but appear to be good candidates for future research; parental monitoring examined with regard to maternal employment is one example.

Across all studies, there is a notable absence of attention to the subjective dimension of family processes. For example, studies examining adolescents' roles in housework have not complemented data on household behavior with information about adolescents' perceptions of the importance of such work or about their understanding of the extent to which their contribution is valued or needed by parents. Similarly, studies of parental monitoring would be strengthened by information on adolescents' perceptions of monitoring. Monitoring could be perceived by adolescents as parental interest, concern, worry, or even intrusiveness.

In reviewing this literature, two limitations stand out most clearly. First, there is very little attention to qualities of the adolescents that influence how they are responded to or how they choose to respond to their particular situation. This limitation is important because, without attention to such person characteristics, these studies convey a very linear set of processes of influence (Lerner & Busch-Rossnagel, 1981). Second, there has been little attention to possible differences in these processes across groups varying in race, class, ethnicity, or family structure. With the exception of the attempt to replicate the Berlin Youth Longitudinal Study among Polish adolescents and their families, there have been no attempts to appraise generalizability of the relationships documented here in different cultural milieus. To encourage attention to these issues, we next address the role of person characteristics and the need to study families from diverse backgrounds.

PERSON CHARACTERISTICS: THE ROLE OF INDIVIDUAL DIFFERENCES

Different children and adolescents will not respond identically to the same circumstances. Yet, few studies of the effects of family economic circumstances on young adolescents have studied person characteristics, other than gender. The only other individual difference dimensions appearing in this literature are physical attractiveness (Elder et al., 1985) and sensitivity to peer evaluation (Silbereisen et al., 1990).

Researchers have proposed several ways to think about person characteristics. Garmezy (1983) and Rutter (1983), working from a stress and coping perspective, focus on "protective factors," "influences, positive or negative, that serve to increase resilience in children exposed to environmental hazard" (Rutter & Quinton, 1984, p. 192). In this framework the interaction of situation and person characteristics is central; characteristics that may protect individuals exposed to stress in one context may be quite unimportant, developmentally, for individuals in another, more supportive context. Several possible protective factors, each of which is relevant for young adolescents who must cope with family reactions to economic circumstances, have been identified, including temperament, biological predispositions to specific types of stressors, intelligence, coping style, and social skills (Garmezy, 1983; Rutter, 1983).

From an ecological perspective, Bronfenbrenner (1989) identified four types of "developmentally instigative characteristics," which constitute another way to think about person characteristics. For Bronfenbrenner these characteristics do not determine the course of development; rather, they "put a spin" on a body in motion, an effect that depends on the other factors in the total ecological system. Borrowing from ideas in behavioral genetics (e.g., Scarr & McCartney, 1983), Bronfenbrenner's first type of developmentally instigative characteristic is "personal stimulus qualities"; such characteristics increase the likelihood that the individual will be responded to in certain ways by others. These include (but are not limited to) temperament and physical attractiveness. The remaining categories in Bronfenbrenner's schema involve various degrees of direct manipulation of the environment. "Selective responsivity" refers to individual differences in individuals' attraction to and selection of activities and stimuli. "Structuring proclivities" are individual tendencies to elaborate and restructure the environment. Finally, "directive beliefs" refer to the individual's conception of his or her own power to reach life goals, a construct similar to locus of control.

Including protective factors or developmentally instigative characteristics in studies of family process would help remedy the linear conceptualizations underlying many studies. During early adolescence, however, the most powerful person characteristics may themselves undergo developmental transformations, a notion that is not emphasized by researchers in either the stress and coping or the ecological tradition. Thus, biological, socioemotional, and cognitive changes are important not only as "outcomes" in studies of adolescence, but also in terms of the mediating role they play as person characteristics, characteristics that themselves are undergoing transformation.

Maccoby (1983) argued, for example, that both cognitive and social cognitive changes are fundamental to alterations in stress appraisal and coping as youngsters move through childhood and adolescence. She noted that internalized coping mechanisms are likely to be more prevalent at older ages and, in addition, a greater diversity of such mechanisms may be available. The development of problem-solving skills including greater planfulness, a greater awareness of the range of possible coping strategies and problem solutions, and a better developed ability to articulate and maintain a commitment to successful problem solution (i.e., a focus on "closure") mean that adolescents who have acquired cognitive abilities such as those Piaget (1972) described as "formal operational" may be better able to cope with stressful events.

Maturing cognitive and social abilities, however, may constitute a double-edged sword. Newly acquired abilities to make social comparisons and to monitor their experiences and emotional status may actually serve to intensify some adolescents' feelings of stress. Many adolescents also begin to move away from the rule-governed behavior and thought of the younger child and to doubt the omniscience of parents and other authority figures. Although these changes represent important milestones in social and cognitive growth, they also mean that adolescents must be able to live with ambiguity.

Pubertal development is another aspect of adolescent change that may mediate the extent to which adolescents respond to family processes, as well as the extent to which adolescents are responded to by other family members. For example, parent–child conflict escalates across the transition to puberty, especially for mothers and sons (Steinberg, 1987). Such conflict may influence the extent to which parents are able to monitor their sons, enlist their sons' participation in household tasks, respond to their sons warmly, and maintain a consistent disciplinary style.

This example also suggests the possible importance of parents' personal characteristics. For example, some parents may be more "at risk" than others to experience job loss as a function of lack of social skills, difficult temperaments, or predispositions to certain problem behaviors such as excessive alcohol use. Similarly, mothers do not enter the labor force completely at random; choice is involved, both about the employment decision itself and, subsequently, specific occupation, extent of temporal involvement in work, and so on. In addition, parents' personal characteristics probably play a role in the extent to which their parenting behaviors are vulnerable to the strains imposed by economic change. Certain parents may be "resilient" and able to buffer their children from stressful circumstances, whereas others crumble under modest levels of strain. More complete models of the interrelationships among economic change, family processes, and adolescent functioning will need to consider the role of individual differences both among adolescents and among their parents.

In short, then, a full picture of the effects of economic social change on young adolescents will not be complete until person characteristics have been included more systematically. Gender is not enough! Furthermore, to better understand young adolescents' reactions to economic changes both within and outside their families, it would be particularly profitable to examine person characteristics that develop during this period. Biological, socioemotional, and cognitive developmental changes from the late school-age through the early adolescent years transform the ways in which some adolescents appraise and react to their environments, as well as the ways in which they are responded to by others (Lerner, 1987). Parents' personal characteristics also deserve attention in that they may reveal important selection effects. The study of the familial economic circumstances of families offers an important, naturally occurring situation in which to examine these basic individual and family processes.

CLASS, COLOR, ETHNICITY, AND FAMILY STRUCTURE: DO FINDINGS GENERALIZE ACROSS DIVERSE GROUPS?

Studies of adolescent development in the context of family life will certainly profit from greater attention to the extent to which family processes are generalizable across different family types and different class, race, and ethnic groups. We have summarized research that reflects the literature and, as such, has been carried out on White, intact, middle-class families. It is certain that some of the relationships examined here do not apply to adolescents growing up in markedly different circumstances. The finding by Walper et al. (1989) that economic strain was related to family cohesion in their Berlin sample, but not in their Warsaw one, illustrates this point.

To our knowledge, there are no studies that have examined the entire set of linkages examined in this chapter (i.e., the connections among economic circumstances, family processes, and early adolescent functioning) in non-White samples or in single-parent families. Indeed, McLoyd (1990) noted that "the links among economic loss, family functioning, and black children's development . . . are virtually uncharted territory," a lacuna she described as "paradoxical" because "without exception, black workers suffer more than white workers during economic recessions" (p. 336).

A few studies have examined pieces of the overall model for adolescents from diverse backgrounds. Such studies are useful because they indicate the extent to which at least some of the relationships of interest are generalizable. Dornbusch, Ritter, Leiderman, Roberts, and Fraleigh (1987) surveyed a diverse sample of over 7,000 high school students from the San Francisco Bay Area about the parenting styles of their mothers and fathers. Using Baumrind's distinctions among authoritarian, permissive, and authoritative parenting (see Baumrind & Black, 1967), Dornbusch et al. examined the relationships among parenting styles and adolescent school performance. The relationship between parenting styles and school performance was quite consistent across the five types of family structures examined. In addition, authoritarian and permissive styles were linked to lower school performance for all four ethnic groups (Asian, Black, Hispanic, and White). The correlation between authoritative (i.e., democratic) parenting and performance was positive for all ethnic groups except Asian females.

When the strength of the relations was examined, however, Dornbusch et al. concluded that, although the model was applicable to adolescents from all four ethnic groups under study, it applied best to Whites and least well to Asian youth. In addition, there were interesting differences for Hispanic males and females. For females there was a strong relationship between authoritarian parenting and lower school performance. For males, although the mean level of authoritarianism was similar, there was virtually no relationship between authoritarianism and performance. These findings imply that parenting processes and person characteristics (i.e., gender) interact differently across different ethnic groups, and highlight the importance of building diverse cultural contexts into studies of early adolescence and family life.

To be useful, such studies would need to go beyond simple comparisons by cultural or ethnic group to include key features of family ecology that might have bearing on the processes under study. As McLoyd (1990) explained:

> Failure to take into account the fact that poor blacks are far more likely than poor whites to live in poor, isolated neighborhoods lacking myriad resources favorable to parenting and children's development may lead researchers to conclude erroneously that differences between blacks and whites . . . are due to stable psychological characteristics or family factors when, in fact, they are rooted in contextual or neighborhood differences. (p. 338)

As Walper et al.'s (1989) Warsaw study pointed out, in addition to neighborhood characteristics, the cultural meaning of economic resources and strains is one ecological feature that needs attention. Other dimensions to keep in mind when making comparisons across cultural or ethnic groups on the links among economic circumstances, family processes, and early adolescent development include the extent to which parents are solely responsible for family socialization or are assisted in that role by grandparents or other family members; parental beliefs about the efficacy of such parenting practices as consistent discipline or close monitoring; and gender role expectations for adolescent and adult males and females. In conducting such research, the goal should not simply be to discover which relationships are generalizable across groups. Indeed, from an ecological perspective, one would expect that processes would not necessarily function similarly under diverse circumstances. Thus, the most interesting findings would identify the conditions under which the linkages from economic conditions to family processes to adolescent development converge and diverge across groups from different backgrounds.

CONCLUSIONS

In challenging economic circumstance, family processes are important influences on adolescent development and well-being. Depending on how parents structure roles, relationships, and activities within the family, adolescents respond differently. In addition, children bring their personal characteristics to the situation, attributes that predispose them to respond in various ways. Indeed, some adolescents actually flourish in seemingly stressful circumstances. The ecological conditions and the personal characteristics that promote such "resiliency" are important from the perspectives of both research and policy.

As we write these remarks, the United States is again experiencing an economic recession, one that promises to raise levels of unemployment, particularly in certain parts of the country and in certain sectors of the economy. At this juncture, it is too early to assess the severity and duration of this economic downturn. For children coming of age in the early 1990s, however, the issues outlined in this chapter may be particularly pertinent. Given this particular sociohistorical context, it may be useful to suggest some promising directions for future research.

Directions for Future Research

The scope of research must expand in several directions. Greater attention needs to be paid to the role of personal characteristics, particularly as these characteristics become transformed throughout the early adolescent years, and to the role of culture as a more general context within which individuals construct and interpret their work and family experiences. In addition, it is important for researchers to examine maternal as well as paternal unemployment.

This area is also a promising one for intervention research. Based on current knowledge, interventions could be targeted to several issues. For example, there has been excellent prevention research in which unemployed men are provided with job-seeking skills, inoculation against setbacks, and social support in an effort to prevent mental health problems such as depression (Caplan, Vinokur, Price, & van Ryn, 1989). Such research could be expanded to include the families of unemployed men in order to explore whether such interventions also prevent disruptions in parent–child relations in such areas as discipline and nurturance. It would also be possible to explore whether children in families in which fathers receive the intervention fare better than children in families in which fathers do not receive such assistance.

Intervention research could also focus on the adolescents themselves by targeting relevant personal characteristics such as coping skills and then assessing whether such training better equips adolescents to deal with trying familial circumstances. Providing support groups to adolescents in similar circumstances would be another way to approach an intervention study.

Some useful intervention strategies focus on aspects of the environment rather than individuals. For example, as workplaces begin to respond to family needs by offering flexible work schedules, flexible benefits, job sharing, and the like, it would be important to assess whether such programs relieve parental strain and, in turn, prevent disruptive parent–child relations (see Greenberger, Goldberg, Hamill, & O'Neil in press). In addition, corporate strategies to deal with economic downturns, such as reducing the hours of all employees as opposed to laying off some employees, could be evaluated for their effects on employees and their families. Finally, at the broadest level, there are policy changes that, if instituted, could be evaluated in terms of their impacts on the processes outlined in this chapter. Perhaps the most obvious of these is the provision of a national health insurance system, a policy that would provide access to health care for all citizens. Such a policy would remove one of the most frightening spectres of unemployment for employees with families—the threat of losing employer-provided health care.

In summary, the course of adolescent development depends in part on the nature of roles, relationships, and activities within the family. These family processes can play an important buffering role when parents experience stressful economic circumstances. When families respond negatively to such extrafamilial stresses, children are vulnerable. Two directions for the next generation of research studies involve expanding and fine-tuning current models and developing interventions designed to support families experiencing stress and enhance the resiliency of children and adolescents.

ACKNOWLEDGMENTS

We thank Avshalom Caspi and Richard M. Lerner for their constructive and useful suggestions.

REFERENCES

Baumrind, D., & Black, A. E. (1967). Socialization practices associated with dimensions of competence in preschool boys and girls. *Child Development, 38,* 291–327.

Bronfenbrenner, U. (1979). *The ecology of human development: Experiments by nature and design.* Cambridge, MA: Harvard University Press.

Bronfenbrenner, U. (1989). *The developing ecology of human development: Paradigm lost or paradigm regained?* Paper presented at the biennial meeting of the Society for Research in Child Development, Kansas City, MO.

Bronfenbrenner, U., & Crouter, A. C. (1982). Work and family through time and space. In S. Kamerman & C. Hayes (Eds.), *Families that work: Children in a changing world* (pp. 39–83). Washington, DC: National Academy Press.

Bronfenbrenner, U., & Crouter, A. C. (1983). The evolution of environmental models in developmental research. In P. Mussen (Ed.), *Handbook of child psychology.* New York: Wiley.

Caplan, R. D., Vinokur, A. D., Price, R. H., & van Ryn, M. (1989). Job seeking, reemployment, and mental health: A randomized field experiment in coping with job loss. *Journal of Applied Psychology, 74,* 759–769.

Conger, R. D., Conger, K. J., Elder, G. H., Jr., Lorenz, F. O., Simons, R. L., & Whitbeck, L. B. (1992). A family process model of economic hardship and adjustment of early adolescent boys. *Child Development, 63,* 526–541.

Crouter, A. C., MacDermid, S. M., McHale, S. M., & Perry-Jenkins, M. (1990). Parental monitoring and perceptions of children's school performance and conduct in dual-earner and single-earner families. *Developmental Psychology, 26,* 649–657.

Crouter, A. C., & McHale, S. M. (in press). The long arm of the job: Influences of parental work on childrearing. In T. Luster & L. Okagaki (Eds.), *Parenting: An ecological perspective* (pp. 179–202). Hillsdale, NJ: Lawrence Erlbaum Associates.

Dishion, T. J., Patterson, G. R., & Reid, J. R. (1988). Parent and peer factors associated with sampling in early adolescence: Implications for treatment. In E. R. Rahdert & J. Grabowski (Eds.), *Adolescent drug abuse: Analysis of treatment research* (Research Monograph No. 77). Rockville, MD: National Institute on Drug Abuse.

Dornbusch, S. M., Ritter, P. L., Leiderman, P. H., Roberts, D. F., & Fraleigh, M. J. (1987). The relation of parenting style to adolescent school performance. *Child Development, 58,* 1244–1257.

Elder, G. H., Jr. (1974). *Children of The Great Depression.* Chicago: University of Chicago Press.

Elder, G. H., Jr., Van Nguyen, T., & Caspi, A. (1985). Linking family hardship to children's lives. *Child Development, 56,* 361–375.

Flanagan, C. A. (1989). *Economic stress in the family: Do the effects for daughters and sons differ?* Paper presented at the biennial meeting of the Society for Research on Child Development, Kansas City, MO.

Flanagan, C. A. (1990). Change in family work status: Effects on parent-adolescent decision making. *Child Development, 61,* 163–177.

Forgatch, M. S., Patterson, G. R., & Skinner, M. (1985, May). *A mediational model for the effect of divorce on antisocial behavior in boys.* Paper presented at the conference The impact of divorce, single parenting, and stepparenting on children, sponsored by the National Institute for Child Health and Human Development, Bethesda, MD.

Galambos, N., & Silbereisen, R. (1987). Income change, parental outlook, and adolescent expectations for job success. *Journal of Marriage and the Family, 49,* 141–149.

Garmezy, N. (1983). Stressors of childhood. In N. Garmezy & M. Rutter (Eds.), *Stress, coping, and development in children* (pp. 43–84). New York: McGraw Hill.

Gold, D., & Andres, D. (1978). Developmental comparisons between ten-year-old children

with employed and nonemployed mothers. *Child Development, 49,* 75-84.
Goodnow, J. J. (1989). Work in households: An overview and three studies. In D. Ironmonger (Ed.), *Household work* (pp. 38-58). Sydney: Allen & Unwin.
Greenberger, E., Goldberg, W. A., Hamill, S., O'Neil, R. (in press). Contributions of a supportive work environment to parents' well-being and orientation to work. *American Journal of Community Psychology.*
Hoffman, L. W. (1989). Effects of maternal employment in the two-parent family. *American Psychologist, 44,* 283-292.
Hogan, D. P., & Kitagawa, E. (1985). The impact of social status, family structure, and neighborhood on the fertility of black adolescents. *American Journal of Sociology, 90,* 825-855.
Kanter, R. M. (1977). *Work and family in the United States: A critical review and agenda for research and policy.* New York: Russell Sage.
Lempers, J. D., Clark-Lempers, D., & Simons, R. L. (1989). Economic hardship, parenting, and distress in adolescence. *Child Development, 60,* 25-39.
Lerner, R. M. (1987). A life-span perspective for early adolescence. In R. M. Lerner & T. T. Foch (Eds.), *Biological-psychosocial interactions in early adolescence: A life-span perspective* (pp. 9-33). Hillsdale, NJ: Lawrence Erlbaum Associates.
Lerner, R. M., & Busch-Rossnagel, N. A. (Eds.). (1981). *Individuals as producers of their development: A life-span perspective.* New York: Academic Press.
Maccoby, E. E. (1983). Social-emotional development and response to stressors. In N. Garmezy & M. Rutter (Eds.), *Stress, coping, and development in children* (pp. 217-234). New York: McGraw-Hill.
McHale, S. M., Bartko, T., Crouter, A. C., & Perry-Jenkins, M. (1990). Children's housework and their psychosocial functioning: The mediating effects of parents' sex role behaviors and attitudes. *Child Development, 61,* 1413-1426.
McLoyd, V. C. (1989). Socialization and development in a changing economy: The effects of paternal job and income loss on children. *American Psychologist, 44,* 293-302.
McLoyd, V. C. (1990). The impact of economic hardship on black families and children: Psychological distress, parenting, and socioemotional development. *Child Development, 61,* 311-346.
Patterson, G. R. (1986). Performance models for antisocial boys. *American Psychologist, 41,* 432-444.
Patterson, G. R. (1988). Family process: Loops, levels, and linkages. In N. Bolger, A. Caspi, G. Downey, & M. Moorehouse (Eds.), *Persons in context: Developmental processes.* New York: Cambridge University Press.
Patterson, G. R., & Stouthamer-Loeber, M. (1984). The correlation of family management practices and delinquency. *Child Development, 55,* 1299-1307.
Piaget, J. (1972). Intellectual evolution from adolescence to adulthood. *Human Development, 15,* 1-12.
Rutter, M. (1983). Stress, coping, and development: Some issues and some questions. In N. Garmezy & M. Rutter (Eds.), *Stress, coping, and development in children* (pp. 1-41). New York: McGraw Hill.
Rutter, M., & Quinton, D. (1984). Long-term follow-up of women institutionalized in childhood: Factors promoting good functioning in adult life. *British Journal of Developmental Psychology, 2,* 191-204.
Scarr, S., & McCartney, K. (1983). How people make their own environments: A theory of genotype-environment effects. *Child Development, 54,* 424-435.
Silbereisen, R., Walper, S., & Albrecht, H. (1990). Families experiencing income loss and economic hardship: Antecedents of adolescents' problem-behavior. In V. McLoyd & C. A. Flanagan (Eds.), *New directions for child development. Economic stress: Effects on family life and child development* (pp. 27-47). San Francisco: Jossey Bass.

Simons, R. L., Whitbeck, L. B., Conger, R. D., & Melby, J. N. (1990). Husband and wife differences in determinants of parenting: A social learning and exchange model of parental behavior. *Journal of Marriage and the Family, 52,* 375-392.

Steinberg, L. (1986). Latchkey children and susceptibility to peer pressure: An ecological analysis. *Developmental Psychology 22,* 433-439.

Steinberg, L. (1987). Impact of puberty on family relations: Effects of pubertal status and pubertal timing. *Developmental Psychology, 23,* 451-460.

Stewart, A. J., & Healy, J. M. (1989). Linking individual development and social changes. *American Psychologist, 44,* 30-42.

Walper, S., Silbereisen, R. K., Albrecht, H. T., & Wiszniewska, A. (1989). *The dynamics of adolescents' reactions to economic deprivation.* Paper presented at the Tenth Biennial Meeting of the International Society for the Study of Behavioural Development, Jyvaskyla, Finland.

6 Early Adolescent Family Formation

Lisa J. Crockett
The Pennsylvania State University

In the United States, adolescent family formation has been considered a major social problem since the late 1970s. The sources of concern are multiple. First, teenage childbearing is associated with risks for the mother and her child, including health problems, reduced life chances, and a greater likelihood of living in poverty. Second, a large and increasing proportion of births to teenagers are nonmarital; this appears to compound these risks. Third, the rate of teenage childbearing in the United States far exceeds those in other Western, industrialized countries (Alan Guttmacher Institute, 1986). The high rate of adolescent pregnancy in the United States results in close to half a million births annually (Pittman & Adams, 1988). These births have huge social as well as personal costs: In 1988, annual public spending to support families begun with an adolescent birth approached $20 billion (Center for Population Options, 1989).

Until recently, little attention was given to early adolescent childbearing, probably because births to girls under age 15 represent a relatively small proportion of teenage births. Social concern increased, however, following reports that the prevalence of sexual activity is increasing in this age group (e.g., Hofferth, Kahn, & Baldwin, 1987). Because young adolescents are especially poor contraceptors, increases in sexual activity are likely to result in higher pregnancy and birth rates for this group.

The prior inattention to young adolescent reproductive behavior has resulted in a paucity of data concerning sexuality and childbearing in youngsters under age 15. This chapter explores the available information on this topic. Initially, data on early adolescent reproductive behavior is reviewed, including findings on sexual activity, contraceptive use, pregnancy, and births, as well as the consequences of early adolescent childbearing. Next, some of the developmental and contextual factors that may contribute to early adolescent family formation are explored. Finally, recommendations for research and policy are discussed. Where possible, existing data on young adolescents are cited. Because most studies have not considered adolescents under age 15 as a separate group, however, it is necessary at times to extrapolate from data on older teenagers.

EARLY ADOLESCENT SEXUALITY AND CHILDBEARING

The rate of sexual activity among young adolescents has increased over the past few decades. Three percent of girls born in 1950–1952 had sex by the time they turned 15, as compared to 13% of girls born 15 years later (Hofferth et al., 1987). Moreover, a national survey conducted in 1983 indicated that 17% of the men born in the early 1960s initiated sex prior to age 15 (Hayes, 1987). In 1988, one third of 15-year-old males reported intercourse experience (Sonenstein, Pleck, & Ku, 1989). Thus, a sizable and increasing proportion of young adolescents are sexually experienced.

This conclusion is sobering in light of young adolescents' poor contraceptive practices. Approximately 30% of girls who initiated intercourse prior to age 15 report having used contraceptives at first intercourse, as compared to more than 50% of those who became sexually active at later ages (Zelnik & Shah, 1983). Moreover, young adolescents are slow to adopt contraception after they become sexually active. According to one national survey, only 23% of girls under age 15 at first intercourse started using a contraceptive method within a month after initial intercourse, whereas 42% delayed contraceptive use for more than 1 year. In contrast, only 15% of 18- to 19-year-olds delayed contraceptive use for over 1 year (Hofferth et al., 1987). Because an estimated half of premarital adolescent pregnancies occur within 6 months after first intercourse (Zabin, Kantner, & Zelnik, 1979), the tendency to delay contraceptive use places sexually active young adolescents at high risk for pregnancy.

Because of these trends in sexual activity and contraceptive behavior, the pregnancy rate for adolescents under age 15 has been increasing over the past few decades. In 1987, 16.6 girls per 1,000 in this age group became pregnant as opposed to 13.5 per 1,000 in 1973. The birth rate for these young adolescents, however, actually declined slightly over the same period, due presumably to increased use of abortion (Henshaw, Kenney, Somberg, & Van Vort, 1989). In the first half of the 1980s, over 50% of pregnancies to girls under 15 were terminated by abortion, a higher proportion than was found among older teenagers. The remaining pregnancies resulted in 10,000 to 12,000 live births each year (Hayes, 1987). Because young adolescents are unlikely to marry to legitimate a pregnancy, almost all of these births occurred out of wedlock. In 1985, over 90% of births to girls under age 15 were nonmarital (Pittman & Adams, 1988).

Evidence suggests that most young adolescents who deliver their babies choose to keep them. In 1982, for example, an estimated 93% of unmarried mothers between the ages of 15 and 19 kept their children (Bachrach, 1986), suggesting that 7% potentially chose adoption. Although separate estimates are not available for adolescents under 15, it is unlikely that their rates are substantially higher than the total figures. Of course, young adolescent girls are not necessarily raising their babies alone. Because very young mothers are more likely to remain with their parents (Furstenberg & Crawford, 1978), they may have more child-care support than do older mothers.

Subgroup Differences

There are striking subgroup differences in rates of adolescent sexual activity, pregnancy, and childbearing. Throughout adolescence, sexual activity rates are higher for boys than for girls, and for African-Americans than for Whites. Black males in particular, report high rates of early intercourse, and some data suggest that prepubertal intercourse is not uncommon in this group (Udry, 1982). Less is known about Hispanic youth, although their rates of sexual activity appear to fall between Whites and African-Americans (Fennelly, chapter 19, this volume). In a 1983 survey of young adults, 12% of White males and 5% of White females reported having intercourse prior to age 15. Among Hispanics, the rates were 19% for males and 4% for females, and among African-Americans they were 42% for males and 10% for females (Hayes, 1987). Recent national data show the same pattern among 15-year-old males: 26% of Whites, 33% of Hispanics, and 70% of Blacks reported having had intercourse (Sonenstein et al., 1989). Pregnancy and birth rates follow a similar pattern, at least among older adolescents. Among 15- to 19-year-old women, the pregnancy rate for African-Americans is two times that for Whites; for Hispanics it is 1.7 times that for Whites. Birth rates for both African-Americans and Hispanics are over twice the rate for Whites (Henshaw et al., 1989). Rates of early sexual activity, pregnancy, and childbearing also vary by socioeconomic status (SES), being higher among poor adolescents (Chilman, 1986).

CONSEQUENCES OF EARLY ADOLESCENT CHILDBEARING

Risks to the Adolescent

There is substantial evidence that early adolescent childbearing entails increased risks for mother and child. Mothers under 15 are at higher risk of health problems: They experience more complications during pregnancy and delivery, more miscarriages and stillbirths, and higher maternal morbidity and mortality. Although many of these health risks could presumably be reduced with adequate nutrition and prenatal care, some negative outcomes appear to result from the mother's physical immaturity. Even with good health care, mothers under age 15 have somewhat higher rates of toxemia, anemia, prolonged labor, premature labor, and mortality (Hayes, 1987).

The negative social and economic consequences associated with teenage childbearing may also be exacerbated among early adolescent mothers. In general, the younger the mother at the time of birth, the lower her educational attainment, although this relationship is stronger for Whites than Blacks (Mott & Marsiglio, 1985). Lack of schooling in turn increases the likelihood of poor employment, poverty, and welfare dependency. Despite the overall relationship between earlier childbearing and lower educational attainment, some data suggest that girls who become mothers before the age of 16 may be more likely to complete high school than those who give birth between ages 16 and 18 (Hayes, 1987). This is probably because very young mothers are less likely than older mothers to make other adult transitions (e.g., getting married, establishing a separate household, getting a job) that make staying in school more difficult (Furstenberg & Crawford, 1978).

Women who begin childbearing prior to age 15 tend to have higher subsequent fertility. This relationship appears to be weaker for African-Americans than Whites, and weaker in recent cohorts than it was in the 1970s (Hayes, 1987). When high fertility co-occurs with low educational attainment the long-term prognosis for adolescent mothers is particularly poor (Furstenberg, Brooks-Gunn, & Morgan, 1987). Therefore, early adolescent childbearers may be at particular risk for long-term difficulties. How long these effects persist may depend on the population. In one long-term follow-up of Black teenage mothers, girls who became mothers at age 15 or less were not worse off in middle adulthood than those who began childbearing at age 16 or 17, once other background variables were controlled (Furstenberg et al., 1987). Teenage mothers as a group, however, fared worse than women who delayed childbearing until their 20s.

Finally, teenage childbearing is associated with marital instability (Hayes, 1987). Although many of these women marry, they are less likely than older mothers to stay married, and are more likely to end up raising their children in single-parent households. These patterns contribute to the young mother's economic distress because economic outcomes tend to be better for teenage mothers who enter stable marital relationships (Furstenberg et al., 1987).

Some research suggests that early parenthood also has detrimental effects on males (Card & Wise, 1978). For example, high school dropout rates are higher for teenage fathers than for other males (Marsiglio, 1987). Although it is unclear whether dropout precedes or follows parenthood, such findings may reflect effects of early parenting. Recent research suggests that educational deficits are greatest for males who move in with their partners (Robbins & Streetman, 1990). Reduced educational attainment should in turn depress the occupational status and earnings of these young males. Virtually nothing is known about males who become fathers in early adolescence. It is not even clear how many boys this includes. Because most girls tend to become involved with somewhat older males (Zelnik & Shah, 1983), the number of young adolescent fathers is probably small.

Risks to the Child

The children born to teenage mothers also appear to be at risk. Babies of teenage mothers, especially mothers under 15, are more likely to be born prematurely or with low birth weight (Hayes, 1987), outcomes that increase the risk of poor health and developmental problems. In early childhood, the children of teenage mothers show poorer cognitive performance and more socioemotional and behavioral problems than do those born to older mothers (Brooks-Gunn & Furstenberg, 1986). These differences are small, however, and are largely accounted for by differences in SES. That is, they appear to be due more to the effects of poverty than to incompetent parenting stemming from the mother's youth. Effects are larger among older as compared to younger children and more common among boys than girls.

The potential significance of these small early deficits is suggested by the few studies that have followed the children of teenage mothers into adolescence. A long-term follow-up of an African-American, urban sample revealed high levels of school failure and misconduct among the adolescent offspring, as well as earlier sexual activity and more illicit substance use (Furstenberg et al., 1987). Thus, early and continued disadvantage may translate into cumulative deficits for the children of teenage mothers.

FACTORS AFFECTING EARLY ADOLESCENT CHILDBEARING

Although some adolescent girls may seek to become pregnant (e.g., Franklin, 1988), intentional pregnancies constitute only a small proportion of all adolescent pregnancies (Zelnik & Kantner, 1980). Data on girls under 15 indicate that virtually all of their pregnancies are unintended (Alan Guttmacher Institute, 1981). Given this, the keys to early adolescent childbearing lie not in factors leading girls to desire a pregnancy, but in the social and individual factors that contribute to early sexual activity, ineffective contraception, and, if pregnancy occurs, a decision to bear the child. In the following sections, factors affecting these decision points are reviewed.

Early Adolescent Sexual Activity

A growing proportion of young people experience their first sexual intercourse during early adolescence. Two main explanations have been offered for this trend, one biological, the other sociocultural. From a biological perspective, the argument has focused on the timing of pubertal development. From a sociocultural perspective, it has been argued that sexual activity among U.S. adolescents is linked to broader demographic shifts and to societal changes in sexual permissiveness (Chilman, 1986).

Several recent studies have documented an association between pubertal development and adolescent sexual behavior. A relationship has been found between androgen levels and sexual activity for White adolescent boys (Udry, Billy, Morris, Groff, & Raj, 1985) and between androgen levels and sexual motivation (but not intercourse) among White adolescent girls (Udry, Talbert, & Morris, 1986). Unfortunately, similar studies with other ethnic groups have not been published.

Pubertal development may also have an effect on sexual behavior, regardless of hormone levels. Some researchers have noted a relationship between level of physical maturity and adolescents' sexual experience, although the strength of the relationship appears to differ by race and gender (Udry & Billy, 1987). Others have found that girls who mature early tend to become sexually experienced at younger ages. These pubertal effects are probably mediated by social responses to the adolescents' appearance. Mature adolescents are more likely to be viewed as attractive sexual partners; they are also more likely to associate with older peers, which in turn is associated with early intercourse (Magnusson, Stattin, & Allen, 1985). In addition, physically mature girls appear to be granted more autonomy by parents, which could increase their opportunities for sexual activity (Brooks-Gunn & Furstenburg, 1989).

Despite the evidence that pubertal development plays a role in early adolescent sexual activity, puberty alone cannot account for the recent trend toward earlier intercourse. Puberty has been occurring at younger and younger ages over the last century (Eveleth, 1986), but this gradual trend toward earlier puberty does not match the dramatic increase in adolescent sexual activity that occurred during the 1960s and 1970s (Petersen & Crockett, in press). Thus, age at pubertal onset may help account for individual differences in the timing of first intercourse but cannot explain the overall trend toward earlier sexual initiation.

An alternative explanation focuses on broader societal changes in sexual attitudes and permissiveness (Chilman, 1986). Chilman noted that the historical shifts in adolescents' sexual attitudes and behavior were accompanied by demographic changes such as a rising divorce rate, an increase in single-parent families, a trend toward later marriage, and an increase in out-of-wedlock births among women of all ages. These changes, as well as more permissive sexual attitudes, probably influenced adolescent sexual behavior. Therefore, the historical increase in early adolescent sexual activity is best understood as an outgrowth of broader societal trends.

Subgroup Differences. As previously indicated, there are substantial subgroup differences in the reported prevalence of early adolescent intercourse. Rates are higher among boys than girls, among low-SES than high-SES groups, and among African-Americans than Whites and Hispanics. Surprisingly little is known about what produces these subgroup differences. Racial differences in timing of puberty, for example, are too small to explain the large differences in sexual behavior. Attempts to explain racial differences in terms of psychological and social variables have also met with limited success. Studies suggest that the racial differences remain when socioeconomic indicators are controlled (Furstenberg, Morgan, Moore, & Peterson, 1985, cited in Hayes, 1987), and even when a broad array of developmental, behavioral, academic, and family variables are controlled (Alexander et al., 1989).

Effects of Poverty. The impact of poverty has been at the heart of theorizing about the early initiation of sexual activity. One prominent hypothesis has been psychological, suggesting that impoverished circumstances offering little hope of future success provide few disincentives for early sexual activity (Chilman, 1986). Other influences may operate at the community or neighborhood level. Hogan and Kitigawa (1985), for example, reported an association between poor neighborhood quality and teenage sexuality rates. The mechanisms for such neighborhood effects are not well understood. One possibility is that poor neighborhoods provide more role models for early sexual activity and nonmarital childbearing. Another is that poor neighborhoods are associated with a lack of effective parental monitoring. Community size may also be a factor because high population density is associated with higher rates of teenage sexual activity (Franklin, 1988).

Sexual Norms. A related explanation for subgroup differences in teenage sexual activity involves differing sexual norms and pressures. Boys, for example, probably feel more peer pressure to be sexually active than do girls, who may experience pressures both to engage in and to delay intercourse. Unfortunately, most of the data are on girls only, providing few opportunities for gender comparisons. Jessor, Costa, Jessor, and Donovan (1983) found that similar personality and contextual variables contributed to timing of sexual initiation for both genders in their White middle-class sample. A study of poor, urban Blacks, however, suggested that the meaning of sex may differ for girls and boys, with early intercourse being associated with more deviant behavior among girls (Ensminger, 1990).

The role of sexual norms in ethnic differences is supported by the finding that a substantial number of African-American boys may experience prepubertal sexual intercourse (Udry, 1982). In such cases, social rather than biological factors appear to govern sexual initiation. Other aspects of adolescent sexual behavior also appear to be governed by social norms. White adolescents, for example, appear to engage in a specific sequence of sexual behaviors prior to initiating intercourse. They progress from holding hands to kissing, to petting above the waist, to genital stimulation, and then to intercourse. African-American adolescents, on the other hand, appear to follow a different pattern, with intercourse coming earlier in the sequence (Smith & Udry, 1985).

Differences in norms could also operate at the community level. Some data indicate that there is a greater perceived tolerance concerning teenage childbearing in Black, urban communities (Hayes, 1987). This tolerance could be interpreted by teenagers as sexual permissiveness. The prevalence of peer sexual activity in the school or community may also influence adolescents' attitudes about appropriate behavior. In one study, African-Americans in segregated schools showed higher rates of sexual activity than those in integrated schools where their rates were closer to those of White students (Furstenberg et al., 1985, cited in Hayes, 1987). Although type of school may have been confounded with SES, there is the intriguing possibility that contact with different sexual norms affected the behavior of the African-American students.

Family Influences. Family socialization factors may also underlie some subgroup differences. Early sexual activity is associated with low parent educational attainment, large family size, and growing up in a single-parent family (Chilman, 1986). These family variables could operate by affecting the values and expectations to which adolescents are exposed, the role models they see, and the amount of supervision they receive. Growing up in a single-mother family, for example, is associated with earlier sexual intercourse for girls (Newcomer & Udry, 1987). The mother may act as a role model for dating and nonmarital sexual relationships. Single mothers may also be less capable of monitoring their daughters' activities, and failure to monitor girls' early dating experiences has been linked to early intercourse (Hogan & Kitigawa, 1985). Other family models of early sex and childbearing may also be important: Early intercourse is more common among girls whose sisters were teenage mothers (Hogan & Kitigawa, 1985) and among adolescents with older siblings (Haurin & Mott, 1990). Finally, a poor parent–child relationship is associated with early sexual activity among girls (Chilman, 1986). Some researchers have suggested that girls who lack adequate support and intimacy at home are more likely to seek close relationships elsewhere.

Sexual Abuse. A final factor contributing to early adolescent sexual activity may be sexual abuse. Recent reports have documented a surprising amount of unwanted sexual experience among American teenage girls (Moore, Nord, & Peterson, 1989). In many cases, the experiences begin prior to or during early adolescence. Thus, a substantial proportion of sexually active young adolescents may have become so due not to their own desires but to factors beyond their control. Nonetheless, these experiences have implications for teenage family formation: Early sexual abuse has been linked to subsequent sexual activity in adolescence and to teenage pregnancy (Butler & Burton, 1990).

Contraceptive Use

As noted earlier, young adolescents tend to be poor contraceptors. Younger girls are less likely than older teenagers and adults to have used contraception and, when they do use it, are less likely to use it consistently and effectively (Kantner & Zelnik, 1972). Younger girls are also more likely to rely on male methods (e.g., condom, withdrawal) and less likely to use a medical method such as birth control pills (Zelnik, Kantner, & Ford, 1981). Similarly, young adolescent males may be less likely than older males to use contraceptives: In a recent national survey, 48% of males who had intercourse between ages 12 and 14 used a condom at first intercourse, as compared to 60% of 15- to 19-year-olds (Sonenstein et al., 1989).

Young adolescents' contraceptive behavior probably reflects a combination of factors, including their cognitive level, the nature of early adolescent sexual activity, and cultural variables that influence their knowledge of and access to contraceptives. One hypothesis focuses on young adolescents' cognitive immaturity. Young adolescents are beginning to develop the capacity for abstract, logical thinking referred to as formal operations (Inhelder & Piaget, 1958). These advances should increase their ability to reflect on their behavior and to consider its possible long-term consequences. However, the capacity for formal reasoning develops gradually and may operate imperfectly, especially in early adolescence when it is just beginning to emerge (Keating, 1990). The use of formal reasoning may also depend on situational variables. Even among adults, the degree of logical thought revealed in a laboratory setting will not necessarily be applied in everyday situations. This is especially true in stressful circumstances or with emotionally "hot" topics. Given that young adolescents' decisions about sex and contraception are likely to involve such hot cognitions, the probability of logical, systematic reasoning is fairly low (Hamburg, 1986).

Research on formal operations also indicates that the consolidation of formal reasoning depends on appropriate environmental stimulation and support (Keating, 1990). In this regard, cross-cultural differences in reasoning about reproduction may be telling. In one study, U.S. and Canadian adolescents lagged behind those in England, Sweden, and Australia in demonstrating formal reasoning regarding "where babies come from" (Goldman & Goldman, 1982). The delay was attributed to the lesser acceptability of teenage sexuality in North America and to the poorer quality of sex education. The impact of cultural context is underscored by cross-national data on teenage sex and pregnancy. Although rates of adolescent sexual activity in other Western, industrialized countries are similar to those in the United States, pregnancy rates are much lower (Alan Guttmacher Institute, 1986). Clearly, some young adolescents are able to use contraceptives effectively, given the right circumstances.

Based on these considerations, it seems probable that many young adolescents reason at the concrete operational level when making decisions about sex. This cognitive limitation could help explain their inconsistent use of contraceptives. For example, many girls seem to underestimate the risk of becoming pregnant. Pregnant girls report believing that they were not at risk because they were too young or had intercourse too infrequently or did not reach orgasm (Shah, Zelnik, & Kantner, 1975). Although misinformation certainly contributes to such beliefs, social cognitive skills may also be involved (Brooks-Gunn & Furstenberg, 1989). In particular, young girls may fail to understand the link between their behavior and possible outcomes or even to consider that such links exist. Or, lacking an extended time frame, they may be unable to imagine how the demands of motherhood would alter their daily lives and future opportunities.

The nature of early adolescent sexual activity may also contribute to ineffective contraception. Because young adolescents are just beginning to be sexually active, intercourse is typically infrequent and unplanned. Lack of planning is in turn associated with unprotected intercourse (Zelnik & Shah, 1983). Young adolescents are probably further disadvantaged by a lack of information about effective contraception. Sex education at the junior high level is less comprehensive than in high school and typically includes less information on contraception (Brooks-Gunn & Furstenberg, 1989). Consequently, misinformation about fertility and contraception may be especially common in early adolescence. Ignorance of pregnancy risks, inaccurate knowledge about the "safe" time of the month, and lack of knowledge about contraceptives, all of which are associated with ineffective contraception, can be attributed in part to lack of adequate sex education. In addition, young adolescents are least likely to have ready access to free, confidential family planning services and to contraceptives. Again, these circumstances are associated with failure to use effective contraception (Hayes, 1987).

Subgroup Differences. African-American adolescents have a higher rate of unprotected intercourse than do Whites. This difference, however, is due primarily to the fact that more African-Americans initiate sexual activity at an early age; once age at initiation is controlled, Blacks and Whites are equally likely (or unlikely) to practice contraception (Hayes, 1987). Contraceptive use is also related to SES (Chilman, 1986). Adolescents with more highly educated parents and those from higher social classes are more likely to use contraception. Other family background variables may also be important, such as parental attitudes and communication about sex and contraception (Moore, Peterson, & Furstenberg, 1986).

Childbearing

Little is known about the decision processes affecting girls' responses to an unintended pregnancy. The girl's reaction may depend on a host of factors such as her educational aspirations, her relationship with the baby's father, her perceptions of family support for keeping the child, and the number of her peers who have become parents (Fox, 1982). Research has identified factors that distinguish girls who choose to keep their babies from those choosing adoption or abortion. These studies indicate that girls who choose to keep their babies tend to have poorer school achievement and lower educational and occupational goals than girls choosing abortion or adoption. They also tend to have less-educated parents and are more likely to come from poor and single-parent families (Hayes, 1987). Family and peer attitudes are also important: Girls who keep their babies come from more religious families than those who choose abortion, are more likely to have friends and relatives who are teenage single parents, and are less likely to have mothers and peers with positive attitudes toward abortion (Furstenberg, Brooks-Gunn, & Chase-Lansdale, 1989). Parental attitudes toward abortion appear to be particularly influential in the case of young adolescents (Hayes, 1987).

These findings suggest several reasons for choosing to keep the child: abortion attitudes and related religious values; role models for early childbearing; and the absence of future goals that would be jeopardized by early parenthood. A family history of teenage childbearing provides both role models and evidence of tolerant attitudes toward early parenthood; a high rate of early childbearing among peers gives similar messages with respect to community norms and fertility values. In some communities, early childbearing may even bring increased status and privileges. Ethnographic studies (e.g., Stack, 1974) describe how early childbearing in a poor, African-American community brings privileges such as entree into the community economic and social network. Indeed, important effects of neighborhood characteristics on adolescent childbearing have been documented. The economic profile of the neighborhood and the prevalence of mother-headed households are both associated with a girl's likelihood of bearing a child out of wedlock, even when family characteristics are controlled (Brooks-Gunn, Duncan, Kato, & Sealand, 1991). In particular, the presence of middle-class neighbors and two-parent families seems to discourage early childbearing. Such neighborhood influences may operate by affecting mothers' ability to monitor their daughters' activities or through the provision of conventional adult role models. Finally, girls without good prospects for the future have little reason to avoid pregnancy, even if they do not actively seek it (Chilman, 1986). This argument is usually applied to girls in restricted economic circumstances, but it may also be important for young adolescents. Because young adolescents' future goals are usually not well articulated, their motivation to avoid an early pregnancy may be reduced.

With younger teenagers, unwillingness to acknowledge the pregnancy may also play a role in early childbearing. The cognitive immaturity that enables some girls to discount the risk of pregnancy may also lead them to deny the reality of an unintended pregnancy. Other young adolescents may simply postpone making a decision until abortion is no longer a viable option. Several reasons for delay have been suggested. Young teenagers may fail to recognize the signs of pregnancy, particularly because many experience irregular menstrual cycles. Others may deny the pregnancy. For some, geographical distance from clinics and hospitals as well as the costs of services may limit access to abortions (Alan Guttmacher Institute, 1981).

Whatever their reasons for continuing the pregnancy, teenagers who decide to bring a child to term tend to become more committed to their decision over the course of the pregnancy (Furstenberg et al., 1989). Family and friends become more supportive over time, and by the end of the pregnancy, most girls report feeling positive (Ooms, 1981). Unfortunately, the sense of well-being may be short-lived; some data indicate that self-esteem and perceived social support increase over the course of the pregnancy but then decline in the first year postpartum (Vicary & Crockett, unpublished data).

Adaptation to Parenthood

Mothers under 15 are thought to be at a disadvantage in assuming the maternal role. Young adolescents tend to be less cognitively and emotionally mature than older teenagers, and this may impair their ability to provide adequate parental care (Petersen & Crockett, 1986). Moreover, the role requirements of parenting conflict with the typical developmental tasks of adolescence (Sadler & Catrone, 1983), which could detract from girls' maternal role performance. Research on adolescent parenting, however, has not provided clear-cut results. Although some signs of inadequate parenting have been identified in young teenage mothers (e.g., McAnarney, 1988), parenting competence is rarely measured directly and is often confounded with effects of low SES. Thus, the issue of maternal competence remains controversial.

In fact, the issue of maternal competence may be less central in the case of young adolescent mothers. Because these mothers are more likely to remain with their parents, they are likely to have the help of more experienced adults in caring for their children. The presence of the grandmother is often associated with better adjustment among the children of adolescent mothers (Kellam, Ensminger, & Turner, 1977).

RECOMMENDATIONS FOR RESEARCH AND POLICY

The preceding account of early adolescent family formation points to numerous gaps in our knowledge that need to be addressed in future research. First and foremost is the paucity of information on adolescents under age 15. Few studies of reproductive behavior focus on this age group. Typically, young adolescents have been either excluded from samples or pooled with older adolescents. Information on boys is particularly lacking. Clearly, if researchers, practitioners, and policymakers are to understand the dynamics of early adolescent family formation, more direct study of this age group is needed. In addition to national statistics concerning rates of sexual activity, contraceptive use, pregnancy, and childbearing among young adolescents, there is a need for more detailed information on the factors influencing their behavior at each of these decision points. For example, more research needs to target young adolescents' thinking about sex and reproduction and the meanings they attach to these behaviors. Such studies will necessarily consider not only the developmental status and individual characteristics of the adolescents but their family circumstances and community environment. In addition, differences related to gender, ethnicity, and social class need to be better understood; therefore, group comparisons should be followed by within-group studies that seek to identify the underlying psychosocial and economic processes affecting reproductive behavior and its outcomes. Finally, the role of sexual abuse in early adolescent sexual activity and pregnancy needs to be examined.

The present account of early adolescent family formation also has implications for social policy. Undoubtedly, one major goal is pregnancy prevention. Recommendations for prevention programs in early adolescence are discussed by Crockett and Chopak (chapter 18, this volume). A second goal is providing ameliorative and support services. Young adolescent mothers and their children confront a unique set of risks related to the mother's cognitive and biological immaturity, lack of experience, and social stage. These mothers are less likely to recognize a pregnancy and less likely to think of appropriate courses of action; consequently, without intervention, they are unlikely to receive adequate nutrition and prenatal care. Without support and assistance, they are unlikely to show the foresight that will enable them to anticipate the child's needs and provide adequate nurturance. Socially, they are relatively inexperienced and may not know how to access services. And their stage of life is still a relatively dependent one, in which they rely on parents economically and emotionally. Therefore, ameliorative programs will need to consider young adolescent mothers' developmental status, as well as their social and economic circumstances.

One priority is the provision of prenatal and postnatal health services (Hayes, 1987). These services need to be familiar to adolescent girls and to their parents so that they will be accessed early in the pregnancy. They also need to be conveniently located and inexpensive. A second priority includes programs that help keep the young mother in school, including flexible class schedules, academic tutoring, and day-care services. Instruction in child development, information on childrearing, and contact with other young mothers would also be useful. A third priority is family planning to avoid a repeat pregnancy. Finally, the tendency for young adolescent mothers to live at home suggests the need for social services that support the family as a whole. The baby brings new family strains not only because of the additional demands for care and nurturance but because of the young mother's ambiguous status in the household as both daughter and parent, child and adult. Under these circumstances, the adolescent issue of autonomy is thrown into high relief, and family tensions may increase. Because parental support is very important in early adolescence, services to strengthen the family are recommended. These might include financial services, comprehensive health care, parenting education, and counseling. Programs that simultaneously enhance family support, improve the health and economic circumstances of the adolescent and her child, and equip the young mother with the academic and vocational skills needed to avoid poverty in the future will go far toward ameliorating the negative consequences of early childbearing.

REFERENCES

Alan Guttmacher Institute. (1981). *Teenage pregnancy: The problem that hasn't gone away.* New York: Author.

Alan Guttmacher Institute. (1986). *Teenage pregnancy in industrialized countries: A study sponsored by the Alan Guttmacher Institute.* New Haven, CT: Yale University Press.

Alexander, C. S., Ensminger, M. E., Kim, Y. J., Smith, J., Johnson, K. E., & Dolan, L. J. (1989). Early sexual activity among adolescents in small towns and rural areas: Race and gender patterns. *Family Planning Perspectives, 21,* 261-266.

Bachrach, C. A. (1986). Adoption plans, adopted children, and adoptive mothers. *Journal of Marriage and the Family, 48,* 243-253.

Butler, J. R., & Burton, L. M. (1990). Rethinking teenage childbearing: Is sexual abuse a missing link? *Family Relations, 39,* 73-80.

Brooks-Gunn, J., Duncan, G. J., Kato, P., & Sealand, N. (1991). *Do neighborhoods influence child and adolescent behavior?* Unpublished manuscript.

Brooks-Gunn, J., & Furstenberg, F. F. (1986). The children of adolescent mothers: Physical, academic and psychological outcomes. *Developmental Review, 6,* 244-251.

Brooks-Gunn, J., & Furstenberg, F. F. (1989). Adolescent sexual behavior. *American Psychologist, 44*(2), 249-257.

Card, J. J., & Wise, L. L. (1978). Teenage mothers and teenage fathers: The impact of early childbearing on the parents' personal and professional lives. *Family Planning Perspectives, 10,* 99-205.

Center for Population Options. (1989, November 5). Americans paid nearly $20 billion to support children born to teens. *Center Daily Times,* E-3.

Chilman, C. S. (1986). Some psychosocial aspects of adolescent sexual and contraceptive behaviors in a changing American society. In J. B. Lancaster & B. A. Hamburg (Eds.), *School-age pregnancy and parenthood: Biosocial dimensions* (pp. 191-217). New York: Aldine de Gruyter.

Ensminger, M. E. (1990). Sexual activity and problem behaviors among black, urban adolescents. *Child Development, 61,* 2032-2046.

Eveleth, P. B. (1986). Timing of menarche: Secular trend and population differences. In J. B. Lancaster & B. A. Hamburg (Eds.), *School-age pregnancy and parenthood: Biosocial dimensions* (pp. 31-52). New York: Aldine de Gruyter.

Fox, G. L. (1982). *The childbearing decision: Fertility attitudes and behavior.* Beverly Hills, CA: Sage.

Franklin, D. L. (1988). Race, class, and adolescent pregnancy: An ecological analysis. *American Journal of Orthopsychiatry, 58*(3), 339-354.

Furstenberg, F. F., Jr., Brooks-Gunn, J., & Chase-Lansdale, L. (1989). Teenaged pregnancy and childbearing. *American Psychologist, 44*(2), 313-320.

Furstenberg, F. F., Jr., Brooks-Gunn, J., & Morgan, S. P. (1987). *Adolescent mothers in later life.* New York: Cambridge University Press.

Furstenberg, F. F., & Crawford, A. G. (1978). Family support: Helping teenage mothers to cope. *Family Planning Perspectives, 10,* 322-333.

Goldman, R. J., & Goldman, J. D. (1982). How children perceive the origin of babies and the roles of mothers and fathers in procreation: A cross-national study. *Child Development, 53,* 491-504.

Hamburg, B. A. (1986). Subsets of adolescent mothers: Developmental biomedical, and psychosocial issues. In J. B. Lancaster & B. A. Hamburg (Eds.), *School-age pregnancy and parenthood: Biosocial dimensions* (pp. 115-145). New York: Aldine de Gruyter.

Haurin, R. J., & Mott, F. L. (1990). Adolescent sexuality activity in the family context: The impact of older siblings. *Demography, 27,* 537-557.

Hayes, C. D. (Ed.). (1987). *Risking the future: Adolescent sexuality, pregnancy, and childbearing* (Vol. 1). Washington, DC: National Academy Press.

Henshaw, S. K., Kenney, A. M., Somberg, D., & Van Vort, J. (1989). *Teenage pregnancy in the United States: The scope of the problem and state responses.* New York: The Alan Guttmacher Institute.

Hofferth, S. L., Kahn, J. R., & Baldwin, W. (1987). Premarital sexual activity among U.S. teenage women over the past three decades. *Family Planning Perspectives, 19*(2), 46–53.

Hogan, D. P., & Kitigawa, E. M. (1985). The impact of social status, family structure, and neighborhood on the fertility of black adolescents. *American Journal of Sociology, 90,* 825–855.

Inhelder, B., & Piaget, J. (1958). *The growth of logical thinking from childhood to adolescence.* New York: Wiley.

Jessor, R. L., Costa, F., Jessor, S. L., & Donovan, J. (1983). Time of first intercourse: A prospective study. *Journal of Personality and Social Psychology, 44,* 608–626.

Kantner, J. F., & Zelnik, M. (1972). Sexual experience of young unmarried women in the United States. *Family Planning Perspectives, 4,* 9–18.

Keating, D. (1990). Adolescent thinking. In S. Feldman & G. Elliot (Eds.), *At the threshold: The developing adolescent* (pp. 54–98). Cambridge: Harvard University Press.

Kellam, S. G., Ensminger, M. E., & Turner, R. J. (1977). Family structure and the mental health of children: Concurrent and longitional community-wide studies. *Archives of General Psychiatry, 34,* 1012–1022.

Magnusson, D., Stattin, H., & Allen, V. L. (1985). Biological maturation and social development: A longitudinal study of some adjustment processes from mid-adolescence to adulthood. *Journal of Youth and Adolescence, 14,* 267–283.

Marsiglio, W. (1987). Adolescent fathers in the United States: Their initial living arrangements, marital experience and educational outcomes. *Family Planning Perspectives, 19,* 240–251.

McAnarney, E. R. (1988). Early adolescent motherhood: Crisis in the making? In M. D. Levine & E. R. McAnarney (Eds.), *Early adolescent transitions* (pp. 139–147). Lexington, MA: D. C. Heath.

Moore, K. A., Nord, C. W., & Peterson, J. L. (1989). Nonvoluntary sexual activity among adolescents. *Family Planning Perspectives, 21,* 110–114.

Moore, K. A., Peterson, J. L., & Furstenberg, F. F. (1986). Parental attitudes and the occurrence of early sexual activity. *Journal of Marriage and the Family, 48,* 777–782.

Mott, F. L., & Marsiglio, W. (1985). Early childbearing and completion of high school. *Family Planning Perspectives, 17*(5), 234–237.

Newcomer, S., & Udry, J. R. (1987). Parent marital status effects on adolescent sexual behavior. *Journal of Marriage and the Family, 49,* 235–240.

Ooms, T. (Ed.). (1981). *Teenage pregnancy in a family context: Implications for policy.* Philadelphia: Temple University Press.

Petersen, A. C., & Crockett, L. J. (1986). Pubertal development and its relation to psychosocial development in adolescent girls: Implications for parenting. In J. B. Lancaster & B. A. Hamburg (Eds.), *School-age pregnancy and parenthood: Biosocial dimensions* (pp. 147–175). New York: Aldine de Gruyter.

Petersen, A. C., & Crockett, L. J. (in press). Teenage sexuality, pregnancy, and childbearing: Developmental perspectives. In M. K. Rosenheim & M. Testa (Eds.), *Early parenthood and the transition to adulthood.* New Brunswick, NJ: Rutgers University Press.

Pittman, K., & Adams, G. (1988). *Teenage pregnancy: An advocate's guide to the numbers.* Washington, DC: Children's Defense Fund.

Robbins, C., & Streetman, L. (1990, November). *The resolution of nonmarital adolescent pregnancy and the transition to adulthood: Educational attainment and financial well-being*. Paper presented at the International Symposium on Public Policies Toward Unwanted Pregnancies, Pittsburgh, PA.

Sadler, L. S., & Catrone, C. (1983). The adolescent parent: A dual developmental crisis. *Journal of Adolescent Health Care, 4,* 100–105.

Shah, F., Zelnik, M., Kantner, J. (1975). Unprotected intercourse among unwed teenagers. *Family Planning Perspectives, 7,* 39–44.

Smith, E. A., & Udry, J. R. (1985). Coital and non-coital sexual behaviors of White and Black adolescents. *American Journal of Public Health, 75,* 1200–1203.

Sonenstein, F. L., Pleck, J. H., & Ku, L. C. (1989). Sexual activity, condom use, and AIDS awareness among adolescent males. *Family Planning Perspectives, 21,* 152–158.

Stack, C. (1974). *All our kin: Strategies for survival in a black community.* New York: Harper & Row.

Udry, J. R. (1982, October). *Socialization of adolescent sexual behavior: A comparison of findings for Blacks and Whites.* Paper presented at the annual meeting of the National Council on Family Relations, Washington, DC.

Udry, J. R., & Billy, J. O. G. (1987). Initiation of coitus in early adolescence. *American Sociological Review, 52,* 841–855.

Udry, J. R., Billy, J. O. G., Morris, N. M., Groff, T. R., & Raj, M. H. (1985). Serum androgenic hormones motivate sexual behavior in boys. *Fertility and Sterility, 43*(1), 90–94.

Udry, J. R., Talbert, L., & Morris, N. M. (1986). Biosocial foundations for adolescent female sexuality. *Demography, 23*(2), 217–230.

Zabin, L. S., Kantner, J. F., & Zelnik, M. (1979). The risk of adolescent pregnancy in the first months of intercourse. *Family Planning Perspectives, 11*(4), 215–222.

Zelnik, M., & Kantner, J. F. (1980). Sexual activity, contraceptive use and pregnancy among metropolitan area teenagers: 1971–1979. *Family Planning Perspectives, 12*(5), 230–237.

Zelnik, M., Kantner, J., & Ford, K. (1981). *Sex and pregnancy in adolescence.* Beverly Hills, CA: Sage.

Zelnik, M., & Shah, F. K. (1983). First intercourse among young Americans. *Family Planning Perspectives, 15*(2), 64–70.

7 Familial Influences on Adolescent Health

Jordan W. Finkelstein
The Pennsylvania State University

The emphasis in this chapter is on the interaction between the family and the adolescent in the context of health. Before examining family health, it is necessary to define health. The World Health Organization (WHO) defines *health* as the optimal state of physical, mental, and social well-being and not merely the absence of disease (WHO, 1978). Health can be envisioned along a spectrum from ideal health on one end to severe illness and death on the other. An adolescent's health status may be positioned anywhere along this spectrum. However, health status may vary because of the different dimensions or levels of health within the same individual. The healthy adolescent will have no physical disease, feel competent, and self-actualized on the psychological level, practice no activities harmful to health on the behavioral level, and engage in appropriate role requirements on the social level (Jessor, 1984). This definition suggests that adolescents with chronic physical health problems might be healthy along the behavioral, psychological, and social dimensions. For instance, an adolescent with insulin-dependent diabetes mellitus who is in excellent metabolic control, who promotes his or her health, who is not experiencing mental health problems, and who is attending school and interacting with family and peers can be considered to be in excellent health despite the diagnosis of diabetes.

The health status of an individual member of a family usually has significant effects on the health status of other members of the family (Blum, 1988). It is therefore essential to consider the developmental status of the individual and the family and the many contexts within which both interact.

Adolescence is a period during which independence from parents is a central task (Havighurst, 1972). Assuming responsibility for management of their own health is an example of a critical task for adolescents (Roberts, Maddux, & Wright, 1984). Therefore, health interactions within the context of the family deserve special consideration. This chapter examines some issues involving adolescent health in the family context. This chapter discusses what is known about adolescents' responsibility for their own health, the health of adolescents with acquired and inherited chronic disease, and the effects of illness in other members of the adolescent's family on teenagers' health. Health promotion for adolescents is considered. Topics and areas to be considered for future investigations are also suggested as are possibilities for changes in policy as it affects adolescent health.

Responsibility for Health: Consent and Confidentiality

Adolescents are usually accompanied by a parent during a visit to a health-care provider. The annual visit for health maintenance by an adolescent may identify no health problems for the teen. However, the issues of consent for medical care and confidentiality will sometimes arise during such visits in early adolescence.

From a developmental point of view, parental permission for adolescents to seek medical care independently can be viewed as providing the adolescent with a level of responsibility that is highly desirable because it allows adolescents to accomplish a major developmental task (Jessor, 1984). However, the developmental stage at which such a significant responsibility should be granted must be carefully assessed. An adolescent who can think abstractly, has good judgment, and can appreciate long-term consequences of current actions may be considered by parents as developmentally appropriate for such a privilege. Parents who agree to such an arrangement give their adolescent a positive message that they recognize the maturity status of the child and are willing to act accordingly. Although most parents who consent to their teens seeking health care independently do so appropriately, some parents who are disinterested in their child's welfare may allow independent health care as an abrogation of their responsibility to their child. Whenever possible, health-care providers should participate in the decision-making process regarding this issue and recognize when it is appropriate. At the present time providers must use their own judgment in regard to providing care for adolescents without parental consent, except in those situations where the law is unambiguous (i.e., emancipated minors, life-threatening emergencies, and in situations involving certain infectious diseases).

There is no clear consensus among providers of medical services to adolescents in regard to which patient, under what circumstances, and for what disorders or situations parental consent is required. Most health-care providers would prefer to have such parental consent, as well as the consent of the teenaged patient. However, some providers feel that many teens would not seek certain services related for example to sexuality, substance use, suicide, and so forth, if they had to seek and obtain consent from parents (Hoffman, 1990). The problem of consent for health care is one that is under close scrutiny by legislators, health-care professionals, parents, and adolescents and there are some legal decisions that have been (Pennsylvania's 1990 Abortion legislation) and will be made in the near future regarding this issue. Legislators and jurists might consider seeking consultation with health-care providers with a developmental background (such as The American Academy of Pediatrics) during considerations of this important policy issue. How legislation or court decisions will affect the provision of health-care services to adolescents is not clear presently. There have been no controlled studies comparing health outcomes for those adolescents who had to seek parental consent to those who did not have to seek such consent. Research comparing these two groups of adolescents might help to resolve this policy issue.

Directly related to the issue of consent is the issue of confidentiality. If parents allow their teenagers to seek medical care independently, will the parents be informed of the content and outcomes of such encounters? Most parents feel it is their responsibility to know of diagnoses (including the diagnosis of excellent health) and management of health issues so that they may monitor their adolescent's health status, as they monitor educational, social, and related statuses.

Many providers of care to adolescents discuss the issues of confidentiality with families sometime in early adolescence. At this time, some teens begin to feel that they cannot discuss certain matters with their parents, or that they do not want their parents to know about some of their personal health concerns. Therefore, if adolescents know that nothing discussed with the provider will be made known to the parents without the adolescent's consent, the teenager may be willing to bring up a topic that they consider important and sensitive. These topics commonly relate to health behaviors that are risky (sexuality, substance use or abuse, parental abuse, etc.). Failure to establish a confidentiality agreement may result in negative health outcomes such as unintended pregnancy because the adolescent may be unable to obtain information about or actually obtain contraceptives (Hoffman, 1990).

Many of the parental refusals with regard to confidentiality are based on the parental assumption that the provider will keep everything confidential. However, most providers would not maintain confidentiality for anything that would put the adolescent at risk for adverse outcomes. For example, adolescents who reveal that they are planning to run away from home would be told that this information cannot be kept confidential, and that their parents must be informed. When these restraints are discussed with parents and adolescents, most will agree to confidentiality arrangements. The American Academy of Pediatrics has recently issued a statement supporting confidentiality arrangements for teens (American Academy of Pediatrics, 1989).

The health-care provider can use the issues of consent and confidentiality to support the development of independence in the adolescent in the family context by providing assistance to families in the decision-making process involved in these issues. Providers can foster normal adolescent development in the area of autonomy and independence by bringing up confidentiality issues at the appropriate time, preferably during early adolescence, and by subsequently treating adolescents as individuals capable of becoming responsible for their own health care. Even if consent or confidentiality arrangements cannot be agreed upon, providers can interact primarily with the adolescent rather than with the parent. If both parent and teen are in the consultation room, the provider can talk primarily to the adolescent, can examine the adolescent without the parent present (parents will usually leave during an exam if asked), can direct instructions to the adolescent, and can hand prescriptions to the adolescent rather than to the parent. These actions will give a strong message to the teen that the provider considers the teen mature, and will tend to support and strengthen teen–provider relations, which will usually result in improved health outcomes for the adolescent and increased satisfaction for the provider. The provider may also serve as a role model for parents, demonstrating effective communications with and how to delegate responsibility to the adolescent.

The Adolescent With Chronic Illness: The Family Context

The number of adolescents with chronic illness in the United States has been steadily increasing. It is estimated that up to 50% of a pediatrician's practice is concerned with chronic illness (Magrab & Calcagno, 1978). The increase in chronic illness has occurred because of the advances in biomedical technology, which allows children who previously would have died of their conditions, to survive. Premature infants of extremely low birth weight (under 1,000 grams) are now surviving, but many of these children have chronic health problems (such as bronchopulmonary dysplasia, a condition similar to chronic obstructive lung disease or emphysema), related to their immaturity at birth or to the technicological procedures used to ensure survival (such as use of high concentrations of oxygen, administered through an endotracheal tube attached to a respirator). Other children with diseases that in the past caused death in childhood (i.e., kidney failure) are now surviving to adulthood because of improved technology and care such as dialysis and transplantation. These adolescents and youth pose new problems for many health-care providers who have previously used only the biomedical model to provide health care. This model assumes that illness can be fully accounted for by a patient's deviation from the norm on measurable biological variables and that even the most complex illness phenomena can be reduced to certain measurable physical abnormalities (DiMatteo, 1991). This model ignores the effects of physical illness on other aspects of the patient's health (psychological, social, and behavioral issues) and on the effects of the health of other members of the adolescent's family. The biopsychosocial model of health requires that all the primary dimensions of health (WHO, 1978)—biological, psychological, behavioral, and social factors—must be included in any attempts to understand and manage all health issues and that these factors must be considered in the context in which they occur—the family (DiMatteo, 1991). Families are the most important support system for children in good health as well as for those children with special health needs (Hutchins & McPherson, 1991). The family's reaction to chronic illness experienced by its members becomes an essential element in the manner in which adolescents are able to cope, adapt to, and manage their own health situations.

Families are diverse in many characteristics such as the number of parents and children, socioeconomic status (SES), marital stability, and ability to cope with a sophisticated health-care delivery system, and so on (Crutcher, 1991). Just as the adolescent has certain developmental characteristics that need to be considered in dealing with health-related problems, every family has its own developmental age, its subsystems (relations between its members), and its emotional structure (which members set the tone for loyalty, who has authority, who cares for whom?) that need to be taken into account when considering familial health issues (Armstrong, 1983). Studies concerning the impact of chronic illness on the family have recently been reviewed by Garrison and McQuiston (1989). They stated that most studies were unidirectional, focused on the effects of families on the child, and on negative outcomes. Few studies have evaluated the effects of children on the family. Data from empirical studies suggested that most children with chronic illness did not manifest intellectual impairments or psychological disturbance, and there was no personality type that characterized the chronically ill child and adolescent population. However, some studies did indicate that there was generally an increased incidence of depression and lowered self-esteem in the child with chronic illness. Certain chronic illnesses were associated with specific psychological problems, and many chronically ill adolescents were at risk for the development of behavioral and adjustment problems. These problems are more likely to be overtly manifested when the biomedical model was used to provide care than when the biopsychosocial approach was utilized. Although families on the whole seem to be functioning well and to show reasonable degrees of resilience for the family in which an adolescent becomes ill, family functioning may become a delicate balancing act (Garrison & McQuiston, 1989).

Adolescents stricken with chronic illness would probably like to assume more responsibility for their own health care, but they would also like to have more privileges. In many instances, chronic illness provides the opportunity for the adolescent to assume more responsibility, but it is hardly the kind of responsibility that the adolescent wishes to assume, and it is often not accompanied by increased, but rather by decreased privileges. This conflict is not easy to resolve. Consider the case of the adolescent with end-stage renal disease who requires hemodialysis for 4 hours, three times a week, and who has to assume responsibility for management of this situation. These responsibilities are enormous because they involve not only the dialysis itself, but a host of other responsibilities (diet control, exercise, participation in school and social activities). Even among those adolescents who are willing and able to assume some or all of those responsibilities, parents may still retain control because they are concerned about, or doubt the teen's ability and willingness to carry out the appropriate tasks. Parental overprotection or resistance to relinquishing responsibility to the adolescent may interfere with the normal developmental tasks of adolescence.

On the other hand, some families are not as concerned with or involved in the management of the adolescent's disease as they should be. Some parents may even sabotage medical care of their chronically ill teenager. Parental behaviors related to adolescents with chronic illness may range from adaptive strain, to difficulties in communication, to noncompliance with management plans, to Munchausen's Syndrome by Proxy (parental deception of providers) (Krener & Adelman, 1988).

Chronically ill adolescents in families that cannot adapt appropriately may not receive adequate support from their family in the management of their health problem. Under these circumstances, teenagers have the opportunity to function autonomously, but they may not be able to do so alone. Insufficient parental support may cause such stress that the adolescent is unable to adequately cope with both the burden of disease and lack of support. The possible result is that the chronic condition may worsen.

Adolescents with a chronic health problem recognize that they are different from their peers (a most undesirable situation to them). They must therefore adjust to this situation. We do not know what proportion of adolescents with chronic illnesses have adjusted well to their problems and research on this topic is sorely needed (Garrison & McQuiston, 1989). It is known that some adolescents with chronic illnesses do not adjust well. For example, some teens with diabetes mellitus do not follow their prescribed regimes of diet and insulin. This noncompliance makes them ill, sometimes so ill that they require emergency hospitalization (Travis, 1987). Although it is recognized that glucose metabolism is somewhat different in normal adolescents compared to younger children or adults (Amul, Sherwin, Simonson, Lauritans, & Tamborlane, 1986) it is not felt that altered glucose metabolism is the reason for repeated hospitalization of this type of teenager with diabetes. Rather, issues related to family conflicts usually are the basis for increased stress, which causes a cascade of complex metabolic events to occur. These hormonally mediated responses to stress result in metabolic derangements requiring hospital treatment. Most of these so-called "brittle" diabetics are teenaged girls. Reasons for the gender difference are unknown and should be explored. Research also is needed to determine what helps many adolescents and their families adapt adequately to chronic illness, and to complete the developmental tasks of adolescence.

The Adolescent With an Inherited Disease

Some of the manifestations of inherited disorders are clearly visible, and anyone can tell the adolescent has such a condition just by looking at him or her, and others are less visible or even impossible for the layperson to detect. The adolescent with a visible deforming condition will have to face the consequences of being easily identified as different at all stages of life. The problem of obvious physical deformity in an adolescent poses potentially difficult adjustments for most adolescents who want to be as like in appearance to their peers as "peas in a pod." Adolescents also tend to be extremely concerned with self-image and with relations with members of the opposite sex, which are often based on appearance.

Diabetes mellitus is an example of an inherited condition that is not easily discernable to the layperson, although the observant person might notice that the affected teenager performs certain "rituals" (such as dietary restrictions and taking of injections) and may therefore suspect that the teenager has a medical problem.

On the other hand, the inherited condition may be such that it is impossible for a layperson to know that an adolescent has an inherited condition because there are no obvious physical or behavioral concomitants of this situation. Such an instance might include congenital hypothyroidism, a condition that is usually diagnosed in the first days of life and for which early treatment results in an adolescent who is generally normal, although he or she must still take daily treatment.

Regardless of the situation of visibility of the disorder to others, the condition is blatantly "visible" to the affected teenagers. They know they have the condition. Many teenagers are so egocentric that they think that they are the center of everyone's attention (Elkind, 1967). They therefore conclude that everyone must know that they have a chronic illness and that everyone "sees" them as different. Providers should consider this issue when planning management strategies for affected teens.

Adolescents with an inherited disease or condition face the problem of dealing with the knowledge that they inherited the disorder from one or both parents. They must face the inescapable fact that their situation is the result of something that they "got" from their parent(s). The issue of teen adjustment to chronic inherited conditions, as reflected in their interactions with their parent(s) from whom they acquired the condition, with other family members such as unaffected siblings, and within the context of school and the workplace, are areas for additional research.

Illness in Other Family Members

Illness in other family members is likely to have significant effects on the adolescent's functioning within the family. The effects vary depending on which family member is affected, what disability is present in the affected member and how much information the adolescent is able to gather about the health problem.

There is little doubt that every adolescent will be upset and worried about illness in a family member. The amount of distress that the adolescent manifests is likely to be strongly related to the degree of emotional attachment between the adolescent and the affected family member. In addition to the emotional issue, the adolescent also may be dependent on the affected person for financial support. Thus, if a wage earner becomes ill, the adolescent may have concerns about family income. This may be a serious problem in families that depend on all of the income generated by all wage earners in order for the family to function effectively. This may be a major problem in single-parent families, especially in those in which alimony or child support is not consistently available. Some adolescents may be forced to consider the possibility of assuming a wage-earning role within the family in order to help financially. This additional responsibility is likely to cause adolescents to work longer hours to accommodate their role as a student and as a wage earner and could adversely affect their health behaviors (such as sleeping or eating) and functioning within the family, school, and with peers.

Although the affected family member may present no obvious physical or functional disability, an adolescent is likely to be concerned that some disability may develop in the future. On the other hand, if the disability is obvious the amount of stress and concern adolescents experience may be great and they may experience anorexia, insomnia, abdominal pain, and so forth, which can be precursors of impaired health (Apley, 1975).

A common family situation is one in which one sibling develops a chronic illness and others do not. Many of the family resources may be redirected toward the care of the ill sibling resulting in neglect of other family members (Sabbath, 1984). Although most of the siblings of chronically ill children adapt well (Garrison & McQuiston, 1989), sibling illness can result in family disruptions of considerable magnitude and may place the adolescent under considerable stress. For instance, the presence of a chronically ill sibling may prevent adolescents from bringing peers into their home, placing them at a social disadvantage (Mass & DeNour, 1975). The incidence of divorce in those families in which a child becomes chronically ill is low, but "marital distress" is increased in families with chronically ill children and adolescents (Sabbath & Leventhal, 1984). Other areas of marital adjustment such as communication, decision making, and role flexibility in these families have received little attention by researchers (Sabbath & Leventhal, 1984).

Information available to the adolescent about illness in another family member may be a factor in determining how the teen will react. It is common practice for physicians to tell only a spouse or parent of a sick person anything at all about a family member's illness. Children and adolescents are usually uninformed about the nature of illness in other family members. In some instances they are given the information by another family member or may overhear bits and pieces of information from which they may deduce (often incorrectly) something about the situation. Insufficient information about the effects of illness on a family member may increase stress and cause illness in the teenager. Little is known about this situation and research is sorely needed in regard to this matter. Policy changes are probably needed so that health providers or adult family members are encouraged to appropriately inform adolescents about significant health problems of other family members. Family members with illnesses may also be reluctant to discuss their health with their adolescent children. It is likely that parental attempts to "protect" their adolescent children from the truth may increase rather than decrease adolescents' concerns.

EFFECTS OF CHRONIC ILLNESS AND FAMILY RELATIONSHIPS ON ADOLESCENTS' HEALTH BEHAVIORS

When adolescents suffer the effects of stress caused by their own chronic illness or chronic illness in a family member, they may react in several ways. Continued stress may cause distress in the adolescent. This distress may be manifested in emotional symptoms such as anxiety or depression, or in physical symptoms, the most common of which are chronic headache or stomachache (Richtsmeier, 1985). Those adolescents presenting with the emotional symptoms of stress are usually easier to diagnose than those presenting with the physical symptoms of stress. However, the emotional symptoms are often not recognized by either parents or health professionals. It is estimated that a substantial number of physicians treating children and adolescents do not adequately identify distressed teenagers' emotional symptoms, do not establish correct diagnoses, and do not institute appropriate management (Starfield et al., 1980). A consequence of failure to diagnose mental illness in adolescents may be the high rate of suicide among adolescents in whom suicide is the second leading cause of death (Gans, Blyth, Elster, & Gaveras, 1990). It is essential that families recognize behavioral symptoms of stress in adolescents and then seek professional help. Part of the problem is that professional help is not so readily available (Gans et al., 1990).

Recognition of the adolescent who manifests stress through the production of physical symptoms is even more difficult (Richtsmeier, 1985). Chronic headache or abdominal pain are two of the most common physical stress-related symptoms in adolescents. It has been estimated that 10% of youngsters have suffered from chronic abdominal pain at some time in their lives (Apley, 1975). These "somatization disorders" result from the conversion of what should be emotional symptoms to physical symptoms. In the past, this group of disorders has been called *psychosomatic* or *conversion* reactions. These symptoms are supposed to relieve stress by preventing the adolescent from doing or participating in something that causes distress. Failure by providers to include the possibility of stress-induced physical symptoms in the evaluation of adolescents presenting with these symptoms may result in extensive, expensive diagnostic procedures, with many laboratory tests, some of which may be invasive. Some patients with abdominal pain have even undergone surgery in order to diagnose their symptoms. These "sick" teens are often unknowingly rewarded by their families for their behaviors. They are taken by parents to many doctors for multiple visits and get a lot of secondary gain from the extra attention focused on them. Recognition of stress-related symptoms in adolescents is essential for appropriate management to be initiated.

Health problems in adolescents may also be caused by family health practices. It is more likely that adolescents will use substances (cigarettes, alcohol, drugs) if their parents are users or abusers of these substances (Brook & Whitman, 1986; Streit, Halstead, & Pascale, 1974). Teen substance use or abuse may result in significant health problems. For instance, accidents are the most common cause of death among adolescents. Most of these are automobile accidents, many of which involve intoxicated teens (Gans et al., 1990). Picture the scenario of the teen who has an argument with his or her parents, uses alcohol to deal with the upset (as a parent has done), and then goes out for a ride to calm down or meet friends. The likelihood of an accident involving this teen is much greater than it would be for a teen who does not drive while intoxicated.

It is estimated that 13.5% of the adult population abuse alcohol (Regier, Boyd, & Burke, 1988). Thus, at least 13.5% of the adolescent population are children of alcoholics (COA). Children of alcoholics suffer from a variety of health problems as a result of their parents' alcoholism. Adverse health outcomes for children and adolescents include death from traffic accidents related to parental drinking and driving, child abuse, fetal alcohol syndrome, dysfunctional family life, and alcoholism (McDonald, 1991). Physician identification of COAs is inadequate because of lack of emphasis in the medical school curriculum, lack of interest by physicians, an unwillingness to "intrude" on personal familial issues, and failure of physicians to recognize potential health-related issues for COAs, (McDonald, 1991). Health effects on adolescents of parental use or abuse of other substances, including prescription drugs, are not well documented and present important opportunities for research.

Some teens who are experiencing significant difficulties in family relations may resort to what has been called "acting-out behaviors," which usually have negative health consequences. These behaviors usually are initially relatively innocuous activities such as refusal to do chores or to participate in customary family activities. If the parents fail to recognize the teen's behavior as an indicator of the presence of a problem, the adolescent's behavior is likely to progress to more serious behaviors such as failing grades in school. Further escalation of attention-seeking, problem behaviors will continue until an outcome occurs that can no longer be ignored by parents. Such outcomes include behaviors associated with high health risks such as substance use and abuse, premature sexual activity with the risk of pregnancy during adolescence, the acquisition of sexually transmitted disease including AIDS, and suicide as a result of unsatisfactory interpersonal relationships with the sexual partner. Recognition of the acting-out syndrome by parents and providers has the potential for establishing early appropriate preventive interventions.

FAMILY HEALTH PROMOTION AND DISEASE PREVENTION

In addition to family reactions to disease states affecting the health of the adolescent and the family, a family approach to disease prevention and health promotion activities is worthy of consideration. Although our society has been focusing on the diagnosis and management of disease (acute illness especially), awareness of the importance of disease prevention and the health promotion has been increasing significantly. The U.S. government has developed a plan for promoting health and preventing disease (Richmond, 1980). Many of the objectives apply to adolescents. More recently, specific objectives for adolescents have been published. The objectives address physical fitness and activity, nutrition, substance use, family planning, mental health, violent and abusive behavior, unintentional injury, environmentally transmitted disease, immunization and clinical prevention (AMA, 1990). Familial involvement in reaching these objectives is not mentioned in either of these documents. The role of the family in promoting health and preventing disease is important. Although some attention has been paid to this aspect of family health (Epstein, Vaolski, Wuy, & McCurley, 1990), it seems likely that adolescents will be dependent on their family for guidance in behaviors that promote health and prevent disease. Research in this area is sorely needed. In addition, third-party payers will only reimburse health providers for their time spent in providing disease prevention services to adults, but not for children (Culhane, 1991). Health promotion services are not reimbursable for either adults or children. Public policies are needed to address these problems.

Families with members who have chronic illness may not engage in health-promoting or disease-preventing activities for many reasons. However, all families should engage in these activities and include the chronically ill person within the limitations imposed by the illness. For instance, even bedridden adolescents may engage in some form of physical activity. To date, there has been little concern with promoting the health of chronically ill adolescents. Most providers managing chronically ill adolescents focus on secondary prevention (prevention of complications) or tertiary prevention (rehabilitation). The only areas of health promotion in children and adolescent with disabilities or handicapping conditions have been related to exercise (Special Olympics) and sexuality (Degen, Strain, & Zumoff, 1983).

There is a great need for new research efforts and demonstration projects in the area of health promotion for teens with chronic illness/disabilities. The concerns to be addressed are the same health issues that are addressed for adolescents without chronic illness. These relate to the common causes of morbidity and mortality among adolescents and include preventing accidents, suicide and homicide, prevention of consequences of premature sexual behaviors (unwanted pregnancy, sexually transmitted disease and "heartbreak"), prevention of substance use and abuse, promotion of exercise programs, appropriate nutritional guidance, good dental hygiene, stress reduction, and so on.

Public Policy for Families

Society has begun to recognize the importance of the family in which there is a child with "special health needs" by developing policies to address familial as well as individual needs (Hutchins & McPherson, 1991). The family is recognized as the most important support system for children and especially for children with chronic illness. According to Hutchins and McPherson, family-centered care is the keystone of this policy issue, whose key elements are as follows:

1. The family is a constant in most children's lives.
2. A parent–health professional relationship must be established.
3. Parents must be provided unbiased information about their child's health.
4. Financial and emotional support programs are required.

5. Families are diverse in regard to many characteristics and these must be considered when developing programs.
6. Children's developmental stage must be considered.
7. Parent to parent support groups are helpful.
8. Programs must be responsive to family needs.

Amendments to The Education of The Handicapped Act (Public Law 92–142) were enacted in 1986 (Public Law 99–457) to address these needs. It is clear that public policy recognizes the needs of the family in managing the problems associated with chronic illness in children and adolescents.

However, public policy in regard to providing health services to adolescents is far from acceptable. A substantial proportion of families with adolescents do not have the financial means to access any health care. In 1989, only 40% of adolescents living in poverty had Medicaid coverage, leaving 3 million poor adolescents without health insurance coverage. Seventeen percent of rural and 13% of urban adolescents had no health insurance (Newacheck, McManus, & Gephart, 1989).

Even in those instances in which some form of public assistance is available to families with adolescents, some providers will not accept patients who are covered because the paperwork involved in applying for reimbursement to governmental agencies is so burdensome, and is often more costly than the fee paid. In some states, this fee is substantially below the "usual and customary" fee charged by providers.

If society is to address the health needs of all adolescents, including those with either acute or chronic altered health states, and address the need to provide health promotion and disease prevention services within the biopsychosocial model of health care, we must ensure that health services are available, accessible, affordable, appropriate, and acceptable. Health professional schools must adjust their curricula to ensure that graduates who become providers, teachers, and policymakers are aware of these issues (McDonald, 1991). However, public policy must also address the problems of making sure that the basic necessities of life—food, shelter, and clothing—as well as health care are available to families. Adolescents who are hungry, homeless, and worried about basic survival issues are sure to be less healthy and less amenable to preventive interventions and health promotion programs than those who are better off.

REFERENCES

Apley, J. (1975). *The child with abdominal pain*. Oxford: Blackwell Scientific Publications.

American Academy of Pediatrics. (1989, April). Policy statement: Confidentiality in adolescent health care. *AAP News* p. 9

American Medical Association. (1990). *Healthy Youth 2000: National health promotion and disease prevention objectives for adolescents.* Chicago: Author.

Amul, S. A., Sherwin, R. S., Simonson, D. C., Lauritans, A. A., & Tamborlane, W. V. (1986). Impaired insulin action in puberty. *New England Journal of Medicine, 315,* 215–219.

Armstrong, S. (1983). Children and adolescents on hemodialysis and transplantation programs. In N. B. Levy (Ed.), *Psychonephrology 2: Psychological problems in kidney failure and their treatment* (pp. 121–126). New York: Plenum Medical Books.

Blum, R. W. (1988). Developing with disabilities: The early adolescent experience. In M. D. Levine & E. R. McAnarney (Eds.), *Early adolescent transitions* (pp. 177–192). Lexington, MA: Lexington Books.

Brook, J. S., & Whitman, M., (1986). Father–daughter identification and its impact on her personality and drug use. *Developmental Psychology, 22,* 743–748.

Crutcher, D. M. (1991). Family support in the home: Home visiting and Public Law 99–457. *American Psychologist, 46,* 138–140.

Culhane, C. (1991, July 8–15). Blues endorse ACD guide in screening schedules. *American Medical News,* p. 6.

Degen, K., Strain, J. J., & Zumoff, B. (1983). Biopsychosocial Evaluation of sexual function in end stage renal disease. In N. B. Levy (Ed.), *Psychonephrology 2: Psychological problems in kidney failure and their treatment* (pp. 45–52). New York: Plenum Medical Books.

DiMatteo, M. R. (1991). *The psychology of health, illness and medical care.* Pacific Grove, CA: Brooks/Cole.

Elkind, D. (1967). Egocentrism in adolescence, *Child Development, 38,* 1025–1034.

Epstein, L. H., Vaolski, A., Wuy, R. R., & McCurley, J. (1990). Ten year followup of behavioral, family based treatment for obese children. *Journal of the American Medical Association, 264,* 2519–2523.

Gans, J. E., Blyth, D. A., Elster, A. G., & Gaveras, L. L. (1990). *America's adolescents: How healthy are they?* Chicago: American Medical Association.

Garrison, W. T., & McQuiston, S. (1989). *Chronic illness during childhood and adolescence: Psychological aspects.* Newbury Park, CA: Sage.

Havighurst, R. J. (1972). *Developmental tasks and education* (3rd ed.). New York: McKay.

Hoffman, A. (1990). Consent and confidentiality: Critical issues in providing contraceptive care. In V. Strasberger (Ed.), *Basic office gynecology* (pp. 59–74). Baltimore: Urban & Schwartzenberg.

Hutchins, V., & McPherson, M. (1991). National agenda for children with special health needs: Social policy for the 1990s through the 21st century. *American Psychologist, 46,* 141–143.

Jessor, R. (1984). Adolescent development and behavioral health. In J. D. Matarazzo, J. A. Herd, N. E. Miller, & S. M. Weiss (Eds.), *Behavioral health* (pp. 69–90). New York: Wiley.

Krener, P., & Adelman, R. (1988). Parent salvage and parent sabotage in the care of chronically ill children. *American Journal of Diseases of Children, 142,* 945–951.

Magrab, P. R., & Calcagno, P. L. (1978). Psychological impact of chronic pediatric conditions. In P. R. Magrab (Ed.), *Psychological management of pediatric problems* (Vol. 1, pp. 18–26). Baltimore: Baltimore University Park Press.

Mass, M., & DeNour, A. (1975). Reactions of families to chronic hemodialysis. *Psychotherapy and Psychosomatics, 26,* 20.

McDonald, D. I. (1991). Parental alcoholism. A neglected pediatric responsibility. *American Journal of Diseases of Children, 145,* 609–610.

Newacheck, P., McManus, P., & Gephart, J. (1989). *Memo.* Institute for Health Policy Studies, University of California School of Medicine, San Francisco, CA.

Reiger, D. A., Boyd, J. H., & Burke, J. D. (1988). One month prevalence of mental disorders in the U.S. based on 5 epidemiologic catchment area sites. *Archives of General Psychiatry, 45,* 977–986.

Richmond, J. B. (1980). *Promoting health and preventing disease: Objectives for the nation.* Washington, DC: Department of Health and Human Services, U.S. Government Printing Office.

Richtsmeier, A. J. (1985). Individual interviews of children with unexplained symptoms. *American Journal of Diseases of Children, 139,* 506–508.

Roberts, M. C., Maddux, J. E., & Wright, L. (1984). Developmental Perspectives in Biobehavioral Health. In J. D. Matarazzo, J. A. Herd, N. E. Miller, & S. M. Weiss (Eds.), *Behavioral health* (pp. 56–68). New York: Wiley.

Sabbath, B. F. (1984). Understanding the impact of chronic childhood illness on families. *Pediatric Clinics of North America, 31,* 47–57.

Sabbath, B. F., & Leventhal, J. M. (1984). Marital adjustment to chronic childhood illness: A critique of the literature. *Pediatrics, 73,* 762–768.

Starfield, B., Gross, E., Wood, M., Pantell, R., Allen, C., Gordon, I. B., Moffatt, P., Brachman, R., & Katz, H. (1980). Psychosocial and psychosomatic diagnoses in primary care of children. *Pediatrics, 66,* 159–167.

Streit, F., Halstead, D. L., & Pascale, P. J. (1974). Differences among youthful users and non-users of drugs based on perceptions of parental behavior. *International Journal of Addiction, 9,* 749–755.

Travis, L. B. (1987). Hyperlabile diabetes. In L. B. Travis, B. H. Brouhard, & B. Schriener (Eds.), *Diabetes mellitus in children and adolescents* (pp. 179–186). Philadelphia: W.B. Saunders.

World Health Organization. (1978). *Primary health care.* Geneva: Author.

II | Early Adolescent Education

Section Editors:

Lynne V. Feagans
Karen Bartsch
The Pennsylvania State University

A Framework for Examining the Role of Schooling During Early Adolescence

Lynne V. Feagans
Karen Bartsch

ADOLESCENCE AND SCHOOLING

In 1989, the Carnegie Corporation Task Force on Education of Young Adolescents addressed the question, "What do we want every young adolescent to know, to feel, to be able to do upon emerging from that educational and school-related experience?" (p. 15). They answered the question with five basic goals that reflected a broad and encompassing view of the role of our educational institutions. These goals require a new conceptualization of the role of education in development even while they reflect our society's growing recognition that schooling may be the most important societal force in shaping future citizens.

The first goal articulated by Carnegie was for adolescents to be intellectually reflective persons. Our youth should develop good analytic skills that would be applied widely to issues ranging from the appreciation of different cultural perspectives to the careful scrutiny of media messages. Skills developed should include coherent writing, articulate verbal expression, and understanding the basics of arts, mathematics, and sciences. Second, youth should emerge as people enroute to a lifetime of meaningful work. An understanding of work as both the means of economic survival and a source of self-definition should be developed. Such individuals would have an appreciation of the rapid technological changes and concomitant training that is needed for the jobs that interest them. Third, youth should emerge as good citizens who accept responsibility for helping to shape their environment, who understand the basic aims and goals of our society and its history, and who appreciate global citizenship and respect the basic differences among cultures. Fourth, youth should become caring and ethical individuals. Youth should learn and understand the difference between good and bad and act for the good in daily life. They should also understand the importance of developing and maintaining close personal relationships with friends and family. Finally, youth must be healthy people. They should be aware of and act on those practices that will develop and maintain a physically and psychologically healthy body (Carnegie Council, 1989).

If we accept these goals for our youth, we will require both a new kind of framework in which to view the developing adolescents and corresponding new emphasis in educational curricula. Although these goals may seem broader than those envisioned by many educators, the American school system has always been seen as a vehicle for social change, a place where broader societal change is reflected (Cremin, 1980; Linney & Seidman, 1989). Recent attempts to improve education do not adequately address these goals. These attempts have included efforts to move "back to basics," increase discipline, improve teacher salaries, and increase testing of students (National Commission on Excellence in Education, cited in Linney & Seidman, 1989). Such narrow and fragmented approaches to education problems may be successful in the short run in achieving some limited objectives, but in the long run these approaches actually thwart efforts to achieve the broader goals as articulated by the Carnegie Council (1989).

Before proceeding with a framework to incorporate the broader goals of schooling, it may be helpful to recall Hyman's (1979) distinction between education and schooling. In an article in the *American Psychologist* Hyman (1979) noted that "Education has to do with the process of learning; schooling is the means by which social, political, and economic factors shape the learning environment" (p. 1025).

It seems clear that the goals that the Carnegie Council (1989) articulated relate more to schooling than to education. Linney and Seidman (1989) lament that more than 10 years later, Hyman's distinction, its implications are still not understood and that little work has been done to create models or frameworks that could incorporate the concept of schooling. Education journals and publications still primarily focus on individual diagnosis and intervention without a view of the broader context and goals of schooling. This chapter presents a framework that incorporates both the goals of Carnegie and the concept of schooling. Our aim is to show how such a framework may be useful for understanding some of the problems in the schooling process, particularly those associated with the period of early adolescence.

Early adolescence, fraught with numerous biological and psychological changes, is a particularly interesting and important time. Hamburg (1990) described the period well.

> Contemporary adolescence now spans at least a decade and comprises three distinctive phases, early, middle, and late. Early adolescence, ages 10 to 15 years, is a time of drastic and superimposed changes in all spheres of functioning (biological, social, and academic). As such, it is a time of maximal discontinuity with the past. Therefore, it represents the developmental period of highest stress and challenge but also a time of maximal opportunity. It is a time of heightened susceptibility to influence and there are possibilities for better or for worse, to change the developmental trajectory in ways that can be sharply different from the past. (p. 16)

Early adolescence constitutes a window of opportunity for real change in the developing child. Yet our schools are generally ill suited to cope with the vulnerability and susceptibility typical of this period, so we as a society are losing the opportunity to promote the goals we have for youth. At the root of many of the problems of schooling during adolescence are tremendous individual differences among children, differences in the biological, social, and psychological realms (Eccles & Midgley, 1989; Lipsitz, 1984). Thus, an adequate framework must take into consideration the changes occurring within the individual adolescent as well as the changes in, and broadening of, the environment in which the adolescent functions.

Clearly, an adequate framework for considering young adolescents in relation to the broad goals we have for them will be one that considers individuals' experiences, perceptions, and beliefs across the multiple contexts in which they are embedded. We propose that such a framework is available in the developmental/contextual perspective (Bronfenbrenner, 1979; Lerner, 1986). Only a broad and complex perspective such as this can provide a useful framework for examining the relationship between early adolescents' experiences and beliefs across multiple contexts and the ability of educational institutions to achieve their goals of preparing students to meet the challenges of living responsibly and independently in adulthood.

A DEVELOPMENTAL/CONTEXTUAL PERSPECTIVE

The developmental/contextual perspective as articulated by Lerner (1986) focuses on a number of concepts that are particularly important for understanding the developing adolescent and schooling. Of particular importance is a focus on intra- and interindividual differences and change. There is emphasis on changes within the individual over time in the same setting as well as changes in the individual in different settings. These two aspects of intraindividual differences are important in understanding the variability within each adolescent as a function of time and setting. Second, differences between adolescents (interindividual) are quite profound during adolescence, both biologically and psychologically (Lerner, 1989; Lipsitz, 1984). These differences between individuals may be critically important in understanding why some adolescents function well through adolescence and why others do not. Defining subgroups of adolescents during this critical period would be important then in understanding their developmental trajectories and in understanding their behaviors and experiences both in and out of school.

In specifying these relationships, Lerner drew upon the work of Thomas and Chess (1977) as well as Schneirla (1957) to conceptualize the "Goodness of Fit" model. This model assumes that each environment in which the adolescent functions has certain demand characteristics and that the individuals who control the setting also have beliefs and perceptions about the functioning of the individuals within it. The adolescent comes to these settings with a certain set of characteristics and the adaptation to the settings is a function of the fit between the individual and the setting. The setting demands and the individuals in the setting give feedback to the adolescent, which in turn affects the individual's behavior, beliefs, and/or perception of adaptation to the situation, creating "circular reactions" of feedback loops (Lerner, 1989). The school that is sensitive to these individual differences and the developmental level of the students is more likely to create constructive feedback loops for all adolescents. Eccles and Midgley (1989) argued that the mismatch between adolescents and their school environments may be causally related to declines in self-esteem and achievement. For example, an adolescent with the belief that literacy skill has little to offer her or him to prepare for the future will encounter a school environment that may mandate that literacy is important for the future. The interaction and feedback between the individual and the school will determine whether the adolescent can maintain self-esteem in the face of this conflict as well as whether the adolescent can come to value the beliefs of both contexts and thus succeed in school.

A particular advantage of the developmental/contextual perspective is that it takes seriously the perceptions, beliefs, and experiences of the individual and those around them in multiple settings. Clearly, the cognitive and life-skill development of early adolescents depends, to a large degree, on the range of experiences, opportunities, and constraints placed upon them in the multiple contexts in which they live. In turn, the nature of early adolescents' in-school experiences are inextricably linked to the *belief systems* that they acquire from their interactions in several key settings, including the home, the neighborhood, and the larger community (e.g., youth organizations).

For example, Stevenson (1988) illustrated the importance of examining parental belief systems in relationship to cognitive achievement in elementary school students. His work points out that a key factor in determining whether certain children are more or less at risk for cognitive deficits in school may be the extent to which children are socialized by their parents to believe that achievement in school is related to effort, and not in-born ability. Children who believe that effort is rewarded will find a better fit with the school because this belief is also found in teachers and other school staff. In a large study of urban youth (Alexander & Entwisle, 1988), parental beliefs about school contributed significantly to the prediction of early school achievement, even when socioeconomic status (SES) was controlled for.

Other studies suggest that when early adolescents believe that their parents are willing to provide them with reassurance, assistance, and support, they are more likely to believe that their effort in school will "pay off" in terms of improved academic performance and more positive self-regard (Comer, 1984; Hess, 1990; Kandel & Lesser, 1972; Marjoribanks, 1978; Stevenson, 1988; Weinhert & Trieber, 1982). Although the family is probably the primary source of influence in shaping belief systems and feelings of competence, the importance of values and expectations coming from individuals outside the family, including the peer group, teachers, and youth leaders, becomes greater as children make the transition from childhood into adolescence (Rosenberg, 1979). In fact, evidence from the social support literature suggests that adolescents who perceive support to be lacking in one domain are likely to seek compensation in the form of more support from the other domains (Weiss, 1976). For instance, adolescents have been found to rely on (and be influenced by) peer relationships more heavily when emotional support from their parents is lacking (Hoffman, Ushpiz, & Levy-Shiff, 1988; Iacovetta, 1975; Larson, 1972; Smith, 1976).

THE DEVELOPMENTAL/CONTEXTUAL FRAMEWORK WITHIN AN ECOLOGICAL PERSPECTIVE

A further elaboration of this framework is necessary to fully address the importance of different contexts themselves. We suggest adopting an ecological perspective that describes the contexts in and out of school in which schooling in the broad sense takes place. The ecological perspective (Bronfenbrenner, 1979) assumes that behavior is in part constrained by expectations of the setting in which the early adolescent operates. According to Bronfenbrenner, behavior and beliefs expected in one setting may or may not coincide with the expectations and beliefs in another setting. Thus, it is important to understand the components of the different settings in which the adolescent is learning. This would include home, school, peer group, and other critical settings.

According to Bronfenbrenner, different levels of settings need to be distinguished. The *microsystem* encompasses the settings in which the individual adolescent is embedded. One of the most important contexts is the molar system of the school that can be subdivided into more microsettings like classrooms, lunchroom, hallways, and sports activities. In addition, the settings of the home, neighborhood, and community activities may play a critical role in the adolescent's development and learning (Rosenberg, 1979). Beliefs and practices about such important school tasks such as literacy may be quite different but valuable in these out-of-school settings. Comer (1984) discussed the conflicts between home and school. "Children may have skills that are useful and valued in their primary social network—housing project, church, neighborhood, and the like—but not highly useful and valuable for school success" (p. 327). There are really two options to help children whose out-of-school microsystems do not fit well with the school microsystem. The school can try to incorporate some of the values and beliefs of the out of school microsystems to help the child see the complementary values of both systems. The school can make clear the differences between home and school and emphasize the importance of the school values. The former strategy would seem the most appropriate from an ecological/developmental perspective but the latter has been the more common strategy in schools. Both Kagan, Schreiber, and Zigler (1984) and Ogbu (1981) called for an understanding of the out-of-school microsystems and an incorporation of the best cultural beliefs and values found there in schooling our children.

The *mesosystem* is central to the ecological framework because it encompasses the connections that link one microsystem to another. These relationships may or may not be facilitative and synergistic. In this perspective, the more facilitative the connections between the microsystems, the better the individual will adapt. For instance, if the literacy practices and beliefs in the home and neighborhood are incongruent with the practices and beliefs in school, strong mesosystems need to be in place so that there is a smooth transition from home to school. Clearly, this is not often the case with minority children or children with special needs (Heath, 1983; Tizard & Hughes, 1984). In adolescence the connections among the microsystems may be particularly important as the peer group and other outside family and school influences begin to emerge. Epstein (1983) agreed that teachers can help build helpful mesosystems by using the peer group. She concluded the following:

> Peer interaction is real, whether teachers accept it, organize it, avoid it, or fear it. Even in the most highly authoritarian, teacher-directed settings, there is a tremendous amount of peer interaction—silently and noisily in the class, before and after class, on the way to and from school. In some schools, teachers and administrators have worked to put the power of peer groups to positive use. They use peer and friendship groups to extend the teachers' resources—to enable students to learn academic skills by assisting one another after the class receives formal instruction from the teacher. They use peer and friendship groups to extend students' social, leadership, and decision-making skills, which require interaction among students and groups. For academic and social skills, peer interaction can be managed so that the teacher can do more educationally than through teacher–student interaction alone. (p. 248)

The *exosystem* contains those settings in which the individual adolescent does not participate directly, but that significantly impact the individual indirectly. For instance, the parents' workplace influences practical aspects of the adolescent's life, like the availability of the parents. It also can affect the beliefs and aspirations of the adolescent. The importance of certain life or job skills (e.g., literacy, mathematics, computer skills) for parents' work can influence the beliefs adolescents hold about the importance of learning such skills in school.

The *macrosystem* includes the institutional and cultural influences of the society in which the individual lives. These values must be taken into account in order to understand the influence of societal values with respect to sexism and racism, as well as the value placed on skills like literacy during early adolescence. Stevenson (1988) examined the effect of living in Asian cultures versus North and South American cultures on parent and child belief systems about the importance of effort in school, and of the role of mathematics versus literacy in contributing to school success. Parents' and children's beliefs about the importance of mathematics and reading were related to the time and effort Chinese, Japanese, and American students were willing to put forth in instruction in these areas during elementary school. Individuals from Asian cultures apparently held stronger beliefs regarding the malleability of human behavior and the importance of effort (rather than in-born ability) in determining accomplishments in school.

THE ECOLOGICAL/CONTEXTUAL FRAMEWORK: THE EXAMPLE OF LITERACY

The usefulness of the ecological/contextual framework can be illustrated by considering the problems of illiteracy and dropout. The relationship between poverty, poor literacy skills, and school dropout has been a major societal problem for the United States (Anderson, Herbert, Scott, & Wilkinson, 1985; Feagans & Farran, 1982). Although a number of programs to alleviate this problem have been successful (Comer, 1980), many of these programs have been geared to general academic improvement through motivation and hard work. The early intervention programs that have tried to prepare students for academics have been successful in preventing retention in grade and placement in special education programs but they have been unsuccessful in improving the literacy skills of the students in the early intervention programs in comparison to control groups without such intervention (Lazar, Darlington, Murray, Royce, & deSnipper, 1982). An examination of the reading scores of children from poverty backgrounds has revealed that these children actually are further behind their peers beginning in elementary school, and fall still further behind by the end of high school. Reports place children of poverty at about the 30th percentile in reading in elementary school and below the 10th percentile by the end of high school.

The reasons for the failure of many programs aimed at increasing literacy skills in children from poverty backgrounds may be the lack of a comprehensive theoretical framework that takes into consideration not immediate and/or proximal skills needed for reading, such as word decoding and word recognition, but the larger context of the literacy experiences of children and the meaning of these experiences in their daily lives.

As a subcomponent of the ecological/contextual framework, the "Goodness of Fit" model is a useful means of examining the relationship between learners and their contexts. The "Goodness of Fit" model in particular enhances our ability to understand literacy in a deeper way for those children who are at risk for failure in reading. This model postulates that individuals bring to each setting a set of characteristics, including behavior and beliefs that either fit or do not fit with the demands of the setting. Schneirla's (1957) notion of circular reactions has also been used to understand the dynamics of the interaction between the individual's characteristics and the demands of the setting. According to Schneirla, individual characteristics—which may include physical characteristics as well as psychosocial ones such as attitudes and belief systems—are reacted to by other individuals in the context, which leads to feedback loops. Positive feedback from key figures in the context is associated with good fit, whereas negative feedback from key socializing others is related to poor fit and negative psychosocial outcomes.

With respect to literacy practices and beliefs, the fit may be quite good for middle-class early adolescents whose parents believe that literacy is important, and also demonstrate by their behavior that literacy is expected in the home. Conversely, for a low-income adolescent, the beliefs and practices in the home microsystem may not fit with the demands of the school microsystem, and the negative feedback loops of circular reactions may lead to poor literacy outcomes.

To fully understand the usefulness of our proposed framework to the educational problems associated with literacy it is important to review what is known about the literacy beliefs and practices in the various contexts in which early adolescents from poverty backgrounds live. A number of ethnographic studies have been conducted in both England and the United States that have focused on the relationship between home and school (Heath, 1983; Tizard & Hughes, 1984).

These studies have contrasted low-income White and Black children to middle-class children. Although most of these studies have involved younger children, the results have implications for programs designed to increase literacy in early adolescence for all children.

CONTEXTUAL AND CULTURAL VARIATION IN LITERACY BELIEFS

Heath (1983) followed a number of White and Black low-income children from infancy through elementary school in the Piedmont area of North Carolina. These children were then compared to a more middle-class sample. Heath's observations were geared toward understanding how each group viewed the use of language and literacy in their everyday microsystems out of school, contrasting this with the use of language and literacy in school. All families in her study, regardless of ethnicity or social class wanted their children to do well in school, yet some of the beliefs and practices at home seemed at odds with the schooling process and contributed to the poorer progress of the children in school.

Heath reported that in low-income Black homes, oral language was very valued and that Black boys were especially encouraged to relate stories and narratives from a very early age. These narratives were more like play acting with much drama and theatrical devices to maintain interest by the listener. On the other hand, this oral tradition was not seen as related to literacy. Children were not encouraged to read except as a practical tool to find items in the grocery store or to read the box scores in a newspaper. Thus, literacy was seen as a practical but minor skill and not one that could enhance the more abstract aspects of the lives of children. Heath observed that these children had great problems relating to the literacy demands in school and gave examples of the few teachers who were successful by making mesosystem connections between home and school. These included using dramatic readings and plays to bridge the gap between oral language at home and literacy practices at school.

Heath's findings have been supported by more traditional psychological research, such as that conducted by Feagans and Haskins (1986), who found that low-income Black children in their home neighborhood spoke as much and about complex and abstract events as very advantaged children. In addition, they found that the measures of language complexity and dialogue complexity were positively related to teacher ratings of school performance for the White middle-class children but there was a negative correlation between high levels of language performance in the neighborhood and teacher ratings in the Black low-income group. This suggests that there may indeed be a conflict between home and school in the practice and beliefs about language and literacy.

The White low-income families in Heath's study were found to speak little. There was not the rich oral tradition found in the Black low-income sample. Adults did not discuss issues at length. Language was used pragmatically to maneuver in the family but not used to relate stories or narratives. However, the families did buy books for their children and encouraged them to begin reading them before kindergarten. These books were often bought through their church and were seen as something the children should do but without enthusiasm. The books were read to the children as though it were a lesson and without expanding on the ideas in the book in conversation. Heath found that these children initially did well in school but like the low-income Black children they also had very poor literacy skills by the end of elementary school. Tizard and Hughes (1984), Wells (1985), and Tough (1977, 1982) have found similar social class differences in England.

Middle-class families appear to demonstrate the relationship between oral and written language by using books as a vehicle to discuss issues with children. In addition, literacy is seen as central to knowledge acquisition in many areas and so as an integral part of their lives in all domains. Thus, for these individuals a strong and positive relationship appears to exist between home and school practices and beliefs.

Implications for Knowledge Acquisition. In order to understand why there is cultural and subcultural variation in literacy practices, we first must address the values and beliefs about literacy and its place in the lives of the people concerned. Literacy practices can have two basic motivations. The first is the acquisition and imparting of new knowledge and the second is the enjoyment of the art form through leisure activities. Both of these motivations are not necessarily important for all activities or for all individuals and groups. It may be helpful to present an example of the possible differences in the value of literacy with respect to the acquisition of new information by the three groups just discussed (White and Black low-income families and White middle-class families) as well as how these beliefs need to be explored in the schooling process.

If, for instance, information was needed about how to fix a car, it is likely that in a middle-class family, a book or manual would be borrowed from the library or purchased in a store. The family might pour over this book talking together to try to understand how this "literacy information" could be the way to new knowledge acquisition. On the other hand, a Black family might find an expert in the community who could merely tell them how to fix the car, someone whose oral language skills on this topic were valued. In further contrast, the low-income White family might find someone to show them how to fix the car, where neither literacy or oral language was the primary way to new knowledge acquisition.

Although this example is overdrawn, it serves to illustrate that the primary vehicle to knowledge acquisition may be different at home versus school in some subcultures and that literacy-based material may not always be the best vehicle to effective knowledge acquisition. As one might imagine, the middle-class family could struggle for days with their car manual, determined to figure out how to fix the car, whereas the low-income White family might short cut this lengthy literacy route by just getting someone to show them how to do it.

If schools value the differences in knowledge acquisition strategies and encourage diversity in certain areas of knowledge acquisition, they can build the necessary mesosystem links between home, school, and community. Adolescents may then be able to better understand the various paths to knowledge acquisition that can be used and that literacy can be an important tool for certain kinds of knowledge.

SUMMARY

This chapter presents a framework for schooling as called for by Hyman (1979). This framework may help us understand better how adolescents learn and think in different contexts as well as how subgroups of adolescents may differ in their beliefs at home and at school. More important, such a framework may hopefully help us to develop better ways to educate all of our youth so that the window of opportunity for change during adolescence will be seized by all of us in forging a better future for youth. Kagan et al. (1984) called for these changes in the 1980s but they are still pertinent today.

> Schools can no longer advance a curriculum change or a piecemeal supplementary program and expect these to provide an optimal learning environment for children. Schools need to view children's home life, culture, and total environment to understand their abilities and performance. This requires a shift in focus from looking at differences between ethnic and socioeconomic groups comparatively to viewing individual differences contextually. (p. 386)

The Carnegie Council (1989) supports these kinds of changes and the growing movement of professionals to build support for the schooling of adolescents through new relationships among schools, families, peer groups, and community institutions. Hopefully by focusing on the broader goals of schooling we can create a better future for all of our youth.

REFERENCES

Alexander, K. L., & Entwisle, D. R. (1988). Achievement in the first 2 years of school: Patterns and processes. *Monographs of the Society for Research in Child Development, 53*(2, Serial No. 218).

Anderson, J. P., Herbert, E., Scott, J. A., & Wilkinson, I. A. G. (1985). *Becoming a nation of readers: The report of the Commission on Reading.* Washington, DC: National Academy of Education.

Bronfenbrenner, U. (1979). *The ecology of human development.* Cambridge, MA: Harvard University Press.

Carnegie Council on Adolescent Development. (1989). *Turning points: Preparing American youth for the 21st century.* New York: Carnegie Corporation.

Comer, J. P. (1980). *School power: Implications of an intervention project.* New York: The Free Press.

Comer, J. P. (1984). Home school relationships as they affect the academic success of children. *Education and Urban Society, 16,* 323–337.

Cremin, L. A. (1980). *American education: The national experience 1783–1876.* New York: Harper & Row.

Eccles, J. S., & Midgley, C. (1989). Stage-environment fit: Developmentally appropriate classrooms for young adolescents. In C. Ames & R. Ames (Eds.), *Research on motivation in education: Vol. 3, Goals & cognitions* (pp. 139–186). New York: Academic Press.

Epstein, J. L. (1983). School environment and student friendships: Issues, implications, and interventions. In J. L. Epstein & N. Karweit (Eds.), *Friends in school: Patterns of selection and influence in secondary school* (pp. 235–253). New York: Academic Press.

Feagans, L., & Farran, D. C. (1982). How demonstrated comprehension can get muddled in production. *Developmental Psychology, 6,* 718–727.

Feagans, L. V., & Haskins, R. (1986). Neighborhood dialogues of Black and White five-year-olds. *Journal of Applied Developmental Psychology, 6,* 27–35.

Hamburg, B. A. (1990). *Life skills training: Preventive interventions for young adolescents.* Report of the Life Skills Training Working Group, Carnegie Council on Adolescent Development. Washington, DC.
Heath, (1983). *Way with words.* Cambridge: Cambridge University Press.
Hess, L. E. (1990). *Family structure, family process and early adolescent functioning in the self, peer, and school domains: A developmental contextual approach.* Unpublished doctoral dissertation, The Pennsylvania State University, University Park.
Hoffman, M. A., Ushpiz, V., & Levy-Shiff, R. (1988). Social support and self-esteem in adolescence. *Journal of Youth and Adolescence, 17,* 307–316.
Hyman, I. A. (1979). Psychology, education, and schooling: Social policy implications in the lives of children and youth. *American Psychologist, 34,* 1024–1029.
Iacovetta, R. G. (1975). Adolescent-adult interaction and peer group involvement. *Adolescence, 10,* 327–336.
Kagan, L. K., Schreiber, E., & Zigler, E. (1984). Recognizing commonalities—respecting differences: Implications for schooling in the 1980's. *Education and Urban Society, 16,* 382–389.
Kandel, D., & Lesser, G. (1972). *Youth in two worlds.* San Francisco: Jossey-Bass.
Larson, L. E. (1972). The influence of parents and peers during adolescence: The situation hypothesis revisited. *Journal of Marriage and the Family, 34,* 67–74.
Lazar, I., Darlington, R., Murray, H., Royce, J., & deSnipper, A. (1982). Lasting effects on early education: A report from the Consortium for Longitudinal Studies. *Monographs of the Societies for Research in Child Development, 47* (2–3, Serial No. 195).
Lerner, R. M. (1986). *Concepts and theories of human development* (2nd ed.). New York: Random House.
Lerner, R. M. (1989). Developmental contextualism and the life-span view of person-context interaction. In M. H. Bornstein & J. S. Bruner, (Eds.), *Interaction in human development* (pp. 217–239). Hillsdale, NJ: Lawrence Erlbaum Associates.
Linney, J. A., & Seidman, E. (1989). The future of schooling. *American Psychologist, 44,* 336–340.
Lipsitz, J. (1984). *Successful schools for young adolescents.* New Brunswick, NJ: Transaction Books.
Marjoribanks, K. (1978). Family environmental correlates on school related affective characteristics. *Journal of Social Psychology, 106,* 181–189.
Ogbu, J. (1981). Origins of human competence: A cultural-ecological perspective. *Child Development, 52,* 413–429.
Rosenberg, M. (1979). *Conceiving the self.* New York: Basic Books.
Schneirla, T. C. (1957). The concept of development in comparative psychology. In D. B. Harris (Ed.), *The concept of development* (pp. 78–108). Minneapolis, MN: The University of Minnesota Press.
Smith, T. E. (1976). Push versus pull—Intra-family versus peer group variables as possible determinants of adolescent orientation toward parents. *Youth and Society, 8,* 5–28.
Stevenson, H. W. (1988). Culture and schooling: Influences on cognitive development. In E. M. Hetherington, R. M. Lerner, & M. Perlmutter (Eds.), *Child development in life-span perspective* (pp. 241–258). Hillsdale, NJ: Lawrence Erlbaum Associates.
Thomas, A., & Chess, S. (1977). *Temperament and development.* New York: Brunner/Mazel.
Tizard, B., & Hughes, M. H. (1984). *Young children learning.* Cambridge, MA: Harvard University Press.
Tough, J. (1977). *Talking and learning: A guide to fostering communication skills in nursery and infant schools.* London: Ward Lock Educational.
Tough, J. (1982). Language, poverty, and disadvantage in school. In L. Feagans & D. C.

Farran (Eds.), *The language of children reared in poverty* (pp. 3–18). New York: Academic Press.

Weinhert, F. E., & Trieber, B. (1982). School socialization and cognitive development. In W. Hartup (Ed.), *Review of child development research* (Vol. 6, pp. 704–758). Chicago: University of Chicago Press.

Weiss, R. S. (1976). The provision of social relationships. In Z. Rubin (Ed.), *Doing unto others*. Englewood, NJ: Prentice-Hall.

Wells, G. (1985). Preschool literacy-related activities and success in school. In D. R. Olson, N. Torrance, & A. Hildyard (Eds.), *Literacy, language, and learning* (pp. 229–255). Cambridge, MA: Cambridge University Press.

8 Adolescents' Theoretical Thinking

Karen Bartsch
The Pennsylvania State University

Is it important for educators to know what adolescents think? Almost certainly any professional in education or psychology would answer "yes." Jean Piaget and other developmental theorists widely acknowledged the cognitive achievements of adolescence, treating them as central marks of the period. Thus, it is perhaps curious that researchers and interventionists in adolescent education focus so little on the cognitive aspects and so much on the social and physiological aspects of adolescence—the "storm and stress" characterizing the period that Hall (1904) referred to as "the infancy of man's higher nature."

The purpose of this chapter is to press for a more balanced treatment of adolescent thought and beliefs in educational research and intervention. This recommendation emerges from a new vision of cognitive development, a vision that places considerably more emphasis on the content, rather than the form, of individual thought. The new view emphasizes the centrality of individuals' beliefs, their theories and concepts, and it is examined in this chapter with an eye to its special implications for adolescent education. It is argued that the adolescent's own views must be assessed and addressed at two levels in any attempts to educate.

A preliminary comment on how this thesis fits into this volume as a whole is in order: A central theme of the volume concerns the benefits to be gained by adopting multidisciplinary approaches to the study of adolescence. Yet the aim of this chapter is to examine the benefits to be gained by considering one perspective, a particular vision of the nature of cognitive development. These themes are not contradictory—in adopting a multidisciplinary perspective, important questions arise regarding the relative contributions appropriately made by each view. This chapter does not have as a goal the conversion of the reader to a particular cognitive developmental perspective; rather, the goal is to urge that, within a multidisciplinary approach to adolescent education, relatively more attention be paid to the students' specific ideas and beliefs. In emphasizing the importance of individual beliefs arising in specific contexts, this chapter endorses a second major theme of this volume.

THE ROLE OF COGNITIVE DEVELOPMENT IN ADOLESCENCE

It is not surprising that in theories of cognitive development, cognitive achievements have been held to play important roles in adolescence (e.g., Baldwin, 1906–1911; Elkind, 1967; Gilligan & Kohlberg, 1978; Hall, 1904; Kohlberg & Gilligan, 1971; Piaget, 1972). Yet current research on adolescence reflects a predominating interest in developments other than, or only indirectly related to, cognitive achievements. Even a brief glimpse at recently published literature is sufficient to convey this impression. For example, of articles published in the journal *Adolescence* from 1988 to 1989, only 7 of 169 titles reflect a primary interest in cognition, thinking, reasoning, or knowledge (e.g., "Cognitive Distortions as Mediators Between Life Stress and Depression"). Surveys of related journals published in the same year reveal similar proportions: *Journal of Adolescence* (2 of 58 titles), *Journal of Adolescent Research* (3 of 59 titles), and *Journal of Youth and Adolescence* (4 of 79 titles). Although such limited and informal surveys do not permit a definitive characterization of the field of adolescent research, they hint that researchers may view adolescence as a time when focal issues concern not cognitive development but rather adjustments in social, emotional, and physical realms.

Two questions arise. First, why in adolescence research are cognitive factors relatively neglected? Second, should cognitive factors be invested with any more importance? In answer to the first, it may be that traditional theories of cognitive development themselves are responsible for the relative lack of attention to cognition by researchers of adolescence. A brief review of Piaget's theory will suggest a historical answer to the first question. Following this, an examination of a new vision of cognitive development will suggest important reasons for treating individual theories and concepts as critical mediators in education, particularly during the period of adolescence.

TRADITIONAL COGNITIVE DEVELOPMENT THEORY

A brief description of Piagetian theory will serve to show how traditional cognitive development theory posits and attempts to account for universal changes in the *form* of individual thought. A central contention is that thinking—regardless of content—develops in a universal, perhaps stage-like fashion (for contemporary discussions of this assumption, see Chapman 1988; Kitchener, 1986). Inhelder and Piaget (1958) described this view with regard to adolescence specifically, contending that adolescence is the time individuals attain the full potential of rationality, the necessary capacity for logical reasoning. Although an infant, according to this view, is limited to sensorimotor thinking, and older children to the mere preliminaries of logical operation, only adolescents are characterized as having ready access to true logical operations. The hallmarks of formal operational thought include thinking about possibilities rather than concrete realities, thinking through hypotheses, thinking ahead, and thinking about thought itself (Broughton, 1983; Inhelder & Piaget, 1958). During this period, it becomes possible for the individual to engage in systematic scientific reasoning, an endpoint reflecting Piaget's view that development is in general a movement away from an egocentric understanding toward a more objective understanding of reality. The changes, of course, are structural, not contingent on a specific content of thought. Such general reasoning powers are held to account for adolescents' penchant for theory construction and emerging concern for social issues.

Of course, this description is oversimplified. In his later writings (e.g., Piaget, 1972), Piaget clearly viewed adolescence as a time of continuing development. Two substages can be identified, an early one in which "the first flush of hypothetical thinking brings with it an unconstrained surge of possibilities which submerges reality" and a later one in which "the individual thinker acquires the ability to test out the practicability of ideals and the truth of hypotheses against brute fact and against the theories of others" (Broughton, 1983, p. 218). In other words, there is an initial overwhelming romance with the ideal of hypothetical thinking, and a later grounding of that ideal in reality. In his later work, Piaget (1972) estimated that a completion of the development of formal operations may not occur until late adolescence (15–20 years of age). But it is Piaget's general conclusion that adolescents are beginning to achieve adult-like thought that has perhaps had the most influence on researchers and educators.

Indeed, for educators this conclusion may have worked to minimize (ironically) the attention paid to cognitive factors during the adolescent period. That is, an implication of Piagetian theory is that the education and socialization of infants and young children should take into account the cognitive limitations of those individuals. The youngster who cannot perform measurements is fundamentally unable to grasp the prerequisite notion of conservation. But adolescents are supposedly relatively unlimited in cognitive terms, so cognitive limitations cannot be held to account for educational or interpersonal problems. Such problems must have a noncognitive source.

NEW VIEW: CHILD-AS-THEORETICIAN

As we have seen, Piaget's account posits fundamental changes in how individuals think, in the form of their reasoning. Recently, a new view has been forwarded that puts emphasis on what individuals think. The following analysis of this new view suggests why, for educators, it is critical to understand students' own views, perhaps particularly during the period of adolescence.

It would be misleading to say that the new view is in fact a single new theory. Rather, it is a general consensus endorsing the usefulness of a particular metaphor for cognitive development—the metaphor of the child as an intuitive scientist or theoretician. The general idea is that, like scientists (T. S. Kuhn, 1977), children and even lay adults make sense of the world by constructing theories about it and revising those theories as new evidence is generated (D. Kuhn, 1989). This view has emerged in work on adult cognition (Holland, Holyoak, Nisbett, & Thagard, 1986; Murphy & Medin, 1985; Nisbett & Ross, 1980) and child cognition (e.g., Carey, 1985a, 1985b, 1986; Kaiser, McCloskey, & Proffitt, 1986; Vosniadou & Brewer, 1987; Wellman, 1990). It reflects the notion that conceptual change occurs through the processes of differentiation and hierarchical integration (Carey, 1985b; Keil, 1979, 1983; Werner, 1948). Unlike a Piagetian account, which focuses on fundamental differences in the form of child versus adult reasoning, this new view emphasizes fundamental similarities in reasoning throughout development. Certainly, children's thinking is not held to be flawless, but differences between the thinking of children (or even lay adults) compared to, say, professional scientists, are attributed primarily to the possession of *different* theories and concepts within specific domains, rather than to a difference in the capacity to have a theory at all. Instead of characterizing children as moving from "pseudoconcepts" to "real" concepts (e.g., Bruner, Goodnow, & Austin, 1956; Piaget, 1962; Vygotsky, 1934/1986), the new approach views individuals as having "real" concepts throughout development, but concepts that may have yet to undergo differentiation and thus theories that have yet to undergo restructuring. The process of cognitive development is seen as a more continuous process, guided by individual experiences and ideas within specific domains.

It is worth noting that in the new view of the child-as-scientist a general constructivism is preserved—that is, the notion that individuals construct their own knowledge and that it is their constructions, rather than the environment itself, which are key to understanding their activities. However, other fundamental assumptions are very different. Especially striking is the abandonment of structural stages that account for thinking similarly across domains in favor of domain-specific thinking and developments.[1]

It is perhaps easiest to motivate and defend the new approach by examining specific instances of it. It is not within the scope of this chapter to fully describe all of the versions of, or rationales for, this new perspective; the goal is merely to illustrate how the new approach offers ideas to researchers and educators. As reflected in the ensuing discussion, empirical research on these topics has so far involved mostly young children. However, the equation of education with theory development is one that should hold across the life span. In the final section of this chapter, reasons for supposing this characterization to be especially important for adolescents are discussed.

One area of cognitive development research that has been significantly influenced by the metaphor of child-as-theoretician is people's understanding of physics. Researchers have suggested that our everyday thinking about physical phenomena is characterized by changes that resemble scientific theory shifts. These shifts are held to account for both childhood errors and also for typical mistakes in adults' theories of motion. For example, Kaiser et al. (1986) showed that school-age children often incorrectly predict a curved path for a ball exiting a curved tube. Kaiser et al. (1986) attributed this error to the acquisition and persistence of motion theory. By adulthood, this theory typically is revised to acknowledge that curvilinear motion requires a continuing external force, resulting in adults' more often correct prediction of a straight path. Vosniadou and Brewer (1989) extended the application of the child-as-scientist metaphor in their work on children's understanding of planetary shape and motion. They report evidence sug-

---

[1]Of course, the shift away from universal stage theory is at least in part due to criticisms made of universal stage accounts, which have come under attack on both theoretical and empirical counts (e.g., Carey, 1985a, 1985b; Fodor, 1972; Gelman & Gallistel, 1978; Mandler, 1983). For example, the apparently sophisticated thinking of young children in areas like social reasoning does not correspond to their ignorance in the physical domain—something for which a domain-general approach like Piaget's cannot easily account (e.g., Bartsch & Wellman, 1989; Gelman & Spelke, 1978).

gesting that children often share a "flat-earth" theory that proves to be pervasive and very resistant to instruction. These researchers suspect that in order to teach children basic information about the solar system, it is essential to address their naive theory in its totality.

A second type of cognitive development, children's growing understanding of people (i.e., children's naive psychology), has also been characterized as a theory-building process. Wellman (1990) noted that adults appear to share an everyday "theory" of human action, one that causally links human actions to mental states, desires, and beliefs. That even young children possess such a naive theory is suggested by their abilities to talk about the mental and emotional states of others (e.g., Bretherton & Beeghly, 1982; Bretherton, McNew, & Beeghly-Smith, 1981; Shatz, Wellman, & Silber, 1983), to attribute to others desires, beliefs, perceptions, and emotions, and to predict and explain others' actions accordingly (e.g., Bartsch & Wellman, 1989; Pillow, 1989; Wellman & Bartsch, 1989; Wellman & Woolley, 1990). These findings challenge the view of Piaget and his followers (e.g., Inhelder & Piaget, 1958; Piaget, 1929) in which children younger than 7 years or so are held to have no real concept of private or subjective mental states or activities, much less a causal theory allowing systematic prediction or explanation.

Wellman (1990) argued that if children do possess such a "theory of mind," then development will consist of concept acquisition within this domain, specifically, in terms of *theory change* within the domain. Because in the area of human action, young children's theory is fundamentally the same as adults', much of their reasoning will resemble that of adults. To the extent that it differs, the differences will reflect differences in the concepts or theory structure. For example, 3-year-olds are notoriously bad at predicting the actions of someone they are told possesses a false belief (e.g., Maxi thinks the cookie is in the red cupboard, but the cookie is really in the blue cupboard. Where will Maxi look?) (e.g., Wellman & Bartsch, 1989; Wimmer & Perner, 1983). It may be that such young children have no concept of belief, although they grasp the other fundamental concepts in a theory of intentional human action, desire, and action. Acquiring the concept of belief, and thus restructuring the previous theory, may account for children's developing reasoning abilities.

Finally, in a third area of cognitive development, biological thinking, young children's thinking is clearly very different from that of adults. But even here, some researchers now argue that it makes more sense to characterize children's early, erroneous thinking as "theoretical" while admitting that their early theories are not very good. Carey's (1985b) work suggests, for example, that children's early theories of biology rest on their early psychological theory. In Carey's studies, young children demonstrated little knowledge about internal organs and often described biological processes such as eating and washing as important for satisfying social (i.e., parental) requirements rather than for maintaining health. Later, children appear to develop an autonomous theory of biological phenomena that supports more adult-like reasoning. However, even the youngest children in Carey's study, 4-year-olds, showed evidence of using some biological knowledge to constrain their categorization. For example, 4-year-old children said that a worm was more likely than a toy monkey to have a spleen (described as a green thing inside people), despite the fact that they thought that a toy monkey was more similar to people than a worm. A variation on Carey's thesis is provided by Springer and Keil (1989), who argued that children's reasoning reflects an even earlier theory of biology, evident in their judgments about inheritance.

The three areas of cognitive development discussed here—physical, psychological, and biological thinking—illustrate how the notion of theory change can characterize the changes in thinking of even very young children. Although empirical research has focused on young children, it is reasonable to suppose that if the thinking of both adults and very young children can be usefully characterized as theoretical, then adolescent thinking should prove no exception. The following discussion of the educational implications of this view notes some empirical support for this extension.

EDUCATIONAL IMPLICATIONS OF THEORY METAPHOR

Although some caution against overextending the analogy between cognitive development and changes in scientific thinking (e.g., D. Kuhn, 1989), there is a growing consensus that cognitive development may be a process characterized, much more than traditional theories suggest, by changes in knowledge within specific domains. This has implications for the education of individuals across the life span. The implications are those of any constructivist paradigm, now construed very specifically. The educator, before attempting to teach anything within any domain, must know what the individual already thinks, specifically, what concepts are embedded in what theories. This is crucial because it is those already present theories that will determine how any new information is processed.[2]

---

[2]Educators may be somewhat relieved to note that the three examples of theory investigation discussed in the previous section suggest that there are *common* erroneous theories, at least in these areas, shared by children at similar points in development, which might ease the burden of needing to address different theories possessed by individual students. However, the extent to which the latter might also be necessary is not known.

The recommendation that educators find out about, and address, their students' existing misconceptions should not be taken lightly or superficially. The child-as-scientist metaphor suggests not simply that children may have false beliefs about various phenomena, but that their beliefs are woven into entire theories in which the actual *concepts* may differ from adult concepts. For example, in a series of studies, Smith, Carey, and Wiser (1985) documented the claim that many students operate with a single concept that includes both heat and temperature, failing to distinguish between what for physicists are two separate concepts. This single concept, for students, is not just a confused concept; it is well adapted to the theory in which it is embedded (Wiser, 1989).

An implication of this characterization is that a simple presentation of new information, even by teachers who are aware that their students might have false beliefs, will not necessarily produce the desired change in thinking. Wiser (1986, 1987) found that traditional instruction about heat and temperature failed to induce reconceptualization in most students, a finding consistent with many studies about mechanics (see e.g., McDermott, 1984). Even interventions aimed at trying to teach specific concepts were unsuccessful. For example, a curriculum focused on topics that should have motivated students to differentiate between heat and temperature (e.g., specific heat and latent heat) fared no better than traditional curricula in fostering conceptual change (Wiser, 1986, 1987).

What is needed, according to Wiser (1989), are curricula designed to facilitate theory change as a whole. Wiser and her colleagues have begun to test such a curriculum in the area of thermal physics, based on computer "conceptual models." These models are designed to present the textbook theories in a self-contained fashion (Wiser & Kipman, 1988). The idea is that such a presentation would allow the students to construct the textbook concepts and principles with "minimal appeal to their own preconceptions, and thus minimal interference from them" (Wiser, 1989, p. 21). Presumably, once students understand the new theory, they would be in a position to recognize its superiority to their own theory. To increase the likelihood of this recognition, metaconceptual lessons about the nature of models and theories, their revisability, and their relation to experimental evidence are also included in the curricula.

Wiser and her colleagues conducted a study among ninth graders to compare the effectiveness of their curriculum with that of a more traditional one (Wiser, Grosslight, & Unger, 1989). Preliminary results indicated that students who received the experimental curriculum learned the textbook theory, including the differentiation between heat and temperature, better than the students who received the control curriculum. The students in the experimental group were better than their control counterparts at solving quantitative problems about the relation of heat, mass, and temperature, and at solving qualitative problems designed to probe their concepts.

THEORIES OF KNOWLEDGE ACQUISITION

The research and interventions described earlier indicate a need for educators to be aware of and address erroneous theories specific to individual domains and maybe even to individual students, whether they are teaching young children, adolescents, or adults. However, the vision of cognitive development as theory change may have special importance for the period of adolescence. This implication arises from the possibility that an understanding of knowledge and knowledge acquisition itself may develop in a theory-like way. Any such epistemological theory would surely have special ramifications for education. Further, there is reason to believe that during adolescence theories of knowledge may undergo major changes.

The claim that even young children have a "theory of mind" (Astington, Harris, & Olson, 1988; Wellman, 1990), as discussed earlier, provides a foundation for the supposition that theories of knowledge themselves may undergo important changes. Empirical research suggests that young children have at least a limited understanding of knowledge and how it is acquired (e.g., Chandler, Fritz, & Hala, 1989; Flavell, 1988; Gopnik & Astington, 1988; Pillow, 1989). Yet is clear that their understanding is indeed limited and has yet to develop into an adult appreciation (e.g., Wimmer & Perner, 1983).

Unfortunately, little is known about the development of theories of knowledge between toddlerhood and adolescence. But those scholars who have commented on the period agree that individuals in middle childhood share a commitment to an objectivist epistemology (e.g., Broughton, 1978, 1983; Chandler & Boyes, 1982; Damon, 1977; Flavell, 1985; Selman, 1980). That is, for individuals in middle childhood, knowledge acquisition is viewed as a simple process of having the objective facts of the world impressed into one's mind in a relatively straightforward way that allows for few differences in interpretation.

At adolescence, this straightforward objectivist theory of knowledge often appears to give way to a more complex, relativistic view—a sort of doubt that true knowledge can be acquired, arising from a recognition of the subjective elements of knowledge acquisition. Unlike younger children, adolescents are "generally held to be capable of representing their own representations" (Chandler, 1987, p. 149), to think about and even compare their own and others' beliefs (Miller, Kessel, & Flavell, 1970). This characterization echoes a Piagetian attribution of the "recognition of the universality of subjectivity" (Inhelder & Piaget, 1958). But for Piaget, the distinction between adolescent and adult thought is in the direction of crediting the adolescent with rather *more* faith in objective knowledge. Piaget (1967, 1972; Inhelder & Piaget, 1958) emphasized the difference between the adolescent's egocentric belief in the omniscient capacity of formal logic and the adult's more equilibrated "reason which reunites intelligence and affectivity" (1967, p. 80). Kohlberg and Gilligan (1971) advanced even further the notion that an individual's personal epistemology is of particular importance during adolescence, but argued that of special importance during this period is "not the logic of formal operations, but its epistemology, its conception of truth and reality" (pp. 1063f). Accordingly, "At its extreme, adolescent thought entertains solipsism and the cogito, the notion that the only thing real is the self" (p. 1063f). Chandler (1987), in a similar vein, contended that adolescents tend to struggle with a view of knowledge acquisition that involves less rather than more objectivity.

The implications of change in the epistemological theories of adolescents have not, it can be argued, been fully acknowledged within a Piagetian perspective. As suggested earlier, perhaps this failure is attributable to an overly simplistic interpretation of Piaget's theory that characterizes adolescents as virtually adult in terms of the capacity to think rationally and scientifically, worrying only about the subjectivity of knowledge insofar as it makes evident the need for a more objective, scientific method for acquiring truth.

However, the larger implications of adolescent epistemological theory change have been explored theoretically. Chandler (1987, p. 150) suggested that adolescents are uniquely plagued by "unassuageable, universal doubts" emerging from the realization of the subjective aspects of knowledge, doubts that "once set in motion, tend to rattle the foundations of the entire knowing process and, if left unchecked, eventually leave no belief standing upon any other belief." Chandler speculated that adolescents, unlike younger and most older persons, are especially plagued by such doubts and that discovering a way out of these doubts is a primary developmental task of the adolescent period.

If adolescents commonly experience such a revision in their theory of knowledge, certain stereotypical traits, such as rebellion toward authority figures, might be seen to reflect their new view. Chandler (1987) hypothesized that in the face of doubt, adolescents may either (a) throw up their hands and go with noncognitive decision making (i.e., do whatever feels good), or (b) turn to a dogmatic strategy, electing, for example, to join a cult or religious sect, perhaps even "alternatively believing without question and questioning all belief in rapid-fire succession" (Chandler, 1987, p. 154).

Chandler's claim is as yet largely unaddressed by research, although a number of studies offer indirect support. For example, Clinchy, Lief, and Young (1977) found that "absolutist" (or objectivist) reasoning is rare even among high school sophomores. In fact, even 10-year-olds resemble college students in their willingness to accept a plurality of opinions (Clinchy & Mansfield, 1985), suggesting an acknowledgment of the relativity of knowledge. Research on belief discrepancy (Enright, Lapsley, Franklin, & Steuck, 1984; Kuhn, Pennington, & Leadbeater, 1983) has demonstrated that the typical teenager is very willing to entertain the possibility that knowledge is inherently subjective. Even the work of Marcia (1976, 1980) and colleagues documents a "moratorium" status common in the teenage years. The claim that epistemological theories continue to develop in later adulthood has found support in the studies of Gilligan and Murphy (1979), Perry (1968), and Kitchener and King (1981).

If indeed theories of knowledge acquisition undergo substantial developments, particularly in adolescence, educators should be aware of these theories, just as they should be aware of individuals' theories within specific domains. It is not obvious what practices would appropriately follow from such knowledge, but adolescents' attitudes toward formal and even informal education are surely contingent on their encompassing epistemological theories. Possibly, educators would do well to address adolescents' concerns in direct or indirect ways, either talking explicitly about relativism or by emphasizing the competition and evaluation of theories within domains. In any case, it seems that the educator who recognizes adolescents' changing ideas about knowledge would be in a better position to deal with their outcomes.

SUMMARY

In this chapter, educators and researchers of adolescents are urged to study the emerging vision of cognitive development as a process of theory change. This new vision has implications for educators of adolescents at two levels. First, the idea that development within specific domains of knowledge, such as physics or biology, occurs through a process analogous to the progression of scientific theory change suggests that educators should discover and address the naive theories of their students, whether the students are 5 or 15 or 50 years old. From this perspective, education is not simply the replacing of ignorance or specific wrong ideas with correct ones, but the process of facilitating the restructuring of entire theories and the concepts embedded within them.

Second, development in terms of theory change has been hypothesized to occur with regard to the domain of knowledge itself, a domain of particular significance for educators. The period of adolescence may be of special importance; both theoretical analysis and indirect empirical evidence indicate that adolescents may experience transition and even crisis with regard to epistemological theory (rather than the happy arrival at rationality suggested by simplistic interpretations of traditional cognitive development theory). If so, educators and education researchers will want to attend to this important cognitive development, developing practices based on such knowledge through further scholarship and empirical research.

REFERENCES

Astington, J. W., Harris, P. L., & Olson, D. R. (1988). *Developing theories of mind.* New York: Cambridge University Press.

Baldwin, J. M. (1906–1911). *Thought and things* (3 vols.). London: Swan Sonnenschein.

Bartsch, K., & Wellman, H. M. (1989). Young children's attribution of action to beliefs and desires. *Child Development, 60,* 946–964.

Bretherton, I., & Beeghley, M. (1982). Talking about internal states: The acquisition of an explicit theory of mind. *Developmental Psychology, 18,* 906–921.

Bretherton, I., McNew, S., & Beeghley-Smith, M. (1981). Early person knowledge as expressed in gestural and verbal communication: When do infants acquire a "theory of mind"? In M. Lamb & L. Sherrod (Eds.), *Social cognition in infancy* (pp. 333–373). Hillsdale, NJ: Lawrence Erlbaum Associates.

Broughton, J. M. (1978). Development of concepts of self, mind, reality, and knowledge. In W. Damon (Ed.), *Social cognition* (pp. 215–266). San Francisco, CA: Jossey-Bass.

Broughton, J. M. (1983). The cognitive-developmental theory of adolescent self & identity. In B. Lee & G. G. Noam (Eds.), *Developmental approaches to self.* New York: Plenum Press.

Bruner, J. S., Goodnow, J. J., & Austin, G. A. (1956). *A study of thinking.* New York: Wiley.

Carey, S. (1985a). Are children fundamentally different kinds of thinkers and learners than adults? In S. Chipman, J. Segal, & R. Glaser (Eds.), *Thinking and learning skills* (Vol. 2, pp. 485–517). Hillsdale, NJ: Lawrence Erlbaum Associates.

Carey, S. (1985b). *Conceptual change in childhood.* Cambridge, MA: MIT Press.

Carey, S. (1986). Cognitive science and science education. *American Psychologist, 41* (Special Issue: Psychological Science and Education), 1123–1130.

Chandler, M. (1987). The Othello effect: Essay on the emergence and eclipse of skeptical doubt. *Human Development, 30,* 137–159.

Chandler, M., & Boyes, M. (1982). Social-cognitive development. In B. B. Wolman (Ed.), *Handbook of developmental psychology* (pp. 387–402). Englewood Cliffs, NJ: Prentice-Hall.

Chandler, M., Fritz, A. S., & Hala, S. (1989). Small scale deceit: Deception as a marker of 2-, 3- and 4-year-olds' early theories of mind. *Child Development, 60,* 1263–1277.

Chapman, M. (1988). *Constructive evolution.* Cambridge: Cambridge University Press.
Clinchy, B., Lief, J., & Young, P. (1977). Epistemological and moral development in girls from a traditional and a progressive high school. *Journal of Educational Psychology, 69,* 337–343.
Clinchy, B., & Mansfield, A. (1985, April). *Justifications offered by children to support positions on issues of "fact" and "opinion."* Paper presented at the 56th annual meeting of the Eastern Psychological Association, Boston.
Damon, W. (1977). *The social world of the child.* San Francisco, CA: Jossey-Bass.
Elkind, D. (1967). Egocentrism in adolescence. *Child Development, 38,* 1025–1034.
Enright, R., Lapsley, D., Franklin, C., & Steuck, K. (1984). Longitudinal and cross-cultural validation of the belief-discrepancy reasoning construct. *Developmental Psychology, 20,* 143–149.
Flavell, J. H. (1985). *Cognitive development.* Englewood Cliffs, NJ: Prentice-Hall.
Flavell, J. H. (1988). The development of children's knowledge about the mind: From cognitive connections to mental representations. In J. Astington, P. Harris, & D. Olson (Eds.), *Developing theories of mind* (pp. 244–267). New York: Cambridge University Press.
Fodor, J. (1972). Some reflections on L. S. Vygotsky's *Thought and Language. Cognition, 1,* 83–95.
Gelman, R., & Gallistel, C. R. (1978). *The child's understanding of numbers.* Cambridge, MA: Harvard University Press.
Gelman, R., & Spelke, E. (1978). The development of thoughts about animate and inanimate objects. Implications for research on social cognition. In J. H. Flavell & L. Ross (Eds.), *Social cognitive development.* Cambridge: Cambridge University Press.
Gilligan, C., & Kohlberg, L. (1978). From adolescence to adulthood: The rediscovery of reality in a postconventional world. In B. Z. Presseisen, D. Goldstein, & M. H. Appel (Eds.), *Topics in cognitive development: Language and operational thought* (Vol. 2, pp. 125–136). New York: Plenum Press.
Gilligan, C., & Murphy, M. (1979). Development from adolescence to adulthood: The philosopher and the dilemma of the fact. In D. Kuhn (Ed.), *New directions for child development: Intellectual development beyond childhood* (pp. 85–99). San Francisco: Jossey-Bass.
Gopnik, A., & Astington, J. W. (1988). Children's understanding of representational change and its relation to the understanding of false belief and the appearance-reality distinction. *Child Development, 59,* 26–37.
Hall, G. S. (1904). *Adolescence* (2 vols.). New York: Appleton.
Holland, J., Holyoak, K., Nisbett, R., & Thagard, P. (1986). *Induction: Processes of inference, learning, and discovery.* Cambridge, MA: MIT Press.
Inhelder, B., & Piaget, J. (1958). *The growth of logical thinking from childhood to adolescence.* New York: Basic Books.
Kaiser, M., McCloskey, M., & Proffitt, D. (1986). Development of intuitive theories of motion: Curvilinear motion in the absence of external forces. *Developmental Psychology, 22,* 67–71.
Keil, F. C. (1979). *Semantic and conceptual development: An ontological perspective.* Cambridge, MA: Harvard University Press.
Keil, F. C. (1983). On the emergence of semantic and conceptual distinctions. *Journal of Experimental Psychology: General, 112,* 357–385.
Kitchener, R. F. (1986). *Piaget's theory of knowledge: Genetic epistemology and scientific reason.* New Haven, CT: Yale University Press.
Kitchener, R. F., & King, P. M. (1981). Reflective judgement: Concepts of justification and their relationship to age and education. *Journal of Applied Developmental Psychology, 2,* 89–116.

Kohlberg, L., & Gilligan, C. (1971). The adolescent as philosopher: The discovery of self in a postconventional world. *Daedalus, C, 4,* 1028-61.

Kuhn, D. (1989). Children and adults as intuitive scientists. *Psychological Review, 96*(4), 674-689.

Kuhn, D., Pennington, N., & Leadbeater, B. (1983). Adult thinking in developmental perspective. In P. B. Baltes & O. G. Brim, Jr. (Eds.), *Life span development and behavior* (Vol. 5, pp. 157-195). New York: Academic Press.

Kuhn, T. S. (1977). *The structure of scientific revolutions.* Chicago, IL: University of Chicago Press.

Mander, J. M. (1983). Representation. In P. H. Mussen (Series Ed.) & J. H. Flavell & E. M. Markman (Vol. Eds.), *Handbook of child psychology: Vol. 3. Cognitive development* (4th ed., pp. 420-494). New York: Wiley.

Marcia, J. E. (1976). Identity six years later: A follow-up study. *Journal of Youth and Adolescence, 5,* 145-150.

Marcia, J. E. (1980). Identity in adolescence. In J. Adelson (Ed.), *Handbook of adolescent psychology* (pp. 159-210). New York: Wiley.

McDermott, L. C. (1984, July). Research on conceptual understanding in mechanics. *Physics Today,* 24-32.

Miller, P. H., Kessel, F. S., & Flavell, J. H. (1970). Thinking about people thinking about people thinking about. . . : A study of social cognitive development. *Child Development, 41,* 613-623.

Murphy, G., & Medin, D. (1985). The role of theories in conceptual coherence. *Psychological Review, 92,* 289-316.

Nisbett, R., & Ross, L. (1980). *Human inference: Strategies and shortcomings of social judgment.* Englewood Cliffs, NJ: Prentice-Hall.

Perry, W. (1968). *Intellectual and ethical development in the college years.* New York: Holt, Rinehart & Winston.

Piaget, J. (1929). *The child's conception of the world.* London: Routledge & Kegan Paul.

Piaget, J. (1962). *Play, dreams and imitation in childhood.* New York: Norton.

Piaget, J. (1967). *Six psychological studies.* New York: Random House.

Piaget, J. (1972). Intellectual evolution from adolescence to adulthood. *Human Development, 15,* 1-12.

Pillow, B. H. (1989). Early understanding of perception as a source of knowledge. *Journal of Experimental Child Psychology, 47,* 116-129.

Selman, R. L. (1980). *The growth of interpersonal understanding.* New York: Academic Press.

Shatz, M., Wellman, H. M., & Silber, S. (1983). The acquisition of mental verbs: A systematic investigation of first references to mental state. *Cognition, 14,* 301-321.

Smith, C., Carey, S., & Wiser, M. (1985). On differentiation: A case study of the development of the concepts of size, weight, and density. *Cognition, 21,* 177-237.

Springer, K., & Keil, F. C. (1989). On the development of biologically specific beliefs: The case of inheritance. *Child Development, 60,* 637-648.

Vosniadou, S., & Brewer, W. (1987). Theories of knowledge restructuring in development. *Review of Educational Research, 57,* 51-67.

Vosniadou, S., & Brewer, W. (1989). *The concept of the earth's shape: A study of conceptual change in childhood* (Tech. Rep. No. 467). Urbana-Champaign, IL: University of Illinois, Center for the Study of Reading.

Vygotsky, L. (1986). *Thought and language.* Cambridge, MA: MIT Press. (Original work published 1934)

Wellman, H. M. (1990). *The child's theory of mind.* Cambridge: MIT Press.

Wellman, H. M., & Bartsch, K. (1989). Young children's reasoning about beliefs. *Cognition, 30,* 239-277.

Wellman, H. M., & Woolley, J. D. (1990). From simple desires to ordinary beliefs: The development of everyday psychology. *Cognition, 35*, 245–275.

Werner, H. (1948). *Comparative psychology of mental development.* New York: International Universities Press.

Wimmer, H., & Perner, J. (1983). Beliefs about beliefs: Representation and constraining function of wrong beliefs in young children's understanding of deception. *Cognition, 13*, 103–128.

Wiser, M. (1986). *The differentiation of heat and temperature: An evaluation of the effect of microcomputer teaching on students' misconceptions* (Tech. Rep. No. 87-5). Cambridge, MA: Harvard Graduate School of Education, Educational Technology Center.

Wiser, M. (1987). The differentiation of heat and temperature: History of science and novice-expert shift. In S. Strauss (Ed.), *Ontogeny, phylogeny, and historical development* (pp. 28–48). Norwood, NJ: Ablex.

Wiser, M. (1989, April). *Does learning science involve theory change?* Paper presented at the biannual meeting of the Society for Research in Child Development, Kansas City, MO.

Wiser, M., Grosslight, L., & Unger, C. M. (1989). *Can conceptual computer models aid ninth graders' differentiation of heat and temperature?* (Tech. Rep. No. TR89-6). Cambridge, MA: Educational Technology Center, Harvard Graduate School of Education.

Wiser, M., & Kipman, D. (1988). *The differentiation of heat and temperature: An evaluation of the effect of microcomputer models on students' misconceptions* (Tech. Rep. No. 88-20). Cambridge, MA: Harvard Graduate School of Education, Educational Technology Center.

9 The Role of Community-Based Youth Groups in Enhancing Learning and Achievement Through Nonformal Education

Judith Semon Dubas
B. Alan Snider
The Pennsylvania State University

> *What we have to learn to do, we learn by doing.*
> —Aristotle (cited in Evans, 1968)

Although considerable attention has been focused on the learning (or lack of learning) that occurs in U.S. public schools, there has been relatively little attention paid to the role of nonformal educational groups in enhancing learning and achievement. Youth groups serve as one means of providing nonformal learning experiences, and most of the activities of these groups provide hands-on practical experiences. Although as early as Aristotle, "doing" has been implicated as playing an important role in learning, the (youth) groups that have used this method have not been adequately studied or evaluated.

It is estimated that over 13 million adolescents participate in organized, community-based youth groups each year. The fact that many well-known organizations, such as 4-H and the Boy Scouts and Girl Scouts, have been in existence since the early 1900s is at least partial testimony for the fact that these groups have a positive impact on the lives of young people. Yet how do these groups function and, more importantly, what are their benefits to society? The Carnegie Corporation recently initiated a national task force to examine youth programs for those who may be at risk for serious problems such as dropping out of school, drug use, and teenage pregnancy.

This chapter reviews the role that these youth groups play in enhancing learning and achievement. Although evaluation of youth group programs has been limited, we (a) discuss the opportunities for learning and achievement that take place in these groups, raising some questions about their efficacy; (b) discuss how these experiences can augment school learning; and (c) suggest ways in which schools might modify their program of instruction (based on youth group practices) to enhance learning. Because of space limitations, we discuss only a limited number of the many programs being offered by our largest national organizations: 4-H, Girl Scouts and Boy Scouts, and Girls' Clubs and Boys' Clubs. Yet it is important to note that other community-based youth groups, such as religious organizations and athletic groups, may also have significant impact on the lives of young people, contributing to changes in learning and achievement (see Price, Cioci, & Trautlein, 1990, for a review).

Adolescence is a time period in which changes are occurring in every important life context (Petersen & Taylor, 1980). The child is experiencing biological changes, cognitive changes, changes in family relationships, changes in school, and changes in peer and friend relationships. Several chapters in this volume discuss the changes that occur in each of these domains. An examination of the role youth groups may play in helping the adolescent deal with all of these coincident changes is especially important because it may be one of the few more stable factors in the individual's life at this time. During early adolescence, the individual is beginning to experience more independence from the family and the school context is becoming more impersonal. Being a member of a close-knit youth group may help in making the bridge from childhood to adolescence an easier one to transverse. Youth groups can also ease the transition to adulthood for older adolescents by offering programs that help the adolescent gain exposure to employment opportunities as well as other adult roles. Hess and Petersen (1990) discussed the role that youth groups, in general, may play in enhancing knowledge about occupations as well as the role that the World Scout Organization, in particular, may play in enhancing employment opportunities for youth by increasing their exposure to various occupational roles. Thus, youth organizations are now receiving considerable attention as important components of the lives of young people. Youth organizations as well are beginning to take an interest in evaluating their own performance in recognition of the changing demands being placed upon them.

WHAT ARE YOUTH GROUPS AND HOW DO THEY OPERATE?

Although each organization has its own specific mission, the overall purpose of youth groups is to provide an opportunity outside of the school and home to bring youth together in order to develop specific subject matter knowledge and life skills. By the term *life skills* we mean skills that enable the individual to be productive in our complex society. Beatrix Hamburg (1990) conceptualized life skills to include a variety of social competencies that afford the adolescent the ability "to cope with academics, to meet fundamental challenges of forming stable human relationships, to maintain hope about the future, to understand and to adopt health-promoting behaviors, to make wise decisions about life options, and to optimize use of social networks" (p. 3). Although each youth group might not address every one of these skills, most youth groups do try to develop at least a few of these competencies. Our conceptualization of learning and achievement is broad, encompassing both important social as well as cognitive skills.

The learning that occurs in youth groups is considered to be nonformal and different from the formal, curriculum-based learning that occurs in school. Resnick (1987a) delineated four somewhat overlapping distinctions between school learning and nonschool learning. First, school learning primarily focuses on the individual, whereas nonschool learning focuses on shared knowledge and activities. The second distinction is that school learning focuses on thought processes, whereas nonformal learning involves the manipulation of tools in addition to pure thought. Third, learning in school is devoid of meaningful context, whereas nonformal learning is based on everyday activities. The last distinction emphasizes that school learning enhances general principles that are believed to transfer to specific situations; nonformal learning is situation-specific. (It should be noted that nonformal education may occur in the school as an unofficial part of the curriculum.) In general, the nonformal learning that occurs in youth groups is "hands-on" and experiential. We discuss specific examples of the learning that occurs in youth groups in a later section.

Changes in family and economic conditions have, and continue to have, influence on the structure and programs of youth-serving organizations. Most of the major programs were founded to bridge the socialization gaps that were appearing between home and school (Erickson, 1986). Even today, many of the arguments that we and others make concerning the role of youth groups in the community are that the groups augment the role of the school and family because of our changing demographic and economic conditions.

Who Belongs?

Youth groups are composed of children and adolescents ranging in age from 4 to 19 years. The bulk of members are between the ages of 8 and

14. Although most studies indicate that over 86% of the youth in these volunteer organizations are from White, middle- or upper middle-class homes (Erickson, 1986), some youth groups target specific less advantaged groups. Boys' Clubs and Girls' Clubs, for example, specifically target lower income and minority populations for membership. Of the girls and women served by Girls' Clubs, 79% were from families with incomes less that $15,000; 32% of their participants are African-American, 10% are Hispanic, and another 2% are other minorities. A recent survey (Louis Harris & Associates, 1989) of 2,000 Grade 4–12 girls found that African-American girls were involved with the Girl Scouts in the same proportion as the national sample, whereas Hispanic girls were underrepresented. 4-H programs serve a wide range of groups—both urban and rural—with 22% of their members in a minority group. Thus, although youth groups still serve the majority population, they are also reaching youth from minority and less advantaged populations. Given the projected increase in minority populations over the next 25 years (Gibbs, Huang, & Associates, 1989), it will be in the best interest of youth groups to attract and meet the needs of culturally diverse youths.

What Are the Advantages for Having Youth Groups as a Means of Enhancing Learning and Achievement?

Youth groups may serve to help in the satisfaction of needs that may not be adequately filled by either family or the school. David Hamburg (1986) eloquently presented the needs of all people for survival and healthy development:

> The need to find a place in a valued group that provides a sense of belonging; the need to identify tasks that are generally recognized in the group as having adaptive value and that thereby earn respect when skill is acquired for coping with the tasks; the need to feel a sense of worth as a person; the need for reliable and predictable relationships with other people, especially a few relatively close relationships—or at least one. (pp. 4–5)

These needs, coupled with the changes that are occurring during early adolescence, may be particularly difficult to satisfy. In addition, youth groups can complement the family and school in providing additional opportunities for success. Therefore, youth groups can serve enrichment as well as (or instead of) remediation functions.

The increasing number of single-parent and working-mother households has significantly reduced the amount of time and energy a parent can expend on enrichment opportunities. In addition, the increasing number of teenage mothers and welfare families also precludes enriching opportunities for learning because of a lack of interest, time, or money, or all three. Community-based youth groups can provide opportunities (such as field trips) and projects that today's parents are too busy for, are not interested in, or cannot afford. It should be noted that recruitment of children from homes in which time and/or income is limited provides impediments to participation in youth groups. Youth groups must turn their attention to the practical matters of actually getting children and adolescents to the meetings. In addition, volunteer leadership for youth groups tends to be parents of the children involved. Youth groups must therefore be concerned with the recruitment of volunteers. Although discussion of these methods is beyond the scope of this chapter, it is important to note that these are important practical issues.

Another potential benefit of youth groups is that participants are in close contact with one or more adult members of the community. These adults could serve as role models, mentors, and friends. Given the erosion of social support networks for families, either as a result of extensive geographic mobility or the rise of single-parent families, many youth may not be receiving the specific attention that they need: The typical child spends about 5 minutes per day alone with his or her father, 40 minutes per day with the mother, and an additional 60 minutes with both parents (Csikszentmihalyi & McCormack, 1986). In homes where both parents work, this time may be even more limited. Research has found that children who seem invulnerable to sustained life stress within the family have had at least one outside source of emotional support—either from a teacher or by being a member of a cooperative group such as 4-H or a church group (Werner, 1984). The increasing size of schools has further reduced the opportunity for a meaningful, personal relationship between student and teacher to develop. In addition, many adolescents will have undergone a transition either to a middle school or a junior high school, resulting in increased anonymity. Youth group participation may provide this needed closeness with peers and/or an adult.

SPECIFIC PROGRAMS AND OPPORTUNITIES

Community Experiences

One of the most powerful strengths of today's youth groups is their ability to maintain focus on issues that are important and relevant to the adolescents they serve. For example, in 1987 the Girl Scouts of America launched itself into the mission of training its leaders for handling issues relevant to girls and young women in today's society. They call this training in "contemporary issues." Contemporary issues deals with potentially sensitive topics such as child abuse, substance abuse, suicide, family crises, teenage pregnancy; topics that are educational, such as math, science, and technology, earth matters; growing up female; and literacy. In addition to these special interest programs, girls work on merit badges that cover a wide range of topics, many of which expose the girls to male-stereotyped activities. For example, a Do-It-Yourself badge workshop focused on developing basic auto mechanic, carpentry, and electrical skills. Other practical skills are developed through weekend campout activities. For example, one weekend seminar focused on developing such skills as reading a bus schedule, knowledge about credit, budgeting, and knowing the best months to buy furniture, appliances, and linens.

In addition to basic skills, most youth groups also have programs for increasing adolescents' knowledge about career possibilities. The Boy Scouts of America offers two programs for increasing adolescents' knowledge of career roles. The first program, Career Awareness Exploring, is a series of in-school seminars in which a number of professional adults from the community speak about their training for and work in their respective occupations. These adults typically include role models from the students' own background, including minorities and women who may be in nontraditional occupations. These seminars were designed to expose youth to a variety of careers in order for youth to understand a number of options available in choosing a career. The second program, Explorer Posts, is designed to give scouts an opportunity to learn about a particular hobby, sport, or general interest area. Most Explorer Posts are career related (Hess & Petersen, 1990). Volunteers from the community are matched with Explorer members according to interest and center their activities around learning about a specific career (Boy Scouts of America, 1990).

The 4-H clubs, whose theme is "Learn by doing," involve youth in a number of projects designed to give them subject matter knowledge. Youth and volunteers are involved in a "Plan-Do-Review" process. As a subsidiary of the U.S. Department of Agriculture and the land grant university, 55% of 4-H's projects fall within the domain of the biological services. For example, youth might be responsible for raising livestock or monitoring the growth of an agricultural product (U.S.D.A., 1987). Other project domains include social science, physical science, and arts and humanities. In addition to subject matter knowledge, projects are designed to provide other learning experiences such as leadership roles, presentations before groups, and social interaction with peers and adults.

Yet when one thinks of the multitude of opportunities and experiences that are possible within the youth group, one must also stop to think about how each of these experiences are implemented. Little empirical work has been done on evaluating the success of many or any of these programs particularly at the specific community group or troop level. Are leaders implementing these programs? How often, for example, is the math, science and technology, contemporary issue of the girl scouts actually implemented, are the leaders primarily focusing on status quo activities such as cooking badges? If the volunteers who run these groups are primarily nonworking mothers who have the extra time to do these activities, what impact will this have on the children whose mothers are too busy to participate because of work and household responsibilities?

Although most youth groups are very much interested in knowing what the needs and interests are of its youth, are they actually implementing these interests into their programs? In a recent survey conducted in the state of Washington, 4-H found that its youth were interested in heterosexual relationships, problems with drugs and alcohol, teen/parent relations, child abuse, nuclear war, and crime (Rude, 1987). Yet whether extension agents working at a specific community monitor the needs and interests of the youth and design programs accordingly remains a research question in need of investigation. There is considerable interest and debate over whether youth groups should offer traditionally or nontraditionally gender-typed activities and whether these should occur in a coeducational or single-gender format (Nicholson, 1984). There are also questions about whether same-gender or different-gender persons acting as models or mentors are equally effective (Price et al., 1990). The Girl Scouts of America have recently confirmed their commitment on keeping the organization a single-gender one.

Not only are youth group activities physically located in the community, many of the programs and projects involve community service (Carnegie Council, 1989). Boy Scouts and Girl Scouts, Boys Club, Girls Club, and 4-H each have various activities that enable youth to interact and give a part of themselves to their community. Activities range from working in a nursing home to beautifying a vacant lot by planting a vegetable garden. These projects are designed to help youth build character and to gain a sense of commitment to their community. In addition, youth gain access to responsibilities and experiences that would otherwise be denied to them. Such activities foster the development of planning skills, working with others, and manual skills that could be valuable for employment opportunities (Hamilton, 1990). Yet community service projects may be implemented in only a few of the groups. Are affluent youth groups providing services to the needy or elderly? Are urban groups working to beautify their own neighborhoods? Are older groups getting involved with mentoring programs for younger groups in their community?

Beyond Community Experiences: State, National, and International Opportunities

In addition to experiences within their own communities, most youth organizations also provide state, national, and international opportunities. For example, the 4-H ambassador program provides opportunities at all four levels. In Pennsylvania, for example, 74 teens (15 to 18 years of age) from throughout the state met at The Pennsylvania State University for a 3-day workshop to develop leadership, communication, and marketing skills. The role of ambassador serves to increase public awareness and interest in the values, opportunities, and benefits of 4-H. At the community level, ambassadors promote the 4-H experience and describe the association between 4-H, cooperative extension, and the land grant university. National ambassadors, who promote 4-H activities to potential donors and legislators in addition to the general public, are selected. Thus, these youth had the opportunity to develop fund-raising skills at a public and private level. The educational objectives of the program were to increase public speaking and communication skills as well as to enhance social skills and self-esteem. Participants engaged in specific seminars that focused on interviewing skills, knowledge about 4-H, personal appearance, and effective presentations. Each participant gave a 2-minute presentation at the end of the program. Social events, such as dances and pizza parties, were also incorporated into the program.

At the national level, 4-H offers the National 4-H Congress, a 6-day annual event held in Chicago, which recognizes a select group of 4-H members for their contributions. In addition to the delegates program, 4-H also offers national competitions and conferences such as the annual National Junior Horticulture Convention and the National Agriculture Engineering Event.

International programs offered by 4-H allow 15- to 19-year-old youths to be ambassadors to different countries. A group of students from a state travel with an American leader and live with host families. Specific programs for 1990 included farming in the Swiss Alps, expressive arts in England, natural resources in Sweden, Norway, and Denmark, and goods and services produced in Italy. Thus, youth are provided with first-hand knowledge of other cultures. For those youth who do not participate in these activities, there are also program booklets available for developing an international project or interest group.

These programs, along with those offered by other organizations, provide youth the opportunity to go beyond their own community to meet and interact with individuals from neighborhoods, states, and cultures different from their own. Yet many of these events are highly competitive and may engender feelings of stress and failure rather than enthusiasm and accomplishment. Moreover, we have to raise the question about who the youth are who participate in these national events. Are they youth from high-achieving families already? Do these opportunities arise for all of the members of the group? What are the characteristics of the youth who are actively involved in these activities versus the youth who do not become as engaged? What characteristics of group leaders foster the greatest participation and most satisfaction?

MEASURING SUCCESS: HOW DO WE KNOW YOUTH GROUPS ARE EFFECTIVE?

Although systematic evaluations of most of these programs are lacking, there is a small body of literature that supports the effectiveness of these programs. Collins (1984) found that youth in 4-H perceived that participation was positively related to the development of life skills. In a study that focused on specific life skills, Heinsohn and Cantrell (1986) found that 4-H members reported that membership had contributed to their leadership skills and their ability to speak in public. In addition to leadership skills, other research has found that participation in 4-H created greater communication and understanding within the family (Abbott, Sutton, Jackson, & Logan, 1976). Also, 4-H participation has been found to enhance dependability and job responsibility (Brown, 1982), self-esteem (Steele & Rossing, 1981), and decision-making skills (Orr & Gobeli, 1986). 4-H alumni report that their involvement with the program influenced their career choices and selection of colleges (Rockwell, Stohler, & Rudman, 1981). Annual program reports by extension agents are smattered with vignettes of individual success stories of getting at-risk youth on a positive life trajectory. One agent wrote about how an 11-year-old girl, who was sexually abused by her father, has renewed her self-confidence and happiness by participating in the 4-H program. She has stopped smoking cigarettes and is engaging in fewer deviant activities.

Recent evidence also suggests that involvement in other youth groups as well as 4-H is associated with the development of life skills (Miller, 1991). Participation in Boy Scouts has been found to provide enrichment opportunities for family relationships and to develop a sense of community responsibility and citizenship (Kleinfeld & Shinkwin, 1983).

There are several problems with most of the evaluation research conducted in this area, however. One primary problem is sample selection. The individuals willing to complete the questionnaires and surveys are probably those individuals who are the most enthusiastic and most involved in the program. Very little research has been conducted evaluating outcome measures on individuals who dropped out of youth groups. Most research that has examined dropouts has primarily focused on why they have left the group (e.g., Hamilton & Kenny, 1988). A second problem is that there are no prospective studies that have examined what factors determine who joins youth groups versus who chooses not to join. A third problem is the nature of the evaluation. Many of the studies discussed here ask the youth to describe whether they felt being in the group has helped them to develop particular qualities such as leadership. Although it is important that participants view their group involvement as helpful, it would also be helpful to know whether these feelings translate into actual leadership behaviors. A fourth problem with the research on youth group evaluation is that it primarily begins with the assumption that all youth groups are good. Researchers have not generally asked questions regarding when youth groups may have deleterious effects on student outcomes. For example, what if youth groups are teaching youth values that are in direct opposition to family values and/or experiences? When is involvement in a youth group too much? Can a youth whose primary goal is to win the blue ribbon at the state fair, be neglectful of their school or family responsibilities? More importantly, under which contexts and for which youth are youth groups most successful? How many youth group activities are too many?

The acquisition and long-term retention of subject matter knowledge remains virtually unevaluated or, at best, is buried in unpublished project reports. Yet we know that youth are learning, as is evidenced by the thousands of merit badges earned each year. Whether youth group participation enhances student achievement in certain school subjects has not been systematically evaluated. Do agricultural experiences in 4-H, for example, translate into success in the science classroom? Systematic evaluation of the programs designed to increase subject matter knowledge is needed together with dissemination of these results to help foster a better understanding of effective and ineffective program content.

WHY DO YOUTH GROUPS WORK?

Youth groups are an important means for empowering youth. By structuring youth groups for the adolescent in a way that allows the members to make their own decisions regarding what the topics are and what the approach will be, a partnership can be established between the youth and their adult leaders. "Such a partnership orientation is more likely to communicate a sense of positive reward and minimize the message that adolescent behavior is inevitably a problem or that young people cannot make important positive contributions" (Price et al., 1990, p. 15).

We believe that youth groups work because they provide an opportunity for youths to meet the basic needs of survival discussed by Hamburg—a sense of belonging, skills with adaptive value (the activities are real-world experiences), a sense of worth (youth contributions are valued), and reliable relationships (group membership). The material that is covered in successful youth group is relevant to their lives, and it is fun. Both Erickson (1988) and Gottlieb (1988) noted that if adolescents do not see a program as relevant to their needs and aspirations, participation will be low. Hess and Petersen (1990) summarized the successful features of youth groups to include "voluntary participation, decision-making activities, or tasks that are rewarding both for their own sake and as a means of achieving future goals, provision of multiple activities to provide opportunities for role experimentation, and shared values among participants and leaders" (p. iii).

STRATEGIES FOR EDUCATION

Augmenting School Learning

There are a number of different ways that youth groups can augment the learning that occurs in school. The first method for augmenting school learning is to coordinate some of the activities in the youth group to complement and enrich the material that is covered in school. Because leaders are based in the community and typically have children who attend the school, the design of certain activities and field trips can complement the school curriculum. This can only be successful, however, if the activities are enjoyable and the values of the school match those of the youth group members.

Several youth organizations with facilities, such as the YMCAs and YWCAs, Girls Clubs, and Boys Clubs, offer daily tutoring sessions and homework assistance programs such as hotlines and clinics (Carnegie Council, 1989).

A third way that youth groups can augment school learning is to provide students with opportunities that may not be available in their schools. There are several organizations that are currently doing just that. The Boy Scouts of America Explorer program provides exposure to adult role models in occupations. Similar occupation-mentoring programs are offered by Girl Scouts, Girls Clubs and Boys Clubs. The Girl Scout contemporary issues on math, science, and technology may give girls an increased interest to the world of mathematics and science. Similarly, 4-H gives youth a number of hands-on lessons in embryology, terrariums, nutrition, and horticulture to name a few.

Programs offered by youth groups can work together with school systems to build on the curriculum and to increase student involvement with school. One innovative program that is meeting with considerable success is the 4-H collaboration with the school system in Philadelphia to enhance science education, called the "4-H Science Environmental Day Camp Program." Twenty-five middle-school youth were participants in a 4-week day camp program designed to improve science literacy skills. The students were recommended by their science teachers and were required to have at least a C average and no discipline problems. The camp included 4-H projects in embryology, hydroponics, terrariums, recycling, woodworking, rocketry, nutrition, and entomology. Three science teachers and one person from the community served as instructors. Several field trips were taken to various science museums, the zoo, and other research facilities. Other fun and social activities were also incorporated into the program, such as arts and crafts, swimming, roller skating, tennis, and trips to the public library. Students learned the scientific method and were encouraged to develop ideas for the next year's George Washington Carver Science Fair. Students are currently being tracked during the school year to monitor their progress in science classes. They meet twice a month to continue to improve their science skills. This program illustrates how youth groups can be an effective means on getting youth excited about school and learning by first "hooking" them into fun, hands-on experiences.

A Government/Leadership training group conducted by 4-H in Philadelphia, in cooperation with the mayor's Commission on Puerto Rican/Latino Affairs, was designed to teach the youngsters that they can have a voice in their families and neighborhoods, as well as within the city. The students participated in mock judicial and voting proceedings, toured city hall, and met with government officials.

Such innovative programs as these encourage the building of links between the community and the school. Other programs help to strengthen the tie to family as well (see Snider and Miller, chapter 28, this volume). By working to establish ties across all domains of the developing adolescent we can help to build "social capital." Social capital refers to the quantity and quality of social relations between youth and adults in their community; such capital helps youth to stay in school and become productive citizens (cf. Colemen, Campbell, Wood, Weinfeld, & York, 1966). According to Ianni (1989), "Coordinated social interventions by a caring community into the life course of adolescents can lead to the joint construction of a shared and mutually acceptable life story which links the past to a believable future" (p. 259).

How can Schools Modify Their Programs of Instruction to Include the Experiential Learning that Takes Place in Community-Based Youth Groups?

Although there has been considerable interest in experiential learning brought about by the work of Bruner in the 1960s (e.g., Bruner, 1960, 1966) as well as the recent educational reform to increase critical thinking skills, hands-on curriculum is being implemented in the classroom. Unfortunately, not all teachers are willing to try these methods, perhaps because of their limited training in these techniques. In teacher education programs, most education majors receive a discussion of these techniques during their introductory educational psychology class taken in their sophomore year. More can be done in the advanced teacher preparation content courses to encourage the use of these methods in the classroom. Evidence that children and adolescents enjoy their youth groups and that they are actively involved members is encouraging—albeit anecdotal—evidence that these techniques work. Although there may be some hesitation in the adoption of these methods because of strict curriculum requirements, hands-on experience coupled with cooperative learning groups can foster an interest in learning that could then make children more interested in direct instruction. There is a very large cognitive literature that supports the idea that meaningful information is attended to and remembered much more efficiently than nonmeaningful information. Experiential, hands-on learning makes the material more meaningful.

Resnick (1987b) found that in-school programs designed to enhance higher order thinking and learning skills share some of the characteristics associated with nonformal learning. The features identified were socially shared intellectual work and direct involvement in the joint accomplishment of tasks—in other words, an experiential, cooperative learning experience. Resnick also noted that successful programs are similar to apprenticeships in that they encourage student observation and make many internal processes overt. It is interesting to note that many of the programs designed to foster an understanding of various occupational roles use this same model. Finally, the most successful in-school programs encourage the development of specific subject matter knowledge rather than general abilities. Thus, as Resnick (1987a) pointed out, schools must redirect their focus to include more "nonformal" methods.

Besides the emphasis on the type of learning, there are at least two important distinctions between the methods of youth groups and the formal educational system. The first is who dictates the content of the material, and the second is in the nature of participation—voluntary versus involuntary. If the model of youth groups is to be used, then these important components that empower the youths to become actively involved in the group are needed.

Although curriculum requirements do focus much of the content that teachers must cover in their classrooms, there should be ways that teachers or schools can provide students with options, both in courses they take and in the means by which learning is achieved. Students must be given the opportunity to have ownership of and responsibility for their own learning. Learning is a process. The major goal of education is to produce students who can think for themselves, solve problems, and become productive citizens. We must start by giving students at least some opportunity for choices in their education both in terms of content and methods. Just as youth groups decide on the topics they cover based on the needs of the community, so, too, should schools ask their students what they think is important. A partnership between schools and the youth they serve could help to build important links within the community, especially one in which the schools and homes are not viewed as having consistent values and views.

4-H began as an educational program of the Cooperative Extension Service to reach adults through training their children with new technical information in agriculture and home economics. Although we typically think of the links between parents and youth or school and youth to be unidirectional (with the arrows pointing toward the youth), we need to recognize, as 4-H did almost 100 years ago, that youth can, and should, influence adult groups. By listening and responding to their needs, schools can give youth a sense of control over their future.

CONCLUSION

Youth organizations provide children with an opportunity to explore a variety of tasks that perhaps they would not have otherwise had an opportunity to explore. The transition into adolescence is one that could be made easier by having a stable network of people who share common goals and interests. The transition out of adolescence can also be made easier if we give youth opportunities to explore adult roles through discussion, mentoring programs, and hands-on opportunities for community service and work experience. Youth organizations can provide these opportunities for many of our youth. The collaborative efforts of youth serving organizations and schools as well as the integration of successful youth group characteristics into the school program can further enhance the development of our youth and strengthen bonds within the community between youth, their families, the schools, and their neighborhoods.

REFERENCES

Abbott, R., Sutton, B., Jackson, M. C., Jr., & Logan, B. W. (1976). *Process and impact evaluation: The Detroit 4-H program* (final report). East Lansing, MI: Michigan State University.

Boy Scouts of America. (1990). *Annual Report, 1989*. Irving, TX: Author.

Brown, L. A. (1982). *A national assessment of the career and occupational development needs of 4-H youth*. Unpublished doctoral dissertation, University of Maryland, College Park.

Bruner, J. S. (1960). *The process of education*. New York: Vintage Books.

Bruner, J. S. (1966). *Toward a theory of instruction*. New York: Norton.

Carnegie Council on Adolescent Development. (1989). *Turning points: Preparing American youth for the 21st century*. Washington, DC: Author.

Coleman, J. S., Campbell, J., Wood, A. M., Weinfeld, F. D., & York, R. L. (1966). *Equality of educational opportunity*. Washington, DC: U.S. Department of Health, Education, and Welfare, Office of Education.

Collins, O. P. (1984). *Life skills development through 4-H: A survey of adolescent attitudes*. Unpublished master's thesis, University of Nebraska, Lincoln.

Csikszentmihalyi, M., & McCormack, J. (1986, February). The influence of teachers. *Phi Delta Kappan*, 417.

Erickson, J. B. (1986). Nonformal education in organizations for American youth. *Children Today*, 17–25.

Erickson, J. B. (1988). A commentary on "Communities and adolescents: An exploration of reciprocal supports." In *Youth and America's future* (pp. 77–87). New York: The Williams T. Grant Foundation.

Evans, B. (1968). *Dictionary of quotations*. New York: Delacorte.

Gibbs, J. T., Huang, L. H., & Associates. (1989). *Children of color*. San Francisco: Jossey Bass.

Gottleib, B. H. (1988). Social support in adolescence. In M. E. Colten & S. Gore (Eds.), *Adolescent stress: Causes and consequences* (pp. 281–306). New York: Aldine de Gruyter.

Hamburg, B. A. (1990). *Life skills training: Preventive interventions for young adolescents* (Carnegie Council on Adolescent Development Working Papers). Washington, DC: Carnegie Council on Adolescent Development.

Hamburg, D. A. (1986). *Preparing for life: The critical transition of adolescence* (annual report). Washington, DC: Carnegie Corporation.

Hamilton, S. F. (1990). *Apprenticeship for adulthood: Preparing youth for the future.* New York: MacMillan.

Hamilton, S. F., & Kenny, S. (1988). Why teenagers drop out: The 4-H experience. *New Designs for Youth Development, 8*(1), 11–13.

Heinsohn, A. L., & Cantrell, M. J. (1986). *Pennsylvania 4-H impact study: An evaluation of teens' life skills development* (final report). University Park: The Pennsylvania State University.

Hess, L. E., & Petersen, A. C. (1990). *Narrowing the margins: Adolescent unemployment and the lack of a social role.* Zurich, Switzerland: Jacobs Suchard Foundation.

Ianni, F. A. J. (1989). *The search for structure: A report on American youth today.* New York: The Free Press.

Kleinfeld, J., & Shinkwin, A. (1983). *Making good boys better: Nonformal education in Boy Scouts* (ERIC Document Reproduction Service No. ED 239815). Fairbanks, AK: Alaska University, Institute of Social, Economic, and Government Research.

Louis Harris & Associates. (1989). *Girl Scouts survey on the beliefs and moral values of America's children.* New York: Girl Scouts of the United States of America.

Miller, J. P. (1991). *Four-H and Non-4-H participants' development of competency, coping, and contributory life skills.* Unpublished doctoral dissertation, The Pennsylvania State University, University Park.

Nicholson, H. J. (1984, March). *From research to practice in youth organizations: Meeting girls' needs in the second decade of life.* Paper presented at the second biennial conference on Adolescent Research: The Second Decade of Life, Tucson, AZ.

Orr, J. D., & Gobeli, V. C. (1986). *4-H teen leadership development in Nebraska.* Lincoln: University of Nebraska, Nebraska Cooperative Extension Service, Institute of Agriculture and Natural Resources.

Petersen, A. C., & Taylor, B. C. (1980). The biological approach to adolescence: Biological change and psychosocial adaptation. In J. Adelson (Ed.), *Handbook of adolescent psychology* (pp. 117–155). New York: Wiley.

Price, R. H., Cioci, M., Penner, W., & Trautlein, B. (1990). *School and community support programs that enhance adolescent health and education* (Carnegie Council on Adolescent Development, Working Papers). Washington, DC: Carnegie Council on Adolescent Development.

Resnick, L. B. (1987a). The 1987 presidential address: Learning in school and out. *Educational Researcher, 16*(9), 13–20.

Resnick, L. B. (1987b). *Education and learning to think.* Washington, DC: National Academy Press.

Rockwell, S. K., Stohler, R. F., & Rudman, L. E. (1981). *4-H's influence on advanced training, careers and leadership roles in adulthood.* Lincoln: University of Nebraska, Nebraska Cooperative Extension Service, Institute of Agriculture and Natural Resources.

Rude, T. L. (1987). *An examination of 4-H youth's needs and interests, and implications for state conference.* Unpublished master's thesis, Washington State University, Pullman, Washington.

Steele, S. M., & Rossing, B. (1981). *How well are 4-H programs attaining century III objectives?* Madison: University of Wisconsin, Extension, Division of Program and Staff Development.

United States Department of Agriculture. (1987). *Science and technology: The 4-H way.* Washington, DC: U.S. Government Printing Office.

Werner, E. E. (1984, November). Resilient children. *Young Children,* 68–72.

10 Academic Achievement Among Early Adolescents: Social and Cultural Diversity

Yoshi Takei
Judith Semon Dubas
The Pennsylvania State University

Variation in academic achievement based on ascribed characteristics such as family background and race has interested many social scientists. The major reason for this interest is undoubtedly the perceived importance of educational achievement for educational attainment, which in turn has a direct bearing on subsequent occupational and status attainment.

Most social scientists who study this topic seek explanations for such variation in the different social and cultural environments over which individuals have little or no control. People, after all, have no say in what families they are born into nor can they, in most instances, readily change their gender, race, or ethnicity. Thus, some of the important environmental factors that can shape people's lives are largely beyond their power to change or modify. This chapter focuses on the influence that social and cultural environments exert on the developing adolescent. We review the research that has examined how categorical differentiation among adolescents can result in differing attitudes and behaviors both in and out of school that then lead to differences in academic achievement. We also pay special attention to the part schools unintentionally can play in creating variations in academic performance.

DIFFERENTIATION AND INEQUALITY AT THE SOCIETAL LEVEL

Creation of Unequal Relationships

The idea that every human society is characterized by some form of differentiation among its members is a truism in social science thinking. Differentiation based on age (adult/nonadult) and gender (male/female) seems to exist everywhere without exception. Societies that utilize means other than hunting and gathering for their subsistence seem to create some form of differentiation based on socioeconomic status (SES). What is interesting about this phenomenon is that most forms of differentiation seem to be associated with some degree of inequality in power, prestige, or wealth. When these disparities become institutionalized, an unequal relationship is created that is often maintained through political and economic institutions.

Unequal relationships become institutionalized to the extent that different sets of norms become established for various categories of people. A category of people who acquire more power will be able to maintain some degree of superiority over the other with minimal coercion if the subordinated group behaves in ways that can be interpreted as revealing the inferiority of the lower status group. Variously referred to as labeling theory, self-fulfilling prophecy, or expectation theory, this line of reasoning suggests that people often become what they are labeled to be or perform as they are expected to perform. Although this theory has been used primarily in explaining changes at the individual level, there is little reason not to utilize it in explaining group differences because groups tend to develop stereotypes of other groups and act on the basis of those stereotypes.

It should not be overlooked, however, that the legitimation of a particular category of people's superordination over another is unlikely to be immutable over time. Subordinate categories of people are capable through collective means to develop alternative definitions of themselves and their relationship with the superordinate category. When this happens, the previously institutionalized unequal relationship may become deinstitutionalized and replaced by a transformed, perhaps more categorically equal relationship. This seems to be occurring in the relationship between husbands and wives in Western societies (Davis, 1984).

How social and cultural factors can affect school performance can be observed in the variations in school-related behaviors among ethnic and racial groups. One of the more notable studies on how the educational performance of African-Americans changed historically to become somewhat lower than that of the White majority is the one conducted by Lieberson (1980) using U.S. Census data. As presented by Lieberson, a comparison of the highest school grade completed early in the 20th century by African-Americans born in the north and U.S.-born children of European immigrants reveal that the educational attainment of Blacks exceeded those of some nationality groups. However, in each succeeding birth cohort, the descendants of European immigrants showed gains in comparison to the African-Americans. For those born after World War II, all nationality groups' educational attainment exceeded that of African-Americans. The major shift toward the educational advantage of the children of European immigrants seems to have taken place among the 1925-1935 birth cohort.

Striking confirmation of Lieberson's findings was reported by Perlmann (1987), who analyzed individual-level data collected from samples of adolescents in Providence, Rhode Island, from censuses conducted between 1880 and 1925. When family status was controlled, the educational achievement (in the form of grade point averages [GPAs]) and attainment of the earlier generations of African-Americans compared very favorably with those of Europeans whose parents had immigrated to the United States.

Both Lieberson and Perlmann pointed out what could be an important factor in the subsequent decline in the educational attainment of African-Americans relative to those of European descent. The occupational attainment and incomes of African-American males were dramatically lower than those of Europeans with similar levels of educational attainment throughout the historical period studied. Such differentiation between Whites and Blacks in rewards for educational attainment has important implications for the subsequent differentiation in educational attainment by race. As Lieberson speculated:

> If, because of discrimination or other forces, the occupational and income rewards of a given educational level differ between Blacks and new Europeans, then both parental support and children's incentives for achieving such levels may differ, and this in turn would lead to differential accomplishments and possibly even a different set of attitudes towards the value and role of education. (p. 237)

This observation incorporates several hypotheses that are based on cultural factors related to racial discrimination that affected African-Americans. Perlmann speculated that Black culture might have come to devalue the importance of education as a result of a long tradition of low rewards to Blacks irrespective of their educational attainment. However, a valid explanation for Black underachievement obviously is more complex than that offered by Perlmann. Black underachievement in schools cannot be adequately explained by relying solely on lower motivation as the causal variable because many studies have shown that Black youths have as high, if not higher, educational and occupational aspirations than White pupils of similar family background (e.g., Coleman, 1966). Ogbu (1978) argued that members of a social group that face severe job discrimination are aware of the situation and this awareness negatively affects the educationally relevant behaviors of the group's young even while the group may value education in the abstract.

Mickelson (1990) found, in analyzing the relationship between attitudes and grades among African-American high school students in the Los Angeles area, that there was almost no relationship between grades and broad, general beliefs about the importance of education. However, she found that skepticism about the instrumental value of education served to explain a fairly substantial amount of variation in GPAs among Black students. Her study illustrates the likelihood that perceptions of anticipated discrimination on the basis of race in attaining jobs lower academic achievement among Black adolescents.

Sue and Okazaki (1990) argued that the educational "overachievement" of Asian-Americans may be largely due to a belief that is a reversal of that of many African-Americans. Asian-Americans are likely, according to Sue and Okazaki, to view education as the most realistic avenue of attaining "success" in this society. This is because Asian-Americans do not believe that the chances of being successful in professional sports or the entertainment world are very good. Furthermore, racial discrimination is also viewed as limiting opportunities for Asian-Americans in craft industries and managerial or executive positions in industry and government. Therefore, Asian-Americans (especially immigrants) are likely to pursue higher education and to concentrate on fields of study involving mathematics and science, because by doing so, they believe they will encounter less discrimination in finding employment. Sue and Okazaki use the term *relative functionalism* to refer to this tendency among Asian-Americans to view achieving success in noneducational endeavors as being problematical—thereby increasing "the *relative* value or function of education as a means of achieving success" (p. 913, italics added). Indirect support for this argument is provided by Ritter and Dornbusch (1989), who found that a strong belief that success in life is dependent on doing well in school was associated with higher grades among Asian-American high school students.

For other ethnic or racial groups whose members perceive the possibility of alternative avenues for socioeconomic success, the relative value of education is decreased. White working-class youths may view doing well in school as being relatively unimportant if they anticipate becoming craftsmen. For African-American youths living below the poverty line, the glamour and money associated with the entertainment industry such as music and professional sports may lower the relative value of education. Thus, in order to improve the educational achievement of youths, it is necessary to identify the various factors salient for each group rather than just one or two if any remediation attempts are going to have a chance in showing any degree of success. In the next section, we focus on environments that are more proximate to the developing adolescent.

DIFFERENTIATION, INEQUALITY, AND UNEQUAL ACADEMIC ACHIEVEMENT AMONG YOUNG ADOLESCENTS

The differentiation and inequalities that are observable at the societal level often penetrate into the lives of the young and cause variations in how they perform in school. This penetration occurs primarily in three sociocultural contexts: the family, the peer group or community, and the schools. The potential effects of these contexts are discussed in turn.

The Family

Most of the research on the family's influence on a person's academic achievement have focused on the family's SES. One of the earliest large-scale studies conducted by Rogoff (1961) on a nationally representative sample of high school seniors in 1958 revealed that family background was a more powerful factor in influencing college-going plans than academic achievement as reflected by test scores. Among the numerous studies on high school pupils, the next major study on the factors affecting academic achievement was conducted by Coleman (1966) in 1965. Based on a nationally representative sample of almost 650,000 students, the finding that subsequently came to be indelibly associated with the Coleman report was that the pupil's family background was the best predictor of how well adolescents perform on written tests (Coleman, 1966).

The identification of family SES as an important factor associated with academic achievement and expected educational attainment spawned a multitude of studies examining how differences in SES affect children's school performance. It is beyond the scope of this chapter to review the voluminous body of academic literature on this topic, thus we briefly summarize the theoretical debates that took place over the most legitimate way to conceptualize the influence of the family's SES on achievement.

The issue became complicated from the outset because the academic performance of certain ethnic and minority children (especially African-American, but American Indian and Mexican-American also), became included in the target population. Most of the earlier research assumed that the opportunities to experience upward social mobility were readily available in this society and, therefore, the twin problems were first, how to improve the academic achievement of children coming from low SES family background or who belonged to a socioeconomically disadvantaged minority group and second, how to raise their educational and occupational aspirations.

These earlier studies can be said to have been based on the assumption of the existence of a cultural deficiency of some kind. The work of Bernstein (1961) in England suggesting that lower class parents used a restricted form of language with their children, which was a disadvantage because teachers used a more elaborated language in the classroom, had a strong influence on the views of U.S. social scientists. When this perspective was used to "explain" the relatively low academic achievement of African-American youngsters in U.S. schools, it sparked a controversy over the question of whether Black English was "deficient" or "different" (e.g., Valentine, 1971).

The proponents of the "deficit" model were more numerous and politically powerful and their view of the problem prevailed, as evidenced by President Lyndon B. Johnson's War Against Poverty programs and, in particular, the establishment of remediation projects like Head Start. Head Start and other early intervention programs are based on the assumption that children born into low SES and minority families are handicapped in life from the very outset due to their lack of exposure to White middle-class culture that forms the basis for much of the curriculum taught in schools. Thus, early intervention is assumed to provide the children a better start in life.

The earlier research seemed to make the assumption that a family's SES more or less represented the family's cultural and material resources that exerted a powerful influence on the pupil's desire and ability to learn. Unfortunately, racial and ethnic identification (i.e., African-American, American Indian, and Hispanic) were often used as surrogates for low SES, even though this was not the case. Furthermore, the initial flood of many middle-class Cuban immigrants after the fall of Batista made it untenable to assume that most Hispanics in this country were of low SES. Later, the stream of highly trained Asian immigrants, especially those from Taiwan, Korea, and India, made it less credible to conceptualize all ethnic and racial minorities as being culturally disadvantaged.

Furthermore, it could be that the influence of family SES on academic achievement may be waning. Goldstein (1967), who reviewed the 80 American studies conducted on the effects of social stratification between 1938 and 1965, concluded that family SES was the most powerful factor in predicting academic achievement. However, more recent studies seem to suggest that school-related attitudes and academic ability are now stronger predictors than family SES in explaining academic performance (e.g., Clark & Takei, 1988; Lee & Bryk, 1988).[1] These results are congruent with Sue and Okazaki's concept of functional relativism. Family SES will not explain variations in achievement across ethnic and racial groups because the groups differ in perceptions of alternative avenues for attaining success (money, power, or prestige). Moreover, within-group variations need to be described in terms of process rather than social address variables.

Another possible approach to the study of academic achievement among adolescents is to examine the nature of their relationship with their parents involving their status. This approach was suggested by West (1979) based on his ethnographic work with adolescents that revealed that the teenagers' stance toward adolescent status largely determined whether they were "straights" or "greasers."

Straights generally accepted their subordinate status as adolescents, although not always without conflict with adults. For them to accept the status of nonadults, they had to have some degree of assurance that their parents (or guardians) would continue to support them financially in the foreseeable future. Under these circumstances, both parents and teenagers "accorded legitimacy to parental control of the adolescent in substantial matters" (p. 140).

The greasers, on the other hand, rejected the status of adolescents and wanted to have the rights of adults. This was probably due to the parental expectation that their children will be independent as early as possible with the result that the adolescents did not automatically defer to adult authority and demanded to negotiate with adults as equals.

---

[1] An analysis of the White students' grades in the High School and Beyond data revealed that family SES explains only .06 of the variation in grades for that subsample. On the other hand, many studies show that family SES remains a strong factor in causing variations in educational attainment. Thus, family background is not only a factor that is strongly associated with college or university enrollment, but it also affects the status of the institution in which a student enrolls. Among those who pursue a higher education, high SES adolescents tend to enroll in more prestigious 4-year colleges or universities and the youths from low SES background tend to attend junior and community colleges.

Continued enrollment in school was not taken for granted and their perspective on school work was highly pragmatic; they evaluated subjects primarily in terms of whether they thought they would be useful in a job.

West's observation is consistent with a recent study of the phenomenon of dropping out of high school in California (Rumberger, Ghatak, Poulos, & Ritter, 1990). An intensive examination of pupils who dropped out showed that unlike those who stayed in school, dropouts came from families that accorded teenagers considerable independence and were characterized by weak emphasis by the adults on doing well in school.

An alternative explanation for variation in academic achievement has been conceptualized as social capital. Bourdieu (1986) defined *social capital* to mean the resources available to individuals as a consequence of being socially integrated into solidarity groups, networks, or organizations. Alternatively, Coleman (1988) defined *social capital* as consisting of the mutuality of obligations and expectations that bind people together, the capacity among people to share information, and the acceptance of norms regulating behavior.

The potential value of the concept rests in the possibility that it may be a fairly good predictor of academic achievement. By using variations in value and normative integration or cohesion as factors that will help shape the early adolescents' attitudes and behaviors, the concept focuses attention of the potential influence of social and cultural contexts on the pupil's school performance. Thus, it might be hypothesized that a pupil with a large amount of social capital whose family does not value school may not excel academically and, similarly, a pupil whose family thinks highly of school, but has little social capital, may exhibit low levels of academic achievement. A pupil who has a considerable amount of social capital and comes from a family that values educational achievement is likely to do well in school controlling for other factors. Social capital may be derived from schools with high expectations for their students, community organizations that promote achievement, or peer groups that value education.

The Peer Group and Community

Perhaps due to researchers' tendency to attribute primary influence on the early adolescent to the family, there has been less interest in the peer group and community's effects on a young person's attitudes and behaviors. The research that has been conducted on this topic supports the expected tendency for the family's ethnic or racial identification and

SES to influence the kind of friends the adolescent associates with outside the family circle. Therefore, the family's influence is usually reinforced by the adolescent's peer group. This pattern is described by Seeley, Sim, and Loosley (1956) for an upper middle-class community in Toronto and by Peshkin (1978) for a rural midwestern town.

An examination of this pattern across ethnic and racial lines, however, show that the adolescents' ethnic or racial identification is associated with differing tendencies. For example, a recent paper by Brown, Steinberg, Mounts and Philipp (1990) reports that peer groups are relatively more influential than parents for Asian and Black students than they are for White and Hispanic youngsters. Yet it also seems to be true that regardless of ethnicity, adolescents whose parents and peers favor school achievement perform better academically than those who have only one source of support (Steinberg & Brown, 1989).

It should be noted that others have reported that adolescents of certain ethnic and racial groups often define teachers and curriculum as representing the dominant White society. Thus, studying and doing well academically are denigrated as cooperating with the enemy. McDermott (1974) argued that school failure is a way for a Black youngster to acquire high status among his or her peer groups because doing poorly in school represents a rejection of the standards of the White group that oppresses their group. Fordham and Ogbu (1986) reported that the Black adolescents they interviewed defined studying and doing well academically as "acting White," and thus many Black pupils who are academically competent do not make the necessary effort to perform well in school.

A number of ethnographic studies report similar beliefs among American Indian pupils. Wolcott (1987) described the Kwakiutl Indian pupils he taught as resisting his authority by various means including accusing him of acting "just like a White man" when he tried to control their behavior. An ambitious anthropological study of an Indian reservation found that pupils in the seventh and eighth grades displayed resistance to school by acting apathetic and feigning incompetence because they are aware that most Whites consider them to be inferior or repulsive (Wax, Wax, & Dumont, 1989).

Some writers who call themselves critical theorists attribute the attitudes and behaviors of some working-class youngsters in terms of the "lived antagonistic experiences of students at the level of everyday life" in a capitalist society (Giroux, 1983). According to the critical theorists, domination by a capitalist class produce a working-class consciousness and culture that contain oppositional aspects. This is manifested in schools by the working-class pupils who actively resist the efforts of teachers to teach middle-class culture and mentality (e.g., McLaren,

1989). Therefore, according to them, the relatively low academic performance of low SES pupils is not due to cultural deficiency, but is an expression of the antagonism of the lower class toward the privileged classes. It is true that many White teenagers refer to those who work hard in schools as "nerds," "brown nosers," or some other derogatory epithet in order to devalue academic achievement and, thereby, reduce the pressure to compete with those who are more academically proficient (Coleman, 1959). Yet the proportion of adolescents who subscribe to the role of a "good student" are higher for Whites and Asian-Americans than for African-Americans and Hispanics (Steinberg & Brown, 1989). Whether the sociopsychological factors that influence the former groups are different from those that affect the latter groups merits further attention. In addition to friends and family, the school context can vary for various ethnic and racial groups.

Schools

There is considerable evidence suggesting that the ways in which schools are structured and the procedures adopted by many schools can cause variations in academic achievement that tend to coincide with the categorization of pupils on the basis of family SES and racial or ethnic identification.

The Coleman report convinced many that differences among schools in terms of physical properties (e.g., number of pupils enrolled in science classes, etc.) had very little influence on academic achievement. Although this might be true for variations in school facilities, the same cannot be said for what might be called differences in "school climate." A major study in England documented the variations in achievement among secondary school students depending on what school they happened to attend (Rutter, Maughan, Mortimore, Ousten, & Smith, 1979). Ethnographic accounts of schools suggest that some schools have very high rates of violence, absenteeism, drug use, and vandalism that probably depress academic achievement (e.g., McLaren, 1989). Such ethnographies also describe the majority of teachers and administrators in those schools to hold low expectations for their pupils.

The "effective school" movement in the mid-1980s was based on the premise that school staff can influence pupils to improve their academic achievement. Largely stimulated by journalistic accounts of schools in economically depressed areas wherein the pupils' averages in standardized test scores were considerably higher than those of other schools enrolling student of similar family backgrounds, there was considerable interest in the question of how these schools were different from the typical schools. Although the elements that made up these exceptional schools varied from school to school, there were broad similarities that enabled educators to describe the common elements among them. These included a principal who accorded high priority to teaching and learning, who sought to develop a consensus among the staff on the importance of emphasizing learning, and who sought to facilitate the efforts of teachers to promote learning (Brookover, Bendy, Flood, Schweitzer, & Wisenbaker, 1979; Edmonds, 1979).[2]

There are two other areas concerning school characteristics that influence learning that merit brief discussion. These are the effects of racial segregation and ability grouping on academic achievement. In the case of the former, the results can be best described as mixed and difficult to synthesize. One of the reasons given in opposition to school segregation was that it violated the equal protection clause in the U.S. Constitution and that racial segregation of schools damaged the self-concept of African-American children and lowered their academic achievement. Indeed, there is considerable evidence that African-American youngsters who attend a school where the majority of pupils are middle-class Whites, score higher on achievement tests, are more likely to attend a White university, and are also more likely to find employment in a predominantly White organization as compared to other African-American pupils who enroll in a racially segregated public school (e.g., McPartland & Braddock, 1981).

On the other hand, there is a possibility that some African-American young people may benefit in some ways from attending a racially segregated school. Perhaps the most notable study in this regard is the study conducted in Baltimore. Rosenberg and Simmons (1972) reported that the interviews conducted with 2,625 pupils ranging from 3rd to 12th grades show that the African-American pupils who attend racially integrated schools scored lower on a self-esteem scale than those who attend a predominantly Black school. The youngsters whose self-esteem showed damage were also likely to report being teased about their race by White pupils. The authors concluded that racial segregation could shield some Black pupils from the sting of racism.

The potential effects of ability grouping and tracking on learning have received considerable attention from researchers. The evidence that ability grouping and tracking can create quite different learning climates and opportunities, not only in a school but also in a classroom by reducing the amount of cognitive material presented to "lower ability" tracks and classes, is fairly convincing (Lee & Bryk, 1988; Oakes, 1985).

---

[2] A more recent analysis using the High School and Beyond data found that organizational differences among schools have a substantial impact on pupils' academic achievement. The average level of pupil achievement is higher in schools that require all pupils to take academically focused courses and offer them fewer options to take a wide variety of courses (Lee & Bryk, 1989).

The key person in this area seems to be the teacher because it is the teacher who controls, to a great extent, the pace of instruction and the amount of material to be covered.

The possibility that some teachers may set in motion a process of self-fulfilling prophecy that dooms most children from low SES families to academic failure caused considerable concern among those interested in the issue of equality of opportunity. Recent work in this area found the effect of teacher bias visible only in classes where a teacher of high-status origin taught lower class children (Alexander, Entwisle, & Thompson, 1987), suggesting that teacher-initiated self-fulfilling prophecy might be more limited than originally proposed. However, the process of assigning youngsters to learning disabled classes and suspending pupils from school for disciplinary reasons do seem to be affected by the race of the young person. African-American pupils seem to be disproportionately represented in mentally retarded classes (Mercer, 1972) and among those suspended or expelled from school (Harris & Bennett, 1982). On the other hand, Asian-American pupils seem to be overrepresented in the college preparatory and gifted classes (Madigan & Takei, in preparation; Tsang & Wing, 1985). This may be partly due to the tendency among teachers to stereotype Asian-American pupils as "model" students (Wong, 1980).

Recent work by Farkas, Grobe, Sheehan, and Shuan (1990) found that teachers assign grades to students in part on factors such as work habits rather than mastery of cognitive material. Among this sample of youngsters in Dallas, Asian-American students were judged by teachers to have more favorable work habits than the others. Thus, within the school context, variations in teacher expectations, biases in assigning students to ability groups, and even biases in grading may all have differential effects for youngsters of different identities.

To summarize this section, it should be noted that researchers should exercise greater care when making a distinction between racially or ethnically related factors from social class factors in conducting future studies in this area. This is important because as some have argued (e.g., Spencer & Dornbusch, 1990), race or ethnicity and SES can interact to magnify group differences so that researchers have attributed racial or ethnic cause to phenomena that may be more a consequence of difference in social class. For example, it is possible that the tendency among many Mexican-American males to view dropping out of school to work full time as a symbol of manhood (Horowitz, 1983) might reflect the working-class culture of the United States not a Mexican-American norm.

Another illustration of the importance of making the distinction is a longitudinal study of a random sample of public school children in

Baltimore that revealed that the standardized test scores in mathematics were almost identical for African-American and White first graders. Two years later, African-American children scored considerably lower on the same test than White children. Further analysis showed that both groups' learning rates were similar while schools were in session, but children from low SES families lost more ground than higher SES children. The researchers found that "summer gains or losses were not very different by race when poverty status was controlled" (Entwisle & Alexander, 1992). Because summer vacations seem to be a strong factor in producing retrogression in learning among low SES children regardless of race, summer school programs for them seem worthy of support.

CONCLUSION

Many people in this society tend to believe that the educational institution offers everyone an equal opportunity to learn. A concomitant belief is that those who excel in learning are the young who not only have more ability but are more motivated to do well academically than others. However, the reasons for some to exhibit higher academic achievement are not that clear and simple. What we have attempted to show in this chapter is that youngsters are embedded in various cultural systems, some of which help youth to do well academically, whereas others may hinder or discourage academic achievement. What is important to remember is that cultural systems related to race or ethnicity often do not offer the adolescent an opportunity to choose the system in which to participate.

It is true that opportunities to choose what cultural system one wishes to participate in increase as the young get older. Therefore, a person who only heard country and western music as a child can become an enthusiastic aficionado of opera as a college student. Conversely, someone raised on symphony music can become an avid listener of hard rock music later in life. However, these are exceptions rather than the rule. Most people find the cultural systems they learned as children comfortable not only because they are familiar, but also because their "kith and kin" continue to interact with each other using those systems.[3]

---

[3]Those who find themselves participating in different cultural systems than the one in which they were raised are compelled to become bicultural or, perhaps, even multicultural in their personal and occupational lives (see Allison & Takei, chapter 4, this volume). It is probable that there will be considerable variation among people in their ability to participate with facility in multiple cultural systems. Because not everyone is a virtuoso in this respect, many people tend to confine themselves to the current cultural system(s) in which they are nested and not seek actively to become integrated into different cultural systems which would require learning new cultural forms and symbols.

It should be acknowledged that we have not discussed all the factors associated with academic achievement. Instead we have chosen to highlight a few that are of interest to us. Moreover, our discussion for the most part has been limited to direct effects rather than to the interaction of different factors. More research on the interaction of various factors is an obvious need. Also research efforts aimed at identifying factors associated with differences in academic achievement within ethnic and racial groups must continue to consider how both distal and proximate social forces affect achievement. Most importantly, future research should be directed toward identifying which factors are most powerful within each group. Adopting educational practices that are effective for one ethnic or racial group might not work for another because other more important social and cultural forces are being overlooked.

REFERENCES

Alexander, K. L., Entwisle, D. R., & Thompson, M. (1987). School performance status relations, and the structure of sentiment: Bringing the teacher back in. *American Sociological Review, 52,* 655–682.

Bernstein, B. (1961). Social class and linguistic development. In A. H. Halsey, J. Floud, & C. A. Anderson (Eds.), *Education, economy, and society* (pp. 288–314). New York: The Free Press.

Bourdieu, P. (1986). The forms of capital. In J. G. Richardson (Ed.), *Handbook of theory and research for the sociology of education* (pp. 241–258). New York: Greenwood Press.

Brookover, W. C., Bendy, C., Flood, P., Schweitzer, J., & Wisenbaker, J. (1979). *School social systems and student achievement: Schools can make a difference.* New York: Praeger.

Brown, B., Steinberg, L., Mounts, N., & Philipp, M. (1990, March). *The comparative influence of peers and parents on high school achievement: Ethnic differences.* Paper presented as part of a symposium entitled Ethnic Variations in Adolescent Experience at the biannual meetings of the Society for Research on Adolescence, Atlanta, GA.

Clark, M. E., & Takei, Y. (1988, December). *High school students and their grades: The relative effects of family background, competence, docility, and school climate.* Paper presented at the 1988 meeting of the Pennsylvania Sociological Society, State College, PA.

Coleman, J. S. (1959, Fall). Academic achievement and the structure of competition. *Harvard Educational Review,* pp. 339–351.

Coleman, J. S. (1966). *Equality of educational opportunity.* Washington, DC: U.S. Government Printing Office (Office of Education).

Coleman, J. S. (1988). Social capital in the creation of human capital. *American Journal of Sociology, 94,* S95–S120.

Davis, K. (1984). Wives and work: The sex role revolution and its consequences. *Population and Development Review, 10,* 397–417.

Edmonds, R. (1979). Effective schools for the urban poor. *Educational Leadership, 37,* 15–27.

Entwisle, D. R., & Alexander, K. L. (1992). Summer setback: Race, poverty, school composition, and mathematics achievement in the first two years of school. *American Sociological Review, 57,* 72–84.

Family Service America. (1987). *The state of families 2: Work and family.* Milwaukee, WI: Author.

Farkas, G., Grobe, R., & Sheehan, D., Shuan, Y. (1990). Cultural resources and school success: Gender, ethnicity, and poverty groups within an urban school district. *American Sociological Review. 55,* 127–142.

Fordham, S., & Ogbu, J. U. (1986). Black students' school success: Coping with the burden of "acting White." *The Urban Review, 18,* 176–206.

Giroux, H. (1983). *Theory and resistance: A pedagogy for the opposition.* South Hadley, MA: Bergin & Garvey.

Goldstein, B. (1967). *Low income youth in urban areas: A critical review of the literature.* New York: Holt, Rinehart & Winston.

Harris, J. J., III, & Bennett, C. (1982). *Student discipline: Legal empirical and education perspectives.* Bloomington, IN: Indiana University.

Horowitz, R. (1983). *Honor and the American dream.* New Brunswick, NJ: Rutgers University Press.

Lee, V., & Bryk, A. S. (1988). Curriculum tracking as mediating the social distribution of high school achievement. *Sociology of Education, 61,* 78–94.

Lee, V. E., & Bryk, A. S. (1989). A multilevel model of the social distribution of high school achievement. *Sociology of Education, 62,* 172–192.

Lieberson, S. (1980). *A piece of the pie: Black and White immigrants since 1880.* Berkeley: University of California Press.

Madigan, T., & Takei, Y. (in preparation). *The probability of college enrollment among Asian Americans and their classmates.*

McDermott, R. P. (1974). Achieving school failure: An anthropological approach to illiteracy and social stratification. In G. D. Spindler (Ed.), *Education and cultural process* (pp. 82–118). New York: Holt, Rinehart & Winston.

McLaren, P. (1989). *Life in schools.* New York: Longman.

McPartland, J. M., & Braddock, J. H., II. (1981). Going to college and getting a good job: The impact of desegregation. In R. Wilson (Ed.), *Race and equity in higher education* (pp. 141–154). Washington, DC: American Council on Education.

Mercer, J. R. (1972). *Labeling the mentally retarded.* Berkeley: University of California Press.

Mickelson, R. A. (1990). The attitude-achievement paradox among black adolescents. *Sociology of Education, 63,* 44–61.

Oakes, J. (1985). *Keeping track: How schools structure inequality.* New Haven, CT: Yale University Press.

Ogbu, J. U. (1978). *Minority education and caste.* New York: Academic Press.

Perlmann, J. (1987). A piece of the educational pie: Reflections and new evidence on Black and immigrant schooling since 1980. *Sociology of Education, 60,* 54–61.

Peshkin, A. (1978). *Growing up American: Schooling and the survival of community.* Chicago, IL: University of Chicago Press.

Rogoff, N. (1961). Local social structure and educational selection. In A. H. Halsey, J. Floud, & C. A. Anderson (Eds.), *Education, economy, and society* (pp. 241–251). Glencoe, IL: The Free Press.

Ritter, P., & Dornbusch, S. (1989, March). *Ethnic variation in the family influences on academic achievement.* Paper presented at the American Educational Research Association meeting, San Francisco, CA.

Rosenberg, M., & Simmons, R. G. (1972). *Black and White self-esteem: The urban school child.* Washington, DC: American Sociological Association.

Rumberger, R. W., Ghatak, R., Poulos, G., & Ritter, P. L. (1990). Family influences on dropout behavior in one California high school. *Sociology of Education, 63,* 283–299.

Rutter, M., Maughan, B., Mortimore, P., Ousten, J., & Smith, A. (1979). *Fifteen thousand hours: Secondary schools and their effects on children.* Cambridge, MA: Harvard University Press.

Seeley, J. R., Sim, R. A., & Loosley, E. W. (1956). *Crestwood Heights: A study of the culture of suburban life.* New York: Basic Books.

Spencer, M. B., & Dornbusch, S. M. (1990). Challenges in Studying Minority Youth. In S. S. Feldman & G. R. Elliott (Eds.), *At the threshold: The developing adolescent* (pp. 123–146). Cambridge, MA: Harvard University Press.

Steinberg, L., & Brown, B. (1989, March). *Beyond the classroom: Family and peer influences on high school achievement.* Paper presented to the Families as Educators special interest group at the annual meetings of the American Educational Research Association, San Francisco, CA.

Sue, S., & Okazaki, S. (1990). Asian American educational achievements. *American Psychologist, 45,* 913–920.

Tsang, S., & Wing, L. C. (1985). *Beyond Angel Island: The education of Asian Americans, 90* (Winter, ERIC/CUE Urban Diversity Series). Oakland, CA: ARC Associates.

Valentine, C. A. (1971). Deficit, difference, and bicultural models of Afro-American behavior. *Harvard Educational Review, 41,* 137–157.

Wax, M. L., Wax, R. H., & Dumont, R. V., Jr. (1989). *Formal education on an American Indian community: Peer society and the failure of minority education.* Prospects Heights, IL: Waveland Press.

West, W. G. (1979). Adolescent autonomy, education and pupil deviance. In L. Barton & R. Meighan (Eds.), *Schools, pupils and deviance* (pp. 133–152). Nafferton, England: Nafferton Books.

Wolcott, H. (1987). The teacher as an enemy. In G. D. Spindler (Ed.), *Education and cultural process* (2nd ed., pp. 136–150). Prospect Heights, IL: Waveland Press.

Wong, M. (1980). Model students?: Teachers' perceptions and expectations of their Asian and White students. *Sociology of Education, 53,* 236–246.

11 Curricular Designs That Resonate With Adolescents' Ways of Knowing

Jamie Myers
The Pennsylvania State University

Any attempt to design curricular experiences that resonate with adolescents' ways of knowing must first consider the research that suggests that current school experiences involve a form of knowing that results in limited understandings of important subject matter. This critical act of recognition of the dominant forms of knowledge and knowing in traditional school experiences is essential to any reinvention of those ways of knowing (Freire & Macedo, 1987). Therefore, this chapter begins by describing research that suggests that most subject matter is treated as a collection of facts, concepts, and generalizations that students mainly reproduce for grades. Given this base, research is presented that conceptualizes a gap between these traditional ways of learning subject matter and the basic needs and ways of learning natural to adolescents. The chapter concludes by providing a proposed curricular design in which knowledge is redefined and the school activities, in which students construct knowledge, are restructured. The form of knowing represented in this proposal simultaneously satisfies the basic needs of adolescents, and engages the students in understanding the subject matter important to school learning. This proposal is reminiscent of Dewey (1938) and the progressive educators, who characterized traditional education in much the same way as current researchers describe today's school practice. Dewey also theorized an insurmountable gap between the traditional methods of learning and behaving in school and children's capacities for experience. He also dealt with many of the same current criticisms that new curricular designs are unmanageable in terms of student activity, and chaotic in terms of the knowledge students must learn.

HOW KNOWLEDGE AND CONTROL ARE CONSTITUTED IN SCHOOL CONTEXTS

The education literature abounds with critiques that elaborate the problems adolescents experience with school curricula. The most recurring image is the traditional lecture situation in which students busily take notes, answer questions, and memorize facts for the upcoming test. This image of the teacher transmitting knowledge to students is extensively supported by both broad national studies of school experience and achievement (Goodlad, 1984; Langer, 1984), and by intensive field-based ethnographic studies (Hamilton-Wieler, 1989; McNeil, 1986; Myers, 1989). Goodlad and his associates (1984) documented school instructional experiences in 129 elementary, 362 junior high, and 525 senior high classrooms across the United States, and painted a rather dismal view of school experiences relatively unchanged over the past several decades. "The picture is of students passively listening, reading textbooks, completing assignments, and rarely initiating anything—at least in the academic subjects" (Goodlad, 1983, p. 10). This description bears an amazing resemblance to Dewey's summation in which "the subject matter of education consists of bodies of information and of skills that have been worked out in the past; therefore, the chief business of the school is to transmit them to the new generation" (Dewey, 1938, p. 17).

Goodlad (1983) highlighted two major deficiencies existing in all school curricula designed for adolescents:

> The first is a failure to differentiate and see the relationships between facts and the more important concepts facts help us to understand. The second, closely related to the first, is a general failure to view subjects and subject matter as merely turf on which to experience the struggles and satisfactions of personal development. (p. 15)

These curricular deficiencies focus on (a) the nature of knowledge, (b) how knowledge is gained and distributed in school, and (c) the relationship of oneself to others and to knowledge. Together, these three aspects of school knowledge characterize how school experiences constitute and define acceptable ways of knowing in school that often differ dramatically with the alternative ways of knowing that adolescents use most to make sense of life experience.

Linda McNeil's (1988) ethnographic study of four schools confirms the definition of knowledge represented by Goodlad; however, it also elaborates in greater depth how the organizational dynamics of schools help shape the experiences that define the patterns of knowing that adolescents must use in school work to be seen as successful by peers and adults.

> Teachers control knowledge in the classroom in order to control students. When teachers perceive that administrators care most strongly that the institution's minimum standards are met, teachers begin to structure their courses in ways that will elicit minimal compliance from their students. They tend to maintain tight control over course content. Rather than allow students to be actively involved in gathering and interpreting information, they lecture and reduce their presentations to lists of terms and unelaborated facts. (McNeil, 1988, p. 334)

When teachers control knowledge and the manner in which it is distributed, in an attempt to control students who are often not aware of any organizational reason why teachers lecture all the time, adolescents define school knowledge as fragmented and disconnected lists of memorizable facts separate from their own experiences. Adolescents become apathetic. And the irony of teacher control is that when adolescents act less engaged, teachers often increase the control—more assignments, stiffer grading requirements—in an attempt to increase the level of engaged learning. These actions, however, can further separate the adolescents from the subject matter as they drill even harder to score high, or choose to resist learning activities, or just do enough to get by while focusing on the real world of friends and activities that is so important in the school context.

The following episode, along with the others that follow, is part of an ethnographic study that examined the social contexts of learning for adolescents in middle school (Myers, 1989). In this rather traditional middle-school experience, knowledge is clearly treated as an objective body of facts and concepts that exist as universal truths, discovered by great scientists and intellectuals, recorded in textbooks, and communicated, not interpreted, in single right answer ways with the teacher as a transmitting representative of authorized knowledge.

In science class:

> Bill: Worksheets are easy. The answers to the questions are in the same order as in the book, so I just read along and answer them.
> Researcher: That's pretty good?
> Bill: Yea. It's also good because the answers on the worksheets are the same as the ones on the tests, so I usually remember stuff during the test if I done the worksheet. Notes help a lot too.

> Researcher: How about these questions at the end of the chapter that you're doing right now?
> Bill: These definitions are bold faced in the chapter, so you just look back.
> Researcher: What are you supposed to do with these sentences? (pointing to the next section in the chapter review)
> Bill: In these, a word might be used wrong, so you have to replace it with the word that makes the sentence correct.
> Jerry: I thought number 2 was wrong because I knew that magnetic force had to do with electric charges and that's not what the sentence said.
> Researcher: How'd you know that?
> Jerry: From reading it in the chapter and from the worksheet. But, I usually look back to double check.
> Bill: I don't look back. Except with something that can be easily mixed up, like gravitational force and gravitational energy.
> Matt: I was doing them all wrong. I was looking up the word and changing the sentence.
> Researcher: Oh.
> Matt: It's easier to look up the words and change the sentence, than to look up the definitions and put in the right word. I still haven't found the information for the first sentence yet, but I did know it was wrong from looking up the word. (Myers, 1989)

Bill, Jerry, and Matt flip through the pages of the textbook to answer the questions on the chapter review. They approach the task differently because they have different capacities to remember or find information in the textbook chapter, but all three demonstrate how knowledge is defined as facts from the text to be memorized and repeated on worksheets, assignments, and tests. Knowledge is not dealt with in any way that would lead adolescents to view it as a social construction of people, including themselves, sharing and negotiating their meanings for world experiences (Berger & Luckman, 1967).

In English class:

> Teacher: You have the trees on the inside of the ditch. [A group of students are holding up their map on the story *Lennigen versus the Ants.*] Why do the trees have to be on the outside? How did the ants get across the ditch?
> Jay: The man on the wheel at the dam was attacked by the ants so the water stopped filling the ditch.
> Teacher: Good. The ants used the leaves to get across the ditch. So the trees have to be on the outside of the ditch where they can get to them. (Myers, 1989)

The teacher asks two questions and Jay answers the second, but the teacher ignores his answer and answers the self-posed question so the class gets the important point. In this traditional recitation class of question–answer–confirmation (Dillon, 1984; Mehan, 1979), no one debated the teacher's incomplete explanation of how the ants got across the ditch. The teacher did not ask for different ideas to negotiate an interpretation. The students memorized the teacher's answer for the quiz the next day. Jay himself explained that he did not say anything else because he just thought in his own mind that both were part of the answer; he said, "I just agreed with the teacher after that."

In social studies class:

[The students are asked to read a chapter about William Jennings Bryan in a supplementary text and given a page of questions to fill out.]
Brent: Do these go in order, like number one, first page, number two, next page, and so on?
[The teacher nods. Students can be seen reading, then stopping to answer a question, then continuing to read.]
Researcher: How are you answering these questions?
Linda: Well, if I know the answer, then I just write it in my own words. If I have to look it up in the book, then I just write down what the book says. Like right now, I'm looking for the word Bryan and reading what it says to find out why he resigned.
Researcher: Is that how you answer all these questions?
Linda: Yes. But, like this question, was it right or wrong, is opinion and that isn't in the book. (Myers, 1989)

Opinion questions are the closest experience for students in the social construction of the knowledge in school; however, this clear distinction between fact and opinion prevents adolescents from conceptualizing how facts as well as personal beliefs are embedded in socially shared views of the world.

At one time in the world's knowledge, the most sophisticated facts detailed the earth standing still as the center of the universe. Fleck (1979) illustrated how scientific facts are social developments embedded in the life situations of the people living at that time. In different ways, Kuhn (1970) and Goodman (1984) illustrated how facts are always determined by theories of reality, not correspondence to any thing that can be experienced as the "real world." Teachers, as all people, adopt a stance toward facts and opinions that reveals the degree to which they believe knowledge is certain, nonhyphothetical, and nonnegotiable (Feldman & Wertsch, 1976); often with students, teachers adopt a stance in which knowledge is far less certain than philosophers of science believe it must be. As a result, knowledge becomes objectified in an external world of reality, and opinion is used to label the everyday sense of knowing that is more accurately the base of all knowledge.

Defining the nature of knowledge as objective truth beyond the realm of everyday experience makes its distribution among students simply achieved by the correct replication of meanings in textbooks, lectures, and predetermined experiments. Subject matter knowledge is divided up into chunks of facts and concepts that can be learned one at a time, then tested. This sets up an experience where students focus on isolated memorization and seldom connect fragmented concepts across time (in one class that meets every day or between different subject matter classes) to construct a broader understanding of the discipline's theory about the world.

In science class:

> [After students complete a quiz on the chalkboard they take out a worksheet done as homework.]
> Teacher: Any questions over the worksheet?
> Jay: How do you identify a base?
> Teacher: What's a base, Sarah?
> Sarah: Bitter?
> Teacher: Uh, uh, go on.
> Sarah: Tastes slippery.
> Teacher: Now what if I give you formulas?
> Sarah: Litmus paper.
> Teacher: No, you can't use litmus paper in a formula.
> Amy: OH.
> George: Didn't have any OH's in there [the quiz].
> Teacher: Because we weren't doing that today.
> Mark: What's the answer to question number 8?
> Teacher: There should be stuff in your reading that is manufactured using sulfuric acid. I'll refer you to the page on that. I'm not going to answer that one for you.
> (Mark opens the book and begins to look for the answer.) (Myers, 1989]

Because the subject matter on acids and bases is fragmented for memorization and testing, Jay and Sarah have a difficult time connecting ideas within the subject matter. George even asks why the quiz didn't have any chemicals with the basic OH molecule. A more serious separation of knowledge from personal experience in the world results when Mark asks for examples of manufactured products involving sulfuric acid and the teacher says it is in the textbook. Again, the textbook of compiled facts becomes the authorized source of knowing, rather than socially shared experience.

This form of knowledge distribution is supported by the structure of time where the day is divided into subject matter periods of such a short length of time that the only efficient way to cover all the concepts and facts jammed into the content of the curriculum is to lecture and assign textbook reading and workbook activities as homework. And this organization of social life is very different from any other social interaction in everyday life, and explains the gap in experience adolescents perceive between school and personal knowing:

> Call up in imagination the ordinary schoolroom, its time-schedules, schemes of classification, of examination and promotion, of rules of order, and I think you will grasp what is meant by "pattern of organization." If then you contrast this scene with what goes on in the family, for example, you will appreciate what is meant by the school being a kind of institution sharply marked off from any other form of social organization. (Dewey, 1938, p. 18)

Given this nature of knowledge and form of distribution in school, memorizing the facts becomes an end in itself. Classroom learning is rarely experienced as an inquiry into how disciplinary perspectives and accumulated subject matter knowledge resonates with the negotiated sense adolescents make of their current life experiences with others. Instead, learning is largely an individualized experience of reproducing an inert body of facts, not for the purpose of self-development or community involvement and growth, but for the purpose of being graded, compared, and stratified. And students try to protect their image among peers by not getting caught not knowing the facts.

In science class:

Teacher: What is meant by concentration?
Janet: Conducts.
Teacher: What?
Janet: Conducts. I don't know, I'm just guessing. (Myers, 1989)

Janet explained this context as one in which she was just trying to act smart for the teacher, but she did not want to risk being wrong in front of the students, so she said she was just guessing. Later in that same science class, while the teacher is discussing the change of color in pH paper according to the concentration, Janet blurts out, "Is that what they use in chlorine?" The teacher ignored her because she spoke without being recognized, so no further discussion of her question ensued. Janet explained that she had helped a friend test the chlorine level in her swimming pool and wondered if that was connected.

Janet's episode demonstrates the fragmentation of knowledge because the teacher made no attempt to connect Janet's knowledge of the conductivity of solutions based on their concentration to the pH value based on concentration. But, perhaps the most striking aspect of the definition of knowledge being constituted for Janet in these classroom experiences is the disconnection of classroom knowledge from the continuity of everyday personal experience. The object of school itself, knowledge, is wrenched from the grasp of the knower, and as a set of abstractions about life experiences beyond the culture of knowing adolescents, becomes the product used to define personal worth, instead of being the tool used to define the world from a position of personal worth.

McNeil (1988) argued that the purpose of school to award diplomas contradicts the purpose of school as a place for learning. Almost every aspect of school life is organized around fulfilling the requirements for a diploma; therefore, just passing, even barely, those requirements becomes the only aim for a majority of students. Large groups of students follow schedules from room to room and ask just what must be done to pass the requirement. These moments in classrooms are meant to be experiences in learning, but they are reduced in meaning to events where students just display the correct procedures to meet requirements (Puro & Bloome, 1987). The life of school is one of giving tests and keeping records on students. Organizational structures in school that should be designed to promote learning, in fact, work against it; this is the central contradiction.

The organizational structure of school constitutes an experience of knowledge as meanings that exist outside oneself. The social context of the classroom devalues the "self," in relationship to others (the experts of the culture), as a source of knowing about science, social studies, and even the meanings for literature. This school context fosters the belief that students fail because of an internal personal inability to learn and transfer ideas from the classroom to life. Yet, the context for instruction reinforces this fragmentation of knowledge as objective fact beyond personal experience by creating a social context in which the hours and days are disconnected moments of truth, full of teacher directions and specific knowledge outcomes everyone must learn and demonstrate on a test or in a discussion.

McNeil (1988) pointed out that students do not understand why teachers lecture all of the time, so they readily conclude that the subject matter is boring, uninformative, and inconsequential compared to the lessons they learn in everyday life outside of school. Although it is probably good that adolescents define knowledge outside of school as more coherent, relevant, and valuable, the definitions they construct for in-school knowledge contribute to the problem just as much as, if not more than, the structures of subject matter and classroom organization used in traditional classrooms.

In science class:

> Mindy: What is number 7? [in reference to quiz question]
> Teacher: [gives the name for the chemical symbols]
> Mindy: Is it acid or base?
> Teacher: As on the quiz, you shouldn't have answered neither.
> Don: But the directions were acid or base.
> Teacher: Then you didn't learn your definitions too well. (Myers, 1989)

As in this quiz, students expect that by following the directions, they will get the answers right and reach the academic achievement being promoted by the whole system of assessment. They do not principally view classroom experiences as learning ones, but as evaluating ones. In this episode the teacher included some problems on the quiz that would not be answered acid or base, but only directed the students to decide if each problem was acid or base. Students did not assume that a problem might be neither. There is nothing wrong with creating situations where students have to think meaningfully about the subject matter, but what is illustrated here is that students do just the opposite; they adhere to the directions and pay little attention to any meaningfulness.

Given that the most common context for social interaction and the social construction of knowledge in the traditional classroom is one of following directions, receiving, and reproducing the authorized meanings beyond your own experientially shared knowing, test situations where students need to think critically are often viewed as a trick questions, not situations to explore the power of sharing ideas to solve problems. Focusing all classroom activity on grades creates a context where students actually become less engaged in meaning as they concentrate on getting right answers to avoid the appearance of not knowing—hardly a good stance for students to take toward knowledge and learning. In most cases, this only pushes the desired cultural knowledge more and more into the authority of teacher and text, and the student only becomes more involved in figuring out what to deliver. The relationship between school knowledge and the adolescent's sense of personal knowing becomes even more disconnected, giving rise to a youth culture in contrast, and often in defiance to the predominating adult culture.

CONTEXTS FOR ADOLESCENTS' WAYS OF KNOWING

> The need for power is the core—the absolute core—of almost all school problems. Even the good students don't feel all that important in school, and the students who receive poor grades certainly can't feel important from the standpoint of academic performance. . . . Literally no one in the world who isn't struggling for bare survival will do intellectual work, unless he or she has a sense of personal importance. (Glasser, 1987, p. 658)

Glasser explained that as students move from the elementary school to the junior high and middle school they begin to experience a school context in which their own concerns and interests become unimportant; they lose a sense of power over the activities in which they create meanings about their experiences in the world. For curricular designs to succeed with adolescents, Glasser suggested that the learning experiences must satisfy the basic needs of power, freedom, love, and fun (Glasser, 1986). The school forms of knowing described earlier at times seem to be purposely designed to suppress the development of these adolescent needs rather than support them. New contexts for learning must promote ways of knowing that are rooted in adolescents' sense of power, freedom, love, and fun.

Adolescents' need for love is satisfied by a sense of belonging, being a member of a club or team. F. Smith (1987) described the powerful and natural learning experiences all people have as members of various clubs. As club members, learning is embedded in valued enterprises in which knowledge is constructed by participation. In schools, the increased use of small group learning activities represents an attempt to incorporate this foundational need for social interaction into subject matter learning; by far, the most popular small group curricular organizational strategy goes by the label of cooperative learning (R. Smith, 1987). This belonging approach to active involvement in subject matter activities transforms the traditional classroom context from the individualized solitary experience of memorizing knowledge to an interactive social experience of constructing knowledge through sharing ideas to generate ways to do things, solve problems, or synthesize ideas. The social activity is purposeful in the experiential lives of the adolescents, and by being so, it fulfills the need for fun.

In several episodes from English class, Arch, Neil, Kevin, and Randy illustrate the ways of knowing based on belonging to clubs that help adolescents meet their needs for love, freedom, power, and fun.

Neil: What rhymes with lazy?
Arch: Hazy.

Neil: I thought of that, it doesn't make sense.
Arch: Here, I'll help you. [Arch moves over to Neil's computer at the next table; he softly reads the poem aloud.] Crazy!
Neil: Yea! [Arch returns to his seat. Neil looks toward me standing close by.] You should read some of his. They're really good. (Myers, 1989)

Neil later explained that Arch's poems are really good because they tell how people feel. They said that they didn't really care what teachers thought of the poems, but decided on their own if they thought they were good or not.

Randy: That's my best poem yet.
Neil: Which one, the wrestling.
Randy: Football.
Neil: That's what I just did!
Randy: [reads his poem aloud, and corrects his own use of the word "ran"]
Neil: Pretty neat! Awesome! I'm doing mine right now.
Randy: [moves over to read Neil's computer screen]. (Myers, 1989)

The coincidence of both boys writing about the same topic gives them a chance to compare what each other thinks about football. They agreed that "writing helps form friendships with those who share interests." Randy extends these friendships to include his father and his friends who play the sport with him. When he printed his poem out, he made a copy to take home to his Dad and one to turn in to the teacher. These students demonstrate their memberships in various clubs with peers, adults, and parents.

As these students socially interact they feel a sense of personal importance in their school activities. Together they explore meanings for experiences that they share in the world, and through this shared exploration they negotiate meanings about those experiences and about their own identity. This gives them a sense of power over their own understanding of themselves and the worlds in which they participate.

In another activity, Kevin and Neil were developing a sports quiz. They debated with each other on the best format for the quiz questions and worked for some time on the project. When it neared time to turn in the quiz for credit the teacher said that they would have to indicate how much each boy had done so grades could be assigned accordingly. The boys did not like this because they felt that it was an equally shared project even though one person might have thought of more questions than another. Neil explained that the "grades split up the group," and so daily work on the sports quiz was dropped. The traditional context of school knowing forced the boys into a comparative relationship in which power could not be equally shared; this disrupted adolescent learning.

In many social relationships in and out of school, adolescents establish contexts where knowledge is defined as the interpretation and negotiation of meaning about shared experiences (Myers, 1989). This way of knowing puts students in control of their culture and as Randy illustrated, adults are welcome members of this culture making process. This contrasts with the typical classroom context where knowledge is defined as the transmission of meaning controlled by authority; here culture is something adolescents must learn to acquire before they can be contributing members. The first definition of knowledge is more resonant with adolescents because it springs from their inherent needs for love, freedom, power, and fun.

This participatory form of knowing also results in a greater focus on the meaningfulness of academic subject matter, instead of just attempting to display the knowledge required for a momentary evaluation. Tracy illustrates this deep attention to meaning instead of just following directions when she constructs a dictionary about whales.

> Tracy: Can I use words like ocean and mountains?
> Researcher: [I remain silent, waiting to see what she thinks.]
> Tracy: She might think they're a little easy.
> Researcher: Why?
> Tracy: Because she [the teacher] said . . . I don't know, because most people know what a mountain is. So could I use stuff like that?
> Researcher: What do you think?
> Tracy: I'll use it because it is an important part of geography. (Myers, 1989)

The teacher repeated several times that students should not include words in their dictionary that they already knew, but Tracy is not willing to ignore the words she believes are important to express a full sense of her topic. Tracy privileges her own thinking and goes against the form authorized by the teacher. She has the power to make this decision because of a strong sense of identity from her membership in a club of inquirers interested in sea life. She also asserts her freedom by implying that the dictionary is not just for the teacher to grade, but for a larger community of readers who might be interested in her thinking about the topic. Tracy reinforces this attention to meaningfulness of ideas when she describes how she goes about reading: "I second guess the stuff I don't agree with. No matter what the topic is, I can pretty much pick out stuff that doesn't make sense and go to other sources." Tracy is deeply involved in negotiating the meaningfulness of the world. She does not read for authorized ideas; instead, she authorizes the ideas she reads in terms of her own knowing and experience embedded in clubs that meet outside school time.

CURRICULAR DESIGNS THAT RESONATE WITH ADOLESCENT KNOWING

Curricular experiences in school must engage students in negotiating the meaning of experiences in terms of their own sense of the world (Macklin, 1978) and their participation with others (Bruner, 1986; F. Smith, 1987). The social contexts created by these curricular experiences should define knowledge as having a source in the student community gathered together to reflect on their interpretations of personal, and socially shared, experiences. Classroom experiences should begin with adolescents' primary experiences in the world, then involve exploring how different interpretations and disciplinary perspectives would make sense of those experiences. This process of constructing meaning involves sharing and negotiating meaning to construct an interdisciplinary knowledge that best represents the collective sense (that may involve very divergent beliefs) about experience. In this sharing, exploring, and negotiating adolescents would find themselves in a connected, active, and personal relationship with each other; knowledge is not the product, but the glue that holds the culture together.

Bruner (1986) described this participatory form of knowing while explaining his own changes in thought over the years about the best structure for learning in school:

> Some years ago I wrote some very insistent articles about the importance of discovery learning—learning on one's own, or as Piaget put it later (and I think better), learning by inventing. What I am proposing here is an extension of that idea, or better, a completion. My model of the child in those days was very much in the tradition of the solo child mastering the world by representing it to himself in his own terms. In the intervening years I have come increasingly to recognize that most learning in most settings is a communal activity, a sharing of the culture. It is not just that the child must make his knowledge his own, but that he must make it his own in a community of those who share his sense of belonging to a culture. It is this that leads me to emphasize not only discovery and invention but the importance of negotiating and sharing—in a word, of joint culture creating as an object of schooling and as an appropriate step

en route to becoming a member of the adult society in which one lives out one's life. (Burner, 1986, p. 127)

To support contexts for such participatory knowing in school classrooms, proposed changes are required in the following three areas of curricular planning: evaluation, materials, and activities.

Evaluation. The evaluation of knowledge constructed by students should be an implicit result of public sharing. No grades should be given for the form or the specific content adequacy in the judgment of a single teacher. If grades must be given, give them for participating in learning events—not participation in an academic game of guessing the right answers, but participation in socially interactive situations where students share ideas from their own experience and the experiences of others. Grading is an unnecessary addition to the power of a community of students to bring out the best in students' thinking.

Materials. Begin with the texts that students already read and write instead of textbooks of factual lists. The disciplines of knowledge—biology, chemistry, history, literature, economics, psychology, and so on—are perspectives or ways of thinking about the worlds represented in writing. This means you could take any collection of student provided texts and think about them in terms of the perspective on the world represented by any discipline. For example, a *Thrasher* magazine has extensive possibilities for learning about the physics of skateboarding, skateboarding history, language, economics, health, culture, and so on all related to world experiences with skateboarding.

The basic principle of materials for school learning shifts from a textbook source of secondary abstractions to a collection of artifacts, primary sources, that can be used to construct knowledge by looking for patterns of ideas and forms for representing those ideas. Texts therefore become generative sources of ideas instead of vessels of fixed meanings students must memorize. The idea of texts must also be broadened to go beyond the printed linguistic texts which dominate school learning to include film, television, gestures, art, music, clothing, dance, sports and all ways in which humans symbolize their experience of the world.

Activities. Every classroom event must have a communicative function in a constructive context aimed at generating knowledge about student posed inquiry. The main activities are the production of artifacts that could take many forms: texts, plays, videos, art, discussion, dance, or music. Class activity is student-directed in predominately small group settings to produce the artifact in answer to an inquiry question of the group. The artifact becomes a part of the class record and can be used as a text for future activities.

In student-directed inquiry learning, students form a small group to learn more about a topic. They would use as many sources of primary data and secondary abstractions about the topic as they could find. They would communicate with each other what they learn about the topic and work together to construct some artifact that represents what the group as a whole has learned. When the different small groups in a particular subject matter class begin to share their learning, the teacher will help organize a discussion of similarities and differences between the ideas of the different groups; these patterns will build over time and repeating cycles of these small group learning clubs into the essential aspects that represent the perspective of the subject matter discipline. Sharing is a central activity because it allows students to get different perspectives on the subject matter, reflect on their own perspective in juxtaposition to others, generate new ideas, and construct the themes and interrelationships that create a genuine intellectual understanding of a subject matter.

In conclusion, the invention of new curricular designs has been desired since at least the progressive movement of the 1930s. Yet the description of the organization of knowing in the classroom has remained relatively the same. By examining recent research into the character of school experiences from the students' points of view, this chapter has recognized some of the contextual forces which maintain traditional forms of knowledge and learning, and put forth a theory on students' ways of knowing upon which curricular reinvention might be based. However, no one curricular design, old or new, can be a static model applied across time and classroom contexts. Each educator must continually strive to recognize how knowing is defined in the particular contexts in which students and teachers interact, then based on that recognition, continually invent the next experience so it establishes continuity in the particular learners' processes of naming and sharing the world.

REFERENCES

Berger, P., & Luckman, T. (1967). *The social construction of reality.* New York: Doubleday.
Bruner, J. (1986). *Actual minds, possible worlds.* Cambridge, MA: Harvard University Press.
Dewey, J. (1938). *Experience and education.* New York: MacMillan.
Dillon, D. (1984, November). Research on questioning and discussion. *Educational Leadership,* 50–56.

Feldman, C., & Wertsch, J. (1976). Context dependent properties of teachers' speech. *Youth and Society, 8,* 227–258.

Fleck, L. (1979). *Genesis and development of a scientific fact.* Chicago, IL: University of Chicago Press.

Freire, P., & Macedo, D. (1987). *Literacy: Reading the word and the world.* South Hadley, MA: Bergin & Garvey.

Glasser, W. (1986). *Control theory in the classroom.* New York: Harper & Row.

Glasser, W. (1987). The key to improving schools: An interview with William Glasser. *Phi Delta Kappan, 68,* 656–662.

Goodlad, J. I. (1983, April). What some schools and classrooms teach. *Educational Leadership,* 8–19.

Goodlad, J. I. (1984). *A place called school.* New York: McGraw-Hill.

Goodman, N. (1984). *Of mind and other matters.* Cambridge, MA: Harvard University Press.

Hamilton-Weiler, S. (1989, October). Awkward comprises and eloquent achievements. *English Education,* 152–169.

Kuhn, T. (1970). *The structure of scientific revolutions.* Chicago, IL: Chicago University Press.

Langer, J. (1984). Literacy instruction in American schools: Problems and perspectives. *American Journal of Education, 93,* 107–132.

Macklin, M. (1978, December). Content area reading is a process for finding personal meaning. *Journal of Reading,* 212–215.

McNeil, L. (1986). *Contradictions of control: School structure and school knowledge.* New York: Methuen/Routledge & Kegan Paul.

McNeil, L. (1988). Contradictions of control, Part I: Administrators and teachers. *Phi Delta Kappan, 69,* 333–339.

Mehan, H. (1979). "What time is it, Denise?" Some observations on the organization and consequences of asking known information questions in classroom discourse. *Theory Into Practice, 18*(4), 285–294.

Myers, J. (1989). *The social contexts of school and personal literacy.* Unpublished doctoral dissertation, Indiana University, Bloomington, IN.

Puro, R., & Bloome, D. (1987). Understanding classroom communication. *Theory Into Practice, 26,* 26–31.

Smith, F. (1987). *Joining the literacy club.* Portsmouth, NH: Heinemann.

Smith, R. (1987). A teacher's views on cooperative learning. *Phi Delta Kappan, 68,* 663–666.

12 Transferring Literacy Between the Classroom and Life: Metacognition, Personal Goals, and Interests

Lori A. Forlizzi
The Pennsylvania State University

Society is changing in ways that are making literacy more important for everyone (Nickerson, 1985). Technological change is largely responsible for the increasing need for literacy in all aspects of life. As the world around us changes constantly, and at an ever-increasing pace, we have to adapt by learning new things all the time. Literacy is an important tool for learning, and thus surviving, in such a society.

The term *literacy* has come to mean more than the ability to decipher and produce print. Currently accepted definitions encompass all cognitive activities that go on as individuals interact with written language (Resnick, 1990; Scribner, 1984). Thus, problem solving, reasoning, communicating, and other cognitive skills are literacy skills, if they are used as people interact with written language. And, print is used and produced in ways that increasingly require these complex cognitive skills (Carnevale, Gainer, & Meltzer, 1989; Carnevale & Schulz, 1988).

Many individuals are unable to meet the increasing literacy requirements of society. Educators and business leaders are, more than ever, reflecting on how we can ensure that individuals are prepared to meet the literacy requirements of our society. They are especially interested in adolescents in the age group about which this volume is written: young adolescents between the ages of 10 and 15 (Anderson, Hiebert, Scott, & Wilkinson, 1985; Cummings, 1989; Kearns & Doyle, 1989).

This chapter provides a perspective on how in-school and out-of school literacy activities can be compared, and eventually integrated, in order to facilitate the development of literacy in this age group. Studying adolescents' knowledge about and use of literacy skills in a variety of contexts can inform researchers and educators about how literacy skills are used in different contexts. It can also suggest ways to provide bridges among the various contexts in which adolescents use literacy. Basic research on metacognition (i.e., knowledge about and regulation of cognitive processes) provides the organization for this discussion.

This chapter first describes how literacy needs are changing in the numerous contexts that define individuals' multiple roles in society. It then documents the growing mismatch between the literacy requirements of society and the literacy abilities of its citizens. It discusses research that indicates that individuals of all ages, particularly adolescents, are better able to effectively apply literacy skills when the setting or task in which they are applying them is directly related to their goals and interests. Finally, it proposes how the concept of *metacognition,* a framework that has been used to study other complex cognitive processes, can be applied to investigate and improve adolescents' literacy skills. The basic idea is that studying how adolescents use literacy in different contexts, and encouraging adolescents to discuss and reflect on how they use literacy in different contexts, can ultimately help them use literacy in a variety of contexts.

THE INCREASING NEED FOR LITERACY

The arena in which the increasing need for literacy has received the most attention is that of the workplace. However, the workplace is just one of many contexts in which the adult functions; and, it is only one of the many contexts that require individuals to interact with written language. Multiple contexts define many roles for individuals, including family member, community member, citizen, and consumer, as well as worker (Hunter & Harman, 1979). Each of these roles requires increasing levels of literacy. Off the job, technological changes have spawned a variety of phenomena including automatic teller machines, more complex billing, the growth of catalogue shopping, and the circulation of detailed credit reports. Computer networks allow people, who might never have come in contact with each other otherwise, to communicate with each other via text in ways that they never would have before. Dealing with these phenomena requires not only an increasing reliance on literacy, but increasingly sophisticated uses of literacy.

In the workplace, technological changes are responsible as well for the increased need for literacy on the part of workers. According to Carnevale and other researchers (Carnevale et al., 1989; Carnevale & Schulz, 1988), technological change has eliminated some jobs that required minimal literacy skills while increasing the range of literacy skills needed to perform the jobs that remain.

In manufacturing occupations, for example, the work of skilled craftspeople, such as tool and die makers, assemblers, repairers, and materials handlers is being taken over by robots. Computers now do many of the tasks that workers in these positions used to do (Carnevale et al., 1989; Carnevale & Schulz, 1988). Advanced technology is also taking over other shop-floor jobs, including laborer, materials handler, operator/assembler, and maintenance worker (Carnevale et al., 1989; Carnevale & Schulz, 1988). A single technician may be responsible for the machinery that does a variety of jobs that once required the efforts of skilled craftspeople. The technician's job, however, requires a wider variety of literacy skills than did any one of the other jobs. Additionally, the technician is responsible for troubleshooting, maintaining machinery, and exercising quality control: All of which require interaction with print materials.

In service occupations, technological change has meant that there is greater product diversification (Carnevale et al., 1989; Carnevale & Schulz, 1988). For example, the banking industry now offers a wider variety of financial services to customers than ever before. Employees must be able to fit available services to the needs of the customer. This requires a greater reliance on print material, both to store the greater amount of information of which any one individual must be in command, and to process a wider variety of documents. In both manufacturing and service occupations, workers have broader roles, more responsibility, and more autonomy, and must rely increasingly on print to be able to do their jobs well (Carnevale et al., 1989).

THE MISMATCH BETWEEN LITERACY REQUIREMENTS AND LITERACY ABILITIES

Concern with adult literacy in our society has increased since the mid-1980s (Chisman, 1989, 1990; Johnston & Packer, 1987). And there is reason to be alarmed: A recent study of the abilities of young adults (between the ages of 21 and 25) to perform literacy activities they would find in work, school, or other social contexts revealed that about half of them had difficulties with the complex information-processing skills required by tasks at the upper end of the scale, such as scanning for information, interpreting information, identifying a theme, or generating prose related to an idea (Kirsch & Jungeblut, 1986; Venezky, Kaestle, & Sum, 1987). These young adults were labeled *mid-level literates* as defined by their performance on the range of tasks presented to them (Kirsch & Jungeblut, 1986; Venezky et al., 1987). Although this is the most recently completed and best survey of literacy performance of adults in the United States at this writing (other surveys are currently underway), it is important to note that this survey sampled only those young adults living in households throughout the United States. Military personnel living on post, street people, and institutionalized young adults were not surveyed (for further information on sampling procedures, see Kirsch & Jungeblut, 1986). Thus, this survey is thought to give a fairly conservative estimate of the literacy skills of young adults in this country.

The one arena in which it has been well-documented that many adults cannot meet literacy demands is that of the workplace. Workplaces are feeling pressure from the inability to find workers who have the literacy skills required to do jobs (Chisman & Campbell, 1990). For example, in a 1982 survey, Henry and Raymond (cited in Mikulecky, Ehlinger, & Meenan, 1987) found that some secretaries had problems reading at the level required by their jobs, whereas some managers and supervisors were unable to write paragraphs free of mechanical errors.

It appears that we are not preparing our citizens to meet the literacy requirements of society. And, as literacy requirements continue to increase, we can expect the mismatch between those requirements and the literacy abilities of our citizens to grow larger—unless we find ways to better prepare them for the high literacy demands of our society. Educators and business leaders are, more than ever, reflecting on how we can better prepare young adolescents to meet the literacy demands of our society.

LITERACY, LEARNING GOALS, AND PERSONAL GOALS

Many educators intuitively know that making literacy and problem-solving skills relevant to students' learning goals and personal goals will help them acquire the skills they need. This intuitive knowledge is supported both by basic research on literacy and mathematical problem solving and applied research on adult literacy instruction.

Basic Research Findings

Several descriptive studies have compared how people use literacy skills and mathematical problem-solving skills in real-life contexts versus school-type environments. These studies reveal that people's performance in the school-type environment is poorer than their performance in the real-life setting, although they are asked to perform similar types of activities.

For example, Carraher, Carraher, and Schliemann (1982, cited in Lave, 1988) observed how 9- to 15-year-old adolescents performed mathematical calculations while selling produce in a Brazilian market. Paper-and-pencil tests requiring performance of the same calculations were then developed and given to the same adolescents. Although the adolescents performed calculations correctly 99% of the time in the market setting, in the school test situation their performance—on problems identical to the ones they had performed in the market—averaged only 74%. In another study targeting adolescents, Herndon (1971) found that junior high students who were failing math classes could efficiently perform many of the same calculations they were asked to do in these classes in the context of hobbies or after school jobs. For example, one student had learned to quickly and accurately complete complicated arithmetic as a scorer for a bowling league.

Other studies have compared adults' use of literacy and problem-solving skills in real-life contexts, such as on-the-job in a dairy, or while grocery shopping, cooking, or dieting, versus school-type environments (Lave, 1988; Scribner, 1984) and have produced similar findings. One speculative interpretation of such findings is that adolescents (and adults) do not perceive the similarity of literacy skills used in school and out-of-school contexts, and thus fail to use the opportunity to transfer skills between the classroom and "real life." Another is that somehow contextual variables in the out-of-school contexts encourage more skillful application of literacy.

Adult Literacy Instruction

Adult literacy instruction is being influenced by research that shows that making literacy skills relevant to learning goals, personal goals, and interests helps adults acquire literacy skills. Adult literacy programs are taking steps to make sure that instruction addresses students' goals and interests.

In traditional literacy programs, adults are taught generic literacy subskills that they then supposedly are able to apply in multiple contexts (Fingeret, 1990). For example, finding the main idea of a paragraph is a skill that literacy practitioners often attempt to teach their students. Students practice the skill on expository passages similar to those found in a textbook. Workbooks exist that purport to develop the "career" reading skills of adults, yet include passages on badgers, quicksand, and witch hunts in colonial times. Learning is assessed with tests that ask them to read another expository paragraph and select the main idea from four choices. It is assumed that application of this subskill in other contexts will occur. The term *basic skills* is often used synonymously with the term *literacy skills* (Chisman, 1990) and may come from the idea that there are basics that can be learned, carried off, and applied in numerous contexts. Traditional literacy programs such as these predominate in the adult literacy scene today (Fingeret, 1990), although this is changing.

There has been a movement in the literacy field since the 1960s to teach literacy skills in the context of adults' goals, needs, and interests (Fingeret, 1990). Job training programs, especially those in the military, have been leaders of this movement (Sticht & Mikulecky, 1984). In these programs, literacy skills are developed as adults need them in their lives. For example, a student may wish to develop literacy skills he or she will need after getting a promotion at work. Learning materials consist of real materials one would find on the job, including memos, manuals, lists of ingredients, or tables. Learning activities consist of practicing job activities that require literacy, such as following directions, reading gauges, or filling out reports. In programs that truly operate from the philosophy that literacy skills are best taught within the context of the needs, interests, and goals of adults, literacy skills are developed as means to a goal, not as end goals themselves. The goal might be obtaining a better job, raising children, or becoming an involved citizen. The literacy skills are secondary to the goal. For example, students in many adult literacy programs are becoming involved in National Issues Forums. The goal of these discussions is to help participants become more involved in the political process. However, preparing for and being involved in the discussions (reading, thinking about the issue, and talking with others about it) develops the literacy skills of the adult literacy student participants. Thus, the idea that literacy skills are tools to be used to achieve personal goals is reinforced (Hurley, 1991).

There is evidence that practices that teach literacy skills in the context of goals, needs, and interests are more successful than traditional programs that attempt to teach generic literacy skills. Sticht (1988) discussed reviews of literature on teaching literacy skills within the context of job training versus generic literacy training. In programs where literacy instruction was integrated with job knowledge development, gains in job literacy were two to three times greater than gains in general literacy. Second, in the same programs, gains made in general literacy were as good as or better than gains made in programs that focused on developing general literacy skills. Third, programs that focused on developing general literacy skills did not make improvements in job-related literacy skills.

Implications of the Findings

This research seems to indicate that individuals of all ages are better able to effectively apply literacy skills when the setting or task in which they are applying them is directly relevant to their goals and interests. But why is this the case? What is different about adolescents' use of literacy skills in the classroom versus the bowling alley? And how can we encourage transfer of skills across these contexts?

We can begin to answer these questions by comparing adolescents' perceptions about and use of literacy skills in different tasks and in different settings. We may identify contextual variables that influence application of literacy. We may discover that adolescents' perceptions of themselves as users of literacy, or of how literacy can be used, differs across contexts. In order to do this, we can borrow a framework that has been used to study knowledge about and application of other cognitive skills. We can apply this framework to (a) explore how adolescents' use of and perceptions about literacy skills differ in various contexts, including school and out-of-school contexts, and (b) apply information about how literacy is viewed and used successfully by adolescents in some contexts to enhance their literacy learning in other contexts.

METACOGNITION: A FRAMEWORK FOR STUDYING COGNITIVE PROCESSES

Researchers have been interested in studying people's knowledge about their cognitive processes and how they regulate them for several years (Garner, 1987; Hare, 1981; Kletzien, 1991; Markman, 1977; Myers & Paris, 1978; Schommer & Surber, 1986). This line of research began with developmental psychologists such as Flavell, who studied the development of memory skills in young children (Flavell & Wellman, 1977). Flavell's research revealed that a 3-year-old child, who is asked to remember a list of items, will appear to listen as the experimenter reads the list, then promptly forget it. A 7-year-old child, however, will repeat the list to him or herself, thus intentionally using a memory strategy. Further investigations revealed that children between the ages of 3 and 7 could tell the researcher that repeating back the list was a way that would help them remember it. They could not, however, necessarily apply the strategy in the appropriate situations (Flavell & Wellman, 1977). The fact that the children had knowledge about a particular strategy did not necessarily mean that they could use that strategy to effectively carry out a cognitive procedure. Thus, Flavell made a distinction between knowledge about a particular strategy and successful application of the strategy. He used the term *metacognition* to refer to both the individual's knowledge about cognitive processes (metacognitive knowledge) and the regulation of those cognitive processes (Flavell, 1979; see also Baker & Brown, 1984).

Metacognitive knowledge consists of knowledge or perceptions about the numerous variables that influence situations where cognitive processing occurs. There are three general categories of variables: person, task, and strategy variables (Flavell, 1979). Each individual has knowledge regarding (a) variables related to him or herself and others as processors (person variables), (b) aspects of tasks that make them more or less difficult (task variables), and (c) knowledge of various strategies and situations in which the strategies are appropriate to use (strategy variables) (Flavell, 1979). Knowledge about self as a processor of information may include such things as, "I cannot read with loud noise in the background," "I remember something better if I find it interesting," or "I am better at writing than at doing math problems." Knowledge about tasks can include such things as, "short lists are easier to remember than long lists," "stories are easier to read than physics textbooks," or "solving a familiar problem is easier than solving an unfamiliar one." Knowledge about strategies includes such things as "rehearsing a list helps me remember it better," "summarizing something in my own words helps me remember it," or "taking notes during a lecture will help me remember what the speaker said" (Flavell, 1979; Garner, 1987). These categories are not neatly defined: For example, when I say, "rehearsing a list helps me remember it better," I indicate something about what I think of my ability to remember things, as well as what I know about rehearsal as a strategy (Flavell, 1979).

Many varied experiences and activities comprise the second component of metacognition: regulation of our cognitive processes (Baker & Brown, 1984; Flavell, 1979). Unlike metacognitive knowledge, which can be articulated outside of an actual cognitive activity, regulation of cognitive processes occurs "on-line" (i.e., as one is involved in a cognitive task). For example, confronted with the complex task of reading a rental agreement, a person may begin reading only to realize five sentences down that he or she is not comprehending. The reader decides to start over, goes back, and begins rereading. He or she has had the metacognitive experience of comprehension failure, and in response, has selected and applied a comprehension repair strategy—rereading. The reader evaluated his or her current cognitive state (misunderstanding) against a goal state (understanding). Sensing a mismatch, the reader attempted to correct the situation by applying a strategy. Evaluation of a cognitive state in relation to a goal, planning what to do next, applying corrective steps, and checking for success of those steps are all examples of regulatory processes (Baker & Brown, 1984).

In the illustration of the rental agreement reader, metacognitive knowledge about the strategy was also activated during the reading episode. In an interview with a researcher, the reader could describe rereading as a strategy he or she would use in response to comprehension failure, revealing metacognitive knowledge. However, regulation of cognitive processes can only be partially observed by an outsider, as a subject engages in some cognitive task (Forlizzi, 1988).

Researchers have developed methodologies with which to study metacognitive knowledge and on-line processing. Metacognitive knowledge is typically studied via interviews. For example, Myers and Paris (1978) asked children in Grades 2 and 6 questions about variables related to reading in order to tap into their metacognitive knowledge about reading. The researchers included questions about person ("What makes someone a really good reader?"), task ("Which is quicker, reading out loud or reading to yourself?"), and strategy ("If you had to read a story very quickly and could only read some of the words, which ones would you try to read?") variables. Gambrell and Heathington (1981) conducted a similar questionnaire study with proficient college student readers and adults enrolled in a program to enhance their reading skills, and Garner and Kraus (1981–1982) conducted such a study with good and poor seventh-grade readers.

Researchers have attempted to discern what happens on-line during cognitive activities, such as reading and writing, by having subjects think aloud as they engage in the task (Flower & Hayes, 1981; Olshavsky, 1976–1977). In research on reading, on-line processing has also been measured by presenting text on a computer, which records movement back and forth through the text, or time spent processing certain sections of text (Baker & Anderson, 1982). Some studies have combined the computer-monitored and read aloud/think aloud procedures (Forlizzi, 1988).

Reflective awareness of cognitive activity is another type of metacognitive knowledge not illustrated in the example of the rental agreement reader. After a task is completed, subjects have knowledge of cognitive processing that went on during that task. Researchers measure this reflective awareness by asking subjects to make a report of the cognitive processes in which they engaged immediately after subjects have completed the task. In reading research, subjects may be asked to report strategies they use to repair comprehension failure (Baker, 1979; Hare, 1981; Hare & Pulliam, 1980; Ngandu, 1977) or strategies they use when directed to specific goals, such as answering questions related to text (Alexander, Hare, & Garner, 1984; Smith, 1967), summarizing what they have read (Garner, 1982), or reading to prepare for a test (Alvermann & Ratekin, 1982). Like other types of metacognitive knowledge, reflective awareness occurs outside of, as well as on-line during, a cognitive activity.

In summary, the metacognition framework consists of two main components: knowledge about and regulation of cognitive processes. The methodologies used to study metacognition are interview, think aloud, and computer monitoring of cognitive activity. Researchers have studied individuals' knowledge about and regulation of many cognitive processes, including memory and reading. This framework and the methodologies used to study it can also be applied by researchers and educators to study and improve adolescents' use of literacy.

APPLYING THE METACOGNITION FRAMEWORK TO INVESTIGATE ADOLESCENTS' LITERACY SKILLS: RECOMMENDATIONS FOR RESEARCHERS

Researchers can compare adolescents' perceptions about literacy in contexts where they successfully apply literacy skills to their perceptions about literacy in contexts where they do not successfully apply literacy skills. For example, a young person who enjoys writing song lyrics may feel very confident of his or her composition abilities outside of school, but feel very unsure of him or herself in English composition class. The young person may understand that writing is a process that takes several attempts in the songwriting context, but not the English class context. He or she may be aware of effective strategies for drafting song lyrics but not English compositions.

Researchers can also compare adolescents' application of literacy skills in contexts where they are successful to those where they are not as successful. They can use a combination of think aloud and reflective awareness methodologies to investigate how variables within different situations might influence use of literacy skills. For example, does an adolescent confidently ask a peer to critique a poster he or she is developing for a fundraiser, yet not think to ask a friend to read and comment on a composition he or she is writing for English class?

Finally, researchers can investigate how adolescents' perceptions about literacy in different contexts might influence application of literacy skills in those contexts. For example, are adolescents who perceive themselves as poor users of school literacy less successful at applying literacy in school?

Research has shown that literacy skills are more efficiently applied in contexts that are relevant to individuals' goals and interests. Researchers can use the metacognition framework to analyze why this is so. They can take an in-depth look at various contexts that require the application of literacy skills. They can look for clues about factors that might influence the use of literacy in contexts where adolescents are successful and those in which they are not successful. They can assess adolescents' metacognitive knowledge about literacy related to different contexts. Eventually, educators can use information gathered from such research to structure learning environments that will maximize adolescents' use of literacy skills. Ideally, these learning environments would also help adolescents transfer literacy skills used in familiar contexts to less familiar contexts.

APPLYING THE METACOGNITION FRAMEWORK TO IMPROVE ADOLESCENTS' LITERACY SKILLS: RECOMMENDATIONS FOR TEACHERS

Good teachers intuitively know that literacy skills are best taught as tools for achieving students' own needs and interests and apply this knowledge in the classroom. Teachers should continue to incorporate students' goals and interests in the classroom and present literacy as a tool for achieving goals and pursuing interests. Teachers can apply the metacognition framework and the methodologies used to study it to more effectively teach adolescents to apply literacy skills.

For example, suppose a teacher in a vocational classroom wishes to show how literacy skills are used in the construction trades. The teacher works with students as they read a chart of pipe dimensions. While students use the chart, the teacher takes a few minutes to explicitly teach strategies for reading charts. The teacher models how he or she uses the chart as he or she works, thinking aloud as he or she demonstrates how to read the chart and how it fits in with other steps in the process of completing a particular job task. The teacher discusses the function of the chart with the students: Because of the chart, they do not have to memorize available pipe sizes. Thus, the chart serves as a memory aid. Students are given opportunities to practice using the chart, and after each chart-reading exercise, are asked to reflect on how they used the chart. The teacher ends the activity by asking students to think of other situations in which they may use charts in similar ways. Learning, use of, and reflection on literacy skills are thus integrated in a context built around a personally relevant goal: succeeding on the job. Taking the next step—encouraging students to reflect on how the same skills are used in other contexts—can provide a bridge for transfer of literacy across several contexts.

Teachers can also use the metacognition framework and associated methodologies to help adolescents reflect on how they use literacy skills outside the classroom (Herndon, 1971). They can ask students to think of a setting outside school where they use reading and writing—perhaps an after school job—and to describe how they use literacy in that setting, how they feel as users of literacy in that situation, and how the reading and writing they do in that situation is similar to and different from the reading and writing they do in school. Activities such as these may show adolescents who are less successful in school that they do successfully use literacy skills in other contexts. They may show adolescents how they can apply in their school activities literacy skills they already use successfully in other contexts. It may give them confidence as individuals who can use literacy as a tool for learning in a variety of situations.

CONCLUSION

People working with adolescents today are faced with the challenge of preparing them for the literacy demands of tomorrow's world. Intuition, research, and successful practice all indicate that presenting literacy as a tool for achieving personal goals and fulfilling interests is a sound strategy for enhancing the development of literacy skills.

Since the 1970s, researchers have been exploring metacognition (i.e., individuals' knowledge about and regulation of cognitive processes, such as memory and reading). The components of metacognition, and the methodologies used to study them, can be applied by teachers immediately to (a) broaden students' conceptions of themselves as users of literacy, and (b) enhance literacy instruction.

Metacognition provides researchers with a framework for exploring why it is most effective to relate literacy to personal goals and interests. Researchers can use the metacognition framework to study adolescents' perceptions about and use of literacy in a variety of contexts. They can study contexts that are interesting and relevant to adolescents, as well as those that are not particularly interesting or relevant to adolescents. They can compare these contexts to discover important similarities and differences among them. Eventually, their findings may indicate additional recommendations for improving literacy instruction.

REFERENCES

Alexander, P. A., Hare, V. C., & Garner, R. (1984). The effects of time, access, and question type on response accuracy and frequency of lookbacks in older, proficient readers. *Journal of Reading Behavior, 16,* 119-130.

Alvermann, D. E., & Ratekin, N. H. (1982). Metacognitive knowledge about reading proficiency: Its relation to study strategies and task demands. *Journal of Reading Behavior, 14,* 231–241.

Anderson, R. C., Hiebert, E. H., Scott, J. A., & Wilkinson, I. A. G. (1985). *Becoming a nation of readers: The report of the Commission on Reading.* Washington, DC: The National Institute of Education, United States Department of Education.

Baker, L. (1979). Comprehension monitoring: Identifying and coping with text confusions. *Journal of Reading Behavior, 11,* 365–374.

Baker, L., & Anderson, R. I. (1982). Effects of inconsistent information on text processing: Evidence for comprehension monitoring. *Reading Research Quarterly, 17,* 281–294.

Baker, L., & Brown, A. L. (1984). Metacognitive skills and reading. In P. D. Pearson, R. Barr, M. L. Kamil, & P. Mosenthal (Eds.), *Handbook of reading research* (pp. 353–394). New York: Longman.

Carnevale, A. P., Gainer, L. J., & Meltzer, A. S. (1989). *Workplace basics: The skills employers want.* Alexandria, VA: American Society for Training and Development.

Carnevale, A. P., & Schulz, E. R. (1988). Technical training in America: How much and who. *Training and Development Journal, 42,* 18–32.

Chisman, F. P. (1989). *Jump start: The federal role in adult literacy.* Southport, CT: The Southport Institute for Policy Analysis.

Chisman, F. P. (1990). Toward a literate America: The leadership challenge. In F. P. Chisman (Ed.), *Leadership for literacy* (pp. 1–24). San Francisco: Jossey-Bass.

Chisman, F. P., & Campbell, W. L. (1990). Narrowing the job-skills gap: A focus on workforce literacy. In F. P. Chisman (Ed.), *Leadership for literacy* (pp. 144–170). San Francisco: Jossey-Bass.

Cummings, J. (1989). Policy and the continuum of change. In J. Cummings (Ed.), *Future choices: Toward a national youth policy* (pp. 3–5). Washington, DC: Youth Policy Institute.

Fingeret, H. A. (1990). Changing literacy instruction: Moving beyond the status quo. In F. P. Chisman (Ed.), *Leadership for literacy* (pp. 25–50). San Francisco: Jossey-Bass.

Flavell, J. H. (1979). Metacognition and cognitive monitoring. *American Psychologist, 10,* 906–911.

Flavell, J. H., & Wellman, H. M. (1977). Metamemory. In R. V. Kail & J. W. Hagen (Eds.), *Perspectives on the development of memory and cognition* (pp. 3–33). Hillsdale, NJ: Lawrence Erlbaum Associates.

Flower, L., & Hayes, J. R. (1981). A cognitive process theory of writing. *College Composition and Communication, 32,* 365–387.

Forlizzi, L. A. (1988). *Relationships among use, predicted use, and awareness of use of comprehension-repair strategies: Converging evidence from different methodologies.* Unpublished doctoral dissertation, The Pennsylvania State University, University Park.

Gambrell, L. B., & Heathington, B. S. (1981). Adult disabled readers' metacognitive awareness about reading tasks and strategies. *Journal of Reading Behavior, 13,* 215–221.

Garner, R. (1982). Verbal report data on reading strategies. *Journal of Reading Behavior, 14,* 159–167.

Garner, R. (1987). *Metacognition and reading comprehension.* Norwood, NJ: Ablex.

Garner, R., & Kraus, C. (1981–1982). Good and poor comprehender differences in knowing and regulating reading behaviors. *Educational Research Quarterly, 6*(4), 5–12.

Hare, V. C. (1981). Readers' problem identification and problem-solving strategies for high- and low-knowledge articles. *Journal of Reading Behavior, 13,* 359–365.

Hare, V. C., & Pulliam, C. A. (1980). College students' metacognitive awareness of reading behaviors. In M. L. Kamil & A. J. Moe (Eds.), *Perspectives in reading research and instruction: 29th yearbook of the National Reading Conference* (pp. 226–231). Washington, DC: National Reading Conference.

Herndon, J. (1971). *How to survive in your native land.* New York: Simon & Schuster.

Hunter, C. S., & Harman, D. (1979). *Adult illiteracy in the United States: A report to the Ford Foundation.* New York: McGraw-Hill.

Hurley, M. E. (1991). Empowering adult learners. *Adult Learning, 2*(4), 1–23, 27.

Johnston, W. B., & Packer, A. E. (1987). *Workforce 2000: Work and workers for the twenty-first century.* Indianapolis, IN: Hudson Institute.

Kearns, D. T., & Doyle, D. P. (1989). *Winning the brain race.* San Francisco: ICS Press.

Kirsch, I. S., & Jungeblut, A. (1986). *Literacy: Profiles of America's young adults* (Rep. No. 16-PL-02). Princeton, NJ: Educational Testing Service.

Kletzien, S. B. (1991). Strategy use by good and poor comprehenders reading expository text of differing levels. *Reading Research Quarterly, 26,* 67–86.

Lave, J. (1988). *Cognition in practice.* Cambridge, England: Cambridge University Press.

Markman, E. M. (1977). Realizing that you don't understand: A preliminary investigation. *Child Development, 48,* 986–992.

Mikulecky, L., Ehlinger, J., & Meenan, A. L. (1987). *Training for job literacy demands: What research applies to practice.* University Park, PA: Institute for the Study of Adult Literacy, The Pennsylvania State University.

Myers, M., & Paris, S. G. (1978). Children's metacognitive knowledge about reading. *Journal of Educational Psychology, 70,* 680–690.

Ngandu, K. (1977). What do remedial high school students do when they read? *Journal of Reading, 21,* 231–234.

Nickerson, R. S. (1985). Adult literacy and technology. *Visible Language, 19,* 311–355.

Olshavsky, J. E. (1976–1977). Reading as problem solving: An investigation of strategies. *Reading Research Quarterly, 12,* 654–674.

Resnick, L. B. (1990). Literacy in school and out. *Daedalus: Journal of the American Academy of Arts and Sciences, 119*(2), 169–185.

Schommer, M., & Surber, J. E. (1986). Comprehension-monitoring failure in skilled adult readers. *Journal of Educational Psychology, 78,* 353–357.

Scribner, S. (1984). Studying working intelligence. In B. Rogoff & J. Lave (Eds.), *Everyday cognition* (pp. 9–40). Cambridge, MA: Harvard University Press.

Smith, H. K. (1967). The responses of good and poor readers when asked to read for different purposes. *Reading Research Quarterly, 3,* 53–83.

Sticht, T. G. (1988). Adult literacy education. In E. Z. Rothkopf (Ed.), *Review of research in education* (pp. 59–96). Washington, DC: American Educational Research Association.

Sticht, T. G., & Mikulecky, L. (1984). *Job-related skills: Cases and conclusions.* Columbus, OH: ERIC Clearinghouse on Adult, Career, and Vocational Education, National Center for Research in Vocational Education, The Ohio State University.

Venezky, R. L., Kaestle, C. F., & Sum, A. M. (1987). *The subtle danger: Reflections on the literacy abilities of America's young adults.* Princeton, NJ: Center for the Assessment of Educational Progress, Educational Testing Service.

13 | Music in the Lives of Adolescents: A Comparison of In-School and Out-of-School Music Experiences and Involvement

Joanne Rutkowski
The Pennsylvania State University

Adolescents' participation in out-of-school nonsupervised music activities and their beliefs about out-of-school music versus in-school music are of particular interest to music teachers. It is during the adolescent years that children often form "garage bands" or engage in music composition. This seems to contradict many adolescents' negative feelings about music class. Middle and or junior high school music teachers often hear "I hate music class" from the same students who live most of their adolescent years with a headset glued to their ears. As reported by Steinel (1984), students in Grades 7–12 rated music class 2.43 on a scale of 1–4, only art and Black studies were rated lower, but the same students' ratings of important activities in everyday life put music second only to sports. In addition, it has been observed that many students who engage in out-of-school music activities are often those who are not involved in traditional school performing ensembles, such as band and chorus. Perhaps the style of teaching presented in school does not fit with these students' best mode of learning. Or perhaps the content or method of presentation is inappropriate for adolescents. Because this same scenario may exist in other disciplines as well, this chapter is intended as a case study in music of in-school and out-of-school learnings. Research findings that give insight to the following questions may provide some transferrable general lessons:

1. Which adolescents are involved in music, both in school and out of school, and what is the nature of that involvement?

2. What factors may contribute to that involvement? What are adolescents' preferences for music activities in-school? What is being taught in school and how is it being taught in school? What factors influence out-of-school involvement?
3. How do adolescents learn music in school and out of school?
4. What research directions seem appropriate for the future?

WHO IS INVOLVED AND HOW ARE THEY INVOLVED?

In-School Involvement

Adolescents' in-school involvement in music usually takes place in a choral, instrumental, and/or general music setting. In a study conducted by Thompson (1986), it was determined that 34% of the responding middle schools had 16%–25% of their students involved in choral programs, whereas 24% of the schools had 26%–35% of their students in choral programs. Involvement in choral music seemed to be at a peak in middle school: In 51% of the high schools less than 10% of the students were involved in choral programs. Instrumental music involvement reflected the same trends but with even fewer numbers of students involved. In 39% of the middle schools responding, 16%–25% of the students were involved in instrumental programs, whereas in 24% of the responding schools, less than 10% of the students were involved. However, the dropout rate from middle school to high school was not as great for instrumental music as for choral music (Frakes, 1984; Thompson, 1986). McDonald (1990) reported that 23 states require general music in junior high school, but only for students not involved in choral or instrumental programs. Unfortunately, general music often becomes "the class for those who can't or don't want to learn about music" (p. 18). To add fuel to this fire, only 8% of the music teachers in Pennsylvania claim to teach middle school/junior high general music for 75% or more of their teaching load (Thompson, 1986). One could infer from these figures that general music is being taught mostly by persons who see their "major" teaching load as other than general music—probably choral or instrumental music teaching.

After school music activities are also available for middle school/junior high students. However, these experiences are usually tailored for those already involved in performing ensembles during the school day. Thompson (1986) reported that 25% of the select choral ensembles in Pennsylvania met after school. Small ensembles, particularly pop/jazz vocal groups, also met after school. A higher percentage of instrumental ensembles meet during the school day, however small ensembles, jazz ensembles, and string ensembles seem more likely to be scheduled before or after regular school hours. The one after school music activity that may attract the student not involved in performing ensembles is the school musical. Perrine (1989) found that participation in a musical production at the middle school had positive effects on students' attitudes toward music activities and seemed to encourage creative thinking skills.

Out-of-School Involvement

Research on adolescents' out-of-school involvement with music is fairly limited. What is consistent among these few sources, however, is the importance of music in the lives of adolescents. From a survey of 11- to 15-year-olds, Leming (1987) found that 46% of them felt music was "very important," 47% felt music was "somewhat important," and only 7% indicated music as "not important at all" to their lives. Frith (1981) said that music is the central activity of youth and that it builds peer group identity. Anyone who has spent any time with an adolescent would certainly not argue that point! Adolescents' out-of-school music participation also seems to shift from organized activities, church choir, and so forth, to more personal activities (i.e., listening, singing to themselves, playing an instrument by themselves; Steinel, 1984). Singing with friends is also a favored activity. Steinel reported that music appears fourth in a ranking of adolescents' hobbies, preceded by sports, reading, and video games. The media provide a means for adolescents' informal, personal involvement with music. The average adolescent listens to the radio 2–3 hours a day and listens to records and tapes 1 or more hours per day (Christenson & Roberts, 1989). Sessions (1987) also reported that younger adolescents actually watch more music videos than older adolescents. A more in-depth discussion of music media and adolescents is presented by Thompson (chapter 23, this volume).

Because band, orchestra, and chorus were second only to sports in adolescents' preferred school activities, it seems that programs are meeting the needs of some students. However, this is less than 35% of the middle school/junior high population. Music is important to the lives of 93% of adolescents but they have ranked music class almost last in preferred subjects in school. It appears obvious that music classes are not meeting the needs of these students. Given their interest in music, music class should be one of the easiest classes to teach in a middle school/junior high setting. Instead, it is one of the most dreaded assignments bestowed on a music teacher. The next sections of this chapter look at the following questions in order to gain some insight to this puzzling contradiction: What factors may contribute to music involvement? How do adolescents learn music? What are their preferences for music activities in school? What is being taught in school and how is it being taught in school? What factors influence out-of-school involvement? How do adolescents learn music out of school?

WHAT INFLUENCES ADOLESCENTS' MUSIC INVOLVEMENT?

In-School Involvement

It would seem that in-school involvement would be influenced by teachers, activities, and perhaps peers. Alpert (1982) surprisingly found that when music teachers and disc jockeys approved of classical music, fifth graders' attitudes toward listening to classical music became more positive, but that when peers approved of classical music the attitudes became more negative. Because fifth grade is often considered to be the beginning of adolescence, it would be interesting to conduct the same study with sixth, seventh, and eighth graders to determine if peers gain more favor and adults less favor as students move through the adolescent years. Characteristics of successful middle school/junior high general music teachers have been of interest. Positive facial expression, positive pacing, positive physical contact, and eye contact appear as similar characteristics among successful teachers (Curtis, 1986). It is unclear, however, if Curtis defined a successful teacher as one whom the students liked, one whom they learned the most from, or both. Adolescents also prefer teachers who are people, rather than academically, oriented (Gerber, 1989): They like teachers who are nice to them. The recent concern for more personal contact between middle school students and teachers seems warranted.

To what adolescents attribute success and failure in music may also influence their in-school involvement. Asmus (1985, 1986), in his work with achievement motivation, found that prior to sixth grade, students mostly attribute success to effort. However, during sixth and seventh grades, success and failure is attributed more to ability. "An interesting problem for future research would be to determine if the shift . . . is a result of music education practice or if the reduced availability of music instruction at higher grade levels is a result of inherent motivational changes in the students" (Asmus, 1986, p. 271).

It is not surprising that the home music environment also significantly influences music achievement and attitude toward school music (Seidenberg, 1986). Because positive attitude toward music class decreases from sixth to eighth grade (Pogonowski, 1985; Seidenberg, 1986), it would seem that this factor plays less of a role with older adolescents. Zimmerman (1986) stated, "The influence of home environment gives way to peer influence and pressure during middle childhood" (p. 31).

It has also been said that academic achievement is a factor in determining involvement with school music performance ensembles. Hill (1987) did find that middle school students who were high achievers in instrumental music groups were also high achievers in academic areas. In addition, students who participated in extracurricular activities also tended to have higher grades and educational aspirations (Parish, 1984). What has not been determined, however, is a cause-and-effect relationship. Are students high achievers academically because of their music involvement or are they involved in music because they are high achievers academically?

What Music Activities do Adolescents Prefer? Several researchers have investigated this question. Johnson (1985) found that adolescents like music around them in school. The presence, but not the type, of music had a positive effect on inner-city junior high school students' behavior. Students also seem to prefer activities where they have some choice (Boswell, 1989). Perhaps this is a reflection of their developing sense of independence from adults. Integrative strategies, where music, visual art, movement, and so forth, are related, have played a positive role in students' academic and attitudinal achievement (McKeon, 1988; Smith, 1984). Special events, such as a school musical production, are also liked by students (Perrine, 1989). A consistent finding among studies has been students' preference for "active" rather than "passive" classroom activities (Boyle, Hosterman, & Noyes, 1981; Gerber, 1989; Thompson, 1991a; Webster, 1990; Wig & Boyle, 1982). Playing guitar or drums, creating, and making tape recordings ("active") were rated high, whereas listening to opera and symphony orchestra, learning about instruments, composers, form, and history ("passive") were rated low. Seventh and eighth graders in the Fall of 1990 completed a questionnaire (Thompson, 1991a) that was previously completed by seventh and eighth graders in 1970 and 1980 (Boyle, Hosterman, & Noyes, 1981). In summarizing his findings, Thompson stated the following:

> the data from this study clearly indicate that throughout the two decades junior high school students preferred general music activities that provide active involvement with the art. They value opportunities to sing and play

instruments and exhibit an increasing desire to be able to create their own music. (p. 8)

The preference for creating music has emerged in other studies as well. Although band/orchestra was the preferred music activity of middle school students in a study conducted by Seidenberg (1986), composition was a strong second. An important aspect of composition/creating is small group or individual work and learning means of expressing that creativity other than singing. Wig and Boyle (1982) found that keyboard learning experiences increased middle school students' attitudes toward music in general and toward their own music and creative skills and abilities significantly more than students not involved in keyboard instruction. It was interesting, however, that these students did not indicate an enjoyment for piano significantly more than the control group. Gerber (1989), in his study of exemplary middle school general music teachers, concluded that students liked teachers who included small group instruction and who gave students opportunities to make their own musical judgments. Even instrumental music students indicated more positive attitudes toward music after participating in small group performance activities rather than only large ensembles (Carmody, 1988).

What is Being Taught in School? After discussing what may influence adolescents' participation in music activities in school and what activities they say they prefer, it seems appropriate to determine what is actually being taught in school and how the material is being presented. Thompson (1991b) analyzed the current music textbooks for Grades 7 and 8. The percentage of each text devoted to various music activities are as follows: songs 23%–49%, listening activities 17%–25%, playing instruments 11%–18%, composing 2%–8%, learning about music 15%–29%, and moving to music .4%–2%. Few studies have investigated the appropriateness or effectiveness of various curricula with middle school/junior high students. Koch (1989) developed a curricula for teaching the elements of music—rhythm, melody, harmony, tone color, form—to middle school students. This content usually falls under the category "learning about music." Various integrated arts and interdisciplinary curricula have been investigated. Lamb (1987) proposed a curricula that emphasized women composers. These strategies have been found to have a positive effect on students' music achievement and attitude (Gibson, 1988; McKeon, 1988; Smith, 1984), although Quay (1987) found that teachers tend to perform differently with different curricula. Perhaps these strategies are successful if the teachers are comfortable with them.

Small versus large group settings have also received some research attention. Nolteriek (1984) found that music teachers use large group settings significantly more than small group settings but recommended that teachers should not be as hesitant to employ small group settings as well. Other studies have dealt mostly with small group settings in instrumental music. Curricula for jazz ensemble instruction at the middle school level that encourage small group and multisensory experiences have been effective (Coy, 1989; Hale, 1988). String players involved in chamber music groups have improved in their intonation skills as well as attitudes toward music (Carmody, 1988). Small group instruction has also been effective with mildly handicapped middle school string players (Van Camp, 1989).

As one might expect, technology and its application in the classroom has been a popular research topic recently. Electronic piano instruction significantly increased sixth graders' music-reading ability (Moss, 1987). McCalla (1989), however, when reporting on the status of class piano instruction in Florida, discovered a philosophical conflict among teachers. Is the purpose of class piano instruction the development of keyboard techniques or the development of general musicianship? Myers (1988) also posed this philosophical question regarding guitar instruction. The computer and commercial software have also been used effectively in middle school/junior high music classes (King, 1988; Nelson, 1988).

Obviously, a scarcity of research exists in this area. A few studies have investigated some isolated curricular issues in music education for adolescents and the textbooks provide some insight regarding what may be being taught in classrooms, but the actual state of affairs has not been documented.

Out-of-School Involvement

Not surprisingly, even less information is available regarding influences on adolescents' out-of-school music involvement. It has been shown that out-of-school experiences in music significantly relate to music achievement in school (Seidenberg, 1986), but the influences on out-of-school experiences have not been widely investigated. One obvious influence is the media. A later chapter of this book discusses that influence specifically, thus only a few relevant issues are presented here. Killian (1990) examined factors affecting junior high students' music preferences, specifically gender and race influences. Black males and females were found to have similar preferences as did White males and females. White students preferred Black performers but, when asked what solo in "We Are the World" they would like to sing, they generally selected a solo performed by a White singer of their gender. It could be concluded that adolescents like music that is not race specific but that they still identify in performance with those of their race and gender. When surveying students in Grades 5, 7, 9, and 11, Boyle, Hosterman, and Ramsey (1981) found that melody, mood, rhythm, and lyrics were the most important factors for selection of a particular piece of music. Interestingly, sociocultural reasons were less important. The melody and instruments were more important for older students, whereas peer influence was more important for the lower grade levels. Parents and siblings have relatively no reported influence for any grade level. Radio was more important for the fifth and seventh graders than for the older students and the younger students as a group agreed more on their choices of familiar songs. The more a student liked pop music, the higher he or she rated lyrics and danceability, whereas friends' views, danceability, and the radio had less importance for those with more music experience.

Christenson and Roberts (1989) reached some different conclusions. They reported that adolescents generally listened to music to control their mood, to fill silence, and for social uses. Lyrical content was unimportant, especially for males, and two thirds of all listening was solitary and personal, although music did have an impact on adolescents' social settings and played a role in defining peer groups.

Although it has been said that "young people use music to resist authority at all levels, assert their personalities and learn about things that their parents and the schools aren't telling them" (Lull, 1987, p. 153), it has also been found that adolescents who achieve in school show significantly more interest than underachieving students in life activities including music (Ciborowski, 1986). This contradiction was noted by Berry (1989) in an investigation of the relationship between pop music and low-income Black adolescents. Rap music was found to play both a role of separation from mainstream society and also a means to legitimize existence within mainstream society.

HOW DO ADOLESCENTS LEARN MUSIC?

The question of how we learn music has been posed for years, however empirical investigation of this question has only just begun. Therefore, the question of how adolescents learn music, although important, seems premature. Some work has begun, however, and those findings are presented here.

Although many believe that one is either talented in music or not, and adolescents attribute success in music more to ability than to effort (Asmus, 1986), an equal distribution of music aptitude among the population has been documented (Gordon, 1965). Therefore, all adolescents have potential for achievement in music. Schmidt and Sinor (1986) found that second graders who were more reflective, were slower to decide about decisions, had higher tonal aptitude than inflective students, but that no differences between these learning styles existed for rhythm aptitude. Is the same true of adolescents? Baer (1987), when investigating motor skill proficiency, found that gross motor skills were related more highly to music aptitude than fine motor skill, but that fine motor skills were related more highly to musical performance achievement. It would seem, then, that many students who felt they were not "talented" in music due to lack of ability to successfully play an instrument (fine motor skills) may actually possess higher music aptitude but may need to seek other avenues of expression of that aptitude. Perhaps that is what those forming garage bands are in fact doing!

Learning music is a complex endeavor. Development of skills in music "hearing" or aural discrimination (audiation as coined by Gordon, 1988), in psychomotor abilities, and in cognitive understanding are all important. However, it is suspected that processes for learning in each of these areas is different (Gardner, 1983). Zimmerman (1986) recommended that aural discrimination learning should precede cognitive understanding but that both are developmental. Gordon (1988) presented a learning sequence for the development of tonal and rhythm skills (audiation). Because he contended that this learning sequence is applicable to all age levels, one would assume that adolescents' music learning is similar.

Students' and teachers' learning styles have been the subject of some recent investigation, although not many in music education. Stone (1981) reported that students achieve better when the teacher is aware of student's cognitive style and adapts instruction to that style. DiStefano (1970) concluded that teachers and students who were matched in cognitive style tended to view each other positively and visa versa. Some contrast, however, may actually be more stimulating to the learning environment. The cognitive styles most closely related to music aptitude are field dependence/field independence and reflection/impulsivity (Schmidt, 1984). Field independent learners performed better on music performance tests and music conservation tasks. Schmidt also found that rhythm training increased students' field independence scores. Teachers should be aware that social interaction, such as class discussions and working in groups, is more important for field dependent students, however, they may actually achieve better in a lecture setting due to the structure it provides.

In a study comparing students' intuitive music ability and rational musical ability with their learning styles, it was found that intuitive music ability and abstract random learning style (imagination, unstructured) were negatively correlated (Moore, 1990). Most music teachers would probably have suspected another outcome! The old saying that "if you're good in music you must be good in math" and visa versa, has not been shown to be valid. Piro (1986) found that an analytic thinking approach used by mathematically gifted students did not appear to cross over to music tasks. The visual processing used by students to solve spatial tasks was not clearly related to their math or music experience (Mason, 1986). Kageff (1984) did find, however, that seventh graders' ability to recognize melodies presented at various levels of abstraction was related to their ability to do other music tasks. And finally, Cutietta (1985), in his analysis of musical hypothesis created by 11- to 16-year-old adolescents, found that these youth grouped musical examples by "properties" and not by "class." For example, they commented on instruments used, tempo, and beat, but not style. They also consistently, but incorrectly, used the terms *opera* and *church:* Opera for anything not sung in a popular style even though no examples of opera were included, and church for any example played by an organ.

Some information is available regarding adolescents' achievement in music. Fifth and sixth graders' kinesthetic responses to rhythm in music can be improved through training (Searle, 1985), as can their rhythmic aural perception and reading recognition (Kluth, 1986), but 6 years of music-performing experience was required before significant development of critical thinking skills could be shown (Deturk, 1988). DeLorenzo (1989), in a study of creative problem-solving processes of sixth graders, found that students at similar levels of decision making showed similar behaviors. She noted that "the student's perception of the problem structure . . . had a far greater effect on the student's perception of choice in the problem situation than the teacher-constructed choices" (p. 195). Perhaps this is related in some way to Asmus' (1986) findings that adolescents begin to attribute success in music to ability rather than to effort. When investigating elementary and junior high school students' melodic composition abilities, Seals (1989) reported similarities among the children's compositions in the areas of tonality, meter, tempo variation, dynamics, modes of attack, pitch movement, rhythmic units, and total duration. However differences were noted in tempo, pitch range, and pitch set. However, boys' and girls' melodic composition ability increased with grade level. These few studies on adolescent achievement in music at least show that music learning does continue throughout the adolescent years. And even those students who drop out of music have significantly more positive attitudes toward music than those who never participated (Frakes, 1984).

Perhaps the area that has received the most research attention has been the adolescent male and female changing voice. It has been shown that boys should continue to sing throughout the voice change period and that stages of change do exist (Barresi & Bless, 1984; Barresi & Russell, 1984; Cooksey, 1977a, 1977b, 1977c, 1978, 1984; Groom, 1984; McKenzie, 1956; Rutkowski, 1984, 1985; Swanson, 1961, 1977). A voice change for females has also been documented, although this change is not nearly as dramatic and, consequently, has not received as much attention (Gackle, 1987).

The question posed, "How do adolescents learn music out of school?" does not seem to have received any research attention. Because it is common knowledge that adolescents figure out how to play an electronic keyboard on their own and often join with groups of friends to create music, the processes they initiate and follow to learn how to make music would certainly have application in the schools.

As illustrated by this potpourri of research, any conclusions drawn at this time about how adolescents learn music would probably be invalid. It is encouraging to see that some researchers have at least begun to investigate this important aspect of music education.

WHAT RESEARCH DIRECTIONS SEEM APPROPRIATE FOR THE FUTURE?

The discrepancies between adolescents' involvement with music out of school and involvement in school are flagrant. Adolescents rate music high on the list of activities important to their life but rate music class third from last on the list of preferred classes in school. Even though adolescents rate band and chorus fairly high, only about 25% of adolescents participate in these ensembles. Furthermore, "while experiences in band, chorus, orchestra, or private instrumental study is desirable for students in upper elementary grades, these factors do not necessarily influence classroom music attitudes" (Pogonowski, 1985, p. 256). Even those who participate in school music ensembles do not like music class!

When comparing adolescents' preferred music activities with those actually included in middle school/junior high music textbooks, it is not surprising that they claim "I hate music class." Students prefer "active" music activities, especially activities in which they can be creative (Thompson, 1991a). These activities comprise only a small portion of those in music textbooks (Thompson, 1991b). Thompson (1991a) concluded:

> throughout the two decades junior high school students preferred general music activities that provide active involvement with the art. They value opportunities to sing and play instruments and exhibit an increasing desire to be able to create their own music. Given this information, one must wonder why so many junior high school general music classes consist exclusively of listening to recordings, filling out work sheets, or taking notes while the teacher lectures. (p. 8)

Geffre (1987) found that junior high students and music teachers differed significantly in their perceptions of preferred music class activities.

The literature certainly confirms these observations. Ferrara (1986) noticed that music teachers present music formally and historically but that students experience music openly and personally. Webster (1990) stated that "being knowledgeable about music is not knowing music" (p. 37). Merrion and Vincent (1988) also concluded that "solid performance based activities remain the most effective and relevant way to engage students in meaningful experiences" (p. 36) but that most teachers stay clear of these experiences in junior high music class. Recommendations to teachers encouraging them to implement this type of instruction are numerous in the literature, specifically use of composition (Myers, 1988; Seidenberg, 1986), large and small group work (Hanshumaker, 1989; Pogonowski, 1987; Webster, 1990), and use of musical instrument digital interface (MIDI) and workstations (Webster, 1990). Composing, improvising, conducting, performing, listening, evaluating, and discussing lead to creative thinking in music and have been shown to stop the decline in attitude toward music class with young adolescents (Pogonowski, 1985). Webster (1990) concluded that teachers who avoid these sorts of instructional strategies actually discourage creative thinking.

The discussion seems to lead back to the teacher who has difficulty implementing instruction that is relevant to the adolescent and that makes the connection between the classroom and real life (Hanshumaker, 1989; Myers, 1988). Perhaps the content traditionally deemed important by the general music teacher is not viewed as important or relevant by the students. McDonald (1990) observed that junior high general music class is often treated casually by the music teacher and, therefore, is treated casually by students and administrators. Teacher training seems an obvious place to initiate change. However, Piperis (1989) found that faculty members in teacher education programs are not very knowledgeable of the characteristics of the middle school child. The paucity of research on adolescents in music compounds the problem.

Where do we go from here? Reimer (1985) recommended that we "cluster our research efforts around significant problems, or topics, or issues" (p. 15) and that there is a "need for large-scale, long-term research, which is notable, in music education, by its almost complete absence" (p. 17). It seems that knowledge about how adolescents learn music, especially when they learn on their own in an out-of-school environment, is crucial. Studies that observe adolescents in "action" in their own settings have not, to my knowledge, ever been conducted. An understanding of these processes would provide a wealth of information for development of curricula and for preservice training of teachers.

The attitudes of music teachers toward general music are also of concern. Although not documented, those involved with teacher preparation in music often find that many music teachers aspire to be choral or instrumental ensemble directors and therefore do not look favorably on general music. A "specialization in music teacher training to include an emphasis in general music for prospective teachers at both public school and college levels" has been proposed (Collins, 1987). However, without appropriate curricula, general music for adolescents will continue to be a problem (McDonald, 1990). The research community must address this issue and influence textbook publishers whose materials often form the core of music curricula in the schools.

With substantial research in the areas of how adolescents learn music out of school, how those processes can be applied to the school setting, teacher training and in-service in general music, and implementation of appropriate curricula and materials for these students, McDonald's (1990) statement that "The 'general music problem' remains one of the challenges of present-day junior high/middle school music education" (p. 18) will no longer be true as we enter the 21st century. Adolescents love music. Let's learn from them and teach them in appropriate ways so they also love music class.

REFERENCES

Alpert, J. (1982). The effect of disc jockey, peer, and music teacher approval of music on music selection and preference. *Journal of Research in Music Education, 30*(3), 173–186.

Asmus, E. P. (1985). Sixth graders' achievement motivation: Their views of success and failure in music. *Bulletin of the Council for Research in Music Education, 85,* 1–13.

Asmus, E. P. (1986). Student beliefs about the causes of success and failure in music: A study of achievement motivation. *Journal of Research in Music Education, 34*(4), 262–278.

Baer, D. E. (1987). Motor skill proficiency: Its relationship to instrumental music performance achievement and music aptitude. *Dissertation Abstracts International, 48*(06A), 1410. (University Microfilms No. AAC8720238)

Barresi, A. L., & Bless, D. M. (1984). The relation of selected variables to the perception of tessitura pitches in the adolescent changing voice. In M. Runfola & L. Bash (Eds.), *Proceedings: Research symposium on the male adolescent voice* (pp. 97–109). Buffalo, NY: Music Department, State University of New York at Buffalo.

Barresi, A. L., & Russell, T. P. (1984). Criteria for selecting appropriate choral literature to assist in the development of the boy's changing voice. In M. Runfola & L. Bash (Eds.), *Proceedings: Research symposium on the male adolescent voice* (pp. 166–181). Buffalo, NY: Music Department, State University of New York at Buffalo.

Berry, V. T. (1989). The complex relationship between pop music and low-income black adolescents: A qualitative approach. *Dissertation Abstracts International, 50*(06A), 1469. (University Microfilms No. AAC8920663)

Boswell, J. (1989, February). *Comparisons of attitudinal assessments in middle and junior high school general music.* Paper presented at the Symposium on Research in General Music, Tucson, AZ.

Boyle, J. D., Hosterman, G. L., & Noyes, W. G. (1981). An inventory of junior high school students' preferences for general music activities, 1970 and 1980. *Pennsylvania Music Educators Association Bulletin of Research in Music Education, 12,* 35–39.

Boyle, J. D., Hosterman, G. L., & Ramsey, D. S. (1981). Factors influencing pop music preferences of young people. *Journal of Research in Music Education, 29*(1), 47–56.

Carmody, W. J. (1988). The effects of chamber music experience on intonation and attitudes among junior high school string players. *Dissertation Abstracts International, 49*(08A), 2140. (University Microfilms No. AAC0563729)

Christenson, P. G., & Roberts, D. F. (1989). *Popular music in early adolescence.* Prepared for the Carnegie Council on Adolescent Development, Washington, DC.

Ciborowski, J. (1986). An examination of interests among achieving and underachieving adolescents. *Dissertation Abstracts International, 47*(02A), 497. (University Microfilms No. AAC8606877)

Collins, I. (1987). General music: A call for reform. *General Music Today, 1*(1), 3–6.

Cooksey, J. M. (1977a, October). The development of a contemporary eclectic theory for the training and cultivation of the junior high school male changing voice, part I: Existing theories. *The Choral Journal,* 5–14.

Cooksey, J. M. (1977b, November). The development of a contemporary eclectic theory for the training and cultivation of the junior high school male changing voice, part II: Scientific and empirical findings: Some tentative solutions. *The Choral Journal,* 5–16.

Cooksey, J. M. (1977c, December). The development of a contemporary eclectic theory for the training and cultivation of the junior high school male changing voice, part III: Developing an integrated approach to the care and training of the junior high school male changing voice. *The Choral Journal,* 5–15.

Cooksey, J. M. (1978, January). The development of a contemporary eclectic theory for the training and cultivation of the junior high school male changing voice, part IV: Selecting music for the junior high school male changing voice. *The Choral Journal,* 5–18.

Cooksey, J. M. (1984). The male adolescent changing voice: Some new perspectives. In M. Runfola & L. Bash (Eds.), *Proceedings: Research symposium on the male adolescent voice* (pp. 4–59). Buffalo, NY: Music Department, State University of New York at Buffalo.

Coy, D. A. (1989). A multisensory approach to teaching jazz improvisation to middle school band students. *Dissertation Abstracts International, 50*(11A), 3508. (University Microfilms No. AAC9010106)

Curtis, S. C. (1986). An observational analysis of successful junior high/middle school general music teachers. *Dissertation Abstracts International, 47*(03A), 821. (University Microfilms No. AAC8611784)
Cutietta, R. (1985). Analysis of musical hypotheses created by the 11-16 year old learner. *Bulletin of the Council for Research in Music Education, 84,* 1-13.
DeLorenzo, L. C. (1989). Field study of sixth-grade students' creative music problem-solving processes. *Journal of Research in Music Education, 37*(3), 188-200.
Deturk, M. S. (1988). The relationship between experience in performing music class and critical thinking about music. *Dissertation Abstracts International, 49*(06A), 1398. (University Microfilms No. AAC8810011)
DiStefano, J. J. (1970). *Interpersonal perceptions of field independent and field dependent teachers and students.* Unpublished doctoral dissertation, Cornell University, Ithaca, NY.
Ferrara, L. (1986). Music in general studies: A look at content and method. *College Music Symposium, 26,* 122-129.
Frakes, L. (1984). Differences in music achievement, academic achievement, and attitude among participants, dropouts, and nonparticipants in secondary school music. *Dissertation Abstracts International, 46*(02A), 370. (University Microfilms No. AAC8507938)
Frith, S. (1981). *Sound effects: Youth, leisure, and the politics of rock 'n' roll.* New York: Pantheon Books.
Gackle, M. L. (1987). The effect of selected vocal techniques for breath management, resonation, and vowel unification on tone production in the junior high school female voice. *Dissertation Abstracts International, 48*(04A), 862. (University Microfilms No. AAC8716155)
Gardner, H. (1983). *Frames of mind.* New York: Basic Books.
Geffre, T. A. (1987). Actual and preferred classroom environment as perceived by North Dakota junior high school general music students and their teachers. *Dissertation Abstracts International, 49*(04A), 756. (University Microfilms No. AAC8805782)
Gerber, T. (1989, February). *The quality quotient for young adolescents: Exemplary general music teachers in the middle grades.* Paper presented at the Symposium on Research in General Music, Tucson, AZ.
Gibson, S. M. (1988). A comparison of music and multiple arts experiences in the development of creativity in middle school students. *Dissertation Abstracts International, 49*(12A), 3543. (University Microfilms No. AAC8906853)
Gordon, E. E. (1965). *Musical aptitude profile.* Boston, MA: Houghton Mifflin.
Gordon, E. E. (1988). *Learning sequences in music.* Chicago, IL: G.I.A. Publications.
Groom, M. D. (1984). A descriptive analysis of development in adolescent male voices during the summer time period. In M. Runfola & L. Bash (Eds.), *Proceedings: Research symposium on the male adolescent voice* (pp. 80-85). Buffalo, NY: Music Department, State University of New York at Buffalo.
Hale, D. J. (1988). A study of recommended techniques and materials for teaching jazz style to the junior high school student. *Masters Abstracts International, 27*(03), 320. (University Microfilms No. AAC1335332)
Hanshumaker, J. (1989, November). Forging instrumental programs for an urban society. *Music Educators Journal,* 33-37.
Hill, W. L. (1987). A comparison of factors related to participation and achievement in instrumental music at the middle school level in the Denver public schools. *Dissertation Abstracts International, 48*(08A), 2013. (University Microfilms No. AAC8723464)
Johnson, J. L. (1985). A use of music to reduce discipline problems in an inner-city junior

high school. *Dissertation Abstracts International, 46*(07A), 1861. (University Microfilms No. AAC8520770)

Kageff, L. L. (1984). Melody recognition at abstract levels and the relationships to contour generation and tonal memory. *Dissertation Abstracts International, 45*(09A), 2793. (University Microfilms No. AAC8428420)

Killian, J. N. (1990). Effect of model characteristics on musical preferences of junior high students. *Journal of Research in Music Education, 38*(2), 115–123.

King, R. V. (1988). The effects of computer-assisted music instruction on achievement of seventh-grade students. *Dissertation Abstracts International, 49*(09A), 2574. (University Microfilms No. AAC8823171)

Kluth, B. L. (1986). A procedure to teach rhythm reading: Development, implementation, and effectiveness in urban junior high school music classes. *Dissertation Abstracts International, 47*, 1643. (University Microfilms No. AAC8617078)

Koch, C. C. (1989). Teaching the elements of music in the middle school general music class. *Masters Abstracts International, 28*(02), 194. (University Microfilms No. AAC1338550)

Lamb, R. K. (1987). Including women composers in music curricula: Development of creative strategies for the general music class, grades 5–8. *Dissertation Abstracts International, 48*(10A), 2568. (University Microfilms No. AAC8721136)

Leming, J. (1987). Rock music and the socialization of moral values in early adolescence. *Youth and Society, 18*(4), 363–383.

Lull, J. (1987). Listener's communicative uses of popular music. In J. Lull (Ed.), *Popular music and communication* (pp. 140–174). Newbury Park, CA: Sage.

Mason, S. F. (1986). Relationships among mathematical, musical, and spatial abilities. *Dissertation Abstracts International, 47*(04A), 1229. (University Microfilms No. AAC8613503)

Merrion, M. D., & Vincent, M. C. (1988, January). Meeting the expressive needs of junior high students. *Music Educators Journal,* 34–37.

McCalla, D. C. (1989). The status of class piano instruction in the public secondary schools of Florida. *Dissertation Abstracts International, 50*(10A), 3175. (University Microfilms No. AAC9007211)

McDonald, D. (1990). General music in education. *Design for Arts in Education, 91*(5), 15–22.

McKenzie, D. (1956). *Training the boy's changing voice.* London: Faber & Faber.

McKeon, S. E. (1988). The effect of an integrated arts program on self-esteem. *Masters Abstracts International, 27*(02), 169. (University Microfilms No. AAC1333762)

Moore, B. R. (1990). The relationship between curriculum and learner: Music composition and learning style. *Journal of Research in Music Education, 38*(1), 24–38.

Moss, R. B. (1987). The effects of electronic piano instruction on sixth-grade middle-school students' music-reading skills. *Dissertation Abstracts International, 49*(07A), 1728. (University Microfilms No. AAC8816354)

Myers, D. (1988). Preparing the way for the lifelong learner. *General Music Today, 2*(1), 14–15, 31.

Nelson, B. J. P. (1988). The development of a middle school general music curriculum: A synthesis of computer-assisted instruction and music learning theory. *Dissertation Abstracts International, 49*(07A), 1728. (University Microfilms No. AAC8816104)

Nolteriek, M. A. (1984). A description of teacher and student behavior within single and multiple group teaching structures in elementary and general music education classrooms. *Dissertation Abstracts International, 45*(08A), 2435. (University Microfilms No. AAC8424727)

Parish, E. A. (1984). Participation in junior high school extracurricular activities and its relationship to academic performance and educational aspirations. *Dissertation Abstracts International, 46*(02A), 319. (University Microfilms No. AAC8507456)

Perrine, V. B. (1989). The effect of participation in a musical theatre production on the self-concept, attitude toward music and music class, and creative thinking skills of middle school students. *Dissertation Abstracts International, 50*(08A), 2419. (University Microfilms No. AAC9000107)

Piperis, J. E. (1989). A survey of the discrepancy between theory and practice in middle school teacher preparation programs. *Dissertation Abstracts International, 50*(06A), 1639. (University Microfilms No. AAC8920998)

Piro, J. M. (1986). Laterality effects for music perception and problem solving among adolescents gifted in music, mathematics and dance. *Dissertation Abstracts International, 50*(01A), 104. (University Microfilms No. AAC8906502)

Pogonowski, L. M. (1985). Attitude assessment of upper elementary students in a process-oriented music curriculum. *Journal of Research in Music Education, 33*(4), 247–257.

Pogonowski, L. M. (1987, February). Developing skills in critical thinking and problem solving. *Music Educators Journal,* 37–41.

Quay, J. S. (1987). The differential effects associated with two music curricula on eighth grade students. *Dissertation Abstracts International, 48*(07A), 1645. (University Microfilms No. AAC8722099)

Reimer, B. (1985). Towards a more scientific approach to music education. *Bulletin of the Council for Research in Music Education, 83,* 1–21.

Rutkowski, J. (1984). Two year results of a longitudinal study investigating the validity of Cooksey's theory for training the adolescent male voice. In M. Runfola & L. Bash (Eds.), *Proceedings: Research symposium on the male adolescent voice* (pp. 86–96). Buffalo, NY: Music Department, State University of New York at Buffalo.

Rutkowski, J. (1985). Final results of a longitudinal study investigating the validity of Cooksey's theory for training the adolescent male voice. *Pennsylvania Music Educators Association Bulletin of Research in Music Education, 16,* 3–10.

Schmidt, C. P. (1984). Cognitive styles research: Implications for music teaching and learning. *Update, 2*(2), 18–22.

Schmidt, C. P., & Sinor, J. (1986). Investigation of the relationships among music audiation, musical creativity, and cognitive style. *Journal of Research in Music Education, 34*(3), 160–172.

Seals, K. A. (1989). A cross sectional investigation of the melodic composition abilities of elementary and junior high school students. *Dissertation Abstracts International, 50*(11A), 3510. (University Microfilms No. AAC9009939)

Searle, J. W. (1985). An investigation of movement to music and rhythmic pattern reading flash-slide training in fifth- and sixth-grade music classes. *Dissertation Abstracts International, 46*(07A), 1862. (University Microfilms No. AAC8520979)

Seidenberg, F. P. D. (1986). Students' preferences and attitudes toward music in school. *Dissertation Abstracts International, 47*(04A), 1231. (University Microfilms No. AAC0558619)

Sessions, G. L. (1987). Adolescent identity formation, regression and music videos. *Dissertation Abstracts International, 48*(08B), 2478. (University Microfilms No. AAC8719839)

Smith, W. F. (1984). Utilizing the arts in general education process to integrate the performing arts into the junior high school (7–9) humanities curriculum plan at the East Harlem Performing Arts School. *Dissertation Abstracts International, 45*(08A), 2435. (University Microfilms No. AAC8424268)

Steinel, D. V. (Ed.). (1984). *Music and music education: Data and information.* Reston,

VA: Music Educators National Conference.
Stone, M. K. (1981). *Teacher adaptation to student cognitive style and its effect on learning.* Unpublished doctoral dissertation, Columbia University Teachers College, New York.
Swanson, F. J. (1961). The proper care and feeding of changing voices. *Music Educators Journal, 48,* 63.
Swanson, F. J. (1977). *The male singing voice ages eight to eighteen.* Cedar Rapids, IA: Laurance Press.
Thompson, K. P. (1986). Status of music in Pennsylvania schools. *Pennsylvania Music Educators Association Bulletin of Research, 17,* 1–24.
Thompson, K. P. (1991a). An examination of the consistency of junior high school students' preferences for general music activities. *Update, 9*(2), 11–16.
Thompson, K. P. (1991b). *A content analysis of junior high general music textbooks.* Unpublished manuscript, The Pennsylvania State University, University Park.
Van Camp, D. J. (1989). An investigation of the effects of a researcher-designed string music curriculum on the playing skills of mildly mentally handicapped middle school students grouped in homogeneous and heterogeneous classes. *Dissertation Abstracts International, 50*(12A), 3884. (University Microfilms No. AAC9011283)
Webster, P. R. (1990). Creative thinking, technology, and music education. *Design for Arts in Education, 91*(5), 35–41.
Wig, J. A., & Boyle, J. D. (1982). The effect of keyboard learning experiences on middle school general music students' achievement and attitudes. *Journal of Research in Music Education, 30*(3), 163–173.
Zimmerman, M. P. (1986). Music development in middle childhood: A summary of selected research studies. *Bulletin of the Council for Research in Music Education, 86,* 18–35.

III | Health Promotion in Early Adolescence

Section Editors:

Patricia Barthalow Koch
Elizabeth J. Susman
The Pennsylvania State University

Health Promotion for Early Adolescents

Patricia Barthalow Koch
Dolores W. Maney
Elizabeth J. Susman
The Pennsylvania State University

DEFINITIONS OF HEALTH

Health, as described by the World Health Organization (WHO, 1987), is a life-long process of sociological, psychological, spiritual, and physical adaptation to organismic and environmental influences. This definition of health, which is considered a standard, necessitates a state of complete physical, mental, and social well-being and not merely the absence of disease. WHO's definition, however, has been criticized because it may be too broad to be realistically attained. Currently, multiple definitions of health are being proposed, all of which emphasize the connections of specific individual, contextual, and cultural components of health. For example, personal health status can be defined as the interrelationships of personal lifestyles with homes, schools, work sites, and health-care contexts; and environmental conditions such as tolerable climate, available nutritious foods, adequate shelter, clean air, and pure water (Edlin & Golanty, 1985). The report of the Joint Committee on Health Education Terminology (Ames et al., 1991) suggests that healthful lifestyles entail a series of "health enhancing behaviors, shaped by internally consistent values, attitudes, beliefs, and external social and cultural forces" (p. 178).

Most laypeople view health as more than simply the absence of illness, including mental, social, and behavioral factors. A more inclusive definition also is considered appropriate by adolescents: Being healthy might include living up to one's potential, functioning physically, mentally, and socially; and experiencing positive emotional states (Millstein & Litt, 1990). In one study of adolescent health conceptions, less than 30% of the participants' descriptions of health were to *not* be sick; with older adolescents having less foci on the absence of disease than did younger ones (Millstein & Irwin, 1987). Adolescents express a wide range of health concerns about such things as nervousness, dental problems, menstrual problems, acne, drugs, sexually transmissible diseases, pregnancy, emotional needs, and social interactions with school, parents, and family (Parcel, Nader, & Meyer, 1977). Overall, adolescents attribute more importance to their health status than most adults believe they do.

HEALTH FOR ADOLESCENTS

Historically, adolescence has been considered a relatively healthy period of the life cycle because diseases typically are not prominent. Today, however, this perception of adolescence no longer seems appropriate. It is quite possible that adolescent health status may be grossly underconsidered because traditional mortality and morbidity estimates are based on biomedical indicators (e.g., hospital discharge rates, physician services, and treatable conditions). Morbidity and mortality among adolescents often results from preventable social, environmental, and behavioral factors (Irwin & Millstein, 1986). For example, preventable mortality among adolescents includes injury, homicide, and suicide. Preventable morbidity, which occurs at much higher rates than adolescent mortality, include injury, unintended pregnancy, and substance abuse. All of these conditions can be moderately to severely debilitating, producing negative health outcomes that are not readily apparent until adulthood. The perception of adolescence as a healthy period of the life span seems inappropriate for other reasons as well. Considering adolescents as a healthy group obscures the heterogeneity among youth and the significantly different health problems for those of differing ages, races, ethnicities, or genders.

The perception of adolescents as a healthy group may be even more inaccurate in the future. Over the next few decades, the health status of adolescents is expected to decline due to the changing sociodemographic composition of youth (Millstein, 1989):

> Compared with adolescents of today, the youth of tomorrow are far more likely to be poorly educated, non-English speaking, and located in metropolitan areas. They are more likely to have been raised in poverty, by a single parent, and to be members of a racial or ethnic minority group. . . .

The well-documented relation between poverty and poorer health status suggests that these sociodemographic changes will have a significant impact on the health of adolescents. (p. 838)

Thus, there is reason for great concern for the current health of adolescents and that of future generations.

The perspective that we propose, in the chapters to follow, is that adolescence is an ideal time for initiating health promotion. Unique developmental changes occur in the second decade of life; all occurring in unique contexts. Periods of rapid change in psychological, physical, and social status provide a window of opportunity for changing adolescents' beliefs and perceptions about their health behaviors, attitudes, and values. In addition, developmental qualities that may contribute to stressfulness of adolescence (e.g., preoccupation with body and self-image) could well be used to promote the health and well-being of adolescents. Thus, adolescents can benefit greatly from the availability of health promotion and disease prevention activities, strategies, and educational programs that are well organized and effectively implemented.

HEALTH PROMOTION

Health promotion has been described as any combination of educational, organizational, economic, and environmental supports for behavior conducive to health (Green, 1984). Specifically, the promotion of health has been viewed as a series of relationships between (a) health education strategies (e.g., health services, health promotion, and health protection), (b) processes of change (e.g., organizing resources; predisposing, enabling, and reinforcing factors; and regulating environments), and (c) objectives for intermediate outcomes (e.g., access to preventive health-care services, behavioral enhancement, and environmental change) (Green & Anderson, 1986). Mechanic (1990) noted that effective health promotion requires a deeper scrutiny of community structures and routine activities of everyday life, as well as strong interventions such as regulatory efforts to restrict adolescents' accessibility to harmful substances such as tobacco, alcohol, and other drugs.

In spite of definitions of health promotion as efforts designed to help individuals make lifestyle changes to acquire optimal health, much of what is classified as health promotion remains oriented toward disease processes (e.g., reducing obesity, high blood pressure, alcohol abuse, and sexually transmissible diseases) (Saunders, 1988). Further, very few of these health promotion efforts have been specifically focused on promoting the health of adolescents. In fact, it has been acknowledged that "one of the most neglected opportunities in disease prevention and health promotion has been the thoughtful exploration of how to reach large numbers of adolescents with preventive approaches" (Hamburg & Takanishi, 1989, p. 826). Often, the health promotion programs offered to early adolescents have resulted in limited success due to the absence of strong theoretical approaches that integrate the developmental, biological, social, and contextual characteristics of adolescence. In addition, the effects of promoting healthful lifestyles during adolescent years for longer term health and development remain a virtually unexplored area of research.

What is clear, however, is that health promotion during the early adolescent years must consider individual adolescent characteristics, the contexts in which adolescents develop (e.g., home, school, community, and peers) and the "goodness of fit" between the two. To this end, the chapters in this section examine ways in which individual adolescent developmental processes (e.g., biological and psychological) interact with the contexts (e.g., family and work) of adolescent development to enhance or impede general and specific health promotion efforts. The theoretical framework for this section is presented in chapter 14 by Susman, Koch, Maney, and Finkelstein. The authors delineate unique developmental changes occurring in adolescence and describe how these create windows of opportunity for health promotion. The rationale for an integrated developmental and contextual approach to adolescent health promotion research, program, and service development and implementation is set forth.

Achterberg and Shannon (chapter 15) highlight some of the major nutritional issues of concern to researchers and practitioners interested in adolescents. The need to promote nutrition education research and programs is emphasized, particularly for special adolescent populations such as those with weight control concerns, eating disorders, undernourished, "out of the mainstream," pregnant youth, alcohol abusers, and athletes.

Vocational and career roles are recognized as core parts of identity, and hence of healthy psychosocial development during adolescence. In turn, "good fits" between the individual's personal characteristics and the demands of the workplace are associated with physical and psychosocial health; poor fits are associated with health problems. Accordingly, Vondracek (chapter 16) integrates theory and research in support of a developmental contextual framework for vocational development in his chapter.

In the final chapter, Koch (chapter 17) examines various aspects of healthful adolescent sexual development and expression, highlighting developmental and contextual influences. Recommendations for future research, as well as the development of policies and programs concerning healthy adolescent sexual development and expression are presented.

REFERENCES

Ames, E. E., Barr, H. H., & Bradford, B. J., Bradley, C. E., Cortese, P. A., Gordon, K. A., Hamburg, M. V., Lackey, C. C., Mico, P., & Seffrin, J. (1991). Report of the 1990 Joint Committee on Health Education Terminology. *Journal of Health Education, 22,* 173–184.
Edlin, E., & Golanty, E. (1985). *Health and wellness.* Boston: Jones & Bartlett.
Green, L. W. (1984). Health education models. In J. Matarazzo, S. Weiss, J. Herd, N. Miller, & S. Weiss (Eds.), *Behavioral health: A handbook of health enhancement and disease prevention* (pp. 181–198). New York: Wiley.
Green, L. W., & Anderson, C. L. (1986). *Community health* (5th ed.). St. Louis: Times/Mirror Mosby College.
Hamburg, D. A., & Takanishi, R. (1989). Preparing for life: The critical transition in adolescence. *American Psychologist, 44,* 825–827.
Irwin, C. E., & Millstein, S. G. (1986). Biopsychosocial correlates of risk-taking behaviors during adolescence. *Journal of Adolescent Health Care, 7,* 82–93.
Mechanic, D. (1990, January/February). Promoting health. *Society,* 16–22.
Millstein, S. G. (1989). Adolescent health: Challenges for behavioral scientists. *American Psychologist, 44,* 837–842.
Millstein, S. G., & Irwin, C. E. (1987). Concepts of health and illness: Different constructs or variations on a theme? *Health Psychology, 6,* 515–524.
Millstein, S. G., & Litt, I. F. (1990). Adolescent health. In S. S. Feldman & G. R. Elliot (Eds.), *At the threshold: The developing adolescent* (pp. 431–456). Cambridge, MA: Harvard University Press.
Parcel, G. S., Nader, P. R., & Meyer, M. P. (1977). Adolescent health concerns, problems and patterns of utilization in a triethnic urban population. *Pediatrics, 60,* 157–164.
Saunders, R. B. (1988, October/November). What is health promotion? *Health Education,* 14–18.
World Health Organization/United Nation Childrens' Fund. (1987). *Youth involvement in health development: Empowering youth for health: A challenge and a beginning.* New York: WHO.

14 Health Promotion in Adolescence: Developmental and Theoretical Considerations

Elizabeth J. Susman
Patricia Barthalow Koch
Dolores W. Maney
Jordan W. Finkelstein
The Pennsylvania State University

As recently as 1972, adolescence as a distinctive and potentially stressful phase of the life span was not adequately recognized (American Medical Association, 1988). Since the early 1980s, however, there has been an immense increase in both the quantity and quality of research on a myriad of topics related to adolescence. Growing out of this research is the recognition that during adolescence, particularly in early adolescence, health-related behavior and health status depends on complex interactions among developing physical characteristics, cognitive abilities, values, attitudes, perceptions, intentions, expectations, morals, and beliefs; and contextual factors. Given the complexity of this developmental period, it is not surprising that the state of theory and research on health promotion is less than ideal.

Yet adolescence is a highly relevant period of the life span in which to promote health. Adolescents become more capable than they were as children of making decisions about the desirability of health-promoting behaviors and acting upon those decisions. It follows that early adolescence may be a most propitious time to encourage youth to adopt healthful lifestyles and related beliefs, attitudes, skills, and intentions. The health behaviors that emerge during this time have the potential for affecting health not just during the adolescent period but throughout the entire life span. These health behaviors and cognitions may influence health in two distinct but related ways. First, behaviors detrimental to long-range health during adolescence may directly contribute to the development of pathologies that are not clinically manifested until adulthood (e.g., cardiovascular disease). Second, adolescents develop specific health perceptions and behavior patterns that they carry into adulthood (e.g., smoking). Yet, the effect of promoting healthful lifestyles during the adolescent years on longer term health remains a virtually unexplored area of research (Bruhn & Parcel, 1982). Thus, there is a lack of empirical findings on health promotion in early adolescence on which to base effective health policies and programs. We propose that future research, policy, and programming is increased in quantity and in quality and is based on theoretical models that feature developmental considerations regarding the uniqueness of adolescence.

In this chapter, a theoretical perspective is advanced suggesting that health promotion for adolescents should be based on efforts to promote total physical, emotional, and environmental health and not merely to prevent disease. A life-span developmental theoretical perspective is proposed that includes considerations of adolescent health promotion as part of a developmental continuum incorporating past health history as well as the future health of the adolescent. Within a life-span developmental perspective, it is possible to develop hypotheses that will incorporate individual adolescent biological and psychological characteristics and contextual factors, their synergisms and interactions that change across the life span, and that explain processes and mechanisms involved in health outcomes. An emphasis on developmental processes leads to considering covariances among health outcomes, rather than single health problems or diseases.

The chapter begins with a discussion of the major developmental changes of adolescence and the implications of these changes for health promotion. Theoretical models for considering health promotion are discussed and a person–contextual life-span developmental perspective is proposed for future health promotion efforts.

MAJOR CHANGES OF ADOLESCENCE

The years between 10 and 20 are replete with physical, physiological, psychological, and social changes. These changes have been described by Steinberg (1989) and others as falling into three categories: biological changes, cognitive changes, and social redefinition.

Biological Changes

The physiological changes of puberty are multiple, resulting from changes in endocrine functioning. The endocrine changes of puberty consist of substantial increases in the concentration of pituitary, adrenal, and gonadal hormones. (See Reiter, 1987, for a review of the major endocrine changes of puberty.)

These hormonal changes trigger the development of primary and secondary sex characteristics. In females, these changes usually begin between 8 and 14 years of age and include pubic and axillary hair growth, breast development, ovarian maturation, changes in body shape and proportions, and eventually menarche. In males, these changes usually occur between 10 and 15 years of age and include pubic and axillary hair growth, voice change, muscle development, spermatogenesis, and change in body shape. Adolescents are acutely aware of these changes in their bodies. New body awareness may increase adolescents' sensitivity to and interest in learning about the structure and function of their bodies and ways to enhance their development, appearance, and health.

The hormone-mediated physiologic and physical changes are accompanied by cognitive and role changes that are described later. Hormonal changes may directly affect adolescent behavior, including health behavior, by acting on the brain. These same changes may indirectly affect adolescent behavior. Peers, parents, teachers, and other adults who perceive the maturational process taking place may begin to behave differently toward adolescents. In turn, adolescents respond to changing expectations by others and modify their behavior to be consistent with the new environmental demands and constraints.

Cognitive Changes

Adolescent thinking is considered different from that of childhood thinking on three levels: (a) basic processing capacity or efficiency, (b) the knowledge base, and (c) cognitive self-regulation (Keating, 1990). Cognitive theories have provided a framework for explaining the development of children's concepts of health and illness. Piaget's theory of cognitive development, for instance, has been used extensively to examine children's modes of thinking about health. Concepts of health and illness change qualitatively with cognitive development in a fashion reflecting the progression from preoperational to concrete to formal operational thought (Kalnins & Love, 1982).

Among young children whose cognitive developmental stage is at a pre-operational level, answers to questions about the definition of health tend to be general, undifferentiated, circular in logic, superstitious, and egocentric. For example, 6-year-old children defined health as a concrete egocentric state that enabled them to play with friends, to go outside, and to be with their families (Natapoff, 1978). In contrast, children whose cognitive developmental stage is at a formal operational level are aware that health is a difficult concept to define, question if it were possible to define it at all, and use internal cues and feelings to describe their own health. Although children of all ages conceptualize health as a state arising from the observation of a series of practices, including eating proper food, getting adequate exercise, and keeping clean, cognitively advanced children go beyond these specific practices to view health as a state resulting from the interaction among body, mind, and environment (Palmer & Lewis, 1976).

The transition from concrete to operational thinking, a transition traversed by some but not all adolescents, has numerous implications for health promotion. With formal operations comes the ability to comprehend that illness may be a result of one's own actions. Adolescents correspondingly develop the recognition that they can influence their health in a positive direction and begin to form hypotheses about the relationship between cause and effect in health and illness (e.g., "If I reduce fats and starches in my diet, I will reduce my weight"). Finally, development of the ability to think abstractly, including thinking about thinking itself, enables adolescents to conceptualize the links between actions, emotions, health, and disease. This conceptual ability provides adolescents with opportunities to explore the interconnectedness of stressful emotional states, physiological processes, and health outcomes. In brief, increased cognitive capacities allow some adolescents to develop a perspective on mind–body interactions, or holistic health.

Social Redefinition

Changes in social status during adolescence involve three primary features: (a) achieving new and more mature relationships, (b) achieving some degree of emotional independence from parents and other adults, and (c) reconstruction of self-concept (Steinberg, 1989). The adolescent gains privileges and rights reserved for adults, including increased autonomy accompanied by increased adult expectations for self-management, personal responsibility, and social interaction. The complex interaction of changing cognitive abilities and socialization experiences contributes to the reconstruction of self-concept. Self-descriptions become less realistic and more differentiated because of pressures from the adolescent's differing social roles: child, student, friend, romantic partner, son or daughter. Adolescents also become more evaluative of self, with physical appearance and peer acceptance significantly impacting their self-esteem.

The implications of social redefinition for health promotion are infinite. Defining oneself as having low self-worth, or low self-esteem, leaves adolescents increasingly vulnerable to negative health outcomes. In an effort to increase self-worth and self-esteem, adolescents may engage in risk-taking behavior (e.g., alcohol and other drug consumption and sexual activities). In contrast, higher self-esteem has been associated with healthful practices (Laing & Bruess, 1989). High self-esteem may motivate adolescents to enhance their appearance through proper diet and exercise, thereby promoting health.

THEORETICAL PERSPECTIVES ON ADOLESCENT HEALTH

Although professionals are cognizant of the major changes happening in the lives of adolescents, health promotion for adolescents constitutes a new endeavor that does not have a strong practical or theoretical heritage. Much of the theoretical and empirical work on adolescent health has approached it from the perspective of prevention of health problems and intervention to reduce risky behaviors. This perspective on adolescent health mirrors the perspectives on adolescent development in general.

Stress and Coping. Stress, coping, and adaptation have played a dominant role in conceptualizations about the development of adolescents. Stress-related physiological processes may even have an effect on the tempo of pubertal development (Susman, Nottelmann, Dorn, Gold, & Chrousos, 1989). The source of the stress is derived both from the rapid physical changes that characterize adolescence and from the normative adolescent need for autonomy, experimentation, and testing the limits of rules and conformity (Millstein & Litt, 1990). Efforts to cope with these stressors consist of risk-taking and potentially health-compromising behaviors: smoking, fast driving, alcohol, and unprotected sex. These health-compromising behaviors also have been viewed as unsuccessful coping strategies.

Problem-Focused Theory. A prominent problem-focused theory to explain adolescent health is the problem behavior theory (Jessor & Jessor, 1977). The theory focuses on the organization of a network of variables and the specification of directions and patterns that constitute a deviance proneness or proneness to engage in problem behavior. The problem behavior theory explains the important transitions that occur during adolescence as behaviors that depart from the regulatory norms that define what is appropriate for the age or stage in life. This theoretical framework consists of three major systems: personality, perceived environment, and behavior. Each system is composed of structures of variables that, in interaction, determine the likelihood of occurrence of deviant or problem behavior (e.g., sexual intercourse, marijuana use, and political activism) as opposed to conforming or conventional behavior (e.g., academic achievement, church attendance, and extracurricular activities). Limitations of this theory for health promotion in adolescence are obvious because its focus is on deviance and problems versus health. In addition, its emphasis on regulatory or adult norms, conflicts with the real-life norms of adolescents (e.g., the majority of adolescents engage in sexual intercourse). The usefulness of a problem behavior theory to explain behavior from the adolescent point of view is questionable.

Cognitive Theory. As was discussed earlier, Piaget's cognitive developmental theory has been used to explain the development of concepts of health in children and adolescents. Most investigations, however, have been preoccupied with studying children's concepts of illness (e.g., Bibace & Walsh, 1980; Millstein, Adler, & Irwin, 1981; Susman, Dorn, & Fletcher, 1987). Kalnins and Love (1982) described the causes and effects of the illness emphasis as follows:

> This emphasis on illness may simply reflect an orientation toward a medical model in which illness (or perhaps more correctly the cost associated with illness) is the problem, and individual prevention seen as the solution. Whatever the reason may be, the result is a dearth of knowledge about what children really think about *health,* how they perceive the relationship between health and illness and their own role in maintaining health. (p. 114)

It should also be recognized that a child's or adolescent's health concepts are influenced by factors other than cognitive abilities. These factors include personality characteristics, health status and contextual variables like family background, and ethnicity (Dielman, Leech, Becker, Rosenstock, & Horvath, 1982). As within the stress and coping approach, a medical model has been used to explain illness as opposed to health processes.

Health Belief Model. The Health Belief Model (HBM; Becker, 1974) has been used much more extensively to examine adult rather than child and adolescent health behaviors. The HBM consists of the following dimensions: perceived susceptibility to the health concern, perceived severity of the health concern, perceived benefits of taking certain actions to avoid the concern or change behavior, perceived barriers to taking such actions, and "cues to action" that help motivate persons to take action. The dimension of the model that has received the most attention in studying children's and adolescents' health beliefs and behaviors has been perceived susceptibility, also termed *perceived vulnerability* (Gochman & Saucier, 1982a, 1982b; Kalnins & Love, 1982). Perceived vulnerability toward illness and accidents has been found to be quite stable throughout childhood and adolescence, leading researchers to conclude that perhaps perceived vulnerability should be viewed as a personality characteristic.

Because the HBM is a psychosocial model, it can only explain the variance in health behavior attributed to attitudes and beliefs. The model appears to be useful when applied to situations where health is highly valued and cues to action are widely prevalent (Janz & Becker, 1984). With regard to children and adolescents, the HBM has been criticized as being less than useful because findings indicate that many young people show little concern for their health (Kalnins & Love, 1982). The HBM also is not developmental in perspective that results in a total disregard for the dynamic processes (e.g., changes in cognition and peer relationships) that influence adolescent health.

To summarize the limitations of past theoretical frameworks, it was concluded from a special conference on the "Health Behavior of Children" that:

> Concepts need to be sharper and clearer, and they need to be integrated with theory. Theory needs to be integrated with programs, measures need to improved, health-related variables need to be widened, and norms and standards to be developed. (Bruhn & Parcel, 1982, p. 247)

Health Promotion: A Person–Contextual Approach. Theories of adolescent development traditionally have focused on characteristics of individuals to explain developmental outcomes. More recent theories of adolescent development suggest that development is a product both of individual characteristics and the influence of specific contexts—families, peer groups, and schools (see Feldman & Elliott, 1990). With the recognition that processes of adolescent development are modified by features of the context, the study of the effects of contexts per se has begun to be considered (Feldman & Elliott, 1990). The life-span perspective of human development is one approach to understanding adolescent development that incorporates processes within the individual as well as processes within the context. We propose a theoretical model for adolescent health promotion based on the following propositions. Health promotion activities should: (a) recognize the dynamic behavioral and physiological developmental processes that characterize adolescence, and (b) take into account the specific contexts in which adolescents develop (e.g., home, peer group, family, school, and community). These two propositions are derived from the life-span perspective on development during the adolescent years (e.g., Lerner, 1987).

Life-Span Developmental Perspective. Since the 1970s, a concept of human development based on theoretical and empirical studies from a number of disciplines has emerged. This new concept has emphasized the continuities and discontinuities in development. From these many studies and theoretical speculations, the life-span perspective has emerged. This perspective involves a set of interrelated ideas that make general predictions about what factors, or set of factors, should be most important in predicting the development of individuals over time. The life-span perspective, with its emphasis on continuities and discontinuities, is particularly relevant to explaining processes involved in adolescent development (Lerner, 1987; see also Lerner, chapter 1, this volume). This perspective is particularly appropriate for examining individual differences in health promotion attitudes, beliefs, intentions, and behaviors as well as health outcomes (see later discussion). Finally, the life-span perspective emphasizes the incorporation of different levels of analysis for understanding outcomes.

The three key concepts of the life-span perspective (Lerner, 1987) that are particularly relevant to our perspective on health promotion are *developmental contextual, embeddedness,* and *dynamic interaction.* The concept of developmental contextualism encompasses the belief that adolescent organismic changes in individual functioning are moderated by social contexts. Embeddedness is the notion that the essence of human life exists at multiple levels (e.g., biological, individual-psychological, dyadic, community, societal, cultural, ecological, and historical). The adolescent's functioning at any point in time is related to the dynamic interaction of all or some of these variables at the various levels (biological to family contextual). The concept of dynamic interaction encompasses the notion that the multiple levels are in constant interaction.

The dynamic interaction of variables at various levels relevant to promoting health can best be illustrated through an example: Iron deficiency is a problem affecting approximately 11% of boys and 17% of girls (NHANES II, 1985). In this case, Deborah Jones became a lacto-ovo-vegetarian at age 13 when her friends convinced her (sociocultural context) that eating the flesh of dead animals is barbaric. Her parents were not pleased but encouraged their adolescent daughter (familial context) to take a multivitamin supplement and iron tablets to prevent nutritional deficiencies (inner-biological). Deborah felt that she was young and healthy enough so she did not take the pills regularly (individual-psychological). She subsequently developed depleted iron stores and became anemic (inner-biological). Fatigue and lethargy was a result of her anemic state and Deborah became too tired to concentrate on her school work. Her grades fell (school context) because her cognitive abilities (individual-psychological) were impaired secondary to iron deficiency.

As demonstrated through this example, the nature of the interactions among variables across multiple levels can be described as circular functions (Schneirla, 1957) or reciprocal interactions. Reciprocal interaction views the individual as entering a situation with certain characteristics. These characteristics are acted upon by the persons and structure of the situation, such that there is feedback to individuals about their characteristics. In turn, individuals are affected and may change some of these characteristics based on the feedback from the situation.

The prediction of outcomes for the adolescent in the previous example with regard to nutrition would involve examining the most potent variables at multiple levels of analysis (main effects) and the interaction among the levels of analysis. The concept of reciprocal interactions between the individual and the environment has been reconceptualized as "goodness of fit" (Lerner, 1987). Adolescents bring individual characteristics to a setting. There are demands placed on the individual by virtue of the physical or social components of the setting. The individual interacts dynamically with the setting resulting in an observable outcome. This model is more predictive of outcomes in the setting when there is an adequate or good fit between the characteristics of the individual and the demands of the setting. For instance, in the school setting, an adolescent who is healthy, has good attention skills, and is eager to learn will likely fit the demands of most traditional schools that require sustained vigilance and a positive attitude toward learning. The feedback that such an adolescent receives would reinforce positive health and social behaviors, so that the circular reactions lead to a good fit for the adolescent. On the other hand, an adolescent who has emotional or health problems and is inattentive may bring to the school setting less than an optimal interest in learning and decreased vigilance. The school context usually reacts to the less healthy adolescent by assigning poor grades and punishment for inattention. Thus, there will not be a good fit between the adolescent and the school context.

The goodness of fit concept is important for understanding the health of adolescents in the various major contexts of development, including home, school, peer, work, and health-care settings. When considering health promotion efforts, the goodness of fit between individual developmental characteristics of adolescents—perceptions of their health, health status, motivation to achieve good health—and the family, peer, workplace, and school environments is likely to influence adolescent health-promoting behaviors. Characteristics of adolescents that might be associated with noncompliance with health-promoting activities (e.g., the main effects of disinterested attitudes toward health) may be modified by characteristics of the peer, school, family, and community contexts (e.g., social support for health-promoting activities). The ultimate aim of health-promoting activities, then, is to improve the goodness of fit between adolescents and the multiple context in which they develop.

RECOMMENDATIONS

To identify the factors that promote adolescent health, the following four recommendations are proposed. First, we suggest the use of a life-span perspective to health promotion. This perspective emphasizes developmental processes incorporating both organismic and contextual factors that interact across the life span to influence health outcomes. Such an emphasis on developmental processes and dynamic interaction leads to a holistic approach to health promotion rather than a focus on single aspects of morbidity or mortality. Past adolescent health research largely focused on specific, presumed independent, health problems including unintended pregnancy, alcohol and other drug abuse, and eating disorders, among others. Little attention was given to considering how one outcome might co-occur with other outcomes. A focus on single-disease outcomes has contributed to fragmentation and inconsistencies in adolescent health-related programs, policies, and services. Within a life-span perspective, optimal health, as well as health problems, are viewed as evolving from interrelated organismic biological, psychological, social, and contextual processes.

Our second recommendation is that interventions should be designed to promote optimal adolescent health and development rather than interventions to change unhealthy behavior or treat illness. Rather than concentrating on the processes of negative health-related behaviors, the American Medical Association (1988) now encourages research and health-promoting activities that will provide adolescents and their families with knowledge, skills, incentives, and necessary supports and choices to enhance adolescent health status. In addition, although the state of perfect health may be an unattainable goal, the achievement of high-level wellness, a state in which individuals find life productive and stimulating is one possible realistic goal of health-promoting activities (Green & Anderson, 1986).

Our third recommendation is to focus research efforts on the adolescents' perceptions of their own health, health beliefs, attitudes, values, and health-related expectations rather than health information alone. Past research efforts into the effects of the acquisition of health information on the promotion of healthy behaviors have shown little positive results (Gold & Kelly, 1988) and there is little evidence that correct or increased knowledge is related to the ultimate adoption of healthy behaviors among children (Rothman & Bryne, 1981). Because adolescent health-related expectations, intentions, values, and cognitions are only now beginning to be studied, it seems critical to examine these processes within their appropriate developmental contexts.

Our last recommendation involves supporting interdisciplinary study of health promotion in early adolescence. The new, exciting, and promising trend is for health professionals to work in collaboration with professionals from fields not usually thought of as health related. Disciplines now collaborating on research, education, program, and policy issues include adolescent medicine, anthropology, endocrinology, health education, human development, nursing, political science, psychology, and sociology. The processes of health promotion are so complex that no single discipline can attend to all of the factors involved.

SUMMARY AND CONCLUSIONS

Health promotion for adolescents has not been a priority for the health of our nation. Professional organizations now, however, are recommending comprehensive health-promoting activities to identify, quantify, prevent, and remediate the broad spectrum of threats to the physical, cognitive, emotional, and social well-being of U.S. adolescents. Although adolescents generally are considered to be a healthy group, this is only true in regard to the absence of major diseases. Adolescents are at risk for health threats from a variety of social, environmental, and lifestyle causes. To adequately promote health in adolescents, a stronger developmental approach encompassing the dynamic changes that occur within individuals (organismic changes), as well as within historical and cultural environments (contexts) is proposed. We propose a life-span developmental perspective that places adolescent health promotion in a developmental continuum, incorporating past history and current health status as well as the future health of the adolescent. Within a life-span developmental perspective, the emphasis also is on identifying the goodness of fit between adolescent organismic and contextual factors and their synergisms and interactions, as they change across the life span to influence health behaviors and health outcomes. The emphasis on organismic and contextual developmental processes leads to focusing on the interrelatedness of health issues during adolescence, rather than on single aspects of morbidity and mortality such as unintended pregnancy, drug abuse, and eating disorders. Optimal health, as well as health problems, evolve from interrelated physiological, psychological, and contextual processes. A perspective that considers only a unitary health problem outcome has contributed to fragmentation and inconsistencies in adolescent health-related programs, policies, and services.

In addition, health promotion interventions for adolescents must be available (programs must exist), accessible (geographically convenient and affordable), appropriate (address issues and use methods relevant to adolescents), and acceptable to adolescents and to the contexts (e.g., home, school, recreation, or community) in which adolescents develop. To accomplish this, health promotion programs must be based on and address the attitudes, beliefs, expectations, values, intentions, and perceptions of adolescents. Health promotion programs built on such foundations will have a greater likelihood of being consistent with adolescent developmental processes and contexts and have a potentially greater positive effect on healthful adolescent development.

To promote adolescent health, providers of health promotion services must be: (a) confident that their efforts are soundly based in theory and supported by empirical research, (b) educated to effectively provide health promotion services, and (c) adequately rewarded (reimbursed by payers) for providing health promotion services to this age group. Finally, society should recognize the need for health promotion services for adolescents and provide both financial and other substantive support for the conduct of research, development of policies, and implementation of health promotion programs for adolescents.

REFERENCES

American Medical Association. (1988, November). *AMA white paper on adolescent health* (abridged and edited). (Available from the AMA Department of Adolescent Health, 535 North Dearborn Street, Chicago, Illinois 60610).

Becker, M. H. (Ed.). (1974). The health belief model and personal health behavior. *Health Education Monograph,* 324–508.

Bibace, R., & Walsh, M. (1980). Development of children's concepts of illness. Pediatrics, 66, 912–917.

Bruhn, J. G., & Parcel, G. S. (1982). Current knowledge about the health behavior of young children: A conference summary. *Health Education Quarterly, 9*(2 & 3), 142–238 & 163–259.
Dielman, T. E., Leech, S., Becker, M. H., Rosenstock, I. M., & Horvath, W. J. (1982). Parental and child health beliefs and behavior. *Health Education Quarterly, 9*(2&3), 156–173.
Feldman, S. S., & Elliott, G. R. (1990). Progress and promise of research on adolescence. In S. S. Feldman & G. R. Elliott (Eds.), *At the threshold: The developing adolescent* (pp. 479–505). Cambridge, MA: Harvard University Press.
Gochman, D. S., & Saucier, J. F. (1982a). Labels, systems, and motives: Some perspectives for future research and programs. *Health Education Quarterly, 9*(2&3), 263–270.
Gochman, D. S., & Saucier, J. F. (1982b). Perceived vulnerability in children and adolescents. *Health Education Quarterly, 9*(2 & 3), 46–59.
Gold, R. S., & Kelly, M. A. (1988). Is knowledge really power? *Health Education, 19*(4), 40–46.
Green, L. W., & Anderson, C. L. (1986). *Community health*. St. Louis: Times/Mirror Mosby College Publishing.
Janz, N. K., & Becker, M. H. (1984). The Health Belief Model: A decade later. *Health Education Quarterly, 11*(1), 1–47.
Jessor, R., & Jessor, S. L. (1977). *Problem behavior and psychosocial development: A longitudinal study of youth*. New York: Academic Press.
Kalnins, I., & Love, R. (1982). Children's concepts of health and illness and implications for health education. *Health Education Quarterly, 9*(2&3), 104–115.
Keating, D. P. (1990). Adolescent thinking. In S. S. Feldman & G. R. Elliott (Eds.), *At the threshold: The developing adolescent* (pp. 54–90). Cambridge, MA: Harvard University Press.
Laing, S. J., & Bruess, C. E. (1989). *Entering adulthood: Connecting health, communication and self-esteem*. Santa Cruz, CA: Network Publications.
Lerner, R. M. (1987). A life-span perspective for early adolescence. In R. M. Lerner & T. T. Foch (Eds.), *Biological-psychosocial interactions in early adolescence: A life-span perspective* (pp. 1–6). Hillsdale, NJ: Lawrence Erlbaum Associates.
Millstein, S. G., Adler, N. E., & Irwin, C. E. (1981). Conceptions of illness in young adolescents. *Pediatrics, 68,* 834–839.
Millstein, S. G., & Litt, I. F. (1990). Adolescent health. In S. S. Feldman & G. R. Elliott (Eds.), *At the threshold: The developing adolescent* (pp. 431–456). Cambridge, MA: Harvard University Press.
Natapoff, J. N. (1978). Children's views of health: A developmental study. *American Journal of Public Health, 68,* 995–1000.
National Health and Nutrition Examination Survey (NHANES II). (1985). National Center for Health Statistics, Washington, DC.
Palmer, B. B., & Lewis, C. (1976). Development of health attitudes and behavior. *Journal of School Health, 46,* 400–402.
Reiter, E. D. (1987). Neuroendocrine control process. Pubertal onset and progression. *Journal of Adolescent Health Care, 8,* 479–491.
Rothman, A., & Byrne, N. (1981). Health education for children and adolescents. *Review of Educational Research, 51,* 85–100.
Schneirla, T. C. (1957). The concept of development in comparative psychology. In D. B. Harris (Ed.), *The concept of development* (pp. 78–108). Minneapolis: University of Minnesota Press.
Steinberg, L. (1989). *Adolescence*. New York: Alfred A. Knopf.
Susman, E., Dorn, L. D., & Fletcher, J. C. (1987). Reasoning about illness in ill and healthy

children and adolescents: Cognitive and emotional developmental aspects. *Journal of Developmental and Behavioral Pediatrics, 8,* 266–273.

Susman, E. J., Nottelmann, E. D., Dorn, L. D., Gold, P. A., & Chrousos, G. P. (1989). The physiology of stress and behavioral development. In D. S. Palermo (Eds.), *Coping with uncertainty: Behavioral and developmental perspectives* (pp. 17–38). Hillsdale, NJ: Lawrence Erlbaum Associates.

15 Nutrition and Adolescence

Cheryl L. Achterberg
Barbara Shannon
The Pennsylvania State University

Nutrition plays a central role in the biological, behavioral, and social changes that characterize adolescence. This chapter highlights some of the major nutrition issues of concern to human developmentalists interested in adolescent populations. In general, the dietary intake of adolescents is a concern because of the short- and long-term effects that their food choices may have on their growth and overall health.

In this context of health promotion and disease prevention, nutrition in adolescence is important from an individual physiological perspective as well as a public health perspective. For example, evidence continues to accumulate indicating that cardiovascular disease, which has a nutritional component, begins in childhood (Lauer & Clarke, 1990). Recently, researchers have also suggested that the typical food intake patterns of adolescents may also lead to diet-related cancers (Slattery, Schumacker, West, Robinson, & French, 1990) as well as osteoporosis (Anderson, 1991). The biggest public health concern, however, is obesity (Anderson, 1991). Food habits and nutrition concerns are also important in the context of interpersonal relationships among peers, family, and ethnocultural groups. For example, what an individual chooses to eat or reject can significantly influence social acceptance either directly or indirectly (through change in weight, appearance, and/or self-esteem). Thus, nutrition is a major factor in adolescent development at both the micro- (physiological and cellular) and macro- (or social) level. In light of this fact, it is surprising how little research has been performed that specifically addresses adolescents' nutrition requirements and dietary habits.

PHYSICAL GROWTH AND DEVELOPMENT

Adolescence is the only time in the postnatal life cycle when the rate of physical growth actually increases and it is second only to infancy in the percent of physical growth accomplished as adolescents gain rapidly in height and weight, alter body composition, and achieve sexual maturation. In terms of growth and physical development, the most important nutrition concerns at the macronutrient level are the extremes of over- and undereating (Anderson, 1991). At the micronutrient level, the most important considerations have not changed over the decades: Adolescent females are at risk for inadequate amounts of dietary calcium and iron (Anderson, 1991).

Menarche is related to height attainment and according to some studies, body weight and total dietary energy intake (Meyer, Moisan, Marcoux, & Bouchard, 1990). Girls who begin menstruation earlier tend to weigh more than their premenarche peers and are already above average weight by age 7 (Forbes, 1991). Underwood (1991) speculated that the causative factor of this phenomenon might be somatomedin. Somatomedin is produced by growth hormone and stimulates growth of bone and certain other tissues. Its production declines with food deprivation and increases with an improved diet. Other researchers, however, note that dietary composition, dietary fat in particular, and total body fat are not associated with the onset of menarche (Meyer et al., 1990).

Unfortunately, relatively little research has been performed on nutrient needs in adolescence from a developmental perspective. Of all the age groups identified in the Recommended Dietary Allowances (RDA), fewer data on nutrient requirements are available for early and middle adolescence than for any other age group in the life cycle (National Research Council [NRC], 1986; U.S. Department of Health and Human Services, 1988). An abundance of data are available on infancy, early childhood, and the college years. Adolescent requirements are, therefore, primarily extrapolated from data on these other age groups (U.S. Department of Health and Human Services, 1988).

Effect of Macronutrient Intake on Growth and Development

Between 5% and 10% of U.S. adolescents are obese and a much greater percent are overweight (Anderson, 1991). A sedentary lifestyle in adolescence is now considered an initial component of the etiology of adolescent obesity (Gortmaker, Dietz, & Cheung, 1990), along with an excessive intake of calories (Underwood, 1991). As Anderson noted, "Because obesity is both a disease in its own right and a precursor to atherosclerotic cardiovascular disease, hypertension, adult-onset diabetes mellitus, and other diseases of adulthood, it represents a significant risk to health when it appears so early in life" (p. 8). The effects of undernutrition are discussed in the section about eating disorders.

Effect of Micronutrients on Growth and Development

Osteoporosis may also be a disease of early life that may, in part, be prevented by an adequate intake of calcium (Anderson, 1991). Matkovic et al. (1979) introduced the concept of peak bone mass as a major factor in protection against later life fractures. Recent studies have also underscored the importance of maximizing bone mass during the early adolescent years (NRC, 1989). Although genetics, endocrine factors, and physical activity play a role in bone mass and osteoporosis, nutritional status is also an integral component (Peck et al., 1988). The skeleton can add up to 7%–8% in bone mass/year during puberty and early adolescence. A difference of only 7% in total bone mass may be responsible for more than a 50% difference in fracture rate later in life. However, calcium intake among teenage girls starts to decline during puberty when requirements are maximal (Matkovic, 1991). Few teenage girls meet their RDA of 1,200 mg of calcium/day (Wright, Guthrie, Wang, & Bernardo, 1991), fewer still achieve suggested intakes of 1,600 mg/day (Matkovic, 1991).

Athletic amenorrhea, low body weight, and anorexia nervosa also have an adverse effect on bone mass, all of which are often linked and are more common in the adolescent female population than in any other group (Henderson, 1991). Numerous studies have documented a 19% decrease in bone mineral mass in the proximal femur, an 11% decrease in the shaft of the radius, and more than a 20% decrease in the lumbar spine among young females diagnosed with anorexia nervosa (Henderson, 1991). It is unknown as yet whether recovery from anorexia nervosa, resumption of normal menses, and an increase in body weight will result in recovery of normal bone density. The significance of delayed menarche due to heavy athletic training on bone mass is also unknown.

When menarche begins in females, menstrual losses of iron must be taken into consideration (Forbes, 1991). Therefore, the RDA for iron in girls aged 11–18 is 15 mg versus 12 mg for boys (NRC, 1986). Because the U.S. diet contains an estimated 6 mg iron/1,000 kcals, it is difficult for adolescent girls to meet their requirement (Marinho & King, 1980), especially if they are disinclined to eat meat. Young males are less problematic because they eat a larger number of calories and have lower iron requirements (Gong & Spear, 1988). However, iron deficiency is prevalent in adolescents of both genders, and in teens of all races and socioeconomic backgrounds (Gong & Spear, 1988).

The growth requirement for nitrogen and minerals during adolescence is lower for girls than boys (Forbes, 1991) because girls are not gaining as much lean body mass. Nevertheless, all mineral requirements are thought to increase during adolescence (Gong & Spear, 1988). There is very little information available, however, on trace mineral requirements for adolescents, in part due to the absence of reliable data on mineral absorption from the gastrointestinal tract (Forbes, 1991). More research is needed to determine adolescents' nutritional needs at different stages of maturation to accommodate variation in growth onset and rate (Gong & Spear, 1988).

Nutrient deficiencies may contribute to growth retardation as well as to the increased risk of ill health in both the short- and long-term development of adolescents (Gong & Spear, 1988). Growth retardation, in turn, may affect psychosocial development, self-efficacy, and self-image. Overnutrition on the other hand, may contribute to early onset of menarche, and other, but equally serious psychosocial sequelae such as stunted psychological development, depression, low self-esteem, low self-efficacy, and dysfunctional coping patterns (Wadden & Stunkard, 1985).

SOCIAL TRENDS AND DIETARY INTAKE

The eating habits of adolescents have changed since the 1950s because of (a) greater freedom of choice, (b) greater purchasing power, and (c) societal changes in general (Underwood, 1991). Some important societal changes include an increase in television watching, a decrease in school physical education requirements, and a decrease in energy expenditure among adolescents (Underwood, 1991).

Dietary intake, food availability, and food preparation responsibilities vary depending on the family's living situation. In 1987, approximately 20% of all children less than 18 years old lived in families with incomes below the poverty line (Cornwell & Curtis, chapter 2, this volume). Where poverty limits financial resources available for food, simple inadequacy of enough to eat or of a variety of foods to eat may limit calorie intake, nutrient intake, or both. With the increased number of women in the labor force, more adolescents in all social classes are left to do food shopping and preparation for the entire family. Thus, their decisions, food shopping, and preparation skills affect not only their own nutritional status, but also the nutritional status of their families. In addition, there is a decided trend (almost 40% in 1987) toward more female-headed and single-parent households where adolescents may carry even greater family-care responsibilities (Cornwell & Curtis, chapter 2, this volume). To complicate the picture even further, it has been estimated that up to half of all U.S. children live in nontraditional family settings as parents separate, divorce, and remarry. In addition, hundreds of thousands of teens set up their own households each year (Cornwell & Curtis, chapter 2, this volume). As economic circumstances change in these situations, food availability may also become more or less critical. All of these situations may exacerbate the nutritional risk that adolescents are exposed to. It should also be noted that educational opportunities about food budgeting, management, preparation, and nutrition in the public school system are shrinking with the increasing demise of home economics programs (Shannon, Ervin, & Bernardo, in press).

Overall, the nutritional status of adolescents as a population group appears to be generally good (Farthing, 1991). With regard to food consumption trends, adolescents tend to consume more milk, fruit drinks, cereal, ice cream, cakes, cookies, snack foods, candy, sugar toppings, and peanut butter than adults but less coffee, tea, alcohol, cheese, and condiments (Wright et al., 1991). They also tend to fall short on dietary fiber because of inadequate intake of fruits, vegetables, whole grains, nuts, and seeds (Anderson, 1991). They are at greatest risk for low or marginal intakes of vitamins A and C, magnesium, calcium, iron, and B-6, with 20% or more of the adolescent population consuming 60% or less of the RDA for these nutrients (Wright et al., 1991). Other studies have indicated that adolescents are at risk for inadequate folacin intake based on serum and erythrocyte folacin values (Clark, Mossholder, & Gates, 1987). Furthermore, inadequate levels were not related to race or income level (Clark et al., 1987). It should be noted that snacks play as important a role in contributing needed calories, iron, and Vitamin A as do meals.

The role the USDA's School Lunch Program plays in setting food behavior patterns (as well as meeting nutrient requirements) needs to be ascertained. Dietary trends will also need to be monitored overall as changes in our food supply (e.g., an increase in the availability of products containing fat substitutes—Olestra and Simplesse—and/or sugar substitutes—aspartame) impact on family and adolescent food choices. Overconsumption of certain nutrients such as saturated fatty acids remains a primary concern, due to the association between dietary fat intake, cardiovascular disease, and certain types of cancer (NRC, 1989; U.S. Dept. of Health and Human Services, 1988). New findings, however, suggest that adolescents may, in fact, be lowering their fat intake similar to adults generally in the United States (Witschi, Capper, & Ellison, 1990).

It is well accepted that cardiovascular disease begins in early adulthood based on autopsy studies done in the Korean and Vietnam wars (Strong, 1986). Only recently has the relation between early childhood plasma cholesterol levels and atherosclerotic streaks in early adulthood been established (Newman et al., 1986). Therefore, a prudent diet (i.e., 30% of calories from fat) for all U.S. citizens over 2 years of age is recommended along with universal cholesterol screening in adults (NCEP, 1988). There is some debate as to when plasma screening should begin due to concerns for the possible psychological sequelae of labeling a youth as "sick" (Newman, Browner, & Hulley, 1990) as well as efficacy of the treatment (Lauer & Clarke, 1990). However, screening by family history alone misses an estimated 25%–50% of individuals with high plasma cholesterol. Because the public health costs are so great, it seems reasonable, therefore, to begin cholesterol screening in adolescence. Adolescents are rapidly approaching adulthood but any adverse physiological changes that their diet may have already wrought should be reversible. Within 5 to 10 years, however, interventions may be considerably less successful because youth are less accessible out of school. In addition, physiological changes may be further advanced and dietary patterns more firmly fixed in early adulthood than they are in adolescence.

SPECIAL POPULATIONS

Adolescent Childbearing. In the last half of the 1980s, about 11% of all female teens aged 15–19 became pregnant, resulting in 470,000 new births in 1987 (National Center for Health Statistics [NCHS], 1989). Pregnant teens are also at greater nutritional risk than any single group of teenagers (Farthing, 1991). The mother's own growth and development may be compromised by her fetus' extra demands. In addition, she will be at increased risk for iron-deficiency anemia, pregnancy-induced hypertension, and premature detachment of the placenta (ADA, 1989). For the baby, there is an increased risk of low birth weight (LBW), birth defects, and increased infant mortality in the first year as well as risks to cognitive and social development later on (Hayes, 1987). Therefore, adolescent pregnancy is considered a major public health problem in the United States.

Although many biological and environmental variables are involved with pregnancy outcome, nutrition is one of the most important, modifiable variables. Appropriate nutrition counseling can decrease the incidence of LBW, birth defects, premature delivery, hypertension, and eclampsia (ADA, 1989). Recent evidence by Skinner and Carruth (1991) indicate that pregnant teens do modify their diets to include more milk products and citrus fruits. However, further education is needed to change iron, calorie, and folacin intakes. Thus, pregnant adolescents should have nutrition intervention early and throughout the duration of their pregnancies (ADA, 1989).

A separate, but related issue is the form of feeding that adolescent mothers may choose for their babies. More data are needed about the effects of choosing breast-feeding versus bottle-feeding on infant growth and development as well as the adolescent mother's growth and development. One study indicates that during 16 weeks of lactation, the adolescent mother may be at risk for bone demineralization because of low intakes of calcium and phosphorus (Chan, Ronald, Slater, Hollis, & Thomas, 1982).

Weight Control/Eating Disorders. As adolescents develop, many become increasingly aware of, and sensitive about, their weight and appearance. Consequently, an estimated 60% or more of U.S. girls have been on a weight-loss diet by the time they reach Grade 9, although most are of normal weight for their height and age at the time (Rosen & Gross, 1987). Yet, obesity is also a legitimate public health concern among adolescents; between 10% and 25% are at least moderately overweight (Hoerr, 1985).

Whatever the motivation, weight-loss diets are of particular concern among this population because they may (a) impair growth and development, (b) impair short-term physical and emotional health, and (c) instill a negative cycling behavioral pattern damaging to long-term physical health and psychosocial development (NRC, 1989). Moreover, a substantial body of research is accumulating that suggests frequent weight fluctuation may be more damaging to health than stabilizing weight at a few extra pounds above the "ideal weight" (NRC, 1989). Although there is little evidence to suggest the precise roles that adolescent weight fluctuations play, it is apparent that such behavior patterns are initiated and learned during this period.

A significant proportion of adolescents (estimated between 2% and 19% depending on the study) also develop more serious pathological eating disorders characterized by anorexic (i.e., self-starvation) and/or bulimic (binge–purge) behaviors that can, if left untreated, lead to psychosocial problems, decreased heart rate, cardiac arrhythmias, hypotension, endocrine changes (Palla & Litt, 1988), and even death from congestive heart failure (Friedman, 1984). Some of those changes are due to reduced lean weight (as well as body fat) (Forbes, 1991). Bone mass may also be reduced (Henderson, 1991). Laboratory abnormalities include anemia, leukopenia (low white blood cell counts), hypoalbunemia (low serum protein values), and mild disturbances of thyroid function (Harris, 1991).

Because of the complexity of eating disorders, a multidisciplinary treatment regimen is best including correction of the medical complications, a refeeding program, family therapy, nutrition counseling, psychotherapy, and sometimes, drug intervention (Casper, 1986; Harris, 1991). A major obstacle to treatment success in anorexia nervosa is the patient's denial that any problem exists (Harris, 1991). Considerably more research is needed to determine how best to screen individuals at risk for developing eating disorders and to understand its occurrence from a developmental perspective. Certainly, social values regarding body image and female thinness play roles, but physiological and psychological explanations must be taken into account as well (Adams & Shafer, 1988). It is important to note that the prevalence of both anorexia nervosa and bulimia appear to be increasing in both male and female adolescent populations (Harris, 1991).

A separate, but related issue is the uncertainty about a biologically appropriate weight-loss regime during adolescence due to the lack of developmentally based data on growth in adolescence. Most programs recommend increased activity while holding caloric intake constant (to avoid growth retardation due to caloric deficits). However, better screening and assessment tools are needed as well as tested intervention strategies to enable adolescents to control their weight appropriately.

Weight gain is also of concern to many adolescent males, especially those who compete in athletic events such as football (Kris-Etherton, 1989). Up to half of these athletes try special diets in order to gain more weight (Rosen & Gross, 1987). In contrast, there is another group of boys who are highly concerned with losing weight, particularly high school wrestlers who try to "make weight" for competition (Forbes, 1991). Both groups may consume disproportionate amounts of protein, certain amino acids, or megadoses of selected vitamins (Kris-Etherton, 1989). These practices can create health risks (ADA, 1987).

Teens Who are "Out of the Mainstream." Relatively little research has been conducted to determine the nutritional status of adolescents who may be characterized as out of the mainstream, such as the homeless, runaways, drug addicts, individuals with AIDS, illegal immigrants, farm migrants, prostitutes, and adolescents living in correctional facilities or similar institutions. These youths are likely to be more vulnerable to undernutrition from of a lack of economic resources and access to food, health services, and education. Documentation of the incidence, severity, and chronicity of malnutrition among these population subgroups is lacking as well as interventions to improve their dietary intake. Due to the potential severity of undernutrition in these populations, research inquiries directed to these populations are essential (Blum, 1987).

Alcohol Abuse. Alcohol use and abuse is increasing in the U.S. teenage population and is recognized as a public health problem of major significance and widespread concern (Story & York, 1987). One recent study reported that over one third of seventh- and eighth-grade children were alcohol users (Farrow, Rees, & Worthington-Roberts, 1987). Other studies indicate that 89% of 10th graders have used alcohol and 38% had five or more drinks during the past 2 weeks (Staff, 1989). There are also at least 3.5 million teenage alcoholics in the United States (California Medical Association, 1990). Story and York (1987) reported that in a sample of native American adolescents, 15% drank alcohol daily.

The impact alcohol has on the nutritional status of adolescents is unclear (Anderson, 1991). Heavy alcohol use appears to be associated with a general pattern of poor dietary intake (as empty calories from alcohol and snack food items displace nutrient-rich foods such as fruit, vegetables, and milk), stunted physical growth, destructive social habits (Farrow et al., 1987), and a low folacin intake (Story & York, 1987). In addition, adolescent alcohol users have abnormally elevated serum iron concentrations, and males also have increased transferrin saturation (Friedman, Kramer, Mendoza, & Hammer, 1988). In adults these abnormalities are the precursors of hepatic iron overload and chronic liver damage. Further research is needed to document the net effect in adolescence (Anderson, 1991).

It also is critical to assess the impact that alcohol consumption has on Fetal Alcohol Syndrome and birth outcome among adolescent mothers. Teens should be educated about the risks of alcohol consumption to unborn children. Due to the severity of these issues, the need for applied research studies in this area is self-evident.

Inherited Diseases. It is beyond the scope of this chapter to discuss the full range of genetic diseases that either impair nutritional status and/or require a therapeutic diet to treat them. In most cases, the first clue to endocrine abnormalities or genetic disorders can be obtained from growth records (Underwood, 1991). The most prominent among the inherited, nutritionally related diseases is diabetes mellitus, affecting 1.6–1.8 of every 1,000 children ages 5–17 (Drash, 1987; National Diabetes Data Group, 1985). Cystic fibrosis, ileitis, and Tay-Sach's disease are other examples. Suffice it to say that diet interventions are critical to maintain life in these instances, but often are more problematic in adolescence as individuals try to assert their independence. Thus, eating restrictions/prescriptions may become battlegrounds in the adolescent's search for self-identity, jeopardizing not only the adolescent's physiological state but also his or her emotional and psychosocial development and family dynamics. Again, there is insufficient information in this domain to draw many conclusions, however, we can anticipate that more and more children will be identified early with genetically related conditions (e.g., hypercholesterolemia) and started on diet regimens in their youth. It is, therefore, essential to gather more information on dietary compliance in adolescence and experiment with various intervention strategies to preserve whatever health gains have been made earlier in childhood.

Athletes. The primary change in dietary requirements for adolescent athletes is an increase in calories, however, there are a number of physiological effects in heavy exercise that may contribute to other increased nutrient needs.

A significant number of female long distance runners as well as some swimmers, ballet dancers, gymnasts, and others suffer from exercise-induced amenorrhea that is also accompanied by decreased bone mineral, predisposing these athletes to osteoporosis (Henderson, 1991). At present it appears that the best treatment is to increase body weight (and specifically the percent of body fat) and to decrease exercise such that these athletes maintain menstruation (Lindberg, Powell, Hunt, Ducey, & Wade, 1987). Calcium supplementation and estradiol treatment need further investigation.

There also is evidence that iron deficiency is not uncommon among runners (whether it is caused by heavy running is still debated), and such deficiency negatively influences performance (Clement & Sawchuk, 1984). As discussed earlier, weight loss and weight gains are also important issues among adolescent athletes. For instance, adolescent wrestlers are considered at high risk for nutritional deficiencies or irregularities because they often engage in extreme dehydration and other weight-cutting procedures on a weekly basis (American College of Sports Medicine, 1976; Steen, Oppliger, & Brownell, 1988). But, the effects of these practices on growth and development have not been explored. Many questions also remain about the overall roles of nutrition in maximizing performance as well as in the repair of body tissue after extreme exertion. In summary, there is a great deal of opportunity for further research in nutrition, exercise, and the adolescent.

NUTRITION INTERVENTION STRATEGIES FOR ADOLESCENTS

Many health promotion, cardiovascular risk reduction, school-based educational interventions for adolescents have been launched in the United States (Farris, Frank, Webber, & Berenson, 1985; Killen et al., 1988; King et al., 1988; Shannon et al., in press; Stone, 1985). In these programs, classroom nutrition instruction has significantly affected, among other things, dietary knowledge, attitudes, and snack food choices. Other, general nutrition curricula have positively affected nutrition knowledge, attitudes, and intentions to include more nutrient-dense foods in the diet (Lewis, Brun, Talmage, & Rasher, 1988). These results suggest that school-based programming may be successful in changing behaviors both at school and in the home under a broad range of conditions (Crockett & Jacobs, 1988).

It should also be noted that adolescents know more about nutrition than they put into practice. Story and Resnick (1986) noted that 900 Minnesota teens did not implement their knowledge because of a lack of time, discipline, and/or a sense of urgency. Farthing (1991) noted, however, that teens may know general nutrition facts but less in terms of how to implement nutrition advice in food choice and food preparation behaviors. Others have noted that adolescents are not a single target audience, rather there are five distinctive subgroups with orientations toward hedonism, social/environmental factors, personal health, peer-supported health, or parent-supported health (Contento, Michela, & Goldberg, 1988). These authors further suggested that it would be beneficial to match nutrition education strategies and messages to specific adolescent subgroups to maximize effectiveness (Contento et al., 1988).

Perry et al. (1988) emphasized the need to incorporate parents with children's school-based nutrition education programming to ensure success. Cooperative Extension and 4-H offer other vehicles for intervening with nutrition education and health promotion programming with some adolescent groups. Media-based television, music, and even telephone approaches have been tested in limited situations, but the results are, as yet, inconclusive in terms of efficacy (Shannon et al., in press). These and many other alternatives to presenting information and motivation need to be explored further because (a) information learned in one setting is not necessarily transferred to other settings, and (b) health promotion messages need to be repeatedly reinforced in various contexts. Thus, a variety of communication strategies may prove more effective than any one by itself.

It is also worth noting the need for continued education among dietitians and others working in the nutrition management of adolescents. In one recent survey, a high majority of dietitians ($n = 549$) reported they had insufficient skills to deal with teens in counseling or educational settings regarding psychosomatic problems (87%), handicapping conditions (82%), sports nutrition (81%), alcohol (80%), or eating disorders (72%). Continuing education methods believed to be most beneficial by these respondents included small conferences, lectures with ample discussion, and "hands-on" workshops (Story & Blum, 1988).

FUTURE PROSPECTS

In summary, there are tremendous gaps in knowledge relative to the food habits and nutrition concerns of adolescence. Three primary foci emerge from this review including the identification of nutrient requirements during adolescence, special needs of the "nutritionally vulnerable" and/or "hard-to-reach" adolescents (i.e., pregnant, eating-disordered and out-of-the-mainstream youth), and appropriate intervention strategies to motivate the adoption and maintenance of life-long, health-promoting dietary habits and lifestyle decisions among normal adolescents.

In nearly all cases, longitudinal and developmental-type data are needed. In the realm of intervention studies, small case control studies are needed to evaluate process variables as well as to test the feasibility and efficacy of various intervention strategies in a broad range of communities and ethnocultural and socioeconomic contexts.

REFERENCES

Adams, L. B., & Shafer, M. B. (1988). Early manifestations of eating disorders in adolescents: Defining those at risk. *Journal of Nutrition Education, 20,* 307–313.

American College of Sports Medicine position stand on weight loss in wrestlers. (1976). *Sports Medicine Bulletin, 11,* 1–2.

American Dietetic Association. (1987). Position of The American Dietetic Association: Nutrition for physical fitness and athletic performance for adults. *Journal of The American Dietetic Association, 87,* 936–938.

American Dietetic Association. (1989). Position of the American Dietetic Association: Nutrition management of adolescent pregnancy. *Journal of The American Dietetic Association, 89,* 104.

Anderson, J. B. (1991). The status of adolescent nutrition. *Nutrition Today, 26,* 7–10.
Blum, R. (1987). Contemporary threats to adolescent health in the United States. *Journal of The American Medical Association, 257,* 3390–3395.
California Medical Association. (1990). *Health tips: Teenage alcoholism.* Index 418, 2 pp.
Casper, R. C. (1986). The pathophysiology of anorexia nervosa and bulimia nervosa. *Annual Review of Nutrition, 6,* 299–316.
Chan, G. M., Ronald, N., Slater, P., Hollis, J., & Thomas, M. R. (1982). Decreased bone mineral status in lactating adolescent mothers. *The Journal of Pediatrics, 101,* 767–770.
Clark, A. J., Mossholder, S., & Gates, R. (1987). Folacin status in adolescent females. *American Journal of Clinical Nutrition, 46,* 302–306.
Clement, D. B., & Sawchuk, L. L. (1984). Iron status and sports performance. *Sports Medicine, 1,* 65.
Contento, I. R., Michela, J. L., & Goldberg, C. L. (1988). Food Choice Among Adolescents: Population Segmentation by Motivations. *Journal of Nutrition Education, 20,* 289–298.
Crockett, S., & Jacobs, D. R. (1988). Parent involvement with children's health promotion. *American Journal of Public Health, 78,* 1156–1160.
Drash, A. L. (1987). *Clinical care of the diabetic child.* Chicago: Year Book Medical Publishers, Inc.
Farris, R. P., Frank, G. C., Webber, L. S., & Berenson, G. S. (1985). A nutrition curriculum for families with high blood pressure. *Journal of School Health, 55,* 110–112.
Farrow, J. A., Rees, J. M., & Worthington-Roberts, B. S. (1987). Health, developmental, and nutritional status of adolescent alcohol and marijuana abusers. *Pediatrics, 79,* 218–223.
Farthing, M. C. (1991). Current eating patterns of adolescents in the United States. *Nutrition Today, 26,* 35–39.
Forbes, G. B. (1991). Body composition of adolescent girls. *Nutrition Today, 26,* 17–20.
Friedman, I. M., Kraemer, H. C., Mendoza, F. S., & Hammer, L. D. (1988). Elevated serum iron concentration in adolescent alcohol users. *American Journal of Diseases in Children, 142,* 156–159.
Friedman, E. J. (1984). Death from ipecac intoxication in a patient with anorexia nervosa. *American Journal of Psychiatry, 141,* 702–703.
Gong, E. J., & Spear, B. A. (1988). Adolescent growth and development: Implications for nutrition needs. *Journal of Nutrition Education, 20,* 273–279.
Gortmaker, S. L., Dietz, W. H., & Cheung, L. W. Y. (1990). Inactivity, diet, and the fattening of America. *Journal of The American Dietetic Association, 90,* 1247–1252.
Harris, R. T. (1991). Anorexia nervosa and bulimia nervosa in female adolescent. *Nutrition Today, 26,* 30–34.
Hayes, C. D. (1987). *Risking the future: Adolescent sexuality, pregnancy and childbearing* (Vol. 1). Washington, DC: National Academy Press.
Henderson, R. C. (1991). Bone health in adolescence. *Nutrition Today, 26,* 25–29.
Hoerr, S. (1985). An overlooked factor in adolescent obesity. *Food Nutrition News, 57,* 3–20.
Killen, J. D., Telch, M. J., Robinson, T. N., Maccoby, N., Taylor, C. B., & Farquhar, J. W. (1988). Cardiovascular disease risk reduction for tenth graders: A multiple-factor school-based approach. *Journal of The American Medical Association, 260,* 1728–1733.
King, A. C., Saylor, K. E., Foster, S., Killen, J. D., Telch, M. J., Farquhar, J. W., & Flora, J. (1988). Promoting dietary change in adolescents: A school-based approach for modifying and maintaining health behavior. *American Journal of Preventive Medicine, 4,* 68–74.

Kris-Etherton, P. M. (1989). Nutrition and athletic performance. *Contemporary Nutrition, 14*, 8.

Lauer, R. M., & Clarke, W. R. (1990). Use of cholesterol measurements in childhood for the prediction of adult hypercholesterolemia, the Muscatine study. *Journal of The American Medical Association, 264*, 3034–3038.

Lewis, M., Brun, J., Talmage, H., & Rasher, S. (1988). Teenagers and food choices: The impact of nutrition education. *Journal of Nutrition Education, 20*, 336–340.

Lindberg, J. S., Powell, M. R., Hunt, M. M., Ducey, D. E., & Wade, C. E. (1987). Increased vertebral bone mineral in response to reduced exercise in amenorrheic runners. *Western Journal of Medicine, 146*, 39–42.

Marinho, D. D., & King, J. C. (1980). Nutritional concerns during adolescence. *Pediatric Clinics of North America, 27*, 125–139.

Matkovic, V. (1991). Diet, genetics and peak bone mass of adolescent girls. *Nutrition Today, 26*, 21–24.

Matkovic, V., Kostial, K., Simonovic, J., Buzina, R., Brodarec, A., & Nordin, B. E. C. (1979). Bone status and fracture rates in two regions of Yugoslavia. *American Journal of Clinical Nutrition, 32*, 540–559.

Meyer, F., Moisan, J., Marcoux, D., & Bouchard, C. (1990). Dietary and physical determinants of menarche. *Epidemiology, 1*, 377–381.

National Center for Health Statistics, Department of Health and Human Services. (1989). Unpublished raw data.

National Cholesterol Education Program. (1988). Report of the National Cholesterol Education Program Expert Panel on detection, evaluation and treatment of high blood cholesterol in adults. *Archives of Internal Medicine, 148*, 36–39.

National Diabetes Data Group. (1985). *Diabetes in America* (Nitt Pub. No. 85-1468). Washington, DC: U.S. Department of Health and Human Services, Public Health Services, National Institutes of Health, National Institute of Arthritis, Diabetes, Digestive and Kidney Diseases.

National Research Council. (1986). *The recommended dietary allowances* (10th rev. ed.). Washington, DC: National Academy Press.

National Research Council, Committee on Diet and Health. (1989). *Diet and health: Implications for reducing chronic disease risk.* Washington, DC: National Academy Press.

Newman, T. B., Browner, W. S., & Hulley, S. B. (1990). The case against childhood cholesterol screening. *Journal of The American Medical Association, 264*, 3039–3043.

Newman, W. P., Freedman, D. S., Voors, A. W., Gard, P. D., Srinivasan, S. R., Cresanta, J. L., Williamson, G. D., Webber, L. S., & Berenson, G. S. (1986). Relation of serum lipoprotein levels and systolic blood pressure to early atherosclerosis. *New England Journal of Medicine, 314*, 138–144.

Palla, B., & Litt, I. F. (1988). Medical complications of eating disorders in adolescents. *Pediatrics, 81*, 613–623.

Peck, W. A., Riggs, B. L., & Bell, N. H., Wallace, R. B., Johnston, C. C., Jr., Gordon, S. L., & Shulman, L. E. (1988). Research directions in osteoporosis. *American Journal of Medicine, 84*, 275–282.

Perry, C. L., Luepker, R. V., Murray, D. M., Kurth, C., Mullis, R., Crockett, S., & Jacobs, D. R. (1988). Parent involvement with children's health promotion: The Minnesota home team. *American Journal of Public Health, 78*, 1156–1160.

Rosen, J. C., & Gross, J. (1987). Prevalence of weight reducing and weight gaining in adolescent girls and boys. *Health Psychology, 6*, 131–147.

Shannon, B., Ervin, B., & Bernardo, V. in collaboration with B. Mullis, Division of Nutrition and D. Poehler, Division of Adolescent and School Health. (in press). *Status of school-based nutrition education in state agencies.* Atlanta, GA: Center for Disease Prevention and Health Promotion, Centers for Disease Control.

Skinner, J. D., & Carruth, B. R. (1991). Dietary quality of pregnant and nonpregnant adolescents. *Journal of The American Dietetic Association, 91,* 718–720.

Slattery, M. L., Schumacker, M. C., West, D. W., Robinson, L. M., & French, T. K. (1990). Food-consumption trends between adolescent and adult years and subsequent risk of prostate cancer. *American Journal of Clinical Nutrition, 52,* 752–757.

Staffs. (1989). Results from the National Adolescent Student Health Survey. *Morbidity Mortality Weekly Report, 38,* 147–150.

Steen, S. N., Opplinger, R. A., & Brownell, K. D. (1988). Metabolic effects of repeated weight loss and regain in adolescent wrestlers. *Journal of the American Medical Association, 260,* 47–50.

Stone, E. (1985). School-based health research funded by the National Heart, Lung, and Blood Institute. *Journal of School Health, 55,* 168–174.

Story, M., & Blum, R. W. (1988). Adolescent nutrition: Self-perceived deficiencies and needs of practitioners working with youth. *Journal of The American Dietetic Association, 88,* 591–594.

Story, M., & Resnick, M. D. (1986). Adolescents' views on food and nutrition. *Journal of Nutrition Education, 18,* 188–192.

Story, M., & York, P. V. E. (1987). Nutritional status of Native American adolescent substance abusers. *Journal of The American Dietetic Association, 87,* 1680–1681.

Strong, J. P. (1986). Coronary atherosclerosis in soldiers: A clue to the natural history of atherosclerosis in the young. *Journal of The American Medical Association, 256,* 2863–2866.

Underwood, L. E. (1991). Normal adolescent growth and development. *Nutrition Today, 26,* 11–16.

U.S. Department of Health and Human Services. (1988). *The Surgeon General's Report on Nutrition and Health* (DHHS Publication No. 88-50210). Washington, DC: U.S. Government Printing Office.

Wadden, T. A., & Stunkard, A. J. (1985). Social and psychological consequences of obesity. *Annals of Internal Medicine, 103,* 1062–1067.

Witschi, C. H., Capper, A. I., & Ellison, R. C. (1990). Sources of fat, fatty acids, and cholesterol in the diets of adolescents. *Journal of The American Dietetic Association, 90,* 1429–1431.

Wright, H. S., Guthrie, H. A., Wang, M. Q., & Bernardo, V. (1991). The 1987–88 Nationwide Food Consumption Survey: An update on the nutrient intake of respondents. *Nutrition Today, 26,* 21–27.

16 Promoting Vocational Development in Early Adolescence

Fred W. Vondracek
The Pennsylvania State University

When reduced to its most basic features, it may be said that the most desirable outcome of the vocational developmental process is the achievement of a good match between the characteristics and needs of the individual, on the one hand, and the characteristics and features of his or her work role, on the other. This, of course, represents the basic proposition of trait-oriented vocational psychologists, such as Holland (1973). He proposed that persons and occupations can be classified through the use of parallel constructs. The more closely a person's personality type matches the person's chosen occupation, the better the person's career choice. Although Holland's theory and the resulting assessment instruments have been the dominant approach in vocational psychology in the United States since the 1970s, there is widespread recognition that Holland's theory is deficient in providing an explanatory framework for understanding the processes by which individuals acquire or develop their personalities and by which they choose their occupations.

Conventional wisdom has maintained that the career decision process occurs mainly during the senior year of high school, when youths are more or less forced to do something about a job or career. Fortunately, this oversimplified view of the vocational development process has been replaced by more sophisticated approaches that recognize vocational development as a life-span process, involving the dynamic interaction between the developing individual and multiple contexts (Dudley & Tiedeman, 1977; Mortimer, 1990; Super, 1980; Vondracek, Lerner, &

Schulenberg, 1983a). These approaches have necessitated a reappraisal of the temporal framework for the study of career development, extending the periods of the life span considered to be salient both downward into the childhood years and upward into old age. In the process, they have called attention to the fact that the knowledge and methods from multiple disciplines need to be integrated to enhance our understanding of the processes involved in vocational development and to permit the development of innovative and effective interventions to promote and optimize vocational development, especially in the critical, but neglected, period of early adolescence.

Theoretical formulations by authors such as Erikson (1963), Havighurst (1964), and Super (1963a) have laid some important groundwork. Erikson proposed eight psychosocial stages, of which three are particularly relevant to the discussion of vocational development during childhood and early adolescence. During the third of his eight stages, which may start around age 5 and which is called the locomotorgenital period, the child finds pleasure in using tools and in caring for younger children which, in Erikson's view, may well sow the seeds of the child's ultimate work identification. Erikson's fourth stage is called the latency stage during which the child begins to be a worker and internalizes the work principle. Simultaneously, this allows the child to overcome feelings of inferiority and to develop a sense of industry. With the advent of puberty/adolescence children reach Erikson's fifth stage, and are faced with the task of developing an identity, a large component of which is what has come to be called vocational identity.

Havighurst (1964) proposed that children during the period of approximately 5 to 10 years of age establish "identification with a worker" primarily through identification with parents or significant other persons. During early adolescence, the period of approximately age 10 to 15, children acquire the basic habits of industry. Havighurst proposed that during this period children learn to do schoolwork and chores, and learn circumstances that are appropriate for work, on the one hand, and play, on the other. Following this period, during late adolescence and early adulthood, individuals acquire identity as a worker, or an occupational identity.

Super (1963a) proposed an extensive developmental theory that included a recognition that vocational concerns develop gradually, starting in late childhood and becoming more salient in early adolescence until they reach their most salient level in late adolescence and early adulthood. He felt that the main task of the early adolescent was the crystallization of a vocational preference, which involves the formulation of ideas about work and self, which could then evolve into an occupational and self-concept. The crystallization of a vocational preference, in turn, would help the individual to make a tentative vocational choice, typically by age 18.

Super (1963b) recognized that the development of the self-concept, including the development of the vocational self-concept, is a continuous process, changing as the individual's life experiences change. The process begins at birth with the child's awareness of self and gradually broadens to create a more elaborate and differentiated understanding of self as distinct from others. Super takes the position that the vocational self-concept is a reflection of the person's overall self-concept, but more specialized in the sense that it has implications for educational and vocational decisions. He recognized that, as the child engages in the process of differentiation of self from others, the child also engages in a process of identification, beginning with identification with same-sex parent. Eventually, through interaction with significant others, including peers, through role-playing and various other kinds of learning, a vocational self-concept becomes established.

One more recent effort to extend career theory downward into childhood is represented by Gottfredson's (1981) circumscription and compromise theory. Harmon and Farmer (1983) suggested that confirmation of Gottfredson's theory would require a reconceptualization of vocational theory and related interventions in order to focus on gender-role socialization processes as a prime determinant of career choice. Although Gottfredson's theory has stimulated considerable interest, much of it has failed to be confirmed (Hesketh, Elmslie, & Kaldor, 1990; Pryor, 1985; Pryor & Taylor, 1989), in part because of serious flaws in assumptions used in the formulation of the theory (Vondracek, Lerner, & Schulenberg, 1983b).

Apart from the theoretical formulations discussed here, relatively little attention has been given to the childhood determinants of career development. One significant exception is represented by the work of Goldstein and Oldham (1979), who conducted a large-scale evaluation of children's socialization to work in a sample of first through seventh graders from middle- and working-class families. They started out from the assumption that career choice and specific occupational attitudes do not simply appear in late adolescence or early adulthood, but that there are childhood antecedents of these processes. Indeed, their study led them to conclude that "such development not only starts early but is far more extensive and rapid than many of us would have otherwise been prepared to believe" (p. 177). Moreover, Goldstein and Oldham concluded that by seventh grade children's work-relevant cognitions, attitudes, and feelings have much in common with those of adolescents and adults.

A common thread that appears to run through most theoretical formulations dealing with childhood and early adolescent vocational development is the recognition that, once children have reached the requisite level of cognitive and physical maturity, they must acquire some knowledge and understanding of work. In other words, they learn about the difference between play and work and they become capable of doing work. Moreover, this advance in children's understanding of work leads to the eventual realization that they, themselves, must find a role for themselves in the world of occupations, they must establish a vocational identity. If this conceptualization is valid (and the findings of Goldstein and Oldham would argue that they are), it would suggest that the promotion of vocational development in early adolescence could focus on (a) helping kids to acquire a sense of industry, and (b) facilitating the processes that may assist them in the acquisition of a vocational identity in later adolescence.

THE EARLY EXPERIENCE OF WORK AND THE DEVELOPMENT OF INDUSTRY

Although the early adolescent's establishment of a sense of industry is dependent on a set of complex factors, including family, peer group, and sociocultural influences, it is likely that early experience with work, and particularly with employment, will significantly contribute to the adolescent's emerging sense of industry. Early adolescents who have positive and rewarding work experiences are probably more likely to establish a firm sense of industry, thereby laying one of the critical foundations for the later successful achievement of vocational identity. Indeed, a longitudinal study, spanning more than three decades, that examined adult outcomes related to a behavioral measure of the degree to which 11- to 16-year-old boys had established a sense of industry found that those graded highest in industry had not only more successful work careers, but generally more successful lives than those who received low scores on the measure of industry (Vaillant & Vaillant, 1981).

One of the questions that remains to be answered, however, pertains to the characteristics of early work experiences that make them likely to be positive, on the one hand, or negative, on the other. Research on this issue is relatively sparse, but a review of the major evidence may lead to some preliminary conclusions. Miller and Yung (1990) found that socialization toward economic issues, including work, may actually predate children's and adolescents' entrance into the world of work. They argued that some features of allowance arrangements among parents and their children (which may or may not include work) may have implications for children's attitudes toward work. They found that those arrangements that encouraged self-direction and egalitarian modes of interaction were most likely to facilitate further achievement.

Goldstein and Oldham's (1979) study remains the most important single study with regard to the work socialization of children and early adolescents. Just as they found that children, as early as fifth grade, had rather sophisticated comprehension of occupations, they also concluded that during the elementary school years children's thinking with respect to work shifted from being egocentric and concretistic to being more abstract and objective. Furthermore, they observed that children's work and earning experiences actually start in early childhood, but on a very small scale, and that they are extremely common and subject to age-related increments. They concluded that, with respect to experiential factors, seventh grade (the middle of early adolescence) represents a turning point in children's direct experiences of work, primarily because of practical considerations rather than the child's readiness, or willingness, to work. Nevertheless, in spite of the fact that children clearly preferred play to work, the great majority of children were found to be overwhelmingly positive about their own work experiences.

Among adolescents, the picture is likely to be more complex and differentiated. Part-time employment among adolescents is normative rather than unusual. Moreover, whereas males accounted for the majority of adolescent employment in past decades, this gender difference has all but disappeared today (U.S. Department of Labor, 1987). The amount of work, however, appears to vary according to age and grade level (Manning, 1990) and social class (Schill, McCartin, & Meyer, 1985).

Manning, citing 1987 census data, reported that of those 16- to 19-year-olds who were still in school, almost 45% were in the active labor force. The very decision, however, of whether they will seek employment during this period may depend, to some extent, on whether they had work experience in early adolescence or even in childhood. In the 1981 National Survey of Children (aged 11 to 16), approximately two thirds reported that they sometimes worked for pay (Yamoor & Mortimer, 1990). The percentage was even higher for some groups, such as nonminority boys. Goldstein and Oldham (1979) reported that the percentage of children who received payment for work outside of the home increased from 13% in first grade to 39% in third grade, 42% in fifth grade, and 75% in seventh grade. This clearly offers further evidence for the conclusion that most children do have some experience with the world of work prior to, or during, early adolescence. The question that remains to be answered is whether this work experience is positive and facilitative of what Erikson called a sense of industry, or whether it is irrelevant or even hinders the emergence of industry.

With few exceptions, the effects of employment on adolescents have been the subject of optimistic speculation based on the assumption that "work is good" (e.g., work creates social and personal responsibility, work keeps kids out of trouble). Work by Phillips and Sandstrom (1990), however, indicates that parents do, in actuality, approve of youth work and report consistently that it fosters independence, greater responsibility, and improved attitudes toward school. Hamilton and Crouter (1980), in their review of the research on the effects of work on adolescents, stated that "we find some evidence that adolescent work experience enhances the socialization (to adulthood) process, but little evidence that it provides either career knowledge or job-related skills that prove advantageous over time" (p. 331).

A different conclusion is reached by Greenberger, Steinberg, and their colleagues (Greenberger & Steinberg, 1981, 1986; Greenberger, Steinberg, & Vaux, 1981; Steinberg, Greenberger, Garduque, Ruggiero, & Vaux, 1982). The overall findings of their research paint a rather negative picture of adolescent employment. For example, they found that, especially among middle-class students, working led to an increase in certain forms of deviant behavior, including money-, substance-, and school-related deviance. There appears to be some additional evidence that adolescents who work especially long hours tend to be more aggressive, are more frequently truant, and more frequently break rules (Bachman, Bare, & Frankie, 1986). Regarding the potential benefits of getting a head start in the job market through early work experience, Greenberger and Steinberg (1986) concluded that "intensive employment during high school may create a short-run advantage in the labor market but set up the conditions for longer-term disadvantage in terms of adult social position and economic attainment" (p. 155). The findings of Greenberger and Steinberg's research, however, should be interpreted with caution because their findings are based on cross-sectional data, which make causal inferences problematic, and that therefore deals with the more immediate consequences of teenage employment (Mortimer & Finch, 1986). It should also be noted that all of their data were collected in four California high schools. One could argue that the generalizability of findings from such a sample is limited.

The findings of a study reported by Mortimer (Mortimer, Finch, Shanahan, & Ryu, 1990) suggest that the impact of work is not nearly as deleterious as has been suggested by previous findings. Most importantly, Mortimer and her colleagues maintained that it is necessary to assess specific features of youth employment in order to fully understand the psychological consequences of working. Moreover, they pointed out that the kind of work most readily available to adolescents, such as minimum-wage, menial jobs in fast-food establishments, has generally been found to have negative psychological consequences for adults. Although further research will be needed to clarify these relationships, their findings suggest the possibility that more positive outcomes of adolescent work experiences might be found if adolescents' jobs were more complex and autonomous and would incorporate some opportunities for independent action. Finally, Mortimer et al. recognized that the various contexts of adolescent development, including family, school, peer group, and workplace interact with one another in determining the adolescent's functioning within each of them (for more extensive discussion of these issues see Dudley & Tiedeman, 1977; Vondracek, Lerner, & Schulenberg, 1986).

Among some of the positive findings reported by Mortimer et al. were the observation that moderate number of hours worked was positively related to expressed higher level of well-being in boys, as well as less substance use and school problem behaviors for both boys and girls. They also reported findings that offered evidence for the view that the specific nature of adolescent jobs and their perceived relationship to present and future life circumstances have important implications for adolescents' mental health. Importantly, they found that "boys' well-being, internal control, self-esteem, and substance use are also dependent on their perceptions of the extent to which their jobs provide skills that will be useful to them in the future" (pp. 29–30). Generally, it was found that, especially for girls, when school and work activities were perceived as being positively integrated, they reported higher self-esteem and well-being and less depressive affect and self-derogation.

Further support for the notion that there are important gender differences in how adolescents respond to early work experience is reported in another study conducted by Mortimer and colleagues (Mortimer, Finch, Owens, & Shanahan, 1990). This is a particularly important issue because, according to Mortimer and her colleagues, virtually nothing is known about the influences that lead boys and girls to initiate paid employment at different ages or about how jobs may differentially affect them as potential sources of vocational development. Examining the work experiences of ninth grade boys and girls, they found significant gender differences in the types of work that boys and girls performed, and they confirmed that boys' wage rates were significantly higher than those of girls. They also found, however, that girls obtained their first jobs earlier than boys, but that boys tended to increase the intensity of their employment more than girls. From the perspective of vocational development, however, it is important to note that Mortimer,

Finch, Owens, and Shanahan (1990) found that the job attributes likely to be experienced by girls tended to be the kinds of work experiences that have the most positive psychological consequences for adults, such as innovative thinking, variety, and challenge. Boys, on the other hand, perceived less opportunity than girls for the development of useful skills in their early job experiences and they perceived more stress on their jobs than do girls. Mortimer and colleagues concluded that adolescent girls may, in fact, have the more developmentally beneficial work experiences.

The overall findings of the research of Mortimer and colleagues offer some cautious support to the notion that early work experience may, in fact, offer some of the positive benefits that had generally been assumed to be present but that have been called into question by a few widely quoted studies. Moreover, it now appears clear that research on the impact of early work experience needs to take a far more differentiated view of adolescent work, both from a quantitative and qualitative perspective, in order to arrive at meaningful conclusions about important developmental consequences. If this holds true, it may yet be possible to demonstrate that early work experience, properly arranged, supervised (Manning, 1990), and integrated into the adolescent's various life contexts (Stern, Stone, Hopkins, & McMillion, 1990), may help the adolescent to develop critical skills that are important later in life, including the ability to successfully develop a sense of industry, a vocational identity, and a successful work career.

THE DEVELOPMENT OF VOCATIONAL IDENTITY

According to Erikson (1968), the successful acquisition of a sense of industry facilitates the adolescent's engagement in a decision-making process that eventually leads to a well-defined sense of self. Erikson postulated that individuals start with a lack of identity (diffusion). In early adolescence (12–16 years) youths become foreclosed (i.e., they are committed to the values, beliefs, and goals of significant others). As life experiences and cognitive sophistication increase, there is greater exposure to a variety of options in the major domains of life, including the vocational domain. This may result in a moratorium period during which the adolescents are struggling with vocational and/or other identity issues. They may be said to be in an identity crisis. The ultimate goal is to resolve the crisis and to achieve an identity, which means that one is pursuing a self-chosen occupational goal or a self-chosen direction in any of the other key domains of identity.

It is important to note that although identity has traditionally been viewed as a more or less global concept, the status of any given individual regarding his or her identity development may vary by domain (Archer, 1989a). Moreover, although Erikson (1968) focused on only three identity domains—vocation, ideology, and family—recent work by Archer and Waterman (1983) focused on the identification of additional domains, including vocational plans, religious beliefs, political ideologies, gender-role orientation, values, and family roles. In this connection, Archer (1989b) raised the possibility that for different people, different domains of identity development may have the greatest salience, and that thus, at any given point in time, they may be quite advanced in their quest for identity achievement in one domain but not in another. Moreover, the progression of individuals toward identity achievement may vary not only according to domain, but also in response to historical and contextual factors (Archer, 1989b).

In light of these considerations, it appears likely that at least some early adolescents are already actively engaged in some of the processes required for the eventual development of a vocational identity. Others may be involved in the acquisition of skills and knowledge that will eventually benefit the career development process, but they may, at the time, not yet understand or appreciate this linkage. Recent research by Blustein, Ellis, and Devenis (1989), for example, has highlighted the multifaceted and complex nature of the processes involved in making an adaptive and committed career choice. Among other things, their research confirmed the presence of significant interindividual differences in the processes and timing of commitment to career choices.

One process that has received considerable attention because of its demonstrated involvement in vocational development (Jordaan, 1963; Jordaan & Heyde, 1979) as well as in identity development (Grotevant, 1987; Marcia, 1989) is the process of exploration. In the process of vocational exploration, individuals are exploring the world of occupations and themselves in relation to the requirements and rewards associated with possible occupational choices. As part of this process they also engage in exploratory activity in order to examine alternatives, but the exploratory activity is broader, encompassing not just the vocational domain but the broader ideological and philosophical issues as well (Grotevant & Adams, 1984).

A recent study by Blustein, Devenis, and Kidney (1989) concluded that individuals are "likely to engage in exploratory activity throughout various stages of both career development and identity formation processes" (p. 200). Although their subjects were college students, it is not unreasonable to assume that their statement may also be true throughout the adolescent period. Marcia (1989) observed that in any effort to promote identity development it would be reasonable to start with the basic underlying processes of exploration and commitment. Moreover, he observed that they are assumed to be present from an early age but that they become developmentally crucial during adolescence. Thus, although individuals in early adolescence may, for the most part, be far removed from any kind of meaningful vocational commitment, they may very well already be involved in some important vocational exploratory activity.

If career or vocational exploration is an important antecedent and/or concomitant of vocational identity achievement, one important question is how it can be promoted in children and early adolescents. Parents can probably play an important role in facilitating exploratory behavior in their children by showing themselves to be open to new information and by encouraging independence of thought and action. They can also be helpful by providing the kind of emotional support that is needed to tolerate ambiguity and lack of closure (Jordaan, 1963). Most important from this perspective may be the provision of a family context in which there is minimal pressure toward foreclosure, and in which an atmosphere of trust and openness favors the relatively guilt- and anxiety-free exploration and consideration of alternatives. Marcia (1989) pointed out, however, that it is important for exploration to go beyond a merely cognitive exercise, and that it must occur at a behavioral level as well.

In a penetrating analysis of both ethical and substantive considerations regarding school-based interventions for identity promotion, Waterman (1989) took the position that identity theory and research have advanced sufficiently since the 1970s to form the conceptual basis for interventions. Thus, he viewed three elements in the process of promoting identity formation: (a) stimulating the consideration of a variety of alternative goals in the various identity domains; (b) facilitating the gathering of relevant information; and (c) fostering the willingness of individuals to make commitments to the goals, values, and beliefs that best express their chosen direction (pp. 390–391).

Within the school context, Waterman envisaged a number of possible interventions. These include:

> Use of social expectations; Exposure to alternatives; Exposure to models undergoing identity crises; Encouragement of social perspective taking; Encouragement of self-reflection through writing activities; Focusing on the development of cognitive skills and decision-making processes; and Deliberate psychological education. (pp. 391–395)

Waterman acknowledged that there may be parental objections to teachers' efforts to facilitate the consideration of identity alternatives that may be perceived to undermine certain parental values. In addition, the precipitation of identity crises (a necessary step toward identity achievement) may be unsettling to both students and their parents. Nevertheless, Waterman concluded that identity-related interventions may be feasible, especially if precautions are taken to minimize the potentially negative effects of intervention.

The promotion of vocational development, discussed thus far, has been conceptualized as an effort to facilitate a developmental process that, ideally, culminates in late adolescence or early adulthood in the establishment of a vocational identity. This would seem to be a worthy objective on its own merit, especially in view of the fact that no less an authority than Erikson (1959) stated that "it is primarily the inability to settle on an occupational identity which disturbs young people" (p. 92). Not surprisingly, therefore, evidence is emerging that the achievement of vocational identity may have demonstrable positive health consequences (Archer, 1989a). Viewed from this perspective it seems self-evident that adolescents who successfully go through the process postulated by Erikson would be in a more desirable position than adolescents who lack vocational direction and commitment. Indeed, there is consistent evidence of positive correlations between identity achievement and various positive psychological outcomes (Archer, 1989a, 1989b).

For example, research by Jones, Hartmann, Grochowski, and Glider (1989) with a group of subjects residing in a rehabilitation center for substance abuse, showed that these subjects were generally lower in their identity achievement and moratorium scores than a matched sample of junior/senior high school students. The implication is that the drug abuse rehabilitation subjects were significantly less psychosocially mature than the high school students. In a similar vein, Jones and Hartmann (1988) reported that students who scored highest on identity diffusion were far more likely to be involved with drugs and alcohol than subjects who fell into the other identity statuses. Matteson (1977), studying a Danish sample of students, found that foreclosures and identity diffusions had significantly lower scores on a measure of autonomy than did identity achievements and moratoriums. Working with adults, Neuber and Genthner (1977) found that identity achievement and moratorium status subjects were much more likely to take personal responsibility for their own lives than were identity diffusion subjects. Marcia (1989), as well as Rotheram-Borus (1989), pointed out, however, that in some cultures identity achievement may not be the most desirable outcome, and several researchers have reported significant differences in identity processes based on gender and gender-role attitudes (e.g., Marcia & Friedman, 1970; Orlofsky, 1978).

In examining the relationships between identity development and well-being, especially as they may apply to younger adolescents, a number of significant cautions, beyond those already mentioned, must be applied. Although there is a great deal of anecdotal evidence that adolescents are, in fact, occupied (if not preoccupied) with achieving an identity of their own, different individuals experience this developmental task in different ways. The various contexts within which adolescents operate can play a major role in how they cope with this experience (see Vondracek et al., 1986). In addition, it is probably necessary to take a much closer look at moderator variables, such as locus of control orientation, social support (Sandler, 1980), temperament, and parental attachment (Greenberg, Siegel, & Leitch, 1983), and how they may influence the health correlates and consequences of different ways of identity formation.

What is clear at this point in time is that in an achievement-oriented, capitalist society such as ours, the demands for a high level of occupational commitment and ever more extensive job training will almost certainly move the process of vocational development into a more prominent position than it has occupied thus far. As major sociological, demographic, and technological changes take place, it will become increasingly apparent that the question: "What do you want to be?" cannot wait until early adulthood. Moreover, there is no reason the vocational development of children and adolescents should be neglected in favor of concentrating on intellectual or motor development. What may be needed, however, is a better understanding of how all aspects of development relate to all other aspects, and how healthy or dysfunctional development in one area may affect health or dysfunction in another.

RECOMMENDATIONS

This review of research related to vocational development in early adolescence suggests that parents and educators could take a more active role in designing and implementing strategies that could facilitate vocational development during this critical period and thereby lay the foundation for the acquisition of a successful vocational identity in late adolescence or early adulthood. There is evidence that parents who encourage self-direction and egalitarian modes of interaction will facilitate the vocational development of their children. Moreover, parents who show themselves open to new information and who encourage independence of thought and action in their children are also likely to provide the kind of positive family context that generates the emotional support necessary for tolerating a certain amount of ambiguity and lack of closure, which are, in turn, required for children to engage in meaningful vocational exploratory activities.

With regard to career education, it may be useful to quote Super's (1984) thoughts on how it could be changed to better reflect current career development theory (and research):

> such a program would recognize individual differences in career development and avoid lockstep curricula; it would seek to foster curiosity (and thus exploratory behavior), autonomy, and time perspective in the elementary years, at the same time that it exposed children to a variety of adult role-models. Exploration in breadth would normally begin in the middle school, would phase into exploration in depth when the individual appeared ready to find focus on one or two groups of occupations, and would phase back into exploring in breadth if depth exploration proved unfruitful. (pp. 223–224)

At the same time, it is clear that simplistic notions, such as "work is good for kids," need to be translated into a much more differentiated view that incorporates the finding that quantitative and qualitative differences in adolescents' jobs may be critical in determining the effects of those work experiences on their vocational development. The research evidence appears to point to the conclusion that adolescents should work moderate hours, especially while they are attending school. The beneficial consequences of holding part-time jobs are much more likely to occur if those jobs offer a certain amount of complexity (Stern & Nakata, 1989) and autonomy and incorporate opportunities for relatively independent action (Mortimer, Finch, Shanahan, & Ryu, 1990). In addition, if part-time jobs contain opportunities for learning skills that are meaningful in the job market, and if work and school responsibilities are sensibly integrated into the adolescents' overall life context, adolescents will feel more positive, not only about their jobs and school, but also about themselves.

ACKNOWLEDGMENT

My thanks go to Jeylan T. Mortimer for helpful comments on an earlier draft of this chapter.

REFERENCES

Archer, S. L. (1989a). Adolescent identity: An appraisal of health and intervention. *Journal of Adolescence, 12,* 341–343.

Archer, S. L. (1989b). The status of identity: Reflections on the need for intervention. *Journal of Adolescence, 12,* 345–359.
Archer, S. L., & Waterman, A. S. (1983). Identity in early adolescence: A developmental perspective. *Journal of Early Adolescence, 3,* 203–214.
Bachman, J. G., Bare, D. E., & Frankie, E. I. (1986). *Correlates of employment among high school seniors* (Monitoring the Future Occasional Paper 20). Ann Arbor, MI: Institute for Social Research.
Blustein, D. L., Devenis, L. E., & Kidney, B. A. (1989). Relationship between the identity formation process and career development. *Journal of Counseling Psychology, 36*(2), 196–202.
Blustein, D. L., Ellis, M. V., & Devenis, L. E. (1989). Monograph: The development and validation of a two-dimensional model of the commitment to career choices process. *Journal of Vocational Behavior, 35,* 342–378.
Dudley, G. A., & Tiedeman, D. V. (1977). *Career development: Exploration and commitment.* Muncie, IN: Accelerated Development.
Erikson, E. H. (1963). *Childhood and society.* New York: Norton.
Erikson, E. H. (1968). *Identity: Youth and crisis.* New York: Norton.
Erikson, E. H. (1959). Identity and the Life cycle. *Psychological Issues, 1,* 18–164.
Goldstein, B., & Oldham, J. (1979). *Children and work: The study of socialization.* New Brunswick, NJ: Transaction Books.
Gottfredson, L. (1981). Circumscription and compromise: A developmental theory of occupational aspirations. *Journal of Counseling Psychology, 28,* 545–579.
Greenberg, M. T., Siegel, J. M., & Leitch, C. J. (1983). The nature and importance of attachment relationships to parents and peers during adolescence. *Journal of Youth and Adolescence, 12,* 373–386.
Greenberger, E., & Steinberg, L. D. (1981). The workplace as a context for the socialization of youth. *Journal of Youth and Adolescence, 10,* 185–210.
Greenberger, E., & Steinberg, L. D. (1986). *When teenagers work: The psychological and social costs of adolescent employment.* New York: Basic Books.
Greenberger, E., Steinberg, L. D., & Vaux, A. (1981). Adolescents who work: Health and behavioral consequences of job stress. *Developmental Psychology, 17,* 691–703.
Grotevant, H. D. (1987). Toward a process model of identity formation. *Journal of Adolescent Research, 2,* 203–222.
Grotevant, H. D., & Adams, G. R. (1984). Development of an objective measure to assess ego identity in adolescents: Validation and replication. *Journal of Youth and Adolescence, 13,* 419–438.
Hamilton, S. F., & Crouter, A. C. (1980). Work and growth: A review of research on the impact of work experience on adolescent development. *Journal of Youth and Adolescence, 9,* 323–338.
Harmon, L. W., & Farmer, H. S. (1983). Current theoretical issues in vocational psychology. In W. B. Walsh & S. H. Osipow (Eds.), *Handbook of vocational psychology: Vol. 1, Foundations* (pp. 39–77). Hillsdale, NJ: Lawrence Erlbaum Associates.
Havighurst, R. J. (1964). *Youth in exploration and man emergent.* In H. Borow (Ed.), *Man in a world at work* (pp. 215–236). Boston: Houghton-Mifflin.
Hesketh, B., Elmslie, S., & Kaldor, W. (1990). Career compromise: An alternative account to Gottfredson's theory. *Journal of Counseling Psychology, 37,* 49–56.
Holland, J. L. (1973). *Making vocational choices: A theory of careers.* Englewood Cliffs, NJ: Prentice-Hall.
Jones, R. M., & Hartmann, B. R. (1988). Ego identity: Developmental differences and experimental substance use among adolescents. *Journal of Adolescence, 11,* 347–360.
Jones, R. M., Hartmann, B. R., & Grochowski, C. O., & Glider, P. (1989). Ego identity and

substance abuse: A comparison of adolescents in residential treatment with adolescents in school. *Personality and Individual Differences, 10,* 625–631.

Jordaan, J. P. (1963). Exploratory behavior: The formation of self and occupational concepts. In D. Super, R. Starishevsky, N. Matlin, & J. P. Jordaan (Eds.), *Career development: Self-concept theory* (pp. 42–78). New York: College Entrance Examination Board.

Jordaan, J. P., & Heyde, M. B. (1979). *Vocational maturity during the high school years.* New York: Teachers College Press.

Manning, W. D. (1990). Parenting employed teenagers. *Youth & Society, 22,* 184–200.

Marcia, J. E. (1989). Identity and intervention. *Journal of Adolescence, 12,* 401–410.

Marcia, J. E., & Friedman, M. L. (1970). Ego identity status in college women. *Journal of Personality, 38,* 249–263.

Matteson, D. R. (1977). Exploration and commitment: Sex differences and methodological problems in the use of identity status categories. *Journal of Youth and Adolescence, 6,* 353–374.

Miller, J., & Yung, S. (1990). The role of allowances in adolescent socialization. *Youth & Society, 22,* 137–159.

Mortimer, J. T. (1990). Introduction. *Youth & Society, 22,* 131–136.

Mortimer, J. T., & Finch, M. D. (1986). The effects of part-time work on adolescent self-concept and achievement. In K. M. Borman & J. Reisman (Eds.), *Becoming a worker* (pp. 66–89). Norwood, NJ: Ablex.

Mortimer, J. T., Finch, M. D., Owens, T. J., & Shanahan, M. (1990). Gender and work in adolescence. *Youth & Society, 22,* 201–224.

Mortimer, J. T., Finch, M., Shanahan, M., & Ryu, S. (1990, March). *Work experience, mental health, and behavioral adjustment in adolescence.* Paper presented at the biennial meeting of the Society for Research on Adolescence, Atlanta, GA.

Neuber, K. A., & Genthner, R. W. (1977). The relationship between ego identity, personal responsibility, and facilitative communication. *Journal of Psychology, 95,* 45–49.

Orlofsky, J. L. (1978). Identity formation, need achievement, and fear of success in college men and women. *Journal of Youth and Adolescence, 7,* 49–62.

Phillips, S., & Sandstrom, K. L. (1990). Parental attitudes toward youth work. *Youth & Society, 22,* 160–183.

Pryor, R. G. L. (1985). Eradicating sex-role stereotypes: An application of Gottfredson's circumscription/compromise theory. *Vocational Guidance Quarterly, 33,* 277–283.

Pryor, R. G. L., & Taylor, N. B. (1989). Circumscription and compromise: Some problems and possibilities. *Australian Psychologist, 24,* 101–113.

Rotheram-Borus, M. J. (1989). Ethnic differences in adolescents' identity status and associated behavior problems. *Journal of Adolescence, 12,* 361–374.

Sandler, R. N. (1980). Social support resources, stress and maladjustment of poor children. *American Journal of Community Psychology, 8,* 41–52.

Schill, W. J., McCartin, R., & Meyer, K. (1985). Youth employment: Its relationship to academic and family variables. *Journal of Vocational Behavior, 26,* 155–163.

Steinberg, L. D., Greenberger, E., Garduque, L., Ruggiero, M., & Vaux, A. (1982). Effects of working on adolescent development. *Developmental Psychology, 18,* 385–395.

Stern, D., Stone, J. R., III, Hopkins, C., & McMillion, M. (1990). Quality of students' work experience and orientation toward work. *Youth & Society, 22,* 263–282.

Stern, D., & Nakata, Y. (1989). Characteristics of high school students' paid jobs, and employment experience after graduation. In D. Stern & D. Eichorn (Eds.), *Adolescents and work: Influences of social structure, labor markets, and culture* (pp. 189–233). Hillsdale, NJ: Lawrence Erlbaum Associates.

Super, D. E. (1963a). Vocational development in adolescence and early adulthood: Tasks and behaviors. In D. E. Super, R. Starishevsky, N. Matlin, & J. P. Jordaan (Eds.), *Career development: Self-concept theory* (pp. 79–95). New York: CEEB Research Monograph No. 4.

Super, D. E. (1963b). Self-concepts in vocational development. In D. E. Super, R. Starishevsky, N. Matlin, & J. P. Jordaan (Eds.), *Career development: Self-concept theory* (pp. 1–16). New York: CEEB Research Monograph No. 4.

Super, D. E. (1980). A life-span, life-space approach to career development. *Journal of Vocational Behavior, 16,* 282–298.

Super, D. E. (1984). Career and life development. In D. Brown & L. Brooks (Eds.), *Career choice and development* (pp. 192–234). San Francisco: Jossey-Bass.

U.S. Department of Labor. (1987). *Employment and earnings* (Vol. 34). Washington, DC: U.S. Government Printing Office.

Vaillant, G. E., & Vaillant, C. O. (1981). Natural history of male psychological health, X: Work as a predictor of positive mental health. *American Journal of Psychiatry, 138*(11), 1433–1441.

Vondracek, F. W., Lerner, R. M., & Schulenberg, J. E. (1983a). The concept of development in vocational theory and intervention. *Journal of Vocational Behavior, 23,* 179–202.

Vondracek, F. W., Lerner, R. M., & Schulenberg, J. E. (1983b). On aspiring to present a developmental theory of occupational aspirations: A reader's guide to Gottfredson. *Journal of Vocational Behavior, 23,* 213–218.

Vondracek, F. W., Lerner, R. M., & Schulenberg, J. E. (1986). *Career development: A life-span developmental approach.* Hillsdale, NJ: Lawrence Erlbaum Associates.

Waterman, A. S. (1989). Curricula interventions for identity change: Substantive and ethical considerations. *Journal of Adolescence, 12,* 389–400.

Yamoor, C. M., & Mortimer, J. T. (1990). Age and gender differences in the effects of employment on adolescent achievement and well-being. *Youth and Society, 22,* 201–224.

17 Promoting Healthy Sexual Development During Early Adolescence

Patricia Barthalow Koch
The Pennsylvania State University

Adolescent sexuality is too often treated as if it "begins with intercourse and ends in pregnancy" (Weddle, McKenry, & Leigh, 1988, p. 251). Sexuality is an integral part of development throughout the life span, involving gender roles, self-concept, body image, emotions, relationships, religious beliefs, societal mores, as well as intercourse and other sexual behaviors. Therefore, to promote healthy development, adolescents should be viewed and accepted as sexual persons by adults, including parents, professionals, and researchers.

Although researchers and developmentalists contend that healthy, satisfying adult sexuality is greatly influenced by the earlier years of sexual development, we know little about healthy adolescent sexual development for a variety of reasons (Diepold & Young, 1979; Jorgensen, 1983; Weddle et al., 1988). First, the study of adolescent sexuality is often grounded in a deviance approach from an adult perspective that focuses primarily on adolescent contraceptive behavior, fertility, and pregnancy. This approach excludes topics such as noncoital behaviors, relationships, and issues of psychosexual development. Second, the study of adolescent sexuality has not been well grounded in developmental theory and has been too often considered outside an inter- or intrapersonal developmental context. For example, Weddle et al. (1988, p. 247) stated that, "while it is widely acknowledged that identity development is the primary developmental task of adolescents, research on identity development has focused primarily on nonsexual components" (e.g., cognitive, vocational, moral, etc.). Third, research has primarily focused on the individual adolescent female, whose sexuality is often treated as problematic. Fourth, there is a lack of understanding of the contextual nature of sexual development and expression in both adolescent females and males. More specifically, there is a dearth of information concerning the interrelationships involved among parental, peer, media, school, religious, and political influences as they impact the sexual development of adolescents. Fifth, research on sexual health promotion policy and program effectiveness generally is lacking or of poor quality. Finally, discomfort among many laypeople, professionals, and researchers with many aspects of sexuality, especially as it is expressed by adolescents, has left adolescent sexuality as a relatively unexplored field of inquiry.

Therefore, in this chapter I examine various aspects of healthy adolescent sexual development and expression based on the limited data available. Developmental and contextual aspects of adolescent sexuality are highlighted. Finally, recommendations for future research, and for the development of policies and programs concerning healthy adolescent sexual development and expression are presented. This approach does not deny that many adolescents do encounter problems in their sexual development (i.e., unintended pregnancies, sexually transmissible diseases, coerced or forced sexual behaviors). However, it does affirm that not all adolescent sexuality is necessarily synonymous with problematic, irresponsible, or unhealthy development and expression.

Describing Healthy Adolescent Sexual Development and Expression

Many believe that "in early adolescence, 'sex' rears its urgent head [and] children burst biologically into puberty . . ." (Sloane, 1989, p. 5). Adults are often so preoccupied with the dangers of adolescent sex—pregnancy, date rape, sexual abuse, sexually transmissible diseases (STDs), acquired immunodeficiency syndrome (AIDS)—that they do not identify healthy and positive aspects of adolescent sexual development. In this section, adult and adolescent perspectives on various ways to describe healthy adolescent sexual development and expression are explored.

Developmental consolidation of an identity has been acknowledged as an important task of adolescence; a core aspect of this consolidation is developing a satisfactory sexual identity. Selverstone (1989) defined this developing process as sexual socialization and described its importance to adolescents.

> It appears to meet many of their needs: their *identity* is validated through their *connectedness* to another person, which provides a sense of *power,*

joy, and *hope.* They feel *lovable* . . . there is no magic age to commence or to cease intimate conduct, what is critical is whether the behavior advances or retards an adolescent's self-esteem and his or her successful completion of [other] developmental tasks. (p. 3)

Because theoretical frameworks have been designed by adults, little is known about the adolescents' perceptions of their own sexual development and expression (Millstein, in press). Definitions of sexual health offered by secondary students in one report ranged from: "not getting knocked up because you were using protection," "feeling comfortable with your own body and all of its good and strange feelings," to "being caring, honest, responsible, respectful, and proud of yourself" (Leight, 1989, p. 10). A common goal for attaining and maintaining sexual health for these adolescents was the assurance of their present and future happiness. They believed that being sexually healthy would allow them more time to concentrate on "finishing school, getting a job, and making 'alotta' money" (Leight, 1989, p. 10). Overall, they viewed sexual health as a means to having more fun and to being a better lover and future parent. Unhealthy sexual encounters were described as those that are physically and/or emotionally harmful, exploitive, or coercive. The adolescents held their parents, followed by the media and peer pressure, most responsible for their sexual health status.

Noncoital Sexuality

Adolescent sexual expression usually develops and progresses from less to more intimate contact. Yet, most research on adolescent sexual behavior has been fertility-based, emphasizing age and frequency of vaginal–penile intercourse, contraceptive use (particularly among females), and unintended pregnancy. Thus, little is known about noncoital or "outercourse" behaviors (those in which the exchange of infected body fluids do not occur). As described by Cross (1991), "Good, erotic courtships may be among the most delicious and memorable experiences of an entire lifetime, and may be invaluable preparation for adult sexual relationships" (p. 9). In addition, nonrisk outercourse behaviors are of increasing importance in the prevention of unintended pregnancies, and STDs, including human immunodeficiency virus (HIV) infection and AIDS.

Although there are little normative data on these various noncoital sexual behaviors, the following results have been reported (Coles & Stokes, 1985):

- Most teens (97%) had their first kiss by age 15; females tended to have their first kiss at a younger age than males.
- 85% of 13- to 18-year-olds had a girlfriend or boyfriend.
- By age 14, 54% of males and 31% of females had participated in breast touching.
- By age 13, 23% of males and 13% of females had participated in vaginal play.
- Of 13- to 18-year-olds, 46% of the males and 24% of the females had masturbated, with percentages increasing with age for males but not age-linked for females.
- 41% of 17- to 18-year-old females had engaged in fellatio and 33% of this age group of males had engaged in cunnilingus.

Another study of southern White adolescents found that slightly more teenagers had given or received oral sex than had had vaginal–penile intercourse (53% vs. 50% for males, 42% vs. 37% for females) (Newcomer & Udry, 1985). Clearly, adolescents are experiencing a wide range of noncoital sexual expression, much of which is overlooked by parents, professionals, and researchers. Therefore, we know little about the role of noncoital sexual activities in adolescent development.

Coital Sexuality

First vaginal–penile intercourse is often viewed by researchers as a pivotal behavior, with statistics regarding (non)virginity, such as percentages and the age of first intercourse, probably being the most recorded sexuality data. Available evidence indicates that the average age of first intercourse for both men and women has been declining for several decades, ranging from 14.0 to 17.6 years depending on the unique personal (e.g., gender, racial/ethnic background) and contextual (e.g., socioeconomic status, urbanicity/rurality) characteristics of the sample being studied (Koch, 1988; Smith, Nenney, & McGill, 1986). Although males, in general, still have first intercourse at an earlier age than do females, females have become more like their male counterparts in the timing of this experience. Research on the prevalence of intercourse experience among adolescents indicates that:

- 14% to 76.4% of 7th to 12th graders, from across the country, have had intercourse at least once (Centers for Disease Control [CDC], 1989; Taylor, Kagay, & Leichenko, 1986).
- 55% of blue-collar midwestern middle and junior high school students have had sexual intercourse at least once, with 7% of

these 7th to 9th graders having intercourse about once a week (Orr, Wilbrandt, Brock, Rauch, & Ingersoll, 1989).
- 15.1% to 42.6% of 13- to 18-year-olds from across the country have had three or more sexual partners (CDC, 1989).

These statistics call into question the inherently "deviant" nature of sexual intercourse among adolescents. Although some researchers (e.g., Donovan & Jessor, 1985) have categorized adolescent intercourse, along with substance abuse and delinquency, as a "problem behavior," does it not depend on the context and outcomes of the intercourse experience as to whether it is problematic to the individuals involved or to society in general?

Understanding any sexual behavior requires qualitative as well as quantitative considerations. Sexuality can be viewed as a pattern of learned human conduct (scripts) involving a set of skills and feelings, with adolescence serving as the first time for people to practice adult sexual scripts (Gagnon, 1977). These scripts involve the "who," "what," "where," "when," and especially the "why" of sexual behavior. These components of sexuality require a substantial amount of interpersonal coordination of the script before, during, and after the actual behavior.

The "when" and "who" of first intercourse has been given considerable attention, yet there is little scientific literature concerning the reasons for and circumstances and conditions under which sexual intercourse occurs for adolescents. This limited research has demonstrated that the affective elements of the first intercourse experience (e.g., motivations for becoming involved, relationship with partner, positive and negative feelings toward the experience) have significantly more impact on the outcomes than the demographic elements (e.g., age) (Koch, 1988). "We have spent much time, effort, and money studying one particular behavioral manifestation of sexuality [vaginal-penile intercourse] as 'seen through the eyes of the researcher' . . . while excluding the *experience of sexuality as seen through the eyes of the adolescent*" (Jorgensen, 1983, p. 146). Thus, researchers need to move from mere "social bookkeeping" (counting virgins) to an understanding of the social contexts and processes that influence coital behavior (Simon, Berger, & Gagnon, 1972).

Same-Gender Sexuality

Not all adolescent sexual activity is between males and females. Regarding same-gender sexual activity among adolescent males, the limited research that exists has indicated a 17%–37% incidence of such activity to orgasm on at least one occasion (Remafedi, 1988; Sorenson, 1973). Same-gender sexual activity does not necessarily indicate a homosexual or bisexual orientation, however, neither does "the homosexual adult, as if by pathogenesis, spring from the heterosexual child at the age of 18 years" (Remafedi, 1987a, p. 222). The weight of evidence from case, prospective, and retrospective studies indicates that the acquisition of a sexual identity (heterosexual, homosexual, or bisexual) is a lengthy process that begins in childhood and extends through adulthood. Approximately 8%–10% of the 30 million U.S. young people will consider themselves gay, lesbian, or bisexual at some point in their lives (D'Augelli, 1988).

During adolescence, some teens identify themselves as gay, lesbian, or bisexual with a well-established affectional/sexual orientation. Studies indicate that the mean age at the time of awareness of same-gender attractions for gay males was approximately 13 years and with self-designation as "homosexual" occurring between the ages of 14 and 21 (Remafedi, 1987b). For lesbians, the average age of awareness of same-gender feelings has been documented at 16 with self-description occurring around 21 years of age (D'Augelli, Collins, & Hart, 1987).

From a White, middle-class, gay male adolescent perspective, homosexuality means more than simply having sex with other males (Ramefedi, 1987b). The majority of gay male adolescents ($N = 25$) who were interviewed viewed homosexuality as a more general affinity toward men, with some regarding it as an indicator of positive qualities like self-awareness and personal strength. Although all these adolescents were able to identify disadvantages attached to being a gay male, 31% were unable to describe any advantages. Most (81%) believed that their affectional/sexual orientation would impact their future lives, with the majority envisioning negative consequences or uncertainties.

Although the road to healthy heterosexual development is fairly well marked, homosexuality is still too often regarded in our society as an illness, moral deviation, or criminal behavior (Remafedi, 1989). "The exuberance of one's first sexual experience, the excitement of one's first serious date, the giddiness of infatuations—all of the critical aspects of sociosexual and affectional development during adolescence—are experienced alone" (D'Augelli, 1988, p. 2), often in crisis by the gay or lesbian teen. It is not possible to accurately assess the number of lesbian and gay youth whose healthy development has been destroyed (e.g., through depression, substance abuse, etc.) due to self-doubt, rejection, discrimination, or outright hatred from others. It is known, for instance, that lesbian and gay youth are two to three times more likely than other teens to attempt suicide and may comprise 30% of all completed youth suicides (Gibson, 1989).

Yet, studies of nonclinical samples of gay and lesbian adults illustrate that healthy development and expression do occur in spite of widespread societal disapproval of this sexual orientation. Remafedi (1989) described healthy sexual development of homosexually oriented persons as having:

1. a positive homosexual core identity and the skills to adapt to other subgroups as well;
2. the ability to achieve emotional and physical intimacy with another person of the same gender, free from sexual scripts that are injurious to self or others, including those behaviors that might transmit HIV; and
3. an affirmative self-concept as a homosexual person, and a sense of being a lovable, respectable, and competent woman or man.

"Ultimately, their developmental progress must not be judged against a heterosexual standard, but by their ability to find unique strategies to bridge divergent and conflicting sexual subcultures" (Remafedi, 1989, p. 8).

Applying the Life-Span Perspective to Adolescent Sexuality

It seems that from both the adolescent and adult perspectives, adolescent sexual expression that maximizes intrapersonal and interpersonal growth while minimizing harm to oneself, to others, and to society is a positive force in development that should be promoted. Therefore, sexuality should only become problematic when its outcomes (pregnancy, STD, abuse) greatly risk an adolescent's, or his or her offspring's, health or life course. As was described in chapter 14, "Health Promotion in Adolescence: Developmental and Theoretical Considerations," the life-span perspective of human development, with its emphasis on holism and promotion, is an approach that is well suited to and much needed in the study of adolescent sexuality.

At the present, "much of what passes for knowledge concerning normal adolescent sexual behavior is best considered as either rumor or mythology" (Diepold & Young, 1979, p. 45). Using a life-span perspective (Lerner, 1987), which incorporates processes within the adolescent as well as processes within the context, as a theoretical base provides a framework for exploring the many unanswered questions about adolescent sexuality. Optimal sexual development should be studied as it evolves from interrelated physiological, psychological, and contextual processes. However, there is a complete lack of understanding of how the various maturational time tables (i.e., cognitive, physiological, social) relate to sexual development (i.e., erotic stimulation, sexual knowledge, attitudes, and behaviors) in young adolescents. For example, the role of hormones and other physiological markers have not been measured in most studies of adolescent sexuality even though there is some evidence that biological factors influence the timing of initial sexual activity (Udry, Billy, Morris, Groff, & Raj, 1985; Udry, Talbert, & Morris, 1986).

Regarding cognitive development and sexuality, cross-cultural studies of children's understanding of "where babies come from" have reported that children in the United States were slower in attaining formal abilities than their peers in England, Sweden, and Australia (Goldman & Goldman, 1982; Koch, 1980). Therefore, it has been suggested that the cultural context of sexuality education influences the levels of cognitive abilities regarding sexual topics. Although four stages of reasoning about sexual behavior in adolescence and young adulthood have been proposed following other cognitive development stage models, they have not been tested (Gfellner, 1986). A life-span perspective would take into consideration these intrapersonal developmental processes.

Not only have researchers failed to study adolescent sexuality within a developmental context, but they also have failed to study it within its sociocultural context. Sexual behavior is clearly an arena in which biological and social forces interact, thus making it ideal for applying a life-span perspective. For example, research on adolescent dating has found that social pressures, based on behavior considered typical and appropriate at various ages, determine the onset of dating, not individual levels of sexual maturation (Dornbusch et al., 1981). One conclusion is that "the social system thus may take biological development into account as it develops and promulgates institutionalized images of appropriate [sexual] behavior" (Dornbusch et al., 1981, p. 184). This one aspect of adolescent sexuality, dating, exemplifies the life-span concepts of:

1. developmental contextual: adolescent organismic changes in individual sexual functioning are moderated by social contexts.
2. embeddedness: sexual development exists at multiple levels (e.g., biological, dyadic, and societal).
3. dynamic interaction: the multiple levels of sexual development are in constant interaction.

Cultural Diversity and Sexuality

We still lack adequate descriptive and inferential data about sexual development and behavior patterns as a function of gender, race, ethnicity, socioeconomic status, family structure, media messages, neighborhood and political environments, and other contextual variables (Hogan & Kitagawa, 1985). It should be noted that sexual development and behavior often differ between adolescent females and males due to biological and sociological forces and these gender-specific developmental issues need to be more systematically researched and addressed (Bolton & MacEachron, 1988; McCaffree, 1989). Further, although there are limited data detailing the sexual behavior patterns of Black adolescents (Belcastro, 1985), we need to make sure that future research includes a life-span approach using comparable representative samples of adolescents from all racial and ethnic backgrounds at all socioeconomic levels in order to disentangle the influences of class versus race/ethnicity. Currently, it is not known what is actual "normative" sexual development and expression among adolescents within various cultures and contexts, such as lower class rural Whites, Hispanic-Americans born within and outside the United States, and adolescents with developmental disabilities or chronic illnesses. Future research on adolescent sexuality should reflect similarities and diversity based on gender, orientation, culture, family structure, class, and geography, as well as other intrapersonal and contextual variables.

DEVELOPING POLICIES AND PROGRAMS TO PROMOTE HEALTHY ADOLESCENT SEXUAL DEVELOPMENT

Sexuality education, in all of its forms, is an important influence on the sexual development of young adolescents, particularly because research indicates that ages 12 and 13 are peak times for learning about many sexual concepts, with 51% of certain sexual information being acquired during this period (Thornburg, 1981). Researchers over the past 50 years have consistently found that adolescents identify their peers as their primary source of sex education, yet the accuracy of the knowledge they receive from other adolescents is questionable. Furthermore, sexually experienced best friends of both sexes have been shown to influence the transition to sexual intercourse of White adolescent females (Billy & Udry, 1985). Thus, friends and peers affect adolescent sexuality in a myriad of ways, many of which are not clearly understood. Yet, we do know that programs facilitated by peers are an effective means of educating adolescents about their sexuality (Planned Parenthood, 1980).

Teenagers also rank the media as a major source of information about sexuality (Haffner & Kelly, 1987). There has been limited research providing conflicting results about the impact of various media messages on adolescents' sexual knowledge, attitudes, and behaviors. Interestingly, although accurate messages about responsible condom use have been restricted on television, an analysis of prime time documented 20,000 scenes of suggested sexual interactions and behaviors in 1 year of evening viewing (Sprafkin & Silverman, 1981). Such mixed messages prompted the National Academy of Sciences to proclaim that the media provides "young people with lots of clues about how to be sexy, but . . . little information about how to be sexually responsible" (Haffner & Kelly, 1987, p. 9). We do not know what messages young adolescents are getting about what it means to be a sexual being and how these messages promote or retard their optimal sexual development.

Research focusing on the sexuality education occurring in the home generally finds it lacking, with most of it focusing on the prevention of sexual health problems (e.g., adolescent pregnancy, AIDS), rather than the promotion of optimal sexual development. For example, it has been found that when parents do talk to their children about sex, the adolescents tend to be less likely to engage in intercourse. If adolescents are engaging in intercourse, they are more likely to use birth control and to have fewer partners than teens who do not talk with their parents (Fox, 1981). Research also indicates that parental strictness and rules have an impact on the sexual attitudes and behaviors of their adolescents in both encouraging and discouraging ways (Hogan & Kitagawa, 1985; Miller, McCoy, Olson, & Wallace, 1986). Thus, there are multiple levels of interaction between the adolescent and his or her family that effect the teen's sexual development. These interactions need to be explored.

Because of the lack of sex education provided in the home and the abundance of misinformation and misconceptions provided by peers and the media, schools have been called upon to fill this educational gap. At present, 20 states and the District of Columbia require sex education in their schools; whereas 32 states and the District of Columbia require AIDS education. A major study concerning the policies of state education departments and large school districts on sex and AIDS education (Kenney, Guardado, & Brown, 1989) concluded that sexuality education has actually suffered from the crisis-driven approach reinvigorated by the AIDS epidemic. Currently, both states and school districts concentrate more financial and human resources and time on AIDS education rather than on a comprehensive, positively focused approach to sexuality education and healthy sexual development.

The quality and extent of the sexuality education being taught in the schools was assessed through an examination of the curricula endorsed by 23 states (deMauro, 1990). The findings included:

- psychosocial aspects of sexuality (e.g., gender identification and gender roles, sexual values and ethical considerations of sexual behaviors, sexual functioning and gratification) were absent
- although the natural and positive function of human sexuality was often noted in a single statement, most curricula concentrated on the negative consequences of sexual behaviors.
- when the sexuality curriculum was written for an autonomous course it was thorough and exact, however, it was minimal when it was written to be integrated into an existing curriculum (e.g., health education or science).

Overall, it was concluded that the increase in numbers of state mandates and curricula on sex education have not resulted in a more comprehensive, developmentally enhancing approach to sexuality in most U.S. schools.

An additional concern is that state and local policies and curricula are not consistently implemented within each individual classroom. Teachers involved in providing sexuality education report large gaps between what they believe should be taught about sexuality and what actually is taught (Forrest & Silverman, 1989). For example, although 97% of Grade 7–12 teachers teaching sex education believed that their students should be taught where they can obtain birth control methods, only 48% were in schools which allowed the communicating of this information. In addition, the abstinence message, which over one third of these teachers believed is the most important concept to teach, seems clearly discrepant with the actual behaviors of many of their students.

The major problems that these teachers said they had in teaching about sexuality were:

1. lack of factual information;
2. lack of appropriate teaching materials and strategies;
3. pressures from parents, community members, or school administrators;
4. students' reactions or lack of interest;
5. lack of time;
6. the manner in which sexuality education is structured within the school; and
7. personal difficulties in dealing with the subject matter.

It seems that these problems could be remedied through the demonstration of *active* support for accurate, developmentally relevant and enhancing sexuality education by policymakers, parents, and community members. Supportive policies need to be explicitly developed on the state and local levels and *comprehensive promotion* (not simply prevention) curricula need to be developed to respond to the students' interests and needs. Finally, teachers need to be provided with training regarding the cognitive, affective, and behavioral aspects of sexuality education.

In conclusion, without knowing what positive or negative roles various sexual expressions may play in differing contexts, we are at an extreme disadvantage in effectively developing policies (e.g., in the home or government) or implementing programs (e.g., in schools or community settings) that will promote healthy sexual and overall development in youth. However, based on what we do know, as previously described in this chapter, there are some general guidelines for providing sexuality education and promoting healthy sexual development during early adolescence (Cross, 1991; Haffner, 1990; Koch, 1992):

1. Adolescents should be taught what they *want* to know, albeit have a *right* to know, about their developing sexuality. Knowledge is better than ignorance for any subject, and sexuality is no exception. Contrary to popular misconception, research indicates that sexuality education does *not* encourage teenagers to initiate sexual activity.

2. Sexuality education should be *integrated* along with other topics into family discussions or academic curricula. Sexuality must be dealt with as a positive and natural aspect of life contributing to the overall development of one's self-esteem.

3. The wide range of sexual attitudes, values, and experiences among youth must be acknowledged. For example, "teens who are not yet dating, teens who choose abstinence, teens who are gay and lesbian, teens who are sexually experienced—all need our support and respect" (Haffner, 1990, p. 13). Programs to promote healthy sexual development must be relevant for diverse participants and encourage young people to be appreciative of each other's differences. A goal of these programs should be to strive to eliminate prejudices (sexism, racism, heterosexism, etc.) from the developing adolescent's view of sexuality.

4. To promote optimal sexual development and understanding among young adolescents, they must be provided with a combination of cognitive, affective, and behavioral learning experiences. Providing adolescents with accurate, up-to-date information on the range of sexual topics is important, but it is not enough. They must also learn to identify and examine their own feelings, attitudes, and values concerning the

wide range of sexual topics because the affective domain often influences behavior. Finally, they must develop and practice the many skills (e.g., communication, assertiveness, decision making, problem solving, etc.) that are necessary for maintaining healthy sexual relationships and for making responsible choices.

5. Adults who impact adolescents in various ways (parents, teachers, youth leaders, clergy, media producers, policymakers, etc.) must become informed about and comfortable with promoting healthy sexual development. Sexuality programs need to be designed and targeted at adults as well as teenagers. Spearheading this advocacy, the Sex Information and Education Council of the United States (SIECUS), along with approximately 50 other professional, community, and youth-serving organizations have formed a coalition to assure that all children and youth receive comprehensive sexuality education by the year 2000. As Debra Haffner (1990), the executive director of SIECUS, challenged:

> All of us need to advocate for teenagers' rights to be sexually literate, sexually educated, and sexually protected. We need to advocate for honesty with young people, not education or public health messages that are veiled moralizing sermons. (p. 14)

We all need to begin by bringing the promotion of healthy adolescent sexual development and expression "out of the closet" in our homes, schools, youth serving organizations, churches, media, policymaking boardrooms, and research centers.

REFERENCES

Belcastro, P. A. (1985). Sexual behavior differences between black and white students. *The Journal of Sex Research, 21*(1), 56–67.

Billy, J. O. G., & Udry, J. R. (1985). The influence of male and female best friends on adolescent sexual behavior. *Adolescence, 20*(77), 21–32.

Bolton, F. G., & MacEachron, A. E. (1988). Adolescent male sexuality: A developmental perspective. *Journal of Adolescent Research, 3*(3–4), 259–273.

Centers for Disease Control. (1989). *HIV/AIDS surveillance*. Atlanta, GA: U. S. Department of Health and Human Services.

Coles, R., & Stokes, G. (1985). *Sex and the American teenager*. New York: Harper & Row.

Cross, R. J. (1991). Helping adolescents learn about sexuality. *SIECUS Report, 17*(4), 6–11.

D'Augelli, A. R. (1988). The adolescent closet: Promoting the development of the lesbian or gay male teenager. *The School Psychologist, 42,* 2–3.

D'Augelli, A. R., Collins, C., & Hart, M. M. (1987). Social support patterns of lesbian women in a rural helping network. *Journal of Rural Community Psychology, 8*(1), 12–22.

deMauro, D. (1990). Sexuality education 1990: A review of state sexuality and AIDS education curricula. *SIECUS Report, 18*(2), 1–9.

Diepold, J., & Young, R. D. (1979). Empirical studies of adolescent sexual behavior: A critical review. *Adolescence, 14,* 45-64.

Dornbusch, S. M., Carlsmith, J. M., Gross, R. T., Martin, J. A., Jennings, D., Rosenberg, A., & Duke, A. (1981). Sexual development, age, and dating: A comparison of biological and social influences upon one set of behaviors. *Child Development, 52,* 179-185.

Donovan, , & Jessor, (1985).

Forrest, J. D., & Silverman, J. (1989). What public school teachers teach about preventing pregnancy, AIDS, and sexually transmitted diseases. *Family Planning Perspectives, 21*(2), 65-72.

Fox, G. L. (1981). The family's role in adolescent sexual behavior. In T. Ooms (Ed.), *Teenage pregnancy in a family context* (pp. 73-130). Philadelphia, PA: Temple University Press.

Gagnon, J. (1977). *Human sexualities.* IL: Scott, Foresman.

Gfellner, B. M. (1986). Concepts of sexual behaviors: Construction and validation of a developmental model. *Journal of Adolescent Research, 1*(3), 327-347.

Gibson, P. (1989). Gay male and lesbian suicide. In A. Adamah (Ed.), *A report of the secretary's task force on youth suicide* (Vol. 3, pp. 110-142. DHHS Pub # 89-1623). Washington, DC: U.S. Government Printing Office.

Goldman, R. J., & Goldman, J. D. G. (1982). How children perceive the origin of babies and the roles of mothers and fathers in procreation: A cross-national study. *Child Development, 53,* 491-504.

Haffner, D. W. (1990). Moving toward a *healthy* paradigm of teen development: Helping young people develop into sexually healthy adults. *SIECUS Report, 18*(4), 12-14.

Haffner, D. W., & Kelly, M. (1987, March/April). Adolescent sexuality in the media. *SIECUS Report,* 9-12.

Hogan, D. P., & Kitagawa, E. M. (1985). The impact of social status, family structure, and neighborhood on the fertility of black adolescents. *American Journal of Sociology, 90*(4), 825-855.

Jorgensen, S. R. (1983). Beyond adolescent pregnancy: Research frontiers for early adolescent sexuality. *Journal of Early Adolescence, 3*(1-2), 141-155.

Kenney, A. M., Guardado, S., & Brown, L. (1989). Sex education and education in the schools: What states and large school districts are doing. *Family Planning Perspectives, 21*(2), 56-64.

Koch, P. B. (1980). A comparison of the sex education of primary-aged children in the United States and Sweden, as expressed through their art. In J. M. Samson (Ed.), *Childhood and sexuality: Proceedings of the international symposium* (pp. 345-355). Montreal: Editions Etudes Vivantes.

Koch, P. B. (1988). The relationship of first intercourse to later sexual functioning concerns of adolescents. *Journal of Adolescent Research, 3*(93-4), 345-362.

Koch, P. B. (1992). Integrating cognitive, affective, and behavioral approaches into learning experiences for sexuality education. In J. T. Sears (Ed.), *Sexuality and the curriculum* (pp. 253-266). New York: Teachers College Press.

Leight, L. (1989). "Golden opportunities" for raising sexually healthy adolescents. *SIECUS Report, 18*(1), 10-12.

Lerner, R. M. (1987). A life-span perspective for early adolescence. In R. M. Lerner & T. T. Foch (Eds.), *Biological-psycholosocial interactions in early adolescence: A life-span perspective* (pp. 9-34). Hillsdale, NJ: Lawrence Erlbaum Associates.

McCaffree, K. (1989). Male and female adolescent developmental needs. *SIECUS Report, 18*(1), 3-4.

Miller, B. C., McCoy, J. K., Olson, T. D., & Wallace, C. M. (1986). Parental discipline and control attempts in relation to adolescent sexual attitudes and behavior. *Journal of Marriage and the Family, 48,* 503-512.

Millstein, S. G. (in press). A view of health from the adolescent's perspective. In S. G. Millstein, A. C. Petersen, & F. O. Nightengale (Eds.), *Promoting adolescent health*. Fairlawn, NY: Oxford University Press.

Newcomer, S. F., & Udry, J. R. (1985). Oral sex in an adolescent population. *Archives of Sexual Behavior, 14,* 41–46.

Orr, D. P., Wilbrandt, M. L., Brock, C. J., Rauch, S. P., & Ingersoll, G. M. (1989). Reported sexual behaviors and self-esteem among young adolescents. *American Journal of Diseases of Children, 143,* 86–90.

Planned Parenthood. (1980). *Peer education in human sexuality*. Washington, DC: Planned Parenthood of Metropolitan Washington, DC.

Remafedi, G. (1987a). Homosexual youth: A challenge to contemporary society. *Journal of the American Medical Association, 258*(2), 221–225.

Remafedi, G. (1987b). Male homosexuality: The adolescent's perspective. *Pediatrics, 79*(3), 326–330.

Remafedi, G. J. (1988). Preventing the sexual transmission of AIDS during adolescence. *Journal of Adolescent Health Care, 9,* 139–143.

Remafedi, G. (1989). The healthy sexual development of gay and lesbian adolescents. *SIECUS Report, 17*(5), 7–8.

Selverstone, R. (1989). Adolescent sexuality: Developing self-esteem and mastering developmental tasks. *SIECUS Report, 18*(1), 1–3.

Simon, W., Berger, A. S., & Gagnon, J. H. (1972). Beyond anxiety and fantasy: The coital experiences of college youth. *Journal of Youth and Adolescence, 1,* 203–222.

Sloane, B. C. (1989). Issues that arise as a young person's sexuality unfolds. *SIECUS Report, 17*(5), 5–6.

Smith, P. B., Nenney, S. W., & McGill, L. (1986). Health problems and sexual activity of selected inner city, middle school students. *Journal of School Health, 56*(7), 263–266.

Sorenson, R. C. (1973). *Adolescent sexuality in contemporary America*. New York: World.

Sprafkin, J. N., & Silverman, L. T. (1981). Update: Physically intimate and sexual behavior on primetime television, 1978–1979. *Journal of Communication, 31*(1), 34–40.

Taylor, H., Kagay, M., & Leichenko, S. (1986). *American teens speak: Sex, myths, TV, and birth control*. New York: Planned Parenthood Federation of America.

Thornburg, H. D. (1981). Adolescent sources of information on sex. *Journal of School Health, 51,* 274–277.

Udry, J. R., Billy, J. O. G., Morris, N. M., Groff, T. R., & Raj, M. H. (1985). Serum androgenic hormones motivate sexual behavior in adolescent boys. *Fertility and Sterility, 43,* 90–94.

Udry, J. R., Talbert, L. M., & Morris, N. M. (1986). Biosocial foundations for adolescent female sexuality. *Demography, 23*(2), 217–230.

Weddle, K. D., McKenry, P. C., & Leigh, G. K. (1988). Adolescent sexual behavior: Trends and issues in research. *Journal of Adolescent Research, 3*(3–4), 245–257.

IV | Preventive Interventions in Early Adolescence

Section Editors:

Bonnie L. Barber
Lisa J. Crockett
The Pennsylvania State University

Preventive Interventions in Early Adolescence: Developmental and Contextual Challenges

Bonnie L. Barber
Lisa J. Crockett
The Pennsylvania State University

Adolescence today is broadly perceived as a more difficult and dangerous period than in previous decades. Those holding this view point to increases in teenage pregnancy and childbearing, sexually transmitted diseases, alcohol abuse, drug addiction, juvenile arrests, depression, and suicide as indicators of changing conditions. Although uncommon in childhood, these problems increase in early adolescence, and they can lead to greater likelihood of negative developmental trajectories. Because young adolescents are at the age when these issues are surfacing, they are a particularly important target group for interventions designed to prevent or delay the onset of negative behavior patterns (Crockett & Petersen, in press). Preventive interventions targeting older youth often start too late, after the onset of the behavior they are designed to prevent. Early adolescence is a good time to intervene, before behavior patterns solidify, increasing the risks of more serious problems.

The goal of this section is to integrate existing research on early adolescent development with the available literature on preventive interventions. The chapters present a discussion of a variety of problems in early adolescence: teenage pregnancy, early childbearing, HIV infection, substance abuse, and depression. In focusing on issues for designing preventive interventions, the authors discuss what content and style of program would be expected to be most effective with young adolescents. Each author had a different amount of prevention research to draw upon. For some of the content areas, there has been a longer history of research and prevention, whereas others are relatively new to prevention efforts. The effectiveness of programs already in place is considered. Suggestions are offered when prevention efforts have not yet been implemented (or have not been evaluated). Rather than attempting a comprehensive review of the prevention literature, the following chapters illustrate several content areas useful for the understanding of the connections between research and application.

Common approaches discussed across most or all of the problem areas include the provision of information, enhancing interpersonal skills, providing increased access to relevant resources, and improving social support. In addition, the chapters recommend that for a program to be successful, it should promote competence that will generalize beyond the specific problem. Multifaceted interventions (i.e., those combining several approaches targeting different dimensions of the problem) appear to be more successful in altering behavior than unidimensional efforts (Perry & Jessor, 1985; Rolf, 1985). For this reason, a number of investigators advocate community-wide interventions that have an impact at multiple levels of the environment.

Key themes highlighted by the chapters include the need to design developmentally appropriate interventions, and the requirement for sensitivity to the cultural setting in which adolescents are growing up. Specifically, the unique characteristics of the early adolescent period should be considered in program planning, as should the competencies and limitations of the targeted individuals. In addition, sensitivity to diversity is crucial, as each racial, ethnic, and cultural group may present particular needs. Sensitivity to community norms and values is also crucial because community support is critical both for mounting a viable intervention program and for maintaining its effectiveness. Programs that undermine community values will meet with strong resistance. Furthermore, in some cases, community agencies such as schools, local media, and service organizations may play active roles in intervention delivery, making community commitment essential.

These issues are first illustrated in the chapter on adolescent pregnancy prevention. Crockett and Chopak emphasize the need to tailor programs to the individual characteristics of adolescents, especially their cognitive and emotional level, as these are influenced by the cultural setting. During early adolescence there is an opportunity to use developmentally appropriate methods to delay the onset of sexual behavior and to instill positive attitudes toward contraception. The authors also highlight the importance of motivation as well as ability in delaying the onset of risk behavior and in using effective contraception. They also stress the importance of recruiting community support for programming.

The chapter on Hispanic adolescent sexuality and childbearing describes the importance of both subgroup diversity and shared cultural values as these affect adolescent childbearing among Hispanics. Fennelly elaborates on the contradictions of the contexts in which young Hispanic adolescents develop. Family and peer group attitudes are conflicting, leading to the need for preventive interventions sensitive to the divergent pressures facing these adolescents.

D'Augelli and Bingham discuss the need for AIDS programs that reflect multiple prevention strategies and multiple levels of prevention based on the salient contexts of adolescence (family, school, community). As in the first two chapters in this section, D'Augelli and Bingham point out that preventing the initiation of risk behavior is preferable to trying to change it once it is established. To reduce the risk of HIV infection, preventive efforts must be focused on both sexual behavior and drug use. Personal skills are highlighted as crucial in prevention efforts, as are the social networks of peers, family, and community.

Individual differences and contextual influences are also important in the etiology of drug use. Swisher's chapter discusses how intrapersonal, interpersonal, and contextual influences converge to affect beliefs about the rewards and risks of substance abuse. Presenting a model that describes these three levels of influence, Swisher suggests that one prevention strategy may be to intervene directly with beliefs and perceptions that are related to substance use. He points out that interventions using simultaneous combinations of individual, interpersonal, and extrapersonal domains have more lasting effects on levels of substance use than those targeting a single domain.

The importance of developmentally appropriate programs is further illustrated in the Kennedy chapter on early adolescent depression. As with other chapters in this section, the importance of the interaction between the young adolescent and the setting is emphasized. Depression is viewed as resulting from a mismatch between the challenges of the early adolescent period and the coping resources of individuals. Prevention efforts then, are geared toward facilitating the mastery of age-related tasks.

By design, the chapters in this section each focus on a single problem. A number of these problems covary, however, and have common antecedents (Dryfoos, 1990). Although research has documented the interrelationships among adolescent problems, only recently have interventions begun to target multiple problems. In this new stage of prevention research and practice, it may be possible to intervene at multiple levels to effect several problems simultaneously.

REFERENCES

Crockett, L. J., & Petersen, A. C. (in press). Adolescent development: Health risks and opportunities for health promotion. In S. G. Millstein, A. C. Petersen, & E. O. Nightingale (Eds.), *Adolescent health promotion*. New York: Oxford University Press.

Dryfoos, J. G. (1990). *Adolescents at risk: Prevalence & prevention.* New York: Oxford University Press.

Perry, C. L., & Jessor, R. (1985). The concept of health promotion and the prevention of adolescent drug abuse. *Health Education Quarterly,* 12, 169–184.

Rolf, J. E. (1985). Evolving adaptive theories and methods for prevention research with children. *Journal of Consulting and Clinical Psychology,* 53, 631–646.

18 Pregnancy Prevention in Early Adolescence: A Developmental Perspective

Lisa J. Crockett
Joanne S. Chopak
The Pennsylvania State University

Although there is widespread interest in preventing teenage pregnancy, few interventions have been directed toward young adolescents. In part this neglect is understandable because adolescents under age 15 account for only a small percentage of teenage pregnancies (Pittman & Adams, 1988). At the same time, the lack of attention to younger adolescents is unfortunate on several counts. First, an increasing number of young adolescents are at risk. Rates of sexual activity have been rising in this group (Hofferth, Kahn, & Baldwin, 1987) and, because young adolescents are typically not consistent or effective contraceptive users, an increasing number of girls are becoming pregnant. Between 1973 and 1987 the pregnancy rate among girls under age 15 increased 23%, from 14 to 17 per 1,000 (Henshaw, Kenney, Somberg, & Van Vort, 1989). In fact, this is the only group for whom pregnancy rates have not declined in recent years. Second, early adolescence represents an important window of opportunity for adolescent pregnancy prevention. During early adolescence, most young people become capable of reproduction and many become sexually active. Thus, prevention efforts need to start by this age if they are to precede the biological and behavioral onset of pregnancy risk. Furthermore, skills and attitudes developed in early adolescence may have long-term benefits, reducing pregnancy risk throughout the teenage years.

Despite the probable benefits of pregnancy prevention in early adolescence, programming for this age group has been limited. Young adolescents receive less extensive sex education in the schools and have less access to contraceptive services than do older adolescents (Hayes, 1987). The limited response reflects societal attitudes toward adolescent sexuality and the belief that frank discussion, detailed information, and access to contraceptives will encourage early intercourse. Public ambivalence thus creates special challenges to developing pregnancy prevention programs for young adolescents. Other challenges derive from the characteristics of young adolescents themselves. These youngsters are typically less knowledgeable, less experienced, and less cognitively sophisticated than older teenagers and adults. Moreover, because of differences in their rates of development, they are frequently at different stages of biological, cognitive, emotional, and social maturity. Finally, young adolescents come from diverse social, economic, and cultural circumstances; thus, they bring differing skills, values, and expectations to sexual and reproductive decision making.

Despite the formidable complexity of these issues, there is growing recognition of the need to create pregnancy prevention programs for young adolescents that are developmentally appropriate (Proctor, 1986) and tailored to the economic and cultural circumstances of the target population (e.g., Roesel, 1987). The multiple factors affecting early adolescent pregnancy are reviewed in a companion chapter (Crockett, chapter 6, this volume). In this chapter, we outline some of the developmental and contextual issues that need to be considered in designing programs for young adolescents, review some existing pregnancy prevention programs, and discuss strategies for reaching a younger audience. We suggest that young adolescents are a unique group with special programming needs.

EARLY ADOLESCENT DEVELOPMENT

Biological Development

At puberty, hormonal increases stimulate changes in physiology, leading to the development of reproductive capability (Petersen & Taylor, 1980). Most girls experience menarche between the ages of 11 and 15, with the average age being 12½ (Eveleth, 1986). Although early cycles are often irregular and infertile, pregnancy is biologically possible for many girls at age 13 or 14. Individual differences in the timing of puberty mean that some girls become fertile at younger ages than others and spend more of their teenage years biologically "at risk" for pregnancy.

Puberty also affects pregnancy risk through its influence on sexual behavior. There is evidence that pubertal increases in particular hormones (androgens) are associated with increased sexual motivation and behavior in both boys and girls (Udry, Billy, Morris, Groff, & Raj, 1985; Udry, Talbert, & Morris, 1986). Hormonal changes may also affect sexual behavior indirectly through their impact on the development of secondary sex characteristics. As adolescents begin to look physically mature, they may experience more opportunity for sexual involvement and more pressure to engage in sex, because they are viewed as attractive sexual partners (Udry et al., 1986).

Implications for Pregnancy Prevention. In early adolescence, girls' inexperience with their menstrual cycles, combined with the frequent irregularity of these cycles, may make them less likely to recognize their fertility and the risk of pregnancy associated with it. Thus, special measures need to be introduced to help girls assimilate the reality of their new reproductive capabilities. Program providers also need to recognize that the sexual interests and motivations of many young people are increasing during early adolescence. To be accepted as relevant, programs need to acknowledge adolescents' own interests, goals, and needs related to sexuality, even if these are not optimal from the perspective of adults. Programs must also consider the developing sexual attractiveness of adolescent girls. There is some evidence that older males are turning to younger girls whom they perceive to be cleaner, free of disease, and less demanding (Newcomer, personal communication, August 1, 1991). Given this situation, girls need to be equipped with the interpersonal skills and knowledge necessary to avoid unwanted sexual experiences. The high rates of nonvoluntary sexual activity among U.S. adolescents (Moore, Nord, & Peterson, 1989) attest to this need. Finally, early maturers may require earlier or more intensive intervention efforts than later maturers.

Cognitive Development

Studies of cognitive development indicate that thinking becomes more sophisticated during adolescence (Keating, 1990). Young people become increasingly able to think hypothetically, understand abstract concepts, and apply a more extended time perspective. These advances should enable them to comprehend risks, reflect on their behavior, and consider the consequences of their actions, all of which should facilitate responsible sexual decision making. There is ample evidence, however, that young adolescents are not proficient in this domain. Relative to older adolescents, they are less competent in decision making and problem solving generally (Weithorn & Campbell, 1982); they are also less likely to use birth control (Hayes, 1987). One reason may be that young adolescents who are just beginning to develop the ability to reason abstractly cannot do so consistently and continue to reason concretely in many situations. Thus, they are less able to generate alternatives, systematically evaluate the consequences of alternative courses of action, and estimate the likelihood of various outcomes, all of which are key features of wise decision making (Keating, 1990).

Even when young adolescents have developed the ability to reason abstractly, they may be unlikely to apply this reasoning in sexual situations. Stressful topics and time-pressured decisions elicit less sophisticated reasoning from adolescents and adults alike (Keating, 1990), and adolescent sexual decision making typically occurs in such a context. In addition, young adolescents' attitudes or beliefs may profoundly shape the decision-making process. Some may not recognize a sexual situation as one involving choice or may prefer not to acknowledge that they have a choice; thus, they fail to go through the decision-making process. Others may be influenced by community values regarding adolescent sexuality and contraception; their decisions may be rational given the cultural system in which they live, but still place them at risk. Finally, some youngsters lack knowledge about birth control methods, the risk of becoming pregnant, or the consequences of early childbearing, and, consequently, base their decisions on faulty information.

Implications for Pregnancy Prevention. There is an obvious need to provide accurate information about pregnancy risk and contraceptive methods to young adolescents. Because abstract reasoning in sexual matters cannot be assumed, however, information about sex and contraception will need to be presented as concretely as possible, with the links between behavior and its consequences carefully and systematically articulated. Short-term consequences may be more salient to young adolescents than long-term ones that require an extended time perspective. In addition, sexual decision making should be modeled and rehearsed, so that adolescents become familiar with the issues they will have to confront in sexual situations and with possible courses of action. Finally, programs must consider young adolescents' beliefs concerning the costs and benefits of sex, contraception, and pregnancy as these are influenced by the norms and values of the communities in which they reside. Improved decision-making skills will only lead to responsible sexual behavior among those who are motivated to avoid unprotected intercourse and who have adequate resources and supports for doing so.

Conceptions of Self

During adolescence, young people become concerned with discovering who they are. In early adolescence, they become more aware of their psychological and emotional characteristics, as well as their talents and values (Harter, 1990). Later in adolescence, young people confront the task of integrating these self-observations into a coherent sense of who they are and who they will be in the future (Erikson, 1968). Young adolescents engaged in learning about themselves need opportunities to uncover their talents, to develop competencies, and to take pride in their accomplishments. They also need to feel accepted and valued by others. Support from family and peers and competence in valued domains both contribute to adolescent self-esteem (Harter, 1990). Young adolescents may also be ready to begin thinking about what they want for themselves in the future.

Implications for Pregnancy Prevention. To engage young adolescents, pregnancy prevention programs need to be sensitive to their interests in self-discovery and personal competence. Discussions can focus on young people's emerging sexual concerns, interests, and values. In addition, skills development and contraceptive use can be presented as dimensions of personal competence. It may also be possible to stimulate thinking about the future. Although young adolescents cannot be expected to have well-articulated career goals, they may be able to identify general hopes as well as outcomes they wish to avoid. The links between unprotected intercourse and blocked opportunities can then be made. In any case, the goal would be to link young adolescents' emerging sense of self to sexual behavior.

CONTEXTUAL FACTORS

Young adolescents' development is intimately connected with the social world in which they are growing up: with their family, peers, school, and community, as well as the broader society. These contexts not only influence adolescent sexual behavior, thereby affecting pregnancy risk; they also define the setting in which prevention programs are to be developed and maintained.

Family Relations

The family continues to be an important source of guidance and support throughout adolescence. Parents provide a set of values, models, and expectations that guide current behavior and shape future goals. Furthermore, most adolescents report that they respect their parents and feel close to them (Offer, Ostrov, & Howard, 1981). Nonetheless, early adolescence is often a period of increasing tension and conflict with parents, as young people negotiate for greater autonomy and more power in the family (Montemayor, 1983). It is important to recognize that, despite such tensions, most adolescents continue to report positive relationships with their parents and to turn to them for advice and support (Steinberg, 1990). Thus, parents can continue to play an important guiding role through communication and through monitoring their children's behavior. Unfortunately, not all parents are successful at these tasks, and this failure affects girls' risk of pregnancy. Lack of monitoring, poor parent–child relationships, and living in a nonintact family increase girls' likelihood of early sexual activity. Poor parent–child communication is also associated with inconsistent use of contraceptives and with early pregnancy (Chilman, 1986).

Implications for Pregnancy Prevention. The data on parent–child relationships suggest that parents can influence early adolescent sexual and reproductive behavior. Parental expectations for their children's achievement, parental monitoring practices, and parent–adolescent communication can be modified to buttress program messages about sex, contraception, and early pregnancy. Conversely, where parent values and practices conflict with these messages, the success of the program is jeopardized. Parents must be convinced that program goals are healthy for their children and do not undercut their own childrearing goals and values. Parents also need to recognize their powerful impact on their children and the crucial role they can play in pregnancy interventions. Parents thus need to be informed and encouraged to participate. They can be recruited to serve on community boards that advise the program developers; they may also become key players in the intervention itself.

Peers

Peers can also exert a powerful influence on adolescent behavior. Although adolescents typically follow parents' values concerning long-term educational and occupational goals, they turn to peers for guidance in the day-to-day activities of being a teenager (Kandel & Lesser, 1972). Thus, peer norms can have important effects, and this may be particularly true in the areas of sexual and contraceptive behavior, where parents often fail to provide guidance and information. A high teen pregnancy rate among peers in the neighborhood or at school, for example, gives the dual message that adolescents are sexually active and that early childbearing is not so deviant. Furthermore, the attitudes and behavior of an adolescent's circle of friends may be influential, especially for girls (Smith, Udry, & Morris, 1985). Finally, romantic partners can be a source of direct pressure to engage in sex.

The influence of peers may be particularly potent in early adolescence when conformity to peer opinion is higher than at any other time (Berndt, 1979). Young adolescents place a great deal of importance on belonging to a peer group and being accepted (Brown, 1989); they are thus especially susceptible to peer group pressure. Because they are relatively inexperienced in the teenage social role, young adolescents may rely heavily on peers as models of appropriate behavior. In addition, the capacity for intimate friendship emerges in early adolescence (Berndt, 1982), and these close, deeply valued relationships may be a powerful force in young people's lives.

Implications for Pregnancy Prevention. In designing pregnancy prevention programs, the importance of peer influence needs to be taken into account. Messages that are not accepted by one's friends are unlikely to be heeded; thus, it may be necessary to intervene directly with peer attitudes or at least with young adolescents' perceptions of peer norms (e.g., Hansen, 1990). On the other hand, peers who promote responsible sexual behavior can be an enormous advantage. Older peer models may be extremely effective in encouraging attitudes and behavior associated with reduced pregnancy risk (Klepp, Halpern, & Perry, 1986).

It may also be possible to target young adolescents' susceptibility to peer influence. Peer resistance skills (e.g., Botvin & Tortu, 1988) can help young people identify and resist pressure to engage in unprotected intercourse. Sexuality can also be discussed as a behavior that requires "true autonomy"; that is, making decisions that are not overly influenced by either parents or peers. Training in decision-making skills may be helpful in facilitating the development of true autonomy.

Community

The neighborhood or community in which family and peers are embedded may exert an additional influence. Communities are characterized by economic resources, ethnic mix, and shared norms and values, each of which may affect adolescent sexual and reproductive behavior. For example, early adolescent intercourse is more common among

Blacks than among Whites or Hispanics (Hayes, 1987). It is also more prevalent among adolescents of lower socioeconomic status (Chilman, 1986) and among adolescents residing in poor neighborhoods (Hogan & Kitigawa, 1985). Thus, the young adolescents at risk for pregnancy are disproportionately poor and from minority populations. Economic resources also influence the quality of schools, employment opportunities, and the array of adult role models to which adolescents are exposed, all of which can affect adolescents' perceptions of opportunities and expectations for the future (Ianni, 1989). In addition, community resources influence the alternative (nonsexual) activities and rewards currently available to adolescents, for example, extracurricular activities and youth groups. Finally, community norms may be important. A high prevalence of nonmarital childbearing and single-parent families may influence adolescents' perceptions of their normal, expectable life course. Expectations for the future may in turn affect current behavioral choices. A recent study found that neighborhood conditions (specifically, the prevalence of single mothers and the absence of middle-class neighbors) affected teenage childbearing even after family socioeconomic status was controlled (Brooks-Gunn, Duncan, Kato, & Sealand, 1991).

Implications for Pregnancy Prevention. Community variables affect both pregnancy risk and the kinds of interventions that are likely to be acceptable. Some communities will tolerate the direct distribution of contraceptives to adolescents; others will be extremely resistant to such programs. Recruiting and maintaining community support is essential for success; thus, showing sensitivity to local values, establishing trust and rapport, and maintaining an ongoing relationship with community leaders and institutions are crucial (SEICUS, 1991).

The Media

The media may also exert an important influence on adolescent sexual behavior. Television programs portray adolescent and young adult sexual relationships with virtually no mention of contraceptive use (although unwanted pregnancy is a common topic). Commercials, magazine advertisements, and MTV also exploit adolescent sexuality through images of young men and women in tight clothes, or in intimate settings. And teen magazines provide endless tales of adolescent love and romance. Although the impact of such images has not been well documented (Frith & Frith, chapter 24, this volume), an effect seems probable. Clearly, more research is needed on this topic.

Implications for Pregnancy Prevention. The media portrayals of adolescent sexuality are likely to arouse young adolescents' interest and curiosity and may also affect their understanding of appropriate teenage behavior. One approach to minimizing the potency of such images is to demystify them by helping young adolescents to analyze the content of the messages and identify the techniques of persuasion employed. Alternatively, it may be possible to recruit the local media to include public service messages on preventing pregnancy (e.g., Vincent, Clearie, & Schluchter, 1987).

PREGNANCY PREVENTION PROGRAMS

How might information on early adolescent development and social contexts inform pregnancy prevention efforts? Pregnancy prevention programs in the United States typically involve one or more of the following strategies: knowledge interventions, access to contraceptives, and enhancing life options (Dryfoos, 1990). A brief review of these strategies is provided, followed by recommendations on how programs could be modified in light of information on early adolescent development and social contexts.

Knowledge Interventions

Knowledge-based programs are those designed to disseminate information on sexuality, reproduction, relationships, and contraception in an attempt to influence adolescents' sexual attitudes and behavior. These programs may be implemented by a variety of community organizations such as schools, churches, boys/girls clubs, and public health agencies (Hayes, 1987).

Most schools offer some form of sex education. By the early 1980s, roughly 75% of all school districts were providing some sex education. Most programs, however, are included in a general health education class and emphasize the basics: anatomy, physiology, pubertal development, and reproduction (Hayes, 1987). Junior high school programs tend to concentrate on puberty, reproduction, and dating, but not on contraceptive methods and family planning, whereas high school programs are more comprehensive. Evaluations of such programs indicate that they increase knowledge about reproduction, especially among younger adolescents. There is little evidence, however, that they affect sexual and contraceptive behavior (Kirby, 1984; Zelnik & Kim, 1982).

Sex education is also provided by some community-based programs that label themselves as family life education programs. These programs not only offer the basics of sex education, they also emphasize roles and responsibilities in the family, social problems within the family, and career and financial planning. Many of these programs have been effective in increasing adolescents' knowledge, both about sexuality and about the consequences of their actions (Hayes, 1987).

Access to Contraception

Contraceptive services are provided to adolescents through school-based clinics, health service organizations such as Planned Parenthood, public health clinics, and private physicians. Most adolescents prefer clinics because they are less expensive than private physicians and because they generally do not require parental consent before prescribing contraceptives, whereas many private physicians do (Hayes, 1987). In addition to contraceptives, many of these family planning clinics offer a wide range of services including testing and counseling for sexually transmitted diseases. School-based clinics operate as comprehensive ambulatory care facilities with many of the same attributes (low cost, convenient, comfortable, confidential) of other family planning agencies. In addition to reproductive health care, these clinics may offer athletic physicals, treatment for nonacute illnesses, laboratory and diagnostic screenings, immunizations, and other services. Preliminary evaluations of school-based clinics indicated that they were associated with decreased adolescent fertility, but the full evaluation has been less positive (Hyche-Williams & Waszak, 1990).

Programs to Enhance Life Options

Life options enhancement programs are designed to increase adolescents' motivation to avoid early pregnancy. By improving decision-making skills, helping young people to set attainable future goals, improving school performance and the value placed on education, enhancing self-esteem, and providing positive role models, these programs seek to introduce alternatives to adolescent childbearing. Programs with these aims have been offered by youth-serving agencies (e.g., 4-H, Boys/Girls Clubs of America). No evaluations of the success of these programs in lowering fertility rates have been completed thus far (Dryfoos, 1990).

Programs With Promise

Most adolescent pregnancy prevention programs are targeted toward teenagers aged 15 and older. Several programs, however, have included younger adolescents. One of the most successful pregnancy prevention programs has been the Self Program in Baltimore, Maryland (Zabin, Hirsch, Smith, Street, & Hardy, 1986a, 1986b). The preventive intervention took place over a 3-year period in one junior high school and one senior high school, with another junior high and senior high serving as control schools. Both treatment schools had an all-Black enrollment, with most students coming from low-income households. The program consisted of school-based sex education combined with access to contraceptive services and counseling. These additional services were offered at a clinic conveniently located between the two treatment schools.

Zabin and her colleagues reported that after almost 2 years' exposure to their program, pregnancy rates had decreased by 23 percentage points in the experimental schools as compared to an increase of 39 percentage points in the control schools. Smaller reductions were seen among the seventh and eighth grade girls than among the older girls, but this difference may be attributed to the smaller proportion of sexually active girls in the lower grades.

Another highly successful program was the School/Community Program for Sexual Risk Reduction Among Teens conducted in South Carolina (Vincent et al., 1987). The strategy in this program was to saturate the community with pregnancy prevention efforts designed to delay the initiation of first intercourse and to promote the consistent use of contraceptives. To accomplish these objectives, the program sought to improve decision-making skills, interpersonal communication, self-esteem, and knowledge about reproduction and contraception. Adults in the community were an important component of the program. Teachers, clergy, church leaders, and parents were included in training to improve their skills as parents and role models in the community. In addition, the local media were used to promote public service messages about preventing pregnancy.

After 4 years, the pregnancy rate among 14- to 17-year-olds in the experimental community was reduced from 61 to 25 (per 1,000), as compared to the control community which experienced an increase from 35 to 50 (per 1,000). Vincent et al. (1987) attributed the success of this program to the complete involvement of all levels of the community. The reduction in fertility, however, may also have been directly influenced by the school nurse who distributed condoms and took girls to the local family planning clinic (Koo, personal communication, October, 1991).

A third program, Reducing the Risk, draws on social learning, social inoculation, and cognitive-behavioral theory and involves setting explicit norms against unprotected intercourse. Initial evaluation results (based on 13 California high schools) indicate that the school-based curriculum significantly increased knowledge about contraception, as well as parent–child communication about abstinence and contraception. Importantly, the curriculum was also associated with significant reductions in initiation of intercourse and in the rate of unprotected intercourse among those who had not initiated intercourse prior to the start of the program (Kirby, Barth, Leland, & Fetro, 1991).

These findings suggest that early adolescent sexual and contraceptive behavior can be influenced by preventive interventions that emphasize norm-setting, interpersonal skills, and access to contraceptives, in addition to knowledge. Enlisting elements of the social context (parents and other community figures and resources) appears to enhance program impact (Dryfoos, 1990).

RECOMMENDATIONS FOR EARLY ADOLESCENT PROGRAMS

Pregnancy is the endpoint of a sequence of events that includes engaging in sexual intercourse and failure to practice effective contraception. Thus, prevention efforts may focus on reducing the frequency of intercourse (through delay or desistance) or on facilitating contraceptive use. Each of these behaviors involves both motivational and ability components (Dryfoos, 1990). Adolescents must have the desire to delay or reduce sexual intercourse or to use effective contraception; they must also have the information and skills needed to translate this desire into action, as well as access to effective contraceptives. Based on these considerations, pregnancy prevention programs need to include direct and honest information about sexuality; access to convenient, confidential, and low-cost family planning services; and options that enhance teenagers' motivation to delay premature pregnancy and childbearing (Haffner & Casey, 1986). When young adolescents are the focus, these tasks are complicated by their biological, cognitive, and social immaturity. Family and community norms, values, and resources introduce additional complexities. To be successful, prevention strategies need to be attentive to this constellation of issues. Our review leads to several specific recommendations for modifying current pregnancy prevention strategies to reach young adolescents.

Improving Knowledge

In addition to the basic information on sexuality that is typically presented in sex education courses, young adolescents would benefit from more explicit information concerning contraception. Information should include instruction in effective contraceptive methods and how to obtain them, as well as instruction and practice in their appropriate use. For knowledge to be useful to young adolescents, all information regarding sex, contraception, and pregnancy should be presented as concretely as possible, with explicit links made to their personal experiences. As an aid to instruction, girls and boys could be encouraged to mentally rehearse the sequence of behaviors they will need to engage in prior to intercourse and should be given opportunities to role-play these behaviors. Of course, such programming will be controversial in many communities; thus, program development will need to include open discussion with parents and other community members and sensitivity to their concerns (SEICUS, 1991).

Enhancing Ability

To improve young adolescents' ability to avoid pregnancy, access to effective contraceptives and instruction in their use is essential. In addition, attention needs to be given to helping boys and girls develop the cognitive and social skills they will need for responsible sexual behavior. Two key areas in which skills are necessary are decision-making ability and resistance to peer influence. Responsible decision making can be hampered by a lack of reflectiveness or an inability to generate alternative courses of action. To counteract these problems, young adolescents must learn to conceptualize sex as involving choice and responsibility. In addition, they need practice in reflecting on their behavior and considering its possible consequences (i.e., thinking before acting), along with practice in generating alternatives to unprotected intercourse. Programs for teaching effective decision making have shown success (Mann, Harmoni, Power, Beswick, & Ormond, 1988) and could be modified to address sexual decision making. Self-management training in which adolescents mentally reward themselves for stopping and thinking during emotionally charged situations (e.g., de Armas & Kelly, 1989) may also be useful, along with role-play of alternative courses of action.

Susceptibility to peer influence can be reduced through peer-resistance training. Adolescents can be taught to analyze peer pressure and to develop the communication and negotiation skills needed to resist it (e.g., Botvin & Tortu, 1988). Practice through role-play is recommended. In addition, the situations in which sexual pressure or force is likely to occur should be discussed, along with strategies for avoiding such situations.

Increasing Motivation

Knowledge and skills will only promote responsible sexual behavior among young adolescents who are motivated to use them. Such motivation requires that adolescents realize they are "at risk" and that pregnancy would bring negative consequences. Techniques like individual charting of the menstrual cycle could be used to increase girls' awareness of their fertility (Klaus, 1987). In addition, the links between current sexual behavior and possible consequences should be carefully elaborated, along with their implications for current activities and future educational and career opportunities. For example, adolescents could be encouraged to imagine what it would be like if they became pregnant or got someone pregnant: how their peers, parents, and teachers would react, and how the imagined reactions of these significant individuals would make them feel. They should then be encouraged to think about how pregnancy would affect their current lives. Short-term negative consequences such as physical changes (e.g., weight gain, stretch marks) and loss of leisure time could be discussed. Finally, negative effects on future opportunities could be introduced. Visual approaches such as videos and role-play might be used to stimulate thinking in these domains. To increase motivation to postpone or reduce intercourse, the risk of contracting sexually transmitted diseases could be discussed, along with possible hassles involved in maintaining a sexual relationship. The general goal of these discussions would be to portray sexual relationships realistically, including costs as well as benefits, and to emphasize the advantages of foregoing these relationships. Clearly, this strategy needs to be combined with other strategies: Interventions that only teach adolescents to "say no" have not been effective in reducing sexual behavior (Christopher & Roosa, 1990).

To ensure that girls and boys have future goals they want to protect, interventions to expand life options are needed (Dryfoos, 1990). Aspirations can be raised by linking young people to educational and occupational opportunities, by providing mentors, and by providing funding for postsecondary education. To realistically expand future opportunities, however, actual competencies that lead to better life chances need to be developed (Newcomer, 1987). For example, academic skills may need to be improved so that high aspirations become more realistic and education becomes a more rewarding activity.

Finally, motivation to delay or desist could be nurtured by providing other rewarding activities that meet young adolescents' needs for intimacy, peer acceptance, and self-enhancement. Involvement in school and in extracurricular or other organized activities meets needs for group belonging and a sense of personal achievement. Volunteer service has also been found to bolster self-worth and to reduce problem behaviors, although the effects appear to be greater for older adolescents (Allen, Philliber, & Hoggson, 1990). With regard to intimacy, it may be possible to help young adolescents develop alternative ways to express affection, feelings of closeness, and physical intimacy; for example, through petting and other noncoital behaviors. Such "functional equivalents" (Jessor, 1984) may be difficult to find in the case of an intrinsically rewarding activity such as sex, especially once it has been experienced. Nonetheless, some adolescents have had sex only once (Zelnick & Kantner, 1980), and others go for long periods between sexual relationships. Thus, encouraging desistance could prove to be a viable strategy in some cases.

Motivation to delay or desist as well as motivation to use contraception will be enhanced if there is peer support for these behaviors. As suggested earlier, peer leaders and models can be employed to promote the message that these behaviors are acceptable alternatives. Ideally, the attitudes of the larger peer group would be changed so that unprotected intercourse is viewed negatively, whereas decisions to postpone sex and to use contraceptives are seen as "adult" choices. The importance of avoiding early pregnancy could be reinforced by parents and by the media.

CONCLUSIONS

The most successful programs will probably be those that simultaneously improve young adolescents' knowledge, ability, and motivation to avoid early pregnancy (Dryfoos, 1990). Fortunately, most of these strategies could be incorporated into currently existing programs and services. For example, more open discussions of sexuality and intimacy could be brought into the sex education curriculum in the junior high schools. More explicit information on contraceptive methods and alternatives to intercourse could also be included in the curriculum, although this would be controversial. Finally, both short- and long-term consequences of unprotected intercourse, including the links between family planning and career opportunities, could be concretely articulated, with the role of choice being emphasized. Sexual decision making and peer-resistance skills could be practiced through role-playing. More generally, formal operational reasoning and decision-making skills could be developed in the broader curriculum, along with academic competence. The latter should boost adolescents' self-esteem and provide a basis for higher educational and occupational expectations. In addition, the school and community could provide alternative activities that are fun, enhance self-confidence, and involve peers. Together, these strategies should decrease the value placed on intercourse (especially unprotected intercourse) and equip youngsters with the skills necessary for responsible behavior.

The actual provision of contraceptives to sexually active young adolescents could be accomplished through conveniently located family planning centers or school-based health clinics. School-based clinics may be preferable because they are situated in or close to the school, provide a range of health services, and have staff familiar to the students. Community clinics located near schools also appear to be successful, however, and have the advantage of being able to hold informal discussions on sexual topics that might be considered too controversial for the school sex education curriculum.

Clearly, the needs of young adolescents will vary considerably from community to community. In middle-class suburban communities where first intercourse tends to occur relatively late, programming might emphasize postponing intercourse in service of future goals. These communities have the resources to provide good academic instruction, and a host of alternative (nonsexual) activities are typically in place. In some poor, inner-city, or rural populations, however, a different approach may be required. A larger proportion of young adolescents will be sexually active, necessitating inclusion of contraceptive services and education. Traditional classroom instructional techniques may not be successful for communicating the necessary information, and more innovative, flexible strategies such as the use of videos and drama may be required (e.g., Roesel, 1987). Finally, safe, alternative activities will need to be provided, along with programs to enhance motivation to avoid early pregnancy.

A basic challenge to mounting pregnancy prevention programs for young adolescents is recruiting community support for what may be a controversial effort. Some of the basic program strategies, such as providing information on contraception and access to effective contraceptive methods, require community approval. In addition, comprehensive, multidimensional programs may need to target both adolescents and aspects of their social environment, such as peers, parents, schools, and local media. For these reasons, pregnancy prevention programs need to engage the community.

REFERENCES

Allen, J. P., Philliber, S., & Hoggson, N. (1990). School-based prevention of teenage pregnancy and school dropout: Process evaluation of the National Replication of the Teen Outreach Program. *Journal of Community Psychology, 18,* 505–524.

Berndt, T. J. (1979). Developmental changes in conformity to peers and parents. *Developmental Psychology, 15,* 608–616.

Berndt, T. J. (1982). The features and effects of friendship in early adolescence. *Child Development, 53,* 1447–1460.

Botvin, G. J., & Tortu, S. (1988). Preventing adolescent substance abuse through life skills training. In R. Price, E. L. Gowen, R. P. Lorian, & J. Ramos-McKay (Eds.), *A casebook for practitioners* (pp. 98–110). Washington, DC: American Psychological Association.

Brooks-Gunn, J., Duncan, G. J., Kato, P., & Sealand, N. (1991). *Do neighborhoods influence child and adolescent development?* Unpublished manuscript.

Brown, B. B. (1989). The role of peer groups in adolescents' adjustment to secondary school. In T. J. Berndt & G. W. Ladd (Eds.), *Peer relationships in child development* (pp. 188–215). New York: Wiley.

Chilman, C. S. (1986). Some psychosocial aspects of adolescent sexual and contraceptive behaviors in changing American society. In J. B. Lancaster & B. A. Hamburg (Eds.), *School-age pregnancy and parenthood: Biosocial dimensions* (pp. 191–217). New York: Aldine de Gruyter.

Christopher, F. S., & Roosa, M. W. (1990). An evaluation of an adolescent pregnancy prevention program: Is "just say no" enough? *Family Relations, 39,* 68–72.

de Armas, A., & Kelly, J. A. (1989). Social relationships in adolescence: Skill development and training. In J. Worell & F. Danner (Eds.), *The adolescent as decision-maker: Applications to development and education* (pp. 84–109). San Diego: Academic Press.

Dryfoos, J. G. (1990). *Adolescents at risk: Prevalence and prevention.* New York: Oxford University Press.

Eveleth, P. B. (1986). Timing of menarche: Secular trend and population differences. In J. B. Lancaster & B. A. Hamburg (Eds.), *School-age pregnancy and parenthood: Biosocial dimensions* (pp. 31–52). New York: Aldine de Gruyter.

Erikson, E. (1968). *Identity: Youth and crisis.* New York: Norton.

Haffner, D., & Casey, S. (1986). Approaches to adolescent pregnancy prevention. *Seminars in Adolescent Medicine, 2*(3), 259–267.

Hansen, W. B. (1990). Theory and implementation of the social influence model of primary prevention. In K. H. Rey, C. L. Faegre, & P. Lowery (Eds.), *Prevention research findings: 1988.* Rockville, MD: Office for Substance Abuse Prevention.

Harter, S. (1990). Self and identity development. In S. Feldman & G. Elliot (Eds.), *At the threshold: The developing adolescent* (pp. 352–387). Cambridge: Harvard University Press.

Hayes, C. D. (Ed.). (1987). *Risking the future: Adolescent sexuality, pregnancy, and childbearing* (Vol. 1). Washington, DC: National Academy Press.

Henshaw, S. K., Kenney, A. M., Somberg, D., & Van Vort, J. (1989). *Teenage pregnancy in the United States: The scope of the problem and state responses.* New York: Alan Guttmacher Institute.

Hofferth, S. L., Kahn, J. R., & Baldwin, W. (1987). Premarital sexual activity among U.S. teenage women over the past three decades. *Family Planning Perspectives, 19*(2), 46–53.

Hogan, D. P., & Kitigawa, E. M. (1985). The impact of social status, family structure, and neighborhood on the fertility of black adolescents. *American Journal of Sociology, 90,* 825–855.

Hyche-Williams, J., & Waszak, C. S. (1990). *School-based clinics: 1990.* Washington, DC: Center for Population Options.

Ianni, F. A. J. (1989). *The search for structure: American youth today.* New York: Free Press.

Jessor, R. (1984). Adolescent development and behavioral health. In J. D. Matarazzo, S. M. Weiss, J. A. Heid, N. E. Miller, & S. M. Weiss (Eds.), *Behavioral health: A handbook of health enhancement and disease prevention.* New York: Wiley.

Kandel, D., & Lesser, G. (1972). *Youth in two worlds.* San Francisco: Jossey-Bass.

Keating, D. P. (1990). Adolescent thinking. In S. Feldman & G. Elliot (Eds.), *At the threshold: The developing adolescent* (pp. 54–89). Cambridge: Harvard University Press.

Kirby, D. (1984). *Sexuality education: An evaluation of programs and their effect.* Santa Cruz, CA: Network Publications.

Kirby, D., Barth, R. P., Leland, N., & Fetro, J. V. (1991). A norms and skills based sex education curriculum: Its impact upon sexual risk-taking behavior. *Family Planning Perspectives, 23,* 253–263.

Klaus, H. (1987). Fertility awareness/natural family planning for adolescents and their families: Report of a multisite pilot project. *International Journal of Adolescent Health, 3,* 103–119.

Klepp, K. I., Halpern, A., & Perry, C. L. (1986). The efficacy of peer leaders in drug abuse prevention. *Journal of School Health, 56*(9), 407–411.

Mann, L., Harmoni, R., Power, C., Beswick, G., & Ormond, C. (1988). Effectiveness of the GOFOR course in decision-making for high school students. *Journal of Behavioral Decision-Making, 1,* 159–168.

Montemayor, R. (1983). Parents and adolescents in conflict: All families some of the time and some families most of the time. *Journal of Early Adolescence, 3,* 83–103.

Moore, K. A., Nord, C. W., & Peterson, J. L. (1989). Nonvoluntary sexual activity among adolescents. *Family Planning Perspectives, 21,* 110–114.

Newcomer, S. (1987, Spring). Teen pregnancy: Not simply a result of adolescent ignorance. *Education Horizons,* 114–117.

Offer, D., Ostrov, E., & Howard, K. (1981). *The adolescent: A psychological self-portrait.* New York: Basic Books.

Petersen, A. C., & Taylor, B. (1980). The biological approach to adolescence: Biological change and psychological adaptation. In J. Adelson (Ed.), *Handbook of adolescent psychology* (pp. 115–155). New York: Wiley.

Pittman, K., & Adams, G. (1988). *Teenage pregnancy: An advocate's guide to the numbers.* Washington, DC: Children's Defense Fund.

Proctor, S. (1986). A developmental approach to pregnancy prevention with early adolescent females. *Journal of School Health, 56*(8), 313–316.

Roesel, R. (1987, Spring). Poor and at risk for pregnancy. *Educational Horizons,* 118–120.

SIECUS. (1991). *Winning the battle: Developing support for sexuality and HIV/AIDS education.* New York: Author.

Smith, E. A., Udry, J. R., & Morris, N. M. (1985). Pubertal development and friends: A biosocial explanation of adolescent behavior. *Journal of Health and Social Behavior, 26,* 183-192.

Steinberg, L. (1990). Autonomy, conflict, and harmony in the family relationship. In S. Feldman & G. Elliot (Eds.), *At the threshold: The developing adolescent* (pp. 255-276). Cambridge, MA: Harvard University Press.

Udry, J. R., Billy, J. O. G., Morris, N. M., Groff, T. R., & Raj, M. H. (1985). Serum androgenic hormones motivate sexual behavior in boys. *Fertility and Sterility, 43*(1), 90-94.

Udry, J. R., Talbert, L., & Morris, N. M. (1986). Biosocial foundations for adolescent female sexuality. *Demography, 23*(2), 217-230.

Vincent, M. L., Clearie, A. F., Schluchter, M. D. (1987). Reducing adolescent pregnancy through school and community-based education. *Journal of the American Medical Association, 257*(24), 3382-3386.

Weithorn, L. A., & Campbell, S. B. (1982). The competency of children and adolescents to make informed treatment decisions. *Child Development, 53,* 1589-1598.

Zabin, L. S., Hirsch, M. B., Smith, E. A., Street, R., & Hardy, J. B. (1986a). Evaluation of a pregnancy prevention program for urban teenagers. *Family Planning Perspectives, 18*(3), 119-126.

Zabin, L. S., Hirsch, M. B., Smith, E. A., Street, R., & Hardy, J. B. (1986b). Adolescent pregnancy prevention program: A model for research and evaluation. *Journal of Adolescent Health Care, 7,* 77-87.

Zelnick, M., & Kantner, J. F. (1980). Sexual activity, contraceptive use, and pregnancy among metropolitan-area teenagers: 1971-1979. *Family Planning Perspectives, 12,* 230-237.

Zelnik, M., & Kim, Y. J. (1982). Sex education and its association with teenage sexual activity, pregnancy, and contraceptive use. *Family Planning Perspectives, 14,* 117-126.

19 Sexual Activity and Childbearing Among Hispanic Adolescents in the United States

Katherine Fennelly
The Pennsylvania State University

Despite widespread interest in adolescent sexual activity and childbearing in the United States, until recently little was known about these behaviors among Hispanic young women or their male partners. This omission is lamentable because social problems often need to be documented before they receive public attention. The lack of data on Hispanic adolescent pregnancy and its impact has reduced the visibility of the problem to many providers and policymakers.

Hispanic adolescents in the United States receive conflicting messages from two cultures regarding standards of sexuality, timing of childbearing, and appropriate roles for women. Although teenagers of all ethnic groups experience some contradictions between family and peer group attitudes toward these issues, the contrasts are often especially sharp for Hispanic girls. This is most likely to be true when they or their parents have been raised outside of the United States. If norms and customs of the society of origin differ greatly from those of the United States, the result is often personal stress and conflicts with parents. This can make parent–child communication about dating, sex, birth control, marriage, and childbearing—never an easy process—especially problematic in Hispanic families.

The paucity of information on Hispanic adolescent childbearing has come about because the surveys from which we traditionally derived data on the fertility of Black and White youth (e.g., the Johns Hopkins' studies of American Youth) included few or no Hispanic adolescents. Conversely, those surveys that have included sizeable numbers of

Hispanics (e.g., High School and Beyond, 1980–1986, or the Hispanic Health and Nutrition Examination Survey, 1982–1984) have included few or no variables measuring sexual activity and reproductive histories. Although several authors have compared the fertility of Hispanic and non-Hispanic adults using census data (see e.g., Bean & Swicegood, 1985; or Jaffe, Cullen, & Boswell, 1980), the preponderance of studies of Hispanic adolescent fertility have employed small, localized samples of Mexican-American teenagers on the U.S.–Mexican border and in the southwestern and western states.

Another barrier to accurate information—and particularly trend data—on U.S. Hispanics is the result of frequent changes in census and survey definitions of this population. Since the 1870s, census information on the U.S. Hispanic population has come from such diverse questions as place of birth, parental place of birth, ancestry and self-identification of origin. In 1980 and 1990 the question asked: "What is the origin or descent of each person in this household?" Persons who responded "Mexican-American, Chicano, Mexican, Puerto Rican, Cuban, Central, or South American or other Spanish" were considered to be "Hispanic." Other definitions based on surnames, language spoken, and interviewer designation of ethnicity have been employed in surveys and vital statistics, although currently self-identification questions are more common.

The availability of information on childbearing among U.S. Hispanics has improved greatly since the late 1980s due to several surveys that have included sufficient numbers of Hispanic adolescents for separate analysis (e.g., the National Longitudinal Surveys of Youth, 1979–1990), and special studies of particular origin groups (e.g., the study of Mexican youth in Los Angeles; Sabagh, 1984), and the addition of Hispanic identifiers to vital statistics data in 23 states.

The purpose of this chapter is to summarize what can be learned from these diverse sources. We begin with an overview of the U.S. Hispanic population in order to describe its diversity, and the socioeconomic context in which Hispanics are raised. This is followed by sections on sexual activity, pregnancy and abortion, childbearing, and birth control among Hispanic adolescents compared with Blacks and Whites. When available, separate data are presented for the major Hispanic origin groups in the United States: Mexicans, Puerto Ricans, and Cubans. We conclude with a discussion of the implications of the data for the improvement of preventive services for Hispanic youth.

OVERVIEW OF THE HISPANIC POPULATION

The 21 million Hispanics who resided in the United States in 1990 represent persons from many countries who differ widely in their background characteristics (Bean & Tiendo, 1987; U.S. Bureau of the Census, 1991). The terms *Hispanic* and *Latino* encompass both recent migrants and families who have lived in the United States for several generations, highly educated professionals and unskilled workers, residents from rural areas and inner cities.

Despite this diversity, it is difficult to find studies that identify Hispanics by specific country of origin except for the largest groups. Because 64% of Hispanics in the United States are of Mexican origin, aggregate statistics on "Hispanics" are heavily influenced by the characteristics of this one group. After Mexicans, the largest Hispanic origin groups are Puerto Ricans (11%) and Cubans (5%) (U.S. Bureau of the Census, 1991). Persons from Central and South American countries make up another large group if considered together. Despite recent waves of immigrants from Salvador, Guatemala, and Nicaragua, very few studies separate out Central Americans by country of origin.

Hispanics currently make up more than 8% of the total U.S. population. As a result of high birthrates and levels of immigration, they are the fastest growing U.S. minority group (see Fig. 19.1), and some researchers predict that they will become the largest U.S. minority by 2010 (Wetzel, 1987).

By several measures, Hispanics are economically disadvantaged. In 1988, 24% of Hispanic families had incomes below the poverty line (less than $11,611 for a family of four) (U.S. Bureau of the Census, 1988). This is three times the poverty rate for non-Hispanic Whites (8%) and

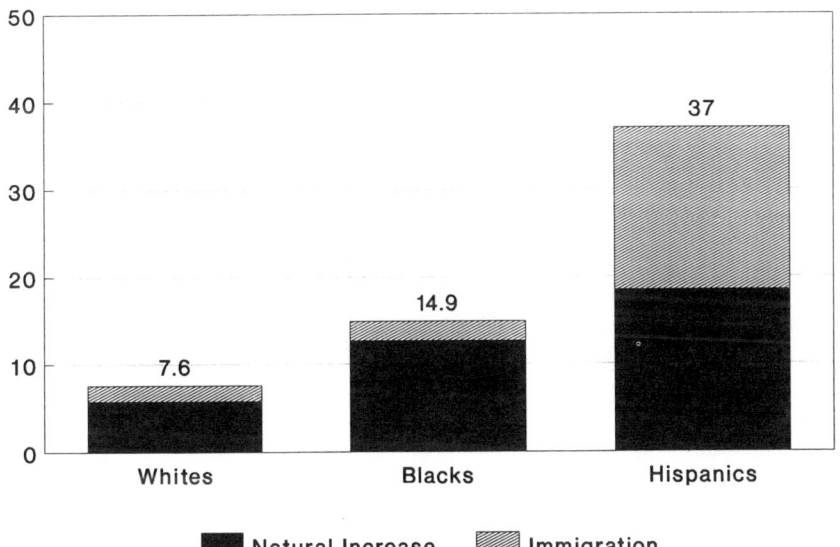

FIG. 19.1 Average annual rates of growth 4/80–7/87 (natural increase and immigration. From U.S. Bureau of the Census, 1989c).

slightly less than the rate for Blacks (28%) (U.S. Bureau of the Census, 1989a).

The contrast between the educational levels of Hispanic and non-Hispanic adults ages 25 and over is also dramatic (see Fig. 19.2). Much of the Hispanic disadvantage is due to school dropout. Almost 50% of Hispanic adults left high school before graduation, compared with less than 25% of the non-Hispanic population. At higher educational levels, Hispanics are only half as likely to go to college (U.S. Bureau of the Census, 1985–1988). Cumulative dropout rates for Grades 9 through 12 are shown in Fig. 19.3.

There are substantial socioeconomic differences among the three largest Hispanic-origin groups on the U.S. mainland. Puerto Ricans are the most disadvantaged in terms of the percentage of single-parent households and the proportion of families with incomes below the poverty level (U.S. Bureau of the Census, 1985–1988). By contrast, Cubans in the United States have higher incomes than others of Hispanic origin and come out better on various measures of education and employment status.

SEXUAL ACTIVITY

High rates of school leaving are often correlated with early sexual activity and fertility because women are left with few alternatives to the

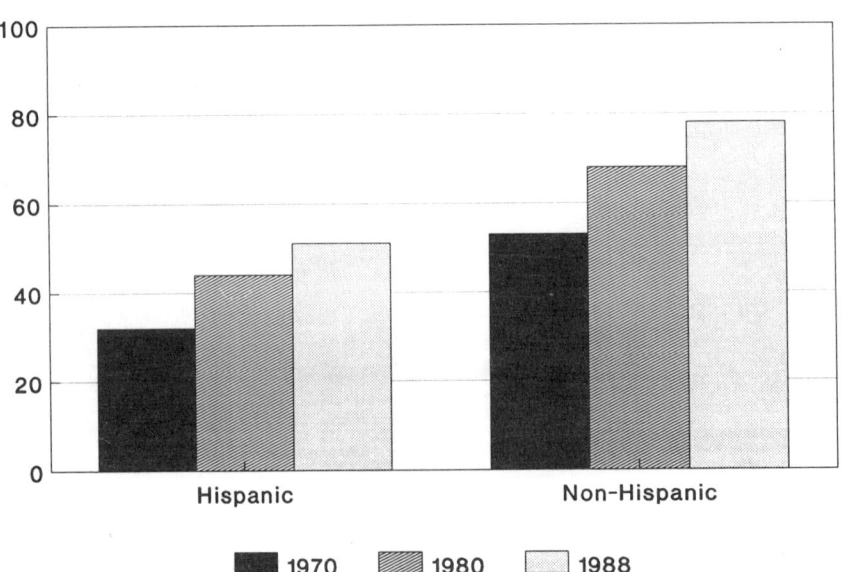

FIG. 19.2 High school graduation: 1970–1988. Percent of persons 25 and older (from U.S. Bureau of the Census, 1989c).

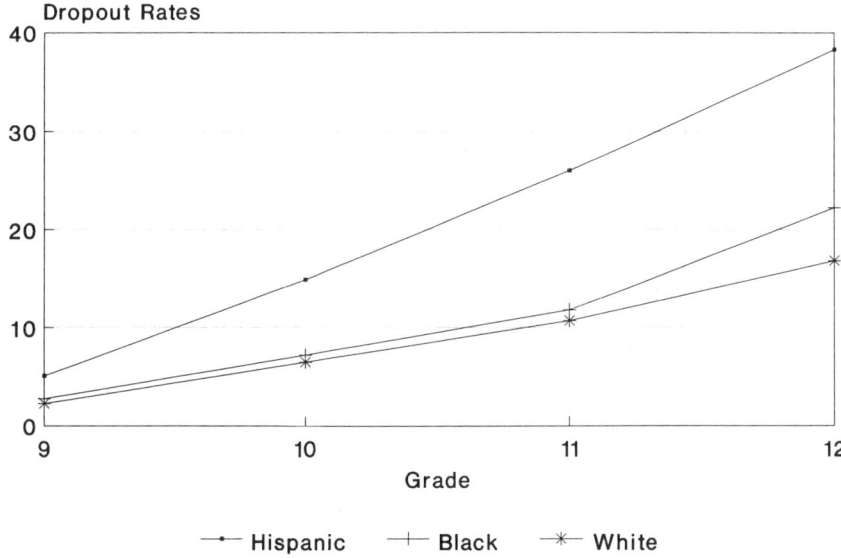

FIG. 19.3 Cumulative high school dropout rates for black, white and Hispanic youth, 1985 (from Kominski, 1990).

parental role (Hogan & Kitagawa, 1985; Michael & Tuma, 1985). Furthermore, the maternal role is highly valued among Hispanics, although much importance is also placed on virginity and women's ability to postpone sexual intercourse until they are married. Some authors describe this as a "cult of virginity" (Garcia, 1980).

In the United States, there is the additional influence of a dominant culture with high rates of nonmarital sexual activity. There are two possible effects of this pressure. On the one hand, it may result in postponement of sexual activity for young Hispanic women; on the other, social pressures may bias their reports of sexual activity. Both of these effects could be operating simultaneously. Whatever the reason, compared to Blacks and Whites, Hispanic teenagers are slightly less likely than Whites to report having had intercourse (Fig. 19.4) (Mott & Haurin, 1988). Data from the 1988 wave of the National Survey of Family Growth suggest that a slight (4 percentage point) difference exists between 18- to 19-year-old White and Hispanic women, but that among 15- to 17-year-olds, 36% of each racial/ethnic group reported ever having had sex (Forrest & Singh, 1990).

When adult Hispanic women are asked to recall whether they had their first sexual experience before or after marriage, a majority (55%) say they lost their virginity before reaching the altar, although this is lower than the corresponding percentages for Whites (65%) and for Blacks (91%) (National Center for Health Statistics, 1985).

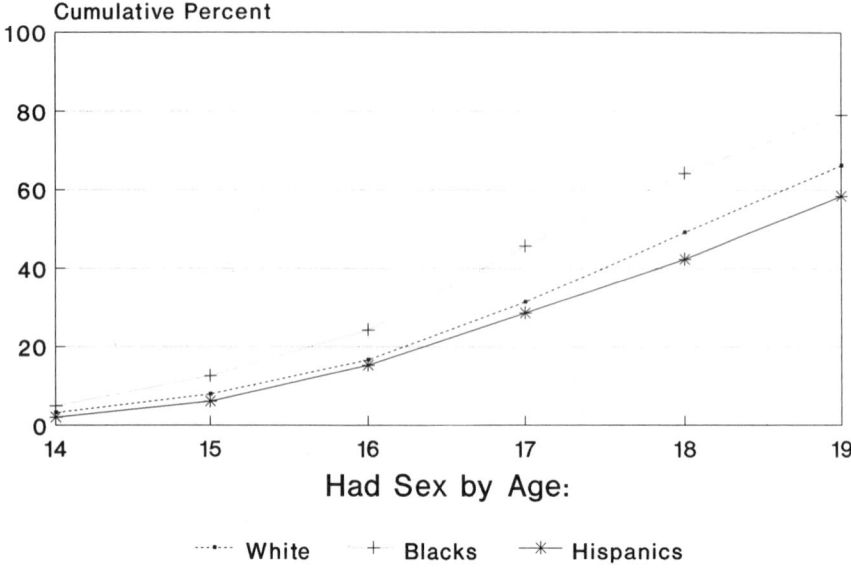

FIG. 19.4 Cumulative percentage of women who had sex by ages 14 to 19 (from Mott & Haurin, 1988).

A clear double standard exists in societal expectations for young Hispanic men and women. Teenage boys are frequently expected, and even encouraged by male relatives and friends to have sex. Although Hispanic girls may have motives for concealing their sexual activity, Hispanic boys may face similar, but opposite pressures to exaggerate their sexual behavior. When the sexual behavior of young Hispanic, Black, and White men is compared, it is the Whites, not the Hispanics, who postpone first intercourse the longest, although rates for young Hispanic and White men are quite similar (see Fig. 19.5). In the 1984 National Longitudinal Survey of Youth, for example, by the time they are 19 years old, 80% of Hispanic males, 76% of Whites, and 94% of Black men report having had sex (Mott & Haurin, 1988). In a more recent survey of U.S. males, Sonenstein, Pleck, and Ku (1989, 1991) found similar rates for each racial/ethnic group. At the youngest ages, similar proportions of White and Hispanic youths had had sex (3%–4% by age 13, 6%–7% by age 14, 16%–19% by age 15). These rates contrast sharply with the much higher figures for Black teens (48% by age 15).

PREGNANCY AND ABORTION

Because a majority of U.S. Hispanic teenagers have sex before marriage, it is not surprising to find that many of them experience premarital

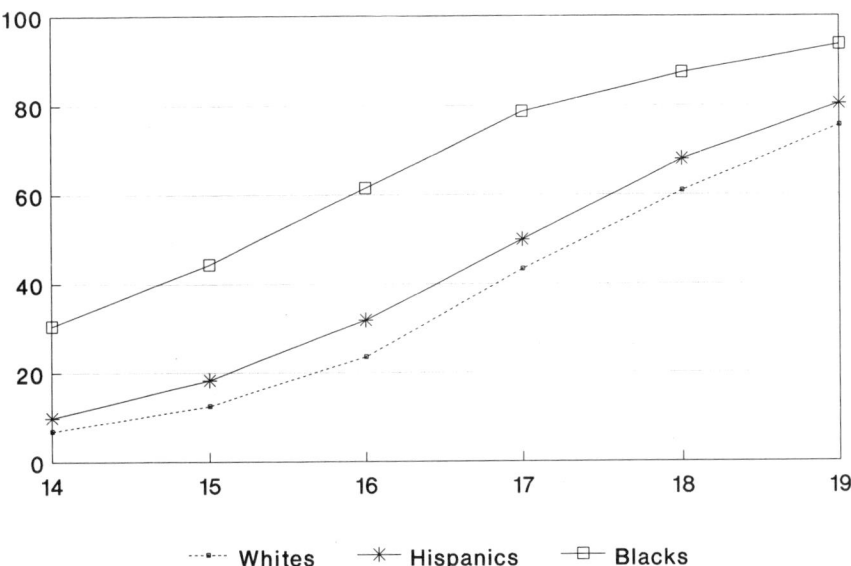

FIG. 19.5 Cumulative percent of men who had sex by ages 14 to 19 (from Mott & Haurin, 1989).

pregnancies. Of unmarried Hispanic teenage women, 15% report having been pregnant (Mott, 1983). This is almost twice the percentage for White teenagers, but it is lower than the figure for Blacks. These figures are likely to be underestimates, however, because of the difficulties in obtaining complete and accurate information on pregnancies that ended in abortions.

Because most Hispanics are Catholic, one might speculate that Hispanic adolescents would have more negative attitudes toward pregnancy termination than do White or Black adolescents (who are predominately Protestant). This does not appear to be the case. In a national study of U.S. teenagers, similar proportions of young White, Black, and Hispanic women said that they would have an abortion if they got pregnant while in school (Louis Harris and Associates, 1986).

Only a few studies provide data on actual abortion behavior, but they also call into question the assumption that Hispanic women are much less likely to seek elective abortions. Henshaw and Silverman (1988) used 1987 service statistics from providers to estimate abortion rates of 43 abortions per 1,000 women for Hispanics and 23 per 1,000 for White women (Fig. 19.6).

In New York, Joyce (1988) found that abortion ratios (abortions per 100 pregnancies) were lower for Puerto Rican teenagers than for Black or White teens. For example, Puerto Rican girls who were age 17 at the

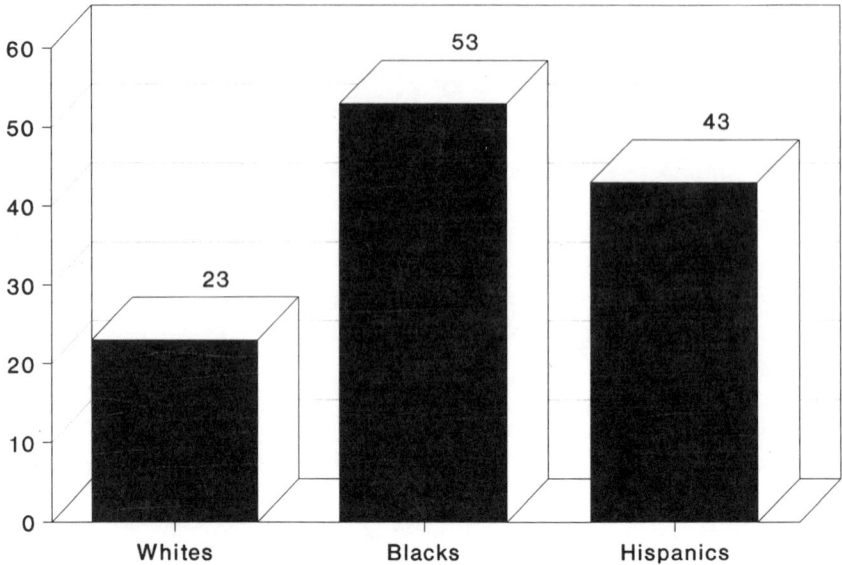

FIG. 19.6 Estimated abortion rates for women ages 15–44 in 1987 (as per 1,000 women. From Henshaw & Silverman, 1988).

time of conception aborted about 44 of every 100 pregnancies. The comparable ratios for non-Puerto Rican Latinos was 32, whereas for White girls it was 69 and 54 for Blacks. However, these differences were narrowed and even reversed when controlling for marital status, general health, previous births, previous abortions, and education. The proportion of pregnancies resulting in induced abortion for an unmarried 17-year-old with no previous live birth, one previous abortion and 10 years of completed schooling was .71 for Puerto Ricans, .71 for Blacks, and .81 for Whites.

On the other hand, Aneshensel, Fielder, and Becerra (1989) compared Mexican-American and non-Hispanic White teenagers who had been pregnant and found that the Mexican-Americans were less likely to report having had an abortion, even after controlling for differences in socioeconomic status.

Some of the differences between the conclusions derived from service statistics (e.g., Henshaw & Silverman, 1988; Joyce, 1988) and surveys of teenagers (e.g., Aneshensel et al., 1989) may be the result of underreporting of abortions by Hispanic young women. Jones and Forrest (in press) analyzed the quality of abortion data from a number of national surveys. In the National Longitudinal Survey of Youth (1979–1990) Hispanic young women (ages 20–24) were considerably less likely than Whites or Blacks to report having had an abortion.

CHILDBEARING

As teenagers, Hispanic women have more children than Whites, but fewer than Blacks of the same age (Fig. 19.7) (U.S. Bureau of the Census, 1985–1988). At older ages, however, they surpass both Blacks and Whites in numbers of children. This is because many Hispanic women have a second child soon after the first (Fennelly Darabi & Ortiz, 1987). In 1988, about 1 in 6 Hispanic-origin births was to a teenaged mother, compared to 1 in 10 among Whites, and 1 in 4 among Blacks. Among Hispanics, the proportion of all births that are to adolescent mothers ranges from a high of 17%–21% among Mexican-origin and Puerto Rican mothers, compared to about 6% of Cuban mothers (USDHHS, 1990).

Although marriage may not reduce the negative consequences of a birth for young parents or their infants, when adolescent childbearing is viewed as a problem, the focus is usually on premarital births. Gross comparisons of births among Black, White, and Hispanic teenagers obscure the fact that a substantial proportion of adolescent births are actually marital births. By age 20, as many as 34% of U.S. Hispanic women are already married, compared to 14% of Blacks and 28% of Whites (Michael & Tuma, 1985). An additional, unknown percentage of Hispanics are living with their partners in informal unions (Fennelly

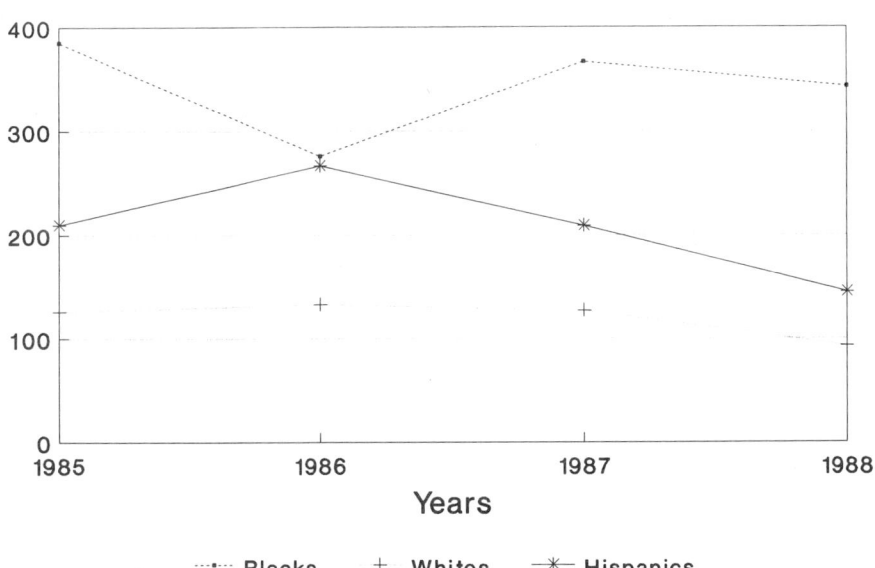

FIG. 19.7 Children ever born per 1,000 women 18–19 (all marital statuses. From U.S. Bureau of the Census, 1985–1988).

Darabi, Kandiah & Ortiz, 1989). These rates vary greatly for women in different Hispanic origin groups (Landale & Fennelly, 1992).

Abrahamse, Morrison, and Waite (1988) asked female high school students whether they would be willing to consider having a child if they weren't married. Forty-eight percent of the Black teenagers, 32% of the Hispanics, and 24% of the Whites said that they would or might be willing to do this. Furthermore, if we look separately at different Hispanic-origin groups, we find that, like Blacks, Puerto Rican teenagers have more births outside of marriage than within (Fennelly Darabi & Ortiz, 1987). Premarital births are less common among women of Mexican and Cuban origin, but are increasing. In 1988, 33% of all Hispanic births and 25% of all non-Hispanic births were to unmarried mothers. This ranges from 53% of Puerto Rican births to 16% of Cuban births (USDHHS, 1990).

An important point to remember in this discussion is that there are always more premarital pregnancies than premarital births, because some women "legitimate" their births by marrying while they are pregnant. White and Hispanic young women are about equally likely to marry during pregnancy (Fig. 19.8), but far fewer Black young women marry before, during, or after pregnancy (U.S. Bureau of the Census, 1989c). Furthermore, although Hispanic and White women have very

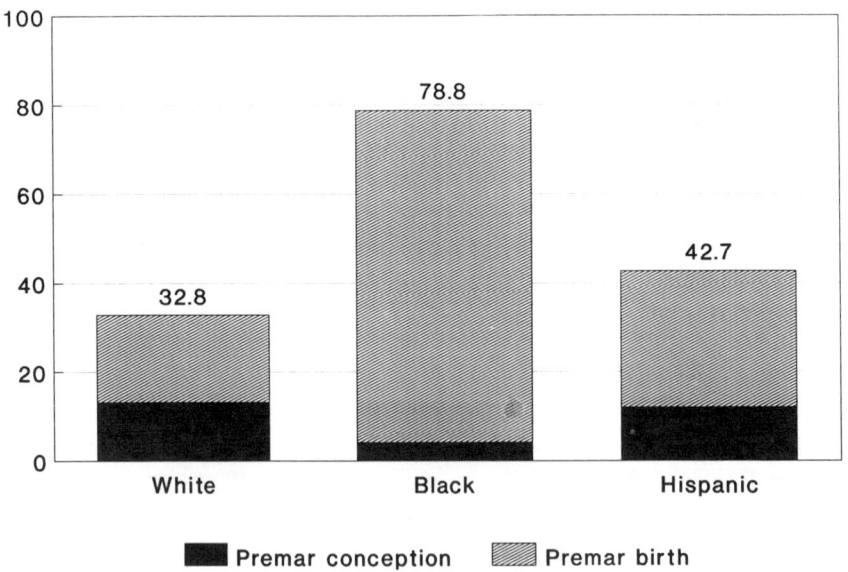

FIG. 19.8 Premarital births and conceptions to women 15–29: 1985–1988 CPS (from U.S. Bureau of the Census, 1989a).

similar rates of premarital conceptions, the former women have more births outside of marriage.

BIRTH CONTROL

Unmarried Hispanic adolescents are as likely or less likely than Whites to report having had sex, but they are more likely to get pregnant. This apparent contradiction seems to be the result of two factors: underreporting of sexual activity and lower rates of contraceptive use by Hispanics. Although underreporting is difficult to measure, findings from studies with widely varying samples and questions document low rates of contraceptive use. Young Hispanic women are consistently less likely than Whites to use birth control, to have used it at first intercourse (Mosher & Bachrach, 1987; Torres & Singh, 1986) or first premarital intercourse (Mosher & McNally, 1991), to have used it before an abortion (Henshaw & Silverman, 1988), or to go to family planning clinics (Mosher & Horn, 1987). Mosher (1988) for example, found that the percentage of unmarried women (or their partners) who used a method at first intercourse was 74% for White Jewish women, 51% among other Whites, 34% among Blacks, and only 27% among Hispanics. Using some of the explanation of the higher fertility of Hispanic than White adolescents may lie in the choice of less effective methods of birth control. Hispanics are least likely to use the pill at first sex (4%), compared to 16% of Blacks and 7% of Whites (Forrest & Singh, 1990). These findings are consistent across several different Hispanic-origin groups.

Even when Hispanic teenagers come into a family planning clinic, they are more likely than other teens to do so for a pregnancy test (Mosher & Horn, 1987) and less likely to adopt a birth control method at the first clinic visit (Torres & Singh, 1986).

The condom is the most popular birth control method reported by unmarried female teens of all racial/ethnic groups when they first have sex (51% of Whites, 35% of Blacks, and 42% of Hispanics) and its use has increased greatly since the early 1980s. These figures are somewhat different when men are the respondents.

Sonenstein et al. (1989) reported similar rates of condom usage among White and Hispanic adolescent males (53%–54%) in their urban sample, compared with 66% of young Black men. Nevertheless, a higher proportion of Hispanic men than either Blacks or Whites were using no method or an ineffective method of birth control.

Some studies describe more negative attitudes toward condom use on the part of Hispanic males, and an unwillingness to assume responsibility for birth control. Hispanic youth workers in New York, for example, cited male embarrassment over the purchase and use of contraceptive methods as a major hindrance to condom use (Fennelly, in press). The providers also noted young women's reluctance to publicly acknowledge that they are sexually active by going to family planning clinics. As one commented, "virgins don't need to come to a clinic."

DETERMINANTS OF ETHNIC DIFFERENCES IN EARLY CHILDBEARING

The preceding sections have shown that Hispanics are at high risk of adolescent childbearing. Despite low rates of reported sexual activity, Hispanic teenagers fall between Whites and Blacks in rates of premarital pregnancy and childbearing.

What accounts for these differences? Clearly, Hispanic youth are less likely than non-Hispanics to use birth control. But what accounts for differences in contraceptive use? Part of the explanation can be found in differences in background characteristics such as education and income. This is shown by the differences in birthrates among Hispanic-origin groups of varying socioeconomic statuses. For example, Cuban teenagers in the United States have both the lowest birthrate of any Hispanic-origin group and the highest socioeconomic status. Incomes and educational levels are much lower among persons of Mexican or Puerto Rican origin (U.S. Bureau of the Census, 1985–1988). Furthermore, a very high percentage of Hispanic families are headed by single females, and poverty rates are most acute among these women and their children. In one national study of high school students, the strongest predictor of premarital childbearing among young Hispanic women was whether or not they grew up in a two-parent household (Marsiglio & Mott, 1986). Some of the differences between young Puerto Rican women and other Hispanic adolescents may also reflect cultural differences between Caribbean and non-Caribbean populations in marriage, household structure, and fertility.

Background factors alone are insufficient to explain all of the differences between Hispanic and non-Hispanic teenagers in the risk of having a first birth, a premarital birth, or a rapid second birth. Rather, the differential must be due to other variables linked to poverty, such as low self-esteem and low educational expectations. Both of these factors have been shown to affect contraceptive use among Hispanic adolescents. Furthermore, differences in basic educational skills and educational plans among high school seniors may explain much of the variation in whether or not a young woman bears a child (Marsiglio & Mott, 1986), especially among Hispanic teenagers (Abrahamse, Morrison, & Waite, 1987). This is because, regardless of ethnicity, teenagers with higher skill levels and aspirations are more aware of academic and employment alternatives to early childbearing than are their peers who do not perform as well in school.

Socioeconomic status and years of education also affect young people's access to information and services. Female Hispanic teenagers may be further limited in this regard because they are less likely than other youth to have taken sex education courses (Marsiglio & Mott, 1986) or to have talked with their mothers about sex or birth control (Lindeman & Scott, 1982).

The motivations for early childbearing and the barriers that limit sex-related communication and access to contraception are likely to be strongest for recent immigrants. They are the most likely to have language difficulties and limited access to health insurance, as well as the most likely to be influenced by the norms of their countries of origin. This effect diminishes as women become acculturated to U.S. society and as their education and income levels improve. In one study in Connecticut, for example, Hispanic adolescent mothers were compared with their peers who did not have children. The young mothers were less likely to have been born in the United States and were less proficient in English (Chung & Sibirsky, 1984). By contrast, Hispanic adolescents of higher status and a greater degree of acculturation may avoid pregnancy or terminate unwanted pregnancies. Those who do undergo abortions appear to be more likely to continue their educations than their peers who carry to term (Ortiz & Vazquez, 1987).

REACHING THE YOUNGEST ADOLESCENTS

In order to plan pregnancy prevention strategies for the youngest adolescents it is useful to examine the special determinants of early childbearing among this population. A strong double standard exists concerning the sexual activities of Hispanic boys and girls. From a very early age, Hispanic girls are taught that female ignorance about sex is equated with purity and innocence. Sexual maturation, sexual intercourse, and the risks of pregnancy are infrequently discussed between Hispanic mothers and their daughters; in contrast, Hispanic boys may be encouraged by male family members to experiment with heterosexual relations soon after they reach puberty. Given these contradictions it is clear that to be successful, pregnancy prevention programs for Hispanic youth must directly involve parents both as planners and participants.

Gender inequality in sexual relationships is exacerbated by the frequent age differences between Hispanic partners. It is not uncommon for female adolescents as young as 13 or 14 to go out with men who are 5, 10, or even 15 years older than they. When such dramatic age differences exist, it is unrealistic to expect the young woman to "just say no" or to imagine that educational sessions promoting strategies for delaying sexual activity can succeed. Instead what are needed are interventions at very early ages that examine gender roles and stereotypes and that encourage adolescents to seek out same-age partners. Such programs might also include segments on future planning and discussions of how to juxtapose educational and career expectations with plans for marriage and childbearing.

Crockett and Chopak (this volume) suggest other components of programs for young adolescents that are applicable to Hispanic youth as well. This involves the promotion of in-school or extracurricular activities that meet young people's needs for intimacy, peer acceptance, and self-enhancement as "functional equivalents" of sexual relationships.

CONCLUSIONS

Because Hispanic teenagers start out disadvantaged on many educational and occupational outcome measures, it is not always easy to distinguish cause from effect, that is, the extent to which poverty and lower educational status lead to early childbearing or vice versa. Both directions of influence are likely to be operating at once. We have found, for example, that more than 66% of Hispanic adolescent mothers dropped out of high school not because of the pregnancy, but before the pregnancy (Fennelly Darabi, 1986). In one analysis of young women who became pregnant while in high school, more than 50% of the Whites and Blacks later secured high school diplomas, compared to only 33% of Hispanics. Among young women who became pregnant after leaving school, the differences were even greater. Fifty-five percent of Hispanics later finished school versus 81%–85% of Blacks and Whites (Mott & Marsiglio, 1985). Hispanic teenage mothers experience many of the same negative consequences of early childbearing that have been extensively documented among Black and White teenagers. These include increased risks of marital disruption (Chung & Sibirsky, 1984), unemployment (Ortiz & Fennelly, 1988), and markedly higher risks of low educational attainment (Mott & Marsiglio, 1985; USDHHS, 1990). Nevertheless, both levels and the determinants of early childbearing vary by racial/ethnic group. Given these differences, it is imperative that culturally sensitive preventive programs be designed for Hispanic youth in collaboration with local community-based organizations. Such programs should offer multiservice centers rather than single service programs so that young people seeking sex-related counseling or birth control do not feel singled out or identifiable to others. Coordination with after school programs can provide access to younger adolescents and exposing them to sex education and information on contraception before they become sexually active. Special attention should also be given to programs that include Hispanic males and that foster examination of gender roles.

Because early sexual activity is most likely among young people exhibiting other "high risk" behaviors, multiservice sites have the advantage of making other needed services more accessible to youth who need them, and of facilitating referrals to and from programs offering health screening, tutoring, and counseling.

To design culturally appropriate services, the first step is to meet with adolescents, parents, teachers, service providers, and heads of community organizations to identify the special local needs of Hispanic youth and to plan interventions that overlap with other service programs.

In addition, efforts are needed to keep young Hispanics in school and to help them develop and work toward realistic educational and occupational goals that may give them an incentive to postpone childbearing. The realization of these aspirations requires the allocation of resources for improvement of the school environment, for teacher training, and for the creation of school-based clinics. It also requires vocational counseling and training programs tied to real possibilities of employment.

Parents play an important role in the socialization of their children. For Hispanics in particular, the quality of a young woman's relationship with her parents is a good predictor of the risk of single parenthood (Abrahamse et al., 1987). If early childbearing is to be discouraged and contraceptive use encouraged, then motivational and educational programs should be designed for parents. The improvement of parent–child communication on sex-related topics is difficult, but urgently needed.

Finally, family planning service providers should take a hard look at their failure to reach many sexually active Hispanic teenagers before the first unwanted pregnancy. Given the lack of bilingual and bicultural staff and educational materials in many institutions, it is hardly surprising that Hispanic youth stay away. Bringing them in will require the improvement of both services and outreach. Successful programs will be those that are perceived to be accessible, confidential, nonjudgmental, and affordable as well as frequented by other Hispanic youth. If these goals are to be accomplished, then federal and state funds must be allotted for the development of bilingual training programs and for the employment of sufficient numbers of providers to staff both counseling and medical services.

Beyond the clinics, nontraditional sources of contraceptive supplies and information must be sponsored. These include condom distribution projects, widespread media campaigns directed at Hispanic youth, and the establishment of in-school and out-of-school sites offering contraceptive counseling and services.

Hispanic youth are an important resource in the United States, but they have received inadequate attention. It is imperative that they be accorded unrestricted access to high quality sex education and family planning services.

REFERENCES

Abrahamse, A. F., Morrison, P., & Waite, L. (1987, April). *Single teenage mothers: Spotting susceptible adolescents in advance.* Paper presented at the annual Population Association of America meeting, Chicago.

Abrahamse, A. F., Morrison, P. A., & Waite, L. J. (1988). *Beyond stereotypes: Who becomes a single teenage mother?* Santa Monica, CA: Rand Corporation publication R-3489-HHS/NICHD.

Aneshensel, C. S., Fielder, E. P., & Becerra, R. M. (1989). Fertility and fertility-related behavior among Mexican-American and non-Hispanic White female adolescents. *Journal of Health and Social Behavior, 30*(1), 56–76.

Bean, F. D., & Swicegood, C. G. (1985). *Mexican American fertility patterns.* Austin, TX: University of Texas Press.

Bean, F. D., & Tienda, M. (1987). *The Hispanic population of the United States.* New York: Russell Sage.

Chung, H. C., & Sibirsky, S. (1984). Needs, goals, and programs for adolescent Hispanic parents in Connecticut. Bridgeport, CT: University of Bridgeport, Urban Management Institute.

Fennelly, K. (in press). Barriers to birth control use among Hispanic teenagers. In B. Bair & S. Cayleff (Eds.), *Wings of gauze: Women of color and the experience of health and illness.* Detroit, MI: Wayne State University Press.

Fennelly Darabi, K. (1986). [Center for Population and Family Health, Columbia University.] Unpublished analysis of data from the 1982 and 1983 National Longitudinal Survey of Youth.

Fennelly Darabi, K., Kandiah, V., & Ortiz, V. (1989). The cross-cultural study of fertility among Hispanic adolescents in the Americas. *Studies in Family Planning, 20*(2), 96–101.

Fennelly Darabi, K., & Ortiz, V. (1987). Childbearing among young Latino women in the United States. *American Journal of Public Health, 77*(1), 25–28.

Forrest, J. D., & Singh, S. (1990). The sexual and reproductive behavior of American women. *Family Planning Perspectives, 22*(5), 206–214.

Garcia, F. (1980). The cult of virginity. In *Program on Teaching and Learning: Conference on the educational and occupational needs of Hispanic women* (pp. 65–73). Washington, DC: National Institute of Education.

Henshaw, S. K., & Silverman, J. (1988). The characteristics and prior contraceptive use of U.S. abortion patients. *Family Planning Perspectives, 20*(4), 158–168.

Hispanic Health and Nutrition Examination Survey (HHANES). (1982–1974). Hyattsville, MD: National Center for Health Statistics.

Hogan, D., & Kitagawa, E. (1985). The impact of social status, family structure and neighborhood on the fertility of black adolescents. *The American Journal of Sociology, 90*(4), 825–855.

Jaffe, A. J., Cullen, R. M., & Boswell, T. D. (1980). *The changing demography of Spanish Americans*. New York: Academic Press.

Jones, E. F., & Forrest, J. D. (in press). Underreporting of abortion in surveys of U.S. women. *Demography*.

Joyce, T. (1988). The social and economic correlates of pregnancy resolution among adolescents in New York City, by race and ethnicity: A multivariate analysis. *American Journal of Public Health, 78*(6), 626–631.

Kominski, R. (1990). Estimating the national high school dropout rate. *Demography, 27*(2), 303–312.

Landale, N., & Fennelly, K. (1992). Informal unions among Mainland Puerto Ricans: Cohabitation or an alternative to marriage?, *Journal of Marriage and the Family, 54*(2).

Lindeman, C., & Scott, W. (1982). The fertility-related behavior of Mexican-American adolescents. *Journal of Early Adolescence, 2*, 31–38.

Louis Harris and Associates (1986). *American teens speak: Sex, myths, TV, and birth control* (fieldwork). New York: Author.

Marsiglio, W., & Mott, F. L. (1986). The impact of sex education on sexual activity, contraceptive use and premarital pregnancy among American teenagers. *Family Planning Perspectives, 18*, 151–161.

Michael, R. T., & Tuma, N. B. (1985). Entry into marriage and parenthood by young men and women: The influence of family background. *Demography, 22*, 515–543.

Mosher, W. D. (1988). Fertility and family planning in the United States: Insights from the National Survey of Family Growth. *Family Planning Perspectives, 20*(5), 207–217.

Mosher, W. D., & Bachrach, C. A. (1987). First premarital contraceptive use: United States 1960–1982, 1987. *Studies in Family Planning, 18*(2), 83–95.

Mosher, W. D., & Horn, M. C. (1987). First family planning visit by young women, 1988, *Family Planning Perspectives, 20*(1), 33–40.

Mosher, W. D., & McNally, J. W. (1991). Contraceptive use at first premarital intercourse: United States, 1965–1988. *Family Planning Perspectives, 23*(3), 108–122.

Mott, F. L. (1983). Fertility-related data in the 1982 National Longitudinal Survey of Work Experience of Youth: An evaluation of data quality and some preliminary analytical results. Columbus: Ohio State University, Center for Human Resource Research.

Mott, F. L., & Haurin, R. J. (1988). Linkages between sexual activity and alcohol and drug use among American adolescents. *Family Planning Perspectives, 20*(3), 128–136.

Mott, F. L., & Marsiglio, W. (1985). Early childbearing and completion of high school. *Family Planning Perspective, 17*(5), 234–237.

National Center for Health Statistics. (1982). Data from the National Reporting System for Family Planning Services. *Vital and Health Statistics*, No. 13.

National Center for Health Statistics. (1985). Marriage and first intercourse, marital dissolution, and remarriage, 1982. *Advance Data from Vital and Health Statistics*, 107. Hyattsville, MD.

National Longitudinal Surveys of Youth (NLSY). (1979–1990). Columbus: Ohio State University.

Ortiz, C. G., & Vazquez, N. E. (1987). Adolescent pregnancy: Effects of family support, education, and religion on the decision to carry or terminate among Puerto Rican teenagers. *Adolescence, 22*(88), 897–917.

Ortiz, V., & Fennelly, K. (1988). Early childbearing and employment among young

Mexican-origin, Black and White women. *Social Science Quarterly, 69*(4), 987–995.
Sabagh, B. (1984, June). *Social Science Quarterly, 65*(2), 594–608.
Sonenstein, F., Pleck, J., & Ku, L. (1989). Sexual activity, condom use and AIDS awareness among adolescent males. *Family Planning Perspectives, 21*(4), 152–158.
Sonenstein, F. L., Pleck, J. H., & Ku, L. C. (1991). Levels of sexual activity among adolescent males in the United States. *Family Planning Perspectives, 23*(4), 162–167.
Torres, A., & Singh, S. (1986). Contraceptive practice among Hispanic adolescents. *Family Planning Perspectives, 18,* 193.
U.S. Bureau of the Census. (1985–1989). Fertility of American women. *Current Population Reports* (Series P-20, Nos. 406, 427, 436) Washington, DC.
U.S. Bureau of the Census. (1989a). Money income and poverty status of families and persons in the United States: 1988. *Current Population Reports,* Series P-60, No. 166.
U.S. Bureau of the Census. (1989b). Population profile of the U.S., 1989. *Current Population Reports,* Special Studies Series, p. 23, No. 159.
U.S. Bureau of the Census. (1991). The Hispanic population in the United States: March 1990 (Advance Report). *Current Population Reports,* Series P-20, No. 449.
USDHHS (1990, August). Advance report of final natality statistics, 1988. *Monthly Vital Statistics Report, 39*(4), Supplement.
Wetzel, J. R. (1987). *American youth: A statistical snapshot. Youth and America's future.* Washington, DC: The William T. Grant Foundation Commission on Work, Family and Citizenship.

20 Interventions to Prevent HIV Infections in Young Adolescents

Anthony R. D'Augelli
C. Raymond Bingham
The Pennsylvania State University

OVERVIEW

HIV illnesses result from infection with the human immunodeficiency virus (HIV). Despite many remaining ambiguities, much has been learned about HIV illnesses since the first cases were reported in 1981. HIV is transmitted in three ways. First, HIV can be transmitted when infected semen or vaginal fluids enter the mucous membranes or the blood of another person. Sexual transmission occurs most efficiently through receptive anal intercourse, but receptive vaginal intercourse is also a transmission mechanism. Sexual transmission from male to male and from male to female are the most common. Second, HIV can be transmitted by blood-to-blood contact, for example, in sharing injection equipment and through transfusions. Third, HIV transmission from mother to infant can occur in utero, perinatally, or possibly during nursing (Mann, Chin, Piot, & Quinn, 1988). Many factors can amplify the likelihood of HIV transmission. For example, sexual transmission of HIV is more probable if the recipient has a history of other sexually transmissible health problems, especially those accompanied by open ulcerations (e.g., syphilis, herpes) that allow ready entry of HIV into the bloodstream. Other factors increasing the risk of sexual transmission include lack of circumcision in men, cervical ectopy, use of an IUD, intercourse during menstruation, and nonulcerative sexually transmissible diseases (such as gonorrhea, chlamydia, trichomonas, and human papilloma virus).

If exposure to HIV is of sufficient intensity, HIV infection occurs. The presence of HIV in the bloodstream leads to immune system decline and illness: 3 to 5 years from infection to illness is common, with a median time of 10 years. The episodic assaults of repeated opportunistic infections will ultimately be fatal, although antiviral and other prophylactic treatments have critically extended postdiagnosis life expectancy (Moss & Bacchetti, 1989). HIV is found in body fluids of infected individuals with highest concentrations in blood and semen (Mann et al., 1988).

HIV/AIDS is an international epidemic. It has rooted itself in distinct populations based on individual differences in gender and racial/ethnic status, sex and drug behavior patterns, and socioenvironmental vulnerability (National Academy of Sciences, 1988; National Research Council, 1989). From 8 to 10 million individuals worldwide are infected with HIV; by the late 1990s, one million new cases of HIV/AIDS illnesses are predicted worldwide (Chin, 1990; Mann et al., 1988; Sato, Chin, & Mann, 1989). In the United States, as of the end of 1991, the Centers for Disease Control (CDC, 1992) reported over 200,000 adult cases of HIV/AIDS, and over 3,400 pediatric cases (under 13 years). Over 60% of the adult and nearly 60% of the pediatric cases have died. Between 1 to 1.5 million Americans are estimated to be infected with HIV (Heyward & Curran, 1988). By 1993, up to 270,000 cases of HIV/AIDS are possible. The scope of the HIV/AIDS pandemic necessitates extensive preventive interventions to forestall new infections.

EARLY ADOLESCENCE AND HIV INFECTION

There are four reasons why comparatively few cases of AIDS among U.S. adolescents have occurred to date. First, the long incubation period of HIV leads to diagnosis many years after infection. Because sexual activity and drug use are the most frequent modes of transmission and they commence after childhood, an infection from the adolescent years would not be diagnosed for many years. Second, the population first infected with HIV in the United States included adults engaging in high-risk sexual activities with other adults. These adults were typically involved in social networks that did not involve adolescents. Third, the use of intravenous (IV) drugs is relatively infrequent among adolescents in the United States. Finally, although many male adolescents engage in same-sex sexual activity, receptive anal intercourse is comparatively infrequent at this age, and the likelihood of a peer sexual partner being infected with HIV is slight.

According to CDC (1992) statistics, there were 424 male and 245 female HIV/AIDS cases among individuals between 5 and 12 years of age at the end of 1991, a total of 669 or .3% of all 206,392 cases. Nearly all are attributed to transmission by transfusion or being born to a mother with HIV illness or at risk for HIV illness. None of these cases are attributed to sexual contact or IV drug use. However, sexual or drug-related transmission of HIV/AIDS is assumed in some of the 789 cases (577 males and 212 females) who were between 13 and 19 years old at diagnosis. Of these, 25% were due to homosexual contact, 13% to IV drug use, and 4% to a combination of homosexual contact and drug use. It is likely that some of the 13- to 19-year-olds were infected during early adolescence. The occurrence of HIV illness among 13- to 19-year-olds indicates that many more adolescents may be infected and could unknowingly infect others. An additional 8,160 (6,765 males and 1,395 females) individuals aged 20-24 have HIV/AIDS. Some of these cases may have become infected during adolescence, although few of this group were likely exposed to HIV during early adolescence. The number of adolescents with diagnosed HIV infections doubles annually (Brooks-Gunn, Boyer, & Hein, 1988; CDC, 1988).

Seroprevalence data about adolescents are limited, and no data on young adolescents (10-13) are available. HIV-seroprevalence rates among recruits for U.S. military service provide data about HIV infection among adolescents (Burke et al., 1990). Between October 1985 and April 1989, over 1.1 million youth under 20 years of age were tested for HIV. Overall prevalence rate was .35 per 1,000 cases. Subpopulation rates per 1,000 were: female, .32; male, .35; White, .17; African-American, 1.00; Hispanic, .52. Seroprevalence varied by state, and by county within states. Age (older), gender (male), race/ethnicity, population density per 1,000 per square mile, and number of HIV positives from the local county were associated with higher HIV-seropositivity. For White and African-American males and for African-American females, age, population density, and county AIDS cases were significant predictors; these variables were not helpful in predicting HIV status in White females, or Hispanic males or females. Data on 60,000 U.S. Job Corps entrants aged 16 to 21 reveal an overall seroprevalence rate of .36%. Seroprevalence was higher among males, among African-Americans and Hispanics compared to Whites, and was higher in the northeast and south than in the midwest and west (CDC, 1990). African-American and Hispanic rates varied by region, whereas White rates did not. Rates among university students, estimated by routine blood sampling at campus health clinics, were found to range from 0% to .9% at 19 campuses (CDC, 1990). Seropositivity averaged .5% for males (range .3%-.7%) and .02% for females (range .002%-.066%) (Gayle et al., 1990). All HIV positive people in this large study were over 18; and, all but 2 of 30 HIV positive students were men. No student under 18 was HIV positive.

RISK FACTORS IN EARLY ADOLESCENCE

Adolescents are a population of great importance for preventing new HIV infections. During adolescence, individuals solidify behavior patterns that can substantially increase the risk of HIV infection throughout their life spans. Interpersonal sexual activity accelerates during adolescence: Vaginal and anal intercourse may be initiated; the number of intercourse experiences increases; and, the number of partners increases. As the sexually active adolescent gets older, his or her partners are older as well, and they bring increasingly complex sexual histories to new sexual exchanges. Drug use, including legal drugs such as alcohol, tobacco (including smokeless), and caffeine (in soft drinks as well as in coffee), as well as illegal drugs such as marijuana, cocaine, and crack, also increases. Considerable escalation of drug use occurs from ages 10 to 13 (Oetting & Beauvais, 1990).

Preventing the initiation of high-risk activities is preferable to attempting to change these behaviors once they have been well practiced. Early adolescence is an ideal time for preventive interventions aimed at promoting the acquisition of cautious sexual behavior and drug use. Forestalling the initiation of problematic sexual and drug habits as early as possible is a wise general strategy, but interventions toward this goal must occur by early adolescence because unlearning sexual and substance patterns after they are developmentally and contextually routinized is exceedingly difficult. For example, it is far easier to learn from the start that "sex" (whether anal, oral, or vaginal) always involves condom use than to begin condom use after years of nonuse. Similarly, there is little doubt that substance avoidance (especially avoidance of physiologically addictive substances) is more effective than eliminating a well-established drug pattern. Interventions must be designed to educate young adolescents about HIV transmission, to encourage the development of competence in sexual matters, to develop resistance to drug habits, and to provide easy access to critical resources such as condoms.

Most adolescents are not well informed about specific aspects of HIV transmission and prevention and their knowledge does not translate into consistent risk reduction (Fineberg, 1988; Price, Desmond, & Kukulka, 1985). In 1988, the CDC surveyed 35,000 youth aged 13 to 18 about their beliefs and behaviors related to HIV (CDC, 1988). Most (over 80%) knew that HIV is transmitted through sexual intercourse and most knew of the dangers of sharing syringes. Many also believed that HIV could be transmitted through giving blood, from mosquito or other insect bites, or by using public toilets. In 1985, DiClemente, Boyer, and Morales (1988) surveyed 14- to 18-year-olds in San Francisco, finding that African-American and Latin adolescents were twice as likely as Whites to misunderstand HIV transmission, although all understood that sex and sharing needles might lead to HIV infection. Far fewer believed that condom use lowered risk of HIV infection. Among 16- to 19-year olds, Strunin and Hingson (1987) found that only 15% altered their behavior due to HIV concerns. Of those who changed, only 10% now used condoms. In a rare longitudinal study, Kegeles, Adler, and Irwin (1988) surveyed 14- to 19-year-old San Francisco medical patients twice in 1 year. Females' views that condoms prevented sexually transmitted diseases (STDs) increased over the year, yet their perception of the importance of condoms decreased. At both times, females were uncertain about males' wanting to use condoms and showed little insistence that partners use them. In contrast, males believed the females expected condom use, and said they planned to use them. Because condoms provide the only predictable protection against HIV for those who engage in sexual intercourse of any kind, their consistent and competent use is crucial. Efforts to ensure such use must be of the highest priority.

Vaginal Intercourse in Early Adolescence

Recent reviews (Brooks-Gunn & Furstenberg, 1989; Voydanoff & Donnelly, 1990) suggest several generalizations about vaginal intercourse in early adolescence. More adolescent females have had intercourse since the 1970s; by age 19, about 60% report having had intercourse at least once. Males have more intercourse experiences than females, beginning earlier and having more partners. Most teenagers have intercourse with one partner, although adolescents report more sexual partners during adolescence than had previously been the case. In addition to cohort and gender, ethnic and racial status and geographical location are related to differences in sexual activity.

In a CDC (1988) high school survey, intercourse rates among 13- to 14-year-olds varied by state and by city. For example, in California, 23% reported having had intercourse, and in Michigan, 35% reported intercourse. By the end of high school, from 29% (San Francisco; 22% of females, 37% of males) to 76% (the District of Columbia; 66% of females, 91% of males) had intercourse. In 1983, 17% boys and 5% girls reported intercourse by age 15 (Hayes, 1987). Of White adolescents, 12% of the boys and 5% of the girls had intercourse; of the African-American adolescents, 42% of the boys and 10% of the girls; of the Hispanic adolescents, 19% of the boys and 4% of the girls. Strunin and Hingson (1987) found 55% of a telephone sample of 16- to 19-year-olds had intercourse, although they report no age or gender breakdown. Stiffman, Earls, Robins, Jung, and Kulbok (1987) studied disadvantaged inner-city 13- to 18-year-old females attending public health clinics. Of the 13-year-olds, 42% had had intercourse. Using 1982 data, Dawson (1986) reported that 46% of female teenagers aged 15–19 had intercourse, with 59% of African-American and 44% of White and other teens reporting intercourse. By 14, 9% of the African-American and 4% of the White teens had experienced intercourse. Rates of intercourse increased to 20% of the African-American and 10% of the White teens by age 15. Dawson found first intercourse at ages 14–16 less likely for females who attend religious services once or more weekly, whose mothers had a 12th-grade education, and who resided with both parents. Exposure to formal instruction was not associated with initiation of intercourse, but was associated with knowledge of contraception and the use of contraception at first and subsequent intercourse. Increased likelihood of contraceptive use within the sexually active group was associated with academic achievement, mothers being at least high school graduates, formal instruction, and being African-American. Less frequent intercourse was associated with lowered likelihood of contraceptive use. Current use of contraception, however, was unrelated to formal intervention, and background variables did not predict current use.

Information about unprotected vaginal intercourse and pregnancy among young adolescents provide crucial data for estimating risk for HIV infection because barrier contraception was either not used or was used incorrectly in these cases. Although contraceptive use has risen among adolescents, over half of all adolescent females initiate intercourse without contraception and 70% of those age 15 use no method at first intercourse (Hofferth, 1990). Of those under 15 who used any method of contraception, 44% used condoms and 14% relied on the pill (which provides no protection against HIV infection). Withdrawal, a risky method, was used by 30% of those reporting any method and rhythm was used by 5%. Also, of those under 15 whose first intercourse was unprotected, only 23% initiated contraceptive use within a month of the first intercourse. Nearly half (42%) of these teenage females delayed initiating contraception for over a year (Hofferth, 1990). Stiffman et al. (1987) found a 4% pregnancy rate among 13-year-old females. (They also found that 7%–8% of the sexually active teenagers aged 13 to 18 reported STDs.) Among sexually active adolescents, more pregnancies were found by Dawson (1986) among older adolescents: 45% of African-American teens and 27% of White teens had been pregnant. Importantly, of these teenagers, 12% conceived within 1 month of initiating intercourse, and 56% within 1 year. Older teenagers were more likely to become pregnant, as were African-American teenagers, those who have frequent intercourse, and those who have been sexually active for longer periods of time. No relationship between involvement in educational programs and premarital pregnancy was found.

Condom use among sexually experienced female adolescents aged 15–19 had stabilized to about 20% in 1982, overshadowed by use of the pill (about 60%; Hofferth, 1990). However, condom use is increasing in response to the HIV epidemic. Supplementing the 1982 data used by Dawson (1986) with 1988 data, Forrest and Singh (1990) found increases in condom use in the sexually active adolescent population, a trend most pronounced in Hispanic teenagers, whose condom use more than doubled from 1982 (22%) to 1988 (54%). At first intercourse, 65% used a contraceptive method, with African-American teenagers reporting less frequent condom use at first intercourse than White teens. Forrest and Singh estimated that 24% of sexually active girls aged 15 to 19 will become pregnant, suggesting a high risk of HIV infection via unprotected vaginal intercourse. High risk is clearly shown even in 1988 data: 35% of all teenage girls did not use contraception at first intercourse. Of the 65% who reported using any contraceptive method, 73% used a condom, 13% used the pill, and 13% used withdrawal (calculations from Forrest and Singh, 1990, Table 5). Thus, 26% of these teenage girls—although protected from pregnancy—were unprotected from HIV infection at their first intercourse. Their actual risk for infection cannot be predicted because partner serostatus is unknown and will vary by context.

Anal Intercourse in Early Adolescence

Little is known about anal intercourse in early adolescence. The extraordinarily rich Kinsey reports (Kinsey, Pomeroy, & Martin, 1948; Kinsey, Pomeroy, Martin, & Gebhard, 1953) do not tabulate heterosexual anal intercourse, while commenting, "As many as half or more of the population may find some degree of erotic satisfaction in anal stimulation" (Kinsey et al., 1953, p. 585). A recent Kinsey Institute estimate is that 39% of women have tried anal intercourse (Reinisch, 1990). Only one study could be located concerning anal intercourse among adolescents. Jaffe, Seehaus, Wagner, and Leadbeater (1988) found that 9% of a sample of African-American and Hispanic American 13- to 15-year-old girls reported anal experiences. Older girls reported higher frequencies: By 18, 25% had anal intercourse and 38% had done so by 21. In contrast to heterosexual activity, Kinsey et al. (1948) did describe anal "play" among male teenagers at different ages. Of the 60% of all preadolescent boys who had any homosexual contact, 17% reported anal experiences.

About 7% of all young adolescent males engage in anal experiences with other males based on these data (Kinsey et al., 1948, Table 27).

Despite gaps in the available knowledge base, the evidence is clear that some initiate vaginal and anal intercourse between the ages of 10 and 12. Involvement in different sexual activities follows different developmental trajectories, depending on gender, sexual orientation, racial/ethnic status, socioeconomic status, family circumstances, and so on. Some subset of these experiences involve risk for HIV infection. As unprotected sexual experiences increase, so does risk for HIV infection.

Drug Use in Early Adolescence

Although the use of alcohol and some other drugs is common in adolescence, IV drug use is relatively rare. Before age 15 (prior to 10th grade), 83% of teenagers have used alcohol and 45% have gotten drunk; of other drugs, 25% have used marijuana, 5% cocaine, 4% crack, 18% inhalants, 13% stimulants, 6% downers, 8% hallucinogens, 4% PCP, 4% heroin, 55% cigarettes, and 30% smokeless tobacco (Oetting & Beauvais, 1990, Table 3). Use of heroin increases to 3% in 7th grade, increases slightly to 4%, and then decreases again to 2% in 12th grade, although underreporting is surely likely. Certainly, it is fair to conclude that 3%–5% of young adolescents inject drugs by age 15; these teens are at direct risk for HIV infection. Use of cocaine, in contrast, increases from 3% in 7th to 5% in 9th and 13% in 12th grade. By the end of high school, 17% of White teenagers and 7% of Black teenagers have used cocaine (Oetting & Beauvais, 1990, Table 4). Use of crack is reported as early as 4th grade, with 1.2% reporting crack use. Crack use increases to 3% in 7th grade, 4% in 9th grade, and 6% in 12th grade. Most of these estimates use school-based self-report surveys, so they likely underrepresent the numbers of heavier drug users and those who begin use at early ages.

Drug use also varies by context. Intravenous drug use among 13- to 14-year-olds varied from 1.4% in San Francisco to 3.2% in Michigan. Males' overall use of IV drugs was twice as high as females' by the age of 18; and, from 3% to 6% of 18-year-olds report IV drug use (CDC, 1988). There is little doubt that significantly higher IV drug use occurs in disadvantaged inner-city neighborhoods. Interestingly, Oetting and Beauvais (1990) documented dramatic differences between three high schools. In one school, 75% of the students were at some risk, and more than 25% were sufficiently frequent drug users to suggest immediate action. In contrast, another school evidenced far less marijuana, cocaine, stimulant, and hallucinogen use. At this school, 4% had used heroin, compared to 26% at the other school.

Summary

Because of their increasing sexual activity and drug use, uncertainties about sexual intentions, reluctance to acknowledge sexual or drug interest or activities, lack of detailed knowledge of HIV and HIV prevention, and difficulties in taking preventive measures, young adolescents are at special risk. This general age-related risk increases substantially in subpopulations with higher rates of HIV-seroprevalence, earlier and more frequent sexual intercourse, earlier and more frequent use of drugs (especially intravenous drugs), less consistent use of contraception (especially condoms), and strong social norms encouraging risky sexual and drug activity. Most early adolescent HIV infections will occur in socially and economically disadvantaged metropolitan areas with high seroprevalence. In such areas, sexual activity is more frequent; there is less condom use; and, the younger average age of first intercourse in this population increases the number of sexual episodes over the life span (Voydanoff & Donnelly, 1990). Also, in such areas, there is greater probability for HIV transmission to adolescents through contact with members of high-risk groups, especially IV drug users. This pattern is exacerbated by the crack cocaine epidemic in urban inner-city neighborhoods. The likelihood of sexual transmission of HIV to adolescents in such contexts is increased by the fact that first sexual partners are typically older than the initiate. This age differential increases the likelihood of the older partner being HIV positive (Bingham, 1989). The use of coercion in age-differentiated sex and drug experiences is yet another factor. Given their relative inexperience and power, younger adolescents may defer to older partners in engaging in high-risk activity. Such socioenvironmental differences demonstrate the need for context-specific preventive programming.

PREVENTION OF HIV INFECTION IN EARLY ADOLESCENCE

Despite the complexity of risk behavior patterns, it is clear that some teens initiate intercourse and IV drug use between ages 10 and 12, and increasing percentages commence these activities between ages 10 and 14. Because relatively few adolescents have initiated intercourse by 12 and even fewer have developed IV drug patterns, the time between the end of Grade 6 and the beginning of Grade 7 seems a critical time for preventive intervention. Teenagers who will soon initiate intercourse must be knowledgeable about HIV transmission and must be competent in condom use. Teens who are continuing to have intercourse are the second highest priority group. Finally, those who are not sexually active and have not begun to use drugs must be helped to develop decision-making skills for considering the place of sex and drugs in their lives.

Prevention of HIV infection entails encouraging the development of personal skills related to sexual behavior and drug usage as well as the maintenance of these patterns over time. Abstinence from sexual activities in which bodily fluids are shared and from injectable drug use are ideal patterns from a risk-reduction perspective. Recognition that abstinence from sexual activity is unlikely has lead to a series of "safer-sex" recommendations, the most important of which involve limiting sexual contact to known partners (and knowing their HIV status) and consistent use of condoms and spermicides in intercourse. Because partners may not know their HIV status or may misrepresent it, routine condom use is required in all forms of intercourse. Forms of sexual expression other than intercourse should also be noted. Those who do not use drugs should be encouraged to avoid developing drug patterns; those who use IV drugs must practice needle hygiene and must be given accessible opportunities for supervised withdrawal. Preventive interventions must not only focus on the individual, but must also be directed to peers and family, relevant neighborhood and community social networks, and local institutions, especially the schools.

Life Development Intervention

Interventions to encourage sexual competence and to deter the development of drug patterns must be tailored to the developmental statuses and ecological contexts of distinct groups of early adolescents. Both patterns can be encouraged by the use of a life development intervention model (Danish, D'Augelli, & Ginsberg, 1984), which identifies critical developmental issues at different points in the life span and promotes personal and social competence. In HIV prevention, personal life goals involving the development of sexual health and drug use competence are identified. Intervention is organized to remove barriers that interfere with personal goal achievement such as lack of current and relevant information about HIV prevention, lack of personal and social skills to avoid risky situations, lack of support from others for the development of competence, and restricted access to critical resources, in this case, condoms and HIV-antibody testing. These barriers can be eliminated by the systematic provision of accurate information, relevant life skills, social support for behavior change, and access to crucial resources.

Both developmental statuses—in this case, the transition to sexual intercourse and the initiation of drug use—and the ecological contexts—the specific communities involved—are crucial to designing effective interventions. The life development model demands a careful analysis of local formal and informal social structures, both in terms of opportunities and barriers, as they impact on the development of knowledge, skills, social support, and resource availability. Special emphasis also needs to be placed on minority early adolescents, both African-American and Hispanic adolescents, and adolescents who self-identify as gay or bisexual, because both groups may experience discrimination of various forms, and because HIV positive rates in certain metropolitan neighborhoods among adult people of color and among adult gay and bisexual populations are unusually high. The life development model forces program development at several levels of impact—individual, family/small group, institutional, and community—consistent with conceptual models of life-span human development. Intervention research is fundamental in suggesting powerful interfaces (between person and family, within families, between families and teachers, between families and community agencies, etc.) that will maintain behavioral norms likely to minimize HIV exposure (D'Augelli, 1990).

Principles of Personal Competence Enhancement

Assuming that individuals shape their own development and that awareness of this encourages feelings of personal competence, the life development model directs program development to approaches that give young adolescents tools for their own competence development. This principle is personal empowerment promotion. Another orienting principle is optimum accessibility without threat. Helping resources must be available in a manner that minimizes fear; in some instances this would dictate anonymous helping systems. Another operating principle is that of assumptive responsibility (i.e., giving adolescents the responsibility to help others). This principle not only solidifies learning and behavior change, but also creates norms of interdependence. The final principle concerns the creation of informal settings in which sensitive personal issues like sexuality and drugs can be explored.

The life development intervention model involves four general kinds of interventions: informational interventions, social skill interventions, social support interventions, and resource access interventions. Planning efforts directed to preventing HIV infections among early adolescents must include all four kinds of interventions. In addition, it is crucial that interventions be designed with an underlying commitment to empowering teenagers, and that they avoid the anti-sex messages contained in so much of the sexuality education directed toward this group (see Fine, 1988).

Informational Interventions. Accurate information about HIV and HIV prevention must be given to all young adolescents. This information must be candid and clear. There must be no doubt concerning what sexual behaviors involve the highest risk of HIV infection. Adolescents should be well informed concerning behaviors that do not increase the risk of HIV infection (i.e., donating blood, casual contact, kissing, hugging, etc.). They should be given instruction about how to obtain and how to use condoms, and condom use should be promoted as both socially acceptable and individually desirable. Finally, adolescents who use IV drugs should be instructed in methods of needle sterilization and risks of needle sharing.

Social Skills Interventions. Personal and interpersonal skills involved in sexual expression and in the avoidance of drug use must be trained for HIV prevention. Young adolescents who have not begun sexual intercourse would benefit from decision-making skills to help them consider when and under what conditions they might begin sexual exploration. Social skills to refuse unwanted sexual contacts would be important as well. In addition, as they get older, adolescents need to know how to talk about sex with potential partners, how to be sexually assertive (vs. aggressive), how to set limits, and how to insist on safer sex. Social skills related to drug use must be similarly developed, except that greater emphasis would be needed on resistance of peer pressure and the development of personal conviction about substance use.

Social Support Interventions. After information and support have been provided by different interventions, it is necessary to maintain the new behaviors that have been learned. Peers and family are critical supports to maintenance, as are teachers, schools, and other important community institutions. A high priority should be placed on peer discussion/support groups in which young adolescents can talk about their changing bodies and their concerns. Older teens can play an important role as facilitators of such groups. Parent discussions of HIV prevention issues would be very useful in maintaining a consistent message about cautious sexual activity and lack of drug use. All teachers should understand the basic interventions used so that they can reinforce the interventions as well. Media programs that encourage the development of social norms are also needed.

Resource Access Interventions. There are two sets of resources to which young adolescents must have access—condoms and HIV testing. Access to condoms has become a controversial issue as several school districts move to provide condoms upon request to high school students. This idea takes advantage of school-based pregnancy information clinics that appear effective in diminishing unwanted teenage pregnancies (Dryfoos, 1988). No research exists to specifically inform the addition of condom distribution to such programs; nor are there any useful data on other methods to provide condoms to adolescents. However, there are data on exposure to sex education efforts, which find no untoward effects on adolescents' development and distinct advantages, such as use of birth control at first intercourse (Dawson, 1986; Marsiglio & Mott, 1986). There is no reason to suppose that consistent condom use would not be enhanced by easy availability for sexually active youth. The high percentages of early adolescents who do not use any contraception at first intercourse is a strong case for making condoms as available as possible so that access is not a reason for nonuse. Interventions that allow privacy and do not force adolescents to acknowledge sexual interests will be the most effective. Programs providing anonymous, personal contact and the means of obtaining condoms and sexual health information discreetly would seem ideal. Parental permission should not be required for condom access because this will discourage access. In addition, such requirements are inconsistent with the concept of empowerment and the development of personal responsibility for the development of one's intimate life.

The second access intervention is voluntary and anonymous HIV testing, which should be available for those who have reason to believe that they have been exposed to HIV. Without testing, many HIV positive people, including adolescents, will transmit HIV to others (Bingham, 1989; Heyward & Curran, 1988; Mann et al., 1988). Anonymous testing (in contrast to confidential testing in which identities are known, although legally protected) encourages testing and diminishes fears of others discovering one's HIV status. As HIV infection becomes more prevalent in the sexually active adolescent population, anonymous testing will become increasingly critical. Providing a way to allow individuals to determine their HIV status not only helps them avoid transmitting it to others, but allows for early medical referral and treatment if required. Testing should also be accessible without parental consent or notification. Otherwise, adolescents will not likely take the multiple risks of testing. All testing must be accompanied by counseling before and after the testing. Posttest counseling is especially crucial for those found to be HIV positive (Bingham, 1989).

CONCLUSION

Preventive intervention directed toward early adolescents will most certainly be met with resistance from individuals who feel that interventions to encourage sexual competence and to educate about drugs might increase sexual activity and drug use. Despite years of practice and much research, there is no evidence supporting these fears. No empirical findings clearly link exposure to sex or drug education to the initiation of sexual activity or drug use, or to escalation of sex and drug patterns begun before exposure. With no evidence to suggest untoward effects and the accumulated information about the increasing numbers of youth at risk for HIV infections (as well as other sexual health problems), there is simply no justification for lack of intervention. Surely some of the hesitancy results from a cultural conviction that merely discussing sex and drugs with young people encourages them to "experiment." All available research points to a very different conclusion. Such interventions produce more informed and prepared individuals, youth who are more competent in making the difficult decisions they will face in developing their sexual identities and in confronting the issues of substance use. Soon the need to candidly discuss HIV transmission will seem superfluous. As the epidemic continues, it is obvious that we cannot afford to maintain our inhibitions about discussing sexual expression and drug use and other factors associated with HIV. Without carefully developed interventions, more and more young people will become infected with HIV.

REFERENCES

Bingham, C. R. (1989). AIDS and adolescents: Threat of infection and approaches for prevention. *Journal of Early Adolescence, 9,* 50–66.

Brooks-Gunn, J., Boyer, C. B., & Hein, K. (1988). Preventing HIV infection and AIDS in children and adolescents: Behavioral research and intervention strategies. *American Psychologist, 43,* 958–964.

Brooks-Gunn, J., & Furstenberg, F. F. (1989). Adolescent sexual behavior. *American Psychologist, 44*(2), 249–257.

Burke, D. S., Brundage, J. F., Goldenbaum, M., Gardner, L. I., Peterson, M., Visintine, R., & Redfield, R. R. (1990). Human Immunodeficiency Virus infections in teenagers:

Seroprevalence among applicants for U. S. military service. *Journal of the American Medical Association, 263,* 2074-2077.
Centers for Disease Control. (1988). HIV-related beliefs, knowledge, and behaviors among high school students. *Morbidity and Mortality Weekly Report, 37,* 717-721.
Centers for Disease Control. (1990). *National HIV seroprevalence surveys: Summary of results, 1989.* Atlanta, GA: Author.
Centers for Disease Control. (1992, January 1). *HIV/AIDS surveillance report.* Atlanta, GA: Author.
Chin, J. (1990). Current and future dimensions of the HIV/AIDS pandemic in women and children. *Lancet, 336,* 221-224.
Danish, S. J., D'Augelli, A. R., & Ginsberg, M. R. (1984). Life development intervention: The promotion of mental health through the development of competence. In S. D. Brown & R. W. Lent (Eds.), *Handbook of counseling psychology* (pp. 520-544). New York: Wiley.
D'Augelli, A. R. (1990). Community psychology and the HIV epidemic: The development of helping communities. *Journal of Community Psychology, 18,* 337-346.
Dawson, D. A. (1986). The effects of sex education on adolescent behavior. *Family Planning Perspectives, 18,* 163-170.
DiClemente, R. J., Boyer, C. B., & Morales, E. S. (1988). Minorities and AIDS: Knowledge, attitudes and misconceptions among Black and Latin adolescents. *American Journal of Public Health, 78,* 55-57.
Dryfoos, J. G. (1988). School-based health clinics: Three years of experience. *Family Planning Perspectives, 20,* 193-200.
Fine, M. (1988). Sexuality, schooling, and adolescent females: The missing discourse of desire. *Harvard Educational Review, 58,* 29-53.
Fineberg, H. V. (1988). Education to prevent AIDS: Prospects and obstacles. *Science, 239,* 592-596.
Forrest, J. D., & Singh, S. (1990). The sexual and reproductive behavior of American women, 1982-1988. *Family Planning Perspectives, 22,* 206-214.
Gayle, H. D., Keeling, R. P., Garcia-Tunon, M., Kilbourne, B. W., Narkunas, J. P., Ingram, F. R., Rogers, M. F., & Curran, J. W. (1990). Prevalence of the Human Immunodeficiency Virus among university students. *New England Journal of Medicine, 323,* 1538-1541.
Hayes, C. D. (Ed.). (1987). *Risking the future: Adolescent sexuality, pregnancy, and childbearing.* Washington, DC: National Academy Press.
Heyward, W. L., & Curran, J. W. (1988). The epidemiology of AIDS in the United States. *Scientific American, 259,* 72-81.
Hofferth, S. L. (1990). Trends in adolescent sexual activity, contraception, and pregnancy in the United States. In J. Bancroft & J. M. Reinisch (Eds.), *Adolescence and puberty* (pp. 217-233). New York: Oxford University Press.
Jaffe, L. R., Seehaus, M., Wagner, C., & Leadbeater, B. J. (1988). Anal intercourse and knowledge of AIDS among minority-group female adolescents. *Pediatrics, 112,* 1005-1007.
Kegeles, S. M., Adler, N. E., & Irwin, Jr., C. E. (1988). Sexually active adolescents and condoms: Changes over one year in knowledge, attitudes and use. *American Journal of Public Health, 78*(4), 460-461.
Kinsey, A. C., Pomeroy, W. B., & Martin, C. G. (1948). *Sexual behavior in the human male.* Philadelphia: W. B. Saunders.
Kinsey, A. C., Pomeroy, W. B., Martin, C. G., & Gebhard, P. H. (1953). *Sexual behavior in the human female.* Philadelphia: W. B. Saunders.

Mann, J. M., Chin, J., Piot, P., & Quinn, T. (1988). The international epidemiology of AIDS. *Scientific American, 259*, 82–89.

Marsiglio, W., & Mott, F. L. (1986). The impact of sex education or sexual activity, contraceptive use, and premarital pregnancy among American teenagers. *Family Planning Perspectives, 18*, 151–162.

Moss, A. R., & Bacchetti, P. (1989). Natural history of HIV infection. *AIDS, 3*, 55–61.

National Academy of Sciences. (1988). *Confronting AIDS: Update 1988.* Washington, DC: National Academy Press.

National Research Council. (1989). *AIDS: Sexual behavior and intravenous drug use.* Washington, DC: National Academy Press.

Oetting, E. R., & Beauvais, F. (1990). Adolescent drug use: Findings of national and local surveys. *Journal of Consulting and Clinical Psychology, 58*, 385–394.

Price, J. H., Desmond, S., & Kukulka, G. (1985). High school students' perceptions and misperceptions of AIDS. *Journal of School Health, 65*, 107–109.

Reinisch, J. M. (1990). *The Kinsey Institute new report on sex.* New York: St. Martin's Press.

Sato, P. A., Chin, J., & Mann, J. M. (1989). Review of AIDS and HIV infection: Global epidemiology and statistics. *AIDS, 3* (suppl. 1), 5301–5307.

Stiffman, A. R., Earls, F., Robins, L. N., Jung, K. G., & Kulbok, P. (1987). Adolescent sexual activity and pregnancy: Socioenvironmental problems, physical health, and mental health. *Journal of Youth and Adolescence, 16*, 497–509.

Strunin, L., & Hingson, R. (1987). Acquired Immunodeficiency Syndrome and adolescents: Knowledge, beliefs, attitudes, and behaviors. *Pediatrics, 79*, 825–828.

Voydanoff, P., & Donnelly, B. W. (1990). *Adolescent sexuality and pregnancy.* Newbury Park, CA: Sage.

21 Early Adolescent Belief Systems and Substance Abuse

John D. Swisher
The Pennsylvania State University

This chapter presents a model for conceptualizing adolescent beliefs about alcohol and other drug use and identifies potential prevention strategies aimed at modifying these beliefs. A central thesis is that adolescents' beliefs about themselves and their peers, parents, and communities are important predictors of their behavior. Consequently, the chapter is organized around adolescents' beliefs about intrapersonal, interpersonal, and extrapersonal influences on alcohol and drug use. I begin by documenting the extent of the problem of alcohol and drug use among young adolescents and then focus on literature related to beliefs, attitudes, and perceptions. Finally, I review interventions related to beliefs that may be effective in reducing substance use. The term *beliefs* refers to attitudes, perceptions, and expectations.

EXTENT OF THE PROBLEM

The U.S. Department of Education (1988) reported that alcohol and other drug use among adolescents is among the top 10 problems facing the nation's schools. Early adolescent use patterns and intentions to use cigarettes, beer, marijuana, and cocaine can be seen in Table 21.1. These data are based on a stratified random sample of school buildings in Pennsylvania (Governor's Drug Policy Council, 1989) that included 7,068 sixth graders, 10,445 seventh graders, 10,392 ninth graders and 10,392 seniors. These data indicate that:

Table 21.1
Self-Reported Regular Use of Substances and Intent to Use Substances, Pennsylvania
1988–1989

Substance	Grade						
	6	7	8	9	10	11	12
Cigarettes, intent to use	16.4	21.9		32.2			36.2
Cigarettes, self-reported use	6.7	11.7		23.2			30.8
Beer, intent to use	27.5	35.1		59.1			72.5
Beer, self-reported use	6.0	10.5		26.3			44.9
Marijuana, intent to use	2.1	4.3		15.5			26.0
Marijuana, self-reported use	0.6	1.4		7.1			13.9
Cocaine, intent to use	1.0	1.3		3.4			6.8
Cocaine, self-reported use	0.2	0.3		0.6			2.4

- alcohol is the most frequently used substance at all grade levels represented
- intentions to use form early
- the percent intending to use any substance is nearly equal to the percent using 2 years later (e.g., 21.9% of seventh graders report intentions to use cigarettes and 23.2% of ninth graders report using cigarettes)
- cocaine intentions and use are very low for early adolescents

Intentions to use are a form of beliefs about future behavior; thus, these data are consistent with the notion that beliefs about future behaviors are related to actual behavior. Furthermore, Wolford and Swisher (1986) found that intentions to use were positively correlated with rates of current use for all substances. These findings are based on cross-sectional data and need to be verified in longitudinal studies.

Longitudinal studies of the consequences of adolescent substance use indicate an association between earlier and heavier use and more frequent problems such as family instability, criminal activity, poor educational achievement, unstable career patterns, and poor mental health (Newcomb & Bentler, 1988; Shedler & Block, 1990). An important finding from these studies was that early adolescent adamant abstainers also experienced problems as young adults but not to the same extent as did early heavy drug users. The best adjusted young adults were those who had some experience but not extensive experience with substances (Newcomb & Bentler, 1988; Shedler & Block, 1990).

Similarly, in a cross-sectional survey of alcohol use, Price (1991) compared ninth graders who drank regularly but did not get drunk with ninth graders who drank regularly and usually got drunk. She concluded that ninth graders who drank but not to drunkenness had better academic records and fewer problem behaviors than their peers who drank regularly and were drunk regularly. Although Price's findings are similar to the longitudinal research just cited, she did not include abstainers or occasional users.

It appears from these studies that early intentions to use are indicative of early use. Furthermore, the earlier and heavier the use, the greater the problems in adolescence and in young adulthood. Ironically, total abstention is also associated with problems, but not to the same degree. Central to these findings is the idea that intentions (beliefs about future use) appear to form before use but correlate positively with use; thus, intentions may be a precursor to adjustment problems in adolescence and adulthood.

THE ROLE OF BELIEFS IN THEORIES OF SUBSTANCE ABUSE

Theories explaining and predicting adolescent involvement with substances can be considered as either disease progression models or psychosocial interaction models. The disease progression models emphasize biological markers and behavior patterns leading to dependency (e.g., Bejerot's, 1980, Tolerance/Withdrawal Theory). Psychosocial models include biological variables and also emphasize contextual variables including perceived peer pressure, perceived family relations, and socioeconomic status (e.g., Jessor & Jessor, 1977, Problem Behavior theory, 1977). The variables focusing on perceived peer pressure and/or family relations are seen as somewhat synonymous with beliefs.

These types of theories consider but do not emphasize the internal perceptual states of the individual, including beliefs, perceived risks, perceptions of parents, attitudes toward the law, and so forth. For example, Jessor and Jessor (1977) assessed perceptions of peer use and found a significant positive correlation between perceived peer use and personal use. For approximately 20 years, psychological research focused more on behaviors than beliefs and, consequently, the realm of beliefs, perceptions, and attitudes has not received adequate attention. There is a need to develop a typology of individual belief systems and to explore more fully their role in decisions made by early adolescents related to substance abuse and other problem behaviors.

BELIEFS DOMAINS RESEARCH: A CONCEPTUAL MODEL

There is some evidence that a variety of individual beliefs, perceptions, and/or attitudes contribute substantially to understanding drug and alcohol use, as well as other social problems such as teen pregnancy, suicide, academic achievement, and delinquency. For example, early adolescent intentions to use alcohol and other drugs are positively correlated with concurrent use (e.g., Wolford & Swisher, 1986). Similarly, the percentage of 7th graders intending to use beer is approximately the percentage of 10th graders who report using beer on a regular basis (Governor's Drug Policy Council, 1989). Because these beliefs about future behavior may influence subsequent use, it is important to gain more insights into how and why these beliefs form. Moreover, because intentions to use often form in early adolescence, and may precede actual use, early adolescence becomes an important period for mounting preventive interventions related to beliefs.

Figure 21.1 presents a matrix for conceptualizing beliefs in terms of the major dimensions that appear to be important in assessment or programming regarding any given social problem (e.g., substance abuse). Although this conceptualization is not limited to early adolescence, I am using it as an overview of the major dimensions to be considered in guiding research or programming for young adolescents. The major categories of beliefs include the adolescent's perceptions of what presently exists, what he or she expects will exist in the future, and what should exist regarding his or her behavior and the behavior of others across the matrix. The matrix presents intrapersonal, interpersonal, and extrapersonal domains (Swisher, 1976) within a contextual model. All of the elements of this model are interactive and overlapping. For example, intrapersonal states are affected by interpersonal interactions, and both are influenced by the environment (e.g., feelings of well-being resulting from having quality family time at a picnic on a sunny day). The literature reviewed for this chapter is organized to the extent possible within the framework of this matrix.

Intrapersonal

The intrapersonal domain includes beliefs about one's biological as well as psychological status. Perceptions of physique and health status are

BELIEFS DOMAINS	CONTEXTUAL						
	INTRAPERSONAL		INTERPERSONAL			EXTRAPERSONAL	
	BIO- LOGICAL	PSYCHO- LOGICAL	PEERS	PARENTS	TEACHERS	COMMUNITY	SOCIO- POLITICAL
WHAT DOES EXIST?							
WHAT WILL EXIST?							
WHAT SHOULD EXIST?							

FIG. 21.1 Matrix for adolescent beliefs regarding contextual influences.

examples of the biological domain, whereas values and decision-making strategies are examples in the psychological domain. These perceptions appear to be related to substance use. For example, Maney (1990) found that college student perceptions of general well-being were negatively correlated with alcohol use. Students with lower perceptions of well-being consumed more alcohol. Chopak, Vicary, and Erickson (1991) found similar results with early adolescents in a rural context in which females who perceived themselves as having poorer health status used more alcohol and cigarettes. The males in this study who reported lower health status also reported more frequent drunkenness. Of course, these results cannot tell us whether perceived health influences substance use or vice versa. In a different vein, Brown (1989) found that adolescents' subjective evaluations of life events were negatively correlated with substance abuse. That is, the more adolescents perceived the event as being disruptive to them, the more they became involved with various substances.

Intrapersonal beliefs also include expectations for future success. Jessor (1990) concluded that adolescent perceptions of future achievement ("making it") differed by ethnic group and by socioeconomic status (SES) within groups. Adolescents with higher expectations for success were found to engage in fewer problem behaviors.

Another type of intrapersonal belief is perceived risk. Bachman, Johnson, O'Malley, and Humphrey (1988) posited that the recent decline in adolescents' use of some substances (e.g., marijuana) is related to perceptions of increased risk (see Fig. 21.2). They concede that their lack of longitudinal data prohibits causal interpretations, but the patterns of data are strong support for their hypothesis: As perceived risks

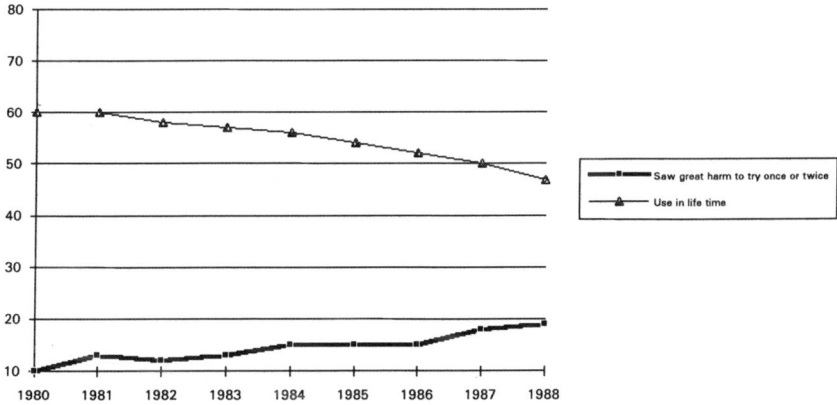

FIG. 21.2 Correlation between marijuana use and perceived harmfulness of marijuana. Statistics from the National Institute on Drug Abuse High School Senior Survey.

of marijuana use and cocaine use (see Fig. 21.3) have increased among senior high school students, lifetime prevalence has decreased. It is not possible to pinpoint the origins of the increase in perceived risks. The increase could be the result of new school initiatives, or it could be an effect of the media portrayal of drugs. In any case, historical changes in beliefs about risk are associated with changes in use.

The longitudinal study of Newcomb and Bentler (1988) also provides insight into the importance of psychological beliefs. They found that adult consequences related to drug use were similar in kind if not in degree for adamant abstainers and heavy users. Shedler and Block (1990) more recently arrived at similar conclusions. Individuals who believe with similar zeal that it is either their "right" to use any drug or that others must be "protected" from using any drug appear to be similar regarding the rigidity and adamancy of their beliefs. This dynamic suggests that something about intensity or rigidity of beliefs may be as important for substance use as the content of the beliefs.

Interpersonal

The interpersonal domain includes adolescents' beliefs about the behavior of their peers and parents, as well as the perceived expectations of peers and parents. This domain also includes perceived self-efficacy to employ various interpersonal skills to refuse drugs (Pentz, 1984).

The importance of interpersonal beliefs was demonstrated by Ashby (1990) who found that students' perceptions of teachers' and parents'

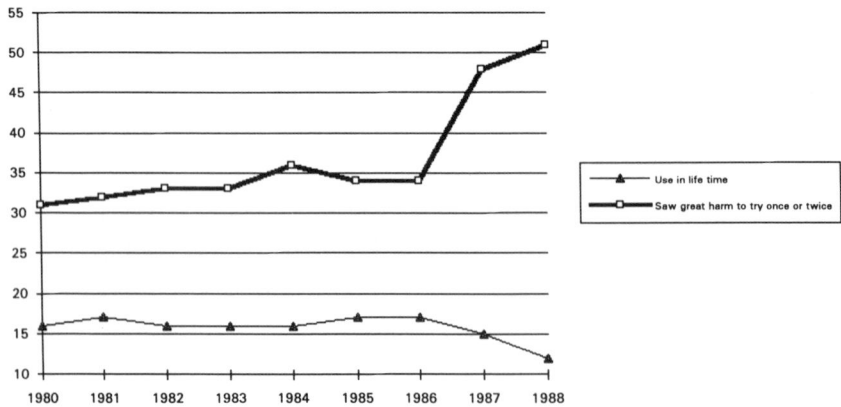

FIG. 21.3 Correlation between cocaine use and perceived harmfulness of cocaine. Statistics from the National Institute on Drug Abuse High School Senior Survey.

academic expectations for them predicted their intentions to use drugs. Although these cross-sectional data do not allow for causal interpretations, they clearly indicate a negative relationship between perceived adult expectations for academic performance and intentions to use drugs.

Focusing on a different set of perceptions, Wilks and Callan (1988) reported that the strongest predictors of alcohol use for males were their perceptions of their fathers' and mothers' drinking, as well as their fathers' actual drinking. Higher perceived drinking was correlated with greater personal use. Similarly, best friends' drinking was positively related to adolescent males' perceptions of themselves as drinkers. Allegrante, O'Rourke, and Tuncalp (1977) reported similar findings for adolescents' perceptions of their parents' smoking. Early adolescent males were more likely to smoke if they believed that either parent smoked. Early adolescent females, however, did not appear to be affected by beliefs about parental smoking.

Perceived lack of parental support and incompatibility between parent and adolescent expectations have been found to be indicative of problem behaviors in general (Petersen & Ebata, 1987). Streit (1973) focused on early adolescents' perceptions of their interactions with parents. Alcohol and tobacco were used by individuals who perceived their parents as being accepting and authoritarian; marijuana users perceived their parents as being accepting and laissez faire; and, hard drug users were those who perceived their parents as being rejecting and laissez faire.

Beliefs about the behaviors and expectations of peers and/or significant adults appears to be associated with adolescents' behavior. In general, the more the adolescents perceive others as using alcohol and other drugs, the greater their own use. Furthermore, the higher the perceived expectations for academic achievement, the lower adolescents' intended use.

Extrapersonal

The extrapersonal domain includes the dynamics of social systems such as organizations, institutions, and communities. It is assumed that what adolescents believe about these social systems influences their behavior. For example, attitudes toward drug laws have been found to correlate significantly with self-reported substance use. Swisher and Horan (1973) asked about adolescents' perceptions of the social origins of laws in general and perceptions regarding who benefits from laws. Eighth graders who believed that laws were made to limit their freedom had higher intentions to use drugs. An adolescent's perceived probability of being caught for drinking and driving also affects compliance with the law (Hingson, Heeren, & Morelock, 1989).

BELIEF DOMAINS INTERVENTIONS

Some research has focused on interventions around specific belief domains. In these interventions altering beliefs was part of the prevention program. This strategy is highlighted in this section, which is organized using the same categories as the previous review of research.

Interventions to Alter Intrapersonal Beliefs

Interventions in the intrapersonal domain focus on variables that are primarily within the individual and do not require others for action. Previous experience with a behavior, current values (regardless of their interpersonal origins), and physical status are examples of intrapersonal variables that may affect substance use. Interventions aimed at modifying beliefs and values concerning personal use of substances fall into this category.

Several early studies led to the position that disseminating only factual knowledge information about drugs had no effect on attitudes toward use or actual use (Swisher & Hoffman, 1975). Consequently, the field of drug education began to emphasize other dimensions (e.g., enhancing self-esteem). Gold and Kelly (1988) recently argued that higher level cognitive processing of information rather than simple factual recall may have a greater impact on health behavior. This type of intervention has not been empirically tested to date. It has been noted, however, that higher levels of perceived risk associated with use of alcohol, tobacco, and other drugs are associated with lower levels of use (Bachman, Johnston, O'Malley, & Humphrey, 1988). Consequently, altering perceptions of risk may represent an effective intervention.

Swisher and Horan (1972) attempted to alter substance use values by inducing dissonance between attitudes toward use and higher order values associated with direct experience in living. In this intervention with college freshmen, students completed questionnaires that assessed the value they placed on direct experience in living (e.g., write to a friend vs. talk to a friend on the phone vs. go to lunch with a friend). After establishing that students valued direct experience, drug use was portrayed as a mediator of experience and therefore inconsistent with the established value of direct experience. Students who generally preferred direct experience with life became more conservative on the posttest. Thus, when students discovered that their attitudes toward drug use were in conflict with higher order values they held, their attitudes toward use became more conservative. Rokeach (1984), upon whose dissonance theory the intervention was based, also reported success in using value dissonance to bring about changes in areas such as racism, ecology, and smoking.

Prior experience appears to make individuals more resistant to interventions. Ellickson and Bell (1990), while reporting general success with a preventive intervention, also reported that their programming had no effect on individuals with prior experience with tobacco. Dielman, Shope, Leech, and Butchart (1989) also found that prior experience with alcohol reduced the effectiveness of a prevention program with early adolescents. Prior experience with a substance apparently has an effect on the individual's psychological filtering of prevention program content.

Interventions to Alter Interpersonal Beliefs

The interpersonal domain has been the focus of most intervention research and has centered on peer and parental influences on use. Interventions that fall into this category include those that seek to modify beliefs about normative use, include testimonials from peers, or attempt to improve the adolescents' ability to resist pressures to use.

Hansen (1990) developed a procedure for modifying perceptions of substance use levels among peers. In discussions with groups of early adolescents, he found most adolescents overestimated peer use of substances. After conducting a survey and presenting results reflecting lower peer use to sixth and seventh graders, he found their subsequent use of tobacco and marijuana was reduced or delayed. This preventive intervention that realigns beliefs about peers has been labeled *normative education.*

Two meta-analyses have focused on the importance of peer models for drug education. Tobler's (1986) analysis of 143 experimentally designed evaluations concluded that peer-led programming that relies on peer modeling as a source of influence had the best results. Bangert-Drowns (1988) also concluded that peer-led programs consistently reduced use. Conversely, Ellickson and Bell (1990) did not find peer-led prevention programs to be more successful except in the case of alcohol use and then only on a short-term basis. Ellickson and Bell concluded that alcohol behavior was more difficult to change because of its widespread social acceptance for adults.

A third technique involves improving refusal skills. Botvin and Tortu (1988) reviewed intervention research on a program known as Life Skills Training that emphasizes intrapersonal and interpersonal beliefs with an emphasis on behavioral rehearsal of refusal skills. Their 14-session program for early adolescents contains information about drugs, advertising resistance, decision-making skills, coping skills, communication skills, and assertiveness training. This program significantly delayed the onset of use of alcohol, tobacco, and marijuana. Moreover, the impact of the program was maintained when five booster sessions were provided in each subsequent year.

The refusal skills models (e.g., Botvin & Tortu, 1988; Pentz, 1984) also target internal beliefs such as self-efficacy (perceiving oneself as being competent to employ the skills learned) and perceived risk. Refusal skill programs are likely to be more effective when individuals perceive that their choices of action will bring rewards from their peers. The effectiveness of a life skills program also depends on how adolescents perceive the skills that are being promoted. A study of assertiveness training for Black adolescents that apparently did not produce desired results concluded that aggression (a negative option) was perceived by the youth to be a more highly valued behavior than assertiveness (Stewart & Lewis, 1986). Although life skills training is based on improved assertiveness skills, it may not be perceived as the most "macho" option for young Black males.

Interventions to Alter Contextual Beliefs

Contextual interventions would include actions such as changing social policies, altering the mass media, or controlling the distribution of alcohol, tobacco, and other drugs. Some recent prevention research has focused on contextual interventions that include comprehensive, coordinated strategies. Pentz et al. (1989) reported success with a prevention program combining classroom instruction, homework involving parents, simultaneous community-wide media documentaries and campaigns, and enforcement of laws regarding sale of alcohol and tobacco to minors. This evaluation focused on 20,000 middle and junior high students and their families in 15 communities. The students were given classroom instruction (information, decision-making, and refusal skills), their parents were involved in homework assignments, and the mass media in these communities presented concurrent documentaries and supplemental information. A comparable sample of control sites was also tested. A 1-year follow-up reported by Pentz et al. (1989) revealed lower levels of cigarette, alcohol, and marijuana use by the experimental students.

Many of the components in this model were previously studied in isolation (e.g., Flay & Sobel, 1984), and the combination was tried in part because of the finding that the individual components were only effective for 1 or 2 years. This type of preventive intervention systematically targets several belief domains simultaneously. In the Pentz et al. (1989) project, all aspects of the intervention were designed to operate simultaneously, thereby impacting intrapersonal, interpersonal, and extrapersonal domains in a coordinated manner.

Goodstadt (1987) also argued for impacting all domains simultaneously:

> Current research suggests that school-based education is a necessary but not sufficient ingredient in preventing drug abuse. Schools provide an opportunity for imparting accurate knowledge, systematically examining values, learning and practicing decision making, and learning to cope with social forces within a controlled setting. Schools by themselves, however, cannot counter the range of powerful forces that operate outside the walls of the classroom and school. Therefore, school-based programs require the support of complementary home-based and community-based programs. (p. 31)

The efficacy of multilevel contextual interventions appears to depend on coordinated, high energy efforts. Scheurich (1986) studied the impact of teams of teachers trained to develop and implement interventions in multiple domains (e.g., school, family, and community) in their home communities. He concluded that the more active teams were better at preventing onset of drug use behavior and reduced use of drugs (i.e., cigarettes, alcohol, marijuana, and drunk driving). Active teams conducted more projects, held more meetings, made more classroom presentations, involved the administration, expanded the original team membership, and obtained additional training.

Swisher and Gorman (1986), in a smaller scale study of multiple domain interventions, compared schools with coordinating teams with control schools and concluded that students in the junior and senior high schools with trained active teams had lower levels of marijuana use. It was also established that the more active teams had administrative support, fiscal support, and worked well as teams. These types of programs were successful when a coordinating group (school team with community members) was given support and recognition, was successful in implementing a variety of programs, included parents in educational activities with their children, involved the media and community agencies in concurrent programming, established community policies such as curfews to protect young people, and assisted law enforcement agencies with monitoring sales to minors and other violations of drug and alcohol laws. More replication studies are needed to verify these patterns of results, but it does appear that multiple domain strategies involving several domains simultaneously have an impact on beliefs.

SUMMARY

The central thesis of this chapter has been that early adolescents' beliefs, perceptions, and attitudes affect behaviors related to alcohol and other drug use. Admittedly, the available literature on this topic is limited; however, the examples cited for basic and applied research representing intrapersonal, interpersonal, and extrapersonal domains provide a rationale for further research. Additional basic research is needed regarding how early adolescents' beliefs about themselves, peers, families, and communities affect their behavior. This research should also incorporate the other major social problems facing early adolescents such as, violence, pregnancy, suicide, and school dropout.

There is also a need to develop applied research that builds upon a better understanding of beliefs and behavior. Programs similar to "normative education" (Hansen et al., 1988) are illustrative of this approach. This type of applied research should also consider the feasibility of including several belief domains and multiple social problem areas simultaneously.

REFERENCES

Allegrante, J. P., O'Rourke, T. W., & Tuncalp, S. (1977). A multivariate analysis of selected psychosocial variables on the development of subsequent youth smoking behavior. *Journal of Drug Education, 7*(3), 237–247.

Ashby, J. S. (1990). *Relative impact of sociocultural variables on adolescent drug and alcohol use.* Unpublished doctoral dissertation, The Pennsylvania State University, University Park.

Bachman, J. G., Johnston, L. D., O'Malley, P. M., & Humphrey, R. H. (1988). Explaining the recent decline in marijuana use: Differentiating the effects of perceived risks, disapproval, and general lifestyle factors. *Journal of Health and Social Behavior, 29,* 92–112.

Bangert-Drowns, R. L. T. (1988). The effects of school-based substance abuse education—A meta-analysis. *Journal of Drug Education, 18,* 243–264.

Bejerot, N. (1980). Addiction to pleasure: A biological and social-psychological theory of addiction. In D. J. Letteiri, M. Sayers, & H. W. Pearson (Eds.), *Theories of drug abuse:*

Selected Contemporary perspectives. (NIDA Research Monograph No. 30). Rockville, MD: National Institute on Drug Abuse.

Botvin, G. J., & Tortu, S. (1988). Preventing adolescent substance abuse through life skills training. In R. Price, E. L. Cowen, R. P. Lorian, & J. Ramos-McKay (Eds.), *A casebook for practitioners* (pp. 98–110). Washington, DC: American Psychological Association.

Brown, S. A. (1989). Life events of adolescents in relation to personal and parental substance abuse. *American Journal of Psychiatry, 146,* 484–489.

Chopak, J., Vicary, J. R., & Erickson, C. (1991). *Risk factors influencing perceived health status among rural adolescents.* Paper presented at the American Association of Health, Physical Education, Recreation and Dance Annual Convention, San Francisco, CA.

Dielman, T. E., Shope, J. T., Leech, S. L., & Butchart, A. T. (1989). Differential effectiveness of an elementary school-based alcohol misuse prevention program. *Journal of School Health, 59*(6), 255–263.

Ellickson, P. L., & Bell, R. M. (1990). Drug prevention in junior high: A multi-site longitudinal test. *Science, 247,* 1299–1305.

Flay, B. R., & Sobel, J. L. (1984). The Role of Mass Media in Preventing Adolescent Substance Abuse. In T. Glynn, C. Leukfeld, & J. Ludford, (Eds.), *Preventing adolescent drug abuse: Intervention strategies* (pp. 5–35). Rockville, MD: National Institute on Drug Abuse.

Gold, R. S., & Kelly, M. A. (1988, August/September). Is knowledge really power? *Health Education,* pp. 40–46.

Goodstadt, M. S. (1987, Winter). Prevention strategies for drug abuse. *Issues in Science and Technology,* pp. 28–35.

Governor's Drug Policy Council. (1989). *Alcohol, drugs and Pennsylvania's youth: A generation at risk. The 1989 survey of Pennsylvania school students.* Harrisburg, PA: Author.

Hansen, W. B. (1990). Theory and implementation of the social influence model of primary prevention. In K. H. Rey, C. L. Faegre, & P. Lowery (Eds.), *Prevention research findings: 1988* (pp. 93–107). Rockville, MD: Office for Substance Abuse Prevention.

Hansen, W. B., Graham, J. W., Wolkenstein, B. H., Lundy, B. Z., Pearson, J., Flay, B. R., & Johnson, C. A. (1988). Differential impact of three alcohol prevention curricula on hypothesized mediating variables. *Journal of Drug Education, 18,* 143–154.

Hingson, R., Heeren, T., & Morelock, S. (1989). Effects of Maine's 1982 .02 law to reduce teenage driving after drinking. *Alcohol drugs and driving, 5,* 25–36.

Jessor, R. (1990, April). *Perceived life chances in the opportunity structure: A generalized expectancy for "making it" among White, Black and Hispanic adolescents.* Paper presented at the Conference on Explanations and Expectations in the Framework of Rotter's Social Learning Theory, California School of Professional Psychology, Los Angeles.

Jessor, R., & Jessor, S. L. (1977). *Problem behavior and psychosocial development: A longitudinal study of youth.* New York: Academic Press.

Maney, D. W. (1990). Predicting university students' use of alcoholic beverages. *Journal of College Student Development, 31*(1), 23–32.

Newcomb, M. D., & Bentler, P. M. (1988). *Consequences of adolescent drug use: Impact on the lives of young adults.* Sage Newbury Park, CA.

Pentz, M. A. (1984). Prevention of adolescent substance abuse through social skills development. *National Institute of Drug Abuse Resource Monograph Service, 47,* 195–231.

Pentz, M. A., Dwyer, J. H., MacKinnon, D. P., Flay, B. R., Hansen, W. B., Wang, E. Y. I., & Johnson, A. (1989). A multicommunity trial for primary prevention of adolescent drug abuse. *Journal of American Medical Association, 261,* 3259–3266.

Petersen, A. C., & Ebata, A. (1987). Developmental transitions and adolescent problem behavior: Implications for prevention and intervention. In K. Hurrelmann, F. Kaufmann, F. Losel (Eds.), *Social intervention: Potential and constraints* (pp. 167–184). New York: Walter de Gruyter.

Price, M. C. (1991). *A comparison of alcohol related problem behaviors of ninth grade students with different drinking patterns.* Unpublished master's thesis, The Pennsylvania State University, University Park.

Rokeach, M. (1984). A value approach to the prevention and reduction of drug abuse. In T. Glynn, C. Leudefeld, & J. Ludfors (Eds.), *Preventing adolescent drug abuse: Intervention strategies* (NIDA Research Monograph 47). Rockville, MD: NIDA

Scheurich, J. (1986). *Evaluation report on the Wichita public schools' team training for substance use prevention, 1985–1986.* Topeka: Kansas Department of Transportation, Office of Highway Safety.

Shedler, J., & Block, J. (1990). Adolescent drug use and psychological health. *American Psychologist, 45*(5), 612–630.

Stewart, C. G., & Lewis, W. A. (1986). Effects of assertiveness training on the self-esteem of black high school students. *Journal of Counseling and Development, 64,* 638–641.

Streit, F. (1973). *A test and procedure to identify secondary school children who have a high probability of drug abuse.* Unpublished doctoral dissertation, Rutgers University, New Brunswick, NJ.

Swisher, J. D. (1976). Mental health—The core of preventive health education. *The Journal of School Health, XLVI*(7), 386–391.

Swisher, J. D., & Gorman, J. (1986). *An evaluation of super teams training.* Research report for Division of Substance Abuse Services, Albany, NY.

Swisher, J. D., & Hoffman, A. (1975). Information: The irrelevant variable in drug education. In B. Corder, R. Smith, J. Swisher (Eds.), *Drug abuse prevention: Perspectives and approaches for educators* (pp. 49–62). Dubuque, IA: William C. Brown.

Swisher, J. D., & Horan, J. (1972). Effecting drug attitude change in college students via induced cognitive dissonance. *Journal of SPATE, 11,* 26–31.

Swisher, J. D., & Horan, J. (1973). Pennsylvania State University evaluation scales. In A. Abrams, E. Garfield, & J. Swisher (Eds.), *Accountability in drug education: A model for evaluation.* Washington, DC: Drug Abuse Council.

Tobler, N. S. (1986). Meta-analysis of 143 adolescent drug prevention programs: Quantitative outcome results of program participants compared to a control or comparison group. *Journal of Drug Issues, 16,* 537–567.

United States Department of Education. (1988). *Drug prevention curricula: A guide to selection and implementation.* Washington, DC: U.S. Government Printing Office.

Wilks, J., & Callan, V. J. (1988). Expectations about appropriate drinking contexts: Comparisons of parents, adolescents and best friends. *British Journal of Addiction, 83,* 1055–1062.

Wolford, C., & Swisher, J. D. (1986). Behavioral intention as an indicator of drug use. *Journal of Drug Education, 16,* 305–327.

22 | Depression as a Disorder of Social Relationships: Implications for School Policy and Prevention Programs

Robert E. Kennedy
The Pennsylvania State University

Depression has been called the "common cold" of psychopathology. Aside from the anxiety problems to which it is closely related, clinical depression has a higher prevalence at any particular point in time and a higher lifetime prevalence (percentage of the population having experienced at least one clinical episode) than any other psychiatric disorder (NIMH, 1981). Estimates of point prevalence for clinical depression among both adolescents and adults range from 4% to 10% and estimates of lifetime prevalence range from 10% to 30%. Of course, at least subclinical levels of depression are a nearly ubiquitous element of human experience following major losses such as the death of a loved one or failure to reach a major life goal. The individual and social costs of both clinical and subclinical depression are enormous. Among adolescents, these costs include school avoidance and failure, substance abuse and other conduct problems, and suicide, which is the second leading cause of death among adolescents after motor vehicle and other accidents (Frederick, 1982).

DEVELOPMENTAL TRENDS

Early adolescence has long been assumed by psychologists, mental health professionals, and laypeople alike to be a period of markedly increasing rates of both depressed affect and episodes of clinical depression. (For a thorough discussion of the distinction between depression as a mood and depression as a clinical disorder, see Angold, 1988.) In fact, results of many cross-sectional studies are consistent with this assumption that adolescents as young as seventh graders are significantly "moodier" than preadolescent children. For example, young adolescents have been found to report lower positive affect and more affective lability than preadolescents (Larsen & Lampman-Petraitis, 1989) and more symptoms of depression within the subclinical range (e.g., Kaplan, Hong, & Weinhold, 1984). Longitudinal studies, on the other hand, have not been as consistent in finding an increase in negative affect from childhood to adolescence. For example, subjects in the Isle of Wight study reported many more depressive symptoms as teenagers than they had as preadolescents (Rutter, 1986). In contrast, however, Petersen, Sarigiani, and Kennedy (1991) found that self-reported affect became more positive as their sample of youngsters from a suburb in the American midwest moved from Grade 6 to Grade 12.

Cross-sectional epidemiological studies of clinical depression, like those of depressive affect, suggest a dramatic increase in rates of this problem from childhood to adolescence. Prior to the mid-1970s, in fact, many authorities held, mostly on the basis of psychoanalytic theory, that preadolescents were incapable of experiencing true clinical depressions. Such depressions were assumed to occur only after the onset of puberty and the development of a stable sense of self, the ability to feel guilt, and other psychological constructs thought to emerge first during early adolescence (Rutter, 1986).

The assumption of no clinical depression during childhood has been abandoned in the face of extensive evidence for childhood depressions that meet the formal criteria for a diagnosis of clinical depression among adults (cf. Angold, 1988). However, the rate of such diagnosable clinical depression seems to be much higher among adolescents than among children. For example, Kashani et al. (1987) found that 8% of a community sample of adolescents whom they interviewed reported depressive symptoms at the time of interview that met standard diagnostic criteria for a depressive disorder. This prevalence was twice that found among 9-year-olds by the same research group (Kashani et al., 1983) and was comparable to the rates commonly found among adults. Retrospective data about the age of onset of depressive disorders also suggest a substantial increase in depression from childhood to adolescence. For example, in one recent study, fewer than 10% of the respondents reporting a depressive disorder sometime in their lives reported that it began before 11 years of age, whereas about 50% indicated that their disorder began during ages 11 through 24 (Sorenson, Rutter, & Aneshensel, 1991). In addition, hypotheses about qualitative differences between clinical depression among children and the analogous disorder among adolescents and adults have not been abandoned (cf. Carlson & Garber, 1986). For example, one crucial difference between depression in childhood and in early adolescence, as discussed later, is that rates of suicide attempts and completions among young adolescents are many times the rates among preadolescent children, who almost never successfully commit suicide and very seldom even attempt it.

No long-term longitudinal study of clinical depression using structured interviews and standard diagnostic criteria in a general population sample has been reported, at least to my knowledge. In the Isle of Wight Study, psychiatric diagnoses of depression were much higher when the participants were interviewed at 14 or 15 than when they had first been interviewed at 10 or 11 (cf. Rutter, 1986). However, this early study does not seem to have used specific diagnostic criteria. Also, diagnoses were apparently based more on information given by the mother than on the adolescent's own report. Probably as a result, the rate of diagnosed depression was extremely low at both times of measurement, limiting the usefulness of this data as information regarding longitudinal increases in clinical depression during the early adolescent transition.

Petersen et al. (1991) asked their subjects in eighth grade and again in twelfth grade whether they had experienced in the preceding years of the study at least one episode, lasting 2 weeks or longer, of depressed affect or loss of interest in most activities. Such an episode is the primary criterion for diagnosis of clinical depression in most contemporary diagnostic systems (i.e., it is the only *necessary* criterion, although it is not *sufficient* by itself for a diagnosis). Almost twice as many of Peterson et al.'s subjects (48%) reported having had such an episode during high school (Grades 9–12) as had reported having had one during junior high (Grades 6–8; 27%). Associated with this increase in number of adolescents reporting at least one episode was a significant increase in the rate of episodes per year from junior high (0.23/person) to high school (0.48/person). Many of the depression episodes reported in this study would undoubtedly not have met the criteria for a diagnosable episode of clinical depression. However, the longitudinal change in the rate of these episodes from junior to senior high, like the increase in nonstandardized diagnoses of depression in the Isle of Wight Study, is consistent with the suggestion from cross-sectional studies that rates of clinical depression increase substantially during adolescence.

Even more dramatic than the increase in clinical depression during adolescence is the increase in suicidal behavior during the same period. Suicide, unlike clinical depression, is exceedingly rare among children below the age of 10 (Shaffer, 1986). It is only during early adolescence that significant numbers of youngsters begin to take their own lives, so that the still relatively low rate of suicide during this period (1.11 per 100,000 population between the ages of 10 and 14) is nevertheless about 50 times the rate for younger children (Frederick, 1985). The suicide rate then continues to increase rapidly during later adolescence (ages 15–19) and early adulthood (20–24; about 10 and 20 times the rate for early adolescence, respectively). In addition, estimates of the prevalence of suicide attempts during adolescence are often startlingly high. For example, Smith and Crawford (1986) reported a lifetime prevalence of 10.5% for suicide attempts among high school students; and Garfinkel, Hoberman, Walker, and Parsons (1987) found a 3% rate for attempts for high school students for the 4 weeks prior to assessment, and 6% for the preceding 6 months.

RELATIONSHIP OF DEPRESSION TO OTHER PROBLEMS COMMON AMONG ADOLESCENTS

There is an intuitively obvious connection between depression and suicide, an association that has received massive empirical support (cf. Buie & Maltsberger, 1989). Less obvious are associations between depression and other behavior problems that also increase substantially during adolescence—namely, drug and alcohol abuse, delinquent behavior, and eating disorders (cf. Lehman, 1985). Actually, conduct problems, including substance abuse, have frequently been considered symptomatic of depression among adolescents and, until recently, were often construed to be forms of "masked" depression or "depressive variants." These indirect or masked expressions of depression through antisocial behavior and substance abuse, problems much more common among males, have often been seen as a possible explanation of the well-documented gender difference in clinical depression that emerges during adolescence (Nolen-Hoeksema, 1987). The assumption in this explanation is that, beginning in early adolescence or even in childhood, males are much more likely than females to express, alleviate, or simply cover up chronically depressed affect through excessive drug or alcohol use or through aggressive, antisocial behaviors. This hypothesis is consistent with evidence that males are much more likely than females to be disapproved of or otherwise socially sanctioned for overt expressions of the emotional components of depression (cf. Oliver & Toner, 1990). Thus, even if the underlying rates of depression are the same for males and females, females are much more likely to express their depression overtly and to be diagnosed as primarily depressed than are males with a depressive disorder, who are more likely to be diagnosed on the basis of the more salient and disruptive conduct problems that stem from their depression (Craighead, 1991). Such conduct problems are more common than behaviors often assumed to be depressive variants among girls, such as bulemia.

Most cases of substance abuse, delinquency, and bulemia or anorexia probably are not the result of an underlying depressive disorder; and many cases of depression actually develop subsequent to the development of one of these other problems rather than prior to them (cf. Rohde, Lewinsohn, & Seeley, 1991). However, there is considerable evidence that, in a substantial minority of individuals, depression does play a primary etiological role in the development of one or more of these other problems. For example, Chiles, Miller, and Cox (1980) found that most of the 28% of recent admissions to a reform school who were diagnosed as suffering from a depressive disorder also reported using antisocial behaviors such as fighting, vandalism, drug-taking, or excessive drinking as methods of coping with dysphoric affect. In addition, Puig-Antich (1982) found that almost all the youngsters in a clinical sample who had been given both conduct disorder and depressive disorder diagnoses showed remission of both the depression and the conduct problems when given therapeutic doses of antidepressant medication. Assessment of recovering alcoholics and drug abusers indicates a very high rate among these individuals of chronic depressive disorders whose onset preceded their substance abuse problems and that, without treatment, remain long after these individuals have begun to be abstinent (cf. Lehman, 1985). Finally, high rates of depressive diagnoses have been found not only among adolescents with eating disorders (cf. Herzog, 1984), but among their first degree relatives as well (e.g., Winokur, March, & Mendels, 1980). Thus, interventions that could prevent the development or intensification of depressive disorders during early adolescence might also indirectly prevent the development of a certain percentage of conduct or delinquency problems, substance abuse problems, and eating disorders as well.

SECULAR TRENDS

The developmental trends of increases in depression and suicidal behavior that begin during early adolescence and continue throughout the adolescent period have been augmented in recent decades by secular trends of substantial increases in these problems among adolescents and young adults. Not only have there recently been secular increases in depression among these younger age groups (Klerman et al., 1985), there has also been a simultanous decrease in the disorder's mean age of onset (Weissman, Lief, Holzer, Myers, & Tischler, 1984). There have also been large increases in suicide rates among younger age groups in the United States and Western countries in the decades between 1950 and 1980, including a 166% increase in the 10–14 age group and a 230% increase among older adolescents (Frederick, 1985). These increases have been part of a long-term change in the age–suicide relationship because only adolescents and young adults have shown substantial increases across the last 40 years, whereas middle-aged adults have shown small increases or none at all, and older adults actually showed substantial decreases (Cross & Hirschfeld, 1986).

Both the developmental and the secular trends for depression and suicidal behavior, as well as the strong continuity across the life span of depressive disorders and suicidal behaviors that begin during early adolescence (e.g., Harrington, Fudge, Rutter, Pickles, & Hill, 1990), point to adolescence, especially early adolescence, as a period of life during which preventive interventions are likely to have powerful effects on the type of developmental trajectory that results in repeated depressions or chronic and ultimately terminal suicidality.

THEORIES OF ETIOLOGY

Depression has often been viewed as an "intrapsychic" disorder, with pronounced depressive affect stemming from negative cognitions about the self, the world, and the future, ineffective methods of modulating negative affect, or a maladaptive attributional style. However, research to date has established only that these cognitive and coping problems are concomitants of depression but not that they are either antecedents of the onset of serious depression or sequelae of episodes of clinical depression that may predispose individuals to further episodes (cf. Barnett & Gotlib, 1988). An alternative theoretical orientation views depression as primarily a result of disturbances in interpersonal functioning. Specifically, theorists with this viewpoint have portrayed depressives as suffering from a paradoxical combination of higher than normal dependence on others for approval and support with greater than normal social introversion and inhibition and poorer than normal social skills. Evidence that problematic interpersonal relationships, lack of social integration, introversion, and abnormal dependence are either antecedents and/or sequelae of depression is much stronger than for the factors presumed by the cognitive theorists to have an etiological role in depression (Barnett & Gotlib, 1988).

Evidence about risk factors for depression comes almost entirely from studies of adults because very few longitudinal data about the development of depression in children have been reported. However, cross-sectional studies have often found depression to be associated with social inhibition and isolation, not only in general population samples of human children and adolescents (e.g., Larson, Raffaelli, Richards, Ham, & Jewell, 1990; cf. Reisman, 1985), but even among other prepubertal primates (Suomi, in press). In addition, clinically depressed children have been found to show pronounced social deficits even after treatment with medication has substantially reduced their depression and associated conduct disorders (Puig-Antich et al., 1985). Social inhibition and anxiety have also been found to characterize a majority of male adolescent suicide completers (Shafii, Carrigan, Whittinghill, & Derrick, 1985) and to be associated with suicidal behavior in the general population (e.g., Smith & Crawford, 1986). Thus, although future longitudinal research may identify other prominent risk factors for depression among children and adolescents (e.g., academic failure, poor self-image), there is already considerable evidence that depressed children and adolescents have the same type of social problems identified as a prominent risk factor among adults.

Theories that link social inhibition and poor social integration to depression are consistent with the wide variety of theories that assume that development of the self-image and of presence or absence of self-esteem depend on others' reactions to the self (e.g., symbolic interactionism, social role theory; cf. Oatley & Bolton, 1985). Socially inhibited individuals may simply be less likely to obtain positive reactions from others, even from parents (cf. Kagan, 1989), resulting in poorer self-image and lower self-esteem that leaves such individuals more vulnerable to depression when they experience a major loss or failure in their lives. (For a detailed discussion of the relationship of interpersonal relatedness, self-concept, and depression, see Blatt & Zuroff, 1992.)

The social deficit theory of depression is also consistent with social support theory and research. For example, Cohen and Wills (1985), in a major review of the social support literature, concluded that a lack of close relationships that can provide coping resources exacerbates the negative mental health effects of stressful life events. Consistent with this conclusion were findings by Kennedy, Miller, and Ding (1990) that major life events (e.g., death in the immediate family) increased rates of 2-week episodes of depressed affect during high school only for girls who had been in the lowest third for reported level of intimacy with their best friend in eighth grade. Intimacy with best friend had no direct or moderating effect on depressive episodes for boys. However, low intimacy with parents had a direct effect on depressed affect for both boys and girls (i.e., the lower the intimacy the higher the rate of subsequent depressive episodes regardless of the number of intervening life events).

The role of social inhibition and isolation in the development of depression may explain part of the large increases in depression and suicide that apparently begin during early adolescence. One of the developmental transitions of the adolescent period is a reduction in reliance on parents for approval, support, and intimacy and an increase in reliance on peers for meeting these interpersonal needs. For example, Kennedy, Rice, and Petersen (1991) found in a recent cross-sectional study that self-reported reliance on parents for advice and support decreased substantially across Grades 6 through 12, whereas reliance on peers increased substantially. In fact, 12th graders reported relying much more on peers than on parents, whereas the reverse pattern was found among sixth graders.

Berndt and his colleagues (e.g., Berndt & Hoyle, 1985) documented in more detail the type of changes in peer relationships that usually occur early in adolescence. Specifically, Berndt has found that during the early adolescent period youngsters move toward a narrower group of friendships that are more intimate and supportive than childhood friendships. This trend is accelerated by the disruptive effect on childhood friendship patterns of the transition from elementary school to middle school or junior high and is especially marked among girls. In addition, of course, early adolescence is the period during which heterosexual relationships and dating usually begin.

Youngsters who are socially inhibited or lacking in social skills can be assumed to make the social transition of early adolescence less successfully. Thus, they are likely either to remain more dependent on their family for social support than are their peers or to experience a decrease in overall support as they begin the process of separating from their parents. Such youngsters are thus likely to be more vulnerable to the depressive effects of major losses and other stressful events. Socially inhibited or unskilled youngsters are also likely to have more problems with dating. Even when such youngsters do date, they may be more likely to have problematic relationships or to have problems with the termination of such relationships because of a dearth of alternative sources of social support. Thus, Petersen and Kennedy (1988) found that among reasons most frequently given by girls for extended episodes of depressed affect during junior and senior high school were lack of friends, rejection by friends, and breaking up with a boyfriend.

The well-documented importance of social isolation in the development of suicidal ideation and behavior (cf. Buie & Maltsberger, 1989) may explain in part the abrupt increase in suicide rates that begins during early adolescence following the virtual absence of completed suicide during childhood. Shaffer (1986) hypothesized that children are relatively invulnerable to depression because they tend to have a rich network of social support from adults. During early adolescence, however, there is a normative decrease in the availability of, or youngsters' reliance on, such support. Many socially inhibited and unskilled youngsters are probably unable to develop adequate alternative support among peers, resulting in a dramatic overall decrease in support and intense feelings of isolation and loneliness, which are frequent precursors of suicidal ideation and behavior.

IMPLICATIONS FOR PREVENTION

Cohen (1985) distinguished between *person-focused* and *situation-focused* preventive interventions. Person-focused interventions assume that the risk of developing an emotional or behavior problem resides in the individual person. Thus, the targets of person-focused interventions are individuals' cognitive, behavioral, or affective deficits or excesses; and intervention strategies usually involve teaching children or adolescents corresponding sets of skills that are assumed to ameliorate or prevent development of significant problems. Situation-focused interventions, on the other hand, assume that characteristics of individuals' environments put them at risk. Such interventions therefore attempt to change whatever specific aspects of the environment are thought to lead to the particular problem. Felner and Felner (1989) extended this distinction by adding the category of *transaction-focused* interventions, which assume that the risk resides in a particular combination of person and situation and in the interactions between them rather than primarily in either one or the other.

A transaction-focused approach to preventive interventions readily accommodates developmental models of psychopathology and is especially relevant to the model of depression as a disorder of social relationships presented earlier. If depression increases during adolescence partly as a result of changes in peer and parent relationships, as hypothesized previously, then the contexts in which those changes take place are, from the transaction-focused viewpoint, an extremely important consideration in developing interventions intended to prevent the development of depression during adolescence.

One of the major contexts in which changes in peer relationships occur during adolescence in the United States is the secondary school. Simmons and Blyth (1987), among others, have documented the stressors that the transition from primary to secondary school presents for young adolescents in most U.S. school systems. For socially inhibited students, this transition is likely to intensify the challenge presented by the more general transition in social relationships that occurs at this time. First of all, secondary schools tend to be much larger than primary schools, several of which usually "feed" a single junior high or middle school. In addition, rather than having most subjects with the same students and with one or two teachers, as in primary school, secondary students tend to change classmates and teachers for each different subject. Thus, the size and structure of secondary schools make it difficult for students to obtain help from teachers and administrators, to maintain previous friendship patterns, and to establish new friendships. These challenges occur at the same time that youngsters are also experiencing the increased academic demands of secondary school, which for many youngsters lead to a significant drop in grades from the level achieved in primary school. The occurrence of such challenges simultaneously has been found to lead to more adjustment problems than the same challenges experienced in a more sequential fashion (e.g., Petersen, et al., 1991).

Changes in secondary and middle school structures that would be likely to reduce the development of depression in their students would be those that would maximize the ability of socially inhibited students to develop new friendships and obtain help and support from school personnel (e.g., schools within schools) or to maintain previous friendships (e.g., maintaining neighborhood groups within the same classes for the first year of secondary school). For example, Felner and his colleagues (cf. Felner & Felner, 1989) have done extensive research on the effects of reducing the scale of the academic and social groups, both student and adult, with which a youngster must interact during his or her first year in secondary school. Positive outcomes have included lower dropout rates, improved academic performance, a reduction in decrements in self-esteem, and lower rates of problem behaviors such as delinquency and illicit drug use. Given these results, it is highly likely that their intervention also produced a reduction in the rate of depressed affect and clinical depression. Documentation of such effects would add to the already compelling arguments for changes in school structure that smooth the transition from primary to secondary school. In addition, future research that assessed the mediating role of peer relationships in the effects of the program would provide an excellent test of the interpersonal model of depression.

It is likely that reducing the scale of secondary schools and increasing the support available from them may reduce the prevalence of depressed affect in the general young adolescent population without reducing the rate of clinical depressions related to quite dysfunctional peer and family relationships (Compas, in press). Finding such a pattern of results in future research on primary prevention strategies like Felner's would suggest the necessity of secondary prevention programs that target adolescents at high risk for depression because of social inadequacies.

Another transaction-focused approach to preventing the potential negative effects of the primary–secondary transition has been that of Elias and his colleagues (e.g., Elias et al., 1986), who have attempted to train elementary school children in various social problem-solving skills that will enable them to cope more effectively with the adaptive challenges presented by the primary–secondary school transition. More toward the person-focused end of the continuum than Felner's restructuring of the school environment, this and similar programs (cf. Weissberg, Caplan, & Sivo, 1989) nevertheless are transaction-focused to the degree that they tailor the program to the actual social environment—middle and junior high schools—in which the children will have to apply their skills.

Depression has not usually been a directly evaluated target of social problem-solving programs. Unfortunately, recent research suggests that this type of program may not have a significant impact on depression among adolescents (Compas, personal communication, July 22, 1990). As was noted regarding the Felner intervention, primary prevention interventions that target entire populations of adolescents, as do most of the problem-solving programs, may not be specific or powerful enough to have a positive impact on serious depression. However, the interpersonal theory of depression provides an additional explanation of why such programs, although successful in preventing problems such as school dropout and substance abuse, are not likely to have significant effects on the development of depression.

The explicit aim of problem-solving programs is to develop social skills. However, the percentage of program time devoted to actual behavioral (rather than cognitive) practice of such skills during the program itself is often surprisingly low. For example, examination of the manual for Elias's curriculum (Elias & Clabby, 1989) suggests that less than 10% of class time in the year-long curriculum is devoted to behavioral practice of social skills. Devoting a preponderance of program time to verbal instruction and cognitive exercises seems unlikely to facilitate the acquisition of social skills among young adolescents when most of them have at best barely begun to think abstractly. Also, the importance of behavioral practice is illustrated by the repeatedly replicated finding that, even among adults, cognitive interventions without major behavioral or experiential components are likely to have limited impact on anxiety problems in general and on pronounced social inhibition in particular (Barlow, 1988). Thus, to the degree that social inhibition contributes to depression, predominantly cognitive/didactic social problem-solving programs are unlikely to have any major impact on the development of depression among young adolescents. On the other hand, Butler, Miezitis, Friedman, and Cole (1980) found that a program for high-risk preadolescents that was comprised largely of the youngsters' role-playing problematic social situations was effective in producing substantial short-term reductions in depression and related problems. In addition, this role-playing program produced significantly greater improvements than both an attention control condition and a "cognitive-restructuring" program that was analogous to cognitive therapy programs used with depressed adults. Subsequent studies that have found "cognitive-behavioral" interventions to be effective in treating the depression of youngsters as young as middle school students (e.g., Lewinsohn, Clarke, Hops, Andrews, & Williams, 1990; Stark, Kaslow, & Reynolds, 1987) have usually involved an experiential or role-playing component.

Programs for reducing the development of depression among adolescents should thus concentrate less on the didactic presentation of guidelines for social interactions and problem solving and more on behavioral interventions, such as assertiveness training, that emphasize the practicing of skills via role-playing. Not only has assertiveness training been shown to be an effective treatment for depressed adults (e.g., Hersen, Bellack, & Himmelhoch, 1980), but role-playing of social interactions has been found among adolescents to reduce another major problem behavior often associated with depression and suicidal behaviors—delinquency (cf. Kennedy, 1984). Role-playing has the additional advantage of allowing peer responses to provide a realistic "setting" in which adolescents can try out specific behaviors and adjust them to their particular environment, making the intervention more transaction-focused than those in which the program or the adult trainer define effective or appropriate behavior.

Another reason that social problem-solving programs may not have a sizable preventive impact on depression is that they are relatively general programs that try to teach a fairly broad variety of skills. At this point, there is little evidence regarding the specific type of social deficits that characterize children and adolescents who are susceptible to depression, other than the evidence that they are characterized by social anxiety and inhibition. In order to provide a more fine-tuned intervention, it would be useful to understand and target the specific social problems related to depression. The value for preventive interventions of evidence regarding specific deficits has been demonstrated in training programs for socially rejected children, who have been found to have particularly pronounced problems in approaching and joining peers at play (cf. Coie, Rabiner, & Lochman, 1989), and in programs for preventing substance abuse among adolescents, which have emphasized peer refusal skills (cf. Botvin & Dusenbury, 1989). General social skills training programs may lead to general improvements among adolescents across a wide variety of indices. However, it will probably be necessary to identify the specific social deficits and excesses that characterize a particular problem such as depression before intervention programs can be designed that will have a powerful effect in preventing that particular problem.

REFERENCES

Angold, A. (1988). Childhood and adolescent depression: I. Epidemiological and aetiological aspects. *British Journal of Psychiatry, 152,* 601–617.

Barnett, P. A., & Gotlib, I. H. (1988). Psychosocial functioning and depression: Distinguishing among antecedents, concomitants, and consequences. *Psychological Bulletin, 104,* 97–126.

Barlow, D. H. (1988). *The anxiety disorders: Theory and treatment.* New York: Guilford Press.

Berndt, T. J., & Hoyle, S. G. (1985). Stability and change in childhood and adolescent friendships. *Developmental Psychology, 21,* 1007–1015.

Blatt, S. J., & Zuroff, D. C. (1992). Interpersonal relatedness and self-definition: Two prototypes for depression. *Clinical Psychology Review, 12,* 527–562.

Botvin, G. J., & Dusenbury, L. (1989). Substance abuse prevention and the promotion of competence. In L. A. Bond & B. E. Compas (Eds.), *Primary prevention and promotion in the schools* (pp. 146–178). Newbury Park, CA: Sage.

Buie, D. H., & Maltsberger, J. T. (1989). The psychological vulnerability to suicide. In D. Jacobs & H. N. Brown (Eds.), *Suicide: Understanding and responding* (pp. 59–72). Madison, CT: International University Press.

Butler, L., Miezitis, S., Friedman, R., & Cole, E. (1980). The effect of two school-based intervention programs on depressive symptoms in preadolescents. *American Educational Research Journal, 17(1),* 111–119.

Carlson, G. A., & Garber, J. (1986). Developmental issues in the classification of depression in children. In M. Rutter, C. E. Izard, & P. B. Read (Eds.), *Depression in young people* (pp. 399–434). New York: Guilford Press.

Chiles, J. A., Miller, M. L., & Cox, G. B. (1980). Depression in an adolescent delinquent population. *Archives of General Psychiatry, 38,* 15–22.

Cohen, E. L., (1985). Person-centered approaches to primary prevention in mental health: Situation-focused and competence-enhancement. *American Journal of Community Psychology, 13,* 31–48.

Cohen, S., & Wills, T. A. (1985). Stress, social support, and the buffering hypothesis. *Psychological Bulletin, 98,* 310–357.

Coie, J. D., Rabiner, D. L., & Lochman, J. E. (1989). Promoting peer relationships in a school setting. In L. A. Bond & B. E. Compas (Eds.), *Primary prevention and promotion in the schools* (pp. 207–234). Newbury Park, CA: Sage.

Compas, B. E. (in press). Promoting positive mental health. In S. G. Milstein, A. C. Petersen, & E. O. Nightingale (Eds.), *Promoting adolescent health.* New York: Oxford University Press.

Craighead, W. E. (1991). Cognitive factors and classification issues in adolescent depression. *Journal of Youth & Adolescence, 20,* 311-326.

Cross, C. K., & Hirschfeld, R. M. A. (1986). Epidemiology of disorders in adulthood: Suicide. In G. L. Klerman, M. M. Weissman, P. S. Appelbaum, & L. H. Roth (Eds.), *Social, epidemiological, and legal psychiatry* (pp. 245-260). New York: Basic Books.

Elias, M. J., & Clabby, J. F. (1989). *Social decision-making skills: A curriculum guide for the elementary grades.* Rockville, MD: Aspen.

Elias, M. J., Gara, M., Ubriaco, J., Rothbaum, P. A., Clabby, J. F., & Schuyler, T. (1986). Impact of a preventive social problem solving intervention on children's coping with middle-school stressors. *American Journal of Community Psychology, 14,* 259-275.

Felner, R. D., & Felner, T. W. (1989). Primary prevention programs in the educational context: A transactional-ecological framework and analysis. In L. A. Bond & B. E. Compas (Eds.), *Primary prevention and promotion in the schools* (pp. 13-49). Newbury Park, CA: Sage.

Frederick, C. J. (1982). Suicide prevention. In C. E. Walker (Ed.), *Clinical practice of psychology* (pp. 189-213). New York: Pergamon.

Frederick, C. J. (1985). An introduction and overview of youth suicide. In M. L. Peck, N. L. Farberow, & R. E. Litman (Eds.), *Youth suicide* (pp. 1-18). New York: Springer.

Garfinkel, B. D., Hoberman, H. M., Walker, J., & Parsons, J. H. (1987). *Suicide attempts in a community sample of adolescents.* Paper presented at the meeting of the American Academy of Child and Adolescent Psychiatry, Los Angeles, CA.

Harrington, R., Fudge, H., Rutter, M., Pickles, A., & Hill, J. (1990). Adult outcomes of childhood and adolescent depression. *Archives of General Psychiatry, 47,* 465-473.

Hersen, M., Bellack, A. S., & Himmelhoch, J. M. (1980). Treatment of unipolar depression with social skills training. *Behavior Modification, 4,* 547-556.

Herzog, D. B. (1984). Are anorexic and bulemic patients depressed? *American Journal of Psychiatry, 141,* 1594-1597.

Kagan, J. (1989). Temperamental contributions to social behavior. *American Psychologist, 44,* 668-674.

Kaplan, S. L., Hong, G., & Weinhold, C. (1984). Epidemiology of depressive symptomatology in adolescents. *Journal of the American Academy of Child Psychiatry, 23,* 191-198.

Kashani, J. H., Carlson, G. A., Beck, N. C., Hoeper, E. W., Corcoran, C. M., McAllister, J. A., Fallahi, C., Rosenberg, T. K., & Reid, J. C. (1987). Depression, depressive symptoms, and depressed mood among a community sample of adolescents. *American Journal of Psychiatry, 144,* 931-934.

Kashani, J. H., McGee, R. O., Clarkson, S. E., Anderson, J. C., Walton, L. A., Williams, S., Silva, P. A., Robins, A. J., Cytryn, L., & McKnew, D. H. (1983). Depression in a community sample of 9-year-old children. *Archives of General Psychiatry, 40,* 1217-1223.

Kennedy, R. E. (1984). Cognitive-behavioral interventions with delinquents. In A. W. Meyers & W. E. Craighead (Eds.), *Cognitive-behavior therapy with children* (pp. 351-376). New York: Plenum Press.

Kennedy, R. E., Miller, S., & Ding, S. (1990). Depressive affect changes in high school as a function of pubertal timing, negative family events, and initial depression level. In B. A. Hamburg (Chair), *Biological, familial, and psychological influences on the development of depressive affect and behavior in adolescence.* Symposium conducted at the meeting of the Society for Research on Adolescence.

Kennedy, R. E., Rice, K., & Petersen, A. C. (1991). *Reports of closeness to, and seeking of support, from best friend and parents among adolescents.* Manuscript in preparation, The Pennsylvania State University, University Park.

Klerman, G. L., Lavori, P. W., Rice, J., Reich, T., Endicott, J., Andreasen, N. C., Keller, M. B., & Hirschfeld, R. M. A. (1985). Birth cohort trends and rates of major depressive disorders among relatives of patients of affective disorder. *Archives of General Psychiatry, 42,* 689-693.

Larson, R., & Lampman-Petraitis, C. (1989). Daily emotional states as reported by children and adolescents. *Child Development, 60,* 1250-1260.

Larson, R., Raffaelli, M., Richards, M. H., Ham, M., & Jewell, L. (1990). Ecology of depression in late childhood and early adolescence: A profile of daily states and activities. *Journal of Abnormal Psychology, 99,* 92-102.

Lehman, L. (1985). The relationship of depression to other DSM-III Axis I disorders. In E. E. Beckham & W. R. Leber (Eds.), *Handbook of depression* (pp. 669-699). Homewood, IL: Dorsey Press.

Lewinsohn, P. M., Clarke, G. N., Hops, H., Andrews, J., & Williams, J. A. (1990). Cognitive-behavioral group treatment of depression in adolescents. *Behavior Therapy, 21,* 385-401.

National Institute of Mental Health (NIMH). (1981). *Science reports: Special report on depression research* (DHS Publication No. ADM 81-1085). Washington, DC: U.S. Government Printing Office.

Nolen-Hoeksema, S. (1987). Sex differences in unipolar depression: Evidence and theory. *Psychological Bulletin, 101,* 259-282.

Oatley, K., & Bolton, W. (1985). A social-cognitive theory of depression in reaction to life events. *Psychological Review, 92,* 372-388.

Oliver, S. J., & Toner, B. B. (1990). The influence of gender role typing on the expression of depressive symptoms. *Sex Roles, 22,* 775-790.

Petersen, A. C., & Kennedy, R. E. (1988). *The development of depression: Is adolescence depressogenic for girls?* Paper presented at the biennial meeting of the Society for Research on Adolescence, Washington, DC.

Petersen, A. C., Sarigiani, P., & Kennedy, R. E. (1991). Adolescent depression: Why more girls? *Journal of Youth & Adolescence, 20,* 247-272.

Puig-Antich, J. (1982). Major depression and conduct disorder in prepuberty. *Journal of the American Academy of Child Psychiatry, 21,* 118-128.

Puig-Antich, J., Lukens, E., Davies, M., Goetz, D., Brennan-Quattrack, J., & Todak, G. (1985). Psychosocial functioning in prepubertal major depression: A controlled study. *Archives of General Psychiatry, 42,* 500-517.

Reisman, J. M. (1985). Friendship and its implications for mental health or social competence. *Journal of Early Adolescence, 5,* 383-391.

Rohde, P., Lewinsohn, P. M., & Seeley, J. R. (1991). Comorbidity of unipolar depression II: Comorbidity with other mental disorders in adolescents and adults. *Journal of Abnormal Psychology, 100,* 214-222.

Rutter, M. (1986). The developmental psychopathology of depression: Issues and perspectives. In M. Rutter, C. E. Izard, & P. B. Reed (Eds.), *Depression in young people: Clinical and developmental perspectives* (pp. 3-30). New York: Guilford Press.

Shaffer, D. (1986). Developmental factors in child and adolescent suicide. In M. Rutter, C. E. Izard, & P. B. Read (Eds.), *Depression in young people: Clinical and developmental perspectives* (pp. 383-398). New York: Guilford Press.

Shafii, M., Carrigan, S., Whittinghill, J. R., & Derrick, A. (1985). Psychological autopsy of completed suicide in children and adolescents. *American Journal of Psychiatry, 142,* 1061-1064.

Simmons, R. G., & Blyth, D. A. (1987). *Moving into adolescence.* New York: Aldine de Gruyter.

Smith, K., & Crawford, S. (1986). Suicidal behavior among "normal" high school students. *Suicide and Life-Threatening Behavior, 16*(3), 313–325.

Sorenson, S. B., Rutter, C. M., & Aneshensel, C. S. (1991). Depression in the community: An investigation into age of onset. *Journal of Consulting and Clinical Psychology, 59,* 541–546.

Stark, K. D., Kaslow, N. J., & Reynolds, W. M. (1987). A comparison of the relative efficacy of self-control therapy and a behavioral problem-solving therapy for depression in children. *Journal of Abnormal Child Psychology, 15,* 91–113.

Suomi, S. J. (in press). Primate separation models of affective disorders. In J. Madden (Ed.), *Adaptation, learning, and affect.* New York: Raven Press.

Weissberg, R. P., Caplan, M. Z., & Sivo, P. J. (1989). A new conceptual framework for establishing school-based social competence promotion programs. In L. A. Bond & B. E. Compas (Eds.), *Primary prevention and promotion in the schools* (pp. 255–296). Newbury Park, CA: Sage.

Weissmann, M. M., Leaf, P. J., Holzer, C. E., Myers, J. K., & Tischler, G. C. (1984). The epidemiology of depression: An update on sex differences and rates. *Journal of Affective Disorders, 7,* 179–188.

Winokur, A., March, V., & Mendels (1980). Primary affective disorders in relatives of patients with anorexia nervosa. *American Journal of Psychiatry, 137,* 695–698.

V | Adolescents and the Media

Section Editors:

Jerome D. Williams
Katherine Frith
The Pennsylvania State University

Adolescents and the Media

Jerome D. Williams
Katherine Frith
The Pennsylvania State University

This section contains three chapters on the interaction between youth and the mass media (i.e., how adolescents use media and how media affects them). Although a critical look at research is stressed throughout all the chapters, policy and program themes with diversity and contextual considerations also receive attention in various individual chapters. For example, particular emphasis is placed on policy implications in the chapter on the processing of health messages. Also, the chapter on alcohol advertising highlights the issue of diversity by focusing on the impact of alcohol-related messages on ethnic minority adolescents.

Perhaps the most significant contribution to this section, however, relates to context. Each chapter demonstrates that many of the generalizations gained from previous empirical literature must be tempered by a consideration of the multitude of contextual settings in which adolescents interact with the media. For example, we know that adolescents spend a significant portion of their time with mass media. However, the direction and degree of the relationship between mass media and changes taking place during adolescence will vary with the context. Also, we know that in many situations mass media have the capacity to influence opinion, beliefs, and behaviors. However, using media as instruments of power in influencing adolescents is very context-dependent.

Each chapter in this section offers a unique contribution by examining the interaction of adolescents and the media related to a specific context (e.g., popular music, health messages, and ethnic minority communities). Before describing each of these contributions, this introduction briefly examines why there is a need for research on media and adolescents, highlights in a succinct fashion several of the historical roots of media research on adolescents, and suggests a theoretical framework in which to place research addressing these concerns.

WHY A NEED FOR MEDIA RESEARCH AND ADOLESCENTS

It is a well-established fact that adolescents spend a significant portion of their time with mass media. It is commonly asserted that the average adolescent spends approximately 8 hours per day with one or more of the mass media, sometimes as a primary behavior, often as a secondary or tertiary activity (Fine, Mortimer, & Roberts, 1989). These media include films, popular comics, television, radio, recorded music, and even encompass video games.

Developing a better understanding of the interaction of adolescents and the media can be placed in the context of a larger, more basic problem. This problem becomes apparent when one reviews the empirical literature and recognizes that since the 1960s, researchers have failed to demonstrate clearly defined media effects. The notion of an all-powerful media has given way to various, more refined paradigms. By rejecting the hegemonic thrust of the message, researchers have taken the opportunity to revisit a number of methodologies developed in previous paradigms in order to better understand how media messages are actually deciphered and used by adolescents in our culture.

Historically, there has been a continuing wave of public concern and controversy over the significance of the media as agencies of social change and their role in social life. Much of this concern has focused on the effects of mass communication, particularly on children and youths. Hence, we felt it important to include a section on media in this volume on adolescents.

A BRIEF HISTORICAL PERSPECTIVE ON MEDIA RESEARCH AND ADOLESCENTS

Delia (1987) traced the history of communication research, providing the context for understanding why emphasis was placed on certain topics. Typically, media research has focused on the study of mass communication phenomena. As each new communication media attained popularity, its growth and audiences quickly became the object of considerable interest by a cadre of researchers. For example, one can trace the successive stages of research dealing with silent motion pictures, radio broadcasting, talking movies, and television as they evolved as social institutions.

Looking solely at movies to illustrate this point, we note that prior to World War I, movies had developed rapidly and were a major source of entertainment activity, particularly for adolescents, and hence, became a topic of considerable research interest. Examples include Healy's (1915) study of movies and delinquency and Phelan's (1919) study of the effects of movie attendance. Also, the Payne Fund studies, published separately in 12 volumes along with an overview volume, were designed to provide objective data on the influence of movie attendance on children. Even the results of these early studies provided the essential understanding of effects that later research would support, and that we have previously alluded to, namely, the lack of any clearly defined all-powerful media effects. These early studies showed that effects are mediated by a host of other individual and situational characteristics (e.g., age, gender, predispositions, perceptions, past behavior patterns and experiences, social backgrounds, parental influence, viewing mates, etc.).

Similarly, another topic that became the object of considerable interest by a cadre of researchers, and particularly noted among the educational community, dealt with the direct effects of mass communication in competition with reading. Consequently, research was stimulated comparing usage levels of communication media and attempts were made to assess the media's impact on reading. Other researchers studied children's programs to discern listeners' evaluation of programs (Longstaff, 1936, 1937). As noted by Wartella and Reeves (1987), however, virtually all of this research on children and the media before 1960 involved the study of one medium at a time and was not cumulative. Hence, today there continues to be a need to extend this earlier research on media and adolescents, both by re-examining previous assumptions and by looking at some broader issues previously neglected.

Although we have already indicated that current research has debunked one previous myth regarding the all-powerful role of media, it is still recognized that in many situations media has the capacity to persuade and effect opinions and beliefs and to influence behavior. In these situations, mass media still can be regarded as an effective instrument of power. Therefore, in dealing with media effects and adolescents, it is important for current researchers to continue addressing questions such as: "How effective are the media in achieving their chosen ends?" and "What variable factors limit or enlarge the power of the media?" (McQuail, 1987). Each of the contributions in this section provides further insight into one or both of these questions.

A THEORETICAL FRAMEWORK TO INVESTIGATE MEDIA RESEARCH AND ADOLESCENTS

As noted by McQuail, a core question concerns the direction and degree of relationship between mass communication and other changes taking place in society (i.e., are media a cause or effect of social change?). Different theories offer different alternative versions of the relationship. One very basic typology that offers a framework for assessing this question is borrowed from Rosengren (1981) and amplified by McQuail (1987). This involves two basic propositions: Society influences the media and media influences society. A cross-tabulation of these two yields four cells. Using Rosengren's labels and applying them to media effects, the following terms can serve as a classification scheme for approaching media effects research:

1. *Interdependence:* Media and society are interactive.
2. *Idealism:* Media molds society.
3. *Materialism:* Media is dependent on society and a reflection of it.
4. *Autonomy:* Media and society vary independently.

McQuail stated there is little point in trying to make a choice among the propositions on grounds of evidence. According to Rosengren, research gives only "inconclusive, partly even contradictory, evidence about the relationship between social structure, societal values as mediated by the media, and opinions among the public" (p. 254). McQuail also stated that a strong possibility exists that each theory may hold under different conditions. In summary, "there can be little doubt that media, either as reflectors or molders of society, are undoubtedly messengers about change, and it is around this observation that the main perspectives on media can best be organized" (McQuail, 1987, p. 102).

SUMMARY OF ARTICLES IN ADOLESCENTS AND THE MEDIA SECTION

In chapter 23, Thompson explores music, an ever present phenomenon in the lives of adolescents. Although *music* may be a generic term encompassing a wide range of expressive sounds, Thompson considers the contextual issue by recognizing that for most adolescents the term has a much narrower meaning (i.e., "popular music"). Therefore, he focuses on the involvement of adolescents with popular music that is accessed through public and personal media such as radio, television, records, tapes, compact discs, and so on.

As noted by Thompson, one of the main concerns about music and adolescents is the view that messages in popular music are contrary to those of "mainstream society." Those holding this view feel such music often glamorizes violence, sex, and substance abuse, and therefore misleads young listeners. However, Thompson observes that there are many individuals who are entrusted with the responsibility of assisting adolescents through their stage of development who look upon this music as *both* a problem and a cure—much of this depends on the context in which it is viewed and the diversity of the life experiences of the listeners. This chapter examines, then, three questions based on an assessment of prior research: "How deeply are adolescents involved with popular music?"; "What influences their decisions to choose musical involvement?"; and "What meanings and gratifications do they derive from their involvement with music?"

Health message and intervention programs are the focal point of chapter 24 by Frith and Frith. By exploring the history of commercial communications in United States, the Frith's show the unfitness of media to effect general social change. This raises issues regarding the applicability of the media for health communications and health education, particularly when one recognizes the myth of the immutability of the message. This chapter explores the link between internal processing of health messages and social experiences. It also explores how the media affect the construction of "healthy" and "unhealthy" messages and compares various research methods that can be used to address these issues, with particular emphasis on participatory research versus social engineering.

As stressed consistently throughout this volume, context is a critical element. Thus, the authors stress the need for participatory research as the most appropriate model of social learning for use by adolescents in the processing of health messages. This involves first of all understanding the adolescent colloquium on health (i.e., the adolescent health construct). Accordingly, the Frith's advocate a systematic exploration of the context of how adolescents process media health messages and create meaning from them.

The final chapter in this section by Williams provides a critical review of the literature on the advertising of alcohol products in the media and the effects on adolescents, especially regarding their susceptibility and vulnerability to marketing efforts. As emphasized in other chapters in this volume, diversity is a significant issue; therefore, this chapter gives particular attention to the effects on minority adolescents. As noted by Williams, a number of political, social, and community organizations have become alarmed over the negative effects of alcohol advertising on adolescents from ethnic minority and other disadvantaged groups. Typically, adolescents from these groups are exposed much more to these messages as alcohol companies tend to advertise their products much more in Black and Hispanic neighborhoods than in other neighborhoods. In response to these marketing practices, there has been a call for specifically targeted intervention programs for adolescents using the mass media as a countermeasure to the efforts of the alcohol companies.

Williams points out that these countervailing media efforts raise a number of questions regarding the effectiveness of each. Using a framework to classify previous studies addressing these issues, Williams reviews the literature to assess how researchers have attempted to answer such important questions as: "Does a direct connection exist between advertising and consumption?" and "What is the effect of the advertising of alcohol products differentially targeted towards minority adolescents?"

Together, these three chapters are representative of perspectives that offer alternative versions of the relationship between adolescents and the media. The approaches and topics exemplify the ever broadening view of media effects on adolescents.

REFERENCES

Delia, J. G. (1987). Communication research: A history. In C. R. Berger & S. H. Chaffee (Eds.), *Handbook of communication science* (pp. 20–98). Beverly Hills, CA: Sage.

Fine, G. A., Mortimer, J. T., & Roberts, D. F. (1990). Leisure, work and mass media. In S. S. Feldman & G. R. Elliott (Eds.), *At the threshold: The developing adolescent* (pp. 225–252). Cambridge, MA: Harvard University Press.

Healey, W. (1915). *The individual delinquent.* Boston: Little, Brown.

Longstaff, H. P. (1936). Effectiveness of children's radio programs. *Journal of Applied Psychology, 20,* 208–220.

Longstaff, H. P. (1937). Mother's opinions of children's radio programs. *Journal of Applied Psychology, 21,* 265–279.

McQuail, D. (1987). *Mass communication theory: An introduction* (2nd ed.). Beverly Hills, CA: Sage.

Phelan, J. J. (1919). *Motion pictures as a phase of commercialized amusement in Toledo, Ohio.* Toledo, OH: Little Book Press.

Rosengren, K. E. (1981). Mass media and social change: Some current approaches. In E. Katz & T. Szecsko (Eds.), *Mass media and social change* (pp. 247–263). Beverly Hills, CA: Sage.

Wartella, E., & Reeves, B. (1987). Communication and children. In C. R. Berger & S. H. Chaffee (Eds.), *Handbook of communication science* (pp. 619–650). Beverly Hills, CA: Sage.

23 Media, Music, and Adolescents

Keith P. Thompson
The Pennsylvania State University

Music is an ever present phenomenon in the lives of adolescents. Although *music* may be a generic term for expressive sounds ranging from the chants of Tibetian Monks to grandiose performances of Wagnerian opera, for most adolescents the term has a much narrower meaning. Music, for most teenagers, is a highly specialized collection of very loud, pulsating sounds created in commercial recording studios and delivered to them through a variety of media and broadly referred to as "popular music." There are, of course, the 20%–30% of this age group that are actively involved in school music ensembles, taking piano lessons, singing in church choirs, and in various ways involved with "other kinds" of music. Adolescent involvement in these activities and with "nonpopular genres of music is discussed by Rutkowski (chapter 13, this volume). It is also pointed out that some teenagers become active performers of popular music in their own "garage bands" and live performances of popular music are available to adolescents through concerts and "teen center" clubs. Because such opportunities to perform and listen are available on a limited basis and to a relatively small percentage of adolescents, they are not considered here. The focus of this chapter is on the involvement of adolescents with popular music that is accessed through public media such as radio and television and the personal media of records, tapes, and compact discs (CDs).

The concern with music and adolescents stems from two broad assumptions. First, adolescents are highly motivated to seek involvement with music and to spend significant amounts of time listening to music; therefore music may be an effective channel through which to communicate information that will enable young people to more effectively deal with personal and social challenges encountered during this phase of development. Music may be a viable intervention for those adolescents experiencing difficulty. Second, music carries powerful verbal and nonverbal "messages." The messages of much popular music are in contradiction to those of mainstream society, glamorizing violence, sex, and substance abuse and therefore misleading young listeners during a critical stage of development. Limiting access to such music may limit the problems encountered by many adolescents.

This chapter examines prior research in an attempt to answer three questions: "How deeply are adolescents involved with popular music?"; "What influences their decisions to choose musical involvement?"; and "What meanings and gratifications do they derive from their involvement with music?"

ADOLESCENTS' INVOLVEMENT WITH MUSIC

It should not be surprising to find that adolescents are heavily involved with music media. Fischer and Powell (1985) estimated that between Grades 7 and 12, teenagers spend 10,500 hours listening to rock music. Verden, Dunleavy, and Power (1989) reported that 78% of southeastern high school students considered music to be "very important" in their lives. Larson, Kubey, and Colletti (1989) concluded that popular music was an important "topic of discussion among adolescents, and is almost invariably background or foreground to the courting behavior that typically occurs during dances, parties, and dating" (p. 597). Roe's (1987) synthesis of research lead to the following conclusion:

> More and more studies show that the whole adolescent milieu is penetrated at many levels by an active interest in music; that many adolescents employ it as a social lubricator; that a great deal of adolescent discourse centers around the language and terminology of rock; and that music provides the core values of numerous adolescent subcultures. (p. 215)

Quantifying music involvement is difficult. On some occasions, listening to music is the primary activity, deliberately chosen and the sole focus of attention. On many occasions, music provides background for other activities and, although teenage listeners would be conscious of its absence, they may not be conscious of its presence. Larson and Kubey (1983) found that adolescents reported involvement in music as a secondary activity six times as frequently as they reported it as a primary activity. Even when listening to music appears to be the primary activity, it may not be the focus of the listener's thoughts and feelings. At times, the musical environment can be controlled: Walkmans provide a highly self-controlled personal sound environment. However, in restaurants, stores, and friends' cars one has little control and may choose not to listen even when subjected to hours of musical exposure. Data on time spent listening must be interpreted with an awareness of these limitations.

Combining all media sources of music, Christenson and Roberts (1989) reported that middle-class California 7th graders listen to music slightly over 2½ hours daily. This level of utilization is generally consistent with other reports, however some researchers (Schlattmann, 1989) report average utilization as high as 6½ hours a day. After reviewing a number of studies, Christenson and Roberts concluded that girls tend to listen to music more than boys; Blacks more than Whites with "Black females being, by far, the most avid listeners, averaging about 7 hours a day with radio" (p. 17).

An important trend was documented by Larson et al. (1989), who compared television viewing with music media involvement and found that between Grades 5 and 9, television viewing declined significantly, whereas at the same time music listening significantly increased. Larson et al. said that, "Adolescents spend proportionately less time absorbing the mainstream adult messages of television and proportionately more time tuned to the teenage focused messages of popular music" (p. 584).

It is not surprising that divergent, even conflicting data are reported in studies examining involvement with particular music media by specific populations of adolescents. Lyle and Hoffman (1972) reported that 92% of 15- to 17-year-olds listen to the radio. In spite of the increased availability and variety of other media since the 1970s, the Radio Advertising Bureau (RAB) still claims that more than 90% of all teenagers listen to the radio (RAB, 1989). Christenson and DeBenedittis (1986) reported that 68% of 11- to 12-year-olds have radios in their rooms and 69% have a favorite radio station. Wade (1971) found that adolescents who received high scores on the Gilford tests of creativity consistently reported less time with media than peers who received lower creativity scores.

Music Television (MTV) represents the newest form of public music media, having begun 24-hour telecasts of music videos on August 1, 1981, with the record-buying consumers (ages 12–34) as its target audience (Wolfe, 1983). It too has a strong adolescent following. Sun and Lull (1986) estimated that MTV reaches 43% of all teenagers weekly and that 80% of a California sample of 9th–12th graders watch MTV an average of 125 minutes a day. This is considerably higher than

Christenson and Roberts' (1989) report of daily music video viewing by 7th graders (41 minutes), 9th graders (32 minutes), and 11th graders (23 minutes). Although Pennsylvania junior high school students were not asked to indicate the duration of viewing, 38% reported watching MTV "every day" and 39% "once in a while" (Thompson, 1991). Walker (1987) examined relationships between MTV viewing and adolescents' use of other media. He reported positive and significant relationships between viewing MTV, listening to music on radio, and listening to records. He concluded that "MTV watching does not substitute for exposure to other forms of rock music, but tends to stimulate interest in them much the same way as radio listening stimulates record purchases" (p. 2). The number of cable channels specializing in music videos is increasing and a home market for music videos is developing. It is reasonable to expect that adolescents' involvement with music delivered by visual media is likewise increasing.

The increased availability of personal media is evidenced by the comparison of 1972 data with that of a more recent study. Lyle and Hoffman (1972) reported that 56% of Grade 6 boys and 48% of Grade 6 girls owned tape recorders. Thompson (1991) found that 90% of Grade 7 youth owned tape recorders. Although some of the 40% difference might be due to the 1-year age difference, most is attributed to increased availability. Thompson also found that 44% of his sample owned CD players and 35% turntables, reflecting the evolving trend in audio technology. Lyle and Hoffman (1972) reported that 49% of their sample had purchased "single" recordings in the preceding month and that 30% had bought albums. Christenson and Roberts (1989) reported average daily record/tape listening by 7th graders as 64 minutes; increasing to 89 minutes for 11th graders.

Larson et al. (1989) pointed out that popular music, unlike other media such as television "is produced by older adolescents and young adults and is generally targeted directly at a teenage audience" (p. 584). Given the level of involvement in music media by adolescents and Frith's (1978) report that 75% of all popular music sold went to customers between 12 and 20 years of age, one must conclude that these producers have been successful in targeting their audience and marketing their products.

The existing research validates the assumption that adolescents have a high degree of music media involvement. Unfortunately most of these studies have been based on the assumptions that "adolescents" represent a homogenous population and that "popular music" is a singular genre. They have also assumed that "listening" through headsets while doing homework provides the same kind of involvement with music as "listening" to radio or MTV while eating popcorn and talking with friends, or "listening" to a new CD with highly focused attention. Scholars of human development now recognize highly individualized patterns of development throughout adolescence. Musicologists recognize many different strands of popular music. Both adolescents and popular music exist in a wide variety of social contexts. There is a need for research that documents the magnitude of individual adolescents' involvement with specific musical styles in specific social contexts. The fact that a high percentage of some adolescents spend a large proportion of their time with some kind of popular music is hardly a basis for making claims about the effectiveness of music as an intervention nor as a deterrent to successful adolescent development.

SOURCES OF INFLUENCE

The next aspect of musical involvement of adolescents considered here is the source of influence for that involvement. Who or what motivates adolescents to choose a particular style of music or to choose music over other activities? Unfortunately there is little empirical data on which to base answers to these questions.

Larson, Kubey, and Colletti (1989) offered the opinion that "rock music, in contrast to much television fare, is associated with peer group values," (p. 585) implying that peers are highly influential in the music involvement of adolescents. After reviewing several studies on the relationship between use of popular music and social popularity, Larson and Kubey (1983) concluded: "At no other period in life does the interplay between media and peer relations seem as crucial as in adolescence. . . . Liking and being able to talk about music is crucial to an adolescent's participation in the world of other youth" (p. 16). Larson et al. (1989) collected empirical data that indicates "the heaviest music listeners spent more time with their friends, less time with their families and significantly less time in class at school" (Larson p. 585).

Working with a sample of older (college-age) adolescents, Dixon (1981) found rankings of 16 classifications of popular music differed for Blacks and Whites as well as for males and females "confirming the existence of taste culture/taste publics . . ." (p. 6). Dixon pointed out that these patterns of taste may result from different degrees of exposure to music industry promotion rather than from intrinsic qualities in the music that appeals to individuals of a particular race or gender. In a study of adolescents in Finland and Sweden, Finnas (1987) found that boys tend to prefer "tough/protesting/rock-oriented" music, whereas girls' preference tended toward "quiet/contemplative/traditional/serious" music. As part of the same study, Finnas found that teenagers of both sexes tend to overestimate their peers' preference for "tough/protesting/rock-oriented" music and underestimate peers' preference for quiet popular as well as for classical music.

An adolescent's family is most likely not a significant direct influence on choices of music. Christenson and DeBenedictis (1986) found that 72% of their young radio listeners were either alone or with young people only during the time period that they listened. Larson et al. (1989) reported that between Grades 5 and 9, there was a decided shift from television viewing as a family activity to music listening as a solitary activity or one shared with age peers. Larson and Kubey (1983) reported that while listening, adolescents "most often reported themselves to be alone, one-quarter of the time they were with their friends, and virtually never were they with their families" (p. 19). Walker (1987) found no significant relationships between MTV viewing and either father's or mother's level of education.

Roe (1987), taking a somewhat unique approach, argued that schools influence adolescents' media choices not through direct teaching but by indirectly assigning students to positions within social class structures that are closely associated with academic success and failure. Each segment of this class structure represents a "taste public" that has its culture, including its own genre of music. "Low achievement leads to a greater involvement with peers, leading to a greater preference for socially disapproved music" (p. 225). Roe carefully pointed out that low school achievement is quite distinct from low social class, even though the two are frequently interrelated. He concluded that "social background influences on most music preferences were very weak. On the other hand, some music factors were related to perceived *future* status" (p. 227).

Schools have attempted to directly influence adolescents' musical values (Music Educators National Conference [MENC], 1986), establishing goals for moving them toward "classical" genres, however, the findings of numerous preference studies (Finnas, 1989) provide little evidence of success in this endeavor leading to the conclusion that neither family nor school curriculum are a significant direct source of influence on adolescents' involvement with music media.

Verden et al. (1989) expressed the opinion of many: Choices of music media are a result of the total adolescent experience rather than a particular person or environment. "Musical preferences are interpreted as following from rather than causing the modes of behavior and kinds of problems associated with adolescence" (p. 74). After reviewing some of the literature included in this report for an article in the *Journal of the American Medical Association,* Brown and Hendee (1989) concluded that: "inasmuch as music can be representative of an adolescent subcul ture, questions about music preference can be corroborating evidence when other affective behavior of the adolescent suggests potentially destructive alienation" (p. 1663).

Accepting the rather strong indications that inherent factors in the "adolescent condition," and peers exert the strongest influence on both the quantity and specific nature of adolescents' involvement with music, attention is turned to the gratifications received and the meanings derived from that involvement.

MEANINGS DERIVED FROM MUSIC

Current aesthetians, Langer (1957) Reimer (1989) view music as symbolic of human feeling. Adolescents apparently agree. At least three studies found that "mood control" was an important reason among teenagers for listening to popular music (Christenson & Roberts, 1989; Gantz, Gartenberg, Person, & Schiller, 1978; Rosenbaum & Prinsky, 1987). Gratifications and "meanings" that may be classified as "affective" have been reported by a number of additional investigators. Larson et al. (1989) found that girls reported lower affective states than boys during music listening and concluded that "it reflects a deliberate use of this media, with its strong emotional message, for remination, reflection upon, and perhaps discharge of negative feelings" (p. 595). Lyle and Hoffman (1972) found that their subjects report the use of music "to help you relax, for situations when someone has hurt your feelings or made you angry." Larson et al. (1989) offered the opinion that "boys appear to use music to pump themselves up, for young adolescent girls the use of music may be driven more by a need to both explore and cope with new concerns and worries that accompany this age period" (p. 576). Burke and Grinder (1966) concluded that teens use music "for a guide or framework for expressing their own feelings or an articulation of their own fantasies" (p. 198). Adolescents apparently use music to "set a mood" for activities, as Larson and Kubey (1983) found that adolescents reported higher motivation, greater excitement, and more openness for activities that are accompanied by music.

Music is also recognized for the inherent value found in patterns of sound (Langer, 1957; Reimer, 1989). There is evidence that some adolescents agree. Verden et al. (1989) reported that 78% of their sample found "beat and sound" to be the most important aspect of a song. Rosenbaum and Prinsky (1987) concluded that to teenagers, the musical beat or overall sound was of greater interest than the lyrics. Christenson and DeBenedictis (1986) reported that 83% of their subjects' reasons for listening to radio could be categorized as "musical."

Similarly Sun and Lull (1986) reported that musical reasons were most frequently offered for MTV viewing by their teenage sample.

In addition to the aesthetic gratifications derived from music, adolescents use their favorite sounds for some utilitarian purposes. Gantz et al. (1978) reported that 91% of adolescents in their study listened to popular music to pass time and to relieve boredom. Rosenbaum and Prinsky (1987) found that among their adolescent sample, "relaxing and taking my mind off troubles" was the primary reason for listening to popular music. Schlattmann (1989) found that his sample of adolescents selected their music "because it was good to dance to."

Recent national attention has been focused on concern over the implied and literal content of the lyrics of some popular music and a number of studies have attempted to examine the degree to which the content of the lyrics of popular music influence the thinking and behavior of young people. Students attending an alternative high school reported that music "influenced the way they thought about an important topic" and both traditional and alternative high school students indicated that music had some degree of influence on the way they dealt with problems (Schlattmann, 1989, p. 27). Wass et al. (1988) identified a sample of students in southeastern high schools that were fans of music that contain themes of "homicide, satanism and suicide" and found that 40% of those students claimed to know all of the lyrics to their favorite music, and that they "often" agreed with those lyrics.

On the other hand, much of the research in this area has found that few students know the lyrics to even their favorite songs and that their interpreted "meanings" are frequently different from those of adults. Greenfield (1987) found that neither 4th-, 8th-, nor 12th-grade students could identify the "meaning" of individual metaphors nor the overall "message" of popular songs that had previously been determined by adults. Robinson and Hirsh (1969) found that fewer than 30% of a group of high school students could write the message allegedly contained in four popular protest songs. They stated "most teenagers made no reference to drugs, sex, or politics when asked to interpret the meaning of songs which we believed said a great deal about each of these subjects" (p. 380). Denisoff and Levin (1971) concluded that the majority of young radio listeners did not understand the meaning of "Top 40" songs and that radio music, for them, served as background noise. Schlattman reported of his high school students: "Even when the message is fairly clear, 2 out of 3 had difficulty interpreting it" (p. 32).

Although one might suspect that the visual element of music videos might convey a more precise meaning, Brown and Schulze (1990) had older adolescents compare two Madonna videos and found that "Viewers differed dramatically in how they interpreted the two videos and did not all agree about even the most fundamental story elements" (p. 7). The data in this study suggest that differences in interpretation of the music's "message" could be attributed to race, gender, and liking for the performing artist. A number of studies (Deiter, 1987; Gunderson, 1985; Hugonnet, 1986; Young, 1987) have compared attitudes, values, and self-concepts before and after viewing selected music videos and have found no changes in pre- and postviewing measures. A separate study by Greeson and Williams (1986) presented qualified evidence that music videos may influence adolescent attitudes toward premarital sex and violence. Hall, Miller, and Hanson (1986) found that Grade 7 students, as well as college-aged students (a) are more attentive to the *visuals* of music videos than they are to the music, (b) prefer music videos in which the visual matches the story line (rather than displaying the musicians performing), and (c) exhibit a rather high degree of confusion about the story line, even when the visual channel does present that story line.

A few authors consider media music as a sociological phenomenon for adolescents. "Rock's meaning as a mass medium is not dependent on its lyrical content, the beat, or the overall sound. It derives instead, from its relationship to specific segments within youth culture" (Frith, 1981, p. 159). Willis (1978) reported "What most of the subcultures had in common was a very strong commitment to some form of popular music. Indeed, in many cases music provided one of the most explicit expressions of group identity."

There appear to be two theoretical models of communication on which research concerning the *"the meaning"* of popular music has been based. In one model, the meaning is inherent in the music, put there by the composer. The listeners' task is to "receive" the meaning. The second theory considers music to be an ambiguous sonic event from which each listener derives a uniquely personal meaning. In either case, parents and others concerned with the welfare of youth should be heartened by the findings of the research if the listener's task is to "decode" the message of popular music, adolescents apparently are not very successful in doing so. If, on the other hand, the listener's task is to discover a personal meaning as a result of the involvement with the music, adolescents' meanings apparently are not as deviant as those of adults.

Parents, teachers, social workers, and others who have assumed responsibility for assisting adolescents through their stage of development, look on music as both a problem and a cure. Existing research support both positions to an extent, but the limitations of the designs of most studies make broad generalizations hazardous. A 12-year-old Hispanic in Miami, a Black youth in Brooklyn, an Asian-American in Falls

Church, and a White adolescent in Sioux Falls may all watch the same music video on MTV on Friday at 4:23 p.m. but what they hear and see will vary greatly, as will the "meaning" they derive from the experience. These differences result from the context in which they view the music, as well as the life experiences they bring to it. Even though popular music is a central part of adolescent culture, it is not necessarily a dependable conduit through which important messages can be "piped in." Although the concerns for the negative influence of music on youth are not completely overridden by the research, it does seem clear that the majority of adolescents do not interpret "messages" in the same way as adults. Those that do, do not accept them unquestioningly. Clearly, there is a need for continued research on the role of music in the developmental process.

REFERENCES

Brown, E. F., & Hendee, W. R. (1989). Adolescents and their music. *Journal of the American Medical Association, 262*(12), 1659–1663.

Brown, J. D., & Schulze, L. (1990). The effects of race, gender, and fandom on audience interpretations of Madonna's music videos. *Journal of Communications, 40*(2), 88–102.

Burke, R., & Grinder, R. (1966). Personality-oriented themes and listening patterns in teen-age music and their relation to certain academic and peer variables. *School Review, 74,* 196–211.

Christenson, P., & DeBenedictis, P. (1986). "Eavesdropping" on the FM band: Children's use of radio. *Journal of Communication, 36*(2), 27–38.

Christenson, P., & Roberts, D. (1989). *Popular music in early adolescence.* Research report for the Carnegie Council on Adolescent Development, New York.

Deiter, P. (1987). *MTV viewing by adolescents and beliefs about violence, sex and sexual violence.* Unpublished master's theses, Michigan State University, East Lansing.

Denisoff, R., & Levine, M. (1971). The popular protest song: The case of "Eve of Destruction." *Public Opinion Quarterly, 35,* 119–124.

Dixon, R. (1981). Musical taste cultures and taste publics revisited: A research note of new evidence. *Popular Music and Society, 8*(1), 2–9.

Finnas, L. (1987). Do young people misjudge each others' musical taste? *Psychology of Music, 15,* 152–166.

Finnas, L. (1989). How can musical preferences be modified? *Bulletin of the Council for Research in Music Education, 102,* 1–59.

Fischer, C., & Powell, S. (1985, October). What entertainers are doing to your kids. *U.S. News and World Report, 23,* 46–49.

Frith, S. (1978). Youth culture/youth cults: A decade of rock consumption. In C. Gillette & S. Frith (Eds.), *Rock file* (Vol. 5). London: Panther, Granada Publishing.

Frith, S. (1981). Sound effects, youth, leisure, and the politics of rock 'n' roll. In R. Middleton & D. Horn (Eds.), *Popular music* (Vol. 1, pp. 159–168). Cambridge: Cambridge University Press.

Gantz, W., Gartenberg, H., Person, M., & Schiller, S. (1978). Gratifications and expectations associated with pop music among adolescents. *Popular Music and Society, 6*(1), 81–89.

Greenfield, P. (1987). What is rock music doing to the minds of our youth? A first experimental look at the effects of rock music lyrics and music videos. *Journal of Early Adolescence, 7*(3), 315–329.

Greeson, L., & Williams, R. (1986). Social implications of music videos for youth: An analysis of the content and effects of MTV. *Youth and Society, 18*(2), 177–189.

Gunderson, R. (1985). *An investigation of the effects of rock music videos on the values and self-perceptions of adolescents.* Unpublished doctoral dissertation, United States International University, San Diego, CA.

Hall, J., Miller, C., & Hanson, J. (1986). Music Television: A perceptions study of two age groups. *Popular Music and Society, 10*(4), 17–28.

Hugonnet, M. (1986). *An experimental study of rock video's impact upon the attitudes and values of normal and emotionally disturbed adolescents.* Unpublished doctoral dissertation, The American University, Washington, DC.

Langer, S. (1957). *Philosophy in a new key.* Cambridge, MA: Harvard University Press.

Larson, R., & Kubey, R. (1983). Television and music: Contrasting media in adolescent life. *Youth and Society, 15*, 13–31.

Larson, R., Kubey, R., & Colletti, J. (1989). Changing channels: Early adolescent media choices and shifting investments in family and friends. *Journal of Youth and Adolescence, 18*(6), 583–599.

Lyle, J., & Hoffman, H. (1972). Children's use of television and other media. In E. Rubenstein, G. Comstock, & J. Murray (Eds.), *Television and social behavior, Vol. 4: Television in day-to-day Life.* Washington, DC: U.S. Government Printing Office.

Music Educators National Conference. (1986). *School music programs: Descriptions and standards* (2nd ed.). Reston, VA: Author.

Radio Advertising Bureau. (1989). *Radio memo* (Press release). New York: Author.

Reimer, B. (1989). *A philosophy of music education* (2nd ed.). Englewood Cliffs, NJ: Prentice-Hall.

Robinson, J., & Hirsch, P. (1969). *Teenage response to rock and roll songs.* Paper presented to the American Sociological Association, San Francisco, CA.

Roe, K. (1987). The school and music in adolescent socialization. In J. Lull (Ed.), *Popular music and communication* (pp. 212–230). Newbury Park, CA: Sage.

Rosenbaum, J., & Prinsky, L. (1987). Sex, violence, and rock 'n roll: Youth's perceptions of popular music. *Popular Music and Society, 11*(2), 79–89.

Schlattmann, T. (1989). Traditional, non-traditional, emotionally/behaviorally disturbed students and popular musical lyrics. *Popular Music and Society, 13*(1), 23–40.

Sun, S., & Lull, J. (1986). The adolescent audience for music videos and why they watch. *Journal of Communications, 36*(1), 115–125.

Thompson, K. (1991). An examination of the consistency of junior high school students preferences for general music activities. *UPDATE, 9*(2), 11–16.

Verden, P., Dunleavy, K., & Power, C. (1989). Heavy metal mania and adolescent delinquency. *Popular Music and Society, 13*(1), 73–82.

Wade, E. (1971). Adolescents, creativity, and media. *American Behavioral Scientist, 14*(3), 341–351.

Walker, J. (1987). The context of MTV: Adolescent entertainment media use and music television. *Popular Music and Society, 11*(3), 1–9.

Wass, H., Raup, J., Cerullo, K., Martel, L., Mingione, L., Speering, A. (1988). Adolescents' interest in and views of destructive themes in rock music. *Omega, 19*(3), 177–186.

Willis, P. (1978). *Profane culture*. London: Rutledge & Kegan Paul.
Wolfe, A. (1983). Rock on cable: On MTV: Music television, the first video music channel. *Popular Music and Society, 9*(1), 41–49.
Young, K. (1987). *The effects of music video violence on the aggression level of emotionally disturbed adolescents*. Unpublished master's thesis, Western Michigan University, Kalamazoo.

24 Creating Meaning From Media Messages: Participatory Research and Adolescent Health

Michael Frith
Katherine Frith
The Pennsylvania State University

MASS MEDIA AND SOCIAL STASIS

Each advance in communications technology made over the past 150 years—from telegraph to satellites—has been accompanied by the promise of liberation and social improvement through the wider accessibility of knowledge. The extent to which the supposedly intrinsic social good in the media has manifested itself is disappointing.

Instead of media technologies serving the broader developmental needs of society, the "needs of a corporate economy prevail over those of the general citizenry" (Wallack, 1989, p. 353). This is hardly surprising. Each form of mass communication technology and virtually every organ of mass media are devised and launched to meet commercial needs. Wallack pointed out that each new media matures to "become a means for reinforcing existing social and economic arrangements, and for providing entertainment rather than stimulating change" (p. 353).

In spite of the emerging recognition that the mass media are unreliable agents for social improvement, many health communicators and educators still try to use the commercial mass media to meet public health and behavior-change goals. This has led to the amassing of conflicting findings on the effects and lack thereof of mass media channels and mediated health messages. Hornik (1989) pointed out that the effects of the various mass communication channels demonstrated under laboratory conditions have seldom, if ever, been satisfactorily correlated with either effectiveness or feasibility beyond the experimental setting. For example, much disappointment has resulted from the poor response to social advertising in public service announcements (PSAs), invariably broadcast infrequently and in off-peak hours. This is symptomatic of air time and space costs preventing health campaigns from attaining the levels of "reach and frequency" required for effective consumer advertising.

Added to the persistent myth of commercial mass media as key to massive social change in the public interest, is the myth of the immutability of the message (Fiske, 1989). The idea that health messages are understood, as transmitted, in a uniform fashion by their target group is another serious impediment to progress in understanding how the media influence the social construct of health. Much laudable effort has been invested in refining audience segmentation and in fine-tuning methods for assuring the relevance of health messages delivered to each psychographic slice of the public health "market" (Plummer, 1974; Wells, 1975). However, scant attention has been paid by media effects researchers (who currently predominate in the mass communication health campaign field) to how these intentional messages are understood by their recipients, especially adolescents. Almost no attention has been given to the internal processing of either incidental or intentional health messages embedded in programming, particularly as perceived by adolescents.

Part of our purpose in this chapter is to advocate the systematic exploration of how adolescents process media health messages and create meaning from them. We consider meaning creation to be an interactive, energy-consuming process rather than a passive reception of messages at the end of a one-way chain of transmission. Our ultimate desire is to refine a practical alternative to the media effects paradigm. This alternative hinges on articulating the process of health-associated self-empowerment developed by some adolescents and helping them popularize it as a means of self-defense against unhealthful persuasion.

THE SOCIAL CONSTRUCTION OF HEALTH

The World Health Organization (WHO) has adopted the definition of *health* in the first article of the Declaration of Alma-Ata, as "a state of complete physical, mental and social well-being, and not merely the absence of disease or infirmity" (WHO, 1978). The inclusion of the phrase "social well-being" has been problematic among Western health workers who cleave to the clinical definition of health disavowed in the second phrase of the definition. The implication that "health" has a social existence that somehow transcends the individual does not easily mesh with the Western belief in individualism.

An important preliminary for health professionals interested in affecting the adolescent construct of health is to understand the cultural arena of adolescent discourse on health. In Western societies, adolescence is primarily a cultural construct. It symbolizes a period of breaking away from the collectivity of home and family and the emergence of the ideal unit of Western democratic societies—the "individual" self. Adolescence involves the rejection of the dominant (adult) culture and the actualization of the individual as "an historical and social construct formed both by his or her material social history and by the discourses through which he or she has experienced that history" (Fiske, 1988, p. 247).

As the product of a unique history, each adolescent is a caught in a web of signification that differs distinctly from those that form the dominant adult culture. Thus, the job of the researcher is essentially semiotic; investigating the meaning of such cultural constructs as "health" within adolescent culture, "sorting out the structures of signification—and determining their social ground and import" (Geertz, 1973, p. 9).

HOW THE MEDIA AFFECT THE CONSTRUCTION OF HEALTH

There are two alternative approaches to employing the mass media to affect the formation of the health construct in the minds of adolescents. The most obvious means of influencing this process, and the one that continues to receive the bulk of attention, is to control the content of the mass media. Consumer movements and public interest groups contend that the instrumental effect of the media on health can be fundamentally altered. By either legislating against "unhealthy" messages (e.g., banning tobacco and alcohol advertising from television, and censoring violence) or inserting healthful messages into the media flow, content determinists believe they can compete with unhealthful commercial interests like tobacco and alcohol. However, economic, political, legal, and many other practical, philosophical, and psychological factors limit the potential for manipulating the health-related content of the mass media.

Although the quality of the health content of the media will never fully satisfy public health interests, we find the efforts of these advocates to limit unhealthful messages in the media commendable. Unquestionably, without the public opinion that these watchdogs lead, U.S. television would still be punctuated by 1950s-style cigarette ads replete with false health claims.

Rather than attempting to change the health content of the media, a second and more promising way to influence the way media messages affect the health construct may be to help adolescents gain conscious control over the way they process media messages. Although the first style of intervention is based on what Carey (1989) called the transmission or control model, the second is based on an alternative concept of communication as a "ritual" process "directed not toward the extension of messages in space but toward the maintenance of society in time; not the act of imparting information but the representation of shared beliefs" (Carey, 1989, p. 18).

For adolescents to gain and maintain control over their own health implies empowerment to create their own health construct. This may be at odds with the commercial interests whose images of medicalized health (e.g., over-the-counter drug use) and mythologized health (e.g., the association of smoking with activities attractive to youth) pervade constitutionally protected commercial free speech. For adolescents, this empowerment may result from learning to monitor and critique the stream of health-related messages, signs, and symbols in the media. Thus, helping youth achieve critical consciousness of the health content of the media may help them develop a heightened sense of health self-efficacy, and refocus the locus of control toward an internal orientation to their well-being. Solomon (1988) suggested the following:

> As long as you are unable to decode the significance of ordinary things, and as long as you take the signs of your culture at face value, you will continue to be mastered by them. But once you see behind the surface of a sign into its hidden cultural significance, you can free yourself from that sign and perhaps find a new way of looking at the world. (p. 8)

In summary, the media effects approach to mass health behavior change in adolescents is in disarray, in major part because (a) it is impractical, if not illegal and unconstitutional, to attempt to influence the content of mass media dictated by commercial interests; (b) at present, public health interests lack the financial clout to increase significantly the health content of the media environment; and (c) scant attention has been paid to what happens after positive and negative health messages are received.

EXPLORING THE ADOLESCENT HEALTH CONSTRUCT

Despite myths like the immutable message and the passive audience, the outcomes of message processing and the construction of meaning are currently beyond prediction. It is clear that although some adolescents accept unequivocally the "preferred" or dominant meaning from media messages, many are equally impervious to, for example, television alcohol advertising and the violent content of some programming. Somehow these individuals are able to construct meanings that may be diametrically opposed to the meaning intended by originators of the messages. Thus, a basic question needs to be explored: "Why do some adolescents accept at face value health-related messages embedded in the mass media, while others selectively evade, reject, or even invert their meanings?"

Understanding how intentionally unhealthful messages are either being ignored or inverted by some adolescents could allow health educators and others to facilitate sharing these skills among other adolescents—particularly those at risk of receiving these messages passively and uncritically. A traditional media effects approach to understanding this process would involve, for example, counting violent episodes on television and attempting to correlate them with adolescent predisposition to violence. The approach we prefer would start, in this example, by understanding why the majority of adolescents are not driven either to acts of violence or to adopt unhealthy addictions in the wake of television viewing. Direct questioning by adults is unlikely to prompt a meaningful answer. To be able to answer this question adequately, adolescents need to become critically conscious of their reflexive relationship with the health elements of their cultural, political, and physical environment.

The development of critical consciousness is a complex process that takes place over a number of years. In the present context, the loss of naivete and the growth of the ability to make oppositional readings to intended media messages results from several gradual developmental processes. This complex growth takes place over time in a cultural matrix and not as a result of isolated, discrete events. As such, these phenomena are more difficult to separate out and study as in a traditional quasi-experimental approach.

As far as we know, the catalyst for critical consciousness of a particular media message must either be embedded in the message (text) or is, more likely, emergent from the psychological interaction (hermeneutic) between text and reader occurring in a specific cultural context. The exposure of young adolescents to these messages, as many parents will attest, is practically uncontrollable. For example, it does not matter if parents exercise control over television viewing and censor print media entering the home because the bulk of cigarette and alcohol advertising is on billboards. Also, with the balance of pro alcohol and smoking persuasion messages in print media and at the point of purchase, no adolescent in the United States (or anywhere else, for that matter) remains unexposed. Under these circumstances, traditional controlled experiments to explore the phenomenon holistically remain impractical.

There is a variety of more promising approaches for adult researchers to understand how and why some adolescents can inoculate themselves against inappropriate persuasion. These methods are, of necessity, explanatory and descriptive. The basic research required could include participant observation and cross-cultural ethnographic studies of the interaction between media and adolescent culture, and psychological studies of the creation and nature of the health construct in individual young people. However, because the social development of health consciousness and health empowerment as a collective phenomenon is the proposed focus of study, participatory research may be the most appropriate. In this research mode, the researcher and the researched collaborate in defining, conducting, and interpreting research whose goal is the simultaneous creation of knowledge and the enhancement of group and individual self-determination.

PARTICIPATORY RESEARCH VERSUS SOCIAL ENGINEERING

Concientization, or empowerment through consciousness-raising, as a theory and practice primarily derived from the work of Freire (1970, 1973), has been blended with the critical sociology of Habermas (1972) by adult educator Jack Mezirow (1978, 1981, 1985, 1990). Although the resulting method, participatory research (Brown, 1985; Dilts, 1983; Frith, 1988; Hall, 1981; Maguire, 1987; Tandon, 1981), has rarely if ever been systematically employed with young adolescents, we show how it holds great promise for this arena of research.

Participatory research is categorized as a method of action research (Oquist, 1977) designed for the construction of social reality, and defined in the *Harvard Educational Review* as: "a people-centered learning process that can transform local patterns of awareness, equalize distributions of power and resources, and increase participation in development activity" (Brown, 1985, p. 70).

Participatory researchers, as educators, are more concerned with the creation and application of group-specific knowledge than with the storage and distribution of universal knowledge. Their emphasis on enabling rather than informing is the most likely reason this mode of research and learning has not migrated from adult education to the traditional school system. In order for adolescents to articulate how they render oppositional readings of the health texts embedded in the media, they have to become conscious of this internal but socially related process in addition to achieving critical consciousness of the actual messages. People becoming critically conscious, according to Freire (1973) and Habermas (1972), alter their social reality in the process of empowerment. If social reality is indeed a human artifact, youth, as much as any other social group, has the potential of changing its own social environment. If our purpose is to study the empowerment of adolescents and then to extend this process to others, participatory research holds the greatest promise of achieving both the learning and action goals simultaneously.

Both because we assume our readers' familiarity with traditional social science, and because a critique of sociological research formed an important impetus for the emergence of participatory research, we have chosen to contrast these approaches with one another. We admit we are drawn philosophically toward participatory research, but although its aims reflect some of our values, we do not intend to suggest that the traditional forms of social research have no utility. On the contrary, there are many important research tasks that could not be attempted without the rigor of traditional and highly objective methodologies. An obvious example is the census, whose findings determine how centrally controlled resources are shared among local governments.

Some of the variables of social research are laid out in Table 24.1, and the salient orientations held by practitioners at the extremes of the two schools of research are listed by each variable. The bulk of actual social research practice and thought lies somewhere between the two. The first column (Traditional) delineates the scientific ideological position of census-takers or social engineers. For proponents of participatory research, the rightmost column lists a set of ideal values and objectives. The term *ideology* is used here in the nonpejorative dictionary sense of the "body of ideas" at the root of a system (or subsystem) of society.

Following is a brief discussion of some of the contrasting values associated with each variable in Table 24.1.

Objectives. The aims of participatory research are the creation of indigenous knowledge and the precipitation of social change. The direction of this action is toward the evolution of society to meet the needs of its constituents rather than adjusting individuals (particularly youth) to fit the needs of an industrial order. Critical sociologists such as Habermas (1972), point out that social scientists continue to hold onto the objectives of prediction and control they transferred from the natural sciences of the industrial revolution to the arena of human behavior—particularly the conditioning of child and adolescent labor to

Table 24.1
The Ideologies of Traditional and Participatory Social Research Compared

	Traditional	Participatory
Objectives	Centralizing social information, maintaining status quo, domestication, assistencial[a]	Creating indigenous knowledge, self-determination social change, emancipation, empowerment
Interests served	Central controlling external	Local self-determining internal
Researcher	Professional, paid remote, expert, source of knowledge and method	Lay, voluntary community member facilitator
Method	Abstractive, quantitative, complex, needs expert interpretation	Praxis[b], creative, reflexive, qualitative, dialogical, open to laypersons
Data	Quantitative numerical, abstract experimental	Qualitative verbal, concrete experiential
Validation	Comparison to fixed reality quality of method	Utility effectiveness of praxis quality of change
Products	Reports, documents policy planning inputs	Process praxis[b] social change
Consumers	Government management external planners	Producers are consumers
Applying knowledge	Banking[c], selective distributive, top-down by edict	Dialogical horizontal, shared from inside out

[a]*Assistencialism* is the term used by Freire (1970) to describe the disempowerment implicit in the helping relationship.
[b]Freire (1973) used *praxis* as a label for the continuous cycle of action and reflection (or theory and practice) that forms the process of experiential learning.
[c]Freire (1970) used this to signify a philosophy of education that conceives the learner as an empty vessel waiting to be filled with knowledge for later withdrawal.
Source: Derived from Frith (1988)

life in the mill. In participatory research, prediction and control to maintain the status quo are replaced by understanding and collaboration as means improving the quality of life.

Interests. The interests served by most traditional sociological researchers (e.g., working to service the needs of government, institutions, brewers, and cigarette and drug manufacturers), tend to be remote and controlling. In contrast, the interests served by participatory research are more localized and aimed at fostering the development of autonomy rather than dependency. This mode of research is in the interest of informed healthful choice in contrast to manipulation and addiction.

Researcher. A participatory researcher is more likely to be a volunteer from within than a paid professional from outside. The traditional social researcher chooses to maintain distance in the interests of objectivity and generalizability, whereas participatory researchers' orientations are toward achieving closeness and empathy for one another. The role of professional social scientists, health workers, or educators as participatory researchers is problematic because they can hardly avoid the intrusion of their personal, organizations', or other external interests into the objectives of research. This potentially destructive influence can be avoided when researchers internalize the ideology of participatory research and elevate, as best they can, their groups' interests above their own.

Method. The methods of traditional social research are, as illustrated by the left-hand column of Table 24.1, opaque. Often, sociologists and others use methods designed to disguise the purpose of research so reactivity is controlled and learning minimized. Traditional methods are more akin to the mining of abstract data than to creating knowledge through action and dialogue.

Data. The "data" of participatory research are more likely to be qualitative in nature: more a verbalization of experience than the encoded tables of numbers, frequencies, and dispersions of traditional social research. Participatory research in the context of youth culture is cast in the dialect of youth rather than in scientific cipher.

Validation. The epistemology of participatory research lies in an indigenous evaluation of the quality of change wrought through its application. The American pragmatism of Dewey and James provides the philosophical support for participatory research, whereas the logical positivism of the natural sciences provides the rationale for traditional social scientism wherein reality is fixed, measurable, and objective. For participatory researchers, truth is a shared vision of reality—an upwardly moving target that changes with each cycle of reflection and action.

Products. The basic product of traditional social research is the report. Scientific reports are often used as input to a planning process. At other times, the process of social evolution implicit in social research is terminated with the filing of a report. Frequently, however, the most important function of a social scientific report is to suggest further studies and not to precipitate remedial action. The distance between the product of research and its application is entirely missing from participatory research, wherein the research process is its own product.

Consumers. Ideally in participatory research there is no separation between researchers and researched. The production and consumption of knowledge are inseparable in a praxis of action and reflection. Although a description of the process and experience of the participants may have inspirational value for others, the conclusions (or actions) are unlikely to be generalizable beyond the immediate environment of the particular participatory research group.

Application. Sociological knowledge tends to be distributed either by statute or textbook. The social knowledge that accrues from the reflexive experience of a participatory research group is more likely shared in discussions and activities undertaken with peers or among the members of a community of interest.

CONCLUSION: PARTICIPATORY RESEARCH AND ADOLESCENT HEALTH

We have argued the importance of adolescent participation in understanding and transferring the process of creating positive meaning from health-related media messages. Our basis has been the match between the purpose of the research (as we have defined it) as a transformational learning process and the ideological position of participatory research. In short, we have tried to show that if indigenous learning and endogenous change are the desired processes and products of this research action, then the most appropriate set of philosophical and practical values are found under the rubric of participatory research. It is possible to find implicit in our position the suggestion that adult intervention in the process of discovery and application of critical consciousness to health messages is neither desirable nor necessary. Here too, Freire (1970) might warn us of the dangers of "assistentialism" or the seeds of disempowerment embedded in the act of assistance. This introduces a paradox: If the intervention of adults undermines the process, how does one start the ball rolling?

Attaining critical control over the meaning of health messages is, as we have pointed out, a gradual developmental process. The study of this process for the purpose of its reproduction by other adolescents, in a participatory research mode, should also be a gradual process that moves participants from dependency on an initiating researcher to self-reliance and empowerment. Thus, the adult initiator, as a *de facto* member of the foreign (adult) culture, must be prepared to unite as much as possible with the adolescents and then let them go as soon as the process gains momentum. Another role for adults might be as observers of the process and reporters to the adult world. In this role, adults would have to adapt the ethnographic methodologies of other cross-cultural communication researchers and avoid creating dependency relationships.

In conclusion, we feel that efforts to improve the quality of health-related messages embedded in the media should be matched by attempts to discover and disseminate the critical methods employed by some adolescents to reject or invert unhealthful messages. Specifically, we advocate an empowerment approach employing participatory research to allow adolescents to discover, articulate, and spread the ability to "inoculate" themselves against unhealthful appeals in the mass media.

REFERENCES

Brown, L. D. (1985). People-centered development and participatory research. *Harvard Education Review, 55*(1), 69–75.

Carey, W. (1989). *Communication as culture: Essays on media and society.* Boston: Unwin Hyman.

Dilts, R. (1983). *Critical theory: Application and field practice.* Unpublished manuscript, Center for International Education, University of Massachusetts, Amherst.

Fiske, J. (1988). Critical response: Meaningful moments. *Critical Studies in Mass Communication, 5,* 246–250.

Fiske, J. (1989). *Reading the popular.* Boston: Unwin Hyman.

Freire, P. (1970). *Pedagogy of the oppressed.* New York: The Seabury Press.

Freire, P. (1973). *Education for critical consciousness.* New York: The Seabury Press.

Frith, M. (1988). Social marketing, nonformal education and participatory research in primary health care: Urban rabies control in Guayaquil, Ecuador. *Dissertation Abstracts International, 49*(5a), 1068.

Geertz, C. (1973). *The interpretation of cultures.* New York: Basic Books.

Habermas, J. (1972). *Knowledge and human interests.* Boston: Beacon Books.

Hall, B. L. (1981). Participatory research, popular knowledge and power: A personal reflection. *Convergence, 14*(3), 6–19.

Hornik, R. C. (1989). Channel effectiveness in development communication programs. In R. Rice & C. K. Atkin (Eds.), *Public communication campaigns* (2nd ed., pp. 309–330). Newbury Park, CA: Sage.

Maguire, P. (1987). *Doing participatory research: A feminist approach.* Amherst, MA: Center for International Education, University of Massachusetts.

Mezirow, J. (1978). Perspective transformation. *Adult Education, 23,* 100–110.

Mezirow, J. (1981). A critical theory of adult learning and education. *Adult Education, 32,* 3–24.

Mezirow, J. (1985). Concept and action in adult education. *Adult Education Quarterly, 35*(3), 142–151.

Mezirow, J. and Associates (1990). *Fostering critical reflection in adulthood: A guide to transformative and emancipatory learning.* San Francisco: Jossey-Bass.

Oquist, P. (1977, April). *The epistemology of action research*. Paper presented at Symposio Mundial Sobre Investigacion Activa y Analisis Cientifico, Cartagena, Colombia.

Plummer, J. T. (1974). The concept and application of lifestyle segmentation. *Journal of Marketing, 38,* 35–42.

Solomon, J. (1988). *The signs of our times.* Los Angeles, CA: Jeremy Tarcher.

Tandon, R. (1981). Participatory research in the empowerment of people. *Convergence, 14*(3), 20–27.

Wallack, L. (1989). Mass communication and health promotion: A critical perspective. In R. Rice & C. K. Atkin (Eds.), *Public communication campaigns* (2nd ed., pp. xxx–xxx). Newbury Park, CA: Sage.

Wells, W. D. (1975). Psychographics: A critical review. *Journal of Marketing Research, 12,* 196–213.

World Health Organization. (1978). *Alma-Ata 1978: Primary health care* (Report of the International Conference on Primary Health Care, Alma-Ata, USSR, 6–12 September 1978, "Health for all" series, No. 1). Geneva, Switzerland: Author.

25 | Minority Adolescents, Alcohol Consumption, and Media Effects: A Review of Issues and Research

Jerome D. Williams
The Pennsylvania State University

The role of alcohol products in the media has come under intense scrutiny and extensive criticism (Jacobson, Atkins, & Hacker, 1983; McMahon & Taylor, 1990; Postman, Mystrom, Strate, & Weingartner, 1987). The alcoholic beverage industry spends approximately $2 billion a year on advertising and promotions in the United States, far exceeding expenditures for prevention and education by government and nonprofit agencies (U.S. Department of Health and Human Services, 1989). This widespread promotion results in consumer expenditures of $44 billion annually, exceeding the $37 billion spent on tobacco products and $40 billion on illegal drugs (Anderson, 1991).

Tobacco and alcohol together as legal drugs cause far more health and economic problems than all illegal drugs combined. Alcohol problems alone result in 100,000 deaths and cost our society even more than smoking—more than $135 billion each year (McMahon & Taylor, 1990). These problems are particularly manifested within minority communities, and especially among Black/African-Americans, which is the primary minority group considered in this chapter. A critical area of concern is how all of this affects adolescents. This chapter addresses this concern by first reviewing three key issues—minority adolescents, alcohol consumption, and media effects—and then reviewing the research using my framework of three aspects of the media and six research approaches. Finally, limitations of past research are discussed, and a concluding comment on direction for future research is given.

A REVIEW OF THE ISSUES

The three main issues discussed in this section are shown in the boxes in Fig. 25.1. Between each box are areas of concern in terms of the relationship between the boxes.

Minority Adolescents

As pointed out in a Carnegie Corporation report (1989), by age 15 a substantial number of U.S. adolescents are at risk. For many adolescents, being at risk is associated with the effects of experiencing alcohol product consumption at an early age and running the risk of permanent addiction.

As noted by Bachman, Wallace, Kurth, Johnston, and O'Malley (1991), it is of particular concern to understand the effects of at-risk behavior on minority adolescents because the nation is undergoing dramatic demographic shifts, and minorities are rapidly becoming the majority in many areas. But more important than the mere demographic shift is the implication of a related shift of health concerns. For example, the National Institute on Alcohol Abuse and Alcoholism indicates that alcohol abuse is the leading health and safety problem in Black America. Although Blacks consume less alcohol (per capita) than Whites overall, drinking in the Black community results in disproportionately higher

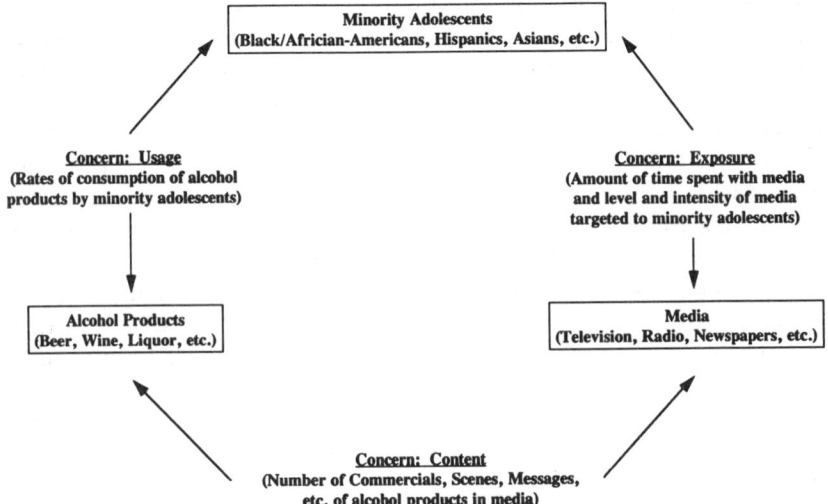

FIG. 25.1 Relationship of issues and concerns.

rates of certain alcohol-related problems such as cirrhosis of the liver. In addition, there are other alcohol-related problems in the form of violence, crime, and accidents that affect Blacks (particularly males) disproportionately (Hacker, Collins, & Jacobson, 1989; McMahon & Taylor, 1990).

Rather than just waiting until the problems are manifested in the adult Black community and dealing with them in a "crisis" mode, it is important to deal with the issues at the adolescent level in a "preventive" mode. We know there is a "crossover" effect of alcohol consumption in the Black community, but little is known about why it occurs, that is, data from surveys comparing Blacks and Whites at various adolescent age levels show much lower usage rates among Blacks compared to Whites, but the differences get smaller in early adulthood, and by middle adulthood, the use/abuse rates are generally higher among Blacks (Bachman, Wallace, O'Malley et al., 1991).

Alcohol Usage

Alcohol is by far the most used and abused drug among young people in the United States today. Many youth first experiment with alcohol during early adolescence. Although the percentage of high school seniors who use illicit drugs is continuing to drop, they continue to show high rates of drinking, with initial experimentation with alcohol occurring at increasingly early ages. For example, 92% of the high school class of 1987 had begun drinking before graduating; of those, 56% had begun drinking in Grades 6 to 9 (Johnston, O'Malley, & Bachman, 1988).

The fact that so many youth are involved with drugs and alcohol at such young ages is alarming because of the "gateway effect," which suggests that experimentation with drugs usually begins with cigarettes, alcohol, or marijuana, and then progresses to other drugs (American Medical Association, 1990; Kandel, 1985). According to Welte and Barnes (1985), the progression of drug use among Blacks was from alcohol, to marijuana, to pills, and finally to "hard" drugs.

As noted earlier, fewer Black adolescents appear to drink alcohol than Whites. According to one recent nationwide survey of senior high school students, the percentages were Black boys (66%) and girls (59%) compared to White boys (81%) and girls (77%) who consumed alcohol at least once a year (Hacker et al., 1989). These low rates by Black students seem surprising, given that alcohol-related mortality and morbidity are higher among Black than White adults. As noted by Bachman, Wallace, O'Malley et al. (1991), however, this may reflect "two worlds" of alcohol use within the Black community: the extremes of abstinence at one end and heavy use/abuse at the other.

Media Effects

A persisting area of concern is the role and effect of the media on adolescent alcohol consumption. As shown in Fig. 25.2, much of the concern stems from the paradigm, adapted from Partenen (1988), that suggests that exposure to alcohol products through the various aspects of the media leads to increased or decreased alcohol consumption behavior, which in turn leads to alcohol misuse/abuse or responsible use, and concomitant health and social effects.

This role in influencing adolescent substance use is substantial in that the media both create and reflect the normative values that shape perceptions of acceptable behavior (Falco, 1988). Many believe that the use of the commercial media by marketers reflects a conscious effort to make alcohol a way of life for people nearing the legal drinking age (Jacobson et al., 1983), although marketers will debate this premise. However, even if the media are not used to consciously target adolescents, young people are primed for a drinking lifestyle before reaching the drinking age by the very existence of alcohol advertising. For this reason, the Surgeon General recently called on the alcohol industry to pull advertising that "could" appeal to young people on the basis of certain lifestyles, sexual appeal, sports appeal, and so on (Stout, 1991).

When adolescents are exposed to alcohol product messages in the media, most researchers acknowledge that there is a differential effect on them compared to adults. For example, Linn, de Benedictis and Delucchi, (1982) found that adolescents can criticize the procedures used to generate the results in product test ads when asked, but they still often believe the results.

In terms of the effects on minority adolescents, there is a great deal of

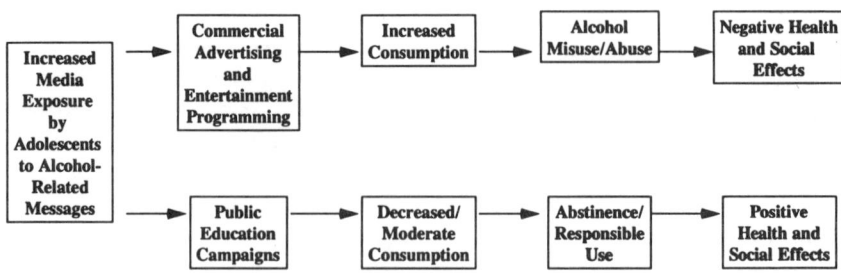

FIG. 25.2 Hypothesized media effects on adolescents of alcohol-related messages.

concern over the targeting of low-income neighborhoods with special alcoholic beverage campaigns. Numerous studies have shown that marketers are pushing these legal drugs much more in Black neighborhoods than in wealthier White ones (McMahon & Taylor, 1990; Schooler & Basil, 1989). This is particularly evident in billboard advertising where the impact is made even before children can read. One 1987 survey conducted by the City of St. Louis found almost 60% of the billboards in Black neighborhoods advertised cigarettes and alcoholic beverages compared to only 36% in White neighborhoods (McMahon & Taylor, 1990). Of 2,015 billboards documented in another study, 70% advertised tobacco or alcohol products and more than 75% of these were in predominantly Black, usually poor, neighborhoods (Scenic America, 1989).

On the other hand, there is some evidence that adolescents most exposed to television, and thus, presumably, to televised alcohol ads, are among those least likely to adopt harmful drinking behavior. For example, Black adolescents watch television more than Whites (Bachman, Johnston, & O'Malley, 1987; Comstock, Chaffee, Katzman, McCombs, & Roberts, 1978), but as was noted earlier, Black adolescents also are more likely than Whites to abstain from alcohol. Also, Chirco (1990) observed that (Moore & Moschis, 1979; Wackman, Reale, & Ward, 1972) adolescents who regard television ads most positively and are most likely to view them for social learning purposes are Black, yet Black adolescents also are more likely to abstain from drinking.

A REVIEW OF THE RESEARCH

Figure 25.3 represents a framework we use to review the literature on the effects of alcohol products in the media on adolescents. Because very few of the studies deal specifically with minority adolescents, I make inferences here based on adolescent studies in general.

Across the top of Fig. 25.3 are three different aspects of the mass media based on a scheme suggested by Partenen (1988). They include advertising, entertainment, and education. Along the side of Fig. 25.3 are various research approaches that can be applied to each of these aspects of the mass media. They include econometrics/modeling, experimentation, quasi-experimentation, surveys, content analysis, and qualitative studies.

On the surface we would expect research to show that adolescent exposure to commercial advertising messages and entertainment programming increases demand for alcoholic beverages, whereas educational campaigns decrease or at least moderate consumption. However,

	Aspects of the Media		
Research Approaches	Commercial Advertising by Marketers	Entertainment Programming	Public Education Campaigns
Econometrics/ Models			
Experimentation			
Quasi-Experimentation			
Surveys			
Content Analyses			
Qualitative/ Discussion Groups			

FIG. 25.3 Literature review framework.

this review shows that there are mixed results in just about every one of the cells of the Fig. 25.3 matrix. This suggests there are still many misconceptions and a lack of a clear understanding of many of the issues surrounding the debate about the link between alcohol messages in the media and adolescent consumption. Because supporters on each side of the debate continue to cite studies supporting their respective position, the conclusion typically drawn under each of the following sections is that there obviously is a need for continued research.

Aspects of the Media

Advertising. Alcohol advertising represents the single greatest source of alcohol education in the United States. Between birth and the legal drinking age, U.S. children see as many as 100,000 television commercials for beer alone (Postman et al., 1987) and close to 1 million in total. However, studies examining the relationship between adolescent day-to-day exposure to advertising and their consumption of alcohol have differed in their conclusions.

In a recent review of empirical studies, Smart (1988) concluded that "alcohol advertising is, at best, a weak variable affecting alcohol consumption" (p. 321). Among his other findings, Smart indicated that advertising bans have little impact on overall sales of alcohol, and those exposed to larger amounts of alcohol advertising are more likely to drink, but the effect of advertising is still small compared to other variables.

In another recent review, however, Atkin (1988) stated that "ads stimulate higher consumption by both adults and adolescents . . . there is a sufficient basis for rejecting the inference of null effects" (U.S. Department of Health and Human Services, 1989, p. 18). An earlier review by Atkin (1987) concluded that advertisements may stimulate alcohol consumption of adults and adolescents to at least a modest degree and may be a significant contributing factor in creating or reinforcing these adverse alcohol use patterns.

We should note that the inconclusiveness of these studies does not prove that no relationship exists. However, it is clear that further research is required to fully understand the role that advertising may play in alcohol consumption among adolescents.

Entertainment. Media entertainment programming, including television, films, videos, books, radio, and recordings, is considered influential in shaping drinking behaviors, particularly among adolescents (Atkin, 1989a, 1989b). This is due to the assertion that alcohol is ubiquitous and taken for granted in the media.

For example, the average child will see alcohol consumed 75,000 times on television before he or she is of legal drinking age, according to one study. Content analyses have documented that 67%–75% of all prime-time television episodes present at least one drinking incident involving characters ordering, pouring, holding, sipping, or talking about alcohol (U.S. Department of Health and Human Services, 1989). In a recent study, Wallack, Breed, and Cruz (1987) reported 10.6 drinks per hour in 1984, continuing a trend that moved upward from 4.8 hourly acts in 1976 to 7.6 in 1978 to 8.7 in 1981. Most of these portrayals are associated with outcomes that are either positive or neutral.

As adolescents are exposed to these frequent media portrayals, it is assumed that the result would be to create social expectations and norms that drinking is expected and appropriate in all situations, thereby increasing both consumption and mistaken beliefs about alcohol and its consequences. However, an examination of the research provides little conclusive evidence that such portrayals actually affect viewers' consumption, hence providing the opportunity for further research.

Education. Although advertising and entertainment would be expected to have a positive relationship with consumption among adolescents, we would expect public education campaigns to have just the opposite effect. However, in the context of health education in particular, there is a growing skepticism within the drug prevention literature about the value of large-scale media campaigns. A number of recent reviews suggest that these campaigns simply are not justified as they have had little or no effect on behavior (Barber, Bradshaw, & Walsh, 1989).

Falco (1988) suggested that some of the reasons why mass media efforts to reduce alcohol use have not succeeded are use of fear-based messages, failure to reach prime-time audiences, infrequency, low exposure, and lack of sophisticated advertising techniques. In addition, she pointed out the ambiguity of using "recovered" celebrities who may be admired because of their success, which included using drugs and being able to overcome any ill effects, while drugs themselves are not necessarily "deglamorized" in the child's perception. Another reason for limited effectiveness of these campaigns is that the assumption implicit in most alcohol education programs is that the way to change an individual's attitudes and behavior is by increasing factual knowledge. However, although the evidence is partially contradictory, the majority of the research suggests that factual drug knowledge is not consistently and significantly correlated with drug attitudes (Kinder, 1975) and much less effective in accomplishing the more important goal of changing behavior (McAlister, 1981).

However, although many campaigns have failed to achieve success in the past, this does not indicate that they cannot be used effectively in the future. Atkin (1981) suggested that through the application of mass communication principles mass media educational campaigns can increase the likelihood of effectiveness.

Approaches to Research

Econometrics/Modeling. Econometric studies have dominated the empirical literature concerned with the effects of advertising on alcohol consumption. However, Kohn and Smart (1984) pointed out that the econometric work has produced a stunning array of conflicting conclusions, including studies showing that advertising has little effect on alcohol consumption and that alcohol advertising modestly increases consumption. For example, Bourgeois and Barnes (1979) found advertising related significantly to per capita consumption for beer, whereas Chirco (1990), using 43 stepwise regression models, found that alcohol use by adolescents is negatively related to media exposure.

In terms of better understanding the effects on adolescents, and more specifically minority adolescents, Smart (1988) noted that a major problem with econometric analysis is the emphasis on aggregate consumption. These types of studies typically examine the correlation of dollars of alcohol advertising with overall alcohol consumption without taking into consideration the different rates of consumption across different groups. Therefore, the effect on adolescents, or for that matter on any target group where there is concern about differential consumption rates and/or media exposure, is obscured in the analysis (Aitken, 1989).

Experimental. Experimental studies also have reported mixed findings. For example, Rychtarik, Fairbank, Allen, Foy, and Drabman (1983) concluded that children aged 8 to 11 who viewed a popular television show with drinking scenes were more likely to name alcohol than water as an appropriate beverage to serve adults, whereas Kotch, Coulter, and Lipsitz (1986), using 43 boys and girls, aged 10–12, found no short-term impact of exposure to a film with alcohol images. In other experimental studies, Kohn et al. found no evidence that either lifestyle or tombstone advertising had any impact on alcohol consumption, whereas Atkin and Block (1983) found that the use of celebrities to endorse alcohol products is highly effective with adolescents, but the impact on older persons was limited.

Smart (1988) noted that none of the experimental studies were ideal methodologically, citing a number of threats to the validity of the results. Therefore, experimental studies do not provide conclusive evidence either way and leave open the door for future research.

Quasi-Experimental. Two quasi-experimental studies reported time-series comparisons between a Canadian province that had banned alcohol advertising and a demographically similar province that had not (Ogborne & Smart, 1980; Smart & Cutler, 1976). Neither study found that banning advertising reduced consumption. However, as noted by Kohn and Smart (1984), both bans were compromised by continued public access to alcohol advertisements in media originating out of the province.

Surveys. Several major correlational surveys provide the most externally valid data on the advertising–consumption relationship. One survey by Strickland (1983) showed a modest positive effect of alcohol advertising exposure on adolescent alcohol consumption. A host of other studies have reached conclusions regarding a positive relationship between advertising and increased consumption (e.g., Atkin & Block 1981, 1984; Atkin, Hocking, & Block 1984; Atkin, Neuendorf, & McDermott 1983; Strickland 1982, 1983).

However, as noted by Kohn and Smart (1984), many of these studies did not convincingly eliminate obvious alternative hypotheses (e.g., selective exposure to alcohol advertising by heavy drinkers). Because survey research only establishes correlations, there are some ambiguities about causal direction (i.e., that perhaps increased drinking produced increased attention paid to advertising rather than vice versa).

Content Analysis. As with the other research approaches, there are mixed findings among content analysis studies. For example, Atkin (1987) showed that lifestyle portrayals are featured along with brand symbolism, as attractive and youthful (but not underage), and characters display enjoyment (but not intoxication). However, Finn and Strickland (1982) concluded there is no reason to believe that underage models are used in advertising to provide peer models for adolescents, and "reliance on anecdotal evidence" has resulted in exaggeration of the amount of "objectionable and controversial" content in the ads. They found little support for the claims that supposedly vulnerable groups, such as minority adolescents, are disproportionately targeted in such advertising.

Qualitative/Discussion Group. All of the above approaches discussed so far tend to focus on quantitative analysis, with the possible exception of content analysis, which is a combination of quantitative and qualitative approaches. Another approach that offers an opportunity to get a more in-depth understanding of the motivation behind adolescents' alcohol consumption behavior and its relationship to advertising is through qualitative techniques such as focus groups and in-depth interviews. Such approaches allow adolescents to use their own words and framework in phrasing the issues rather than approaching the issue from an adult researcher's point of view.

In one such study, Aitken (1989) conducted discussion groups in Scotland with a sample of 150 adolescents aged 14–16. The groups discussed television alcohol commercials and under-age drinking. He concluded there was a positive relationship between advertising and increased consumption. Based on these discussions, television alcohol commercials become increasingly salient and attractive over the years 10–14. Also, drinkers tended to be more adept at recognizing and identifying brand imagery and tended to be more appreciative of alcohol commercials. This study suggests that although other influences such as peer group pressure are probably more important, the effects of advertising on under-age drinking cannot be ignored as they reinforce under-age drinking.

LIMITATIONS OF PAST RESEARCH

There are a number of limitations of the research conducted to date examining alcohol products in the media and the effect on adolescent consumption. Most of these limitations can be grouped into four major areas dealing with effects that researchers have failed to adequately consider.

Interaction Effects

Many studies fail to consider the multiple causes (e.g., price, availability, peer pressure, social influence, habits of parents and friends, curiosity, scholastic abilities, where and with whom adolescents spend spare time, etc.) of alcohol consumption and the interaction of alcohol with these other variables. For example, few researchers claim that the role of alcohol products in the media is the only influence in initiating or establishing drinking patterns among adolescents. However, even when a significant relationship is found, it is important to recognize that advertising effects actually are small compared to the impact of the other variables that in most cases are likely to be more dominant in determining adolescent attitudes toward alcohol (Bruun et al., 1975; Graham, Marks, & Hansen, 1991; Ornstein & Hanssens, 1985; Smart, 1988).

Holder (1988) reinforced this point by noting that advertisements are part of a complex interaction of real-world factors leading to alcohol-related problems that is unlikely to be replicated in a laboratory. Similarly, as emphasized by Hansen (1988), the causes of excessive drinking are always multiple and interactive and that any single-factor model of causation is not only wrong in theory, but in practice will lead to inappropriate responses to the individual, and to imperfect social policies.

Cumulative/Long-Term Effects

Many of the studies fail to consider that some effects of media exposure are cumulative and long term and may not be apparent for months or years. Studies based on short-term viewing of one clip are highly problematic (Hansen 1988; Smart 1988). Merely seeing a single beer commercial (the methodology employed in many studies) is unlikely to cause an adolescent to begin a habit of long-term consumption. However, what is more likely to have an effect is seeing thousands of commercials over time at an age when adolescents are forming their conceptions of society and the association of alcohol products with good times, relaxation, friends, and success (Jacobson et al., 1983).

Unfortunately, there have been few longitudinal studies of a lifetime of exposure to alcohol advertising (Smart, 1988). More research is needed that assesses the impact of thousands of advertisements over decades on the drinking of adolescents.

Contextual Effects

Many of the studies have ignored the contextual emphasis in understanding the media effects on adolescent alcohol consumption, particularly minorities. Braucht (1980) indicated that one cannot separate the person from the environment in the interaction process; therefore, the unit of analysis should be the person–environment. By ignoring this, the "decontextualized and 'clinical' nature" of many studies do not recreate real-life situations (Smart, 1988).

By isolating advertising or program content from one another, or from the influence of other social and cultural contexts in which they take place, many studies fail to show that the effects found may be generalized beyond the social vacuum of the research laboratory to the larger social context. Because the portrayal of alcohol and drinking in the media does not reach adolescents as a series of disjointed, or decontextualized images, but rather as integral parts of narratives and symbolic message structures, it is unlikely that alcohol portrayal out of context has much meaning (Hansen, 1988).

At an individual level, Hansen (1988) stressed that much of the research does not allow sufficiently for the active, interpretive process that goes on in the meeting between viewer and message. In terms of adolescent implications, he also pointed out that the research insufficiently accounts for the fact that media messages may be inflected through factors such as age that may be more important. Therefore, there is a need for more qualitative/in-depth interviewing type studies where adolescents can negotiate, select, interpret, and use what they see and make sense out of it. Such approaches would allow researchers to gain greater insight into, not so much influences of the message on the viewer, but the social context in which the messages are interpreted and used in making sense of the social environment.

Alternative Explanations and Theories

Many of the studies have failed to give enough attention to investigating alternative explanations (e.g., social, cultural, environmental factors) and alternative theories. For example, Kohn and Smart (1984) observed that previous studies in many instances did not convincingly eliminate obvious alternatives to the hypothesis that advertising affects consumption and did not rule out all possible effects of advertising (e.g., studies by Atkin & Block, 1979, and Kohn, Smart, & Ogborne, 1984).

One theory that offers an alternative explanation of advertising effects but that has been largely ignored is commodity theory (Brock,

1968). For example, in applying the theory to informational commodities such as persuasive messages, it has been suggested that a commodity should be perceived as less available, and hence more valuable when there are greater efforts involved to withhold or supply it and when there are greater restrictions on the possession of the commodity. In marketing this is often referred to as the "mystique factor," as when demand for a product might be higher in geographic regions where it is not available than at a later time when the marketer makes it available. Similarly, attempts to restrict adolescents from information about sex, or the expressing of strong concerns by parents and others about certain music or reading material, actually has had an opposite than intended effect. The degree to which commodity theory holds true regarding media messages received by adolescents about alcohol could be investigated as an alternative to current paradigms, such as the one suggested in Fig. 25.2.

DIRECTION FOR FUTURE RESEARCH AND CONCLUSION

Given these aforementioned limitations of past research, it is recommended that future research focus on better designs and procedures that are most likely to provide better answers to questions about adolescents, particularly minorities, alcohol consumption, and media effects. It seems that studies that emphasize the following areas would be most useful in achieving this aim:

1. interaction of media with the host of other factors that are likely to affect consumption;
2. cumulative, long-term effects of several years of media exposure, especially beginning with adolescents in the years when they are starting to drink;
3. the person–environment context, including the media environment and individual interpretive meaning of messages in making sense of the social environment; and
4. alternative explanations and theories.

Obviously more and better research is needed before we have a full and proper understanding of the relationships between media representations of alcohol and the impact on adolescents, both minority and nonminorities. Hopefully, this chapter has provided some guidelines that should prove useful to researchers in taking further steps down this path.

REFERENCES

Aitken, P. P. (1989). Television alcohol commercials and under-age drinking. *International Journal of Advertising, 8,* 133–150.
Anderson, P. (1991, June 20). Billions spent on illegal drugs. *Centre Daily Times,* p. 2A.
American Medical Association. (1990). *Healthy youth 2000: National health promotion and disease prevention objectives for adolescents.* Chicago, IL: Author.
Atkin, C. K. (1981). Mass media information campaign effectiveness. In R. E. Rice & W. J. Paisley (Eds.), *Public communication campaigns* (pp. 265–280). Beverly Hills, CA: Sage.
Atkin, C. K. (1987). Alcoholic-beverage advertising: Its content and impact. In H. D. Holder (Ed.), *Control issues in alcohol abuse prevention: Strategies for states and communities* (pp. 267–287). Greenwich, CT: JAI.
Atkin, C. K. (1988). *A critical review of media effects on alcohol consumption patterns.* Report prepared for the Alcoholic Beverage Medical Research Foundation, Baltimore, MD.
Atkin, C. K. (1989a). Television socialization and risky driving by teenagers. *Alcohol, Drugs, and Driving, 5*(1), 1–11.
Atkin, C. K. (1989b). Effects of television alcohol messages on teenage drinking patterns. *Journal of Adolescent Health Care, 9*(2), 121–134.
Atkin, C., & Block, M. (1979). *Content and effects of alcohol advertising* (Report 1: Overview and summary of project). Unpublished manuscript, Michigan State University, East Lansing.
Atkin, C. K., & Block, M. (1981). *Content and effects of alcohol advertising* (prepared for the Bureau of Alcohol, Tobacco, and Firearms, Pub. No. PB82-123142). Springfield, VA: National Technical Information Service.
Atkin, C., & Block, M. (1983). Effectiveness of celebrity endorser. *Journal of Advertising Research, 23,* 57–62.
Atkin, C. K., & Block, M. (1984). The effects of alcohol advertising. In T. C. Kinnear (Ed.), *Advances in consumer research,* (Vol. 11, pp. 688–693). Provo, UT: Association for Consumer Research.
Atkin, C. K., Hocking, J., & Block, M. (1984). Teenage drinking. Does advertising make a difference? *Journal of Communication, 34,* 157–167.
Atkin, C., Neuendorf, K., & McDermott, S. (1983). The role of alcohol advertising in excessive and hazardous drinking. *Journal of Drug Education, 13,* 313–325.
Bachman, J. G., Johnston, L. D., & O'Malley, P. M. (1987). *Monitoring the future: Questionnaire responses from the nation's high school seniors, 1986.* Ann Arbor, MI: Institute for Social Research.
Bachman, J. G., Wallace, J. M., Jr., Kurth, C. L., Johnston, L. D., & O'Malley, P. M. (1991). *Drug use among Black, White, Hispanic, Native American, and Asian-American high school seniors (1976–1989): Prevalence, trends, and correlates.* Ann Arbor, MI: Institute for Social Research, The University of Michigan.
Bachman, J. G., Wallace, J. M., O'Malley, P. M., Johnston, L. D., Kurth, C. L., & Neighbors, H. W. (1991). Racial/ethnic differences in smoking, drinking, and illicit drug use among American high school seniors, 1976–89. *American Journal of Public Health, 81,* 372–377.
Barber, J. G., Bradshaw, R., & Walsh, C. (1989). Reducing alcohol consumption through television advertising. *Journal of Consulting and Clinical Psychology, 57*(5), 613–618.
Bourgeois, J. C., & Barnes, J. G. (1979). Does advertising increase alcohol consumption? *Journal of Advertising Research, 19,* 19–30.

Braucht, G. N. (1980). Psychological research on teenage drinking: Past and future. In F. R. Scarpitti & D. K. Datesman (Eds.), *Drugs and the youth culture* (pp. 190–143). Beverly Hills, CA: Sage.

Brock, T. C. (1968). Implications of commodity theory for value change. In A. G. Greenwald, T. C. Brock, & T. M. Ostrom (Eds.), *Psychological foundations of attitudes* (pp. 243–275). New York: Academic Press.

Bruun, K., Edwards, G., Lumio, M., Makela, K., Pan, L., Popham, R. E., Room, R., Schmidt, W., Skog, O. J., Sulkunen, P., & Osterberg, E. (1975). *Alcohol control policies in public health perspective* (Vol. 25). Helsinki: Finnish Foundation for Alcohol Studies.

Carnegie Corporation. (1989). *Turning points: Preparing American youth for the 21st century*. New York: Carnegie Council on Adolescent Development.

Chirco, A. P. (1990). *An examination of stepwise regression models of adolescent alcohol and marijuana use with special attention to the television exposure–teen drinking issue*. Unpublished doctoral dissertation, Syracuse University, Syracuse, NY.

Comstock, G., Chaffee, S., Katzman, N., McCombs, M., & Roberts, D. (1978). *Television and human behavior*. New York: Columbia University Press.

Falco, M. (1988). *Preventing abuse of drugs, alcohol, and tobacco by adolescents*. Paper commissioned for the Carnegie Council on Adolescent Development, Washington, DC.

Finn, T. A., & Strickland, D. (1982). A content analysis of beverage alcohol advertising, #2. Television advertising. *Journal of Studies on Alcohol, 43*, 964–989.

Graham, J. W., Marks, G., & Hansen, W. G. (1991). Social influence processes affecting adolescent substance use. *Journal of Applied Psychology, 76*, 291–298.

Hacker, G. A., Collins, R., & Jacobson, M. (1989). *Marketing booze to Blacks*. Washington, DC: Center for Science in the Public Interest.

Hansen, A. (1988). The contents and effects of television images of alcohol: Towards a framework of analysis. *Contemporary Drug Problems, 15*, 249–279.

Holder, H. D. (1988, Spring). A review of research opportunities and issues in the regulation of alcohol availability. *Contemporary Drug Problems*, 47–66.

Jacobson, M. F., Atkins, R., & Hacker, G. (1983). Booze merchants cheer on teenage drinking: The marketing of alcohol is increasingly focusing on youth. *Business and Society Review, 46*, 46–51.

Johnston, L. D., O'Malley, P. M., & Bachman, J. G. (1988). *Illicit drug use, smoking and drinking by America's high school students, college students, and young adults: 1975–1987* (DHHS Publication No. [ADM] 89-1602). Washington, DC: U.S. Government Printing Office.

Kandel, D. B. (1985). Effects of drug use from adolescence to young adulthood on participation in family and work roles. In R. Jessor (Chair), *Longitudinal Research on Substance Use in Adolescence*. Symposium conducted at the meeting of the International Society for the Study of Behavioral Development, Tours, France.

Kinder, B. N. (1975). Attitudes toward alcohol and drug abuse II: Experimental data, mass media research, and methodological considerations. *International Journal of the Addictions, 10*, 1035–1054.

Kohn, P. M., & Smart, R. G. (1984). The impact of television advertising on alcohol consumption: An experiment. *Journal of Studies on Alcohol, 45*(4), 295–301.

Kohn, P. M., Smart, R. G., & Ogborne, A. C. (1984). Effects of two kinds of alcohol advertising on subsequent consumption. *Journal of Advertising, 13*, 34–40.

Kotch, J. B., Coulter, M. L., & Lipsitz, H. (1986). Does televised drinking influence children's attitudes toward alcohol? *Addictive Behaviors, 11*(1), 67–70.

Linn, M. C., De Benedictis, T., & Delucchi, K. (1982). Adolescent reasoning about advertisements: Preliminary investigations. *Child Development, 53*, 1599–1613.

McAlister, A. (1981). Antismoking campaigns: Progress in developing effective communications. In R. E. Rice & W. J. Paisley (Eds.), *Public communication campaigns* (pp. 265–280). Beverly Hills: Sage.

McMahon, E. T., & Taylor, P. A. (1990). *Citizens' action handbook on alcohol and tobacco billboard advertising.* Washington, DC: Center for Science in the Public Interest.

Moore, R. L., & Moschis, G. P. (1979). *The role of advertising in adolescent consumer learning* (ERIC Document Reproduction Service No. ED 173793). Washington, DC: U.S. Department of Education.

Ogborne, A. C., & Smart, R. G. (1980). Will restrictions on alcohol advertising reduce alcohol consumption? *British Journal of Addiction, 75,* 293–296.

Ornstein, S. I., & Hanssens, D. M. (1985). Alcohol control laws and the consumption of distilled spirits and beer. *Journal of Consumer Research, 12,* 200–213.

Partanen, J. (1988). Communicating about alcohol in the mass media. *Contemporary Drug Problems, 15*(2), 281–309.

Postman, N., Mystrom, C., Strate, L., & Weingartner, C. (1987). *Myths, men and beer: An analysis of beer commercials on broadcast television.* Falls Church, VA: American Automobile Association.

Rychtarik, R. G., Fairbank, J. A., Allen, C. M., Foy, D. W., & Drabman, R. S. (1983). Alcohol use in television programming: Effects on children's behavior. *Addictive Behaviors, 8,* 19–22.

Scenic America. (1989). *Billboards in Baltimore: A blight on beauty and a scourge on health in our city.* Washington, DC: Author.

Schooler, C., & Basil, M. D. (1989). *Alcohol and cigarette advertising on billboards: Targeting with social cues.* Paper presented at International Communication Association Conference, Dublin, Ireland.

Smart, R. G. (1988). Does alcohol advertising affect overall consumption? A review of empirical studies. *Journal of Studies on Alcohol, 49,* 314–323.

Smart, R. G., & Cutler, R. E. (1976). The alcohol advertising ban in British Columbia: Problems and effects on beverage consumption. *British Journal of Addiction, 71,* 13–21.

Stout, H. (1991, November 5). Surgeon general wants to age alcohol ads. *Wall Street Journal,* p. B1.

Strickland, D. E. (1982). Alcohol advertising: Orientations and influence. *International Journal of Advertising, 1,* 307–319.

Strickland, D. E. (1983). Advertising exposure, alcohol consumption and misuse of alcohol. In M. Grant, M. Plant, & A. Williams (Ed.), *Economics and alcohol: Consumption and controls* (pp. 201–222). New York: Gardner Press.

U.S. Department of Health and Human Services. (1989). *Surgeon general's workshop on drunk driving: Background papers* (December 14–16, 1988). Washington, DC: Author.

Wackman, D. B., Reale, G., & Ward, S. (1972). Racial differences in responses to advertising among adolescents. In E. A. Rubenstien, G. A. Comstock, & J. P. Murray (Eds.), *Television and social behavior, Vol. 4. Television in day-to-day life: Patterns of use* (pp. 543–553). Washington, DC: U.S. Government Printing Office.

Wallack, L. Breed, W., & Cruz, J. (1987). Alcohol on prime-time television. *Journal of Studies on Alcohol, 48,* 33–38.

Welte, J. W., & Barnes, G. W. (1985). Alcohol: The gateway to other drug use among secondary-school students. *Journal of Youth and Adolescence, 14,* 487–498.

VI | Research, Policy, and Programs: Toward an Integrated Approach

Section Editors:

Bea Mandel
Wayne Schutjer
The Pennsylvania State University

Research, Policy, and Programs: What Works in Today's Society

Bea Mandel
Wayne Schutjer
The Pennsylvania State University

Issues and challenges of early adolescence have been placed high on this nation's agenda and are becoming more evident as worldwide concerns. Increased attention to the problems of homelessness, malnutrition, drug abuse, violent crime, teenage pregnancy, and families that are disrupted by war, marital discord, or severe poverty have become almost commonplace. All of these concerns point to a national, if not worldwide, need for using knowledge gained through research and practice to make a significant impact on our most vital resource—the next generation.

Carnegie Corporation's Council on Adolescent Development (1989) identified "the need to clarify facts [to] provide a needed synthesis of knowledge that cuts across disciplinary and professional boundaries" (p. 2). The synthesis is needed as the basis for developing more informed approaches to program development, for stimulating creative and effective youth policies at all levels of government, and for enhancing the understanding of practitioners and the public about the youth development process.

The focus of this volume on young adolescents, ages 10 to 15, emphasizes a particularly critical stage in the development of youth, because this age period is one of increased vulnerability, potential risk, and special opportunities. Thus, early adolescents are a prime group to benefit from political processes that direct experience, knowledge, and research bases toward the implementation of constructive programs and policies serving the greatest numbers of young people as they face the challenge of this period and gradually find their way to adulthood.

How to bring knowledge to bear on policy decisions is not a new issue. As Amitai Etzioni noted, Plato reflected upon the question and concluded that the solution was to unify in one person both analysis and policymaking by crowning a philosopher king (Majchrzak, 1984). Today's solutions to the problem tend toward the use of consultants, the development of "think tanks" such as the Brookings Institution and the Heritage Foundation, and the development of program and policy analysis capacities within government agencies, legislative bodies, and worldwide youth-serving organizations such as scouting and 4-H programs.

Within the array of entities seeking to influence policy and program decisions, how can the research and analysis of university-based researchers most effectively impact the process? More specifically, how can the results of research on the complex forces shaping adolescent behavior—identified in this volume and in the Carnegie-supported volume edited by Feldman and Elliott (1990)—become important components of public policy?

In the introductory chapter to this volume, Lerner noted the critical importance of both creating academic legitimacy for policy analysis and the acceptance of a multidisciplinary paradigm as central to scholarly participation in public policy formulation and evaluation. In this section, we focus more broadly on the role of academic research in the policy and program process and seek to demonstrate by description and example that the integration of research, policy, and intervention can result in more positive outcomes and can contribute to enhancing the well-being of young people through building self-esteem, increasing successful experiences, and breaking the cycle of failure and disadvantage. The chapters in this section provide only a beginning discussion of "What Works in Today's Society," utilizing some of the recent research findings and knowledge about early adolescence as the basis for policies and programs to benefit youth within their diverse contexts—family, community, and society in general. More is yet to be done and analyzed.

At the most basic level, the relationship between the policy analyst and the policy program process is governed by the philosophy of policy formulation held by the participants. As Reich (1990) noted:

> Beneath the daily activities of elected officials, administrators, and their advisers and critics, and beneath the public's tacit decision to accord legitimacy to specific policy decisions, exist a set of first principles that suggest what good policymaking is all about. They comprise a view of human nature, of how people behave as citizens. They also reflect a view of social improvement, of why we think that society is better in one state

than another. And they offer a view of the appropriate role of government in society—given human nature, our aspirations for social improvement, and our means of defining and solving public problems. (p. 1)

Instrumentally, *policy research* is defined as the conduct of research or analysis of a fundamental social problem that is designed to provide decision makers with pragmatic, action-oriented recommendations for alleviating the problem (Majchrzak, 1984). This definition is clearly most consistent with a policy philosophy that defines the public interest as a mathematical aggregation of the individual preferences of a self-interest seeking public. Within this view, the central responsibility of program formulators and of policy analysts who serve them is to determine the extent of need for public intervention and to select the policy action that maximizes the welfare of the average citizen (Reich, 1990). This approach to policy emphasizes the optimal allocation of scarce program resources toward competing ends. To achieve an optimal allocation, those responsible for the development of policy must specify an objective, define alternative strategies for meeting the objective, and evaluate the costs and benefits of each alternative. This process, in turn, provides the basis for a decision that maximizes the net benefits to the group being served (Majone, 1990).

A broader, less restrictive view of policymaking places a higher value on the need for the policy process to include consideration of what "is good for society" in developing the public agenda. Within this context, it is not satisfactory for public policy decisions to be based exclusively on a quantitative determination of what people want for themselves and on an analysis of the most efficient path to that end. Rather, it is the responsibility of the policy process to provide alternative visions of what is both good and possible, to stimulate deliberation about options and their underlying value structure and in this way "to broaden the range of potential responses and deepen society's understanding of itself" (Reich, 1990, p. 4). The central task for policy researchers in support of this broader philosophy of policy formulation is to provide data and analysis that contribute to the quality of public discourse (Majone, 1990).

Both models of policy analysis and formulation have relevance for current youth development program needs. Society is clear in its interest and commitment to reducing levels of teen suicide, drug abuse, high school dropout rates, teen pregnancy, and other social problems associated with youth. The development of youth policy within this context requires the analysis of the potential of alternative programs to accomplish the goals regarding teenage problems, so as to maximize both the impact of programs and minimize the amount of resources devoted to meeting the goals. At the same time, the current youth program structure and overall level of resource commitment to youth programs reflects societal judgments regarding legitimate approaches to youth problems and about appropriate levels of resource commitment. Both the definition of acceptable approaches and the level of resource commitment that should be devoted to youth programs are issues that must be continuously reviewed. Research on problems of youth that is properly formulated and introduced into the policy process can greatly enhance the quality of public debate on both issues.

At a working level, it is important for scholars of the youth development process to note that alternative policy formulations reflect the perspective of decision makers that "using policy research" can be a much broader notion than applying the results of analysis to a specific problem (Weiss, 1980). Enlightened policymakers see research as having multiple functions including support for a particular political agenda and the generation of awareness of needs and problems.

Similarly, not all research is viewed as being of equal value by policymakers. Decision makers at all levels are exposed to numerous research reports, lobbying efforts, and in-house studies. In coping with this deluge of data and information, policymakers must decide which studies are to be used. In making that decision, the first concern is the relevance of the study, that is, the match between the topic of the research and the individual's responsibility (Weiss & Bucuvalas, 1980). According to Weiss and Bucuvalas, research that meets the "relevance criteria" is subjected to a "truth test" (Is the research trustworthy?) and a "utility test" (Does the research provide direction?). In evaluating the scientific integrity of the analysis, Weiss and Bucuvalas suggested that policymakers rely not only on their evaluation of the scientific approach but the conformity of the findings to their expectations (i.e., Do the results seem reasonable?). Similarly, Weiss and Bucuvalas found that for research to be judged to have utility, it must provide the basis for action. The research must show how to introduce feasible change or it must offer information to challenge the conventional wisdom or status quo.

For university-based researchers, the relationship between the research methodology and the acceptance of results by the policy process is of equal importance. Studies of the methodology–result acceptance relationship suggest that policymakers appreciate the complexity of the real world in which policy must operate (i.e., the environment for social policy). And as a result, policymakers are more receptive to analyses that reflect the complexity of the real world through the use of methods that include qualitative dimensions and do not rely exclusively on assumption-laden quantitative models that define away the qualitative dimensions of the problem (Oman & Chitwood, 1984).

For many academic researchers, active participation in the policy process from a disciplinary perspective is a new professional arena. Researchers accustomed to academic debate of concepts, data, and assumptions may feel less at home in discussions when the quality of the scholarship is assumed and emphasis is placed on generalizing the results to the particular issue being discussed. Scholars seeking to be effective in the policy arena need to accept that research results are not politically neutral. Results impact on the political agendas of the participants, and in any policy discussion it is likely that numerous political agenda are represented. Schon (1983) argued that professionals, whether economists, engineers, biologists, or educators, can increase their effectiveness by operating as reflective practitioners. Reflective practitioners are professional experts who consciously reflect on what they are doing and are willing to change their view and input in light of the particular cultural, interpersonal, political, and social circumstances surrounding a given problem situation. This reflection-in-action allows the professional practitioner to learn from other participants involved in sorting out the issue, to incorporate the knowledge of others into their discussion and analysis of the situation, and to adapt this discussion and activities on the spot to more responsively address the issues at hand. Alter (1987) provided an application of Schon's (1983) principles to the role of academics as public policy educators.

Social psychologist, Lisbeth Schorr (1988), in her book, *Within Our Reach: Breaking the Cycle of Disadvantage,* presents the conviction that social policy can significantly strengthen or weaken a family's ability to instill appropriate values within its children. Further, in an age of economic uncertainty, working mothers, protective services, foster care, high teenage unemployment, and ubiquitous street drugs, the need for rallying resources, skills, and commitment to the world's adolescents becomes even more critical.

It has also been acknowledged, in a recent report on adolescent health conducted by the National Adolescent Health Resource Center, that "problem behaviors of youth are often symptoms of other problems or strains in the community" (Blum, Resnick, Harris, & Bennett, 1990, p. 10). Therefore, it becomes even more important to develop a broader understanding of how the social system overall impacts adolescents as, to a certain extent, these influences can be redressed through education, social programs, other types of programs and, particularly, through changes in policy—at a local, state, and national level.

The perspectives and programs presented in the following chapters represent approaches to supporting the premise that we must apply what we have learned in integrative and innovative ways in order to change the futures of our vulnerable youth.

In chapter 26, Ruby Takanishi provides an agenda for researchers and child development professionals to more effectively link research and policy. Takanishi points out that success in achieving a national policy agenda is dependent on steady work over a period of time, acknowledgment of early adolescence as a vital period within the life span, and that public support and agreement must be garnered in order to move forward in a manner that will address a broad-based spectrum of issues confronting the youngsters of the 1990s.

Takanishi calls for a model that is "fluidly bidirectional" regarding knowledge to practice connections and the integration of key institutions and systems in an adolescent's ecology. These include family, schools, communities, and the health-care system. Finally, she calls for much more work to be done to articulate a specific policy agenda and a total commitment to linking research with policy for early adolescence.

In chapter 27, Patricia Best reviews the use of research and policy analysis within a formal school system. In her case study, Best describes the process undertaken by a local community in which the issues of change became a focus for developing professional growth for educators, broadening understanding for community members, parents, and administrators and increasing the appreciation of the complexity and magnitude of integrating policy with research and programs.

Although the perspective represented in this chapter by Best may be seen as unique to the geographic area (i.e., resources, public support, access to a university, and an above average student body), the experiential lessons to be learned are generalizable to school districts nationwide, whether or not in university situated environs. Specifically, Best points to the fact that researchers must become better acquainted with life as it is lived in classrooms; that there are specified criteria for implementing innovation in a school (any school); and that there are steps involved in planning school improvement which, in order to be effective, require adaptation to the local school district. Best also points to the political, economic, and social forces that affect any community in today's climate of budget cutbacks, taxpayer unrest, educational uncertainties, and changing social climate for youngsters and their families.

In the last chapter, Alan Snider and Jeff Miller focus on 4-H programs as an example of a nonformal youth program based on the interaction of youth with volunteers. The increasing impact and importance of nonformal education has not only far-reaching implications for participating youth, but also for youth workers and teachers on many different levels.

The demands for innovative and creative approaches to the needs of young adolescents is a growing trend, perhaps best exemplified by 4-H in the past. Today, 4-H reflects the increasing similarities of issues prevalent among inner-city urban, suburban, and rural youth and the need to incorporate research into programs to ensure ongoing effectiveness. Additionally, it becomes apparent that in order to provide more meaningful programs for young adolescents, sufficient training of youth workers, adult volunteers, and teachers is a critical contributor to their success. Looking toward the future is a challenge and, as presented by Snider and Miller, one worthy of the best resources research and practice have to offer.

These chapters further clarify the overall challenge presented to policymakers, researchers, and interventionists and to those who care about the future generation.

REFERENCES

Alter, T. R. (1987). Increasing our effectiveness as public policy educators. *Increasing understanding of public problems and policies.* Oak Brook, IL: The Farm Foundation.

Blum, R. W., Resnick, M. D., Harris, L., & Bennett, S. (1990). *Conducting an adolescent health survey.* Minneapolis: National Adolescent Health Resource Center, Adolescent Health Programs, University of Minnesota.

Carnegie Council on Adolescent Development. (1989, June). *Turning points: Preparing American youth for the 21st century* (The Report of the Task Force on Education of Youth Adolescents). Washington, DC: Author.

Carnegie Council on Adolescent Development. (1989, April). A pamphlet on the program of Carnegie Corporation of New York. Washington, DC.

Feldman, S. S., & Elliott, G. R. (Eds.). (1990). *At the threshold: The developing adolescent.* Cambridge, MA: Howard University Press.

Majchrzak, A. (1984). *Methods for policy research.* Newbury Park, CA: Sage.

Majone, G. (1990). Policy analysis and public deliberation. In R. B. Reich (Ed.), *The power of public ideas* (pp. 157–178). Cambridge, MA: Howard University Press.

Oman, R. C., & Chitwood, S. R. (1984). Management evaluation studies: Factors affecting the acceptance of recommendations. *Evaluation Review, 8*(3), 283–305.

Reich, R. B. (Ed.). (1990). *The power of public ideas.* Cambridge, MA: Howard University Press.

Schon, D. A. (1983). *The reflective practitioner: How professionals think in action.* New York: Basic Books.

Schorr, L. (1988). *Within our reach: Breaking the cycle of disadvantage.* Garden City, NY: Doubleday.

Weiss, C. H. (1980). Knowledge creep and decision accretion. In C. H. Weiss (Ed.), *Knowledge: Creation, diffusion, utilization* (pp. 697–705). Newbury Park, CA: Sage.

Weiss, C. H., & Bucuvalas, M. J. (1980). Truth tests and utility tests: Decision makers' frames of reference for social science research. *American Sociological Review, 45*(2), 302–313.

26 An Agenda for the Integration of Research and Policy During Early Adolescence

Ruby Takanishi
Carnegie Council on Adolescent Development

In policy discussions, early adolescence is a developmental phase caught between early childhood and late adolescence. Since the 1970s, the critical importance of the early childhood years, including the prenatal period, has risen steadily on the public policy agenda (U.S. General Accounting Office, 1990). The youth policy agenda is still dominated by late adolescence, specifically concerns about transition from school into the workplace. Thus, debates rage over national educational standards and examinations, vocational education, and job training and employment programs. Early adolescence, although gaining some visibility because of the realization that adolescent problems occur at earlier ages (Carnegie Council on Adolescent Development, 1989), is still in the foreground in discussions about policy development for children and youth.

As an observer of efforts since the 1970s to place early childhood education and child care higher on the national agenda, I believe we must take a long-term view regarding policy development and young adolescents. Considerable time is needed for any developmental period to gain ascendance on the policy agenda; most importantly, steady work leads to concrete results.

As a necessary, but not sufficient prerequisite, a pervasive consensus that early adolescence is a special and critical period within the life span that merits public support must enter the realm of "public ideas" (Reich, 1988). This widespread public acceptance has been accomplished for the early childhood years, although the actual allocation of funds to the period remains problematic.

Within the early adolescence research field, cogent arguments attest to the criticality of this period of life for healthy and productive adulthood (B. Hamburg, 1974; D. Hamburg, 1989; Susman, Koch, Maney, and Finkelstein, chapter 14, this volume). Even for those adolescents who have no previous history of problems, the early adolescent years (ages 10–15) are crucially formative in terms of increased vulnerability, potential risk, and special opportunities. Young adolescents experience biological, cognitive, and psychological changes that contribute to a reappraisal of themselves and their relationships to their families and communities (Feldman & Elliott, 1990). These changes are often accompanied by disengagement from school; the onset of experimentation with alcohol, tobacco, and other drugs; and unprotected sexual activity. The loss of human potential is reflected in school dropouts, injuries, homicides, suicides, unwanted or unplanned pregnancies, substance abuse, and depression.

A wider, more public knowledge and acceptance of these ideas, and a strong case made for widespread attention to this developmental phase are required. Once the case is made, what naturally follows are the specific strategies by which we can prevent future adolescent problems and create conditions for healthy development, making early adolescence the crucial link between the early childhood years and late adolescence.

CREATING CONNECTIONS BETWEEN RESEARCH AND POLICY

The connections between research and policy can be roughly divided into two realms: science policy or research opportunities and youth support policy. Although these two policy areas are interlinked, increasingly so in the formation of research agendas in the future (see later), for purposes of this discussion they are presented separately.

Science Policy. The status of a research field and the identification of research opportunities occurs internally in the scientific community (Dornbusch, Petersen, & Hetherington, 1991) and externally in response to societal concerns and priorities that drive research funding (Langenberg, 1991; Office of Technology Assessment, 1991a). The Carnegie Council on Adolescent Development, among other entities, conducts inquiries into the state of knowledge and identifies research opportunities during adolescence with a focus on the early adolescence period (Feldman & Elliott, 1990).

What is clear from these research syntheses (Feldman & Elliott, 1990; Millstein, Petersen, & Nightingale, in press) are a number of themes that reverberate in this volume. The gap between the conduct of basic and applied research in adolescent development remains wide. Equally wide is the gap between what is known from research and what is used in actual practice with adolescents. A few examples have emerged in the work of the Council: the research on peer group relations (Brown, 1990; Savin-Williams, & Berndt, 1990) and peer-mediated interventions are not well connected; research on parent–adolescent relations and approaches to support families as their children become adolescents are not adequately integrated (Small, 1990); research on perception and assessment of risk among adolescents and preventive intervention programs to reduce risk of problem behaviors, particularly injury prevention, remain isolated from each other (Beyth-Marom, Fischhoff, Jacobs, & Furby, 1989; Furby & Beyth-Marom, 1990).

This listing does not exhaust the rich opportunities to conduct fundamental research that integrates basic and applied strands of scientific activity (Lerner, chapter 1, this volume), but present barriers to such connections continue and must be directly addressed. What must be challenged is unidirectional thinking that we must proceed from knowledge to practice; what is needed is a model that is fluidly bidirectional regarding knowledge-to-practice connections.

A very troubling gap is the paucity of research on the diverse racial and ethnic backgrounds that characterize the adolescent population in the United States (Spencer & Dornbusch, 1990). Studies repeatedly neglect to represent adequately the diversity of adolescents, their families, their community contexts, and economic circumstances (Feldman & Elliott, 1990). The flip side of this lack of scientific knowledge about diversity is that we lack an understanding of what might be the universally shared aspects of the adolescent experience, which has significant implications for generic approaches to prevention (D. Hamburg, 1992). The rapidly changing demography of the adolescent population, particularly in racial and ethnic backgrounds (Fuchs, 1990), is likely to generate more studies looking at commonalities and differences among adolescents of color (see, e.g., Bachman, Wallace, Kurth, Johnston, & O'Malley, 1990).

Federal support for research on adolescence is still relatively small (Langenberg, 1991; Office of Technology Assessment, 1991a), but is likely to grow as a result of efforts of the Council on Adolescent Development and other entities to identify specific opportunities for increasing our understanding of development during the second decade linked to national priorities. New initiatives that span three federal research and health agencies, the National Institute of Child Health and Human Development, the National Center for Nursing Research, and the National Institute of Mental Health, to support exploratory centers in adolescent health promotion are promising.

The entire research enterprise in the United States is ripe for restructuring (Langenberg, 1991; Office of Technology Assessment, 1991a). Congress no longer views science as "the endless frontier" with no limits to its share of federal expenditures. The competition within the various sciences for funds is real. Priorities must be set, and it is unclear who will be involved. Integral to that review will be researchers who can identify priorities for publicly supported research that are consonant with broad national goals that transcend traditional disciplinary and professional boundaries. In the field of adolescent development, such priority setting has been rare (see Feldman & Elliott, 1990) because of the reluctance, if not opposition of the research community, to find alternatives to the free enterprise model of setting research agendas. In practice, priority setting has always occurred within the public and private agencies and has driven research in specific directions.

One of the challenges, then, facing the research community in adolescence specifically and the research community in general, is the role it will play in the setting and justification of research priorities, particularly in the competition for public and private research support with other research fields. Such priorities will undoubtedly be tied to national goals and needs such as international competitiveness (Langenberg, 1991; Office of Technology Assessment, 1991a).

Youth Support Policy. A comprehensive youth support policy must involve the key institutions in an adolescent's ecology: families, schools, community organizations, and the health-care system. The integration of these institutions and systems remain a singular challenge for the future.

Family Support Policy. The vast majority of discussions on family policies in the United States is exclusively focused on families with young children. Very few have considered what forms policies regarding families with adolescents might take (Family Resource Coalition, 1990; Small, 1990). One reason may be that, consistent with traditional theories of adolescent development (Apter, 1990; Steinberg, 1990), parents and families tend to see adolescence as a time of disengagement from their children. Certainly, the low levels of parental involvement in the education of their adolescents (Dornbusch & Ritter, 1988), and in other realms of activity (Coles, 1989), attest to this detachment on the part of parents of adolescents for a variety of reasons.

Significantly, however, in surveys, informal and formal using a variety of methods, adolescents express a very strong desire to have more contact and guidance from their parents, even though they acknowledge that present levels of interaction are unsatisfactorily low (Coles, 1989).

The integration of research with preventive strategies and policies concerning families presents great opportunities. A number of specific policies regarding parents and families of adolescents have been articulated and should be seriously considered:

- Preventive intervention programs for parents and families, particularly as their children become adolescents are needed. The transition into adolescence for both parents and children is a crucial time for intervention and anticipatory guidance (Hill & Holmbeck, 1986). Yet the numbers of efforts in family support during adolescence (Family Resource Coalition, 1990) are scattered and relatively little is known about their scope and effectiveness (Small, 1990). Approaches that are widespread among parents of young children (e.g., parent support groups and networks), may also be desirable for and adapted to the early adolescent period (Louv, 1990).
- Parental leave and flextime should be extended to parents of adolescents to enable them to be involved in schools, as volunteers in youth organizations, and to spend more time than they now do with their adolescents. These leave policies are now limited to parents of young children and to those with elderly parents, and a case needs to be made for including parents of young adolescents.
- The child-care tax credit should be extended to the early adolescent period so that families will benefit from placing their young adolescents in high quality after-school programs.

Education of Young Adolescents. Although much of past education reform efforts have focused on early education and the senior high schools, more recent efforts have turned to the education of young adolescents in junior high, intermediate, and middle schools (Carnegie Council on Adolescent Development, 1989). These efforts are relatively new and are currently being assessed.

There are major needs in a number of areas that research could contribute to and where the connection between research and practice could be strengthened:

- The development of curricula in a number of subject areas for young adolescents that is based on knowledge of the cognitive

capacities (Keating, 1990) of young adolescents is urgently needed. Developmentally appropriate curricula with a strong content base are lacking, partially because the middle grade years have not typically been considered as a time of strong academic focus (Carnegie Council on Adolescent Development, 1989).
- The preparation and education of teachers for young adolescents remains at a very rudimentary stage. The National Board for Professional Teaching Standards is focusing on the voluntary certification of teachers of young adolescents in selected subject areas. Although teacher preparation and certification are beginning to be addressed, no state has requirements for teachers of young adolescents in the same way such requirements exist for elementary and secondary education.
- Research on the characteristics of effective school environments for young adolescents and their outcomes remain at an early stage (Petersen & Epstein, 1991). Most research has focused on elementary and secondary schools (Entwisle, 1990).
- Effective ways to engage parents in the education of young adolescents are in a gestational phase. Although there are promising efforts to involve young adolescents and their families in schools and supporting education, such efforts are in an experimental phase and are not widespread (Small, 1990).
- Innovative ways in which schools can provide before- and after-school programs linking education, health, and youth service, in some cases with the cooperation of community-based organizations, should be carefully examined. Many of these programs can be involved in youth community service as part of their approaches (see, e.g., Rural Clearinghouse for Lifelong Education and Development, 1991) in which young adolescents experience a genuine, meaningful contribution to addressing community needs as part of their after-school experience (Schine, 1989). Other approaches might address health promotion and educational enrichment, extending the learning experiences of young adolescents (see also section on community organizations). Understanding how these approaches work and their benefits for adolescent development is at a promising, but early stage (Heath & McLaughlin, 1991). These approaches, undoubtedly, can provide a welcome alternative to unsupervised, often hazardous activities engaged by young adolescents left to their own devices.

Community Organizations and Contexts. The neglect of contextual variables and their essential interactions with individual variables in development during the second decade is often lamented (Feldman & Elliott, 1990; Lerner, chapter 1, this volume). Research activity in the diverse community contexts of adolescent development is beginning to flourish (for notable exceptions, there is the promising work of the MacArthur Network on Successful Adolescence in High-Risk Settings, see Jessor, 1991; Ianni, 1989; the Chicago Study of William Julius Wilson and Marta Tienda, see Wilson, 1987). The experience of being an adolescent varies in different economic, cultural, social, and geographical settings (Ianni, 1989). We can learn a great deal by examining those communities in which adolescents are growing up healthy, becoming responsible citizens, and preparing to be productive workers. In these communities, there are good schools that match the needs of adolescents, involved parents who have a strong interest in their adolescent's well-being (Hansell & Mechanic, 1991), safe places where adolescents can choose activities they are genuinely interested in with caring adult supervision and guidance (Heath & McLaughlin, 1991).

The roles of nonschool, community-based, voluntary organizations in the healthy development of adolescents is only beginning to be scrutinized. The efforts of the Rockefeller Foundation's initiative on community foundations and high-risk youth, the Chicago Community Trust's Children, Youth, and Families Initiative, and the Carnegie Council's Task Force on Youth Development and Community Organizations, among others will likely increase our knowledge and our options for action in the near future.

Health of Adolescents. In 1991, a Congressional support agency, the Office of Technology Assessment (OTA), released the first landmark national study of the health status of American adolescents (OTA, 1991a, 1991b, 1991c). As a comprehensive study of adolescent health, broadly defined, this report provides opportunities for national, state, and local action in the science policy and youth support arenas. Among the contributions of the OTA effort is its critique of the collection of national health statistics on adolescents, a review of federal agency programs and budgets for adolescents, and a detailed rendering of options for program and policy action for national, state, and local government.

The core trio of options in the OTA report provide many opportunities for the integration of research and practice:

- OTA offers for Congressional consideration specific strategies to improve adolescents' access to appropriate health services. One such strategy is the school-linked or community-based health and youth services center (Millstein, 1988). As OTA notes, much needs to be learned about whether these centers really improve adolescents' health and social outcomes. Other strategies include increasing legal access to health services through changes in consent and confidentiality regulations (see Gittler, Quigley-Rick, & Saks, 1990, for the research base for changes); support for training of health providers for adolescents and the evaluation of training approaches, and strategies to include the perspectives and input of adolescents in the design of delivery systems.

- OTA suggests that there be a new locus for a strong federal role in adolescent health and a strengthening of federal agency roles in research, collection of national statistics, and program development. The research community, working through scientific and professional societies, can become active nationally in the research agenda-setting process, in improving the collection of statistics on adolescents and their environments, and in assuring that research informs policy and program development.
- OTA urges improvement in the social environment of adolescents including increased support to families of adolescents (see section earlier on family-friendly policies); limitations on access to firearms; the expansion of recreational opportunities for adolescents (see section on community organizations); and the evaluation of the National and Community Service Act of 1990.

PROSPECTS FOR CONNECTING RESEARCH AND POLICY IN EARLY ADOLESCENCE

What needs to happen for early adolescence to become higher on the policy agenda? What strategies might concerned researchers, professionals, and policymakers fashion to assure the emergence of this stage of life as a public policy concern? The elements of such a strategy include:

- Public education to highlight the "critical nature" of the early adolescent years. Strong and continuing linkage between the various media and the research community is crucial.
- Clear articulation of public policy agendas for young adolescents linking health, education, and family support.
- Education and preparation of researchers to address effectively questions of policy regarding the early adolescent period.

Public Education and Media Policy

Television, radio, music, and film can play powerful roles in reinforcing, reflecting, and shaping public perceptions of the adolescent years. The steady infusion of research-based knowledge about adolescents into the various media (television, film, music videos, radio, teen magazines, and other print media) should be a high priority among those who aim for early adolescence to be higher on the public policy agenda. Various mediating institutions, such as the Scientists' Institute for Public Information, the Los Angeles-based office of the Center for Population Options, and the media activities of the Carnegie Council on Adolescent Development, are actively involved in the transfer of knowledge to the media community.

What might be considered to be accepted knowledge among small communities of researchers and practitioners involved with the age group may not be known outside these circles. As one critical example, the need of young adolescents to renegotiate rather than sever their relationships with their parents has a powerful preventive message. If more parents understood the need of young adolescents to remain close to them, more opportunities for guidance might be taken.

Articulating a Public Agenda for the Early Adolescent Years

In contrast to other developmental periods, the public policy agenda for the early adolescent years remains at the stage of infancy. *Turning Points* (Carnegie Council on Adolescent Development, 1989) was one effort to articulate a broad multi-institutional strategy, involving schools, families, health, and community organizations, in the education of young adolescents. In that report, the focus was exclusively on young adolescents. The OTA (1991b) report on adolescent health, on the other hand, makes very little reference to the early adolescent years and focuses on the broad adolescent period from 10 to 18 years of age. As such, the report missed an opportunity to make a case that the early adolescent period constitutes prime time for prevention for a variety of adolescent health-related problems.

What is still missing from all of our policy discussions related to young adolescents is what specific policies, strategies, and approaches are uniquely suited to this developmental phase. Some examples have been offered in the course of this chapter, but much more needs to be done to articulate a policy agenda for young adolescents. Policymakers respond to specific courses of action, not to broad principles or general concepts. It is these action plans that must be clearly articulated with supporting cases.

Education and Preparation of Researchers

The early childhood field provides solid precedent for preparing researchers and child development professionals for forging linkages between research and policy (Takanishi & Melton, 1987). Consonant with the aspirations of the adolescent development field (Lerner, chapter 1, this volume), linkages have been multidisciplinary and multiprofessional in practice.

With significant philanthropic support from the Foundation for Child Development and the W. T. Grant Foundation (Brim, & Dustan 1983), the Congressional Science Fellowship Program enabled individuals for almost two decades to work in Congress and its support agencies. Many of these fellows continue to work in Congress, in the intersection of scientific and professional societies and policy, in American philanthropy, and in academe. The Bush Foundation also supported several generations of established researchers and new ones in preparing individuals in graduate education for various roles in the policy arena.

Most importantly, the Congressional Science Fellowship program and the Bush Centers created a network of individuals, at different stages of their careers, whose primary commitment is to the linkage of research and policy in a variety of arenas: national and state governments, foundations, scientific societies, advocacy and nonprofit organizations. Almost all of these individuals work in the early childhood area, although a few have migrated into the adolescent arena. However, nothing near a critical mass of individuals whose major work arena is in the linkage of adolescent development research and policy currently exists. This should be a high priority in graduate education institutions and internship programs in the near future.

SUMMING UP

We stand at the threshold of genuine prospects to link research, practice, and policy during the early adolescent period. Rich opportunities for integration are before us. The child development field provides an excellent precedent for what can occur during the adolescent period (Takanishi & Melton, 1987). The major issue that must be strategically addressed is that resources are constricted and hence a competition for scarce resources among developmental periods is necessary. What must be cogently communicated is that although investment in the early childhood years has demonstrated effects, even for the most resilient, the challenges of adolescence, particularly early adolescence, can be turning points for even the best and the brightest (Kotlowitz, 1991). Immunization is a very effective analogue for disease prevention, but is not the appropriate one for the prevention of adolescent problems. The human capital approach that invests in the development of people has to be extended to the entire period of vulnerability, from early childhood through adolescence, during which society and its adult members have clear responsibilities for the nurture of all young people. This sea of change in public ideas (see Reich, 1988) is vitally needed for American society to invest seriously in all its children and youth, but particularly in the still neglected early adolescent period.

REFERENCES

Apter, T. (1990). *Altered loves: Mothers and daughters during adolescence.* New York: St. Martin's Press Inc.

Bachman, J. G., Wallace, J. M., Jr., Kurth, C. L., Johnston, L. D., & O'Malley, P. M. (1990). *Drug use among Black, White, Hispanic, Native American, and Asian American high school seniors (1976-1989): Prevalence, trends, and correlates.* Ann Arbor, MI: Institute for Social Research, The University of Michigan.

Beyth-Marom, R., Fischhoff, B., Jacobs, M., & Furby, L. (1989). *Teaching decision making to adolescents: A critical review.* Washington, DC: Carnegie Council on Adolescent Development Working Paper Series.

Brim, O., & Dustan, J. (1983, January). Psychology in the public forum. *American Psychologist,* 85-90.

Brown, B. B. (1990). Peer groups and peer cultures. In S. S. Feldman & G. R. Elliott (Eds.), *At the threshold: The developing adolescent* (pp. 171-196). Cambridge, MA: Harvard University Press.

Carnegie Council on Adolescent Development. (1989, June). *Turning points: Preparing American youth for the 21st century* (The Report of the Task Force on Education of Young Adolescents). Washington, DC: Author.

Coles, R. (1989). *Girl Scouts survey on the beliefs and moral values of America's children.* New York: Girl Scouts of the United States of America.

Dornbusch, S. M., Petersen, A. C., & Hetherington, E. M. (1991). Projecting the future of research on adolescence. *Journal of Research on Adolescence, 1*(1), 7-18.

Dornbusch, S. M., & Ritter, P. L. (1988). Parents of high school students: A neglected resource. *Educational Horizons, 66*(2), 75-77.

Entwisle, D. R. (1990). Schools and the adolescent. In S. S. Feldman & G. R. Elliott (Eds.), *At the threshold: The developing adolescent* (pp. 197-224). Cambridge, MA: Harvard University Press.

Family Resource Coalition. (1990). *Report* (Vol. 9, No. 1). Chicago, IL: Author.

Feldman, S. S., & Elliott, G. R. (Eds.). (1990). *At the threshold: The developing adolescent.* Cambridge, MA: Harvard University Press.

Fuchs, L. H. (1990). *The American kaleidoscope: Race, ethnicity, and the civic culture.* Hanover: Wesleyan University Press.

Furby, L., & Beyth-Marom, R. (1990). *Risk taking in adolescence: A decision-making perspective.* Washington, DC: Carnegie Council on Adolescent Development Working Paper Series.

Gittler, J., Quigley-Rick, M., & Saks, M. J. (1990). *Adolescent health care decision making: The law and public policy.* Washington, DC: Carnegie Council on Adolescent Development Working Paper Series.

Hamburg, B. (1974). Early adolescence: A specific and stressful stage of the life cycle. In G. Coelho, D. A. Hamburg, & J. E. Adams (Eds.), *Coping and adaptation* (pp. 102-124). New York: Basic.

Hamburg, D. A. (1989). *Early adolescence: A critical time for interventions in education and health*. New York: Carnegie Corporation of New York.

Hamburg, D. A. (1992). *Today's children: Creating a future for a generation in crisis*. New York: Times Books, Random House.

Hansell, S., & Mechanic, D. (1990). Parent and peer effects on adolescent health behavior. In K. Hurrelmann & F. Losel (Eds.), *Health hazards in adolescence* (pp. 43–65). New York: Aldine De Gruyter.

Heath, S. B., & McLaughlin, M. W. (1991). Community organizations as family: Endeavors that engage and support adolescents. *Phi Delta Kappan, 72*(8), 623–627.

Hill, J., & Holmbeck, G. (1986). Attachment and autonomy during adolescence. In G. Whitehurst (Ed.), *Annals of child development* (Vol. 3, pp. 145–190). Greenwich CT: JAI Press.

Ianni, F. A. J. (1989). *The search for structure: A report on American youth today*. New York: The Free Press.

Jessor, R. (1991). *Risk behavior in adolescence: A psychosocial framework for understanding and action*. Paper prepared for the Seventh Cornell Health Policy Conference on "Adolescents at risk: Medical–social perspectives," Cornell University Medical College, New York.

Keating, D. P. (1990). Adolescent thinking. In S. S. Feldman & G. R. Elliott (Eds.), *At the threshold: The developing adolescent* (pp. 54–89). Cambridge, MA: Harvard University Press.

Kotlowitz, A. (1991). *There are no children here: The story of two boys growing up in the other America*. New York: Doubleday.

Langenberg, D. N. (1991). Science, slogans, and civic duty. *Science, 252*(5004), 361–363.

Louv, R. (1990). *Childhood's future*. Boston: Houghton Mifflin Company.

Millstein, S. G. (1988). *The potential of school-linked centers to promote adolescent health and development*. Washington, DC: Carnegie Council on Adolescent Development Working Paper Series.

Millstein, S. G., Petersen, A. C., & Nightingale, E. O. (Eds.). (in press). *Promoting adolescent health*. Oxford: Oxford University Press.

Office of Technology Assessment. (1991a). *Adolescent health volume I: Summary and policy options* (OTA-H-468). Washington, DC: U.S. Government Printing Office.

Office of Technology Assessment. (1991b). *Adolescent health volume II: Background and the effectiveness of selected prevention and treatment services* (OTA-H-468). Washington, DC: U.S. Government Printing Office.

Office of Technology Assessment. (1991c). *Adolescent health volume III: Crosscutting issues in the delivery of health and related services* (OTA-H-467). Washington, DC: U.S. Government Printing Office.

Petersen, A. C., & Epstein, J. L. (1991). Development and education across adolescence: An introduction. *American Journal of Education, 99*(4), 373–378.

Reich, R. B. (Ed.). (1988). *The power of public ideas*. New York: Ballinger Division, Harper & Row.

Rural Clearinghouse for Lifelong Education and Development. (1991). *Accommodating change and diversity: Linking rural schools to communities*. Manhattan: Kansas State University.

Savin-Williams, R. C., & Berndt, T. J. (1990). Friendship and peer relations. In S. S. Feldman & G. R. Elliott (Eds.), *At the threshold: The developing adolescent* (pp. 277–307). Cambridge, MA: Harvard University Press.

Schine, J. (1989). *Young adolescents and community service*. Washington, DC: Carnegie Council on Adolescent Development Working Paper Series.

Small, S. A. (1990). *Preventive programs that support families with adolescents*. Washington, DC: Carnegie Council on Adolescent Development Working Paper Series.

Spencer, M. B., & Dornbusch, S. M. (1990). Challenges in studying minority youth. In S. S. Feldman & G. R. Elliott (Eds.), *At the threshold: The developing adolescent* (pp. 123–146). Cambridge, MA: Harvard University Press.

Steinberg, L. (1990). Autonomy, conflict, and harmony in the family. In S. S. Feldman & G. R. Elliott (Eds.), *At the threshold: The developing adolescent* (pp. 255–276). Cambridge, MA: Harvard University Press.

Takanishi, R., & Melton, G. B. (1987). Child development research and the legislative process. In G. B. Melton (Ed.), *Reforming the law: Impact of child development research* (pp. 86–101). New York: Guiford Press.

U.S. General Accounting Office. (1990). *Children's issues: A decade of GAO reports and recent activities.* Washington, DC: Author.

Wilson, W. J. (1987). *The truly disadvantaged: The inner city, the underclass, and public policy.* Chicago: The University of Chicago Press.

27 | Integrating Research, Policy, and Practice: One School District's Approach to Improving Middle-Level Education

Patricia L. Best
State College Area School District, State College, Pennsylvania

In a recent National Association of Secondary School Principals' publication, *Inside Grade Eight: From Apathy to Excitement* (Lounsbury & Clark, 1990), one educational researcher described a telling interaction with a perceptive sixth grader. The researcher was explaining to a class of middle-level students, the results of a nationwide shadow study on the day-to-day educational experiences of eighth grade students in 161 schools. In concluding his talk, the researcher told the class that these studies had been done before over the past 20 years and mostly confirmed what is already known about what needs to be done to improve schools. One student raised his hand and asked politely, "But if you know all those things, how come it doesn't change?"

How come, indeed? It is the purpose of this chapter to address some of the concerns with and opportunities for a more productive relationship among educational researchers, policymakers, and practitioners as seen through the lens of the public school teacher and administrator. I believe, based on our school district's experience with a planned change process for school improvement, that such a relationship can be productive and can result in improved learning experiences for middle-level students.

It is the dramatic or unusual that captures the interest of the media and often the attention of policymakers as we all look for creative solutions to identified problems in public schools. It is our belief that we must not only pursue the creative and innovative but we must also continue those incremental steps that lead complex social institutions like schools in the direction of authentic transition.

This chapter discusses just such a process in one junior high school in a public school district in Pennsylvania. This process is one that can be carried out in any school district in the nation with productive results.

THE CONTEXT FOR CHANGE

Among the specific issues receiving increased attention nationally is the quality of educational programming for young adolescents. The publication of *Turning Points* in 1989 by the Carnegie Council on Adolescent Development focused on the characteristics and needs of junior high and middle school students and recommended changes in schooling to improve their learning.

In addition to the signs of interest in early adolescence on the part of researchers, the perception of professional educators is slowly changing. Once an assignment in a junior high or middle school was viewed as time served before "moving up" to a high school position. Slowly, professional educators are recognizing middle-level education as a significant and crucial period in the psychological, social, emotional, and educational development of students. This shift is an important step in focusing the profession's attention on the need for change and specialization. For teachers and administrators whose professional goal is to make a difference in the lives of children, work with middle-level students is emerging as a fertile field of specialization.

In our school district, we are finding that junior high teachers have a great deal of pride in what they have accomplished during the past 5 years with their school improvement process. Teachers are no longer seeking reassignment to the high school as routinely as they once did. In fact, their senior high colleagues are beginning to attend some of the inservice sessions presented by the junior high faculty on the teaming concept and cooperative learning strategies. We believe this shift in teacher awareness is one result of our conscious efforts through our district improvement process to integrate policy, research, and practice in bringing about improvement for all students.

Research, Policy, and Practice. In the past, achieving a productive dialogue among researchers, policymakers, and practitioners has been problematic for a number of reasons. The context in which each functions is governed by very different factors. Communication is difficult when a common language does not exist. The language of policymakers is one of compromise, negotiation, trade-offs, and competing interests. The language of the educational researcher revolves around definitions, controls, manipulations, and carefully qualified results and implications. The practitioner's language is one that reflects expectations, applications, performance, compliance, and assessment. Unlike policymakers and researchers, much of the language of the practitioner is imposed from outside the classroom or school. But the most basic difference is that for educational policymakers and researchers children are most often discussed and viewed in the abstract. For teachers and administrators in public schools, however, children are very real identifiable individuals.

Given the differences in their worlds, it is not surprising that policymakers, researchers, and practitioners frame questions differently, set priorities differently, acquire information differently, and apply knowledge to problem solving differently (Mitchell, 1988). Consequently, one critical issue in addressing the specific needs of middle-level learners in public schools is finding a more effective way for these three entities to share knowledge and to define a common agenda.

Educational research has, for the past 85 years, produced a large body of correlational and experimental studies. However, the majority of teachers and administrators in public schools, and possibly professors of education in universities, would probably be hard pressed to explain their classroom practices in terms of what has been demonstrated in the literature.

Eisner (1985) suggested that changes in school practices are more likely to take place because an idea or approach is intuitively attractive to practitioners than because a databased set of research conclusions indicates such a change is desirable. To increase the utility of educational research for practitioners, researchers must become better acquainted with life as it is lived in classrooms and cease conducting "educational commando raids to get the data and to get out" (p. 264).

In the developing body of research on change in schools, however, it is becoming clear that introducing, implementing, and sustaining an innovation in instructional practice is not simply a function of how attractive the idea is. For example, Fullan (1982) described four criteria that affect the degree to which an innovation is implementable in a school: recognized need for change, clarity of purposes and procedures, complexity (i.e., degree of change required by the innovation), and practicality (i.e., degree to which the change can be put into practice).

The experience with educational innovation in our school district would also suggest that the static, one-way concept of research informing practice is neither very useful nor a reflection of reality. In reconceptualizing the relationship, what comes to mind is a lesson from elementary school mathematics about constructing a Mobius strip. The children take a long, narrow strip of construction paper, and by turning one end over and taping the two ends of the paper together, they have converted a one-dimensional flat surface into a two-dimensional, continuous loop. In a productive, dynamic relationship, research informs practice as practice informs research.

To accomplish this, schools that are undertaking improved learning experiences for middle-level students need to actively seek out what research information is available, to determine its applicability to the local situation, to establish networks with university faculty who specialize in the field, and to share their classrooms with researchers who are interested in establishing the kind of working relationship that Eisner suggests. It was this kind of approach that was useful to our junior high faculty.

Educational policymaking at every level is an inherently political process. It is, in general, characterized by the presentation of diverse personal and special interest agendas, a variety of conflicting perspectives and value systems, and the resolution of dissent through compromise.

Elmore (1983) described what happens in the gap between policy enactment by policymakers and policy implementation by local practitioners as "the power of the bottom over the top." For meaningful change to occur at the school level, a marriage between, in Elmore's terms, the power of the top and the power of the bottom is essential. With this nexus we can get to the heart of change that is how school time, space, and resources are allocated, how classroom routines and instructional practices are devised and evaluated, how student learning outcomes are formulated, and how faculties and administrators are held accountable for student learning.

In our school district, we have an agenda for improving middle-level education that was developed within the context of the overall school district school improvement planning process. Within this framework, our teachers and administrators tapped and applied educational research, were supported by local school board policy, and undertook a planned change effort. The work of this faculty and administration is still evolving.

INITIATING SCHOOL-BASED CHANGE

State College, Pennsylvania, is a community with a population of 65,000 located in the geographical center of the state. It is a thriving university community situated in the midst of a rural region. The State College Area School District draws its 6,000 students from a 150-square mile attendance area. The school system includes 11 elementary buildings (K–6), a junior high school (7–8), a high school (9–12), and an alternative program (7–12). The percentage of graduates who attend 4-year colleges after graduation increased from 52% in 1982 to 65% in 1990.

The student body is increasingly diverse, with the minority population having doubled since 1980 from 5% to more than 10%. In addition, the student body includes a sizable rural population as well as international students. More than 23 language groups are represented among the children in district English as a Second Language (ESL) classes.

This description is not about a school district in crisis; it is, however, about examining past instructional practice for its continuing suitability for today's students. In some ways, it is more difficult for schools that are viewed as doing what they do well to stop and ask the disconcerting question, "Should we be doing this at all?"

Planning for Change. The change process in the school district began with the adoption in 1985 of a mission statement by the Board of School Directors.

The superintendent assigned the responsibility for formulating an approach to implementing an improvement process to a central office administrator in charge of strategic planning and research. She posed three questions to guide the initial process development:

1. What do we know about good schools?
2. What do we know about managing change effectively?
3. What do we know about indicators that change efforts produce the desired results?

In looking to educational research for help with the first question, central office administrators and principals examined the effective schools literature. During the 1980s, the effective schools research began to provide descriptors of schools that produce positive student outcomes (Purkey & Smith, 1985). This growing body of research represents one perspective on school change and improvement efforts.

In addressing the second guiding question, a review of the literature on planned organizational change was undertaken by the planning director. Fullan (1982) described attempting change in schools as a "complex, dilemma-ridden, technical, sociopolitical process" (p. 391). In retrospect, he was being optimistic.

Especially useful in developing the change process was the work of Corbett, Dawson, and Firestone (1984). They identified eight local school conditions that affect the outcomes of change efforts. The two most important variables were accessibility of school resources and provision and quality of incentives and disincentives for innovation. They also cited current instructional and administrative practices and previous experience with change projects as influential. As the steps of the process were formulated, local school conditions related to these variables were informally assessed by the planning director.

John Goodlad (1984) pointed out another barrier to meaningful change, which addressed the third guiding question in the district's approach to process development. He observed that schools rarely know what they need to know to change. Data are usually lacking in such areas as exactly what the school's functions are; how relevant instruction is to student and community needs; how resources are distributed across learning areas; how access to knowledge varies for different students; how much time is actually spent on instruction; and, finally, what a school's practices are.

The Planning Process for School Improvement. Based on conclusions from the preliminary work described here on developing a school improvement process, six important guidelines were developed:

1. The process is to be school-based.
2. The process is to provide for shared decision making.
3. The process is to be goal driven.
4. The process is to be research based.
5. The process is to provide district level support.
6. The process is to result in improved student learning.

It was at this juncture that crucial conversations with the Board of School Directors took place. The superintendent and planning director shared with the board their synthesis of the educational research that had been reviewed, described how this knowledge could be used to develop an improvement process tailored to the State College Area School District, indicated how this process would support the mission statement and goals adopted by the board, and requested monies to support the initiation and implementation of the process.

As might be expected, the discussion was lively and challenging, with reactions ranging from skepticism to enthusiasm. The result, however, was the agreement of the policymakers to support the efforts of the practitioners to improve services. The application of selected research was useful in presenting the various facets of the problem to the school board.

Improving the Middle-Level Program. Within the framework of the district's overall improvement process, the junior high school

(Grades 7–8) identified as its primary target the improvement of the educational program to better meet the developmental and educational needs of middle-level students. The focus of the change effort would be to align both the curriculum of the school and teacher expectations for student performance with the growing knowledge of the developmental needs of middle-level students.

Led by an energetic and committed principal, the faculty undertook a year of study. Using the literature presented some difficulties. Research studies of the same practice sometimes present conflicting results or the context of a study is so narrowly drawn that generalizing the findings to the local junior high is difficult. In addition, the teachers were working across a number of discrete areas of research (e.g., cognitive maturation of early adolescents, factors in building self-esteem, authentic assessment techniques, instructional methods for promoting critical thinking skills, etc.). Integrating the information in a way that provided clear guidelines for developing practice proved challenging.

The degree of commitment on the part of the faculty to the process grew out of their clear sense of ownership for the direction they were exploring. Issuing a directive from the central office to make significant changes in their program would have met with resistance rather than the active and widespread involvement that was characteristic of the first year.

During the second year, committees went to work examining the junior high curriculum and program for areas that were counter to the descriptions of effective middle-level approaches. A number of areas were identified (e.g., large size of the school, rigid scheduling, and homogeneous grouping in major subject areas).

A university consultant specializing in middle-level education was hired to provide staff development and to advise on planned program changes. She was chosen for her expertise, but also because she was familiar with the day-to-day functioning of junior highs and middle schools through continued contacts across the state. Her credibility with the faculty was high. The consultant also participated in several parent education programs. Informing parents of the possibility of change and the reasons for it was a critical step in the process.

Teams of teachers and the principal visited middle schools that had been recognized as exemplary and returned with ideas for improving the structure of the junior high program. These visits gave teachers the opportunity to see in practice some of the changes that were suggested in the literature and by the consultant. Talking with other practitioners and observing students in action were powerful motivators for change. In the spring, the faculty developed a proposal for a pilot project.

In 1988–1989, 125 seventh graders, approximately one third of the class, were randomly assigned to an interdisciplinary team of teachers. The team consisted of teachers of English, mathematics, social studies, science, art and music, and a counselor. The goals for the pilot were to encourage teachers and students to form a learning community through creating a smaller group of students that would spend most of the day together, to ease the transition from the neighborhood elementary schools, to improve communication with the home, to develop consistency in academic and behavioral expectations among teachers, and to examine more effective instructional practices for middle-level students.

The pilot project provided the teachers on the team with a common planning time, which was used to coordinate academic work and to discuss student progress. In addition, the team devised a flexible schedule, moved toward homogeneous grouping except in mathematics, initiated regular parent contacts during the year, added cooperative learning to their repertoire of instructional methods, and incorporated a student group community service project into the program. Tackling a multidisciplinary approach to subject matter areas proved too complicated for the pilot. Although some curriculum units were taught in tandem, the team did not develop a fully integrated multidisciplinary approach to the curriculum.

At the end of the school year, parents of all seventh graders were surveyed. The results indicated that parents of students who were involved in the interdisciplinary teams were more positive in their responses to questions about their child's junior high experience than parents of students in the traditional program. Teacher and student comments were also positive. Although the academic achievement of students in the pilot was consistent with the rest of the student body, the difference was in their more positive attitudes toward school. As a result, the pilot continued for a second year.

During the 1989–1990 school year, *Turning Points* was released. A number of the recommendations affirmed the initial directions taken by the junior high; for example, dividing a large school into smaller units or teams, reviewing the core curriculum for its fit to the learning needs of early adolescents, examining teacher expectations for students and student grouping practices, involving parents, and linking schools and the community in the educational process. Following the second year of the pilot program in interdisciplinary teaming, the junior high decided to extend the approach to the entire seventh grade during the 1990–1991 school year.

Currently, the issue before the school is the extension of the concept to the eighth grade. The availability of staffing and classroom space have become issues for expanding the team concept. Additional costs will be involved in the expansion. The educational benefits are competing with some local economic realities in the form of budget cutbacks and taxpayer unrest.

The Politics of Change. Although the junior high was engaged in a deliberate process of program improvement for middle-level students, another process was being played out at the district level. The growing enrollments of elementary students forced consideration of facilities expansion. Into a highly politicized community environment came the discussion of realigning the K–8 structure and creating two Grade 6–8 middle schools.

The Board of School Directors appointed a citizens' advisory committee to examine the philosophy of middle-level education and to recommend a possible course of action. The advisory committee consisted of district personnel, including the junior high principal and several teachers, Pennsylvania State University faculty knowledgeable about middle-level education, community representatives, and parents. The committee worked diligently over a 9-month period to review the research, to understand the current efforts at the junior high, to visit schools with different grade alignments, and to formulate a recommendation for the school board. A public meeting was sponsored by the committee, during which several recognized experts in middle-level education made presentations and responded to questions.

During this period, parent concern about removing sixth graders from the elementary schools surfaced. Letters were written to the local newspaper and to the school board asking that such a move not be undertaken. At a public hearing, a number of parents adamantly objected to the change.

Nevertheless, when the advisory committee presented its recommendation, the suggestion was to create two smaller Grade 6–8 middle schools that embodied the middle-level learner philosophy in their educational programming. The report provoked renewed objections from some concerned parents of sixth graders. In addition, the teachers' union took a position against the Grade 6–8 structure despite the participation of teachers on the advisory committee.

In the end, the careful, methodical work of the citizens' committee was not sufficient to convince the school board to move to a Grade 6–8 middle school structure. Neither the educational research nor the testimony of experts that there were compelling instructional benefits for sixth graders in a middle school configuration swayed the board.

Although refusing to move sixth graders from the elementary schools, the Board of School Directors affirmed its support of the middle-level philosophy as it was being developed and implemented at the Grade 7–8 junior high school. The policy decision reflected the school board's approach to dealing with the sharp division between those parents and faculty who supported and those who opposed the recommendation.

Implications for Future Action. Are schools changing? The events in our school district since 1987 are one indication that the answer is a qualified yes. The degree of change in curriculum and instruction within our junior high is more modest than we would like, but the impetus for continued improvement has become part of the annual cycle of the school year through the school improvement planning process.

From our experience, students benefit when practitioners become better consumers of educational research and more active participants in policy development. It is also clear that the needs of practitioners are best served when researchers and policy makers understand the dynamic ebb and flow of life in a junior high or middle school. Building better bridges among practitioners, researchers, and policymakers committed to improving the quality of learning experiences provided by the public schools for middle-level learners is essential.

REFERENCES

Carnegie Council on Adolescent Development. (1989). *Turning points: Preparing American youth for the 21st century.* Washington, DC: Task Force on the Education of Young Adolescents.

Corbett, H. D., Dawson, J. A., & Firestone, W. A. (1984). *School context and school change: Implications for effective planning.* New York: Teachers College, Columbia University.

Eisner, E. W. (1985). *The art of educational evaluation.* Philadelphia, PA: The Falmer Press.

Elmore, R. (1983). Complexity and control: What legislators and administrators can do about implementing policy. In L. S. Shulman & G. Sykes (Eds.), *Handbook of teaching and policy* (pp. 342–369). New York: Longman.

Fullan, M. (1982). *The meaning of educational change.* New York: Teachers College Press.

Goodlad, J. (1984). *A place called school.* New York: McGraw-Hill.

Lounsbury, J. H., & Clark, D. C. (1990). *Inside grade eight: From apathy to excitement.* Reston, VA: National Association of Secondary School Principals.

Mitchell, B. (1988). Research, policy, practice: Where are we headed? *Theory Into Practice, 27*(2), 90.

Purkey, S. C., & Smith, M. S. (1985). School reform: The district policy implications of the effective schools literature. *The Elementary School Journal, 85*(3), 353–389.

28 | The Land-Grant University System and 4-H: A Mutually Beneficial Relationship of Scholars and Practitioners in Youth Development

B. Alan Snider
The Pennsylvania State University

Jeffrey P. Miller
Community CARES, National 4-H Council

The land-grant university system was created to provide all people with opportunities and access to research and new knowledge—knowledge that is applied to meet societal needs, solve problems, and enrich the lives of people in the United States and around the world. Land-grant institutions have provided the impetus for growth and change through their uniquely blended roles in teaching, research, and public service. In its early history, in what was a more agrarian society, the land-grants' greatest impacts on progress were in the areas of agriculture and the mechanical arts. But just as society has changed over the past 125 years, land-grant institutions have changed. They continue to adapt the land-grant mission to meeting the needs of a complex, diverse, and rapidly changing world. On the verge of the 21st century, change will become more rapid as a result of society's problems that are becoming more complex and challenging.

The working classes, bypassed by other educational institutions, were the clientele for these new universities. That legacy can be seen today in a variety of community activities, involving university extension offices in 3,100 counties of the United States. The models undergirding these outreach efforts have been emulated and exported throughout the world, and some believe the land-grant universities are the most influential innovation in U.S. higher education (P. A. Miller, 1988).

Families and youth have been important clientele in the land-grant movement. Virtually all these universities have been major educators of school teachers at all levels. A number of these have been part of special initiatives with public schools to enhance learning. Today that challenge is greater than ever before as evidenced by current statistics.

> One in every five children lives in poverty. Four of every ten girls will become pregnant during the teen years. One in five will bear a child. One-half of all welfare payments are made to women who gave birth while in their teens. The infant mortality rate in the U.S. is the highest among 22 industrialized nations and is most frequently associated with teen parenthood. One in four children attending high school today will not graduate. In 1985, two million children were reported as victims of abuse and neglect to state child protective service agencies. Each year 500,000 teens will attempt to kill themselves, of which 5,000 will succeed. Nearly 50% of the nation's high school seniors say they have used illegal drugs during the past year. Over 30% of high school seniors get drunk once a week. More than three million teenagers are chronic alcoholics. Every five seconds a teenager is involved in an alcohol or drug-related traffic accident. (United States Department of Agriculture/Extension Service [USDA/ES], 1989a, p. 3)

Many of these statistics may sound all too familiar, and in fact it is easy to become unmoved by numbers and forget the human tragedy that they represent. The central problem is not any of these issues in isolation. These are the symptoms of the problem: our national neglect of children. There is a crucial need for a national commitment to invest in children and youth if they are to help create a productive and human future (USDA/ES, 1989a). The youth crisis is nothing short of a national tragedy. This country cannot afford to waste so much human capital and expect our democratic way of life to continue (Brown, 1987).

When viewed from a developmental perspective, societal issues affecting youth often seem to stem from the same roots. Emerging research on prevention of antisocial behavior shows that educators, whether formal or nonformal, must place a greater emphasis on self-esteem enhancement and on the acquisition and practice of life skills (Shrum, 1987). Experiential youth development education programs are powerful delivery methods for creating positive development in youth. These programs can link education (knowledge transfer) with prevention programming (addressing societal issues) through learning experiences that directly build on the developmental tasks the young person must successfully achieve (Snider, 1988).

The Cooperative Extension 4-H programs of land-grant universities have a long history of providing services to society, and especially to youth and families, and are a considerable resource in implementing solutions to problems youth face. Whatever the solutions may be to the youth crisis, enlightened public policies, community service based on quality research, and dedicated efforts of professional and volunteer workers are all essential ingredients to help youth reach their potential.

The long-standing techniques that land-grant universities have successfully utilized need to be incorporated into an extended partnership capable of devising a national program of service for U.S. youth. Families and schools are fundamental to every child. Beyond them, however, lie a variety of supporting institutions, organizations, and collective experiences that influence the social, emotional, and intellectual development of young people. The 4-H youth development program is an educational component of the land-grant university outreach program that can be an instrumental force in addressing the youth crisis.

This chapter demonstrates how the land-grant institutions in general and 4-H youth development education in particular contribute to the "welfare of youth" and can address the present youth crisis. The chapter details the importance of stronger linkages between youth development researchers and practitioners who are providing educational leadership through delivery of youth development programs in local communities to meet the needs of youth and their families.

EVOLUTION OF 4-H AS A YOUTH DEVELOPMENT ENTERPRISE

> I pledge my Head to clearer thinking,
> My Heart to greater loyalty,
> My Hands to larger service,
> My Health to better living,
> for my club, my community, and my country[1]

In 1927, at the first National 4-H Camp, these words by Otis Hall of Kansas were officially adopted as the 4-H pledge (Reck, 1951). Although this formally recognized the philosophical base of the agricultural and home economics club work being conducted in most states, 4-H's roots can be traced to early in the century.

In the early 1900s educators in a number of states were discovering the need to give rural children a new type of education that could be applied to the practical arts of living, and would help keep the children interested in school. Very few farm boys enrolled in high school, and only about 1 in 500 went on to college. Additionally, rural children also had poor self-images, thinking of themselves as second-class citizens

---

[1] The words "and my world" were later added to recognize the cross-cultural and global perspective of the 4-H program (Wessel & Wessel, 1982).

(Reck, 1951). Several of these rural educators (independent of one another) spoke of an educational experience that utilized the three Hs as well as the three Rs (Graham, 1958; McCormick & McCormick, 1984; Reck, 1951; & Stewart, 1969). They each promoted a nonformal, out of school type of education that used the teaching of agricultural concepts based on the philosophy of the three Hs (Reck, 1951; Stewart, 1969). The fourth H was later added to represent Health; resisting disease and encouraging the enjoyment of life. Each of these nonformal educational programs were meant to complement, not replace, the school curriculum.

These nonformal educational programs evolved into agricultural corn clubs for boys and homemaking canning clubs for girls. The nationwide expansion of these clubs was supported by the U.S. Department of Agriculture. The purpose of the federal government's involvement in sponsoring these clubs was twofold. First, to encourage rural people to take a more active interest in education, and second to introduce, through the children, new and improved agricultural practices being developed by land-grant schools of agriculture, which farmers were slow to adopt. The goal was to make farm life more attractive and profitable to rural people (Reck, 1951).

Passage of the Smith-Lever Act in 1914 formally established the partnership between federal, state, and local governments in extending the work of the colleges of agriculture and home economics to all counties in the country, thus forming what today is known as Cooperative Extension, of which the 4-H program is a major component (Reck, 1951). From 1914 until the start of World War II, 4-H groups began to organize outside of the public schools.

Clubs became community centered as adults realized that the lessons of 4-H programs were reinforcing values they wanted their children to possess. The community focus of the 4-H groups also provided a support network for individuals during the Great Depression. The 4-H effort continued to grow, and club members made major contributions to national efforts during both world wars. Some of these efforts included planting gardens, food preservation, and preparation, as well as the production of clothing for the needy. Campaigns to collect paper, scrap metal, and fat; war bond support, and overall conservation and community cooperation efforts highlighted youngsters contributions to the war efforts. All of the efforts undertaken helped instill the importance of recycling, teamwork, and citizen participation (Lang & Gerwig, 1989).

Following the war years and into the 1970s, with the changing social scene, the emphasis of 4-H programs changed. As society began to place more emphasis on individuality, individual skills that enabled young people to adjust to the changing adult world were taught. Although agriculture and home economics were still the basis of the 4-H program, members were given opportunities to develop themselves as leaders and citizens. In addition, further expansion of the involvement of volunteer leaders took place, becoming an integral part of the successful 4-H educational process. Similarly, as U.S. society was becoming less rural, the 4-H program took on a much larger role in urban areas. Nutrition education, handicrafts, and care of the domestic environment were viewed as means of expanding 4-H programs to youth of inner cities. Many of the urban programs were also designed to support family unity by encouraging the participants and their parents to work together (Wessel & Wessel, 1982). The 4-H program also felt the strains of the civil rights movements of the 1960s, and subsequently desegregated all of its educational activities (Stewart, 1969; Wessel & Wessel, 1982).

The post-Vietnam War years brought an increase of career awareness and training to 4-H educational materials and programs. Efforts were undertaken to strengthen and expand the recruitment, training, and management of 4-H volunteers. An increased emphasis on the teaching of basic skills useful for everyday living, and the incorporation of science and scientific concepts into the curriculum were made with a national effort launched to provide more and better training for volunteers (Lang & Gerwig, 1989; Wessel & Wessel, 1982). More 4-H educational activities were designed with the explicit objective of helping youth to feel good about themselves and give them a sense of accomplishment rather than teaching specific knowledge or skills.

On the brink of the 21st century, major initiatives have been undertaken that address issues that youth are facing. School dropout, substance use and abuse, sexually transmitted diseases, teenage pregnancy, and poor self-esteem are just a few of the problems being addressed by Extension 4-H professionals. The original reasons given by early 20th-century educators for starting the forerunners of 4-H still apply today: problems with youth completing their education and their feelings of helplessness and inferiority. An example of a program used then was the 4-H corn club. Youth dealt with a real situation for which they had responsibility, clear goals pointing to accomplishment, and that helped to motivate them to stay in school while strengthening their self-worth. A major difference today is the focus of 4-H is not just on rural youth; it is on all youth, yet the programs' goals remain equally applicable. The 4-H program currently reaches over 5 million youth each year, with a 50–50 distribution of participants in metropolitan and rural areas, including minority and racially diverse youngsters (USDA/ES, 1991).

The 4-H philosophy, with its beginnings in the early 1900s, is still relevant. Giving young people a chance to develop good feelings about themselves, instilling a sense of pride, and educating them with skills that will enable them to become self-directing, productive, and contributing members of society is still the primary goal of 4-H educational programs.

The 4-H program continues to carry out this mission using a nonformal educational delivery system that is organized through the land-grant university in each state, with community-based local extension offices. For instance, at The Pennsylvania State University, field-based faculty provide educational leadership to the educational programs of the university (including 4-H) in each of the 67 counties of the commonwealth. Volunteers play a key role in the delivery of 4-H programming, which uses the "learn-by-doing" experiential approach. As a result, the groups involve parents and other adults in the community through their commitment to making 4-H happen. Without interested volunteers, parents, community leaders, educators, and others who are willing to work with youth, 4-H would not exist. This historical overview of 4-H over the past 80 years, serves to demonstrate how 4-H has evolved in response to changes in the social economic environment of U.S. families.

THE "GENIUS" OF 4-H EDUCATIONAL PROGRAMS

Based on sound developmental theories, 4-H educational programs contain many of the key elements found in all successful youth education programs (J. P. Miller, 1991). A national task force on out-of-classroom education suggested that 4-H embodies a certain genius and demonstrated effectiveness, causing it to be worthy of expansion to more youth (USDA/ES, 1980). The genius of 4-H as stated by these educators includes these educational concepts:

1. provides co-educational learning experiences that contribute to both personal and social development;
2. uses real-life work experiences, letting youth set their own goals for achievement;
3. encourages individual initiative and provides opportunities for young people to experience success which in turn raises the level of their aspirations and contributes to a feeling of self-worth;
4. incorporates the "learning-by-doing" methodology directed toward personal development;
5. provides laboratory situations for individual learning in practical projects and activities;

6. provides opportunities for young people to practice democratic group action and social development through local clubs and group experiences;
7. provides for natural progression from simple to more complex tasks;
8. provides opportunities to become part of a program that benefits the community;
9. provides for effective youth–adult relationships that help integrate youth into society, and keeps adults in tune with the needs and interests of youth;
10. utilizes the dynamics of positive peer-group influence; and
11. extends the influence of homes, schools, and churches through its complementary relationships.

DESIGN ELEMENTS OF 4-H EDUCATIONAL PROGRAMS

The basis of the principles on which 4-H is based have evolved over time from experiences of practitioners and with the application of research. The essential design elements for an effective 4-H learning experience are constructs that account for readiness, need, motivation, and individual differences. These elements have been derived from theories that comprise the academic base for 4-H (USDA/ES, 1984). An effective 4-H curriculum utilizes these elements in each experience, and are to be clearly identifiable in the curriculum materials as well as staff development. The experiences are to be practical, realistic, useful, and helpful applications of subject matter wherever possible. The design elements that maximize the potential for success of a 4-H learning experience are:

1. *Action*-related activities based on the idea that young people enjoy doing new things that are fun, exciting, and result in learning.
2. *Interaction* in a 4-H experience provides young people opportunities for learning to talk to and work with all kinds of people (adults and youth, friends and strangers—across ages, roles, and cultures); learning to examine new ideas and to apply them to the way they live; and learning to use such things as equipment, libraries, bicycles, fabric, magazines, lakes, animals, the backyard, or a computer.
3. *Decision making* experiences are provided when youth are involved in clarifying the need, setting goals, planning to achieve their goals, finding the help they need, doing the things

they planned, assessing their progress, and sharing results and accomplishments.
4. *Recognition* can provide reinforcement for learning by pats on the back from friends, parents, and leaders; as well as awards and rewards.
5. *Public affirmation* experiences are provided to publicly share what has been made, learned, believed, or accomplished through demonstrations, speaking, exhibitions, and performing.
6. *Leadership (helpership)* experiences can provide people (both youth and adults) with opportunities for learning to help each other by enabling them to show someone how to do something without doing it for them; observe and listen; support with encouragement; show sincere interest, help a person do things his or her way; and give praise when needed and earned.
7. *Flexibility* of 4-H experiences can provide situational and individual alternatives for people in learning opportunities, policies, and requirements, roles, role definitions, job descriptions, ways to be involved, and expected outcomes.
8. *Utilization of resources* experiences in 4-H can help people recognize and use resources around them such as (a) themselves—their natural abilities, working with their hands, solving problems, expressing ideas, sharing with others, being a helper to others, and learning from others; (b) other people—parents, brothers and sisters, friends, leaders, and people in their community (neighbors, policemen, grocery store owners, and librarians); and (c) items in their home and the various items in their neighborhood.

In addition, 4-H has developed a number of design elements that recognize the close relationships between youths' development and their family environment. Thus, 4-H programs seek to capitalize on the home and family setting as a naturally occurring center for 4-H learning. "Natural" family activities are used for 4-H learning experiences. Family members, friends, and neighbors are natural helpers for 4-H learning. This is becoming especially important for single-parent families and for families where both parents work.

Traditionally, 4-H has been a part of the community and program planners have found these efforts to be enhanced when the use of common resources is facilitated; assistance is provided in assessing community needs; accepting community responsibilities is encouraged; becoming involved in community activities is encouraged; community improvement is planned for; the community is viewed as a natural center for learning; natural community activities are used as learning opportunities; community members are involved as natural helpers to each other; and 4-H activities promote and support community (USDA/ES, 1984).

All of these elements just mentioned are equally important for all youths regardless of circumstances or membership in 4-H or other youth organizations. These elements need to be integrated into overall learning experiences. They also need to be considered regarding their implications for youth policies.

In summary, the success of 4-H in large part has been through the holistic view of the youth in their environment (i.e., personal development, the family, and the community). Today this emersion model is gaining widespread acceptance among individuals designing youth intervention programs (Swisher, 1988). The 4-H model has also been implemented in over 80 countries around the world demonstrating a worldwide commitment to young people everywhere.

ROLE AND RELATIONSHIP OF SCHOLARS AND PRACTITIONERS

An acknowledgment and focus on the necessity to enhance and broaden knowledge about youth points to the need for increased interdisciplinary collaboration. Researchers and practitioners are a powerful team that can accomplish the multifocal goals for young people and those who work with them. The research-scholar has the understanding of theory and concepts in their discipline. The practitioner-educator has real-life field work experience and expertise with youth in their various environments. Each can contribute to the work of the other.

As centers of knowledge and providers of talent, colleges and universities must be among those who forge the needed partnerships that will address the complex dimensions of the youth crisis. Throughout their history, land-grant universities integrated the results of research with delivery of educational services, and in a manner that enhances the capabilities of people and their groups in the community at large. Grounded in research and tested in practice, this history constitutes a major resource that can be put to greater use. In helping children and youth move toward self-confident adulthood, it is recognized that early adolescence is a critical juncture in determining the social and intellectual development of youth. (P. A. Miller, 1988.)

Retrieving and sharing existing knowledge, conducting applied research, and systematically evaluating and documenting joint youth development efforts continue to be important. The land-grant universities can play an important role in the more formal aspects of research, and, in so doing, take the lead in mobilizing the full range of interdisciplinary and professional resources. Practitioners and researchers as partners must be involved in conceptualizing and assessing research strategies. This focus of information sharing will help people apply knowledge to the problems of youth with an increased likelihood of positive outcomes.

Like most collaborations, strengthening the partnerships between researchers and practitioners will take some time and in some instances may be difficult to accomplish. However, the difficulty can be minimized through the development of commitment to the common goal of helping youth develop their potential and the realization of the mutually beneficial relationship.

Norman A. Brown (1987), president of the W. K. Kellogg Foundation, a former administrator and youth development professional at two land-grant universities (Michigan State and Minnesota) offered the following suggestions regarding the needs that he felt land-grant universities should specifically be able to address. These institutions are able to:

1. Provide problem-solving research in areas of youth development, such as child and adolescent health, leadership development, social behavior, and parenting;
2. Develop family and community-based program models to address such problems as alcohol and drug abuse, teenage pregnancy, juvenile delinquency;
3. Provide expertise in communities on housing, crime prevention, economic development, etc.;
4. Revitalize the university curricula that prepare professionals who will work in youth and community development efforts;
5. Increase access by workers in preschools, K-12 schools, and non-school youth programs to relevant, dynamic continuing education programs;
6. Build on the demonstrated strength of the Cooperative Extension Service in management of volunteer systems;
7. Improve efforts to provide university students with a greater understanding of, exposure to, and experience in volunteerism. (pp. 3–4)

Brown further stated that the knowledge is available in the United States to radically change the youth trends. He called for unprecedented action programs by land-grant universities to help solve problems of modern youth. He said land-grant universities can not only help the United States solve a problem of crises proportions, but in the process can regain the respect they once had because they were seen by taxpayers as helping people solve their problems. Brown added that unless land-grant universities start working harder at being pro-active and responsive to the problems that need to be solved in the United States (and start looking outward rather than simply to their peers in the disciplines), the United States is going to create new institutions that will do the job that is needed.

YOUTH-AT-RISK PROGRAMMING

Toward this end, extension programs and 4-H are currently expanding the land-grant university leadership with "youth-at-risk" programming. Significant need for youth-at-risk programming is defined in terms of risk factors contributing to youth not meeting their full potential. An example of this effort has recently occurred at The Pennsylvania State University. Collaborations are being formed between faculty members of the College of Agriculture and the College of Health and Human Development to strengthen the linkages between researchers and the providers of nonformal youth education programs. Joint faculty appointments, field-based research activities, graduate seminars, conferences, and workshops, are some of the approaches being used. One example of efforts within this relationship was a one-day inservice education workshop with 50 field-based and campus faculty as well as researchers on the topic of "Enhancing Self-Esteem of Youth: Dialogue Between Agents and Researchers." A resultant follow-up meeting with a work group of field-based faculty, program specialists, and researchers was held to initiate the development, implementation, and evaluation of an educational curriculum on the topic of "Enhancing Self-Esteem Through Life Skill Development," and a major contribution to youth development programming is the anticipated outcome.

Educational programs addressing some of the causes of antisocial behavior in youth are also being introduced. New programs that are to be implemented along with ongoing 4-H programs are after-school programs, leadership skills, parenting and health issues, child care, and enhancement of self-esteem. These programs are being implemented with a three-tiered approach: (a) youth development education, (b) parent education, and (c) community education. The community education component will require collaboration with other youth service agencies. Some of the proposed projects for the communities involve: (a) targeting communities that have a high number of risk factors, (b) involving youth as resources for the community, (c) developing volunteers as mentors for youth, (d) instituting school-age child-care education programs, and (e) improving literacy and employability in communities (USDA/ES, 1989b).

One example of such a program is "On My Own and O.K." This program is targeted to 9- to 12-year-olds who can benefit from or who spend time alone and can benefit from self-care education. In Wilkes-Barre, Pennsylvania, Christine Tomascik, the field-based faculty member in Luzerne County, worked with the school district and others to identify an area with the majority of low-income families and who had concerns about youths being at home alone. About 100 youth were involved and completed the program with successful outcomes. An assessment of youths' self-care skills by pre- and postsurvey showed an overall increase in competency of 18%. Some of the largest increases were a 30% increase in the ability of youth to act in emergency situations, a 26% increase in the ability of youth to deal with boredom, 20% increase in the ability of youth to deal with fears when home alone and to handle things in the kitchen, 18% increases in the ability of youth to deal with brothers and sisters and to organize after-school activities while home alone. Thirty-eight parents attended two educational meetings that dealt with discipline techniques. Learn-at-home discipline packets were sent to all (50) parents of the children in the after-school program. Parents' evaluations of their children's self-care abilities and of their discipline techniques show increases in both child and parent competencies. Overall, this program demonstrates the 4-H comprehensive approach utilizing youth, parent, and community involvement to address a problem.

Another example of 4-H adapting to the changing needs of youth and specifically addressing identified at risk youth can be illustrated by the "Step in the Right Direction" program in Johnstown, Pennsylvania. Gary Washington, a field-based faculty member with youth-at-risk programming responsibilities, working with Lisa Acruio, Juvenile Probation Officer of the Cambria County court system, has involved adjudicated youth in a personal development, 4-H club meeting program. The goal of the program is to identify the children's strengths as individuals, increase their self-esteem and sense of responsibility toward themselves and others, and identify important and influential people in their lives. Only 1 of the 24 youth involved with the program in 1991 has since gotten into trouble and reentered the court system. Although only a first "step," those involved agree overwhelmingly that it is definitely in the right direction.

To more effectively deal with the youth crisis, 4-H is also fostering partnerships with agencies, businesses, and others in communities. The problems now confronted by U.S. youth are so pervasive that unilateral efforts yield limited results. Individual organizations must focus their efforts and resources on those problems they are best qualified to solve. But it is of special importance in the local community that programs bring into concert the concerns and actions of parents, schools, local governmental officials, community organizations, social welfare agencies, churches, planning councils, businesses, industry, trade unions, and others. As an outreach component of the land-grant university, 4-H can bring, among other resources, a knowledge base of youth development and programming to any community partnership.

The 4-H program has encountered some problems as it moved to urban programming and most recently targeting at risk youth and family constituencies. An example of an obstacle or barrier was the reluctance of some field-based and campus faculty and administrators to accept high-risk youth as a 4-H clientele and to move in that direction. Earmarked 4-H funding in the 1960s for urban programming helped to encourage states and counties to do expanded programming, particularly in urban areas, where 4-H had not been introduced extensively. More recently with the youth-at-risk initiative, again the USDA/ES funds provided incentives for states to address and expand the clientele base.

In Pennsylvania for example, 20% of the counties were provided with additional funds in 1989 to be used for piloting effective approaches for expansion of 4-H programs addressing specific youth issues and needs. Field-based faculty experimented with taking the "basic" 4-H program to an at-risk youth audience in communities of counties they worked with. In some cases, the Expanded Food and Nutrition Educational Program (EFNEP), a low-income educational program conducted by The Cooperative Extension System was already working with at-risk families. Reports of accomplishments by agents at the end of the second year of a 3-year commitment, indicated that field and campus-based faculty had adjusted the 4-H program to the newer audiences. One of the major adjustments was the increased collaboration with other human service agencies (i.e., county probation office, child development council, state hospital, private industry council, etc.) to reach low-income, disadvantaged youth and families. The various projects dealt with subjects of interest to the youth such as leadership development, gardening, and foods and nutrition. An observation of the process suggests that appropriate adjustments are made providing an understanding of program goals is present. The goal remains—to meet the needs and interests of youth.

The introduction of and subsequent emphasis on at-risk youth was met with mixed responses. Some field-based faculty were hesitant to do programming with at-risk youth and families. Some were not comfortable in working with the clientele. Others expressed time problems with additional time needed to adequately start the development of coalitions when they were already committed to "150% of their time." There was also an uncertainty as to whether or not "administration" would support them. These factors were discovered through a series of visits with field-based faculty in 14 counties by the faculty member assigned the responsibility for educational leadership for the youth-at-risk programming in Pennsylvania. Field-based faculty also expressed the need for additional staff development opportunities on understanding and developing programs for at-risk youth and families (Snider & Coslett, 1989).

Another obstacle 4-H has tried to overcome over the years is its rural image. Various communication approaches are being introduced to provide messages on youth development education. One of the more effective methods has been personal contact and involving people with the 4-H youth development education program. Nonrural people are recognizing that 4-H is more than "cows and cooking." An ongoing approach that has been helpful is the publishing and distribution of written materials illustrating the urban approaches and successes of 4-H. One example is the article in the Spring–Summer, 1989, issue of *Penn State Agriculture, "New Faces, New Places. Involving City Kids in Contemporary 4-H Programs."* In addition, on the national level are the two new national 4-H publications that focus on nonrural programs; *The 4-H You Know and the 4-H You Don't Know* and *The Difference We Make*. These publications are being well received nationally.

Recent expanded private and public dollars for youth-at-risk programming has been a key factor influencing the 4-H youth development ability to implement programs with at-risk youth and families. In 1990, a $5.9 million project was funded by the W. K. Kellogg Foundation called Community CARES. CARES is the acronym for Creating Action for Responsibility, Education, and Support. The funding was granted to the consortium of Extension Service, USDA, and the National 4-H Council to help enhance the capacity of the Cooperative Extension System to efficiently and effectively deliver programming to a broad spectrum of the nation's youth. Seven Centers for Action in Youth at Risk Programming are located at land-grant institutions around the country. They are providing training and technical assistance to the federally funded youth-at-risk community programs and other extension youth programs around the country (National 4-H Council, USDA/ES, 1990).

In fiscal year 1991, 70 targeted youth-at-risk sites were funded through a new federal budget initiative of $7.5 million. These community sites target at-risk youth with three program foci: school-age child care education, collaborations that support youth at high risk, and science–technical and reading literacy. Significant need for at-risk youth programming was defined by the request for applications in terms of risk factors contributing to youth not meeting their full potential. Need is significant when two or more risk factors interact. Risk factors include poverty, substance abuse, teen pregnancy, illiteracy, school dropouts, AIDS, homeless youth.

To aid communities in addressing needs of at risk youth, the Cooperative Extension System has implemented targeted prevention and intervention programs to improve the opportunities for youth and to reduce the conditions causing risk. Programming objectives for this new federal funding include:

1. Forming coalitions of private and public support in communities in support of youth;
2. Increasing self-confidence and skills toward productive adulthood;
3. Involving parents in building positive parenting skills;
4. Reducing long-term costs to society by producing competent youth moving into adulthood; and
5. Increasing the employability of youth (USDA-ES, 1990).

For Fiscal year 1992, $10 million was allocated in President Bush's budget for the youth-at-risk initiative administered by USDA/ES, with $15 million being proposed for fiscal year 1993.

As the Cooperative Extension System with other educational organizations expand their efforts to reach more families and youth at risk, there is an even greater demand for enhanced knowledge to deal with the youth crisis. This points out the importance of strengthening the collaborative role of researchers and practitioners in their discovery and application of new knowledge that can help provide successful outcomes for all families and youth.

THE FUTURE

As one looks to the future, what will the successful youth development education program be like? Insight to this question was provided by John A. DiBiaggio, President of Michigan State University, in a presentation to youth development administrators and faculty of land-grant universities in 1989. DiBiaggio (1989) suggested that the youth development organization of the future:

1. does not operate in a vacuum. This organization recognizes the necessity of working collaboratively with people inside and

outside of universities, to create programs and garner support for continued efforts;
2. pulls together the creative minds of faculty and specialists in many campus departments—not only those that they've worked with in the past—to help design broadened youth programs that are informative and relevant to today's kids;
3. recognizes that it is not only in the business of educating youth—but that it can also make a significant impact on parents, teachers, youth development professionals, and adult and teen volunteers who work with kids;
4. works in partnership with schools and sees its mission as helping educate youth by providing high-impact, hands-on, experiential learning environments for kids;
5. teams up with the "youth development champions" who are currently working in business and industry—and there are more of them than you may realize—talented professionals who would relish the opportunity of sharing what they know with interested youngsters;
6. creates opportunities for young people to succeed, recognizing that one of the most precious gifts one can offer a child is positive self-worth;
7. provides ways for kids to experience that learning is fun—and works with kids to help them develop into life-long learners who can be active participants and leaders in a changing world;
8. works with children holistically—focusing on the total child, who is part of a family, a community and a planetary society;
9. helps young people develop life skills for the future—including helping them get excited about science, expose kids to global issues, and help kids develop personal coping skills, and show them how they can invent their own futures;
10. creates environments where people can have a lot of fun—while they learn—using innovative curricula that include video, computers, satellite communications, and interactive video to mention a few. (pp. 3–6)

Many of the characteristics DiBiaggio suggested are starting to become a reality with some land-grant institutions, such as at The Pennsylvania State University. This indicates that these elements are realistic for a successful youth development educational program. Some are saying at The Pennsylvania State University, in fact, that the future is "now."

There is a need for basic and applied research initiatives to help tailor outreach and resident instruction programs built on a scientifically sound knowledge and experience base. Research needs must be prioritized so that resources can be directed to critical concerns.

Needed research will require interdisciplinary models involving collaborative efforts among sociology, psychology, anthropology, education, law, health sciences, public administration, political science, and other disciplines contributing to youth development. Priority research areas need to be identified with input from practicing youth development professionals as well as other professionals, researchers, community and business leaders, government officials, and parents who have an interest in educational environments for youth. The Professional Research and Knowledge (4-H PRK) taxonomy for youth professionals provides a useful framework for classifying research needs and identifying gaps in this developing research field. Developed through a grant from USDA/ES at The Ohio State University and Mississippi State University the five major areas for classifying youth development research and knowledge in 4-H PRK are communication, educational design, youth development, youth program management, and volunteerism (Hastings, Rennekamp, & Gerhard, 1988). Further research and application efforts are underway to support and strengthen what we know works and to expand, enhance, and enlighten us in those areas in which we have much to learn.

As was said in the beginning of this chapter, the responsibility of land-grant universities is to provide all people with opportunities to access research and new knowledge that will enrich their lives. In addition, it is being demonstrated that researchers and practitioners make a powerful team that can develop the knowledge needed to apply to youth needs; and at the same time provide mutually beneficial outcomes. Researchers will benefit through experiencing the application of scholarly work in a very real environment. Practitioners will benefit through a better understanding of concepts and thus will be more effective with their efforts. Communities will benefit through increasing quality of life and reducing risk-taking behaviors on the part of their youth. Best of all, youth will benefit through development of their full potential.

It is expected that additional partnerships will be developed in the future to address the many needs of youth. Furthermore, it is anticipated that collaborations formed by 4-H youth development programs and faculty can indeed be a vehicle for community partnerships in order to more fully bring the research and knowledge base of the university to communities. The combined resources of land-grant universities can be a powerful influence in helping to solve the youth crisis that the United States faces, and in paving the way to more positive outcomes for young people around the world.

FINAL COMMENT

An essential genius of the 4-H program has been the development of conceptually sound youth development programs that are programmatically based in real-world problems facing youth and the families of which they are a part. As our understanding of youth development processes has emerged and the social economic environment of U.S. families has changed, 4-H has responded, and today continues as the nation's largest nonformal educational youth-serving program. The challenges of the 1990s, however, are great, and maintenance of a strong, viable, and relevant youth development education program within land-grant universities will require the development of stronger links between the emerging youth development research base and holistic programs that draw heavily on the wide variety of resources available within communities and other organizations that value the upcoming generation of young people.

REFERENCES

Brown, N. A. (1987, October 26). *Youth development in the land-grant university* (McDowell Lecture). University Park: The Pennsylvania State University, Department of Agricultural and Extension Education.

DiBiaggio, J. A. (1989, October 4). *Vision and challenges for 4-H and youth development in the future.* Presentation made to assistant directors of extension; State 4-H resource development directors, and Extension Service/United States Department of Agriculture staff, Chevy Chase, MD.

Graham, A. B. (1958). *Beginnings of the 4-H program* (recorded interview by MaryLou Pfeiffer, WRFD radio, Worthington, OH). Columbus: Ohio State University 4-H Office Archives.

Hastings, S., Rennekamp, R., & Gerhard, G. (1988). *The 4-H professional research and knowledge base (4-H PRK) executive summary.* Washington, DC: Extension Service/United States Department of Agriculture.

Lang, C. L., & Gerwig, J. L. (1989). The ever growing clover. *NAE4-HA News and Views, 42*(4), 6–8.

McCormick, V. E., & McCormick, R. W. (1984). *A. B. Graham: Country schoolmaster and extension pioneer.* Worthington, OH: Cottonwood Publications.

Miller, J. P. (1991). *Four-H and non-4-H participants' development of competency, coping, and contributory life skills.* Unpublished doctoral thesis, The Pennsylvania State University, University Park.

Miller, P. A. (1988). *To our colleagues in the land-grant universities: A statement on the crisis of youth in America.* Unpublished manuscript.

National 4-H Council, USDA-ES. (1990). *Request for proposals, Community CARES Centers for Action.* Chevy Chase, MD: Author.

Reck, F. M. (1951). *The 4-H story: A history of 4-H club work.* Ames: The Iowa State College Press.

Shrum, G. A. (1987). *Extension commitment to youth.* Chevy Chase, MD: National 4-H Council.

Snider, B. A. (1988). *Preparing youth for responsibility: An implementation strategy for extension faculty and staff.* Concept paper for the National Initiative, Building Human Capital, Extension Service/United States Department of Agriculture, Washington, DC.

Snider, B. A., & Coslett, L. (1989). *Summary of responses to discussion questions from the youth at risk fact finding meetings with 14 counties in Pennsylvania, Fall 1989.* Unpublished manuscript, The Pennsylvania State University, University Park.

Stewart, G. H. (1969). *A touch of charisma: A history of the 4-H club program in West Virginia.* West Virginia 4-H All Stars. Morgantown, WV.

Swisher, J. D. (1988). *What works?* Prevention research, Findings: 1988, Office of Substance Abuse Prevention, monograph-3, Rockville, MD.

United States Department of Agriculture, Extension Service (USDA/ES). (1980). *Four-H in century III* (Report by Task Force on 4-H in Century III to Extension Committee on Organization and Policy). Washington, DC: Author.

United States Department of Agriculture, Extension Service (USDA/ES). (1984). *Building blocks for curriculum design in 4-H program development.* Washington, DC: Author.

United States Department of Agriculture, Extension Service (USDA/ES). (1989b). *New dimensions in youth development education* (A report by the 4-H youth development subcommittee of the Extension Committee on Organization and Policy) Washington, DC: Author.

United States Department of Agriculture, Extension Service (USDA/ES). (1989a). *The American agenda* (A report of the National Initiative Task Force on Youth at Risk). Washington, DC: Author. Irby, J. E., & O'Brien, S. Cochairs.

United States Department of Agriculture, Estension Service (USDA/ES). (1990). *National announcement youth at risk extension funding program, requests for applications.* Washington, DC: Author.

United States Department of Agriculture, Extension Service (USDA/ES). (1991). *Cooperative extension system, national 4-H statistics, 1990.* Washington, DC: Author.

Wessel, T., & Wessel, M. (1982). *4-H: An American idea 1900–1980: A history of 4-H.* Chevy Chase, MD: National 4-H Council.

Author Index

A

Abbott, R., 167, *173*
Abraham, K. G., 61, *66*
Abrahamse, A. F., 344, 347, 349, *350*
Adams, G. R., 42, 44, 47, *48*, *50*, 93, 95, *109*, 285, *290*, 315, *332*
Adams, L. B., 268, *272*
Adams, R. G., 59, *68*
Adelman, R., 116, *125*
Adelson, J., 3, 4, 11, 17, 18, *22*
Adler, N. E., 357, *367*
Aitken, P. P., 440, *444*
Albrecht, H. T., 72, 78, 82, 85, 86, *90*, *91*
Alder, N. E., 252, *259*
Alexander, C. S., 100, *108*
Alexander, K. L., 133, *140*, 186, 187, *188*, *189*
Alexander, P. A., 215, *218*
Allegrante, J. P., 375, *380*
Allen, C. M., 120, *126*, 439, *446*
Allen, D. M., 45, *48*
Allen, J. P., 329, *331*
Allen, V. L., 99, *109*
Alpert, J., 224, *233*
Alter, T. R., 453, *455*
Alvermann, D. E., 216, *219*
Ames, E. E., 241, *245*

Amul, S. A., 117, *125*
Anderson, C. L., 243, *245*, 257, *259*
Anderson, J. B., 261, 262, 263, 265, 269, *273*
Anderson, J. C., 384, *396*
Anderson, J. P., 136, *140*
Anderson, P., 431, *444*
Anderson, R. C., 207, *219*
Anderson, R. I., 215, *219*
Andreasen, N. C., 387, *397*
Andres, D., 77, *89*
Andrews, J., 394, *397*
Aneshensel, C. S., 342, *350*, 384, *398*
Angold, A., 384, *395*
Apley, J., 119, 121, *124*
Apter, T., 460, *467*
Archer, S. L., 285, 287, *289*, *290*
Armstrong, S., 115, *125*
Ashby, J. S., 374, *380*
Ashton, G. C., 55, *68*
Asmus, E. P., 224, 224, 229, 229, 230, *233*
Astington, J. W., 151, *154*, 155
Astone, N., 28, 32, *33*
Atkin, C. K., 437, 438, 439, 440, 442, *444*
Atkins, R., 431, 434, 441, *445*
Austin, G. A., 146, *154*

501

B

Bacchetti, P., 354, *368*
Bachman, G. G., 65, *66*
Bachman, J. G., 282, *290*, 373, 376, *380*, 432, 433, 435, *444, 445*, 459, *467*
Bachrach, C. A., 95, *108*, 345, *351*
Baer, D. E., 229, *234*
Baker, L., 214, 215, *219*
Baldwin, J. M., 144, *154*
Baldwin, W., 93, 94, *109*, 315, *332*
Baltes, P. B., 1, 11, 12
Bandura, A., 17, *22*
Bangert-Drowns, R. L. T., 377, *380*
Barber, J. G., 438, *444*
Bare, D. E., 282, *290*
Barlow, D. H., 393, *395*
Barnes, G. W., 433, *446*
Barnes, J. G., 438, *444*
Barnett, P. A., 388, *395*
Barr, H. H., 241, *245*
Barresi, A. L., 231, *234*
Barth, R. P., 326, *332*
Bartko, T., 80, *90*
Bartsch, K., 147, 148, *154, 156*
Basil, M. D., 435, *446*
Bauman, K. E., 58, *67*
Baumrind, D., 85, *89*
Bean, F. D., 336, 337, *350*
Beauvais, F., 356, 360, *368*
Becerra, R. M., 342, *350*
Beck, N. C., 384, *396*
Becker, M. H., 59, *69*, 252, 253, *258, 259*
Beeghley, M., 148, *154*
Beeghley-Smith, M., 148, *154*
Bejerot, N., 371, *380*
Belcastro, P. A., 301, *305*
Bell, N. H., 263, *274*
Bell, R. M., 377, *381*
Bellack, A. S., 394, *396*
Bell-Scott, P., 62, *66*
Belsky, J., 17, *22*
Bendy, C., 185, *188*
Bennett, C., 186, *189*
Bennett, S., 453, *455*
Bentler, P. M., 370, 374, *381*
Berenson, G. S., 266, 271, *273, 274*
Berger, A. S., 297, *307*
Berger, P., 194, *205*
Berman, L. B., 41, *48*
Bernardo, V., 263, 265, 271, *275*

Berndt, T. J., 321, *331*, 390, *395*, 459, *468*
Bernstein, B., 180, *188*
Berry, V. T., 228, *234*
Beswick, G., 327, *332*
Beyth-Marom, R., 459, *467*
Bibace, R., 252, *258*
Billy, J. O. G., 98, 99, *110*, 300, 301, *305*, 307, 317, *333*
Bingham, C. R., 361, 365, *366*
Birkel, R., 19, 20, *22*
Black, A. E., 85, *89*
Blatt, S. J., 389, *395*
Bless, D. M., 231, *234*
Block, J., 3, 11, 370, 374, *382*
Block, M., 439, 442, *444*
Bloome, D., 198, *206*
Blum, R. W., 111, *125*, 269, 272, 273, 275, 453, *455*
Blustein, D. L., 285, *290*
Blyth, D. A., 4, 12, 59, *66*, 120, 121, *125*, 391, *397*
Bogart, K., 39, *48*
Bolton, F. G., 43, *48*, 301, *305*
Bolton, W., 389, *397*
Bordieu, P., 64, *67*
Boswell, J., 225, *234*
Boswell, T. D., 336, *351*
Botvin, G. J., 321, 328, *331*, 378, *381*, *395*
Bouchard, C., 262, *274*
Bourdieu, P., 182, *188*
Bourgeois, J. C., 438, *444*
Bouterline-Young, H., 54, *69*
Bowman, P. J., 54, *67*
Boyd, J. H., 121, *126*
Boyer, C. B., 355, 356, *366*, 367
Boyes, M., 151, *154*
Boylan, F., 41, *50*
Boyle, J. D., 225, 226, 228, *234*, 238
Brachman, R., 120, *126*
Braddock, J. H., II, 185, *189*
Bradford, B. J., 241, *245*
Bradley, C. E., 241, *245*
Bradshaw, R., 438, *444*
Brandon, J., 42, 43, *50*
Braucht, G. N., 442, *445*
Breed, W., 437, *446*
Brennan, M., 6, 7, 11
Brennan, T., 42, *48*
Brennan-Quattrack, J., 389, *397*

Bretherton, I., 148, *154*
Brewer, W., 146, 147, *156*
Brim, O., 466, *467*
Brittain, C. V., 17, *22*
Brock, C. J., 297, *307*
Brock, T. C., 442, *445*
Brodarec, A., 263, *274*
Bronfenbrenner, U., 19, *22*, 52, 67, 72, 77, 83, *89*, 131, 134, *140*
Brook, J. S., 121, *125*
Brookins, G. K., 6, 11
Brookover, W. C., 185, *188*
Brooks-Gunn, J., 3, 4, 8, 12, 17, 19, *22*, 29, 30, *34*, 96, 97, 98, 99, 103, 104, 105, *108*, 322, *331*, 355, 357, *366*
Broughton, J. M., 145, 151, *154*
Brown, A. L., 214, 215, *219*
Brown, B. B., 183, 184, *188*, *190*, 321, *331*, 459, *467*
Brown, C. H., 57, 59, 67, *68*
Brown, E. F., 412, *416*
Brown, J. D., 58, 67, 414, *416*
Brown, L., 302, *306*
Brown, L. A., 167, *173*
Brown, L. D., 424, *429*
Brown, N. A., 482, 490, *498*
Brown, S. A., 373, *381*
Brownell, K. D., 270, *275*
Browner, W. S., 266, *274*
Bruess, C. E., 251, *259*
Bruhn, J. G., 248, 253, *259*
Brun, J., 271, *274*
Brundage, J. F., 355, *366*
Bruner, J. S., 146, *154*, 171, *173*, 203, 204, *205*
Brunswick, A. F., 57, *67*
Bruun, K., 441, *445*
Bryam, O. W., 56, *67*
Bryk, A. S., 181, 185, *189*
Buccuvalas, M. J., 452, *455*
Buie, D. H., 386, 390, *395*
Bumpass, L., 28, 32, *34*
Burgess, A. W., 43, *49*
Burgos, W., 56, *67*
Burke, D. S., 355, *366*
Burke, J. D., 121, *126*
Burke, R., 413, *416*
Burton, L. M., 58, *67*, 102, *108*
Busch-Rossnagel, N. A., 82, *90*
Butchart, A. T., 377, *381*
Butler, J. R., 102, *108*

Butler, L., 394, *395*
Buzina, R., 263, *274*
Byrne, N., 257, *259*

C

Calcagno, P. L., 114, *125*
Call, V., 32, *34*
Callan, V. J., 375, *382*
Campbell, J., 171, *173*
Campbell, S. B., 318, *333*
Campbell, W. L., 210, *219*
Canton, D., 43, 46, *49*
Cantrell, M. J., 167, *174*
Caplan, M. Z., 393, *398*
Caplan, R. D., 88, *89*
Capper, A. I., 266, *275*
Card, J. J., 97, *108*
Carey, S., 146, 147, 148, 150, *154*, *156*
Carey, W., 422, *429*
Carlsmith, J. M., 300, *306*
Carlson, G. A., 384, 385, *395*, *396*
Carmody, W. J., 226, 227, *234*
Carnevale, A. P., 207, 208, 209, *219*
Carrigan, S., 389, *397*
Carruth, B. R., 267, *275*
Casey, S., 326, *331*
Casper, R. C., 268, *273*
Caspi, A., 72, 73, 75, 80, 82, *89*
Catrone, C., 106, *110*
Cattell, R. B., 1, 12
Caudill, W., 63, *67*
Cerullo, K., 414, *417*
Chaffee, S., 435, *445*
Chan, G. M., 267, *273*
Chandler, M., 151, 152, 153, *154*
Chapman, M., 145, *155*
Char, W. J., 55, *68*
Chase-Lansdale, L., 104, 105, *108*
Cheatham, H. E., 61, *67*
Chess, S., 20, *22*, 132, *141*
Cheung, L. W. Y., 262, *273*
Childers, K. W., 58, *67*
Chiles, J. A., 387, *395*
Chilman, C. S., 96, 98, 99, 100, 101, 104, 105, *108*, 320, 322, *331*
Chimezie, A., 53, *67*
Chin, J., 353, 354, 365, *367*, *368*
Chirco, A. P., 435, 438, *445*
Chisman, F. P., 209, 210, 212, *219*
Chitwood, S. R., 453, *455*

Chopak, J., 373, *381*
Christenson, P. G., 223, 228, *234*, 409, 410, 412, 413, *416*
Christopher, F. S., 328, *331*
Christopherson, V. A., 61, *66*
Chrousos, G. P., 251, *260*
Chung, H. C., 347, 348, *350*
Ciborowski, J., 228, *234*
Cioci, M., 160, 165, 169, *174*
Clabby, J. F., 393, *396*
Clancy, M. A., 44, *48*
Clark, A. J., 265, *273*
Clark, D. C., 471, *480*
Clark, M. E., 181, *188*
Clarke, G. N., 394, *397*
Clarke, W. R., 261, 266, *274*
Clark-Lempers, D., 72, 74, *90*
Clarkson, S. E., 384, *396*
Clearie, A. F., 323, 325, *333*
Clement, D. B., 270, *273*
Clinchy, B., 153, *155*
Coasta, F., 100, *109*
Coates, D. L., 59, *67*
Cohen, E. L., 46, *50*, 391, *395*
Cohen, R., 47, *48*
Cohen, S., 391, *395*
Coie, J. D., *395*
Cole, E., 394, *395*
Coleman, J. S., 63, *67*, 171, *173*, 178, 179, 182, 184, *188*
Coleman, P. P., 57, *67*
Coles, R., 295, *305*, 460, 461, *467*
Collentti, J., 408, 409, 410, 411, 412, 413, *417*
Collins, C., 298, *305*
Collins, I., 233, *234*
Collins, O. P., 167, *173*
Collins, R., 433, *445*
Comer, J. P., 133, 134, 136, *140*
Compas, B. E., 393, *395*
Comstock, G., 435, *445*
Conger, J. J., 37, *48*
Conger, K. J., 75, *89*
Conger, R. D., 74, 75, *89*, *91*
Connor, J. W., 54, 63, *67*
Connors, M. E., 61, *67*
Contento, I. R., 271, *273*
Cooksey, J. M., 231, *234*
Coombs, N. R., 45, *48*
Cooper, C., 39, *48*
Corbett, H. D., 475, *480*

Corcoran, C. M., 384, *396*
Cortese, P. A., 241, *245*
Costlett, L., 494, *499*
Coulter, M. L., 439, *445*
Cox, G. B., 387, *395*
Coy, D. A., 227, *234*
Craighead, W. E., 387, *396*
Crawford, A. G., 95, *108*
Crawford, S., 386, 389, *398*
Cremin, L. A., 130, *140*
Cresanta, J. L., 266, *274*
Crockett, L. J., 99, 105, *109*, 311, *314*
Crockett, S., 271, *273*, *274*
Cross, C. K., 388, *396*
Cross, R. J., 295, 304, *305*
Crouter, A. C., 72, 77, 80, *89*, *90*, 282, *290*
Crutcher, D. M., 115, *125*
Cruz, J., 437, *446*
Csikszentmihalyi, M., 163, *173*
Culhane, C., 123, *125*
Cullen, R. M., 336, *351*
Cummings, J., 207, *219*
Curran, J. W., 354, 355, 365, *367*
Curtis, S. C., 224, *235*
Cutietta, R., 230, *235*
Cutler, J., 38, *50*
Cutler, R. E., 439, *446*
Cytryn, L., 384, *396*

D

Damon, W., 151, *155*
Danish, S. J., 362, *367*
Darlington, R., 136, *141*
D'Augelli, A. R., 298, *305*, 362, 363, *367*
Davies, M., 389, *397*
Davis, K., 176, *188*
Dawkins, M. P., 56, *67*
Dawson, D. A., 358, 359, 365, *367*
Dawson, J. A., 475, *480*
de Armas, A., 327, *331*
DeBenedictis, P., 409, 412, 413, *416*
De Benedictis, T., 434, *445*
Degen, K., 123, *125*
Deiter, P., 415, *416*
Delia, J. G., 402, *406*
DeLorenzo, L. C., 230, *235*
Delucchi, K., 434, *445*
deMauro, D., 303, *305*
Dembo, R., 56, *67*

Denisoff, R., 414, *416*
DeNour, A., 119, *125*
Derrick, A., 389, *397*
Desmond, S., 356, *368*
deSnipper, A., 136, *141*
Deturk, M. S., 230, *235*
Devenis, L. E., 285, *290*
DeVos, G., 63, *67*
Dewey, J., 191, 197, *205*
DiBiaggio, J. A., 495, *498*
DiClemente, R. J., 356, *367*
Dielman, T. E., 252, *259*, 377, *381*
Diepold, J., 293, 299, *306*
Dietz, W. H., 262, *273*
Dillon, D., 195, *205*
Dilts, R., 424, *429*
Dimatteo, M. R., 115, *125*
Ding, S., 389, *396*
Dishion, T. J., 75, 76, *89*
DiStefano, J. J., 229, *235*
Dixon, R., 411, *416*
Dolan, L. J., 100, *108*
Donnelly, B. W., 357, 361, *368*
Donovan, J., 100, *109*, 297, *306*
Dorn, L. D., 251, 252, *259*, *260*
Dornbusch, S. M., 6, 13, 60, *69*, 85, *89*, 178, 186, *189*, *190*, 300, *306*, 458, 459, 460, *467*, *469*
Douvan, E., 3, 11, 17, 18, *22*
Doyle, D. P., 207, *220*
Drabman, R. S., 439, *446*
Drash, A. L., 270, *273*
Dryfoos, J. G., 9, 11, 313, *314*, 323, 324, 326, 328, 329, *331*, 365, *367*
Ducey, D. E., 270, *274*
Dudley, G. A., 277, 283, *290*
Duke, A., 300, *306*
Dumont, R. V., Jr., 183, *190*
Duncan, G. J., 105, *108*, 322, *331*
Dunleavy, K., 408, 412, 413, *417*
Dusenbury, L., *395*
Dustan, J., 466, *467*
Dwyer, J. H., 378, 379, *381*

E

Earls, F., 357, 358, *368*
Ebata, A., 375, *382*
Eccles, J. S., 131, 132, *140*
Edelbrock, C., 42, *49*
Edlin, E., 241, *245*

Edmonds, R., 185, *188*
Edwards, G., 441, *445*
Ehlinger, J., 210, *220*
Eisner, E. W., 473, *480*
Elder, G. H., Jr., 71, 72, 73, 75, 80, 82, *89*
Elias, M. J., 393, *396*
Elkind, D., 118, *125*, 144, *155*
Ellickson, P. L., 377, *381*
Elliot, D. S., 42, *48*
Elliott, G. R., 3, 8, 11, 253, *259*, 450, 455, 458, 459, 460, 463, *467*
Ellis, M. V., 285, *290*
Ellison, R. C., 266, *275*
Elmore, R., 474, *480*
Elmslie, S., 279, *290*
Elster, A. G., 120, 121, *125*
Endicott, J., 387, *397*
Englander, S. W., 42, *48*
Enright, R., 153, *155*
Ensminger, M. E., 57, 59, *67*, *68*, 100, 106, *108*, *109*
Entwisle, D. R., 133, *140*, 186, 187, *188*, *189*, 462, *467*
Epstein, J. L., 135, *140*, 462, *468*
Epstein, L. H., 122, *125*
Erickson, C., 373, *381*
Erickson, J. B., 161, 162, 169, *173*
Erikson, E. H., 54, *67*, 278, 284, 285, 287, *290*, 319, *331*
Ervin, B., 265, 271, *275*
Evans, B., 159, *173*
Eveleth, P. B., 99, *108*, 316, *331*

F

Fairbank, J. A., 439, *446*
Falco, M., 434, 438, *445*
Fallahi, C., 384, *396*
Fanshel, D., 39, *48*
Farkas, G., 186, *189*
Farmer, H. S., 279, *290*
Farnworth, M., 57, *67*
Farquhar, J. W., 271, *273*
Farran, D. C., 136, *140*
Farris, R. P., 271, *273*
Farrow, J. A., 269, *273*
Farthing, M. C., 265, 266, 271, *273*
Feagans, L. V., 136, 138, *140*
Featherman, D. L., 1, 11
Feldman, C., 195, *206*

Feldman, S. S., 3, 8, 11, 253, *259*, 450, *455*, *458*, 459, 460, 463, *467*
Felner, R. D., 391, 392, *396*
Felner, T. W., 391, 392, *396*
Fennelly, K., 344, 346, 348, *350*, *351*
Fennelly Darbi, K., 343, 344, 348, *350*
Ferrara, L., 232, *235*
Ferro, D. L., 39, *49*
Fetro, J. V., 326, *332*
Fielder, E. P., 342, *350*
Finch, M. D., 282, 283, 284, *289*, *291*
Finch, S., 39, *48*
Fine, G. A., 402, *406*
Fine, M., 364, *367*
Fineberg, H. V., 356, *367*
Fingeret, H. A., 211, 212, *219*
Finn, T. A., 440, *445*
Finnas, L., 411, 412, *416*
Firestone, W. A., 475, *480*
Fischer, C., 408, *416*
Fischhoff, B., 459, *467*
Fisher, B., 45, *48*
Fisher, C. B., 6, 7, *11*
Fiske, J., 420, 421, *429*
Flanagan, C. A., 71, 78, 79, *89*
Flavell, J. H., 151, 152, *155*, *156*, 213, 214, *219*
Flay, B. R., 378, 379, *380*, *381*
Fleck, L., 195, *206*
Fletcher, J. C., 252, *259*
Flood, P., 185, *188*
Flora, J., 271, *273*
Flower, L., 215, *219*
Fly, J. W., 56, *67*
Foch, T. T., 17, *23*
Fodor, J., 147, *155*
Forbes, G. B., 262, 263, 264, 268, *273*
Ford, D. H., 19, *22*
Ford, K., 102, *110*
Fordham, S., 183, *189*
Forgatch, M. S., 76, *89*
Forlizzi, L. A., 215, *219*
Forrest, J. D., 303, *306*, 339, 342, 345, *350*, *351*, 359, *367*
Foster, S., 271, *273*
Fox, G. L., 104, *108*, 302, *306*
Foy, D. W., 439, *446*
Frakes, L., 222, 231, *235*
Fraleigh, M. J., 85, *89*
Frank, G. C., 271, *273*
Frankie, E. I., 282, *290*

Franklin, C., 153, *155*
Franklin, D. L., 98, 100, *108*
Frederick, C. J., 383, 386, 388, *396*
Freedman, D. S., 266, *274*
Freeman, E. W., 58, *67*
Freire, P., 191, *206*, 424, 425, 426, 428, *429*
French, T. K., 261, *275*
Friedman, E. J., 268, *273*
Friedman, I. M., 269, *273*
Friedman, M. L., 287, *291*
Friedman, R., 394, *395*
Frith, M., 424, 426, *429*
Frith, S., 223, *235*, 410, 414, *416*
Fritz, A. S., 151, *154*
Fuchs, L. H., 459, *467*
Fudge, H., 388, *396*
Fullan, M., 473, 475, *480*
Fullerton, C. S., 41, *48*
Furby, L., 459, *467*
Furstenberg, F. F., 19, *22*, 29, 30, *34*, 95, 96, 97, 98, 99, 103, 104, 105, *108*, *109*, 357, 366

G

Gackle, M. L., 231, *235*
Gagnon, J. H., 297, *306*, *307*
Gainer, L. J., 207, 208, 209, *219*
Galambos, N., 71, 79, *89*
Gallistel, C. R., 147, *155*
Galloway, A. N., 39, *49*
Gambrell, L. B., 215, *219*
Gans, J. E., 120, 121, *125*
Gantz, W., 413, 414, *416*
Gara, M., 393, *396*
Garber, J., 385, *395*
Garcia, C. R., 58, *67*
Garcia, J., 339, *350*
Garcia-Tunon, M., 355, *367*
Gard, P. D., 266, *274*
Gardner, H., 229, *235*
Gardner, L. I., 355, *366*
Garduque, L., 282, *291*
Garfinkel, B. D., 386, *396*
Garmezy, N., 82, 83, *89*
Garner, R., 213, 214, 215, *218*, *219*
Garrison, W. T., 115, 116, 117, 119, *125*
Gartenberg, H., 413, 414, *416*
Gates, R., 265, *273*
Gaveras, L. L., 120, 121, *125*

Gayle, H. D., 355, *367*
Gebhard, P. H., 359, *367*
Geertz, C., 421, *429*
Geffre, T. A., 232, *235*
Gelman, R., 147, *155*
Genthner, R. W., 287, *291*
Gephart, J., *124*, *126*
Gerber, T., 224, 225, 226, *235*
Gerhard, G., 497, *498*
Gerwig, J. L., 485, *498*
Gfellner, B. M., 300, *306*
Ghatak, R., 182, *190*
Gibb, S., 6, 7, 11
Gibbs, J. T., 56, 67, 162, *173*
Gibson, P., 66, 67, 299, *306*
Gibson, S. M., 226, *235*
Gil, E., 39, *48*
Gilligan, C., 144, 152, 153, *156*
Gilliland-Mallo, D., 41, *48*
Ginsberg, M. R., 362, *367*
Giroux, H., 183, *189*
Gittler, J., 464, *467*
Glass, G., 39, *49*
Glasser, W., 200, *206*
Glazer, N., 63, *67*
Glider, P., 287, *290*
Gobeli, V. C., 167, *174*
Gochman, D. S., 253, *259*
Godfrey, W., 42, 47, *50*
Goetz, D., 389, *397*
Golanty, E., 241, *245*
Gold, D., 77, *89*
Gold, P. A., 251, *260*
Gold, R. S., 257, *259*, 376, *381*
Goldberg, C. L., 271, *273*
Goldberg, W. A., 88, *90*
Goldenbaum, M., 355, *366*
Goldman, J. G., 102, *108*, 300, *306*
Goldman, R. J., 102, *108*, 300, *306*
Goldstein, B., 181, *189*, 279, 281, *290*
Gong, E. J., 264, *273*
Goodlad, J. I., 192, *206*, 476, *480*
Goodman, N., 195, *206*
Goodnow, J. J., 81, *90*, 146, *154*
Goodrich, W., 41, *48*
Goodstadt, M. S., 379, *381*
Gopnik, A., 151, *155*
Gordon, E. E., 229, *235*
Gordon, I. B., 120, *126*
Gordon, K. A., 241, *245*
Gordon, S. L., 263, *274*

Gorman, J., 379, *382*
Gortmaker, S. L., 262, *273*
Gotlib, I. H., 388, *395*
Gottfredson, L., 279, *290*
Gottleib, B. H., 169, *173*
Graham, A. B., 484, *498*
Graham, J. W., *380*, *381*, 441, *445*
Grandon, G., 56, *67*
Grasso, A., 41, *50*
Green, L. W., 243, *245*, 257, *259*
Greenberg, G., 1, 2, 13
Greenberg, M. T., 288, *290*
Greenberger, E., 88, *90*, 282, *290*, *291*
Greenfield, P., 414, *417*
Greeson, L., 415, *417*
Grinder, R., 413, *416*
Grobe, R., 186, *189*
Grochowski, C. O., 287, *290*
Groff, T. R., 98, *110*, 300, *307*, 317, *333*
Groom, M. D., 231, *235*
Gross, E., 120, *126*
Gross, J., 267, 268, *274*
Gross, R. T., 300, *306*
Grosslight, L., 150, *157*
Grotevant, H. D., 285, *290*
Grundy, J., 39, *48*
Guardado, S., 302, *306*
Guiterres, S. E., 43, *48*, *49*
Gulotta, T., 44, *48*
Gunderson, R., 415, *417*
Gunther, D., 44, *50*
Gurry, S. E., 41, *49*
Guthrie, H. A., 263, 265, *275*

H

Habermas, J., 424, 425, *429*
Hacker, G. A., 431, 433, 434, 441, *445*
Haffner, D. W., 302, 304, *305*, *306*, 326, *331*
Hagen, J. W., 6, 7, 11
Hala, S., 151, *154*
Hale, D. J., 227, *235*
Hall, B. L., 424, *429*
Hall, G. S., 143, 144, *155*
Hall, J., 415, *417*
Halpern, A., 321, *332*
Halstead, D. L., 121, *126*
Ham, M., 389, *397*
Hamburg, B. A., 17, *23*, 102, *108*, 131, *141*, 161, *173*, 458, *467*

Hamburg, D. A., 162, *174*, 244, *245*, 458, 459, *468*
Hamburg, M. V., 241, *245*
Hamilton, S. F., 166, 168, *174*, 282, *290*
Hamilton-Weiler, S., 192, *206*
Hammer, L. D., 269, *273*
Hammill, S., 88, *90*
Hansell, S., 463, *468*
Hansen, A., 441, 442, *445*
Hansen, W. B., 321, *331*, 377, 378, 379, *380*, *381*
Hansen, W. G., 441, *445*
Hanshumaker, J., 232, *235*
Hanson, J., 415, *417*
Hanssens, D. M., 441, *446*
Hardy, J. B., 325, *333*
Hare, V. C., 213, 215, *218*, *219*
Harman, D., 208, *220*
Harmon, L. W., 279, *290*
Harmoni, R., 327, *332*
Harrington, R., 388, *396*
Harris, J. J., III, 186, *189*
Harris, L., 453, *455*
Harris, Louis, 162, *174*, 341, *351*
Harris, P. L., 151, *154*
Harris, R. T., 268, *273*
Hart, M. M., 298, *305*
Harter, S., 319, *331*
Hartmann, B. R., 287, *290*
Harwicke, N. J., 39, *49*
Haskins, R., 138, *140*
Hastings, S., 497, *498*
Hates, C., 29, *34*
Haurin, R. J., 101, *108*, 339, 340, 341, *351*
Havighurst, R. J., 112, *125*, 278, *290*
Hayes, C. D., 94, 95, 96, 97, 100, 101, 103, 104, 107, *108*, 266, *273*, 316, 318, 322, 323, 324, *331*, 357, *367*
Hayes, J. R., 215, *219*
Healey, W., 403, *406*
Healy, J. M., 71, *91*
Heath, 134, 137, *141*
Heath, S. B., 462, 463, *468*
Heathington, B. S., 215, *219*
Heeren, T., 376, *381*
Heimer, K., 57, *68*
Hein, K., 355, *366*
Heinsohn, A. L., 167, *174*
Helton, J., 44, *50*

Hendee, W. R., 412, *416*
Henderson, R. C., 263, 268, 270, *273*
Henshaw, S. K., 95, 96, *108*, 315, *331*, 341, 342, 345, *350*
Herbert, E., 136, *140*
Hernandez, D. J., 29, *34*
Herndon, J., 211, *218*, 220
Hersen, M., 394, *396*
Herzog, D. B., 387, *396*
Hesketh, B., 279, *290*
Hess, L. E., 133, *141*, 160, 164, *174*
Hetherington, E. M., 458, *467*
Heyde, M. B., 285, *291*
Heyward, W. L., 354, 365, *367*
Hiebert, E. H., 207, *219*
Hill, J. P., 59, *66*, 388, *396*, 461, *468*
Hill, W. L., *235*
Himmelhoch, J. M., 394, *396*
Hines, A. M., 56, *67*
Hingson, R., 357, *368*, 376, *381*
Hirsch, M. B., 325, *333*
Hirsch, P., 414, *417*
Hirschfeld, R. M. A., 387, 388, *396*, *397*
Hoberman, H. M., 386, *396*
Hochstadt, N. J., 39, 40, *49*
Hocking, J., 439, *444*
Hoeper, E. W., 384, *396*
Hoerr, S., 267, *273*
Hofferth, S. L., 93, 94, *109*, 315, *332*, 358, 359, *367*
Hoffman, A., 113, 114, *125*, 375, 376, *382*
Hoffman, H., 409, 410, 413, *417*
Hoffman, L. W., 72, *90*
Hoffman, M. A., 133, *141*
Hoffman, M. L., 52, *67*
Hogan, D. P., 58, *67*, 76, *90*, 100, 101, *109*, 301, 302, *306*, 322, *332*, 339, *351*
Hoggson, N., 329, *331*
Holder, H. D., 441, *445*
Holland, J. L., 146, *155*, 277, *290*
Hollis, J., 267, *273*
Holmbeck, G., 461, *468*
Holyoak, K., 146, *155*
Holzer, C. E., 387, *398*
Hong, G., 384, *396*
Hopkins, C., 284, *291*
Hops, H., 394, *397*
Horan, J., 376, *382*
Horn, M. C., 345, *351*
Hornik, R. C., 419, *429*

Horowitz, R., 186, *189*
Horvath, W. J., 252, *259*
Hosterman, G. L., 225, 228, *234*
Howard, C., 54, *67*
Howard, K., 320, *332*
Hoyle, S. G., 390, *395*
Hsu, J., 55, *68*
Huang, L. H., 162, *173*
Huggins, G. R., 58, *67*
Hughes, M. H., 134, 137, 138, *141*
Hugonnet, M., 415, *417*
Huiinga, D., 42, *48*
Hulley, S. B., 266, *274*
Humphrey, R. H., 373, 376, *380*
Hunt, M. M., 270, *274*
Hunter, C. S., 208, *220*
Hurley, M. E., 212, *220*
Hutchins, V., 115, 123, *125*
Hyche-Williams, J., 324, *332*
Hyman, I. A., 130, 139, *141*

I

Iacovetta, R. G., 133, *141*
Ianni, F. A. J., 171, *174*, 322, *332*, 463, *468*
Ingersoll, G. M., 297, *307*
Ingram, F. R., 355, *367*
Inhelder, B., 102, *109*, 145, 148, 152, *155*
Irvine, J., 41, *49*
Irwin, C. E., Jr., 242, *245*, 252, *259*, 357, *367*
Irwin, L., 47, *48*

J

Jackson, M. C., Jr., 167, *173*
Jacobs, D. R., 271, *273*, *274*
Jacobs, M., 459, *467*
Jacobson, M. F., 431, 433, 434, 441, *445*
Jaffe, A. J., 336, *351*
Jaffe, L. R., 359, *367*
Janus, M. D., 43, *49*
Janz, N. K., 253, *259*
Jassett, R. L., 60, *68*
Jaudes, P. K., 39, 40, *49*
Jennings, D., 300, *306*
Jessor, R. L., 100, *109*, 111, 112, *125*, 251, *259*, 297, *306*, 312, *314*, 329, *332*, 371, 373, *381*, 463, *468*

Jessor, S. L., 100, *109*, 251, *259*, 371, *381*
Jewell, L., 389, *397*
Johnson, A., 378, 379, *381*
Johnson, C. A., *380*, *381*
Johnson, J. L., 225, *235*
Johnson, K. E., 100, *108*
Johnson, K. W., 243, *245*
Johnson, N. S., 43, *49*
Johnston, C. C., Jr., 263, *274*
Johnston, L. D., 65, *66*, 373, 376, *380*, 432, 433, 435, *444*, *445*, 459, *467*
Johnston, W. B., 209, *220*
Jones, E. F., 342, *351*
Jones, R. M., 287, *290*
Jordaan, J. P., 285, 286, *291*
Jorgensen, S. R., 293, 297, *306*
Joyce, T., 341, 342, *351*
Judd, P., 41, *48*
Jung, K. G., 357, 358, *368*
Jungeblut, A., 209, 210, *220*

K

Kadushin, A., 39, *49*
Kaestle, C. F., 209, 210, *220*
Kagan, J., 389, *396*
Kagan, L. K., 134, *140*, *141*
Kagay, M., 296, *307*
Kageff, L. L., 230, *236*
Kahn, J. R., 93, 94, *109*, 315, *332*
Kaiser, M., 146, 147, *155*
Kaldor, W., 279, *290*
Kalnins, I., 249, 252, 253, *259*
Kandel, D. B., 17, *23*, 65, *68*, 133, *141*, 320, *332*, 433, *445*
Kandiah, V., 343, 344, *350*
Kanter, J. F., 352
Kanter, R. M., 74, *90*
Kantner, J. F., 94, 97, 98, 102, 103, *109*, 110, 329, *333*
Kaplan, S. L., 384, *396*
Kashani, J. H., 384, *396*
Kaslow, N. J., 394, *398*
Katchadourian, H., 17, *23*
Kato, P., 105, *108*, 322, *331*
Katz, H., 120, *126*
Katzman, N., 435, *445*
Kauffman, M. B., 19, *23*
Kearns, D. T., 207, *220*
Keating, D. P., 102, *109*, 249, *259*, 317, 318, *332*, 462, *468*

Keeling, R. P., 355, *367*
Kegeles, S. M., 357, *367*
Keil, F. C., 146, 149, *155*, *156*
Kellam, S. G., 57, 59, 67, 68, 106, *109*
Keller, M. B., 387, *397*
Kelly, J. A., 302, *306*, 327, *331*
Kelly, M. A., 257, *259*, 376, *381*
Kennedy, R. E., 384, 385, 389, 390, 392, 394, *396*, *397*
Kenney, A. M., 95, 96, *108*, 302, *306*, 315, *331*
Kenny, S., 168, *174*
Kessel, F. S., 152, *156*
Kidney, B. A., 285, *290*
Kilbourne, B. W., 355, *367*
Killen, J. D., 271, *273*
Killian, J. N., 227, *236*
Kim, Y. J., 100, *108*, 323, *333*
Kinder, B. N., 438, *445*
King, A. C., 271, *273*
King, J. C., 264, *274*
King, P. M., 153, *155*
King, R. V., 227, *236*
Kinlow, M. R., 39, *49*
Kinsey, A. C., 359, 360, *367*
Kipman, D., 150, *157*
Kirby, D., 323, 326, *332*
Kirsch, I. S., 209, 210, *220*
Kitagawa, E. M., 58, 67, 76, *90*, 100, 101, *109*, 301, 302, *306*, 322, *332*, 339, *351*
Kitano, H., 63, *68*
Kitchener, R. F., 145, 153, *155*
Klaus, H., 328, *332*
Kleinfeld, J., 168, *174*
Klepp, K. I., 321, *332*
Klerman, G. L., 387, *397*
Kletzien, S. B., 213, *220*
Kluth, B. L., 230, *236*
Knapp, J. R., 17, *23*
Koch, C. C., 226, *236*
Koch, G. G., 58, *67*
Koch, P. B., 296, 297, 300, 304, *306*
Kohlberg, L., 52, *69*, 144, 152, *156*
Kohn, P. M., 438, 439, 442, *445*
Kominski, R., 339, *351*
Kostial, K., 263, *274*
Kotch, J. B., 439, *445*
Kotlowitz, A., 466, *468*
Kraemer, H. C., 269, *273*
Kraus, C., 215, *219*
Krener, P., 116, *125*

Kreppner, K., 18, *23*
Kris-Etherton, P. M., 268, *274*
Kroupa, S. E., 41, *49*
Ku, L. C., 94, 95, 102, *110*, 340, 345, 351, *352*
Kubey, R., 408, 409, 410, 411, 412, 413, *417*
Kuehl, R. O., 61, *66*
Kuhn, D., 146, 149, 153, *156*
Kuhn, T. S., 146, *156*, 195, *206*
Kukulka, G., 356, *368*
Kulbok, P., 357, 358, *368*
Kunfeldt, K., 43, 44, *49*
Kurth, C. L., 271, *274*, 432, 433, *444*, 459, *467*

L

Lackey, C. C., 241, *245*
Laing, S. J., 251, *259*
Lamb, R. K., 226, *236*
Lamborn, S. D., 60, *69*
Lampman-Petraitis, C., 384, *397*
Landale, N., 344, *351*
Lang, C. L., 485, *498*
Langenberg, D. N., 458, 459, 460, *468*
Langer, J., 192, *206*
Langer, S., 413, *417*
LaPaille, K., 40, *49*
Lapsley, D., 153, *155*
Larson, L. E., 133, *141*
Larson, R., 384, 389, *397*, 408, 409, 410, 411, 412, 413, *417*
Lauer, R. M., 261, 266, *274*
Lauritans, A. A., 117, *125*
Lave, J., 211, *220*
La Voie, L., 56, *67*
Lavori, P. W., 387, *397*
Lazar, I., 136, *141*
Leadbeater, B. J., 153, *156*, 359, *367*
Leaf, P. J., 387, *398*
Lee, C. C., 59, 60, *68*
Lee, V., 181, 185, *189*
Leech, S. L., 252, *259*, 377, *381*
Lehman, L., 386, 387, *397*
Leichenko, S., 296, *307*
Leiderman, P. H., 85, *89*
Leigh, G. K., 293, *307*
Leight, L., 295, *306*
Leitch, C. J., 288, *290*
Leland, N., 326, *332*

Leming, J., 223, *236*
Lempers, J. D., 72, 74, *90*
Lerner, R. M., 1, 2, 3, *4*, 5, 8, 12, 17, 18, 19, 20, *22*, *23*, 82, 85, *90*, 131, 132, *141*, 254, 255, *259*, 277, 278, 279, 283, 288, *292*, 299, *306*
Lesser, G. S., 17, *23*, 65, *68*, 133, *141*, 320, *332*
Leventhal, J. M., 119, *126*
Levine, J., 29, 30, *34*
Levine, M., 414, *416*
Levy-Shiff, R., 133, *141*
Lewinsohn, P. M., 387, 394, *397*
Lewis, C., 250, *259*
Lewis, J. M., 58, *68*
Lewis, M., 271, *274*
Lewis, W. A., 378, *382*
Lieberson, S., 177, *189*
Lief, J., 153, *155*
Ligbow, E., 44, *49*
Lindberg, J. S., 270, *274*
Lindeman, C., 347, *351*
Linn, M. C., 434, *445*
Linney, J. A., 130, *141*
Lipsitz, H., 439, *445*
Lipsitz, J., 131, 132, *141*
Litt, I. F., 251, *259*, 268, *274*
Litt, L. F., 242, *245*
Lochman, J., 58, *69*
Logan, B. W., 167, *173*
Longstaff, H. P., 403, *406*
Looney, J. G., 58, *68*
Loosley, E. W., 183, *190*
Lorenz, F. O., 75, *89*
Lounsbury, J. H., 471, *480*
Louv, R., 461, *468*
Love, R., 249, 252, 253, *259*
Luckman, T., 194, *205*
Luepker, R. V., 271, *274*
Lukens, E., 389, *397*
Lull, J., 228, *236*, 409, 414, *417*
Lumio, M., 441, *445*
Lundy, B. Z., *380*, *381*
Lyle, J., 409, 410, 413, *417*
Lyman, S. M., 59, *68*

M

Maccoby, E. E., 83, *90*
Maccoby, N., 271, *273*
MacDermid, S. M., 77, *89*

MacEachron, A. E., 301, *305*
Macedo, D., 191, *206*
MacKenzie, R., 46, *50*
MacKinnon, D. P., 378, 379, *381*
Macklin, M., 203, *206*
MacNamara, D. E. J., 45, *49*
Maddux, J. E., 112, *126*
Madigan, T., 186, *189*
Magnusson, D., 4, 6, 12, 13, 18, *23*, 99, *109*
Magrab, P. R., 114, *125*
Maguire, P., 424, *429*
Majchrzak, A., 450, 451, *455*
Majone, G., 451, *455*
Makela, K., 441, *445*
Maloney, P., 45, *49*
Maltsberger, J. T., 386, 390, *395*
Malveaux, J., 62, *68*
Mandler, J. M., 147, *156*
Maney, D. W., 373, *381*
Mann, J. M., 353, 354, 365, *368*
Mann, L., 327, *332*
Manning, W. D., 281, 284, *291*
Mannio, F. V., 44, *49*
Mansfield, A., 153, *155*
March, V., 387, *398*
Marcia, J. E., 153, *156*, 285, 286, 287, *291*
Marcoux, D., 262, *274*
Marinho, D. D., 264, *274*
Marjoribanks, K., 133, *141*
Markman, E. M., 213, *220*
Marks, G., 441, *445*
Markstrom-Adams, C., 6, 13
Marotta, T., 45, *48*
Marsiglio, W., 58, *68*, 96, 97, *109*, 346, 347, *351*, 365, *368*
Martel, L., 414, *417*
Martin, C. G., 359, 360, *367*
Martin, J. A., 300, *306*
Masiglio, W., 347, 348, *351*
Mason, S. F., 230, *236*
Mass, M., 119, *125*
Matkovic, V., 263, *274*
Matsueda, R. L., 57, *68*
Matteson, D. R., 287, *291*
Matthews, B., 42, 47, *50*
Maughan, B., 184, *190*
McAlister, A., 438, *445*
McAllister, J. A., 384, *396*
McAnarney, E. R., 106, *109*

McCaffree, K., 301, *306*
McCalla, D. C., 227, *236*
McCarthy, J., 30, *34*
McCartin, R., 281, *291*
McCartney, K., 83, *90*
McCloskey, M., 146, 147, *155*
McCombs, M., 435, *445*
McCormack, A., 43, *49*
McCormack, J., 163, *173*
McCormick, R. W., 484, *498*
McCormick, V. E., 484, *498*
McCoy, J. K., 302, *306*
McCurley, J., 122, *125*
McDermott, J. F., 55, *68*
McDermott, L. C., 150, *156*
McDermott, R. P., 183, *189*
McDermott, S., 439, *444*
McDonald, D. I., 121, *124*, *125*, 222, 232, *233*, *236*
McGee, R. O., 384, *396*
McGill, L., 59, *69*, 296, *307*
McHale, S. M., 72, 77, 80, *89*, *90*
McKenry, P. C., 293, *307*
McKenzie, D., 231, *236*
McKeon, S. E., 225, 226, *236*
McKnew, D. H., 384, *396*
McLanahan, S., 28, 32, *33*, *34*
McLaren, P., 183, 184, *189*
McLaughlin, M. W., 462, 463, *468*
McLeod, J., 57, *68*
McLoyd, V. C., 52, 61, *68*, *69*, 71, 85, 86, *90*
McMahon, E. T., 431, 433, 435, *446*
McManus, P., *124*, *126*
McMillion, M., 284, *291*
McNally, J. W., 345, *351*
McNeil, L., 192, 193, 198, *206*
McNew, S., 148, *154*
McPartland, J. M., 185, *189*
McPherson, M., 115, 123, *125*
McQuail, D., 404, *406*
McQuiston, S., 115, 116, 117, 119, *125*
Mead, M., 6, 12
Mechanic, D., 243, *245*, 463, *468*
Medin, D., 146, *156*
Meenan, A. L., 210, *220*
Mehan, H., 195, *206*
Meier, J., 39, *48*
Melby, J. N., 74, *91*
Melton, G. B., 466, *469*
Meltzer, A. S., 207, 208, 209, *219*

Mendels, 387, *398*
Mendoza, F. S., 269, *273*
Mercer, J. R., 186, *189*
Merrion, M. D., 232, *236*
Messeri, P., 57, *67*
Meyer, F., 262, *274*
Meyer, K., 281, *291*
Meyer, M. P., 242, *245*
Mezirow, J., 424, *429*
Michael, R. T., 339, 343, *351*
Michela, J. L., 271, *273*
Mickelson, R. A., 178, *189*
Mico, P., 241, *245*
Midgley, C., 131, 132, *140*
Miezitis, S., 394, *395*
Mikulecky, L., 210, 212, *220*
Miller, B. C., 302, *306*
Miller, C., 415, *417*
Miller, J. P., 168, *174*, 280, *291*, 486, *498*
Miller, M. L., 387, *395*
Miller, P. A., 481, 489, *498*
Miller, P. H., 152, *156*
Miller, S., 389, *396*
Millstein, S. G., 242, *245*, 251, 252, *259*, 295, *307*, 459, 463, *468*
Milner, J., 39, *49*
Mingione, L., 414, *417*
Mitchell, B., 473, *480*
Moffatt, P., 120, *126*
Moisan, J., 262, *274*
Montemayor, R., 320, *332*
Montero, D., 54, *68*
Moore, B. R., 230, *236*
Moore, J., 62, *69*
Moore, K. A., 101, 104, *109*, 317, *332*
Moore, R. L., 435, *446*
Morales, E. S., 356, *367*
Morelock, S., 376, *381*
Morgan, D. L., *33*, *34*
Morgan, S. P., 96, 97, 98, *108*
Morris, N. M., 98, *110*, 300, *307*, 317, 321, *332*, *333*
Morrison, P., 344, 347, 349, *350*
Mortimer, J. T., 277, 281, 282, 283, 284, 289, *291*, 292, 402, *406*
Mortimore, P., 184, *190*
Moschis, G. P., 435, *446*
Mosher, W. D., 345, *351*
Moss, A. R., 354, *368*
Moss, R. B., 227, *236*
Mossholder, S., 265, *273*

Mott, F. L., 29, *34*, 96, 101, *108*, *109*, 339, 340, 341, 346, 347, 348, *351*, 365, *368*
Mounts, N., 60, *69*, 183, *188*
Mullis, R., 271, *274*
Munroe, G., 42, *48*
Munson, R. F., 40, *49*
Murphy, G., 146, *156*
Murphy, M., 153, *155*
Murray, D. M., 271, *274*
Murray, H., 136, *141*
Mussen, P. H., 54, *69*
Myers, D., 227, 232, *236*
Myers, J., 192, 193, 194, 195, 196, 197, 199, 201, 202, *206*
Myers, J. K., 387, *398*
Myers, M., 213, 215, *220*
Mystrom, C., 431, 436, *446*

N

Nadar, P. R., 242, *245*
Nakamura, C. Y., 55, *69*
Nakata, Y., 289, *291*
Narkunas, J. P., 355, *367*
Natapoff, J. N., 250, *259*
Nathanson, C. A., 59, *69*
Nelson, B. J. P., 227, *236*
Nenney, S. W., 296, *307*
Nesselroade, J. R., 1, 11, 12
Neuber, K. A., 287, *291*
Neuendorf, K., 439, *444*
Newacheck, P., *124*, *126*
Newcomb, M. D., 370, 374, *381*
Newcomer, S. F., 101, *109*, 296, *307*, 328, *332*
Newman, T. B., 266, *274*
Ngandu, K., 215, *220*
Nguyen, N. A., 55, *69*
Nicholson, Heather J., 165, *174*
Nickerson, R. S., 207, *220*
Nightingale, E. O., 459, *468*
Nimmo, M., 43, 44, *49*
Nisan, M., 52, *69*
Nisbett, R., 146, *155*, *156*
Nolen-Hoeksema, S., 386, *397*
Nolteriek, M. A., 227, *236*
Nord, C. W., 101, *109*, 317, *332*
Nordin, B. E. C., 263, *274*
Nottelmann, E. D., 251, *260*

Noyes, W. G., 225, *234*
Nye, F. I., 42, *49*

O

Oakes, J., 185, *189*
Oatley, K., 389, *397*
Oetting, E. R., 356, 360, *368*
Offer, D., 3, 12, 17, *23*, 320, *332*
Ogborne, A. C., 439, 442, *445*, *446*
Ogbu, J. U., 64, *69*, 134, *141*, 178, 183, *189*
Okazaki, S., 178, *190*
Oldham, J., 279, 281, *290*
Oliver, S. J., 386, *397*
Olsen, L., 44, *49*
Olshavsky, J. E., 215, *220*
Olson, D. R., 151, *154*
Olson, T. D., 302, *306*
O'Malley, P. M., 65, 66, 373, 376, *380*, 432, 433, 435, *444*, *445*, 459, *467*
Oman, R. C., 453, *455*
O'Neil, R., 88, *90*
Ooms, T., 105, *109*
Opplinger, R. A., 270, *275*
Oquist, P., 424, *430*
Orlofsky, J. L., 287, *291*
Ormond, C., 327, *332*
Ornstein, S. I., 441, *446*
O'Rourke, T. W., 375, *380*
Orr, D. P., 297, *307*
Orr, John D., 167, *174*
Ortiz, C. G., 347, *351*
Ortiz, V., 343, 344, 348, *350*, *351*
Osterberg, E., 441, *445*
Ostrov, E., 320, *332*
Ousten, J., 184, *190*
Overstreet, E. J., 41, *50*
Owens, T. J., 283, 284, *291*

P

Pachon, H., 62, *69*
Packer, A. E., 209, *220*
Palla, B., 268, *274*
Palmer, B. B., 250, *259*
Pan, L., 441, *445*
Pantell, R., 120, *126*
Parcel, G. S., 242, *245*, 248, 253, *259*
Paris, S. G., 213, 215, *220*

Parish, E. A., 225, *236*
Parke, R. D., 19, *23*
Parmelee, D., 47, *48*
Parsons, J. H., 386, *396*
Partanen, J., 434, 435, *446*
Pascale, P. J., 121, *126*
Patterson, G. R., 75, 76, *89*, *90*
Paul, B., 6, 7, 11
Pearson, J., *380*, *381*
Peck, R., 43, *49*
Peck, W. A., 263, *274*
Pennbridge, J., 46, *50*
Penner, W., 160, 165, 169, *174*
Pennington, N., 153, *157*
Pentz, M. A., 374, 378, 379, *381*
Perlmann, J., 177, *189*
Perner, J., 148, 151, *157*
Perrine, V. B., 223, 225, *237*
Perry, C. L., 271, *274*, 312, *314*, 321, *332*
Perry, W., 153, *156*
Perry-Jenkins, M., 77, 80, *89*, *90*
Person, M., 413, 414, *416*
Peshkin, A., 183, *189*
Peters, D. F., 59, *69*
Petersen, A. C., 1, 2, 3, 4, 8, 12, 17, *22*, 99, 105, *109*, 160, 164, *174*, 311, *314*, 316, *332*, 375, *382*, 384, 385, 390, 392, *396*, *397*, 458, 459, 462, *467*, *468*
Peterson, G. W., 59, *69*
Peterson, J. L., 101, 104, *109*, 317, *332*
Peterson, M., 355, *366*
Peterson, N., 39, *48*
Peterson, W., 59, *69*
Pfeiffer, S. I., 41, *49*
Phelan, J. J., 403, *406*
Philipp, M., 183, *188*
Philliber, S., 329, *331*
Phillips, S., 282, *291*
Piaget, J., 84, *90*, 102, *109*, 144, 145, 146, 148, 152, *155*, *156*
Pickles, A., 388, *396*
Pillow, B. H., 148, 151, *156*
Piot, P., 353, 354, 365, *368*
Piperis, J. E., 232, *237*
Piro, J. M., 230, *237*
Pittman, K., 93, 95, *109*, 315, *332*
Pleck, J. H., 94, 95, 102, *110*, 340, 345, *352*
Plummer, J. T., 420, *430*
Pogonowski, L. M., 225, 231, 232, *237*
Pomeroy, W. B., 359, 360, *367*

Popham, R. E., 441, *445*
Postman, N., 431, 436, *446*
Poulos, G., 182, *190*
Powell, M. R., 270, *274*
Powell, S., 408, *416*
Power, C., 327, *332*, 408, 412, 413, *417*
Prentice-Dunn, S., 40, *50*
Price, J. H., 356, *368*
Price, M. C., 370, *382*
Price, R. H., 88, *89*, 160, 165, 169, *174*
Prinsky, L., 413, 414, *417*
Proch, K., 39, *49*
Proctor, S., 316, *332*
Proffitt, D., 146, 147, *155*
Pryor, R. G. L., 279, *291*
Puig-Antich, J., 387, 389, *397*
Pulliam, C. A., 215, *219*
Purkey, S. C., 475, *480*
Puro, R., 198, *206*

Q

Quay, J. S., 226, *237*
Quigley, Rick, M., 464, *467*
Quinn, T., 353, 354, 365, *368*
Quinton, D., 82, *90*

R

Rabiner, D. L., *395*
Raffaelli, M., 389, *397*
Raj, M. H., 98, *110*, 300, *307*, 317, *333*
Ralph, N., 58, *69*
Ramsey, D. S., 228, *234*
Rasher, S., 271, *274*
Ratekin, N. H., 216, *219*
Rauch, S. P., 297, *307*
Raup, J., 414, *417*
Reale, G., 435, *446*
Reck, F. M., 483, 484, *498*
Redfield, R. R., 355, *366*
Rees, J. M., 269, *273*
Reese, H. W., 1, 11
Reeves, B., 403, *406*
Reich, J. W., 43, *48*, *49*
Reich, R. B., 450, 451, *455*, 457, *467*, *468*
Reich, T., 387, *397*
Reid, J. C., 384, *396*
Reid, J. R., 75, 76, *89*
Reid, P. T., 6, 12

Reiger, D. A., 121, *126*
Reimer, B., *233*, *237*, 413, *417*
Reinisch, J. M., 359, *368*
Reisman, J. M., 389, *397*
Reiter, E. D., 249, *259*
Remafedi, G. J., 298, 299, *307*
Rennekamp, R., 497, *498*
Resnick, L. B., 161, 171, 172, *174*, 207, 220
Resnick, M. D., 271, 275, 453, *455*
Reynolds, W. M., 394, *398*
Rice, J., 387, *397*
Rice, K., 390, *396*
Richards, M. H., 389, *397*
Richmond, J. B., 122, *126*
Richtsmeier, A. J., 120, *126*
Rickels, K., 58, *67*
Riggs, B. L., 263, *274*
Ritter, P., 178, *189*
Ritter, P. L., 85, *89*, 182, *190*, 460, *467*
Robbins, C., 97, *109*
Roberts, A., 44, *49*
Roberts, D. F., 85, *89*, 223, 228, *234*, 402, *406*, 409, 410, 413, *416*, 435, *445*
Roberts, M. C., 112, *126*
Robilland, A. B., 55, *68*
Robins, A. J., 384, *396*
Robins, L. N., 357, 358, *368*
Robinson, J., 414, *417*
Robinson, L. M., 261, *275*
Robinson, T. N., 271, *273*
Rockwell, S. K., 167, *174*
Roe, K., 408, 412, *417*
Roesel, R., 316, 330, *332*
Rogers, M. F., 355, *367*
Rogoff, N., 179, *189*
Rohde, P., 387, *397*
Rokeach, M., 377, *382*
Rolf, J. E., 312, *314*
Ronald, N., 267, *273*
Room, R., 441, *445*
Roosa, M. W., 328, *331*
Rosen, J. C., 267, 268, *274*
Rosenbaum, J., 413, 414, *417*
Rosenberg, A., 300, *306*
Rosenberg, M., 133, 134, *141*, 185, *189*
Rosenberg, T. K., 384, *396*
Rosengren, K. E., 404, *406*
Rosenstock, I. M., 252, *259*
Rosenthal, J., 39, *49*
Ross, L., 146, *156*

Rossing, B., 167, *174*
Rothbaum, P. A., 393, *396*
Rotheram-Borus, M. J., 287, *291*
Rothman, A., 257, *259*
Royce, J., 136, *141*
Rude, T. L., 165, *174*
Rudman, L. E., 167, *174*
Ruggiero, M., 282, *291*
Rumberger, R. W., 182, *190*
Russell, T. P., 231, *234*
Rutkowski, J., 231, *237*
Rutter, C. M., 384, *398*
Rutter, M., 82, 83, *90*, 184, *190*, 384, 385, 388, *396*, *397*
Rychtarik, R. G., 439, *446*
Ryu, S., 282, 289, *291*

S

Sabagh, B., 336, *352*
Sabbath, B. F., 119, *126*
Sadler, L. S., 106, *110*
Saks, M. J., 464, *467*
Sandler, R. N., 288, *291*
Sandstrom, K. L., 282, *291*
Sarigiani, P., 384, 385, 392, *397*
Sato, P. A., 354, *368*
Saucier, J. F., 253, *259*
Saunders, R. B., 243, *245*
Savin-Williams, R. C., 459, *468*
Sawchuk, L. L., 270, *273*
Saylor, K. E., 271, *273*
Scarr, S., 83, *90*
Schacter, J., 39, 40, *49*
Schaffer, D., 43, 46, *49*
Scheurich, J., 379, *382*
Schill, W. J., 281, *291*
Schiller, S., 413, 414, *416*
Schine, J., 462, *468*
Schlattmann, T., 409, 414, *417*
Schluchter, M. D., 323, 325, *333*
Schmeidler, J., 56, *67*
Schmidt, C. P., 229, *237*
Schmidt, W., 441, *445*
Schneider, K., 39, *49*
Schneirla, T. C., 2, 12, 132, 136, *141*, 255, *259*
Schommer, M., 213, *220*
Schon, D. A., 453, *455*
Schooler, C., 435, *446*
Schorr, L., 453, *455*

Schreiber, E., 134, *140*, *141*
Schulenberg, J. E., 277, 278, 279, 283, 288, *292*
Schulz, E. R., 207, 208, 209, *219*
Schulze, L., 414, *416*
Schumacker, M. C., 261, *275*
Schuyler, T., 393, *396*
Schweitzer, J., 185, *188*
Scott, J. A., 136, *140*, 207, *219*
Scott, W., 347, *351*
Scriber, S., 207, 211, *220*
Sealand, N., 105, *108*, 322, *331*
Seals, K. A., 230, *237*
Searle, J. W., 230, *237*
Seehaus, M., 359, *367*
Seeley, J. R., 183, *190*, 387, *397*
Seffrin, J., 241, *245*
Seidenberg, F. P. D., 225, 226, 227, 232, *237*
Seidman, E., 130, *141*
Selman, R. L., 151, *156*
Selverstone, R., 294, *307*
Sessions, G. L., 223, *237*
Shafer, M. B., 268, *272*
Shaffer, D., 385, 391, *397*
Shafii, M., 389, *397*
Shah, F., 103, *110*
Shah, F. K., 94, 97, 103, *110*
Shanahan, M., 282, 283, 284, *289*, *291*
Shannon, B., 265, 271, *275*
Shatz, M., 148, *156*
Shedler, J., 370, 374, *382*
Sheehan, D., 186, *189*
Sherwin, R. S., 117, *125*
Shinkwin, A., 168, *174*
Shinn, E. B., 39, *48*
Shope, J. T., 377, *381*
Shore, M. F., 44, *49*
Shrum, G. A., 482, *498*
Shuan, Y., 186, *189*
Shulman, L. E., 263, *274*
Sibirsky, S., 347, 348, *350*
Siegel, J. M., 288, *290*
Silber, S., 148, *156*
Silbereisen, R. K., 71, 72, 78, 79, 82, 85, 86, *89*, *90*, *91*
Silva, P. A., 384, *396*
Silverman, J., 303, *306*, 341, 342, 345, *350*
Silverman, L. T., 302, *307*
Sim, R. A., 183, *190*

Simmons, R. G., 4, 12, 185, *189*, 391, *397*
Simon, W., 297, *307*
Simonovic, J., 263, *274*
Simons, R. L., 72, 74, 75, *89*, *90*, *91*
Simonson, D. C., 117, *125*
Simpson, G., 54, *69*
Singh, S., 339, 345, *350*, *352*, 359, *367*
Sinor, J., 229, *237*
Sivo, P. J., 393, *398*
Skinner, J. D., 267, *275*
Skinner, M., 76, *89*
Skog, O. J., 441, *445*
Slater, P., 267, *273*
Slattery, M. L., 261, *275*
Sloane, B. C., 294, *307*
Small, S. A., 459, 460, 461, 462, *468*
Smart, R. G., 436, 438, 439, 441, 442, *445*, *446*
Smith, A., 184, *190*
Smith, C., 150, *156*
Smith, E. A., 100, *110*, 321, 325, *332*, *333*
Smith, F., 200, 203, *206*
Smith, H. K., 215, *220*
Smith, J., 100, *108*
Smith, K., 386, 389, *398*
Smith, M. S., 475, *480*
Smith, P. B., 59, *69*, 296, *307*
Smith, R. S., 20, *23*, 200, *206*
Smith, T. E., 133, *141*
Smith, W. F., 225, 226, *237*
Smyer, M. A., 19, 20, *22*
Snider, B. A., 482, 494, *499*
Sobel, J. L., 379, *381*
Solomon, J., 422, *430*
Somberg, D., 95, 96, *108*, 315, *331*
Sonenstein, F. L., 94, 95, 102, *110*, 340, 345, *352*
Sorenson, R. C., 298, *307*
Sorenson, S. B., 384, *398*
Soth, N., 41, *49*
Spaights, E., 54, *69*
Spanier, G. B., 1, 2, 12, 17, *22*
Spear, B. A., 264, *273*
Speck, N., 44, *49*
Speering, A., 414, *417*
Spencer, M. B., 6, 13, 186, *190*, 459, *469*
Spillane-Grieco, E., 43, *50*
Sprafkin, J. N., 302, *307*
Springer, K., 149, *156*
Srinivasan, S. R., 266, *274*

Stack, C., 104, *110*
Starfield, B., 120, *126*
Stark, K. D., 394, *398*
Stattin, H., 4, 6, 13, 99, *109*
Steele, S. M., 167, *174*
Steen, S. N., 270, *275*
Steinberg, L. D., 60, *69*, 77, 84, *91*, 183, 184, *188*, *190*, 248, 250, *259*, 282, *290*, *291*, 320, *333*, 460, *469*
Steinel, D. V., 221, 223, *237*
Stern, D., 284, *289*, *291*
Steuck, K., 153, *155*
Stevenson, H. W., 133, 135, *141*
Stewart, A. J., 71, *91*
Stewart, C. G., 378, *382*
Stewart, G. H., 484, 485, *499*
Stewart, J. B., 61, *67*
Sticht, T. G., 212, *220*
Stiffman, A. R., 357, 358, *368*
Stivers, M. E., 59, *69*
Stohler, R. F., 167, *174*
Stokes, G., 295, *305*
Stone, E., 271, *275*
Stone, J. R., III, 284, *291*
Stone, M. K., 229, *238*
Story, M., 269, 271, 272, *275*
Stout, H., 434, *446*
Stouthamer-Loeber, M., 75, 76, *90*
Strain, J. J., 123, *125*
Strate, L., 431, 436, *446*
Street, R., 325, *333*
Streetman, L., 97, *109*
Streit, F., 121, *126*, 375, *382*
Strickland, D. E., 439, 440, *445*, *446*
Strobino, J., 38, *50*
Strong, J. P., 266, *275*
Strunin, L., 357, *368*
Stunkard, A. J., 264, *275*
Sue, S., 55, 60, *69*, 178, *190*
Sulkunen, P., 441, *445*
Sum, A. M., 209, 210, *220*
Sun, S., 409, 414, *417*
Suomi, S. J., 389, *398*
Super, D. E., 277, 278, 279, *289*, *291*, *292*
Surber, J. E., 213, *220*
Susman, E. J., 251, 252, *259*, *260*
Sutton, B., 167, *173*
Swanson, F. J., 231, *238*
Sweet, J., 28, 32, *34*
Swicegood, C. G., 336, *350*

Swisher, J. D., 370, 372, 375, 376, 379, *382*, 489, *499*

T

Taber, M., 39, *49*
Takanishi, R., 244, *245*, 466, *469*
Takei, Y., 181, 186, *188*, *189*
Talbert, L. M., 300, *307*, 317, *333*
Talmage, H., 271, *274*
Tamborlane, W. V., 117, *125*
Tandon, R., 424, *430*
Taylor, B. C., 12, 160, *174*, 316, *332*
Taylor, C. B., 271, *273*
Taylor, H., 296, *307*
Taylor, N. B., 279, *291*
Taylor, P. A., 431, 433, 435, *446*
Taylor, R. L., 62, *66*
Taylor, R. W., 56, *67*
Telch, M. J., 271, *273*
Thagard, P., 146, *155*
Thiel, K. S., 59, *66*
Thomas, A., 20, *22*, 132, *141*
Thomas, M. R., 267, *273*
Thomas, T., 58, *69*
Thompson, K. P., 222, 225, 226, 231, 232, *238*, 410, *417*
Thompson, M., 186, *188*
Thornburg, H. D., 301, *307*
Tiedeman, D. V., 277, 283, *290*
Tienda, M., 337, *350*
Timberlake, E. M., 38, 39, *50*
Tischler, G. C., 387, *398*
Tizard, B., 134, 137, 138, *141*
Tobach, E., 1, 2, 13
Tobler, N. S., 377, *382*
Todak, G., 389, *397*
Toner, B. B., 386, *397*
Torres, A., 345, *352*
Tortu, S., 321, 328, *331*, 378, *381*
Tough, J., 138, *141*
Trautein, B., 160, 165, 169, *174*
Travis, L. B., 117, *126*
Trieber, B., 133, *142*
Tripodi, T., 41, *50*
Tsang, S., 186, *190*
Tseng, W., 55, *68*
Tsukashima, R., 54, *68*
Tuma, N. B., 339, 343, *351*
Tuncalp, S., 375, *380*

Turner, J., 57, *68*
Turner, R. J., 106, *109*

U

Ubbriaco, J., 393, *396*
Udry, J. R., 95, 98, 99, 100, 101, *109*, 110, 296, 300, 301, *305*, *307*, 317, 321, *332*, *333*
Underwood, L. E., 262, 263, 264, 269, *275*
Unger, C. M., 150, *157*
Upchurch, D., 30, *34*
Ushpiz, V., 133, *141*

V

Vaillant, C. O., 280, *292*
Vaillant, G. E., 280, *292*
Valentine, C. A., 180, *190*
Van Camp, D. J., 227, *238*
Van Nguyen, T., 72, 73, 75, 80, 82, *89*
van Ryan, M., 88, *89*
Van Vort, J., 95, 96, *108*, 315, *331*
Vaolski, A., 122, *125*
Vaux, A., 282, *290*, *291*
Vazquez, N. E., 347, *351*
Venezky, R. L., 209, 210, *220*
Verden, P., 408, 412, 413, *417*
Verdieck, M. J., 39, *50*
Vicary, J. R., 373, *381*
Vincent, M. C., 232, *236*
Vincent, M. L., 323, 325, *333*
Vinokur, A. D., 88, *89*
Visintine, R., 355, *366*
Vondracek, F. W., 277, 278, 279, 283, 288, *292*
Voors, A. W., 266, *274*
Vosniadou, S., 146, 147, *156*
Voydanoff, P., 357, 361, *368*
Vygotsky, L., 146, *156*

W

Wackman, D. B., 435, *446*
Wacquant, L. J. D., 64, *69*
Wadden, T. A., 264, *275*
Wade, C. E., 270, *274*
Wade, E., 409, *417*
Wagner, C., 359, *367*
Wait, R. B., 59, *69*
Waite, L., 344, 347, 349, *350*

Walker, J., 386, *396*, 410, 412, *417*
Wallace, C. M., 302, *306*
Wallace, J. M., Jr., 432, 433, *444*, 459, *467*
Wallace, R. B., 263, *274*
Wallack, L., 419, *430*, 437, *446*
Walper, S., 72, 78, 82, 85, 86, *90*, *91*
Walsh, C., 438, *444*
Walsh, M., 252, *258*
Walton, L. A., 384, *396*
Wang, E. Y. I., 378, 379, *381*
Wang, M. Q., 263, 265, *275*
Ward, S., 435, *446*
Wartella, E., 403, *406*
Washington, E. D., 61, *69*
Wass, H., 414, *417*
Waszak, C. S., 324, *332*
Waterman, A. S., 285, 286, *290*, *292*
Wax, M. L., 183, *190*
Wax, R. H., 183, *190*
Webber, L. S., 266, 271, *273*, *274*
Webster, P. R., 225, 232, *238*
Weddle, K. D., 293, *307*
Weinfeld, F. D., 171, *173*
Weingartner, C., 431, 436, *446*
Weinhert, F. E., 133, *142*
Weinhold, C., 384, *396*
Weisberg, D. K., 45, *48*
Weiss, C. H., 452, *455*
Weiss, R. S., 133, *142*
Weissberg, R. P., 393, *398*
Weissmann, M. M., 387, *398*
Weisz, J., 47, *48*
Weithorn, L. A., 318, *333*
Wellman, H. M., 146, 147, 148, 151, *154*, 156, *157*, 213, *219*
Wells, G., 138, *142*
Wells, W. D., 420, *430*
Welte, J. W., 433, *446*
Werner, E. E., 20, *23*, 163, *174*
Werner, H., 146, *157*
Wertsch, J., 195, *206*
Wessel, M., 483, 485, *499*
Wessel, T., 483, 485, *499*
West, D. W., 261, *275*
West, W. G., 181, *190*
Wetzel, J. R., 52, *69*, 337, *352*
Whitbeck, L. B., 74, 75, *89*, *91*
Whiting, B. B., 6, 13
Whiting, J. W. M., 6, 13
Whitman, M., 121, *125*

Whittaker, J. K., 41, *50*
Whittinghill, J. R., 389, *397*
Wig, J. A., 225, 226, *238*
Wilbrandt, M. L., 297, *307*
Wilkinson, I. A. G., 136, *140*, 207, *219*
Wilks, J., 375, *382*
Williams, H. L., 55, *69*
Williams, J. A., 394, *397*
Williams, R., 415, *417*
Williams, S., 384, *396*
Williamson, G. D., 266, *274*
Willis, P., 415, *418*
Wills, T. A., 391, *395*
Wilson, D. R., 40, *50*
Wilson, W. J., 64, *69*, 463, *469*
Wimmer, H., 148, 151, *157*
Windle, M., 45, *50*
Wing, L. C., 186, *190*
Winokur, A., 387, *398*
Wise, L. L., 97, *108*
Wisenbaker, J., 185, *188*
Wiser, M., 150, *157*
Wiszniewska, A., 78, 85, 86, *91*
Witschi, C. H., 266, *275*
Wolcott, H., 183, *190*
Wolfe, A., 409, *418*
Wolford, C., 370, 372, *382*
Wolk, S., 42, 43, *50*
Wolkenstein, B. H., *380*, *381*
Wolters, C., 6, 7, 11
Wong, M., 186, *190*
Wood, A. M., 171, *173*

Wood, M., 120, *126*
Woolley, J. D., 148, *157*
Worthington-Roberts, B. S., 269, *273*
Wright, H. S., 263, 265, *275*
Wright, L., 112, *126*
Wurtle, S. K., 40, *50*
Wuy, R. R., 122, *125*

Y

Yamoor, C. M., 281, *292*
Yates, A., 54, *69*
Yates, G., 46, *50*
York, P. V. E., 269, *275*
York, R. L., 171, *173*
Young, K., 415, *418*
Young, P., 153, *155*
Young, R. D., 293, 299, *306*
Young, R. L., 42, 47, *50*
Yung, S., 280, *291*

Z

Zabin, L. S., 94, *110*, 325, *333*
Zelnik, M., 94, 97, 98, 102, 103, *109*, *110*, 323, 329, *333*
Zigler, E., 134, *140*, *141*
Zimmerman, D. P., 41, *50*
Zimmerman, M. P., 225, 229, *238*
Zimo, D. A., 39, 40, *49*
Zumoff, B., 123, *125*
Zuroff, D. C., 389, *395*

Subject Index

A

Ability grouping, 185–186
Abortion, 104
  among Hispanics, 340–342
  increase rate of, 95
  race/ethnicity and, 341–342
Academic achievement, *see also Education; School(s)*
  and child bearing, 96, 97
  of children in single parent households, 28, 29–30
  differentiation and inequality at the societal level, 175–179
  in different racial-ethnic and socioeconomic groups, 59–60
  effect of schools on, 184–187
  effects of family on, 179–182
    economic stress and, 76
    structure, 32–33
  effects of peer group and community on, 182–184
  effects of poverty on, 31
  reasons for low, of racial/ethnic groups, 183–184
  social capital and, 63–64
Acculturation, 54–55

Adaptation, 251
Adolescent-context relations, model of, 19–20
Adolescents, *see also Children; Early Adolescence*
  acting-out behaviors in, 122
  and adjustment to change, 2–3
  parenthood, 105–106
  childbearing of, 29–30, 93–107
    risks to, 96–97
  and chronic illnesses, 114–117, 119–120, 120–122
  cognitive development in, 143–154
  common cause of death in, 121
  cultural context of, 51–66
  deriving meanings from songs and videos, 413–416
  effects of bi-culturality on, 53–55
  effects of familial economic stress on, 71–88
  health promotion for, 241–245
    developmental and theoretical concerns for, 247–258
  nutrition, 261–272
  sexual development, 293–305
  vocational development as part of, 277–289
  households headed by, 27, 119

521

522 | SUBJECT INDEX

illness in other family members and, 118–120
influence of family on health of, 111–124
with an inherited disease, 117–118
involved in prostitution, 45
literacy in, 207–218
living arrangements of, 26–28, 31–33
    nonfamily and alternative settings, 37–48
major changes in
    biological, 248–249, 316–317
    cognitive, 249–250, 317–318
    social redefinition, 250–251
with more social capital, 63–64
music involvement of, 221–233
and media, 407–416
poverty among, 30–31
reasons for keeping child, 104–105
runaway, 41–47
and youth groups, 159–173
Adoption, 104
Adult literacy instruction, 211–212
Advertising
    alcohol, 431–443
African-Americans, *see also Race/ethnicity*
    academic achievement of, 177, 178
    family structure of, 57
    parent-adolescent conflicts and, 65
    racial segregation of schools and, 185
    rates of sexual activity and childbearing, 95, 96
Age
    and contraceptive use, 102
    of first intercourse, 296–297
    and suicide, 385–386, 387–388
AIDS, *see also HIV infections*
    education about, 302, 313
    reasons for few cases among adolescents, 354
Alcohol abuse, *see also Drug abuse; Substance abuse*
    belief systems and, 369–380
    deaths related to, 431, 433
    effects on identity achievement, 287
    health problems related to, 433
    nutrition and, 269
Alcohol advertising
    minority adolescents and, 431–443
        approaches to research, 438–440
        aspects of media, 436–438
        effects on alcohol use, 433–435
        future research, 443
        limitations to research, 440–443
Amenorrhea, 263, 270
Anal intercourse
    and transmission of HIV infections, 356, 359–360
Androgen levels, 98
Anorexia nervosa, 263, 267–268
Anxiety
    chronic illness and adolescents', 120
Asian-Americans, *see also Race/ethnicity*
    academic achievement of, 55–56, 178
    parenting and performance, 86
Assertiveness training, 394
Assimilation, 54–55
Athletes
    nutrition and, 270–271
Audiation, 229
Authoritarian parenting style, 85–86
Authoritative parenting style, 85–86

B

Behavior problems
    acting-out, 122
    of adolescents in residential or institutional placement, 40–41
    of children in foster care, 39
    and depression, 386–387
Belief systems, 133
    substance abuse and
        belief domains interventions, 376–380
        belief domains research, conceptual model for, 371–376
        impact of all domains used simultaneously on, 379–380
Bi-culturality, 53–55, 335
Biological change, 248–249, 316–317
Biomedical model of health, 115, 116
Biopsychosocial model of health, 115, 116
Birth control, 318, *see also Contraceptive use*
    among Hispanics, 345–346
    race/ethnicity and, 345–346
Blacks, *see also Race/ethnicity*
    academic achievement of, 177–178
    family structure of, 57
    literacy and, 137–138, 139

living arrangements of, 27
parenting and performance, 86
sexual activity and childbearing, 95, 96–97
Bone mass, 263, 268
Boy and Girl Scouts, 159–160, 164, 165–166, 168, 170
Boys' Clubs, 160, 162, 165, 169, 170
Bulimia, 267–268

C

Calcium, 263, 270
Cardiovascular disease, 266
Career Awareness Exploration, 164
Career guidance programs, 244
 of youth groups, 164
Case Family program, 39–40
Child-as-theoretician view, 146–151
 three areas of cognitive development and, 147–149
Childbearing, early adolescent, 93–94
 adolescent, 29–30
 consequences of
  risks to adolescent, 96–97
  risks to child, 97–98
 factors affecting
  adaptation to parenthood, 105–106
  contraceptive use, 102–104
  deciding whether or not to keep the child, 104–105
  early adolescent sexual activity, 98–102
 increased rate of, 93
 in different racial-ethnic and socioeconomic groups, 58–59, 343–345, 346–347
 nutrition and, 266–267
 recommendations for research and policy, 106–107
 sexual activity and, 94–96
  among Hispanics, 335–350
Child care, 31
 tax credit needed for, 461
Children, *see also* Adolescents
 depression in, 384–386
 early adolescent childbearing risks to, 97–98
 familial economic stress and family roles of, 79–81
 family roles in household work, 79–81

in foster care, 37–40
group home vs. foster care, 39
homeless, 30–31
in self-care, 77
in single parent households, 28, 29–30
work socialization of, 279–281
Children of alcoholics (COA), 121
Child sexual abuse
 effects on early adolescent sexual activity, 101–102
 runaways and, 43
Cholesterol screening, 266
Choral programs, 222
Cocaine, 360
Cognitive development, 143–144, 249–250, 317–318
 child-as-theoretician view on, 146–149
 educational implications of, 149–151
 and contraceptive use, 102–103, 318
 and music performance, 229
 role of, in adolescence, 144
 and sexuality, 300
 theories of knowledge acquisition, 151–153
 three areas of, 147–149
 traditional Piagetian theory of, 145–146, 249, 252
Cognitive-restructuring program, 394
Coital sexuality, 296–297
Community
 clinics, 330
 effects of on academic achievement, 182–184
 pregnancy prevention and, 321–322
Community organizations
 research and policy concerning, 462–463
Computers
 effects of, on literacy, 208–209
Condom, use of
 to prevent HIV transmission, 356–357, 359, 362, 365
 race/ethnicity and, 345–346
Confidentiality, issue of
 concerning medical care, 112–114
Congenital hypothyroidism, 118
Consent, issue of
 concerning medical care, 112–114
Contraceptive use, 102–104, 318, 327, 330, 358–359, *see also* Birth control

poor practices in, 94
pregnancy prevention and access to, 324
Cooperative learning, 200
Coping, 251
Correctional facilities, 40, 41
Crack, 360
Crime
  runaways involved in, 45–46
Critical consciousness, 423
Cultures
  conflicting messages from two, 335
  research directions regarding, 63–66
    on racial-ethnic groups, 56–63
  variations in, 51–56
    academic achievement, 175–188
    adolescent sexuality, 301
    literacy beliefs, 137–139
    meanings of economic stress, 78
Curricular designs
  participatory form of knowing, 203–205
    activities, 204–205
    evaluation, 204
    materials, 204
    student-directed inquiry learning, 205
  that resonate with adolescent knowing, 191–205

D

Daughters
  fathers' unemployment and behavior toward, 73–74
Decision making, 364
  about sex, 317–318
Delinquency
  depression and, 386–387
  familial economic stress and, 75–76
Demographic context, 25–26, 31–33
  living arrangements of U.S. adolescents, 26–28
  significant changes in family characteristics, 28–31
Depression
  in children, 384–386
    chronic illness and adolescent, 120
    developmental trends in, 383–386

fathers' unemployment and, 74
masked, 386
prevention of, 391–395
problem-solving programs to reduce social inhibition, 393–395
relationship to other adolescent problems, 386–387
runaways and, 46
secular trends in, 387–388
social deficit theory of, 389–390
social support theory of, 389–390
theories of ethiology concerning, 388–391
transition from primary to secondary school and, 391–395
Depression, The Great
  development of 4-H program during, 484
  impact on youth, 73–74
Developmental/contextual perspective, 1, 5, 19–20, 254, 300
  advantage of, 132–133
  with an ecological perspective, 133–135
  regarding adolescent and schooling, 131–135
Diabetes mellitus, 117, 118, 270
Disease
  adolescent with inherited, 117–118
  nutrition and, 269–270
  prevention, 122–124
    HIV infections, 353–366
    sexually transmitted, 295
Disease progression models
  regarding substance abuse, 371
Drop outs, 32, 135–136, 182
  race/ethnicity and, 338–339
Drug abuse, *see also* Alcohol abuse; Substance abuse
  adolescent health problems caused by parents', 121
  belief systems and, 369–380
  effects on identity achievement, 287
  familial economic stress and, 75–76
  influence of family on ethnic/racial group adolescent, 56–57
  intravenous (IV), 46, 360
  runaways and risk of, 45–46
  and transmission of HIV infections, 360–361
Dynamic interaction, 254–255, 300

E

Early adolescence, *see also Adolescence*
  biological and psychological changes in, 131
  childbearing in, 93–107
  depression and, 383–395
  integrating research, policy, and intervention for, 1–11, 17–22, 457–467
  preventing HIV infections in, 353–366
  role of schooling during, 129–140
  scientific information about, 4
  social and cultural diversity in academic achievement, 175–188
Eating disorders
  depression and, 386–387
  nutrition and, 267–268
Ecological/contextual perspective
  regarding adolescent and schooling, 133–137
Economic stress, familial, 71–88
Education, *see also Academic achievement; School(s)*
  on AIDS, 302, 313
  child-as-theoretician view and, 149–151
  distinguished from schooling, 130
  Hispanic level of, 338
  influence on alcohol use, 437–438
  integrating research and policy to improve
    context for change, 471–474
    initiating school-based change, 474–480
  level and adolescent childbearing, 346–347
  normative, 377
  on nutrition, 271
  programs for teachers, 171
  self-care skills, 492
  sex, 103, 300, 301–305, 323–324, 330
  special programs, 136
  of young adolescents, 461–462
  youth-at-risk programming, 491–495
  youth groups, 159–173
Education of the Handicapped Act, 124
Effective school movement, 184
Embeddedness, 254, 300
Employment
  gender differences in adolescent, 281, 283–284
  need for parental leave/flextime, 461
  part-time adolescent, 281–284
  potential benefits of adolescent, 282–283
Entertainment programs
  influence on alcohol use, 437
Environment, 132
Erikson, eight psychosocial stages of, 278
Ethnicity/race. *See Race/ethnicity*
Exercise
  nutrition and heavy, 270–271
Exosystem, 52, 135
Expanded Food and Nutrition Education Program (EFNEP), 493
Experiential learning, 171–172
Exploration, vocational, 285–286
Explorer Posts, 164
Extrapersonal beliefs, 375–376

F

Familial economic stress, 71–72
  children's family roles in times of, 79–81
  class, race, ethnicity, and family structure concerning, 85–87
  directions for future research in, 87–88
  effects of illness on adolescent, 119
  effects on parent-child interaction patterns, 73–79
  nutrition and, 264–265
  role of individual differences in, 82–85
  study of Warsaw youth, 78
Family, *see also Father; Mother; Parents*
  adolescents living in alternative settings to, 37–48
  attitudes on abortion and childbearing, 104
  conflict and runaways, 42, 44
  cultural context of adolescents and, 51–66
  definition of, 18
  dysfunctional, 38
  effects of on academic achievement, 179–182
  formation, early adolescent, 93–107
  foster care, 37–40
  impact of chronic illness on, 115–117
  influence on early adolescent sexual activity, 101
  influence on ethnic/racial group adolescents, 56–60

influences on adolescent health, 111–124
involvement in residential treatment, 41
pregnancy prevention and, 319–320
role of in adolescence, 17–19, 22
significant changes in characteristics of, 28–31
single-parent, 28–31
single- vs. dual-earner, 80–81
structure, 32–33, 47
and academic performance, 32–33
effect on delinquency, 57
functional role of, 18–19, 22
Family-centered care, 123–124
Family planning services, 324, 349–350
Family support policy, 107, 460–461
Fathers, *see also* Parents
loss of income and parenting behavior of, 73–75
Fertility and childbearing, 96
Fetal Alcohol Syndrome, 269
4-H program, 22, 159–160, 164–165, 166–168, 170–171, 172, 454–455
ambassador, 166
community service in, 165–166
design elements of education in, 487–489
effectiveness of, 167
functions of, 486–487
history of, 483–486
international programs offered by, 166–167
land-grant university system and, 481–498
future directions for, 495–497
methods for augmenting learning in school, 170
national level projects of, 166
Professional Research and Knowledge program of, 497
youth-at-risk programming
examples of programs, 492–493
obstacles encountered with, 493–495
three-tiered approach to, 491–492
Formal operational stage, 145, 250
Formal reasoning, 102
Foster care, 37–40
behavioral problems of children in, 39–40
children at risk for multiple placement, 39
compared to group home care, 39

G

Gay youth, 297–299
Gender
activities in youth clubs and, 165
adolescent employment and, 281, 283–284
and career choice, 279
children's family roles in household work and, 79–81
and contraceptive use, 102, 356–357, 359
differences in Hispanic sexual behavior, 340
differences in iron requirements, 263–264
drug use and, 360–361
early adolescent childbearing and, 96–97
economic hardship causing parental conflict and, 79
effects on depression, 386–387
girls in residential treatment, 40–41
influence of family on ethnic/racial group adolescents and, 56–57
influence of on music involvement, 227–228, 409, 411–412
prostitution and, 45
runaway youth and, 42
sexual activity and, 95, 357
first intercourse, 296–297
and weight control, 268
Girl and Boy Scouts, 159–160, 164, 165–166, 168, 170
Girls' Clubs, 160, 162, 165, 169, 170
Goodness of Fit model, 132, 136–137, 258
adolescent health and, 244, 255–256
Grade level, school
music involvement and, 409–410
Group home care
compared to foster care, 39
Group learning activities, 200
Group quarters, 27–28

SUBJECT INDEX

H

Head Start, 180
Health
 for adolescents, 242–243
 effects of media
  on construction of, 421–422
  and social stasis concerning, 419–420
 biomedical and biopsychosocial models of, 115, 116
 definition of, 111, 241–242, 420–421
 early adolescent childbearing and, 96, 97
 exploring adolescent construct for, 422–424
 familial influences on adolescent
  adolescent with chronic illness, 114–117
  adolescent with inherited disease, 117–118
  chronic illness and family relationships, 120–122
  consent and confidentiality, 112–114
  illness in other family members, 118–120
  major changes in adolescents and, 248–251
 participatory research and adolescent, 424–429
 promotion and disease prevention for families, 122–124
 research and policy concerning adolescent, 463–464
 social construction of, 420–421
 theoretical perspectives on adolescent
  cognitive theory, 252
  Health Belief Model (HBM), 252–253
  life-span developmental perspective, 254–256
  person-contextual approach, 253–254
  problem-focused theory, 251–252
  stress and coping, 251
Health Belief Model (HBM), 252–253
Health-care providers
 issues of consent and confidentiality effecting, 112–114
Health promotion, 247–248
 nutrition, 261–272
 programs for adolescents, 243–245
 recommendations for, 256–257

 sexual development, 293–305
 vocational development as part of, 277–289
Hispanics *see also Race/ethnicity*
 birth control use of, 345–346
 childbearing, 343–345
  determinants of ethnic differences in, 346–347
  negative consequences of, 348
  rates of sexual activity and, 95
 living arrangements of, 27
 overview of population of, 336–338
 parenting and performance, 86
 pregnancy
  and abortion regarding, 335–336, 340–342
  prevention strategies for, 347–348
  programs and services to help, 349–350
  sexual activity of, 335–336, 338–340
 value of virginity for, 339
HIV (Human Immunodeficiency Virus) infections, *see also AIDS*
 anonymous testing for, 365–366
 early adolescence and, 354–355
 limited data on rates, 355
 prevention of, 295, 361–362
  life development intervention model, 362–363
  personal competence enhancement, 363–366
 risk factors in early adolescence, 356–357
  anal intercourse, 359–360
  drug use, 360–361
  vaginal intercourse, 357–359
 runaways and risk of, 46
 transmission of, 353–354, 355
Homeless adolescents
 nutrition and, 268–269
Homosexuality, 297–299
Hormones, 249
 growth, 262
 increase in, at puberty, 316–317
 role of, in sexuality, 300
Household work
 children's family roles in, 79–82
Human development
 biological, 248–249, 316–317
 cognitive, 249–250, 317–318
 developmental contextualism approach to, 1, 5

four levels of ecological context in, 52–53

I

Identification, 184
  ethnic and racial, 180, 183
  with family's socioeconomic status, 179
  with a worker, 278–279
Identity
  sexual, 294–295
  vocational, 278, 280, 284–288
Identity crises, 287
Identity development, 54
Illiteracy. *See Literacy*
Illness
  chronic
    adolescent with, 114–117
    effects of, and family relations on adolescents, 120–122
  perceived vulnerability toward, 253
Individual differences, 4, 6, 7
  developmentally instigative characteristics, 83
  drug use and, 313
  familial economic stress and, 82–85
Industry
  early work experience and development of, 280–284
Infants
  form of feeding chosen for, 267
  HIV infection transmitted to, 353
  premature, 115
  at risk for low birth weight (LBW), 266–267
Informational interventions, 364
Institutional placement
  of adolescents, 40–41
Interpersonal beliefs, 374–375, 377–378
Interpretive validity, 61
Intervention programs
  integrating policy, research, and, 1–11, 17–22
Intrapersonal beliefs, 372–374, 376–377
Intravenous (IV) drug use, 46, 360
Iron deficiency, 270
  requirements, 263–264

J

Japanese-Americans, 55, *see also Race/ethnicity*

success and social capital regarding, 63–64
Job training programs
  for literacy, 212

K

Knowledge
  acquisition, 151–153
    literacy and, 138–139
  control of, in classroom, 192–199
  of effective contraceptive methods, 327
  for pregnancy prevention, 323–324

L

Land-grant university system
  and 4-H, 481–498
  functions of, 481–482, 483
  future directions for 4-H and, 495–497
  scholars and practitioners involved in, 489–491
Laws
  health promotion, 124
  pertaining to runaway and homeless youth, 46
Learning
  about music, 228–231
  experiential, 171–172
  from group activities, 200
  literacy skills, 207–218
  participatory form of knowing and, 203–205
  school vs. nonschool, 161
  student-directed inquiry, 205
Lesbian youth, 297–299
Life development intervention model
  for prevention of HIV infections, 362–363
Life options enhancement programs, 324
Life skills, 161, 378
Life-span developmental perspective, 248, 254–256, 257–258
  applied to adolescent sexuality, 299–300
  three key concepts of, 254–255
Literacy
  adult instruction for, 212
  cultural variations in beliefs on, 137–139
  definition of, 207

increasing need for, in the workplace, 208–209
training programs for, 212
in manufacturing and service occupations, 209
learning and personal goals concerning, 210–213
metacognition and, 213–218
mismatch between requirements and abilities regarding, 209–210
problems involving poor skills in, 135–137
traditional programs for instruction, 211–212
Living arrangements, 26–28, 31–33
nonfamily and alternative settings, 37–48

M

Macronutrient intake, 261–263
Macrosystem, 52–53, 135
Manufacturing occupations
regarding needs for literacy, 209
Marital difficulties
fathers' unemployment and, 74
Marital distress
chronically ill family member and, 119
Maternal employment, 72, 74
Media
adolescent music involvement and, 227–228, 404–405, 407–416
and adolescents, 401–402, 404–406
historical perspective on, 402–404
reasons for research, 402
theoretical framework for, 404
effects on minority adolescents and alcohol use, 431–443
and health messages, 405–406
participatory research regarding, 419–429
impact on reading, 403
nutrition education programming and, 271–272
policy and public education, 464–465
pregnancy prevention and, 322–323
Medical care
issues of consent and confidentiality concerning, 112–114
Menarche, 262, 316
Menstruation, 262, 270

Mesosystem, 52, 134–135
Metacognition
applied to investigating adolescents' literacy skills, 216–218
as a framework for studying cognitive process, 213–216
reflective awareness type of, 215–216
three categories of variables in, 214–216
Micronutrient intake, 261–262, 263–264
Microsystem, 52, 134
Minority adolescents, *see also Race/ethnicity*
effects of media on alcohol use, 431–443
advertising, 436–437
approaches to research on, 438–440
educational programs, 437–438
entertainment programs, 437
future research on, 443
limitations to research on, 440–443
Mothers, *see also Parents*
adolescent, reasons for keeping child, 104–105
fathers' unemployment and parenting behavior of, 74
Motor skills
and music performance, 229
Multidisciplinary approach, 143
to diversity and context for research, policy, and intervention, 2–8
Music involvement, 221–222, 407–411
adolescents' reasons for, 413–414, 415
changing voices and, 231
defining music for adolescents, 407
factors influencing, 224–228
future research directions in, 231–253
in-school, 222–223, 224–227
activities preferred by students, 225–226
current methods used, 226–227
successful teachers in, 224
three types of, 222–223
learning skills for, 228–231
meanings derived from music, 408, 413–416
out-of-school, 223–224, 227–228
sources of influence on, 411–413
Music Television (MTV)
compared to listening to radio or records, 410–411

daily viewing of, 409–410
messages derived from, 414–416

N

National Longitudinal Surveys (NLSY), 33
National Statistical Survey on Runaway Youth, 43
National Survey of Children, 281
National Survey of Families and Households (NSFH), 32
Noncoital sexuality, 295–296
Normative education, 377
Nutrition, 244
   adolescent childbearing and, 266–267
   athletes and, 270–271
   effects of social trends on, 264–266
   impact of alcohol abuse on, 269
   impact on physical growth and development
      macronutrient intake, 261–263
      micronutrient intake, 263–264
   and inherited diseases, 269–270
   intervention strategies for adolescents, 271–272
   out of the mainstream teens and, 268–269
   weight control/eating disorders, 267–268

O

Obesity, 262–263, 267
Objectivist theory of knowledge, 151–152, 151–153
Occupational identity, 278–279
Occupations
   regarding needs for literacy for various, 208–209
On My Own and O.K. program, 492
Osteoporosis, 263, 270

P

Parental-adolescent relationships
   among various ethnic/racial groups, 59, 64–65
   economic hardship and, 73–79
Parental belief systems, 133
Parental leave/flextime, 461

Parental monitoring, 81–82
   risk for pregnancy in lack of, 320
   in single- vs. dual-earner families, 76–77
Parenthood
   adolescents adapting to, 105–106
Parenting style
   familial economic stress and, 85–86
Parents, *see also Family; Father; Mother*
   adolescent health problems caused by drug abuse of, 121
   Caucasian vs. Navajo, 60–61
   child care and working, 31
   of chronically ill teenagers, 116–117
   Danish vs. U.S., 64–65
   depression and adolescent less reliance on, 390
   facilitating vocational exploratory behavior in children, 286
   Hispanic, socialization of children, 349
   influence of on music involvement, 412
   influences on substance abuse, 377
   issues of consent and confidentiality effecting, 112–114
   of runaways, 42–43
   sex education and, 302
   single, 28–31, 32, 76, 101, 119
Participatory research, 424–429
Peer-resistance training, 327–328
Peer-resistance training, 330
Peers
   depression and adolescent reliance on, 390–391
   effects of on academic achievement, 182–184
   influence of on music involvement, 411
   influences on substance abuse, 377
   pregnancy prevention and, 320–321
   as primary source for sex education, 301–302
   selection of, in adolescence, 17–18
Perceived risks, 373–374
Permissive parenting style, 85–86
Personal competence enhancement
   four kinds of interventions, 363–364
   for prevention of HIV infections, 363–366
Person characteristics, 82–85, 87, 88
   developmentally instigative, 83
Person-focused interventions, 391, 393
Physical deformities, 117–118

Physical growth
    effects of macronutrient intake on, 262–263
    effects of micronutrient intake on, 263–264
Piagetian theory
    on cognitive development, 145–146, 152, 249, 252
Poland
    study of economic stress in, 78
Policy
    concerning family health promotion and disease prevention, 122–124
    integration of research, programs, and, 1–11, 17–22, 449–455, 457–458, 466–467
        articulating a public agenda for adolescents, 465
        community organizations and contexts, 462–463
        education and preparation of researchers, 465–466
        education of young adolescents, 461–462
        family support policy, 460–461
        health of adolescents, 463–464
        improving middle-level education, 471–480
        public education and media policy, 464–465
        science policy, 458–460
        youth support policy, 460
    regarding early adolescent childbearing, 106–107
    to promote healthy adolescent sexuality, 301–305
Policy research, 452
    definition of, 451
Poverty
    adolescent childbearing regarding, 346
    among adolescents, 30–31
    effects on early adolescent sexual activity, 100
    Hispanics rate in, 337–338
    and illiteracy, 136
Pregnancy
    among Hispanics, 340–342
    in different racial-ethnic and socioeconomic groups, 58–59
    increase rate of, 94–95
    nutrition and adolescent, 266–267
Pregnancy prevention, 295
    contextual factors involved in
        community, 321–322
        family relations, 319–320
        media, 322–323
        peers, 320–321
    early adolescent development and, 316–319
    need for, 315–316
    programs for, 323–326
        access to contraception, 324
        enhance life options, 324
        knowledge interventions, 323–324
        recommendations for, 326–329
        successful, 325–326
        strategies for Hispanics, 347–348
Preventive intervention programs, 311–313
    childbearing among Hispanics, 335–350
    common approaches used in, 312–313
    for depression, 383–395
    effectiveness of, 312
    HIV infections, 353–366
    for parents and families, 461
    pregnancy, 315–331
    substance abuse, 369–380
Problem-focused theory, 251–252
problem-solving programs, social, 393–395
Professional Research and Knowledge program, 497
Programs, intervention
    for Hispanics, 349–350
    integrating research and policy in, 1–11, 17–22, 449–455
    to promote healthy adolescent sexuality, 301–305
Prostitution
    adolescent male vs. female, 45
    runaways involved in, 45–46
Psychoanalytic theory, 384
Psychosocial functioning
    children's family roles in household work and, 80
    models regarding substance abuse, 371
Psychosocial stages of Erikson, 278
Psychosomatic disorders
    chronic illness and adolescent, 121
Puberty, 84

age of onset, 99
effect on sexual behavior, 98–99
pregnancy risk at, 316–317

R

Race/ethnicity, *see also* Minority
  anal intercourse and, 359–360
  bi-culturality and, 53–55
  childbearing and, 346–347
  differences in contraceptive use, 103–104, 345–346, 358–359
    condoms, 356–357, 359
  diversity in academic achievement and, 175–188
  dropping out of school, 338–339
  drug use and, 360
  early adolescent sexual behavior and, 99–100
    and childbearing among Hispanics, 335–350
    intercourse experiences, 357–358
    norms regarding, 100–101
  familial economic stress and, 85–87
  feelings about abortion and, 341–342
  influence of on music involvement, 227–228, 409, 411
  membership to youth clubs regarding, 162
  premarital childbearing regarding, 343–345
  research on adolescents and families regarding, 56–63
    new directions for, 63–66
    problems with, 60–63
  risk for pregnancy and, 321–322
Racial segregation of schools, 185
Reciprocal interaction, 255
Reducing the Risk program, 326
Reflective awareness, 215–216
Reform schools
  depression and, 387
Refusal skills models, 378
Relative functionalism, 178
Researchers
  education and preparation of, 465–466
Research
  applying metacognition to investigate literacy, 216–217
  integration of policy, intervention, and, 1–11, 17–22, 449–455, 457–458, 466–467
    articulating a public agenda for adolescents, 465
    community organizations and contexts, 462–463
    education and preparation of researchers, 465–466
    education of young adolescents, 461–462
    family support policy, 460–461
    health of adolescents, 463–464
    improving middle-level education, 471–480
    public education and media policy, 464–465
    science policy, 458–460
    youth support policy, 460
    regarding early adolescent childbearing, 106–107
Residential treatment, 40–41
  family involvement in, 41
Resource access interventions, 365–366
Risks, perceived, 373–374
Role-playing, 328, 330, 394
Roles
  for adolescents in different racial-ethnic and socioeconomic groups, 57–58
  familial economic stress and children's family, 79–81
Runaway and Homeless Youth Act (RHYA), 46
Runaways, 31, 41–47
  adjustment issues for, 45–47
  classification of, 43–45
  depression and suicide attempts of, 46
  family conflict, 42
  involved in illegal activities, 45–46
  nutrition and, 268–269
  reasons for leaving home, 42–43
  repeat offenders, 44–45
  at risk for HIV infection, 46

S

School/Community Program for Sexual Risk Reduction Among Teens, 325–326
Schooling, 129–131

developmental/contextual perspective for, 131–133
  example of literacy, 135–139
  with an ecological perspective, 133–135
  distinguished from education, 130
  five basic goals in, 129–130
School(s), *see also Academic; Education*
  ability grouping in, 185–186
  curricular designs that resonate with adolescent knowing, 191–205
  dropping out of, 32, 135–136, 182
  effects of on academic achievement, 184–187
  effects of poverty on achievement in, 31
  grade level and music involvement and, 409–410
  health clinics, 324, 330
  importance of group learning activities in, 200
  learning methods distinguished from youth groups, 161, 172
  modifying programs to include experiential learning, 171–172
  music involvement in, 222–223, 224–227, 229–233, 412
  nutrition education programming in, 271
  programs needed to keep adolescent mothers in, 107
  racial segregation of, 185
  sex education in, 302–305
  single parent households and, 28, 29–30
  teaching literacy skills in, 207–218
  transition from primary to secondary, 391–395
  youth groups' methods for augmenting learning in, 169–171
School Lunch Program (USDA), 265–266
Science policy, 458–460
Segregation of schools, racial, 185
Self-care skills, 492
Self-concept, 250
  vocational, 278–279
  pregnancy prevention and, 319
Self-esteem
  children's family roles in household work and, 80
Self Program, 325

Sensorimotor thinking, 145
Service occupations
  regarding needs for literacy, 209
Settings, 132, 136
  different levels of, 134–135
Sex education, 103, 300, 301–305, 323–324, 330
  and parents, 302
  peers as primary source for, 301–302
  in schools, 302–305
Sexual activity, 98–99
  abstinence from, 362
  among Hispanics, 335–350
  applying life-span perspective to adolescent, 299–300
  childbearing and early adolescent, 94–96
  coital, 296–297
  contraceptive use during, 102–104
  cultural diversity in, 301
  developing policies and programs to promote healthy, 301–305
  effects of hormonal changes on, 317
  effects of poverty on, 100
  family influences on, 101
  healthy development in expression of, 294–295
  increased rate of, 94
  increasing motivation to reduce or postpone, 328–329
  limited knowledge on healthy adolescent, 293–294
  noncoital, 295–296
  norms concerning, 100–101
  same-gender, 297–299
  sexual abuse as an contributing factor to early, 101–102
  subgroup differences in, 99–100
  and transmission of HIV infections, 353–354, 356, 357–360
Sexual decision making, 318–319, 330
Sexually transmitted diseases
  and HIV infection transmission, 353
  prevention of, 295
Sibling
  chronically ill, 119
Single parents, 28–31, 32, 76, 101, 119
Situation-focused intervention, 391, 393
Smith-Lever Act, 484
Social capital, 171, 182
  academic achievement and, 63–64

definition of, 63, 182
Social deficit theory of depression, 389–390
Social inhibition, 392
  leading to development of depression, 389–391
  problem-solving programs to reduce, 393–395
Socialization, sexual, 294–295
Social problem-solving programs, 393–395
  goal of, 393
  role-playing in, 394
Social redefinition, 250–251
Social skills interventions, 364
Social support interventions, 364–365
  for Hispanics, 349–350
  need for, 107
Social support theory of depression, 389–390
Social trends
  and dietary intake, 264–266
Societal rejects, 44
Socioeconomic status (SES), 52
  adolescent childbearing regarding, 346–347
  effects of on academic achievement, 176, 179–181, 184, 187
  of Hispanics, 338
  risk for pregnancy and, 321–322
Somatization disorders
  chronic illness and adolescent, 120–121
Somatomedin, 262
Sons
  fathers' unemployment and behavior toward, 73–74
Special education programs, 136
Step in the Right Direction program, 492
Stress, 251
  chronic illness and adolescent, 120–121
Substance abuse, *see also Alcohol abuse; Drug abuse*
  belief domains interventions for, 376–380
  beliefs domains research model, 371–376
    extrapersonal, 375–376
    interpersonal, 374–375
    intrapersonal, 372–374
  effects on depression, 387
  impact of all domains used simultaneously on, 379–380
  peer and parental influences on, 377
  problem of, 369–371
  role of beliefs in theories of, 371
Suicide, 389, 391
  among homosexual teens, 298–299
  chronic illness and adolescent, 120
  increase in, 385–386, 387–388
  runaways and, 46

T

Teachers
  applying metacognition to investigate literacy, 217–218
  biasness of, 186
  controlling knowledge in classrooms, 193
  educational programs for, 171, 462
  music, 224–225, 226–227, 229–230, 232–233
  teaching sex education
    guidelines for, 304–305
    problems faced by, 303–304
Theoretical thinking, 143–154
Throwaways, 44
Transaction-focused intervention, 391, 393
Transitional Living Grant Program for Homeless Youth, 46

U

Unemployment
  familial economic stress, 71–88
U.S. Bureau of the Census
  Current Population Survey (CPS), 25–26
U.S. Department of Agriculture, 164

V

Vaginal intercourse
  and transmission of HIV infections, 356, 357–359
Virginity
  Hispanic value of, 339
Vocational development, 164, 244, 277–280
  early work experience and development of industry, 280–284
  Erikson's eight psychosocial stages for, 278
  identification and, 278–279

process of exploration, 285–286
recommendations for, 288–289
vocational identity and, 278, 280, 284–288
vocational self-concept and, 278–279
Voice, changing of, 231

W

Weight control
nutrition and, 267–268
Whites, *see also Race/ethnicity*
childbearing in, 96
literacy and, 137–138, 139
living arrangements of, 27
parenting and performance, 86
rates of sexual activity and childbearing, 95
Work
increasing need for literacy at, 208–209
need for parental leave/flextime, 461

Y

Youth-at-risk programming, 491–495
Youth groups
4-H program, 22
advantages of, 162–163
career guidance programs of, 164
distinguished from school learning, 161
effectiveness of, 167–169
examples of, 159–160
functions of, 160–161
involvement in enhance life options programs, 324
land-grant university system and 4-H, 481–498
learning methods distinguished from school, 161, 172
members of, 161–162
problems in evaluating, 168
role of, in enhancing learning and achievement, 159
specific programs and opportunities
community experience, 163–166
state, national, and international opportunities, 166–167
strategies for education
augmenting school learning, 169–171
modification of schools to include experiential learning, 171–172
Youth support policy, 460